Winds of Hope, Storms of Discord

In brisk and engaging prose, this comprehensive introductory textbook traverses the broad sweep of US history since 1945. *Winds of Hope, Storms of Discord* explores how Americans of all walks of life – political leaders, businesspeople, public intellectuals, workers, students, activists, migrants, and others – struggled to define the nation's political, economic, geopolitical, demographic, and social character. It chronicles the nation's ceaseless ferment, from the rocky conversion to peacetime in the early aftermath of World War II; to the frightening emergence of the cold war and repeated US military adventures abroad; to the struggles of African Americans and other minorities to claim a share of the American dream; to the striking transformations in social attitudes catalyzed by the women's movement and struggles for gay and lesbian liberation; to the dynamic force of political, economic, and social conservatism. Carrying the story to the spring of 2022, *Winds of Hope* also shows how dizzying technological changes at times threatened to upend the nation's civic and political life.

Salim Yaqub is Professor of History at the University of California, Santa Barbara, where he directs the Center for Cold War Studies and International History. He is the author of two previous books: *Containing Arab Nationalism: The Eisenhower Doctrine and the Middle East* and *Imperfect Strangers: Americans, Arabs, and US–Middle East Relations in the 1970s.*

Winds of Hope, Storms of Discord

The United States since 1945

Salim Yaqub
University of California, Santa Barbara

CAMBRIDGE
UNIVERSITY PRESS

University Printing House, Cambridge CB2 8BS, United Kingdom

One Liberty Plaza, 20th Floor, New York, NY 10006, USA

477 Williamstown Road, Port Melbourne, VIC 3207, Australia

314–321, 3rd Floor, Plot 3, Splendor Forum, Jasola District Centre, New Delhi – 110025, India

103 Penang Road, #05–06/07, Visioncrest Commercial, Singapore 238467

Cambridge University Press is part of the University of Cambridge.

It furthers the University's mission by disseminating knowledge in the pursuit of education, learning, and research at the highest international levels of excellence.

www.cambridge.org
Information on this title: www.cambridge.org/highereducation/isbn/9781108496728
DOI: 10.1017/9781108654524

First published 2023

Printed in the United Kingdom by TJ Books Limited, Padstow, Cornwall, 2023

A catalogue record for this publication is available from the British Library.

Library of Congress Cataloging-in-Publication Data
Names: Yaqub, Salim, author.
Title: Winds of hope, storms of discord : the United States since 1945 / Salim Yaqub, University of California, Santa Barbara.
Other titles: United States since 1945
Description: Cambridge, United Kingdom ; New York, NY : Cambridge University Press, 2023. | Includes bibliographical references and index.
Identifiers: LCCN 2022024947 | ISBN 9781108496728 (hardback) | ISBN 9781108721882 (paperback) | ISBN 9781108654524 (ebook)
Subjects: LCSH: United States – History – 1945– | United States – Politics and government – 1945–
Classification: LCC E741 .Y37 2023 | DDC 973.918–dc23/eng/20220616
LC record available at https://lccn.loc.gov/2022024947

ISBN 978-1-108-49672-8 Hardback
ISBN 978-1-108-72188-2 Paperback

Additional resources for this publication at www.cambridge.org/yaqub

To my students

Contents

Figures

Maps

Preface

This book is a general, synthetic history of the United States since 1945. Its coverage is comprehensive, surveying politics, economics, culture, political and social movements, foreign relations, demographic change, technological transformation, and other topics. The volume is pitched to upper-division undergraduates and thus is accessible to educated general readers as well. Its treatment features the verve and "attitude" of an engaged individual author, while striving throughout for fairness and empathy.

The themes of the book are key to understanding the unfolding of US history since 1945 and remain vitally important today. They include: differing, and at times sharply clashing, visions of the national government's proper role in the domestic economy and society; constantly changing understandings of gender, sexuality, and family; the struggles of traditionally marginalized groups to share more fully in the benefits of citizenship; the dynamic, disruptive, and sometimes corrosive impact of rapid technological, social, and economic change; and the unending and often bitter debate over the United States' appropriate role in the world.

Four qualities set this book apart from most others in the genre. The first, as suggested above, is its comprehensiveness. The second is its newness: the manuscript takes the narrative up to mid-March 2022. It thus covers all of the Donald Trump years and the first fourteen months of Joseph Biden's administration, along with recent societal events that have transcended official politics and governance, such as the "Me Too" movement, the Covid-19 pandemic, and responses to the 2020 murder of George Floyd. It also includes the early weeks of the Russian invasion of Ukraine launched in February 2022. The third quality of the book is relative concision; it consists of fifteen chapters, most of them ranging in length from 12,000 to 15,000 words. The combination of comprehensiveness and brevity makes, I hope, for a special kind of reading experience. Because the typical chapter contains a wide range of subjects, the connections between different realms of American experience come readily to the fore. We see, for example, how struggles for racial justice at home dovetailed with the drive for decolonization abroad, and how both phenomena, in turn, transformed the cold war. Similarly, we trace the impact of US military and diplomatic intervention abroad on changing patterns of immigration to the United States, and the profound influence of immigration debates on domestic American politics.

The fourth feature is a diversity of narrative approach. Although most of the chapters proceed in a generally chronological fashion, some, like the chapters on the 1950s, the 1970s, and the 1980s, present a range of patterns and vignettes in a more synchronic manner. A few chapters, such as the one on the revival and end of the cold war, feature a relatively narrow range of topics, whereas most of the others present several subjects whose *interrelation* constitutes the main theme. I have opted for such variety partly because I believe it will be more interesting to readers than a more uniform approach would be. But I also want to expose them to different ways of understanding and representing the past. Grasping a causal sequence is one form of historical knowledge; taking in a panorama constitutes another.

To carry the readers across such wide and varied terrain, I have striven for a prose style that is brisk and authoritative, blending narrative with analysis, illustrative detail with digestible statistics. Here, a key objective is to convey the significance, vitality, poignancy, diversity, and contemporary relevance of modern US history – to arouse the curiosity of readers and encourage them to delve more deeply into the many topics featured in the book. Each chapter is followed by a list of suggested readings highlighting up-to-date scholarship on the subjects at hand, along with older historical works that remain indispensable. The book offers a distinct perspective but is, as well, an invitation to further exploration.

The volume features a substantial number of illustrations – mostly photographs, but also maps and a political cartoon. Instead of serving as deliberate detours from the primary text (as textbook illustrations often do), these visual materials are integral to the main narrative and designed to keep the reader's attention focused on it.

Most instructors assigning the book will probably wish to have their students read it all the way through, in order. Its organization easily lends itself to a one-chapter-per-week reading schedule in a semester-long course. Yet the chapters are sufficiently thematic that each can stand on its own. Instructors may alter their sequence within a course, or assign a smaller selection of them. A set of reading questions at the end of each chapter underscores its themes and encourages critical reflection on some of the author's claims. Instructors, students, and other interested readers may visit www.cambridge.org/yaqub to find relevant documents that further illuminate the book's contents.

Acknowledgments

I did not set out to write this book. Between projects, I received an email from Deborah Gershenowitz, then a senior editor at Cambridge University Press, urging me to consider authoring a post-1945 history of the United States. At first it seemed out of the question that I would undertake such a daunting assignment, for which I felt so unqualified and unprepared. But Debbie's vision and enthusiasm won me over, and I agreed to give it a try. Debbie has since moved on to another press, but I remain indebted to her for launching me on this unexpected, challenging, and rewarding journey.

Unlike my previous book projects, this one has drawn almost entirely on secondary literature. So I must acknowledge the scores of historians, journalists, social scientists, memoirists, and others (only some of them listed in the short bibliographies following the book's chapters) who produced the vivid, detailed, textured, and insightful accounts that I have synthesized here. I am also grateful to the librarians at the University of California, Santa Barbara, and other institutions who made these published works available to me so quickly and efficiently. Covid-19 struck midway through the project. Overall, the pandemic's impact on me and my family has been tiny compared with the trauma, disruption, misery, and heartbreak inflicted on millions around the globe. But the crisis did significantly alter my work on this book, requiring me to rely much more heavily on digital materials. I am thankful to the countless archivists and technicians who digitized and posted so many of the books, journals, newspapers, and other printed materials on which this account is based.

UC Santa Barbara and its extraordinary Department of History furnished a highly congenial environment for pursuing this project: brilliant and supportive colleagues, sharp and inquisitive students, humane teaching loads, survivable committee assignments, and a leave of absence in the fall of 2020. A post-World-War-I US history survey course I developed at UCSB allowed me to cobble together the preliminary framing for many of the book's chapters.

At Cambridge University Press, Cecelia Cancellaro, Maggie Jeffers, and Rachel Norridge have served as the main overseers of the project, and working with them has been a delight. Joe LeMonnier, Mike Richardson, Peter Buckles, and many others at Cambridge whose names I don't know have labored with skill, dedication, and professionalism to bring out this volume. The anonymous outside readers caught many errors and offered invaluable suggestions for improving the book. Generous colleagues and friends – especially Mark Bradley, Miroslava Chávez-García, Nathan Citino, Ann Gordon, Laura Kalman, Douglas Rossinow, Kelly Shannon, and Elizabeth Teare – discussed the project with me, read portions of the manuscript, or otherwise helped to make it better.

Brief portions of this manuscript appeared in my 2016 book *Imperfect Strangers: Americans, Arabs, and US–Middle East Relations in the 1970s*. I am grateful to Cornell University Press for granting permission to reprint those passages.

For nearly six decades, my parents and siblings have extended unconditional love and support. Over a shorter span of time – and, for me, an undeservedly happy one – my wife, Elizabeth Teare, and my daughter, Dorothy Teare Yaqub, have sustained me in ways I cannot begin to recount.

Introduction

In April 1946, the USS *Missouri* glided into the port of Istanbul. The American battleship received a warm welcome from the Turkish government and press, as well as from ordinary city dwellers, thousands of whom crowded into the old Ottoman forts overlooking the harbor to cheer the ship's arrival. Turkey's main tobacco company had manufactured 30,000 commemorative cigarette packets, labeled "Missouri," to be presented as gifts to the visiting Americans. The *Missouri* came bearing the body of Turkey's late ambassador to the United States, Mehmet Münir Ertegün, who had died in Washington, DC, in 1944, while World War II still raged. With the hostilities now ended, it had become possible to exhume the deceased diplomat from his temporary resting place in Arlington National Cemetery and furnish him a dignified voyage home for final burial.

To informed people around the world, the name "USS *Missouri*" was instantly recognizable. Seven months earlier, in Tokyo Bay, representatives of Japan had boarded that vessel and formally surrendered to the United States and its allies, bringing World War II to a close. In using the *Missouri* to repatriate Ertegün's remains, the US government not only signaled its esteem for a strategically located nation (Turkey abutted the Mediterranean Sea, bordered the Soviet Union, and contained the narrow straits connecting the Mediterranean and Black Seas) but also appeared to send a warning to Moscow. For some months, the Soviet Union had pressured Turkey to cede border territories and permit the establishment of Soviet bases on the Turkish straits. The Turks had resisted these demands, and the administration of Harry S. Truman had quietly backed their position. Turkey's government and much of its public now interpreted the *Missouri*'s visit as a bolder indication of US support – hence the enthusiastic reception. President Truman and his advisers may not have fully intended to send a saber-rattling message (there were sound logistical reasons for employing the *Missouri* in this errand), but in the coming months they grew more forceful in their pro-Turkish stance, and official policy soon caught up with optics. In March 1947, Truman urged Congress to appropriate $400 million to help Turkey and neighboring Greece resist communist pressures, issuing an early salvo in what was to be a decades-long cold war.

Stateside, another kind of legacy was taking shape. Ambassador Ertegün's widow and daughter returned to Turkey, but his two sons stayed in America. The younger of them, twenty-three-year-old Ahmet Ertegun, pursued a passion that would closely enmesh him in the life of his adopted country. Since boyhood, Ahmet had been mesmerized by jazz and blues, spending the late 1930s and the war years – a period coinciding with his father's US ambassadorship – frequenting the theaters and music halls of Washington's Black neighborhoods. On weekends, he and his brother converted the Turkish embassy into an open house for visiting jazz musicians, challenging the social mores of segregated Washington. The brothers met renowned African American performers such as Duke Ellington and Lena Horne, and they assembled a record collection numbering some 15,000 items. Following the ambassador's death, Ahmet Ertegun borrowed $10,000 from a Turkish dentist and launched his own record company in New York, Atlantic Records. After struggling in obscurity for a couple of years, Atlantic scored a string of hits with Ruth Brown, the pioneering rhythm and blues singer, and then with Ray Charles, the pianist, singer, and composer whose irresistible blend of jazz, blues, gospel, and R&B came to define for many the early "Atlantic sound." By the late 1950s, that sound featured considerable technological innovation. Atlantic was the first record company to use eight-track tape machines, which enabled richer, more intricate, and more textured recordings, and one of the first to exploit stereophonic sound.

Initially, Atlantic Records catered mostly to Black audiences. But in the mid-1950s, as R&B enjoyed cross-racial success and shapeshifted into rock and roll, Ertegun, too, branched out, pitching recordings by Black artists to the burgeoning white teenage market. Later in the decade, he found he could also make stars of white performers, such as the singer Bobby Darin. For the rest of the century, Ertegun continued his ceaseless and seldom erring quest for The Next Big Thing, divining the commercial potential in musicians as varied as Otis Redding, Aretha Franklin, Sonny & Cher, Crosby, Stills, & Nash, Led Zeppelin, Phil Collins, and Kid Rock. He played a leading role in establishing the Rock and Roll Hall of Fame, which opened its doors in Cleveland, Ohio, in 1986. Following a public campaign by Ruth Brown, Ertegun belatedly acknowledged the unjust terms imposed on many of Atlantic's early performers and, by extension, on Black artists across the recording industry. Atlantic reached monetary settlements with Brown and other performers, and in 1988 Ertegun helped to found the Rhythm and Blues Foundation, which supported needy musicians and urged record companies to enact royalty reform. When Ertegun died in 2006 at the age of eighty-three – of complications resulting from a backstage fall at a Rolling Stones concert – few areas of popular music had been left untouched by this Turkish American impresario born in the final year of the Ottoman Empire.

Yet Ertegun's own empire was hardly an untroubled one. This was the music business, after all, an industry notorious for its gargantuan egos, rampant self-indulgence, and casual exploitation of those deemed expendable. Most remembered Ertegun as an exuberant, fun-loving, and generous soul. In 2018, however, a former Atlantic Records executive named Dorothy Carvello claimed in a memoir that, when starting out as Ertegun's young secretary, she had fended off crude and unwelcome sexual advances from her boss, who had also violently manhandled her in a nonsexual way. Carvello thus joined the "Me Too" movement, a wave of allegations by women in the late 2010s, many but not all of them in the

Figure I.1 Soul singer Aretha Franklin, Franklin's husband and manager Ted White, and Atlantic Records founder and president Ahmet Ertegun, 1968. Source: The Estate of David Gahr / Premium Archive / Getty Images.

United States, about the predatory sexual behavior of powerful men in the entertainment industry, the news media, business, politics, and other realms. Ertegun was no longer around to respond to the accusations, and no public legal proceedings unfolded to shed light on the matter. Yet few if any of Ertegun's devoted friends stepped forward to object that the charges couldn't be true, and as of the fall of 2021 reputable filmmakers were working with Carvello to turn her memoir into a television "docuseries." The disturbing allegations had become an inescapable part of the music man's legacy.

Ertegun's biography was illustrious and idiosyncratic, but it reflected circumstances that told the story of the nation as a whole in the decades after 1945: commanding power on the world stage, unprecedented prosperity and social mobility, rapid technological change, increasing ethnic diversity, and the flourishing of new cultural expressions that gestured toward rebellion and challenged old racial hierarchies and taboos. Yet his life also signified the persistence of injustice and exploitation in postwar America, and the relentless efforts by the victims of such offenses to bring them to light and force a public reckoning.

***

This book chronicles the history of the United States since the end of World War II. It is an intricate and many-sided story, combining politics, economics, foreign relations, demographic change, social transformations, new technologies, popular culture, and political and social movements. The narrative unfolds in a broadly chronological fashion, but five central themes recur throughout the text.

The first theme concerns the varying, and highly contested, ways in which the national government interacted with the private economy. During World War II, Washington had pumped tens of billions of dollars into the domestic economy, by concluding contracts with private companies to provide the goods and services needed for waging the conflict. Into the postwar years, the federal government remained invested in the private economy (albeit at a lower level), and it continued key New Deal programs such as Social Security, agricultural subsidies, laws facilitating union organizing, progressive federal tax rates, and regulations of certain industries. With hiccups and slumps here and there, the combination of robust government intervention and dynamic market mechanisms enabled, over the next quarter-century, a steady expansion of the US economy and a dramatic increase in overall prosperity. Still, the nation's incomes and wealth were distributed highly unequally, and tens of millions remained trapped in poverty, with African Americans and other people of color disproportionately numbered among the poor and working-class. An ambitious "War on Poverty," launched by Washington in the 1960s, helped to bring the official US poverty rate down from over 20 percent of the population at the start of the decade to about 12 percent ten years later. (It has fluctuated between around 11 and 15 percent ever since.) Yet the effort failed to vanquish poverty in the manner its name implied, and it was sharply attacked from several political directions. Meanwhile, a global economic crisis taking hold at the start of the 1970s signaled an end to America's postwar economic boom.

In the late 1970s and early 1980s, after several years of economic turmoil, Washington shifted toward more market-friendly approaches, inaugurating a new era that, arguably, continues in some form to this day. Congress began scaling back federal regulations of key industries, and Republican President Ronald Reagan, who served from 1981 to 1989, used executive orders to weaken surviving regulations, a practice emulated by later Republican presidents. Through a series of congressional tax reforms, the top individual earners went from paying a 70 percent tax on their marginal income in the late 1970s to paying a 37 percent marginal rate by 2022 (though the closing of earlier tax loopholes made the contrast somewhat less stark than it appeared on the surface). President Bill Clinton (1993–2001), although a Democrat, gave voice to the new zeitgeist, proclaiming in his January 1996 State of the Union address, "The era of big government is over." Later that year, Clinton signed legislation ending welfare as a federal entitlement. Wealth and income disparities, which had steadily narrowed since the late 1920s, began widening again in the late 1970s. (To take just one index: in 1929, the top 1 percent of US households held more than 44 percent of the nation's wealth; by 1976, the top 1 percent held under 20 percent; by 2021, that figure was back up to about 32 percent.) Labor unions, which had slowly lost clout since the 1950s, experienced a precipitous decline after the 1970s, as the unionized share of the workforce dwindled and employers shipped manufacturing jobs overseas and reduced wages and benefits.

Liberal political leaders struggled to mitigate these trends, with mixed success. Clinton immediately followed his "era of big government" statement with the comment "But we cannot go back to the time when our citizens were left to fend for themselves." In 1997, partly to address the baneful consequences of the previous year's welfare reform, he signed legislation creating the Children's Health Insurance Program, a federal–state partnership to assist children in families not already covered by the Medicaid program. In 2009–2010, Democratic President Barack Obama persuaded Congress to pass the Affordable Care Act, an ambitious reform of the health insurance system that had eluded liberal leaders and policy advocates for generations. Obama also signed into law new banking legislation to correct abuses resulting from the deregulation policies of previous decades. These and other liberal programs were innovative and resourceful, but they only partially blunted the surge of market-oriented federal policies.

The second theme is Washington's geopolitical engagement, marking a sharp break with its stance prior to World War II. In the early postwar years, the United States became locked in a cold war with communist nations: the Soviet Union, the People's Republic of China (PRC), and lesser powers allied with them. The global contest was to last for more than four decades. In waging it, the United States built up a massive and permanent military establishment and forged alliances with likeminded nations around the world, chief among them the North Atlantic Treaty Organization (NATO), centered in Western Europe. The United States fought two hot wars against communist foes, in Korea in the early 1950s and in Vietnam in the 1960s and early 1970s, the latter conflict bitterly dividing Americans. Meanwhile, the US Central Intelligence Agency (CIA) secretly battled foreign governments and movements seen as communist or procommunist. The culture of secrecy surrounding such activities made it harder for Americans to ask penetrating questions about their government's behavior abroad. Even more corrosive to domestic political life, especially in the first postwar decade, were exaggerated, though not always unfounded, suspicions that domestic radicals were subverting the nation's institutions on behalf of the Soviet Union or other communist nations. Throughout the cold war, and indeed in the years thereafter, a nuclear arms race between the United States and the Soviet Union, and then Russia, cast a pall of terror over all of humankind.

In the late 1980s and early 1990s, the cold war ended with the rapid decline and collapse of the Soviet Union and with Eastern European nations' dramatic rejection of communism. (The PRC remained nominally communist, and genuinely authoritarian, while increasingly embracing capitalism at home and abroad.) The United States continued, however, to wield vast military, economic, diplomatic, and cultural power across the globe. As the sole remaining superpower, it saw itself as the main enforcer of the "new world order" emerging after the cold war and, often, as the chief mediator of destabilizing international disputes. Political turmoil in the oil-rich Persian Gulf region, and in other parts of West and Central Asia, prompted the United States to launch military interventions, especially after Islamist militants based in Afghanistan staged stunningly destructive attacks against American civilians on September 11, 2001. An ensuing twenty-year military occupation of Afghanistan, and a shorter but far more divisive war in Iraq, left many Americans eager to curtail their nation's overseas entanglements. For some, this mood expressed itself in greater suspicion of foreigners.

For a few years after the end of the cold war, the United States had some hope of forging cordial ties with post-Soviet Russia. But the subsequent expansion of NATO to include several Eastern European nations, combined with the determination of Vladimir Putin, Russia's official or de facto leader since 1999, to dominate neighboring states that had once been Soviet republics, placed ever greater strain on US–Russian relations. Meanwhile, the PRC emerged as an increasingly formidable geopolitical and economic rival of Washington. With the apparent exhaustion of the United States following its demoralizing ventures in the Muslim world, and with the growing assertiveness of other nations, hostile and friendly alike, the unipolar system prevailing in the 1990s and 2000s was giving way by the 2010s to a more multipolar one. In early 2022, Russia launched a full-scale invasion of Ukraine, a shocking development that threw much of the global community into turmoil and seemed destined to reshuffle countless international arrangements and assumptions.

The third theme of the book is demographic transformation. In the 1940s, non-Hispanic whites made up about 88 percent of the US population. By 2020, that figure had declined to around 58 percent, a change accompanied by dramatic increases in the numbers of Americans of Hispanic, Asian, and Middle Eastern origin. In the mid-1960s, the US Congress eliminated decades-old quotas that had favored immigrants from Northern and Western Europe, allowing substantial immigration from nonwhite areas of the globe. A separate issue, but one often linked in the public mind with the nation's changing racial makeup, was the rapid increase in the number of undocumented immigrants, most of them Mexican. In 1980, an estimated two million undocumented immigrants lived in the United States, mainly in California and the Southwest. By 2006, their numbers had risen to eleven million, and they remained at about that level in the years thereafter. From the 1990s on, the immigration question sharply divided the nation. Another controversy swirled around the status of American Muslims, both immigrant and native-born, numbering perhaps two and a half million in the early 2000s. Amid a climate of fear of Islamist terrorism – most pervasive in the aftermath of the 9/11 attacks but present at other times, too – many Muslim Americans were treated as unwelcome intruders in their own country.

This brings us to our fourth theme: powerful and ongoing disagreement among Americans. Throughout the postwar period, the two-party system has been the main forum for expressing and adjudicating political differences, with the Democratic Party generally favoring stronger federal regulation of the private economy and a more expansive government safety net, and Republicans urging greater deference to the private sector and tighter restraints on social spending. In foreign affairs – with important exceptions – Republicans have tended to be more supportive than Democrats of using military force abroad. All that said, in the early postwar decades each party was more ideologically diverse than it would be later. Each contained liberals, moderates, and conservatives, and the Democratic Party was home to both northern African Americans and southern white segregationists. In the 1960s, however, as the national Democratic Party embraced civil rights reform (and took other stances that offended conservatives), southern whites started to abandon the party, turning the South by century's end into a Republican-dominated region. During those same years, each party became more ideologically uniform, with Democrats clustering at the liberal end of the spectrum and Republicans growing more conservative. Increasingly, Democrats and Republicans came to regard each other as enemies; Republicans were especially prone to such thinking.

For all the durability of the two-party system, some of the most dynamic political struggles unfolded outside of it (while at times helping to redraw the battle lines between the parties). Struggles by African Americans for political and legal equality, civic dignity, and economic opportunity, waged most intensively in the South but not only there, gained national and even global attention in the second half of the 1950s. By the mid-1960s, the civil rights movement had won judicial and legislative victories that outlawed nearly all forms of de jure discrimination, although securing the implementation of these rulings and laws remained a challenge. Campaigns for African Americans' rights continued into the ensuing decades, focusing mainly on combating de facto discrimination, as seen in the disproportionate levels of poverty, unemployment, urban blight, police violence, crime, incarceration, and similar ills plaguing Black communities. A host of other political and social movements – to oppose the Vietnam War and other military adventures abroad, to uphold women's rights, to overcome societal taboos against same-sex intimacy, to insist that Latino, Asian, and other "Third World" Americans had their own vibrant cultures and need not adhere to the norms of the white-dominated society, to halt the degradation of the natural environment – gathered critical momentum in the late 1960s and early 1970s and provided templates for future progressive struggles. Activists engaging in these movements gained footholds in the Democratic Party, contributing to its leftward drift.

Conservative activists, too, were highly vocal and influential in the postwar period. Stern anticommunists fueled the red scares of the late 1940s and early 1950s, decried Washington's failure to pursue all-out victory in the Korean and Vietnam Wars, and chastised Republican and Democratic presidents alike for trying to ease US–Soviet tensions from the 1950s through the 1980s. White defenders of the racial status quo, in the South and elsewhere, resisted the integration of schools, neighborhoods, and public accommodations and opposed later government efforts to remedy past discrimination through affirmative action programs. Social conservatives, active throughout the postwar years but nationally consequential from the mid-1970s on, fought pitched battles against secularists, feminists, gay rights activists, civil libertarians, and other foes of traditionalism. Critics of big-government liberalism organized state-level "tax revolts" in the late 1970s and a national "Tea Party" in the late 2000s and early 2010s. Many Tea Party enthusiasts joined a preexisting movement demanding stricter limits on illegal immigration. Like their counterparts on the left, right-leaning activists increasingly found a home in, and hardened the line of, the adjacent major party.

More diffusely, working-class whites also gravitated toward the Republican Party. In the early postwar decades, a powerful labor movement had drawn such Americans toward the Democratic Party. But unions' rapid decline after the 1970s helped to dissolve this loyalty, leaving blue-collar whites more receptive to the Republican Party's appeals to patriotism, "law and order," respect for religious institutions, adherence to traditional gender roles, and other conservative values. Indeed, a substantial minority of working-class nonwhites, especially in Latino communities, also found this formula attractive.

The fifth and final theme is rapid, ceaseless, disruptive, and sometimes frightening technological change. In the late 1940s and, especially, the 1950s, television took hold of the nation, altering the rhythms of family life and helping to create a national consumer culture. Over those same years, a headlong expansion in the capabilities of nuclear weapons, acquired by the United States in 1945 and the Soviet Union in 1949, forced people everywhere to contemplate the obliteration of entire cities and even nations, and beyond that the extinction of the human species. A technological breakthrough in the late 1950s eventually joined these two realms. Both superpowers developed powerful rockets that could not only fire nuclear payloads at distant continents but also put artificial satellites into earth orbit. Satellites, in turn, could transmit televised images from one side of the globe to the other. In the 1960s, satellite broadcast linkups were cumbersome and infrequent, reserved for special occasions such as President John F. Kennedy's funeral procession in 1963 or the 1967 multinational concert program *Our World*, on which the Beatles famously performed their countercultural anthem "All You Need Is Love." But by the 1970s such transmissions were a regular feature of American news and sports broadcasting. Meanwhile, other media had become more vivid and engaging. Vinyl records were now routinely issued in stereo; magazines, movies, and television shows were a kaleidoscope of color.

In the following decade, the nation entered the digital age in earnest. A novelty item in 1980, the personal computer was a necessity for tens of millions of Americans by decade's end. Vinyl gave way to digital compact discs. By the start of the new millennium, sound recordings were increasingly consumed via portable digital files, which untethered content from physical discs of any kind. With the widespread adoption of email in the early 1990s, and the rise of the commercial internet a few years later, personal computers became portals onto an endlessly expanding universe of communication, information, commerce, and entertainment. Optimism about the digital revolution's democratizing potential, earnestly voiced in the 1990s and early 2000s, later turned into dismay over its corrosive qualities – over the havoc new technologies played on users' attention spans; over the growing ability of commercial vendors to compile intimate virtual dossiers on the habits and yearnings of their customers (or of unsuspecting web grazers they hoped to convert into customers); over the ever-present threat that a foolish youthful photograph or posting, eternally archived in cyberspace, might resurface to destroy an adult reputation or career; and, eventually, over the thoroughness with which social media platforms such as Facebook, Twitter, Instagram, and TikTok supplanted traditional news outlets as sources of information about current events.

This last phenomenon allowed millions of Americans to sequester themselves in ideological "echo chambers" that exclusively affirmed their political predispositions, making them less and less tolerant of opposing views. Worse, it left many of them peculiarly susceptible to false or misleading news stories and "memes" (some circulated deliberately by online saboteurs) that clouded their civic judgment. From the mid-2010s on, the societal costs of such mis- and disinformation were all too obvious. The problem was most glaring in the tsunami of falsehoods that swept Donald Trump to victory in the 2016 presidential election and, a few years later, prevented many of his supporters from taking common-sense measures to protect themselves from a deadly pandemic. Yet liberals spun their own cocoons of fact-free self-righteousness. In January 2019 in Washington, DC, a group of mostly white high school boys from Kentucky, some wearing shirts and caps inscribed with pro-Trump slogans, got into a tense and awkward standoff with Native American protesters near the Lincoln Memorial. Brief video clips of the encounter, misleadingly edited to make the boys appear to be the sole offenders, circulated on liberal social media, provoking a chorus of fulminations against "racist white privilege" and threats of violence against the boys. The fuller video record later revealed a more complicated event in which the young Kentuckians, though obnoxious, arguably were more sinned against than sinning.

There was, of course, a much more beneficial side to the digital and online revolutions. In ways inconceivable just a few decades earlier, the internet placed vast stores of knowledge, imagery, and sound within instantaneous reach of ordinary people. When harnessed by smartphones, global positioning systems made it possible for drivers to reach unfamiliar destinations with hardly any mental effort (a dramatic quality-of-life improvement for me and countless other incompetent map readers). Far more significantly, smartphones enabled the wide dissemination of videos of excessive police violence and other forms of official misconduct, shining a national and sometimes global spotlight on injustices previously visible only to their immediate victims and witnesses. The viral notoriety of such incidents, combined with the new organizing strategies made possible by social media networks, spawned powerful protest movements that occasionally won key political reforms or led to broader cultural and social change. It is difficult to imagine the "racial reckoning" that has occurred since the summer of 2020 – a salutary endeavor, despite some excesses – without the horrifying, and widely shared, video of George Floyd's brutal murder in May of that year.

***

The postwar era now exceeds three-quarters of a century. Writing about it comprehensively and at humane length keeps getting harder and harder. I have rendered this history in fifteen chapters, most of them combining multiple aspects of American life: politics, foreign relations, economics, culture, demographics, and so on. Such an approach has been largely dictated by necessity; granting each of these areas the focused, singular, and sustained attention it deserves would add hundreds of more pages to the book. Yet multi-themed chapters do offer some advantages. They allow us to observe how different facets of US history affected each other – how, for example, cold war politics abroad influenced civil rights protests at home, and vice versa. They also replicate the simultaneity of American public life in these years. Even in the case of coinciding events that had little to do with one another – say, the 1954 Geneva Conference on Vietnam and Elvis Presley's recording debut – knowing that they *did* coincide tells us something about what it was like to experience an era.

This book has turned out longer than I planned. Still, I have labored to keep it to manageable dimensions, with the result that many topics are addressed cursorily, and some not at all. I have tried to be both provocative and insightful, to tell a story of postwar America that is vibrant, textured, reasoned, and compassionate. Yet no history can be considered the final word on the subjects it addresses, least of all this one. So readers should treat the volume as a starting point, as an invitation to delve deeply into the suggested readings listed at the end of each chapter, and into other texts they may discover on their own.

***

Before we begin our story, it will be helpful to consider the broad outlines of the nation's history over the decade and a half preceding 1945 – the events and patterns lodged in the memory of most adult Americans as World War II drew to a close. The onset of the Great Depression at the very start of the 1930s was a national calamity. Tens of thousands of businesses failed, and by 1933 a quarter of the workforce was unemployed. Hundreds of thousands were homeless, hungry, and desperate. Democratic President Franklin D. Roosevelt (FDR), elected in 1932, worked with a heavily Democratic Congress to enact federal policies, collectively known as the New Deal, that dispensed relief, hired the unemployed to work on government projects, subsidized agriculture, regulated industries, and, in the middle years of the decade, established the beginnings of a government social safety net and made it easier for workers to unionize.

These measures appreciably eased Americans' suffering, brought the national unemployment rate down to under 15 percent by 1937, and restored a measure of public confidence. But they did not address the main driver of the Great Depression, which was a lack of sufficient purchasing power among the public; ordinary Americans couldn't buy enough goods and services to sustain the national economy. Politically, however, Roosevelt's ebullient personality and tireless efforts to address the national emergency struck a chord with the electorate, facilitating a historic realignment of the parties. FDR presided over the forging of a broad political coalition attracting farmers, laborers, professionals, intellectuals, political progressives, ethnic minorities, northern African Americans, southern whites, and other strange bedfellows, all united in seeing the Democratic Party as a vehicle for their own advancement or for causes they supported. This coalition would remain a dominant force in American politics for the next three decades. The Roosevelt administration made few efforts to combat racial discrimination and oppression. In the southern states, it allowed plantation owners and other racist white elites to administer local New Deal programs, at the expense of poor sharecroppers of all backgrounds, but especially African Americans. Across the country as a whole, however, Black Americans significantly benefited from the New Deal. Where permitted to vote, they gravitated toward the Democratic Party, a loyalty that continued into the postwar decades and was overwhelming after the mid-1960s.

The outbreak of World War II in September 1939 threw the United States into political turmoil, especially after the late spring of 1940, when Nazi Germany rapidly conquered and occupied nearly all of Western Europe. Although most Americans agreed that their nation should not enter the war as a direct belligerent, they were sharply divided over whether to provide military and other aid to Great Britain, the last major holdout against Nazi Germany in Western Europe. Self-described "internationalists" argued that helping Britain withstand the Nazis would allow the United States to stay out of the war. "Isolationists" countered that Britain was a lost cause and that Americans should muster their defenses and resources at home. Over the course of 1940, internationalists gained the upper hand, permitting President Roosevelt, a strong (though sometimes secretive and devious) advocate of that position, to win an unprecedented third term in the November presidential election.[1] In March 1941, he persuaded Congress to pass the Lend Lease program, whereby the United States "loaned" Britain warplanes, ships, tanks, munitions, foodstuffs, and other goods without specifying the timing or manner of Britain's return of, or payment for, these items. Lend Lease aid was also extended to the Soviet Union, following Nazi Germany's invasion of that country in June 1941. Isolationists excoriated these moves. Although they continued to lose public support, their increasingly vitriolic attacks against Roosevelt's policies roiled the body politic, creating a mood of domestic strife at a time of grave international peril.

By now, FDR believed the United States would have to enter the war. A victory by the Axis powers – Germany and its allies, Italy and Japan – would be intolerable. Nearly all of Eurasia would become a vast trading bloc that excluded the United States, and advances in air power would eventually enable Axis aircraft to strike the Western Hemisphere. To survive in such a world, the United States would have to regiment itself in ways that threatened the liberal and democratic institutions that, however violently and inequitably, had taken root in American soil. In the summer and fall of 1941, FDR secretly authorized the US Navy to skirmish with German submarines in the Atlantic Ocean. He hoped to provoke an "incident" that he could portray as German aggression, thus justifying America's entry into the war.

In the end, of course, the *casus belli* came in the Pacific, not the Atlantic, and on a much more destructive scale. On December 7, 1941 – after a decade of deteriorating relations stemming from US opposition to Japan's efforts to create a sphere of domination in East Asia and the western Pacific – Japanese aircraft struck the US naval base at Pearl Harbor, Hawaii, destroying much of America's Pacific fleet. The attack was part of a broader campaign in which Japan attacked and occupied the Philippines, then a US colony, the US territories of Guam and Wake Island, and the British imperial holdings of Hong Kong, Malaya, and Singapore. On December 8, Roosevelt requested and received a congressional declaration of war against Japan. Three days later, Germany declared war against the United States, bringing it into the European conflict, too.

The US entry into World War II profoundly altered American domestic life. It was the war effort, not the New Deal, that finally ended the Great Depression. In the 1930s, some economists had advised that massive federal investment in the private economy could grant citizens the purchasing power necessary to restore national prosperity. Roosevelt took modest steps in this direction but held back from ambitious strides, fearful of getting the federal budget too far out of balance and alarming members of Congress or the public. And so the Depression persisted throughout that decade and into the next. After Pearl Harbor, however, FDR had no choice but to call for massive federal expenditures. He had vowed

[1] Serving more than two presidential terms would not be constitutionally prohibited until the ratification of the Twenty-second Amendment in 1951. But there had been an unbroken tradition limiting presidents to two terms that dated back to George Washington's insistence on stepping down after completing his second presidential term in 1797.

on December 8 that the nation would "win through to absolute victory" against Japan, and he later made similar promises about vanquishing Germany and Italy. His administration would have to spend whatever it took to redeem those solemn pledges. During the war years, total federal spending reached $320 billion (between about $5 trillion and $6 trillion in 2022 dollars), more than twice as much as the government had spent in all previous years combined. Most of that money circulated in the private economy by means of government contracts with private corporations, which furnished a staggering array of products and services needed for the war: guns, planes, tanks, ammunition, uniforms, food, medical supplies, vehicles, housing, and on and on. The effort to meet the government demand put millions of American to work, all but eliminating the curse of joblessness. As late as 1940, 15 percent of the workforce had been unemployed. By 1944, unemployment was a mere 1.2 percent.

The war modestly recast US social relations. More than six million women joined the paid workforce, meeting a labor shortage created by the widespread conscription of men into the military. By 1945, 37 percent of female adults were working outside the home, up from about 28 percent in 1940. This was a notable transformation, but its social meaning was more limited than some later imagined. Although the iconic female worker of wartime propaganda posters was "Rosie the riveter" – a robust, no-nonsense, bandana-clad white woman confidently doing a man's job on a defense plant assembly line – only about 10 percent of female employees of any background labored in military production. Most did "women's work" as domestic servants, housecleaners, schoolteachers, nurses, secretaries, and the like, with women of color disproportionately clustered in menial occupations. And within manufacturing, where wages tended to be higher, women in 1945 earned only about 65 percent of what men did. Women between the ages of twenty and thirty-four (that is, in their peak years of childbearing and -rearing) were the least likely to join the workforce, partly as a consequence of inadequate child care services.

Meanwhile, hundreds of thousands of southern African Americans left rural and small-town communities to take war-related jobs in urban areas, sometimes elsewhere in the South but mostly in the North and West. Like other Americans, they benefited from the wartime prosperity, and those leaving the South found themselves in less oppressive (though hardly equitable) surroundings. About a million African Americans, nearly all of them male, served in the armed forces. Military units were segregated, and Black enlistees were mostly confined to menial and support roles, though some received combat assignments in the latter stages of the war as casualties among white soldiers mounted. Racial discrimination pervaded American society and institutions, and few civil rights victories were won in these years. At home and abroad, however, the conditions of wartime gave African Americans an expanded sense of what was possible, and a stronger basis for demanding equality, justice, dignity, and opportunity in the years ahead.

For some, the nation's entry into the war brought disaster. In the weeks after Pearl Harbor, there were widespread and unfounded fears, especially on the West Coast, that people of Japanese descent, US citizens and legal residents alike, would commit acts of sabotage to aid Japan. Catering to the hysteria, which drew on decades-old reserves of anti-Asian bigotry, and which many white politicians, business leaders, and civic activists exploited,

President Roosevelt issued an executive order authorizing military commanders to declare portions of the country military areas "from which any and all persons may be excluded." In the spring of 1942, the US Army proclaimed military zones in the states of Arizona, California, Oregon, and Washington and forcibly relocated more than 100,000 Japanese Americans and Japanese residents to inland internment camps, where most remained until the final stages of the war. Many of the camps were hastily constructed military-style barracks; some lacked plumbing facilities and were plagued by overcrowding and poor sanitation. In 1944, the US Supreme Court upheld the legality of Japanese internment. But in 1988, following a years-long campaign by Japanese American activists, Congress passed legislation apologizing for the injustice and authorizing reparations payments to surviving internees.

Overseas, US forces actively engaged in both of the main theaters of World War II: the European/Mediterranean theater, in which their chief partners were Britain and the Soviet Union; and the Asian/Pacific theater, where Britain and China were the principal allies. (The Soviet Union did not declare war on Japan until August 1945, just days before Japan announced its surrender.) In Europe, the Soviet Union bore the brunt of Nazi military power for most of the war. Joseph Stalin, the Soviet leader, repeatedly called for the establishment of an Anglo-US front in Western Europe to ease the pressure on the Soviet Union. Roosevelt and Winston Churchill, Britain's prime minister, recognized the necessity of opening a second front in German-occupied France, but logistical challenges and Anglo-US disagreements over tactics prevented this from happening for two and a half years. Stalin was outraged by what he saw as a deliberate Anglo-US policy of stalling on a second front so that the Soviets and the Nazis could battle each other into submission, a suspicion that would fuel cold war animosities after Germany's defeat.

But Anglo-US forces were not idle. In 1942 and 1943 they landed in North Africa and, aided by a separate British force pushing westward from Egypt and Libya, overran Nazi Germany's military encampment in Tunisia. From there, the Americans and the British invaded the island of Sicily and then proceeded to the "toe" of the Italian "boot." They fought their way up the Italian peninsula, battling mainly against occupying German forces, for Italy's government by then had surrendered and switched over to the Allied side. In June 1944, British, US, Canadian, and other troops mounted the long-awaited amphibious landings on the beaches of Normandy. After gaining this foothold, they liberated the rest of France from Nazi occupation and moved eastward into Belgium and Germany itself.

Meanwhile, Soviet forces, thrown back on their heels by Germany's invasion in mid-1941, had regained the initiative and begun driving the Nazis back across the broad expanse of Eastern Europe. By the end of 1944, nearly all of Eastern Europe was under Soviet occupation. By early 1945, the Soviets were pushing into Germany itself, where later that spring they linked up with the Anglo-US forces that had entered Germany from the west. As they closed in on their common foe, Soviet and Anglo-US forces liberated several Nazi death camps in German-occupied portions of Eastern Europe and within Germany itself. Some six million European Jews, and millions of others the Nazis deemed undesirable, had been worked to death at slave labor or exterminated outright. The surviving prisoners were living skeletons, and many perished in the weeks after liberation. Germany surrendered on May 8, 1945.

In the Pacific theater, US, British, and other Allied forces steadily contracted the scope of Japanese power, waging savage campaigns to oust Japanese forces from a string of Pacific islands. From air bases established on some of those islands, the United States launched hugely destructive firebombing raids against Tokyo and other Japanese cities. These air attacks culminated in America's dropping of two atomic bombs on Japan on August 6 and 9, 1945, causing tens of thousands of Japanese, most of them civilians, to die horribly and inaugurating the nuclear age. (The Soviet entry into the war against Japan occurred between the first and the second atomic bomb attacks.) On August 15, Japan's Emperor Hirohito announced his nation's surrender over the radio. On September 2, Japanese government and military representatives signed instruments of surrender aboard the USS *Missouri*.

More than sixteen million Americans served in uniform during World War II, the vast majority of them men. About 350,000 women served in various noncombat auxiliary units. Only a small fraction of male troops saw direct combat, but those who did often found themselves in hellish conditions, enduring, perpetrating, and witnessing barbarities that would haunt them for the rest of their lives. More than 400,000 American soldiers and sailors were killed and nearly 700,000 wounded, a staggering toll nonetheless dwarfed by the casualties of other nations. Up to three million Japanese, around six million Poles, some five million Germans, as many as twenty-seven million Soviets, and, in a conflict with Japan that began in 1937, perhaps twenty million Chinese lost their lives. Unlike the United States, each of these countries, and many others, incurred enormous civilian casualties. The war was a formative experience for Americans who lived through it and especially those who served in uniform, casting a long shadow into the postwar decades. In every presidential election from 1952 through 1996, at least one of the major-party candidates had served in the military during the war.[2] The 2000 election, whose two main contenders were born in 1946 (George W. Bush) and 1948 (Al Gore), was the first presidential race since 1948 with no World War II veteran on the ballot.

Of course, an experience as vast as World War II yielded multiple meanings, lessons, and legacies for Americans. In the broadest terms, however, the war lingered in the collective memory as a righteous endeavor in which Americans of all walks of life, on the battlefield and the home front, pulled together and, as FDR predicted they would, "won through to absolute victory." Much, far too much, was obscured in this telling: the racism, sexism,

[2] In the following pairings of major-party presidential candidates, World War II veterans are indicated in bold type: 1952 – **Dwight D. Eisenhower** versus Adlai Stevenson; 1956 – **Eisenhower** versus Stevenson; 1960 – **John F. Kennedy** versus **Richard M. Nixon**; 1964 – **Lyndon B. Johnson** versus **Barry Goldwater;** 1968 – **Nixon** versus Hubert H. Humphrey; 1972 – **Nixon** versus **George McGovern**; 1976 – **Gerald Ford** versus **Jimmy Carter**; 1980 – **Carter** versus **Ronald Reagan**; 1984 – **Reagan** versus Walter Mondale; 1988 – **George H. W. Bush** versus Michael Dukakis; 1992 – **Bush** versus Bill Clinton; 1996 – Clinton versus **Robert Dole**. With a slight stretching of the definition ("served militarily" as opposed to "served *in* the military"), the 1944 and 1948 elections could also be included. In each race, an incumbent president who had served as commander-in-chief of the armed forces during the war (first Franklin D. Roosevelt and then Harry S. Truman) ran against nonveteran Thomas E. Dewey.

homophobia, and vengefulness pervading American society and institutions, the ease with which the nation's political and military leaders ordered the slaughter of enemy civilians, the coercive banality of American patriotic discourse, and other pitfalls typical of a powerful nation in the thrall of total war. Yet there was enough truth to the myth to give it an enduring hold on the nation's public imagination. Ultimately, the problem with the inspiring World War II story lay less in its slight resemblance to actual events than in its meager relevance to the vexing challenges and murky triumphs Americans would face in the decades to come.

1 Wake Up Willie

From War to Postwar, 1945–1948

Introduction

It was November 1945, with autumn in full swing. Professional baseball's spring training was just weeks away, and soon after that the first postwar season would begin. *The Sporting News* ran a story about several white patrons of a barbershop, in an unnamed city, discussing reports that the Brooklyn Dodgers had just signed a Black ballplayer. Jackie Robinson would start at one of the Dodgers' farm teams in the minor leagues. If he did well, he would become the first African American in major league baseball since the late nineteenth century. Some of the barbershop customers jokingly groused about the change, predicting that the New York Yankees' club would be "turned into a minstrel show" and that white players would "have to cork up" – wear blackface – "to stay in the major leagues." But one patron spoke up in favor of integration. Black athletes had already competed in the Olympics, the National Football League, and professional boxing, he said; why not in major league baseball, too? "Well, it ain't never been done before," one of his companions objected. "We never threw an atomic bomb before either," came the retort. "Wake up Willie, this is 1945."

The scene was imaginary, an invention of the sports columnist Dan Daniel (born Daniel Margowitz; the Jewish writer knew something about prejudicial barriers to professional success). But it hinted at the new world of startling, promising, and frightening possibility awaiting Americans as their nation shifted from war to peace. By the international standards of late 1945, the country was truly fortunate. Unlike most other industrialized nations, the United States had escaped physical devastation during World War II. In fact, it had grown far more prosperous and powerful by waging it. Its military might dwarfed that of most other countries, and it was the sole possessor – and user – of the atomic bomb. American soldiers and sailors had experienced, and participated in, unspeakable violence, but the nation's civilians had been spared the carnage of war. In the coming years, they and the returning veterans would enjoy unprecedented prosperity, comfort, opportunity, and escapist pleasure.

By no means, however, were those blessings equally shared. In the early postwar years, as in previous eras, American society was deeply stratified along lines of race, class, and gender – realities that held back, and all too often harshly oppressed, millions of citizens.

The nation as a whole was scarred, even traumatized, by the recent memory of the Great Depression. Yet the imperative of mobilizing the society to wage global war had reshuffled domestic arrangements, restoring prosperity on a wide scale and creating opportunities for disadvantaged Americans to challenge long-standing inequities. And now, as peace returned, several key questions loomed. How could the nation ensure that the good times kept going? Should the federal government continue its recent interventions in the private economy, or draw back from them? Did wartime changes in the experiences of African Americans, wage laborers, women, and others augur more sweeping transformations in the postwar era? What role should the national government play in addressing *those* issues? Americans were deeply, often bitterly, divided on such questions, making the early postwar years a time of ceaseless and angry contention at home.

Overseas, America's relations with the Soviet Union, its wartime ally, rapidly deteriorated. Within a couple of years these two nations, each heading a coalition of European states, were locked in a cold war. The new crisis abroad profoundly shaped American domestic life. Fears of Soviet-inspired subversion at home – some of them justified, many of them overblown – caused the executive branch, Congress, state and local governments, and numerous private institutions to cast a suspicious and punitive gaze on many thousands of Americans. The resulting investigations, interrogations, loyalty hearings, and purges did turn up some actual subversives and spies. They also ruined countless lives. The climate of fear and hypervigilance had a chilling effect on American culture and public discourse, making it difficult, and sometimes dangerous, to offer challenging critiques of dominant institutions and views.

A central actor in most of these dramas was President Harry S. Truman, who was thrust into office by Franklin D. Roosevelt's sudden death in April 1945, just a few weeks before Germany's surrender. Truman had served as Roosevelt's vice president for under three months, and in that brief time he had been nowhere near FDR's inner circle. He knew little more about his government's policies than what he could read in the newspapers. Truman's prior experience as a county judge in Missouri and then a US senator from that state afforded him little expertise in foreign policy. He now had to guide the nation through the closing stages of a global war, a task of enormous complexity. He would then face the equally daunting challenge of overseeing a massive and intricate transition back to a peacetime economy. Truman was unadorned and plainspoken, blunt and irritable, almost wholly lacking in his predecessor's charm, expansiveness, cheerful deviousness, and ability to inspire. To many, he seemed too small for the job. Later generations would view Truman far more kindly. During his presidency, however, the palpable disappointment he aroused in many Americans, even those who preferred him to any of the available alternatives, contributed to the sour atmosphere enveloping so much of the nation's public life.

Postwar Dislocations

Across the country in mid-August 1945, Americans boisterously celebrated the news of Japan's surrender, creating the scenes of jubilation – parading, dancing, toasting, embracing – that have marked the occasion in the nation's public memory. But a mood of somberness also hung in the air, borne of the enormous destruction the war had inflicted around the world, and of the realization that the United States would be intimately involved in efforts to reorder the chaos. In brief remarks to well-wishers from the porch of the White House, President Truman said, "This is the great day … the day for the democracies," but "[w]e are faced with the greatest task we ever have been faced with. The emergency is as great as it was on Dec. 7, 1941" – the day Japan had attacked Pearl Harbor. Looming large in many minds were the two atomic bombs the United States had just dropped on Japan, each powerful enough to devastate an entire city. In the coming months, as more information about the fates of Hiroshima and Nagasaki emerged, that awareness would turn into genuine, and sometimes acute, anxiety.

Most Americans, though, were preoccupied with the here and now. The early postwar months were a time of widespread change, some of it welcome, some of it painful, almost all of it disorienting to greater or lesser degree. Hundreds of thousands of soldiers were coming home. Comparable numbers of laid-off defense plant workers, and dismissed employees of other industries no longer requiring their labor, were seeking new jobs and, in some cases, returning to the cities, towns, and farms they had inhabited before the war. Government and business planners had not expected a sudden Japanese surrender and were unprepared to execute such a rapid conversion to a peacetime economy. Americans thus contended with a severe housing shortage, labor unrest, bouts of runaway inflation, and temporary disappearances of consumer goods as companies readjusted their production lines to meet new patterns of demand. On the positive side, wartime rationing was ending. Better still, servicemen's families no longer had to follow war news with gnawing worry.

Some of the most dramatic changes occurred in the employment status of American women. During the war, over six million women had entered the paid labor market, largely to meet the new production needs generated by the military effort. As peace returned, war-related industries drastically reduced their workforces, laying off women at a much higher rate than men. At the peak of wartime production, women constituted 40 percent of the aircraft industry's employees; by 1948, that figure was 12 percent. Women also left jobs that were less directly connected to the war. In automobile manufacturing, women's share of the workforce shrank from 25 percent in 1944 to just 7.5 percent in 1946. There was broad societal support for the female exodus from the paid workforce. Opinion leaders in government, journalism, business, and advertising repeatedly exhorted working women to step aside so that returning servicemen could find jobs. Most Americans seemed to accept such thinking. In a fall 1945 opinion poll, 57 percent of women and 63 percent of men said that married women should not work outside the home. Many female employees willingly left their jobs to assume more purely domestic roles.

But many other women wished or needed to keep working, and in some quarters the pro-employment sentiment was overwhelming. A 1946 US Labor Department study found that, in ten wartime production areas across the country, an average of "about 75 percent of the wartime-employed women … expected to be part of the postwar labor force." A female steelworker frontally challenged the reigning assumptions: "I don't see why [women] should give up their position to men . . . . The old theory that a woman's place is in the home no longer exists. Those days are gone forever."

This was, of course, wishful thinking. From clergy, educators, psychologists, advice columnists, fashion designers, and others, there was growing social pressure on women (especially, but not only, those who were middle-class and white) to avoid paid employment, marry and have children early, concentrate on family needs, and be more "feminine" in appearance. In large measure, the population was moving in these same directions. First the Great Depression and then the war had caused many young people to hold off on marrying and having children. The arrival of peace reversed this trend, producing a surge of marriages and a "baby boom," which officially lasted from 1946 to 1964. During the Depression, the nation's annual birth rate had dipped below nineteen births per 1,000 members of the population; in 1947, it reached a postwar high of more than twenty-six births for every 1,000 people.

Even so, many women remained in the workplace, shortly returned to it, or soon entered it for the first time. After an immediate postwar plunge in female employment, the number of women workers began rising again. By 1950, 32 percent of women were in paid employment, four percentage points higher than in 1940. Rates of female employment continued their steady rise, matching the 1945 rate of 37 percent by 1962. These increases were not incompatible with the turn toward female domesticity. In the late 1940s and early 1950s, the largest cohort of women entering or staying in the workforce were aged forty-five to fifty-four, typically well past the early childrearing years.

One issue, though, threatened to make Americans' concerns about work, marriage, family, and everything else entirely moot. From the first terse bulletins about the atomic incineration of Hiroshima on August 6, 1945, large numbers of Americans recognized that a new, frightening stage of human history had begun. There was, to be sure, plenty of ghoulish *schadenfreude* over reports that Japan had suffered such a crippling blow. Almost immediately, however, American opinion leaders began voicing the obvious caveat. "We must assume," observed NBC radio news commentator Hans von ("H. V.") Kaltenborn on the evening of the 6th, "that with the passage of only a little time, an improved form of the new weapon we use today can be turned against us." Far from downplaying or sanitizing the problem, mainstream news outlets bore down on it relentlessly in the coming weeks and months. Detailed, ghastly eye-witness reports of the atom bombs' impact on Hiroshima and Nagasaki were presented in Congress and received wide coverage in the news. In November 1945, *Life* magazine ran a lengthy speculative article, with lurid illustrations, imagining atom bomb attacks on thirteen major American cities, including New York and Washington, DC, killing ten million Americans. Similar pieces ran in smaller periodicals around the country. From such appalling scenarios, it was but a short step to contemplate the utter extinction of humanity, a premonition that transcended American society and stirred peoples across the globe.

What to do? For millions of Americans, salvation now lay in the dissolution of squabbling national governments and in the establishment of a global sovereignty that could exert rational, humane control over the atom's terrifying power. "World government" was hardly a new idea, but the advent of "the Bomb" lent new urgency to the cause, which enjoyed its American heyday in the first eighteen months or so of the postwar era. Across the country, an impressive array of world-government clubs, conferences, lecture series, and publications sprang to life, nurtured by educators, journalists, church leaders, peace activists, and scientists. In that last category, wielding a special, poignant authority, were leading nuclear physicists who had helped to create the atomic bomb and now gazed in horror at their handiwork. The benevolent, disheveled figure of the émigré physicist Albert Einstein, whose pioneering research decades earlier had enabled later atomic breakthroughs, was a frequent presence in these discussions. Other influential one-worldists were *Nation* editor Freda Kirchwey, *Saturday Review* editor Norman Cousins, and University of Chicago president Robert Hutchins.

Some world-government advocates found encouragement in the emergence of the United Nations, which held its inaugural session in San Francisco in June 1945. The UN's advent, they said, demonstrated that the peoples of the world were ready for cooperation on a global scale. But most one-worldists criticized the UN for validating the nation-state as the primary unit of world politics. They were especially dismayed that the five permanent members of the UN Security Council – the United States, the Soviet Union, Britain, France, and China (which was not yet communist) – had the ability to veto that body's resolutions. Such arrangements only magnified the power of certain governments, rather than promoting true collective decision-making.

Drawing on opinion surveys, the historian Paul Boyer estimates that in 1945–1946 the world-government idea "won at least passive support from a third to a half of the American people," an impressive evolution for a population so recently immersed in the nationalistic dogmas of wartime mobilization. Much depended, however, on how the opinion surveys were worded. Typically, if a survey question spelled out the elements of sovereignty the United States would have to relinquish to make world government possible, support for the idea diminished. This vigilant outlook grew more pronounced over time, in response to a darkening international scene. In the early postwar months, many one-worldists were heartened by the fact that the world's second-greatest military power, the Soviet Union, had recently fought alongside the United States. But by late 1946 that alliance seemed a distant memory, and the makers of US foreign policy, who of course had no use for the world-government movement, felt practically no political pressure from that earnest quarter.

Early Tensions with the Soviet Union

The cold war began not because an America preferring to mind its own business finally felt compelled to counter aggressive Soviet moves. It began because Soviet actions disrupted existing US plans for reshaping the postwar world. Even if there had been no Soviet Union, the United States would have heavily involved itself in international affairs after 1945. Although the Truman administration intended to conduct a substantial drawdown of US forces, it insisted on keeping a formidable military machine in place. "We have learned the bitter lesson," Truman said in an October 1945 speech, "that the weakness of this great Republic invites men of ill-will to shake the very foundations of civilization all over the world." The nation must never again be vulnerable to a surprise attack in the manner of Pearl Harbor. Robust armed forces would also enable the United States to uphold the UN's mission of maintaining collective security – "to support a lasting peace," as Truman put it, "by force if necessary."

Economic considerations, too, pushed Washington to continue its active global role. The war effort had required the US government to spend massively; those outlays stimulated the domestic economy in ways that finally ended the Great Depression. But what would happen once the war and the related federal spending ended? Many feared a return of economic hard times. American government and business leaders generally agreed that this danger could be averted by expanding the scope of US economic engagement with the world. If more and more areas of the globe were open to US trade and investment, the American economy could keep growing and provide ample employment for its citizens. The only alternative to such a postwar system, Assistant Secretary of Commerce William Clayton warned in 1943, would be "to turn our country into an armed camp, police the seven seas, tighten our belts, and live by ration books for the next century or so." American leaders repeatedly argued, and in most cases probably genuinely believed, that an open international system would benefit people everywhere, but they were primarily concerned about their own nation's well-being. As the US economy was already so huge and dominant, it was bound to prosper in any system based on a "level playing field."

More immediately, at war's end the United States militarily occupied Germany and Japan, the former in concert with Britain, France, and the Soviet Union, the latter along with some British Commonwealth forces. In addition to having been major military powers, both of those defeated nations had, for decades, served as the economic and industrial hubs of their surrounding regions. Despite some uncertainty and internal debate in the war's closing months, US policy-makers increasingly agreed that Germany's and Japan's economic and industrial capabilities (though not their military power) had to be, somehow, revived and harnessed. Without those nations' active participation, it would be extremely difficult, and perhaps impossible, to construct a US-friendly global economic order.

In Japan, the United States was the dominant occupying power. In Germany, and in Europe as a whole, things were more complicated. By the time of Germany's surrender in May 1945, Soviet forces occupied the nations of Eastern Europe and a major portion of eastern Germany. Over the previous century and a half, Russia had endured repeated invasions by Western European powers using Eastern Europe as a staging area. Twice in the last thirty years those attacks had originated in Germany. Joseph Stalin, the Soviet leader, was adamant about preventing a repetition of that history. His favored strategies were crude: to ensure, by force if necessary, that all the governments of Eastern Europe were friendly to Moscow; and to keep Germany in a permanently weakened and deindustrialized state.

American leaders could live with Soviet domination of Eastern Europe. Although they would have much preferred to have full commercial and financial access to that region, its participation was not, in the end, vital to the success of their global economic vision.

Similarly, while the growing authoritarianism of Eastern Europe's pro-Soviet governments offended democratic principles, that issue alone did not call for a massive geopolitical reorientation. Western Europe was another story. Despite all the destruction it had suffered, Western Europe greatly exceeded Eastern Europe in industrial plant, capital accumulation, technological development, and prior cultural, trade, and banking ties to the United States. American leaders generally agreed that their nation's postwar prosperity – indeed, its chances of escaping another Great Depression – depended on the ability of American economic actors to trade with and invest in Western European countries. And Western Europe's economic revival, in turn, required the engine of Germany industry, which happened to be concentrated in the western portions of the country occupied by the United States, Britain, and France.

At its core, the US–Soviet cold war occurred because each superpower had plans for Germany that the other saw as profoundly threatening. Washington's (and London's) determination to rebuild German industry caused Stalin to fear that a resurrected Germany would again menace the Soviet Union. Moscow's desire to keep Germany down imperiled Western Europe's economic recovery, in which the United States had a vital stake. True, there were fundamental ideological disagreements between the two superpowers, one a capitalist democracy and the other a socialist dictatorship whose authoritarianism and brutality had grown especially severe under Stalin. Such differences were bound to cause considerable friction between the two nations, as indeed had happened before they became allies in World War II. Equally true, in the coming decades the cold war struggle would be waged on a vast range of issues and fronts: espionage, propaganda, internal subversion, decolonization, trade, and competition for supremacy in nuclear weapons and space. The zero-sum clash over Germany and Europe, however, formed the crux of the cold war standoff.

It would take a few years for the political struggle over Europe to emerge in its full dimensions. Not until early 1948 would Stalin's drive to extinguish all internal dissent in Eastern Europe become unmistakable (though evidence of this intention had started accumulating in the closing months of World War II); the final rupture over Germany happened in 1948–1949. In the meantime, the superpowers probed one another's intentions in disputes over Europe, the Middle East, atomic weapons, and other matters, each growing more convinced of the other's hostility and bad faith.

Tensions increased markedly in the spring of 1946. In a February 9 speech, Stalin urged Soviet citizens to rededicate themselves to the Marxist struggle in a world dominated by hostile capitalism. Rhetoric of this sort had emanated frequently from Moscow prior to its entry into World War II in 1941, but some American opinion leaders professed alarm to hear the resumption of such talk so soon after the Soviet Union had fought alongside the United States. *Time* magazine called the speech the most "warlike pronouncement uttered by any statesman since V-J [victory against Japan] Day." Supreme Court justice William O. Douglas, who opined frequently on public affairs, was even more hyperbolic, claiming that Stalin had issued a "Declaration of World War III." Other American commentators dismissed these reactions as overblown.

On February 22, George Kennan, an experienced diplomat at the US embassy in Moscow, sent Washington an 8,000-word analysis of the Soviets' outlook and behavior. Dubbed the "Long Telegram," it described the Soviet government as "a political force committed fanatically to the belief that with US there can be no permanent modus vivendi." Instead, Moscow saw the West as implacably hostile and was driven to foment constant crises with it. Kennan believed, however, that the Soviets did not want war and would retreat whenever they encountered firm resistance. If the Western nations made it clear they would defend their interests, and erected figurative barriers against the further extension of Moscow's power and influence, the Soviet system would lose vitality and then either collapse or mellow over time. The Long Telegram strongly resonated with US officials back home, as it offered both a plausible analysis of the Soviet challenge and an apparently realistic plan for meeting it. Kennan's recommended approach became known as the "containment" doctrine.

In early March, just days after Kennan sent his telegram, another disturbing assessment of Soviet behavior emerged, this time in public. Former British prime minister Winston Churchill, who had been voted out of office several months earlier, spoke at Westminster College in Fulton, Missouri. He declared that "an iron curtain" had "descended across the continent" of Europe; the nations to the east of it were subject "to a very high and increasing measure of control from Moscow." Churchill called for a Western alliance to check the expansion of this new Soviet-dominated sphere. Although Truman's presence on the stage with Churchill communicated tacit approval of these sentiments, the president stopped short of an explicit endorsement, partly to avoid antagonizing more liberal elements of the Democratic coalition, many of whom did criticize Churchill's remarks as unduly provocative.

Even so, the steady drift of US policy was toward a harder line on Soviet behavior, as soon became evident in a standoff over Iran. During the war, British and Soviet troops had jointly occupied Iran to keep that oil-rich nation out of Axis hands and to maintain an Allied supply route from the Persian Gulf to the Soviet Union (some of whose southern republics bordered Iran). The occupying powers had pledged to withdraw their forces by March 1946, and Britain observed its end of the agreement. But the Soviets, hoping to use their presence in northern Iran to pressure the Iranian government to grant them oil-drilling rights, refused to follow suit. The US Department of State vigorously protested Moscow's stance, and in short order Soviet forces did pull out. Although this outcome probably had as much to do with shrewd diplomacy by Iranian prime minister Ahmad Qavam as it did with Washington's tough talk, Truman and his advisers believed their firmness had paid off.

Another question of grave concern in 1946 was what international controls, if any, should be placed on the atomic bomb. As we saw, the shocking introduction of that weapon in the previous year had aroused widespread revulsion and alarm both at home and abroad. The UN had established an Atomic Energy Commission (AEC) to regulate the new technology, and it was politically imperative that the Truman administration cooperate with that body. Still, US officials worried about the consequences of relinquishing their nation's atomic monopoly. So they hedged their bets: they granted atomic scientists a significant role in drafting a scheme for international control but then toughened up the proposal in ways that left many of those scientists angry and disillusioned.

Figure 1.1 Director of Office of War Mobilization (and future Secretary of State) James Byrnes, President Harry Truman, and Secretary of Commerce Henry Wallace, 1945. Source: PhotoQuest / Archive Photos / Getty Images.

In a June 1946 submission to the AEC known as the Baruch Plan (named after Bernard Baruch, the prominent American financier charged with presenting it), the United States called for the establishment of an International Atomic Development Authority that would control all the raw materials and facilities needed for producing nuclear energy. Once this authority was in place, the United States would destroy its atomic weapons. Because Washington insisted on maintaining its nuclear monopoly in the interim, however, the Soviets rejected the Baruch Plan, and many American leftists and some liberals dismissed it as insincere (even as conservatives objected that it conceded too much). An opportunity for early arms control had slipped away.

By the summer of 1946, there was near-unanimity within the Truman administration about the futility of seeking further cooperation with the Soviet Union. The last significant holdout was Secretary of Commerce Henry Wallace. A staunch progressive, Wallace had served as secretary of agriculture in the 1930s and as vice president from 1941 to 1945. Many considered him FDR's true political heir, a sentiment sharpened by the realization that Wallace would now be president himself had Democratic Party bosses not booted him off the ticket in 1944 and replaced him with the centrist Truman. The commerce secretary thus had a stature in American politics out of keeping with his current cabinet rank. Wallace was dismayed by what he saw as a growing bellicosity in Washington, an attitude he feared would provoke unnecessary conflict with the Soviet Union. In a September 1946 speech before a left-leaning audience at New York's Madison Square Garden, Wallace warned that a "get tough with Russia" approach would be futile and dangerous. He also insisted that the Soviets had a legitimate sphere of interest in Eastern Europe, a position at odds with US policy.

An outraged James Byrnes, Truman's secretary of state, said he would resign unless the president repudiated Wallace's statements. Truman was in a ticklish position, for he had approved the controversial speech in advance. Clearly, the president had read the text too hastily, but Wallace had significantly departed from it, too. Once it had become clear that many audience members were boisterously pro-Soviet, the commerce secretary omitted some lines critical of Moscow and ad-libbed the statement "The danger of war is much less from communism than it is from imperialism – whether it be of the United States or England." After the speech, Truman extracted what he believed was a pledge from Wallace to stop speaking out on foreign policy. When Wallace made it clear he planned to keep on opining, Truman asked for his resignation. "He wants us to ... trust a bunch of adventurers in the Kremlin Politbureau," the president fumed in his diary. "I do not understand a 'dreamer' like that." Though unavoidable under the circumstances, Wallace's departure from Truman's cabinet further sharpened the anti-Soviet thrust of US policy.

Domestic Politics, 1945–1946

For liberal Democrats, Wallace's sacking was the latest in a string of disappointments emanating from the Truman administration, most of them touching on domestic policy. At the time of Truman's elevation, there had been little progressive legislation over the previous several years. This dearth had resulted first from conservative gains in the 1938 congressional elections and later from US involvement in World War II, during which Washington had sought the cooperation of big business rather than pressure it to give ground to workers and consumers. As the war neared its end, most liberals expected President Roosevelt to resume and expand New Deal policies upon the achievement of victory. Labor leaders harbored heady visions of a postwar industrial order in which workers not only enjoyed substantially increased wages and benefits but also cooperated with management on an equal footing to establish work conditions, production goals, and even the broad contours of the national economy. Roosevelt fed liberals' hopes by promising, in early 1944, a "Second Bill of Rights" guaranteeing housing, medical care, education, and gainful employment to all citizens. In September 1945, just weeks after Japan's surrender, Truman conspicuously endorsed FDR's vision when he presented Congress with a twenty-one-point program consisting of public works, hospital and housing construction, a national health insurance system, aid to education, an expansion of Social Security, continued federal protection of labor unions, and similar measures.

Although liberals applauded this ambitious agenda, by 1946 many of them were souring on Truman. The president hadn't helped his case by appointing centrists and conservatives to his cabinet and businessmen and corporate lawyers to other federal positions. Worse still, he got precious little of his 1945 program through the Congress, which, though still Democratically controlled, was under the sway of a coalition of Republicans and conservative southern Democrats. The few bills that did survive passed in gutted form. A case in point was the misnamed Full Employment Act, which authorized federal measures to achieve "maximum" rather than "full" employment, a provision allowing for a substantial unemployment rate. A proposed hospital construction bill emerged from the congressional sausage factory as a boon to builders and contractors. Given the political realities on Capitol Hill, Truman's program was bound to be an extremely hard sell; FDR himself would have had difficulty achieving it had he lived. But liberals blamed the disappointing results on the new president's political ineptitude or alleged lack of conviction. Conservatives, of course, resented Truman for even proposing these liberal measures; his failure to enact them turned their displeasure into contempt.

Compounding Truman's political woes was the vexing challenge of returning the nation to a peacetime footing, a massive undertaking for which neither experience nor ideology offered much useful guidance.[1] With the war now over, the US public expected a rapid demobilization of the twelve million soldiers and sailors in the armed forces. Across the country, families clamored for the immediate return of their loved ones in uniform. Especially vocal were servicemen's wives struggling under the burden of raising their children alone. Yet Truman's military advisers insisted that a large residual force was needed for occupying Germany and Japan. His economic advisers warned that the private economy could not absorb the sudden influx of millions of new jobseekers. In January 1946 the president voiced his opposition to full demobilization, sparking a furious public reaction, including protests by soldiers at overseas bases. "No boats, no votes," was their rallying cry, directed at both Truman and members of Congress. "You put us in the Army and you can get us out," a soldier wrote to his Oklahoma representative. "Either demobilize us or, when given the next shot at the ballot box, we will demobilize you." Bowing to the pressure, Truman worked with Congress to achieve a brisk drawdown of troops, who by June 1947 numbered just 1.6 million. (A year later, however, cold war tensions would prompt the administration and Congress to start building the armed forces back up.)

Although many had feared a crippling resumption of unemployment after the war, this did not happen. Instead, inflation posed the most immediate economic challenge. During the war, the short supply of consumer goods had created enormous pent-up demand; after Japan's surrender, Americans rushed to spend their accumulated savings. But new consumer items were slow to appear, driving up the prices of the goods that did materialize. To combat the problem, in early 1946 Truman asked Congress for authority to continue the federal price controls imposed during the war. When Congress granted Truman only some of the requested powers, he vetoed the legislation. The sudden lifting of price controls produced a sharp spike in inflation and a torrent of anger from US consumers. A chastened Truman requested, and promptly signed, another price control bill, this one not much different

[1] The United States did, of course, have to execute a transition to peacetime after World War I. But both the scale and the duration of America's participation in the Second World War greatly exceeded those of its participation in the First.

from the first. In October, he and Congress ended price controls for good, causing a further inflationary surge. Although supply soon caught up with demand and the scourge of inflation eased, the president's fumbling responses drew widespread ridicule. "To err is Truman," critics chortled.

This was also a period of extraordinary labor militancy. About five million American workers went on strike between August 1945 and August 1946. In some cases, they struck for the right to share in management decisions. More often, they sought increased wages and benefits at a time when rampant inflation threatened hard-won gains from previous labor struggles. As a rule, business owners adamantly refused to grant workers any decision-making role but proved willing to make concessions on wages, cost-of-living increases, job security, and pensions. Indeed, they compromised on the latter issues largely to avoid having to give ground on the first one. Workers striking in major industries gained, on average, an 18 percent wage increase in 1946. Their strikes disrupted, and sometimes threatened to paralyze, the nation's largest and most vital industries, such as coal, shipping, railroads, and auto manufacturing. Truman was generally sympathetic to labor but drew the line at actions that seemed to imperil the national economy. When the United Mine Workers went on strike that spring, he seized control of the coal mines and forced a settlement. Around the same time, he responded to a nationwide railroad strike by asking Congress for the authority to draft idle rail workers. (Coincidentally, news of the strike's settlement arrived just as Truman was addressing Congress.) The president's actions enraged many union members and their liberal allies. The New York leader of the transportation workers' union called Truman "the number one strike breaker of the American bankers and railroads."

As wrenching as all of these disruptions were, they appear in retrospect as the short-term convulsions of a fundamentally sound economy undergoing a massive conversion from war to peace. War-related prosperity had equipped the broad American public with unprecedented purchasing power. Once industry completed its transition back to producing civilian goods, the economy embarked on a long-term expansion during which, by most measures, Americans' standard of living dramatically improved. Inflation became manageable, and, over the following decade, the unemployment rate mostly stayed under 5 percent. The federal government stoked the prosperity by implementing the Servicemen's Readjustment Act, popularly known as the GI Bill of Rights, which Congress had passed in 1944. The GI Bill provided veterans with low-interest loans for purchasing homes and starting businesses and with public grants for seeking job training and postsecondary education. By 1956, 7.8 million veterans had availed themselves of the program. The benefits were hardly bestowed equitably. Banks dispensing the government-backed loans often denied service to African American veterans. Many colleges and universities, especially in the South but not only there, blocked admission to Black applicants. Yet, for all these limitations, the GI Bill lifted millions of Americans into the middle class, creating a deep reserve of purchasing power that would sustain the US economy for decades to come.

In 1946, however, American society was in genuine turmoil, and few were satisfied with the drift of events. The Democrats, who had held the presidency and both houses of Congress for nearly fourteen years, seemed particularly vulnerable as the 1946 midterm elections approached. Truman had alienated the party's liberals without winning appreciable support from centrists or conservatives. By September, his approval rating had sunk to 33 percent. The Republicans' pithy slogan for the midterms was "Had enough?" That question, writes the historian Mark S. Byrnes, "was brilliantly designed to mean all things to all people. It captured both short-term frustration with Truman, and a longer-term sense that the Democrats had held the reins of power for too long." In November, Republicans surged to victory in both chambers, gaining fifty-five seats in the House and twelve in the Senate. Truman seemed so discredited by the outcome that Senator J. William Fulbright, an Arkansas Democrat, urged him to appoint Senator Arthur Vandenberg, a Michigan Republican with a reputation for bipartisanship, secretary of state; Truman should then resign and make Vandenberg president. (There was no vice president from 1945 to 1949, and until 1947 the secretary of state was next in the line of presidential succession.) Truman dismissed the advice, calling its purveyor "Halfbright." It was indeed premature to count the president out.

A Deepening Cold War

Both at home and abroad, 1947 and 1948 were years of continued turmoil. The difference was that, whereas the domestic realm remained subject to bitter partisan strife, foreign relations provided an occasion for significant, and highly consequential, bipartisan cooperation. In February 1947, British officials informed their US counterparts that severe financial difficulties were forcing Britain to end its economic assistance to Turkey and to withdraw its troops from Greece. This was worrisome news to Truman and his advisers. Turkey faced diplomatic pressure from the Soviet Union, which demanded a role in policing the Turkish straits connecting the Black Sea to the Mediterranean, as well as the cession of some Turkish land bordering the Soviet Union. The Soviets had tried to intimidate Turkey by deploying troops near its territory and issuing menacing statements. In Greece, a conservative monarchy battled a leftist insurgency dominated by local communists. The Soviet threat was clear enough in the first case but mostly conjectural in the second. Stalin had declined to aid the Greek insurgents, in keeping with an earlier pledge to recognize Britain's preeminence in that country. If the rebels nonetheless prevailed, however, they might willingly orient Athens toward Moscow.

To prevent the Soviets from gaining a foothold in the Mediterranean, from which, conceivably, they could further extend their influence into Western Europe or the Middle East, the Truman administration decided to ask Congress for $400 million in aid to Turkey and Greece. The challenge was persuading the House and Senate, both now under the control of tight-fisted, and in some cases isolationist, Republicans, to appropriate such a substantial sum (the equivalent of about $5.2 billion in 2022 dollars). In a March 1947 address to a joint session of Congress, Truman situated the Turkish and Greek crises within a worldwide struggle between freedom and totalitarianism. He warned that Congress's failure to help Turkey and Greece could cause both countries to fall under totalitarian control. In a statement pundits called the Truman Doctrine, the president declared, "I believe that it must be the policy of the United States to support free peoples who are resisting attempted subjugation by armed minorities or by outside pressures." Congress voted the money for Turkey and Greece, both of which remained squarely within the Western camp (in Greece's case after a vicious civil war in which both the US-supported regime and the leftist insurgents committed numerous atrocities). Beyond the Mediterranean, Truman's stark language promoted a black-and-white view of the cold war struggle ill suited to the morally ambiguous international challenges that Americans would actually face in the decades ahead.

Even as it secured congressional aid to Greece and Turkey, the Truman administration was preparing a plan for Europe as a whole. As of the spring of 1947, Western Europe remained crippled by wartime devastation and suffered major shortages of coal, oil, food, and other staples. Industry was nearly paralyzed. These bleak conditions strengthened the appeal of local communist parties, which, by blaming the economic misery on the failings of capitalism, could compete successfully in democratic elections. Once in power, US officials feared, the communists would turn toward the East bloc, permitting a peaceful Soviet takeover of Western Europe. If Moscow's domination of Eastern Europe was already dismaying to American leaders, the loss of Western Europe would be intolerable. As noted, Washington's plans for a congenial economic climate worldwide, and thus its hopes for continued prosperity at home, depended on the ability of American economic actors to trade with and invest in the more economically advanced nations of Western Europe. The surge of popular support for Western European communists now threw that prospect into doubt.

The Truman administration's answer to the threat was to try to ease the economic deprivation that seemed to benefit local communists. In what became known as the Marshall Plan – because it was unveiled in a June 1947 speech by former army chief of staff General George Marshall, who had recently succeeded James Byrnes as secretary of state – the United States pledged billions of dollars to aid Europe's economic recovery. The central idea of the plan, which Congress approved in March 1948, was for European nations to take the lead in reviving their economies. If they did so on terms promoting private enterprise, transparency, and liberalized trade, they could count on generous US assistance. At least in theory, the Soviet Union and the Eastern European nations were eligible to receive Marshall Plan aid. As Marshall had stated in his 1947 speech, "Our policy is directed not against any country or doctrine but against hunger, poverty, desperation, and chaos." Still, US officials expected that the Soviets would balk at the plan's underlying conditions and turn down the aid. Sure enough, the Soviets not only rejected the Marshall Plan but pressured Eastern European nations to do so as well. The Truman administration had shrewdly maneuvered the Soviets into bearing the onus of spurning a constructive international initiative.

Meanwhile, Western European nations enthusiastically accepted US aid, which from 1948 to 1952 amounted to $13 billion. The Marshall Plan achieved its main objectives. The economies of Western Europe rapidly recovered, and communist influence there correspondingly waned. The initiative was also of considerable benefit to American business, as the US assistance enabled Europeans to purchase more and more American goods. With some justification (especially if one didn't look too closely at the Greek case), US officials saw themselves as "doing well by doing good" – as anchoring their own nation's security and prosperity in the contentment of millions of ordinary Europeans.

Even so, American leaders were not above engaging in a little subversion when it suited them. In the spring of 1948, Italy held parliamentary elections. The country's communist party, widely respected for its years of resistance to Benito Mussolini's Fascist regime, seemed capable of unseating the incumbent Christian Democratic Party, a centrist formation. Washington threw its weight behind the Christian Democrats. Although much of this effort unfolded publicly, a key element was a covert operation mounted by the Central Intelligence Agency, which had come into being the previous year. Secretly, the CIA funneled cash into the campaign coffers of the Christian Democrats, who in April decisively won the elections. The result owed less to American clandestine meddling than to the Vatican's open denunciation of the communists – a decisive political intervention in that overwhelmingly Catholic country – but American spooks quietly congratulated themselves on a job well done. This would not be the last US covert action to combat a real or fanciful communist threat.

Geopolitically, the Marshall Plan's main impact was to accelerate and harden the division of Europe. The more the plan succeeded in revitalizing Western Europe, the more alarmed Stalin became about the security of the Eastern sphere. In reacting, the Soviet leader badly overplayed his hand. He clamped down so tightly on Eastern Europe that the United States and its Western European partners, which until now had mostly limited themselves to economic and political forms of containment, began resorting to significant military measures as well.

Stalin's first overreaction was in Czechoslovakia, where since 1945 communists and noncommunists had shared power in a coalition government. In February 1948, with Moscow's approval, the communists seized exclusive control of the government, extinguishing what remained of Czechoslovakia's democratic institutions.

Stalin's second overreaction – and a far more consequential blunder – occurred in Germany. Because of western Germany's enormous industrial potential, the United States and Britain had worked to revive that region and facilitate its integration into the Western European economy. (France, which over the last several decades had far more directly borne the brunt of German military power, was less enthusiastic about Germany's economic revival.) In early 1948, Washington and London took the first steps toward establishing a separate West German state, eventually including the introduction of a new currency for use in the Western occupation zones. This move intensified Stalin's fear that a revived Germany, even if confined to a western rump, would again be poised to threaten the Soviet Union. His response was to squeeze the Western allies in Berlin. Though well within the Soviet zone, Berlin, like Germany as whole, was occupied by all four of the victorious powers. The US, British, and French sectors were located in the western half of the city, forming an enclave of Western governance in the heart of eastern Germany. The Western allies were able to provision their sectors via guaranteed overland access routes. In June 1948, the Soviet government announced a land blockade around Berlin, barring train and automobile traffic from entering the city from the west. Evidently, Stalin sought either to pressure the Western

Figure 1.2 Children in West Berlin cheering the flight of a US cargo plane, *c*. 1948. Source: Bettmann / Getty Images.

powers to abandon their plans for a West German state or, if this failed, to expel them from Berlin and thereby consolidate the Soviet zone in Germany.

The Truman administration pondered its options. Acceding to the blockade seemed out of the question. That would undermine Western Europeans' confidence in US leadership and imperil the effort to harness West Germany's economic and industrial potential. A retreat from Berlin, Marshall warned, would spell the "failure of the rest of our European policy." It would also make Truman seem weak at home just as he was preparing to seek election in his own right that November. (He was still serving out FDR's fourth term.) How, then, to resist the Soviet move? Some US military leaders advocated challenging the blockade on the ground, predicting that the Soviets would back down and let the Western trucks and trains through. Of course, if Moscow did *not* back down, the resulting clash could well ignite a general shooting war. Another option, provisioning West Berlin by air, seemed a much safer bet. This could be done without automatically bringing rival militaries into physical contact, as a blockade-busting convoy obviously would do. To disrupt an aerial supply effort, the Soviets would have to shoot down food-bearing cargo planes. Western leaders calculated – correctly, it turned out – that their adversaries would be unwilling to go that far.

And so, for nearly a year, a brisk rotation of US and British planes ferried food, coal, and other necessities into two airfields in Berlin. At the peak of the operation, a plane landed every ninety seconds, a pace that stunned and disheartened Soviet military officers stationed in the city. As one of them recalled years later, "[A plane] would appear overhead, another would disappear over the horizon, and a third emerge, one after another, without interruption, like a conveyor belt." Soviet aircraft occasionally harassed the US and British planes, but they never fired on them. Throughout the crisis, Washington and London foregrounded the humanitarian nature of the Berlin airlift. Nonetheless, Truman subtly threatened the

Soviets by sending sixty B-29 bombers capable of carrying atomic weapons (though not actually outfitted with them) to British airbases.

In May 1949 Stalin lifted the blockade, tacitly conceding that the Western powers could remain in Berlin. That same month, a separate West German state came into existence, to be followed in October by the establishment of East Germany. The country's division was replicated in Berlin, though as yet no physical barrier ran through the city.

In the spring of 1949, the United States joined with Canada, Britain, France, Italy, and several other Western European nations to form the North Atlantic Treaty Organization (NATO). The member states were bound by a mutual defense agreement; an attack on one would be treated as an attack on all. (For the time being, West Germany was kept out of the alliance; it became a member in 1955.) In July 1949, the US Senate approved the treaty by an 82–13 vote. The establishment of NATO, to which the East bloc later responded by creating the Warsaw Pact, sealed Europe's hostile division for the next four decades.

In the Middle East, a bitter impasse of far longer duration – indeed, one that remains unresolved today – was also taking shape at this time. Here again the US role was decisive. In early 1947, Britain announced it would soon withdraw its forces from Palestine, which it had governed under a League of Nations mandate since the early 1920s, and allow the United Nations to adjudicate the competing claims of Zionist Jews and Palestinian Arabs. The Zionist cause had gained powerful impetus and broad international sympathy following the revelation of Nazi Germany's murder of six million Jews during World War II. The Palestinian Arabs' perspective was less well understood around the world. A special UN committee investigated the issue and proposed that Palestine be divided into a Jewish and an Arab state. The Zionists accepted the proposal, but the Arab states and the Palestinians, seeing the Zionists as European colonists of Arab land, adamantly rejected the partition plan. In November 1947, the UN General Assembly approved partition. Violence erupted between Zionists and Palestinians, with Zionists eventually gaining the upper hand. In May 1948, the Zionists proclaimed the independent state of Israel, prompting several surrounding Arab countries to go to war against the new state. Israeli forces handily rebuffed the attacks and seized a larger share of Palestine than had been initially allotted to the Jewish state. By the time an armistice was reached in early 1949, about 750,000 Palestinian civilians had fled or been driven from their homes in what became Israel, most of them settling in refugee camps in neighboring countries. The Israeli government barred their return.

Against the advice of top State Department officials, who worried about antagonizing Arab countries, Truman strongly supported Israel's creation, first by vigorously endorsing the UN partition plan and then by immediately recognizing the newly proclaimed Jewish state. In part, the president sought to please American supporters of Zionism, Jews and gentiles alike, whose gratitude might bolster his 1948 election prospects. In part, he hoped to validate the work of the UN, a heavily US-dominated institution in those days. Mostly, however, Truman acted out of humanitarian concern for Jewish Holocaust survivors and because he saw no workable alternative to partition. Both political parties and the bulk of US public opinion warmly celebrated Israel's creation. Few Americans understood the Arabs' – or, for that matter, the State Department's – objections to Zionism, even though

Map 1.1 The Cold War in Europe, 1949–1955. Source: Created by Joe LeMonnier.

the most powerful of those critiques drew on a principle Americans had long championed: the right of national self-determination. A lopsided majority of Palestine's population clearly and vehemently rejected the proposal to convert 56 percent of the country into a Jewish state. (Jews then constituted only about a third of Palestine's population.) With Washington's forceful backing, the international community was imposing partition anyway. Truman's actions aroused deep anger in the Arab world, complicating US Middle East policy for decades to come.

The Struggle for Civil Rights

A key facilitator of the Arab–Israeli armistice was an American political scientist-turned-diplomat named Ralph Bunche. In 1948–1949, Bunche was the UN's chief mediator of the Middle East conflict. In 1950, he became the first person of African descent to receive the Nobel Peace Prize. Taking his own measure of the diplomat's talents, in the spring of 1949 Truman offered to appoint Bunche assistant secretary of state for Near Eastern affairs. Bunche declined the job, citing, among other reasons, his unwillingness to relocate from New York City to Washington, DC, where strict racial segregation prevailed. "It's extremely difficult for a Negro to maintain even a semblance of human dignity in Washington," he told a reporter. "At every turn he's confronted with places he can't enter because of his color – schools, hospitals, hotels, restaurants, theatres, bars, lunch counters, and rest rooms, not to mention widespread job barriers." If Bunche's renown suggested a new world of possibility for Black Americans in the early postwar years, his indignant recitation of Jim Crow[2] realities in the nation's capital underscored the hard limits on the era's racial progress. It also signaled African Americans' growing determination to surmount those obstacles.

Most African Americans, of course, enjoyed none of Bunche's privileges. Yet World War II had brought new opportunities and prospects for change. More than a million Blacks had served in uniform during the war, gaining skills useful in peacetime and, in many cases, a new sense of civic entitlement. They had bled for freedom and democracy abroad; who now dared deny them those blessings at home? The fact that one of the main enemies in the war, Nazi Germany, was fanatically committed to racist doctrines gave a further boost to American critiques of racial discrimination. Stateside, war-related job opportunities caused hundreds of thousands of African Americans to migrate from rural areas in the South to urban centers throughout the country. Those leaving the South escaped Jim Crow oppression and found themselves in more fluid, though still highly stratified, circumstances. Unlike southern Blacks, who were kept away from the polls by a web of law, custom, intimidation, and deadly violence, African Americans in the North could vote, and they became a constituency the major parties could not entirely ignore. North and South, a more urbanized Black population formed a consumer market for businesses to court. Urban African Americans

[2] "Jim Crow" laws and customs enforced racial segregation and discrimination in the South, the term "Jim Crow" being a pejorative term for a Black person.

were also better equipped (such as by the proliferation of Black-run newspapers and radio stations) to publicize racial injustice and organize to combat it.

During the war, the National Association for the Advancement of Colored People (NAACP) and other civil rights groups had mounted broad-based antiracism campaigns. With the return of peace, these efforts intensified. Across the South, returning Black veterans tried to register to vote and encouraged other African Americans to do the same. White vigilante groups, often with the blessing of law enforcement, brutally resisted these efforts. Medgar Evers, a young army veteran who later became a key NAACP officer, joined four other Black veterans in trying to vote in Decatur, Mississippi, only to be driven off from the polling place by several white men wielding pistols. In Taylor County, Georgia, four white men shot and killed Maceo Snipes, another Black army veteran, after he voted in that state's 1946 Democratic primary election. Police forces, too, joined in the violence. In the first six weeks of 1946, officers reportedly killed five Black veterans for attempting to register others to vote. Beyond overt violence, white authorities had countless ways to keep African Americans from voting, including the threat of job loss, eviction, or denial of credit and the blatantly unfair administering of literacy tests. Still, the voter registration drives met with some success. By 1947, 12 percent of Black adults were registered in the South, up from just 2 percent in 1940.

But voter suppression was only part of the story. Repeatedly in those early postwar months, African Americans were viciously disciplined for other perceived infractions against the racial order. At a bus station in Bateson, South Carolina, police officers savagely assaulted Isaac Woodard, a Black army veteran who had exchanged sharp words with a white bus driver. The officers clubbed and jabbed Woodard with their nightsticks, blinding him for life. At the Moore's Ford Bridge east of Atlanta, Georgia, a white mob tied two young Black married couples to an oak tree and shot them dead. One of the lynched men had allegedly stabbed and wounded his white landlord. The other was a war veteran. "Up until George went into the army," one of his murderers later said, "he was a good n-----. But when he came out, they thought they were as good as any white people."

Another pattern of racist oppression in the South, one that had unfolded for generations but that civil rights activists were better able to publicize by the 1940s, was sexual violence against African American women. Throughout the decade, local NAACP offices received numerous reports of white men abducting Black women, sometimes by luring them with offers of employment, and taking them to secluded areas and raping them. In 1947, a white businessman in Meridien, Mississippi, promised a Black teenaged girl a babysitting job but took her to a tavern instead of his home. When the girl refused to enter the establishment with him, he beat her unconscious, raped her, tied her to the bumper of his car, and dragged her through the town. Miraculously, the girl survived. Civil rights organizations and Black newspapers raised enough publicity about such assaults to oblige county prosecutors to put some of the alleged perpetrators on trial. Almost invariably, however, all-white juries refused to convict.

Civil rights advocates realized there was little prospect of quelling the violence without federal support, and they relentlessly pressured President Truman to take a stand. In the

Figure 1.3 Isaac Woodard with his mother, Eliza Woodard, at a benefit show in his honor in New York City, 1946. Source: FPG / Archive Photos / Getty Images.

summer of 1946, members of the National Association of Colored Women's Clubs picketed the White House; "Speak! Speak! Mr. President," demanded one of their signs. The NAACP and other groups formed the National Emergency Committee Against Mob Violence, which staged a 15,000-person march to the Lincoln Memorial. A native of Missouri, where slavery had existed until 1865, Truman was culturally in tune with many white segregationists. Yet he also recognized African Americans' growing importance to the Democratic coalition, and as a senator he had supported some civil rights legislation. The president was genuinely disturbed, moreover, by the upsurge of supremacist violence in the South, especially when its targets were war veterans. In late 1946, he convened a panel of distinguished civic and business leaders – thirteen whites and two African Americans – to examine the issue. The report of this Civil Rights Committee, issued in October 1947, condemned the racial status quo. It called for the desegregation of the armed forces, antilynching legislation, congressional action to uphold voting rights, the establishment of a civil rights division within the Department of Justice (DOJ), and similar measures. Truman promptly endorsed the report. Months earlier, he had become the first American president to address the NAACP, pledging to "make the Federal Government a friendly, vigilant defender of the rights and equalities of all Americans." Any bid for US global leadership, he noted, "should rest on practical evidence that we have been able to put our own house in order."

Truman's gestures pleased many civil rights activists, but his record of concrete follow-up was mixed. The president did ask Congress to act on many of the Civil Rights Committee's recommendations, but he declined to press the case vigorously on Capitol Hill, where he knew segregationist forces were deeply entrenched. In July 1948, largely in response to a threat by the Black labor leader A. Philip Randolph to organize a massive civil disobedience campaign, Truman issued an executive order desegregating the armed forces. The desegregation order was a significant achievement, though it was not implemented until after the outbreak of the Korean War in mid-1950. As much as Truman wished to assure African Americans of his sympathy and support, he worried about antagonizing the white supremacists who remained so dominant in his party.

For the nation at large, race relations unfolded most visibly on the baseball diamond. Although Black athletes had played on white-dominated teams in the nineteenth century, organized baseball had been strictly segregated since the 1890s. Barred from competing in both the major and the minor leagues, Black ballplayers performed in an assortment of Negro Leagues. During World War II, baseball came under a version of the integrationist pressures operating on the wider society. Here, the chief proponents of change were African American players, sportswriters, and fans and white urban politicians responsive to growing Black constituencies (and capable of coercing teams by threatening to withhold city permits). Beyond baseball, the wide celebrity of Jesse Owens, track-and-field star of the 1936 Olympic Games in Berlin, and Joe Louis, world heavyweight boxing champion from 1937 to 1949, showed that many whites would now cheer for Black athletes. At war's end, most white baseball team owners and executives opposed hiring Black players. An exception was Branch Rickey, president of the Brooklyn Dodgers, whose motives were at once noble and self-serving: to strike a blow against unreasoning prejudice and to attract Black spectators to Dodgers games. In October 1945 Rickey signed Jackie Robinson, an army veteran playing in the Negro National League, to join the Montreal Royals, the Dodgers' main farm team, and thus break the minor leagues color line. In April 1947, Robinson made front-page news when he debuted for the Dodgers, becoming the first major-league Black ballplayer of the twentieth century.

Robinson's highly public reintegration of the majors demanded every ounce of his forbearance and self-control, all the more so because the athlete was naturally proud and short-tempered. Several of his own teammates initially shunned him, though the obvious fact that their professional success was bound up with his soon brought them around. Opposing players, of course, had every incentive to stay nasty. From the dugouts, they taunted Robinson with racial epithets. When he batted, pitchers threw fastballs at his head. On the infield, sliding base runners aimed spikes at his shins. The rookie seethed inside but almost never let it show, realizing that any display of emotion on his part could bring the entire experiment to an end. While traveling out of town, Robinson was sometimes barred from staying at the same hotels as his teammates. He received death threats in the mail.

Overall, though, public reactions were favorable. Robinson became a folk hero to many African Americans, and fans of all backgrounds flocked to Dodgers games. At first, it appears, white spectators were drawn mainly by curiosity, but this increasingly gave way to appreciation of the athlete's abilities. Robinson was an outstanding infielder and an even better hitter and base runner, delighting crowds with his audacity in stealing bases, and sometimes home plate. The Baseball Writers' Association of America named him Rookie of the Year for 1947. Outside the South, the white-dominated press gave Robinson friendly coverage, celebrating his rise as an American success story. This portrayal was well intentioned, but it seriously understated the racism he had encountered throughout his life. (Robinson grew up in Southern California, which many whites fancifully saw as an egalitarian idyll.) Four other Black players joined the major leagues in 1947. Although baseball's integration in subsequent years proceeded more slowly than many expected, Robinson's initial breakthrough did help to foster, in society at large, a new sense of what was possible. The spectacle of a Black athlete stoically enduring racist abuse, while doggedly refusing to be deterred from his quest, caught the attention of millions of white Americans and surely made some of them more receptive to future efforts to combat racial injustice.

The Red Scare

Even as restrictions loosened in one realm, they grew more rigid and onerous in another. For decades, American conservatives had charged that progressive social and economic policies (whether enacted or merely proposed) were tainted by communist influence. In part, this was a self-serving and disingenuous way to stigmatize ideas opposed on other grounds. But it also reflected the plain fact that American communists, many taking their cues directly from Moscow, were active in US politics and labor organizing. The Communist Party of the United States of America (CPUSA) enjoyed its greatest influence in the 1930s, a consequence of the Great Depression, which discredited capitalism, and of the rise of fascism in Europe, which caused many left-of-center Americans to seek a more militant creed with which to combat the far right. In the mid- to late 1930s, the Soviet government instructed communist parties abroad to suspend their revolutionary rhetoric and join with noncommunists in an antifascist "Popular Front." When American communists heeded this call, they became more respectable in progressive and liberal circles. By late 1938, the CPUSA had about 82,000 members. Hundreds of thousands of other Americans never joined the party but worked alongside it to advance a host of progressive causes, such as antifascism, antiracism, social welfare, and workers' rights.

The Popular Front era abruptly ended in the fall of 1939, when, after the Soviet Union signed a nonaggression pact with Nazi Germany (an event that helped to trigger the outbreak of World War II), the CPUSA dropped its antifascist campaign and called for US neutrality in the ensuing conflict. The party's standing among liberals and progressives waned. But Germany's military attack against the Soviet Union in June 1941, and Japan's bombing of Pearl Harbor the following December, brought the United States and the Soviet Union into the war on the same side. The two nations' alliance over the next three and a half years permitted American communists to regain much of their domestic influence.

War's end brought another political reversal, as the onset of the cold war dramatically inflamed the old American suspicions about domestic communism. As in earlier times, the attitude reflected both opportunism and reality. It was certainly convenient for business advocates, segregationists, and critics of the New Deal to allege that labor unions, civil rights organizations, and the whole federal bureaucracy were lousy with communist agitators. That said, communists *were* at the helm of some unions, and their secretive and dogmatic behavior had at times alienated others in the labor movement. More explosively, there were charges of espionage and other serious security breaches. In June 1945, an (illegal) Federal Bureau of Investigation (FBI) raid on the offices of *Amerasia*, a small scholarly journal with some communist associations, turned up classified State Department documents, stirring allegations that communist-sympathizing government officials had leaked the materials. In the spring of 1946, newspapers reported that several Canadian communists in their government's employ had been caught passing atomic secrets to the Soviet Union, and that the spy ring might extend to US atomic facilities. Meanwhile, FBI agents were secretly interviewing an ex-communist named Elizabeth Bentley. She alleged that dozens of federal employees, many of them New Dealers with Popular Front ties, had shared sensitive military information with Soviet officials during the war. Although Bentley's charges would not become public until July 1948, the FBI passed the names of some of the suspect employees to selected members of Congress conducting their own antisubversion investigations.

Of the congressional committees looking into domestic communism, the best known was the House Committee on Un-American Activities, whose initial letters journalists rearranged to form the more pronounceable "HUAC." Established in 1938 to address the twin threats of fascist and communist subversion, HUAC had become exclusively preoccupied with the latter. And, as the Republicans took control of Congress in early 1947, the red-hunting committee kicked into high gear. That fall, HUAC captured the nation's attention by subpoenaing figures from the movie industry to testify about communist infiltration of Hollywood. Although most witnesses cooperated, ten directors and screenwriters, all current or former CPUSA members, refused to discuss their political affiliations, citing their First Amendment right of free association. Several of these hostile witnesses engaged in shouting matches with their interrogators, and federal marshals physically hauled some of them away from the witness table. The Hollywood Ten, as they became known, were convicted of contempt of Congress and received one-year prison terms. Scores of other Hollywood figures tainted by communist association found themselves on a private blacklist that barred them from working openly in the film industry. Over the next several years, HUAC and other investigating bodies turned their sights on numerous American industries and institutions, grilling thousands of Americans about political activities and associations that, just ten or fifteen years earlier, had raised few eyebrows.

The system tended to be forgiving of ex-communists who fully cooperated with their interrogators by confessing and repudiating their communist pasts – and by fingering others who may have belonged to the party. But ex-communists not wishing to "name names" faced excruciating dilemmas. After the Hollywood Ten and other witnesses failed to find cover under the First Amendment, ex-communists increasingly relied on the Fifth Amendment's protection against self-incrimination. Yet this provision, too, often proved unavailing. If witnesses, pleading the Fifth, declined to answer any questions at all, they might escape a

Figure 1.4 The House Committee on Un-American Activities opening its investigation into communist influence in Hollywood, 1947. Representative (and future President) Richard M. Nixon is seated at the questioners' table, second from right. Source: Bettmann / Getty Images.

finding of contempt, but they were widely assumed to be guilty of communist affiliation and risked losing their jobs or being placed on professional blacklists. If they agreed to testify about themselves but not others, then they *could* be prosecuted for contempt, as courts usually forbade such selective invocation of the Fifth. And if they did name names, they had to live with the shame of betraying old friends. Although most witnesses followed this last course, many others suffered severe legal, professional, social, and personal repercussions for running afoul of the inquisitions in some way. A handful committed suicide.

Truman was annoyed by the Republicans' investigative zeal, seeing it more as a vehicle for partisan grandstanding than as a sincere effort to safeguard the nation. True, galling security breaches had come to light, but most of those had occurred during the war, when Americans and Soviets were fighting on the same side. The CPUSA's membership was now rapidly dwindling. Still, Truman saw the danger of letting Republicans monopolize the issue. In March 1947, he issued Executive Order 9835, which empowered the government to investigate the loyalty of federal employees and remove those belonging to "totalitarian, fascist, communist, or subversive" organizations or harboring a "sympathetic association" with such groups. Historians generally agree that Truman's "loyalty-security program" did far more harm than good. The vagueness of the "sympathetic association" language cast a cloud of suspicion over a wide swath of federal employees, many of whom had to answer to murky charges by anonymous accusers. From 1947 to 1951, 212 employees were dismissed under the program and several thousand pressured to resign. The latter included scores of suspected homosexuals, purged either because they were considered vulnerable to blackmail or because many believed sexual "deviancy" was closely linked to the political variety. None of these ousted employees was found guilty of espionage.

Nor did Truman's action prevent the Republicans from exploiting the communist issue. To the contrary, it lent credence to their suspicions, emboldening them to step up their investigations.

Truman's Rebound, 1947–1948

Although the loyalty-security program clearly was a misstep, it was part of a broader political strategy that helped Truman regain his footing after the disastrous 1946 midterm elections. One component of that strategy was, indeed, to crack down on domestic communism. The others were to take credit for the emerging bipartisan containment policy abroad; to appeal to northern Black voters; to embrace and promise to build on the legacy of the New Deal; and to condemn the Republicans as heartless reactionaries scheming to erase that legacy. The strategy, which coalesced somewhat haphazardly in 1947 and 1948, suited the president's centrist outlook and combative temperament. (Later generations of political observers would use the term "raging moderate" as a droll oxymoron, but that's literally what Truman was.) The strategy also positioned Truman favorably for the 1948 election, though this was not widely evident until after the votes had been counted.

In essence, Truman sought to claim a broad expanse of center-left terrain. He largely achieved this by tangling with adversaries to both his right and his left. His main conservative foil was the Republican-controlled Eightieth Congress. In the summer of 1947, Truman successfully vetoed two Republican tax cut bills, insisting that they unduly favored the rich. Around the same time, Congress passed the Taft–Hartley bill, a labor law named for its Republican sponsors, Senator Robert Taft of Ohio and Representative Fred Hartley of New Jersey. Taft–Hartley prohibited "closed shops" (rules mandating that all new employees belong to unions); barred unions from contributing to political campaigns; expanded the president's power to intervene in strikes; and required all union members to sign affidavits asserting that they were not communists. Again, Truman vetoed the Republican legislation, calling it a gross violation of labor's rights, but this time Congress overrode his veto. Taft–Hartley significantly eroded labor's bargaining power. The affidavit requirement in particular triggered a purge of communists from official union positions that bitterly divided and further weakened the union movement. Truman, however, politically benefited from the law's passage. By fighting a vigorous, though losing, battle against Taft–Hartley, he drew a stark contrast with congressional Republicans and regained much of the labor support he had lost the year before. There was another way that Truman hoped to win by losing: in his January 1948 State of the Union address, he called for a host of liberal programs, fully aware that congressional Republicans would ignore the proposals and enable him to condemn their inaction.

On the left, Truman's chief antagonist was Henry Wallace. Since departing the administration in 1946, Wallace had panned the president's anticommunist initiatives, such as the Truman Doctrine and Executive Order 9835. After initially supporting the Marshall Plan, he swung sharply against the program, portraying it as a scheme by bankers and militarists to capture foreign markets and split the world into two warring camps. In late 1947, Wallace launched a third-party run for Truman's job, drawing support from liberals, trade unionists, pacifists, communists, and others on the left. Truman denounced "Henry Wallace and his Communists" and charged that "Communists are using and guiding the third party." Wallace was his own man, but he had independently concluded that antagonizing the Soviets could spark a dangerous superpower confrontation. This stance created the appearance that communists were calling the shots – needless to say, a highly damaging impression. Wallace's refusal to criticize the February 1948 communist coup in Czechoslovakia caused many liberals to drift back to, or stay in, the Democratic mainstream. In a key setback for Wallace, the Congress of Industrial Organizations, the main coalition of progressive unions, endorsed Truman. Even so, the president's election faced long odds.

At the Democratic National Convention in Philadelphia in July, Truman won his party's nomination, despite many delegates' obvious dissatisfaction with him. The fiercest debate in Philadelphia concerned the party platform's language on civil rights. Truman had favored a mild plank – strong enough to satisfy northern Blacks and liberal whites, but not so strong as to repel southern segregationists. When the delegates instead passed a much more robust plank, Truman shifted course and embraced the new language, hoping to maximize Black and liberal support (and to win back those who had defected to Wallace, himself a forceful advocate of civil rights). In response, the delegations of four southern states bolted the Democratic Party, forming the segregationist States' Rights Party, commonly known as the "Dixiecrats," and making Governor Strom Thurmond of South Carolina their presidential nominee.

With the Democratic Party now split in three, Truman's path to election remained extremely daunting, especially given the lack of open dissension among Republicans and the fact that their nominee, Governor Thomas Dewey of New York, consistently led in the polls. Actually, the Republicans themselves were deeply divided – between isolationists and internationalists and between fierce opponents of the New Deal and those resigned to its perpetuation in some form. Dewey was on the latter side of each debate, but he found it prudent to downplay intraparty disagreements and confine himself to platitudes, such as "Your future is ahead of you," and "Our streams should abound with fish." Truman, by contrast, had already opted to accentuate divisions among Democrats; he could proclaim his positions much more clearly and forcefully. In a frenetic whistle-stop campaign around the country, he mostly ignored Thurmond but continued to denounce Wallace as soft on communism. Even more lustily, the president lambasted the "do-nothing" Republican Congress. He said the letters GOP (an abbreviation of "Grand Old Party," a nickname for the Republican Party) actually stood for "Gluttons of Privilege." He warned that Dewey would revive the bad old days of Herbert Hoover, a charge Dewey could not answer without offending some portion of his constituency. It was a valiant effort on Truman's part, but nearly everyone assumed it would fall short.

On Election Day, however, Truman won a stunning upset victory, receiving 49.5 percent of the popular vote to Dewey's 45.1 percent, and 303 Electoral College votes to Dewey's 189. The Democrats took back both houses of Congress. Wallace and Thurmond each got about 2.5 percent of the popular vote for president. Wallace won no states or electoral votes, but

Thurmond, whose support was regionally concentrated, carried Alabama, Louisiana, Mississippi, and South Carolina and won thirty-nine electoral votes. Although Truman swept the remaining southern states, Thurmond's strong showing foreshadowed the price Democrats would pay in future decades for upholding the rights of Black Americans.

***

At last, Truman would be president in his own right. During his long occupancy of Franklin Roosevelt's fourth term, he had arrived at what he considered a successful formula for governance: a vigorous but measured containment policy abroad, coupled with stern measures against communist subversion at home; maintenance of a vibrant and expanding capitalist economy, tempered by robust federal regulation and generous social welfare; and an ongoing, though modest, commitment to combating racial discrimination and oppression. On a very general plane, this formula did enjoy wide public support. Yet Truman's actual policies in the coming years would prove unexpectedly controversial, at times arousing furious and devastating opposition.

Eliciting the sharpest attacks would be his administration's actions and attitudes regarding the anticommunist struggle, both abroad and at home. A series of international shocks on the cold war front, including the outbreak and expansion of a grinding, bloody war, would sharply intensify the domestic red scare. Consuming the remainder of Truman's presidency and extending well into the term of his successor, the panic would disrupt the lives of thousands and inflict significant damage on the nation's civic life.

READING QUESTIONS

1. Between the fall of 1945 and the summer of 1949, what circumstances and issues pushed the United States and the Soviet Union toward cold war? Do you find that either or both of these nations missed, or shunned, opportunities for compromise?
2. Why were liberals and progressives so often disappointed with President Harry S. Truman's handling of domestic policy issues from 1945 to 1948? How might Truman have defended his domestic record to these constituencies?
3. How did US participation in World War II enable African Americans to strive to improve their economic, social, and political circumstances? In what ways did they continue these struggles into the early postwar years, and what were the most daunting obstacles they faced?
4. Suppose you are living during the early postwar red scare. You are a former member of the Communist Party of the United States who now teaches in a public school. You have been called to testify before the House Committee on Un-American Activities. You no longer support communist ideology and are willing to testify about your own history with the CPUSA. But you are loath to "name names" and thereby cause harm to your former associates. What options do you have? What consequences might flow from taking each of those options?

SUGGESTIONS FOR FURTHER READING

Boyer, Paul. *By the Bomb's Early Light: American Thought and Culture at the Dawn of the Atomic Age*. New York: Pantheon, 1985.

Byrnes, Mark S. *The Truman Years, 1945–1953*. New York: Longman, 2000.

Dallek, Robert. *Harry S. Truman*. New York: Times Books, 2008.

Devine, Thomas W. *Henry Wallace's 1948 Presidential Campaign and the Future of Postwar Liberalism*. Chapel Hill, NC: University of North Carolina Press, 2013.

Doherty, Thomas. *Show Trial: Hollywood, HUAC, and the Birth of the Blacklist*. New York: Columbia University Press, 2018.

Gergel, Richard. *Unexampled Courage: The Blinding of Sgt. Isaac Woodard and the Awakening of President Harry S. Truman and Judge J. Waties Waring*. New York: Farrar, Straus and Giroux, 2019.

McGuire, Danielle. *At the Dark End of the Street: Black Women, Rape, and Resistance – A New History of the Civil Rights Movement from Rosa Parks to Black Power*. New York: Knopf, 2010.

Schrecker, Ellen. *Many Are the Crimes: McCarthyism in America*. Princeton, NJ: Princeton University Press, 1998.

Spalding, Elizabeth Edwards. *The First Cold Warrior: Harry Truman, Containment, and the Making of Liberal Internationalism*. Lexington, KY: University Press of Kentucky, 2006.

Steil, Benn. *The Marshall Plan: Dawn of the Cold War*. New York: Simon & Schuster, 2018.

Tygiel, Jules. *Baseball's Great Experiment: Jackie Robinson and His Legacy*. New York: Oxford University Press, 1983.

Whitfield, Stephen J. *The Culture of the Cold War*. Baltimore: Johns Hopkins University Press, 1991.

2 We May Not Now Relax Our Guard

Hot War Abroad and Cold War at Home, 1949–1954

Introduction

She did not mention the object of her criticism by name. She didn't have to. When Margaret Chase Smith of Maine, the only woman in the US Senate, stood up in that body on June 1, 1950, and decried "the reckless abandon in which unproved charges have been hurled from this side of the aisle," everyone knew she meant the actions of her fellow Republican, Senator Joseph R. McCarthy of Wisconsin. Since February, McCarthy had issued charge after lurid charge, claiming that American diplomats, bureaucrats, academics, and others were knowingly betraying their country to international communism. His evidence for these allegations, though at times superficially impressive, almost invariably wilted under closer scrutiny. Even so, millions of Americans thrilled to McCarthy's audacity. Smith recognized the Wisconsinite's newfound popularity and, like any good Republican, wished for her party's electoral success. "But I do not want to see the Republican Party ride to political victory on the Four Horsemen of Calumny – Fear, Ignorance, Bigotry, and Smear," she told her Senate colleagues. Smith's "Declaration of Conscience," as her speech was called, received glowing plaudits in the nation's press, along with some criticism. Inevitably, neither supporters nor detractors could resist highlighting her sex. The *Boston Post* opined that all Americans "can rejoice that a woman had tied on her dust cap, seized a broom, and launched a housecleaning" of the nation's politics. Another Massachusetts newspaper, the *Fitchburg Sentinel*, grumbled that the chorus of praise for the Maine senator seemed "to have gone to her pretty head."

Smith was hardly a reluctant anticommunist. Since the start of the cold war, she had called for vigorous action to contain Soviet power abroad; her Declaration of Conscience included criticism of the Truman administration's alleged "complacency to the threat of communism here at home." During the Korean War, which erupted a few weeks after her Senate speech, Smith repeatedly insisted that the United States must spare no effort to defeat its two communist foes in that conflict, North Korea and the People's Republic of China. Soon after an armistice was concluded in the summer of 1953, she publicly urged that if war resumed the United States should "drop the atomic bomb on these barbarians who obviously

Figure 2.1 Senator Margaret Chase Smith, 1950. Source: Bettmann / Getty Images.

in their past atrocities have proved that they have no concept of or desire for decency." That same year Smith and other lawmakers tried, unsuccessfully, to pass legislation stripping communist "conspirators" of citizenship. Surely savoring the irony, the left-leaning journalist I. F. Stone charged that Smith and her colleagues were "outdoing McCarthy" in this "betrayal of American democracy."

It was for her Declaration of Conscience, though, that Senator Smith would be remembered, mainly because forceful Republican criticism of McCarthy was so rare in 1950. (Such sentiment was of course far more prevalent in the opposing party, although plenty of Democrats either supported the Wisconsin senator or found it advisable to soft-pedal their opposition to him.) True, six other Republican senators, men of generally moderate leanings, endorsed Smith's Declaration, prompting McCarthy to dismiss the whole group as "Snow White and the six dwarfs." Within weeks, however, after getting an earful from pro-McCarthy voters back home, five of those six had melted away. Smith herself never retreated from her anti-McCarthy position and from time to time publicly restated it. Still, she was prudent enough to refrain from waging a full-scale campaign against her demagogic colleague. She, too, found a path of lesser resistance.

Smith's thwarted rebellion was a small, disheartening skirmish in a wider set of political struggles unfolding in the late 1940s and early 1950s. During those years, cold war animosities scarily intensified both internationally and domestically. The communist takeover of China, the Soviet acquisition of the atomic bomb, and the outbreak and subsequent expansion of the Korean War all suggested that the contest with international communism would be far longer, bloodier, and more dangerous than previously feared. Escalating crises abroad dramatically raised the stakes of anticommunist politics at home. Politicians and pundits could now claim that domestic traitors were contributing to the deaths of American soldiers on Asian battlefields and hastening the day when the American heartland itself might endure nuclear attack. In truth, the threat of Soviet infiltration of US institutions had been practically eliminated during the first couple of years of the postwar era. But the perilous international situation after 1949 could not help heightening fears of domestic subversion. Joe McCarthy, whose anticommunist rampages lasted from 1950 to 1954, brutally exploited this psychological reality. He both symbolized and exacerbated a preexisting panic that upended the lives of thousands of Americans and coarsened the national culture for tens of millions more. Granted, such distortions of democracy paled alongside the harsh and even murderous repression occurring at that time within the Soviet Union. This was meager consolation, however, to the victims of the American hysteria.

In time, McCarthy overplayed his hand, and he received a wounding rebuke from his own Senate colleagues. American conventional wisdom settled around the notion that it was possible to take anticommunist suspicion too far, an outlook reinforced by a modest easing of cold war animosities after 1953. Nonetheless, an anticommunism shorn of its most divisive excesses continued to serve as the nation's civic religion. There would be no repudiation of the senator from Maine.

The Truman Administration and the Deepening Red Scare

On January 20, 1949, Harry Truman took the oath of office and became, for the first time, president in his own right. His ensuing term would be one of frequent disappointment, frustration, and aggravation. In an irony that must have maddened Truman, the Democrats' across-the-board victory in the 1948 elections had done little to strengthen his administration's domestic political position and, in some ways, had even weakened it. Republicans were livid over their surprise election defeat and determined to exact revenge; they would fight the administration's domestic initiatives (and foreign ones, too) with fresh intensity. Moreover, the transfer of power on Capitol Hill meant a resumption of Democratic control of congressional committees. Many of the restored committee chairmen, especially in the Senate, were southern segregationists who could now resist civil rights legislation even more effectively than in the previous Congress. They would also join with Republicans to stymie other liberal initiatives. In his January 1949 State of the Union address, Truman presented Congress with a liberal wish list, including expanded Social Security benefits, an increase in the minimum wage, repeal of the Taft–Hartley Act, creation of a new welfare department, federal support for housing construction, and a

$4 billion tax increase to pay for it all. Congress passed some of Truman's requests, such as the minimum wage increase and part of the Social Security expansion, but rebuffed the president on most of the rest.

In foreign affairs, the bipartisan mood lingered just long enough to ensure Senate approval of the North Atlantic Treaty Organization in July 1949, and evaporated soon thereafter. Republicans now generally agreed that their presidential nominee in 1948, New York Governor Thomas Dewey, had erred in refraining from harshly criticizing Truman's foreign policies; the president would no longer benefit from such restraint. More importantly, 1949 and 1950 brought a series of startling setbacks, abroad and at home, that exposed the Truman administration to the charge that it was dangerously soft on communism. It would have taken superhuman forbearance for Republicans to resist the urge to pounce on these opportunities, and forbearance was not exactly the GOP's strong suit.

By mid-1949, US officials could be reasonably satisfied with the situation in Western Europe. Its nations were on a US-guided path to economic recovery, and they had just created a mutual defense organization in which Washington played a leading role. East Asia was another story. Since the 1920s, China's Nationalist government, led by Chiang Kai-shek, had vied with Mao Tse-tung's (Mao Zedong's) Chinese Communist Party (CCP) for control of the country. The civil war somewhat abated during World War II, as both sides concentrated on fighting Japan, only to resume with a vengeance after Japan's defeat in 1945. The United States, which had long supported Chiang, encouraged him to reach an accommodation with the CCP. But the US mediation effort failed, and in the ensuing struggle the Nationalists, though still backed by Washington, steadily lost ground to Mao's forces, which had strong support among China's huge peasant population. In the summer and fall of 1949, the Nationalist government collapsed and the communists seized power, declaring the People's Republic of China (PRC) on October 1. Chiang and his supporters fled to the island of Formosa (later called Taiwan), where they established the Republic of China, claiming it to be the true government of all of China.

The communist takeover in China sparked a bitter American debate over who was responsible for this geopolitical debacle. The Truman administration blamed Chiang, arguing that his government had been too corrupt, unpopular, and lethargic to fend off the CCP. In a 1,054-page "White Paper" publicly issued weeks before Mao's triumph, the State Department recounted its extensive but futile efforts to bolster the Nationalists. Republicans denounced the White Paper as a shameful attempt to deflect responsibility. The real culprits, they said, were incompetent, defeatist, and perhaps even traitorous State Department officials who had betrayed the Nationalists and abandoned China to communism. Truman and Dean Acheson, who had replaced George Marshall as secretary of state in January 1949, firmly rebutted these charges. In one respect, however, they gave crucial ground to conservative critics: they readily accepted the claim that the PRC marched in lockstep with the Soviet Union and banished any thought of recognizing the former, instead regarding the Formosan government as the legitimate sovereign over all of China. The US government would adhere to that diplomatic position for more than twenty years.

In September 1949, in the midst of the Nationalists' collapse on the mainland, the American public received another shock: the Truman administration revealed that the Soviet Union had successfully tested an atomic bomb. Moscow's achievement of this milestone was hardly unexpected, but it occurred several years earlier than many experts had predicted. The only plausible explanation for such rapid progress, some commentators argued, was that Soviet spies had stolen atomic secrets from US laboratories. Republicans echoed this theme, castigating the Truman and Roosevelt administrations for their lax security procedures. As if to validate these critiques, in February 1950 British authorities announced that Klaus Fuchs, a German-born physicist who had worked on the Manhattan Project, had confessed to passing sensitive nuclear information to the Soviets. Historians and nuclear physicists estimate that Fuchs's espionage sped up the Soviet atom bomb program by a year to eighteen months. In the wake of the Soviet bomb test, US officials debated whether to develop a new, more devastating weapon – the hydrogen bomb, which could be up to a thousand times as powerful as the atomic bomb. Many prominent nuclear scientists opposed taking this step, fearing it would lead to an uncontrollable arms race – a worry echoed by some administration officials. But in January 1950 Truman overruled the objections and authorized a crash program to develop the hydrogen bomb.

If the Chinese Revolution and the Soviet bomb test threw the Truman administration on the defensive, a concurrent domestic controversy was proving to be even more discrediting. It had started at a House Committee on Un-American Activities hearing in August 1948, when an ex-communist named Whittaker Chambers accused Alger Hiss, president of the Carnegie Endowment for International Peace and a former high-ranking diplomat in the Roosevelt and Truman administrations, of having been a CPUSA member in the mid- to late 1930s. Hiss indignantly denied the charge, and several prominent Democrats, including members of the Truman administration, leapt to his defense. Truman himself publicly dismissed the accusation as a "red herring," aimed at distracting Americans from the Republicans' meager legislative record. Many HUAC members were inclined to drop the case, but a young California Republican on the committee named Richard M. Nixon, who had received secret tips from the FBI lending credence to Chambers's story, urged his colleagues to keep digging.

In late 1948, Chambers made an explosive new claim: that in the late 1930s, when working for the State Department, Hiss had conspired with Chambers to pass sensitive information to the Soviet Union. Chambers furnished copies of classified State Department documents, most famously by producing strips of microfilm hidden in a hollowed-out pumpkin on his Maryland farm. Some of the documents, it turned out, had been typed on a typewriter belonging to Hiss. Truman's Department of Justice, which had tried to bury the case, now was obliged to indict Hiss for perjuring himself before HUAC (the statute of limitations on espionage having since expired). In January 1950, Hiss was convicted and sentenced to a five-year prison term.

The Hiss case was highly consequential. It made a national figure of Congressman Nixon, who would be elected to the Senate in 1950 and achieve even higher office in the years thereafter. It boosted the reputation of HUAC, whose heyday continued until the mid-1950s.

Most importantly, it appeared to vindicate Republicans' claims that communist agents had deeply infiltrated the US government and that the Truman administration was more interested in shielding them than in exposing them. The totality of evidence suggests that Hiss probably did secretly assist Moscow before and during World War II. The stage was now set, however, for the hurling of far less credible accusations of Democratic complicity with international communism.

Joseph McCarthy and McCarthyism

In February 1950, Senator Joseph McCarthy of Wisconsin, a first-term Republican, addressed the Women's Republican Club of Wheeling, West Virginia. Charging that the State Department was "thoroughly infested with Communists," he held up a sheet of paper that he claimed was a list of 205 communist agents currently working in that department. He also mentioned, by name, several individual diplomats and civil servants he said were guilty of subversion. In the coming days McCarthy spoke in several other cities, making similar allegations at each stop. The claim of communist infiltration of Foggy Bottom was by now standard fare in Republican circles. The novelty lay in the senator's willingness to cite specific numbers and names, even though both changed from one speech to the next. McCarthy's information grew out of a distorted reading of State Department personnel records from 1946 and 1947. The senator took the number of employees the department had placed under investigation as security risks (for a range of reasons, suspected procommunist sympathy being just one), subtracted from it the number of employees subsequently let go, and concluded – automatically – that all the rest had to be communists still working in government. The publicity-craving senator had stumbled into a cause that garnered him instant headlines. And instant notoriety: barely a month after the Wheeling speech, the political cartoonist Herblock (short for Herbert Block) coined the term "McCarthyism" to describe the practice of hurling baseless accusations of communist affiliation or sympathy.

A hallmark of the McCarthy style was to make sensational allegations and then scramble to find evidence to support them. In the weeks after Wheeling, as reporters peppered him with questions about his claims, the senator was almost comically desperate for assistance. "What am I gonna do? You gotta help me," he pleaded to William Randolph Hearst, Jr., editor-in-chief of Hearst Newspapers. A motley assemblage of avid anticommunists flocked to McCarthy's aid: rightwing journalists, former FBI agents and congressional staff members, loyalty-security investigators, ex-communists who had previously testified before HUAC, and others. Most of these figures had been involved in, or possessed information about, earlier anticommunist investigations that in their view required further probing. Plied with documents by his new allies, McCarthy made haphazard attempts to substantiate his accusations but could not resist the temptation to lodge fresh ones, sometimes wildly misstating or exaggerating the information contained in the documents.

The brazenness of the charges ensured wide news coverage. Plainly, McCarthy was indifferent to the accuracy of his own statements. This shocked many reporters and commentators, yet it fascinated them, too, and they gave his utterances wide currency. Apparently intuitively (for the senator was the opposite of studious), McCarthy grasped and ruthlessly exploited the logistical, economic, and social incentives driving American journalism. He fed reporters' insatiable hunger for information by producing a seemingly inexhaustible supply of press releases and documents, often furnishing the most explosive "revelations" shortly before filing deadlines. Lacking the time to examine the material fully, but unwilling to be outflanked by rival news outlets, newspapers would print the senator's unvetted accusations. McCarthy also made himself unusually accessible to journalists. He kept his office door open and was available at all hours to go out for drinks or play cards. Gregarious and fun-loving, he exuded a crude charm that won reporters over in spite of themselves. One of them recalled, "You knew very well that he was a bum – still, you liked this kind of bum." Journalists tried to be fair; their stories about McCarthy usually quoted people critical of him. But the refutations paled alongside the eye-catching charges.

Numerous others, of course, enthusiastically supported McCarthy. A network of conservative publications and journalists – newspapers such as the *Chicago Tribune* and the dailies churned out by the Hearst chain, as well as columnists like Walter Winchell, George Sokolsky, and Westbrook Pegler – championed the senator's cause. McCarthy also gained a devoted following among millions of ordinary citizens, especially lower-middle-class whites (and most especially fellow Irish Catholics, many of them Democrats), who delighted in his skewering of "striped pants" diplomats and government bureaucrats.

The reaction of the Republican Party, while varied and complicated, was ultimately favorable, too. Rightwing anticommunists in the party loved McCarthy, but more moderate figures, along with some conservatives, found him vulgar and unscrupulous and worried that his antics would backfire on the party. On the other hand, the Wisconsin senator was getting results, thanks to the sheer volume of his efforts. True, most of his accusations went nowhere and were quietly dropped without explanation or apology. But some of them did compel the Truman administration to launch new investigations, or reopen old ones, into the political associations of figures working for or contracting with the federal government. And, even if *those* cases dragged on without legal conclusion, Republicans of all stripes could relish watching Truman and Acheson squirm. In a more serious vein, some Republicans were genuinely distressed by the communist victory in China and keen on learning where and how, exactly, the Truman administration had failed. If anything could shake answers loose, they reasoned, surely it was McCarthy's relentless pounding. And so, with the notable exception of Margaret Chase Smith's futile rebellion, Republicans sat back and let the boorish upstart have his way, occasionally emitting audible cheers from the sidelines.

Democratic opposition to McCarthy was ineffectual. If anything, it only strengthened him. In the spring and summer of 1950, Senator Millard Tydings, a Maryland Democrat, chaired a Senate subcommittee charged with looking into McCarthy's allegations about communist infiltration of the Truman administration. Hoping to nip the Wisconsinite's challenge in the bud, Tydings and the other Democrats on the subcommittee authored a report that dismissed McCarthy's claims as groundless; Tydings himself called them a "fraud and a hoax." But the Republicans on the subcommittee refused to sign the report, making the whole investigation look like a partisan exercise. That fall, Tydings lost his reelection bid after McCarthy aggressively campaigned against him in Maryland. Even more strikingly, McCarthy went after the Senate majority leader, Scott Lucas of Illinois, who had recruited Tydings to chair the subcommittee, and Lucas, too, lost his seat in November. In each case, the Democratic senator had been in serious political trouble at home before McCarthy injected himself into the reelection campaign. But to all appearances the Wisconsin senator had inflicted harsh vengeance on his foes. Truman himself mostly declined to rebuke McCarthy by name, instead voicing generic criticisms of wild and unfounded attacks. Going any further, the president reasoned, would only rile up the demagogue's devoted followers.

One of the more prominent victims of McCarthy's early rampages was a China expert named Owen Lattimore, who had served as the US government's liaison to Chiang Kai-shek during World War II but was mostly an outside analyst of Asian affairs. An acerbic critic of Chiang and the Nationalists, Lattimore had drawn the ire of Chiang's American supporters, some of whom charged – falsely, as far as available evidence shows – that he was a Soviet spy. In the spring of 1950 McCarthy surfaced the allegation, which Lattimore vehemently denied. The specialist then endured a grueling Senate investigation into his loyalty, followed by federal perjury charges stemming from his Senate testimony. In 1955, a judge dismissed the charges as insubstantial, but Lattimore's academic career was stunted for years thereafter.

The Outbreak of the Korean War

June 1950 brought yet another international jolt – one that briefly stalled, then powerfully impelled, McCarthy's reckless crusade. The shock emanated from the Korean Peninsula, whose crisis had its proximate origins in the immediate aftermath of World War II. Following Japan's defeat in 1945, the United States and the Soviet Union jointly occupied Korea, which Japan had colonized since 1905. Korea was divided at the 38th parallel, with US troops stationed to the south of that line and Soviet troops to its north. By 1949, both superpowers had withdrawn their forces, leaving behind a situation of de facto partition. Two rival regimes had emerged: pro-US South Korea, led by President Syngman Rhee, and communist North Korea, under President Kim Il-sung. Each leader hoped to reunite the entire peninsula under his own government's control. Circumstances enabled Kim to act: South Korea was beset by internal conflict and turmoil, and prior consultations revealed that both Mao and Joseph Stalin, the Soviet leader, were willing (albeit reluctantly) to bless a North Korean operation. On June 25, 1950, North Korean troops surged across the 38th parallel, overwhelming South Korea's poorly equipped forces and advancing quickly southward. So began a three-year war that would kill more than 33,000 Americans, over 150,000 Chinese, and as many as three million Koreans.

Truman and his advisers were stunned by the attack, which they saw as the brainchild of Stalin himself. Although they had not previously considered South Korea essential to US security in the Pacific, they immediately agreed that the provocation could not go unanswered. Failing to act would not only call US global leadership into question but also

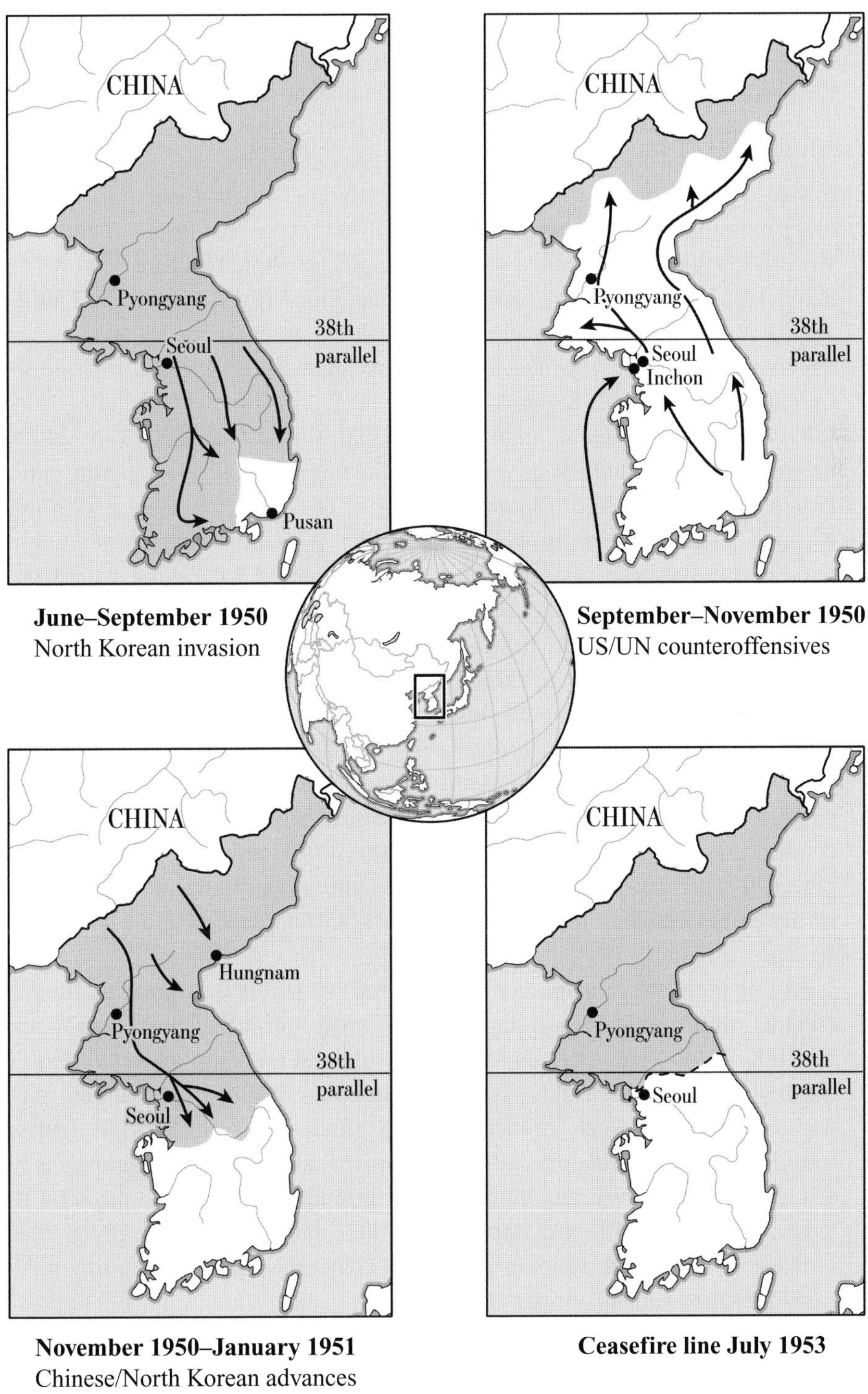

Map 2.1 The Korean War, 1950–1953. Source: Created by Joe LeMonnier.

further inflame the administration's domestic rightwing critics. American officials hastened to the United Nations Security Council and persuaded it to pass a resolution condemning the North Korean attack and authorizing collective military action to defend South Korea. The Soviets were then boycotting the UN over its decision to award China's seat to Formosa rather than the PRC. Thus they were not present to veto the resolution, which, in essence, provided UN cover for a US-run campaign to repel North Korean forces. Although several other nations, most notably Britain and Turkey, took part in the operation, US and South Korean troops would do most of the fighting. The whole UN force, known as the UN Command, was led by US Army General Douglas MacArthur, a prominent military figure from World War II's Pacific campaigns, who took his orders from Truman (or was supposed to, anyway) rather than from the UN secretary general. By the end of June 1950, US troops were in action in South Korea.

Truman did not seek a congressional declaration of war. At a June 29 press conference, he said that the United States was merely helping "to suppress a bandit raid" against South Korea. A reporter asked if it was "correct ... to call this a police action under the United Nations." The president answered, "Yes. That is exactly what it amounts to." Although a requested declaration of war almost certainly would have passed the Congress, Truman hoped to avoid opening his entire East Asia policy to lawmakers' questioning and criticism. He also wanted to have the flexibility to turn away from Korea should communists launch a more central offensive elsewhere.

For the rest of that summer, things went terribly for the UN Command. North Korean troops overran nearly all of South Korea, corralling their adversaries into the southeastern corner of the peninsula. In September, however, MacArthur's forces executed an audacious amphibious landing at Inchon, on South Korea's northwestern coast. This action, combined with a ground offensive from the south, caught the North Korean troops in a pincer, forcing some to surrender en masse and others to flee northward to the 38th parallel. By early October, all of the active North Korean troops had been expelled from South Korea.

At this point, having successfully restored the status quo prior to June 25, the Truman administration could have declared its mission accomplished and ceased operations. But the North Koreans were scattered and on the run, and the temptation to continue the offensive north of the 38th parallel, and extinguish the communist regime that had started the conflict, was overpowering. Such an offensive, US officials reasoned, would deprive international communism of valuable real estate and show Stalin that overstepping his bounds came at a steep cost. Moreover, any failure by the Truman administration to seize this opportunity would expose it to withering Republican attack, hardly a welcome prospect as the 1950 midterm elections loomed. Truman authorized General MacArthur to push northward and seek to reunify the peninsula under UN authority.

One problem with the plan was that it might place American forces close to the Chinese border and provoke a violent PRC response. Truman understood this danger and ordered that US troops keep their distance from the border areas. But MacArthur, who never suffered from a lack of self-confidence, disregarded the order and pushed northward toward the frontier. In what turned out to be a major blunder, Truman declined to press the matter

Figure 2.2 A US infantryman comforts a fellow soldier whose friend has been killed, South Korea, 1950. Source: Corbis Historical / Getty Images.

with MacArthur, whose prestige was sky-high in the aftermath of the Inchon landing. At a mid-October meeting on the Pacific island of Wake, to which the president flew over 6,000 miles to consult with the general, MacArthur assured Truman that the Chinese would not intervene but that, even if they did, the US military would easily defeat them. "[I]f the Chinese tried to get down to Pyongyang," MacArthur said, referring to North Korea's capital, "there would be the greatest slaughter." This prediction proved to be accurate in ways that MacArthur probably did not intend.

Days later, small numbers of PRC troops began crossing the Yalu River into North Korea, where UN troops were already deployed and advancing northward. Tens of thousands of additional Chinese troops soon followed. In late November, the PRC army struck in full force. Up to 300,000 soldiers hurled themselves against the US-led coalition, inflicting heavy casualties and forcing it to turn back to the 38th parallel. It was a miserable retreat for the UN troops, conducted in a sub-zero blizzard along narrow, treacherous mountain roads. Chinese troops ambushed them as they fled, often in the dark of night. News of the debacle sent a current of alarm through the US government and public. At a November 30 press conference, Truman suggested that the United States might use atomic weapons against the Chinese, causing an international uproar. The White House quickly downplayed the statement, and Truman privately assured Britain's prime minister that he had no current plans to use nuclear weapons. But the situation in Korea was desperate and getting worse. By the New Year, the UN Command had been driven back into South Korea.

Finally, in late January, the UN forces halted the Chinese advance. Over the next several weeks, they retook the offensive and, once again, pushed their adversaries north of the 38th parallel. This time, a wised-up Truman ordered the troops to stop at or near the original demarcation line and signaled his openness to a ceasefire. General MacArthur, however, bridled at the notion of leaving communists in power in Pyongyang – or Beijing, for that matter. In March 1951, the general made public statements advocating a widening of the conflict. Truman was outraged at the insubordination but hesitated to move against the popular general. In April, House Minority Leader Joseph Martin, a Massachusetts Republican, published a letter from MacArthur advocating an expanded war with China. "[I]f we lose the war to Communism in Asia," the general warned, "the fall of Europe is inevitable.... There is no substitute for victory." For Truman, this was the final straw. Days later he announced the firing of MacArthur, explaining that, under the nation's system of government, military leaders must submit to civilian authority.

Truman was on rock-solid constitutional ground. But MacArthur, the hero of the Inchon, had enormous stature among Americans, and his sacking drew howls of protest. Angry letters and telegrams, running twenty to one against the firing, inundated the White House. Enraged citizens also wrote to members of Congress, demanding the president's removal from office: "IMPEACH THE IMBECILE"; "IMPEACH THE RED HERRING FROM THE PRESIDENTIAL CHAIR"; "WE WISH TO PROTEST THIS LATEST OUTRAGE ON THE PART OF THE PIG IN THE WHITE HOUSE." (Displaying her characteristic blend of hawkishness and principle, Margaret Chase Smith shared MacArthur's desire to widen the war but reluctantly agreed that his indiscretion merited removal.) Truman's approval rating sank to the mid-twenties.

MacArthur came home to a hero's welcome, riding in ticker-tape parades and making numerous public speeches. His most famous address was before a joint session of Congress, where he chastised those "who ... would appease Red China," clearly implying that Truman belonged in that category. The general quoted a line from an old army ballad, "Old soldiers never die; they just fade away," and announced that he, too, would now "just fade away – an old soldier who tried to do his duty as God gave him the light to see that duty." MacArthur then embarked on what the historian Eric Goldman called the "noisiest fading away in history": more parades and speeches, a return to Capitol Hill to testify before a Senate committee, even an appearance at the New York Polo Grounds to throw out the first ball in a Giants–Phillies game. There was excited talk, which MacArthur pretended not to notice, of a presidential run in 1952.

But he really did fade away. At Senate hearings on the general's dismissal, top military leaders upheld Truman's decision and systematically demolished MacArthur's Asia policy. If the latter's view prevailed, they said, the United States would find itself in a full-scale war with China and perhaps also the Soviet Union, a nation now armed, however primitively, with atomic weapons. Some of MacArthur's congressional champions began having second thoughts. News reports of the hearings encouraged more sober reflection among the public, too. In a July 1951 poll, 74 percent of respondents favored peace talks over Korea.

Yet wanting peace and achieving it were two different things. The Korean conflict was no longer a war of movement, as the two sides had settled into a grinding stalemate along a battle line approximating the 38th parallel. Still, US aircraft heavily bombed North Korea, laying waste to much of the country and causing massive military and civilian casualties. The Soviet government facilitated truce talks between the United States and the PRC (there being no official relations between the two antagonists), but agreement foundered over the fate of prisoners of war (POWs). Both the PRC and North Korea called for the repatriation of all POWs, whereas the UN Command (which, practically speaking, meant the United States) stood on the principle that Chinese and North Korean POWs unwilling to return to their countries should not be forced to do so. The issue remained unresolved, and the war dragged on.

The Korean War's impact on US cold war policy was both immediate and far-reaching. American officials generally assumed that North Korea's attack on South Korea was part of a broader enemy offensive masterminded from Moscow. The event thus vindicated and intensified previous US steps to combat international communism. Several months prior to the war's outbreak, some Truman administration officials had drafted a secret policy document called National Security Council Paper no. 68 (NSC-68). Produced in reaction to the Chinese Revolution and the Soviet atom bomb test, NSC-68 stated that the United States had entered into a desperate, long-term struggle against international communism, a force bent on world conquest and responsive only to the language of force. The document called for a massive buildup of conventional and nuclear forces, including development of the hydrogen bomb, and urged Americans to recognize "that the cold war is in fact a real war in which the survival of the free world is at stake." Washington had to set aside any scruples it might have about engaging in morally questionable behavior: "The integrity of our system will not be jeopardized by any measures, covert or overt, violent or nonviolent, which serve the purpose of frustrating the Kremlin design."

NSC-68 could not become national policy until the president signed it, and it was initially controversial within the administration. Although Secretary of State Acheson championed the document, other high-ranking officials warned it would dangerously ratchet up international tensions. Truman shared this concern; he was also reluctant to divert resources from domestic social programs. Into the summer of 1950, he declined to sign off on NSC-68, saying he needed to give it more study. But the Korean War removed his doubts, and in September 1950 he endorsed the document. In keeping with its recommendations, US defense spending increased from $17 billion in 1950 to $50 billion in 1952. The administration also sped up a re-expansion of the armed services it had begun in 1948. In that year, some 1.4 million personnel served in the US military; by 1952, the figure exceeded 3.6 million.

Across the globe, the administration assumed a militant posture toward world communism that would dominate US policy-making for years to come. Within days of the North Korean attack, Truman declared that the United States would physically oppose any PRC effort to take over Formosa, and he ordered the US Navy to patrol the narrow strait separating Formosa from mainland China. The United States began giving Chiang

Kai-shek's government significant military and economic aid. Recognizing that Japan would serve as the main logistical base for waging the Korean War, Washington invested billions of dollars in building the necessary infrastructure in that country, thereby helping to revitalize its economy. In September 1951, the United States concluded a peace treaty with Japan that formally ended the postwar US occupation. Japan allowed the United States to operate military bases on its soil and promised not to forge close economic ties with the PRC. In Western Europe, the Truman administration beefed up its commitment to NATO, augmenting the US troops stationed on the continent. Greece and Turkey were admitted into the alliance, partly in recognition of their contribution to the UN effort in Korea, partly to block any Soviet moves into the Near or Middle East. Meanwhile, US scientists and technicians raced to develop hydrogen bombs, successfully testing the first one in November 1952 by obliterating a Pacific islet.

McCarthyism at Full Tide

For a few weeks after the North Korean attack of June 1950, Americans rallied behind their president. The public's appetite for vitriolic criticism of the government markedly diminished, and Joe McCarthy found it prudent to hold his tongue. "My only forum is page one," he admitted to a reporter. "I don't have that now, so I'll keep quiet." But by mid-summer the supportive mood was dissipating, thanks largely to the terrible war news prior to Inchon (soon after which, of course, the terrible war news would resume). Indeed, the fighting gave fresh urgency to charges of communist infiltration, for it could now be claimed that American turncoats were directly responsible for the deaths of American boys on the battlefield. And many believed that the crisis transcended East Asia. In an August 1950 Gallup poll, 57 percent of respondents agreed that "the United States is now actually in World War III."

That summer, the FBI arrested a married couple, Julius and Ethel Rosenberg, accusing them of passing atomic secrets to the Soviets as part of the same spy ring in which Klaus Fuchs had operated. Historians generally agree that the Rosenbergs were guilty, though their espionage was far less consequential than Fuchs's, and Ethel's role appears to have been especially minor. But because the Rosenbergs were American, and because one of them was female and the mother of young children, their case commanded much greater public attention than Fuchs's did. (The Rosenbergs' Jewishness, too, was a subject of some consternation. Many American Jews worried that the couple's alleged misdeeds would provoke reprisals against the entire community, whereas others, especially on the left, charged that anti-Semitism had already manifested itself in authorities' singling out of the Rosenbergs. Both concerns were somewhat mitigated, however, by the fact that the judge and the chief prosecutor in the couple's federal trial were Jewish as well.) In the spring of 1951, the Rosenbergs were convicted of espionage. Pronouncing the sentence of death, Judge Irving Kaufman inflated the defendants' offense and endowed it with world-historical significance. "I consider your crime worse than murder," he said. "… I believe your conduct in putting into the hands of the Russians the A-bomb years before our best scientists predicted Russia would perfect the bomb has already caused … the Communist aggression in Korea." In 1953, following a vigorous but futile international campaign for clemency on their behalf, both Rosenbergs would die in the electric chair.

Against the alarming news backdrop of 1950–1951, anticommunist sentiment reached a new pitch of intolerance. A judge sentenced five activists to six months in prison for writing "PEACE" on a wall in a Brooklyn, New York, park. Congress passed the Internal Security Act of 1950, which required vaguely defined "Communist-action organizations" to register with the Department of Justice and authorized the president, in times of emergency, to detain people deemed prone to subversive activity. Truman vetoed the bill as excessive, but Congress overrode him. "In a bizarre scene," writes the historian David Oshinsky, "Speaker [of the House] Sam Rayburn had to plead for quiet in order to have the veto message read aloud. Angry members chanting 'Vote! Vote!' didn't want to hear it." In the 1950 midterm elections, Congressman Richard Nixon faced fellow House member Helen Gahagan Douglas, a former stage and film actor with a prominent liberal profile (including strong opposition to HUAC), in a race for one of California's seats in the US Senate. Invoking the anticommunist credentials he had earned in his takedown of Alger Hiss, and perhaps playing on voters' doubts that women belonged in the Senate, Nixon charged that Douglas was "pink right down to her underwear." Combining those two appeals with faith in voters' racial animus, his campaign mailed out postcards reading "Vote for our Helen for Senator. We are with her 100%," signed by the fictitious "Communist League of Negro Women." Nixon handily defeated Douglas that November. (In the midterms as a whole, Democrats kept their majorities in both houses of Congress, but by slimmer margins.)

Within state governments, too, the anticommunist fervor intensified. In early 1951, a delegation of mostly liberal governors (including Democrats Adlai Stevenson of Illinois, Frank Lausche of Ohio, Elbert Carvel of Delaware, and Gordon Browning of Tennessee) asked FBI director J. Edgar Hoover for confidential information about alleged subversives on their state payrolls. Such intelligence, the governors hoped, would enable them to take the initiative in anticommunist investigations and keep rightwingers in their state legislatures from monopolizing the issue. Hoover obliged by launching the "Responsibilities program," whereby the FBI furnished governors and other state officials with "blind memoranda" – reports typed on sheets of paper displaying no letterheads, watermarks, or other indications of their origin – about suspect individuals, many of them teachers in public schools or state universities. The governors believed the FBI director shared their goal of tamping down anticommunist hysteria. Actually, Hoover's outlook was much closer to McCarthy's than to their own (though Hoover did increasingly resent McCarthy's notorious lack of discretion, which drew public attention to activities Hoover preferred to conduct in private). Over the next few years, the "blind memoranda" went out to an ever-expanding list of recipients, some of them clearly more interested in pursuing political witch hunts than in preventing them. Hundreds of public employees were fired or forced out. The Responsibilities program, writes the historian Kenneth O'Reilly, "proved to be more of an asset to the McCarthyites than to vulnerable liberal governors." Governor Stevenson himself was placed on a mild form of FBI surveillance, partly on account of his professional association with Alger Hiss in the 1930s and 1940s.

Popular entertainment amplified the rancorous mood. Hollywood movies such as *I was a Communist for the FBI* (1951), *Big Jim McLain* (1952), and *My Son John* (1952) valorized HUAC and portrayed communists as ruthless infiltrators seeking to cripple the nation's industries, exacerbate its racial and ethnic conflicts, and control the minds of its youth. These were part of a series of films released in the late 1940s and early 1950s to assure HUAC and other watchdog organizations that Hollywood took the communist threat seriously – and thus stave off federal regulation or private sector boycotts. The anticommunist movies mostly failed at the box office, but that wasn't the point, writes the historian Thomas Doherty. The films "were protection payments in 35mm."

The film blacklist, precipitated by the 1947 Hollywood Ten case (see Chapter 1), had by now spread to the broadcast industry. In the summer of 1950, the process became more visible and systematic with the publication of *Red Channels*, a book-length compilation of information about the alleged communist affiliations of 151 writers, actors, musicians, and other entertainers in radio and television. Issued by American Business Consultants, a private company headed by former FBI agents, *Red Channels* became the blacklisters' bible of the airwaves, despite containing some questionable or downright false information. By 1951, the television networks and their sponsors refused to hire anyone listed in it. The banned artists included the film director Orson Welles, the writers Langston Hughes and Lillian Hellman, the musicians Aaron Copland and Pete Seeger, and the singer, actor, and dancer Lena Horne.

Artists in other genres loudly cheered on the anticommunist crusade, sometimes with frank bloodlust. "There'll be fire, dust, and metal flying all around," twanged the country singer Jackie Doll in 1951, "And the radioactivity will burn them to the ground/If there's any Commies left they'll be all on the run/If General MacArthur drops an atomic bomb." In Mickey Spillane's pulp novel *One Lonely Night* (1951), which sold more than three million copies, the hero-detective Mike Hammer turns his vengeance on domestic communist subversives. "I killed more people tonight than I have fingers on my hands," Hammer brags. "I shot them in cold blood and enjoyed every minute of it.... They were Commies.... They were red sons-of-bitches who should have died long ago."

His brutal politics back in vogue, Senator McCarthy resumed his antisubversive campaign, and by 1951 was aiming it at the highest levels of government. In a Spillanian flourish of his own, he called Truman a "son of a bitch" who must have been drunk when he fired MacArthur. Discussing the plight of a severely disabled Korean War veteran named Bob Smith – maimed, the senator charged, by Dean Acheson's traitorous foreign policy – McCarthy suggested that, when Smith "gets his artificial limbs, he first walk over to the State Department and call upon the Secretary.... He should say to him, 'Dean, ... if you want at long last to perform one service for the American people ... you should remove yourself from this country and go to the nation for which you have been struggling and fighting so long.'" In his wildest attack – the more shocking for tarring a figure widely seen as a patriot above politics – McCarthy proclaimed on the Senate floor that former Secretary of State George Marshall, who had returned to serve the Truman administration as secretary of defense, was at the center of "a conspiracy so immense ... as to dwarf any previous venture in the history of man." McCarthy's sliming of Marshall received widespread criticism, including from Senate Republicans. Some of the latter backtracked, however, once it became clear that the Wisconsin senator's hold on Republican voters remained as strong as ever.

The McCarthyite assault raised the stakes of controversies that in recent years had unfolded less urgently. A few weeks after McCarthy's February 1950 speech in Wheeling, another Republican senator, Styles Bridges of New Hampshire, compelled the State Department to confirm in public something it had already privately disclosed to members of Congress: that, of the many department employees fired or pressured to resign since 1947, ninety-one were suspected homosexuals. The revelation produced a flurry of panicky stories in the press and gleeful denunciations by congressional Republicans. An antihomosexual purge that had been largely confined to the State Department was now extended more broadly across the federal government. Police in Washington, DC, cracked down on the city's gay and lesbian nightclubs and on "cruising areas" within the public parks – an intensification of a campaign, begun a few years earlier, to stamp out a semipublic gay subculture that had flourished in the nation's capital since the 1930s. (See Chapter 8 for more on gay and lesbian life in the 1950s, and beyond.)

Similarly, shortly after the outbreak of the Korean War, the State Department revoked the passport of Paul Robeson, a world-renowned Black singer and actor who strongly sympathized with the Soviet Union. Visiting Paris a year earlier, Robeson had been quoted – inaccurately, he claimed – as saying that African Americans would not willingly fight in a war against the Soviet Union. The remark drew widespread condemnation back home, including from mainstream Black civil rights leaders anxious to shield their movement from charges of disloyalty. The baseball star Jackie Robinson appeared before HUAC and called Robeson's statement "silly." Violent white mobs wielding baseball bats and hurling rocks prevented Robeson from singing at an outdoor concert in Peekskill, north of New York City; thirteen people suffered serious injuries. In blocking Robeson from further foreign travel, the State Department did more than simply inconvenience him. It closed off sources of income for Robeson just as stateside gigs were quickly drying up. It also physically hindered his efforts to rally international criticism of the US government. At a time when long-distance communication was rudimentary and cumbersome, there was no substitute for a celebrity's actual presence at an event to drum up support for a political cause.

Such a cause was afoot in the following year, and US officials were surely thankful they had grounded the charismatic artist. In December 1951, the Civil Rights Congress (CRC), a procommunist organization with which Robeson was allied, submitted a 237-page appeal to the UN entitled "We Charge Genocide." It claimed that the US government's toleration of Jim Crow subjugation, and especially its willingness to let numerous lynchings go unpunished, amounted to genocide as defined by a recently adopted UN protocol. To overcome a predicted US media blackout, the CRC's national secretary, William Patterson, presented the statement at a UN meeting in Paris, rather than at the UN's New York headquarters. Robeson would have liked to accompany Patterson but, barred from leaving the country, was obliged to submit his copy in New York. Once Patterson returned home, the State Department revoked his passport, too. Meanwhile, the department enlisted several mainstream

Figure 2.3 Stone-throwing protesters try to obstruct supporters of Paul Robeson approaching the concert grounds at Peekskill, New York, 1949. Source: Bettmann / Getty Images.

African American leaders, including Ralph Bunche at the UN and National Association for the Advancement of Colored People (NAACP) executive secretary Walter White, to criticize the CRC statement. The leaders obliged, but not without some quiet misgivings. Yes, the claim of genocide was hyperbolic, but the CRC's evidence of government-sanctioned oppression and murder, much of it compiled by the NAACP itself, was truly damning. As NAACP assistant secretary Roy Wilkins privately wondered, "How can we 'blast' a book that uses our records as source material?" As expected, the US-dominated UN took no action on the CRC's complaint, but the document gained widespread and favorable international notice, including in Western Europe.

The 1952 Presidential Election

Truman was eligible to seek reelection in 1952,[1] but in March of that year he announced that he would not do so. His approval rating was under 30 percent, and he would be getting

[1] The Twenty-second Amendment, ratified in February 1951, states that no person may be elected to more than two presidential terms. It also bars anyone who has served as president "for more than two years of a term to which some other person was elected President" from being elected president more than once. This latter provision describes the experience of Truman, who served for nearly all of Franklin D. Roosevelt's fourth term. But the amendment goes on to say that the restriction does not apply to anyone serving as president at the time of the amendment's proposal by Congress or final ratification by the states. Truman, therefore, was exempted from the restriction.

nearly two terms anyway. Painfully aware that the ongoing Korean War accounted for much of his unpopularity, Truman stepped up the military pressure against North Korea and the PRC, hoping to force their acceptance of the UN Command's ceasefire terms and thus end the conflict before he left office in January 1953. In the summer of 1952, the US Air Force escalated an ongoing bombing campaign against North Korea, reducing Pyongyang and many other cities to rubble and inflicting tens of thousands of civilian casualties. American bombing attacks on hydroelectric plants along the Yalu River deprived North Korea and parts of the PRC of electrical power. But those two nations held firm to their negotiating position, and the war ground on.

His own political ambitions foreclosed, Truman sought to ensure that another Democrat would succeed him. In December 1951, already seeing the handwriting on the wall, he had secretly reached out to US Army General Dwight D. Eisenhower, the hero of D-Day, then serving as the military commander of NATO, to gauge his interest in running for president as a Democrat. Little was known about Eisenhower's views on the issues, but Truman was hardly alone among Democrats in supposing that, if the enormously popular general could just keep the White House in Democratic hands, the politics would somehow sort themselves out. As it happened, prominent Republicans were making their own overtures to Eisenhower, who soon signaled his preference for the GOP. In July, he received the Republican nomination; Senator Richard Nixon became the party's vice-presidential nominee. That same month, the Democrats nominated Illinois's Governor Stevenson for president and, to ensure that white southerners fully supported the ticket this time, awarded the vice-presidential nomination to Senator John Sparkman of Alabama, a staunch segregationist.

Stevenson essentially ran on the Truman program, though with a greater reluctance to speak out on civil rights. His chief political assets were his eloquence, wit, and earnest demeanor, all of which charmed liberal intellectuals. Yet Stevenson faced daunting challenges: the extraordinary appeal of General Eisenhower (affectionately known as "Ike"), the electorate's unhappiness with the war in Korea (which Eisenhower pledged to visit, thereby heightening public expectations that he would quickly end the conflict), and voters' fatigue after nearly two decades of Democratic rule. Stevenson also had to contend with the "communists in government" issue, which Eisenhower and especially Nixon ruthlessly exploited, and with the fact that Truman had been slow to dismiss some self-dealing officials in his administration. A Republican campaign slogan that year, "K_1C_2" – for Korea, communism, and corruption – stated the anti-incumbent case with impressive economy.

One incident during Eisenhower's 1952 presidential campaign left a sour taste in the mouths of observers at the time and historians years later. Privately, Eisenhower despised Joe McCarthy. He was especially appalled by the senator's smearing of George Marshall, who had mentored, supported, and rapidly promoted Eisenhower in the army during World War II. At the same time, Eisenhower's campaign aides recognized McCarthy's hold on the Republican Party's right wing and urged the candidate not to alienate those voters by criticizing the senator. Instead, they persuaded Eisenhower to appear alongside McCarthy at some campaign events in Wisconsin. Determined to stick up for his old boss, Ike inserted a paragraph praising Marshall into a speech he intended to deliver in Milwaukee, "right in McCarthy's backyard." Word of the planned tribute spread through Republican circles and eventually reached, and infuriated, McCarthy himself. As the campaign train chugged toward Milwaukee, Eisenhower's aides pleaded with the candidate to remove the offending passage. Keeping it in, one of them revealingly warned, would be like calling on the Pope and "telling him what a fine person Martin Luther was." Eisenhower relented, rationalizing that he had praised Marshall "in Denver two weeks ago, and there's no real reason to repeat it tonight." The Marshall incident quickly became public knowledge, and Eisenhower received some criticism in the press. Although he seems to have paid no political price for failing to defend Marshall, Eisenhower was personally chagrined by his own lapse. Harry Truman was livid.

Election Day was a rout for the Democrats. Eisenhower won 55.2 percent of the popular vote to Stevenson's 44.3 percent, and 442 electoral votes to his opponent's eighty-nine. For the first time since Herbert Hoover's ignominious ouster two decades earlier, a Republican would occupy the White House. Eisenhower's party also regained control of both the Senate and the House.

As Truman exited the presidency, his approval ratings remained stuck in the low thirties. He had failed to end the Korean War, and McCarthy's wild accusations, though deplored by many, had eroded the president's standing. Yet these negative assessments were hardly the last word on Truman. No one knew it at the time, but the fighting in Korea would end, and McCarthy's influence markedly decline, early in Eisenhower's presidency. Ultimately, Truman's historical reputation would rest on broader results, ones that professional observers and ordinary citizens alike would remember as notable accomplishments: managing a successful, if rocky, transition from war to peace; nurturing a robust and growing private economy; ensuring the survival of the New Deal's core elements (albeit not achieving the major expansion of the program that liberals and progressives desired); establishing a foreign policy infrastructure that vigorously contained Soviet influence while avoiding the reckless ventures urged by some; and making modest efforts to uphold the rights of Black Americans. Of course, this record was subject to criticism. Liberals and progressives would lament Truman's timidity on civil rights and his complicity in the construction of an overweening national security state. Conservatives would flay the president as too enamored of government intervention in the economy and too complacent about the communist menace at home and abroad. For better or worse, though, Truman's governing formula would persist in broad outlines for the next quarter-century – an outcome few Americans could have predicted as the outgoing, and largely accidental, president boarded the train back to Missouri.

Toward Armistice in Korea

The next chapter contains an overview of President Eisenhower's domestic and foreign policies. The remainder of this one examines how the vexing issues of Korea and McCarthy unfolded, and wound down, during Eisenhower's first two years in office. In December 1952, the president-elect made his promised visit to South Korea. A brief survey of the scene confirmed his view that the status quo was untenable. He was already contemplating a strategy for coercing the PRC and North Korea to accept peace on US terms. That same month, the UN General Assembly passed a resolution authorizing the creation of a neutral commission that could take custody over POWs refusing repatriation, thus offering a possible formula for breaking the diplomatic impasse. Taking office in January 1953, Eisenhower did not immediately embrace the UN plan. Instead, his administration beefed up US forces on the peninsula, increased military aid to South Korea, and signaled that it would support Formosan military action against mainland China. But the United States also made a small conciliatory gesture: in late February Mark Clark, the US Army general now heading the UN Command, proposed an interim exchange of sick and wounded POWs.

In early March, Joseph Stalin died. This event would alter the entire course of the cold war, ultimately permitting a more diplomatically oriented, though still highly dangerous, rivalry between the superpowers. Regarding the Korean conflict, the milestone's most immediate consequence was to enable the PRC and North Korea to pursue conciliatory leanings of their own. By now, both nations were extremely eager to end the war, which had imposed devastating human and economic costs on them. Stalin had repeatedly discouraged them from seeking peace; now he was gone. In late March, the PRC and North Korea accepted Clark's POW proposal, and the PRC endorsed the UN resolution on a neutral commission. In April, truce talks resumed at Panmunjom, a town bordering the two Koreas where sporadic negotiations between a PRC/North Korean team and a UN Command delegation had taken place since 1951. Over the next few months, the parties haggled over implementation details. Significant concessions from the communist side placed a final agreement within reach, but a new obstacle arose when Syngman Rhee, South Korea's president, voiced his opposition to any deal that left the North Korean regime in place. Rhee threatened to remove South Korean troops from the UN Command (thus freeing them to launch independent military attacks) and to release all POWs in South Korean custody who opposed repatriation to North Korea or the PRC.

The Eisenhower administration was not about to grant Rhee's wish for an indefinite prolongation of the Korean War. But it *was* prepared to heat up the conflict temporarily so as to gain his acquiescence in an armistice. At the Panmunjom talks in May, the UN Command negotiators, at Washington's behest, insisted that the communists make a number of additional concessions favorable to South Korea. To underscore these demands, the US Air Force destroyed North Korean irrigation dams, railway lines, bridges, and farmland. Meanwhile, John Foster Dulles, the new US secretary of state, warned Indian President Jawaharlal Nehru, who was in direct contact with PRC leaders, "that if the armistice negotiations collapsed, the United States would probably make a stronger rather than a lesser military exertion, and that this might well extend the area of conflict." Both Eisenhower and Dulles later portrayed this statement as a veiled nuclear threat that compelled the PRC to accept an armistice on US terms. Nehru denied, however, that he had conveyed the message to the Chinese.

The purpose of all these belligerent moves was to win enough concessions from the communists to persuade Rhee that his regime could survive in a post-armistice environment. The strategy did succeed in extracting concessions, for, even if the Chinese received no specific nuclear threat from Dulles, the overall situation was sufficiently menacing to make them and the North Koreans downright desperate to end the fighting. In early June, they accepted nearly all of the UN delegation's demands; a final agreement was tantalizingly close. Rhee, however, remained unappeased. In mid-June, he permitted the escape of 25,000 Chinese and North Korean POWs who had opposed repatriation. Eisenhower was outraged by this move, which he feared would scuttle the armistice talks. The PRC and North Korean negotiators were furious as well, accusing the United States of complicity in Rhee's action – but they kept talking at Panmunjom. Swallowing his indignation at Rhee, Ike now concentrated on cajoling him to accept the armistice. In July 1953, after receiving offers of generous US military and economic aid and promises of a US–South Korean mutual defense agreement, Rhee finally dropped his opposition. The UN Command conveyed Rhee's acceptance to the PRC/North Korean delegation and pledged that, in the event South Korea resumed the war, the United States would cut off all assistance to that country. On July 27, the parties signed the Korean armistice agreement.

Formally, the conflict had not been resolved, merely paused by a truce. The opposing Korean parties were almost exactly where they had been before the fighting began. "We have won an armistice on a single battlefield, not peace in the world," Eisenhower said in a television address on the evening of the agreement. "We may not now relax our guard nor cease our quest." General Clark was equally somber, telling reporters, "I cannot find it in me to exult at this hour." Few ordinary Americans could, either. Grim relief, not wild jubilation, was the dominant public mood.

The Fall of McCarthy

In pushing through the Korean armistice, Eisenhower defied those congressional Republicans who, much as General MacArthur had done two years earlier, demanded total victory in the war. On another anticommunist front, the president was more accommodating to the Republican right. The same caution that had prevented Eisenhower from antagonizing Joe McCarthy during the 1952 campaign now carried over into his presidency. And McCarthy still required appeasing. Although political observers had assumed that the Republicans' capture of the White House would cause McCarthy to drop the issue of communists in government, he continued to press it after January 1953. "Like a little wind-up toy that bumps into objects but cannot stop until it runs down," the historian Ellen Schrecker writes, "the Wisconsin senator could not keep from attacking the nation's top officials." His drinking, always excessive, was becoming more so, making him even less careful than before.

Moreover, the Republican takeover in Congress now enabled McCarthy to chair the Senate Government Operations Committee's Permanent Subcomittee on Investigations and to use it as an instrument for harassing the executive branch. His biggest governmental target was the State Department, which he insisted remained a hotbed of communist subversion. Secretary of State Dulles sought to placate McCarthy and other hardliners by purging the department of diplomats who had aroused their ire (and had somehow survived earlier loyalty investigations). The department also ordered its overseas libraries to stop carrying titles "by any controversial persons, Communists, fellow travelers, etcetera," an ominously capacious standard – especially in the "etcetera" – that soon led to the removal of books by the NAACP leader Walter White, the detective writer Dashiell Hammett, the popular journalist Theodore White, and Dulles's own cousin, the historian Foster Rhea Dulles.

McCarthy wasn't satisfied. He complained that one of the ousted diplomats got to keep his pension. In the spring of 1953, the senator's top aide, twenty-six-year-old Roy Cohn, traveled to Europe with David Schine, a young heir to a hotel chain fortune whom McCarthy had hired at Cohn's urging. Cohn and Schine conducted a highly publicized inspection tour of US overseas libraries, to ascertain that those facilities were indeed free of subversive material. Cohn later lamented that the trip was a "colossal mistake" that allowed McCarthy's critics "to spread the tale that a couple of young, inexperienced clowns were hustling about Europe, ordering State Department officials around, burning books, creating chaos wherever they went, and disrupting foreign relations." Apart from the reference to burning books – the young men had yanked them off shelves, not put them to the torch – this was a fair rendition of the episode and its diplomatic impact. In Paris, for example, US diplomats had been quietly urging French officials to remove alleged communists from sensitive government positions. The Cohn–Schine visit, an American diplomat later recalled, "just made anti-Communists look ridiculous, and we couldn't get the French to do anything further about it."

Though disgusted by the McCarthyite tactics, Eisenhower refrained from denouncing them in public for fear of splitting the Republican Party. He also believed that his stature would be diminished by an open feud with the Wisconsin senator. "I will not get into the gutter with that guy," the president vowed. But such reticence only further emboldened McCarthy, who in the fall of 1953 began charging that the US Army, of all institutions, was soft on communism. McCarthy was already pushing his luck by badgering a Republican administration, a move that obviously limited his value as a partisan asset. Now, he was attacking a military branch that *Life* magazine called "the heart of Ike's heart." The senator's first gambit was to investigate allegedly lax security measures at the US Army Signal Corps laboratory at Fort Monmouth, New Jersey. When nothing came of that probe, McCarthy pivoted to a more inviting army target. An army dentist named Irving Peress had received a routine promotion even after questions had arisen about his loyalty. (The army intended to discharge Peress and eventually did so, but the dismissal was delayed through bureaucratic error.) In February 1954, McCarthy grilled Peress's commanding officer, Brigadier General Ralph Zwicker, about this "Communist coddling." When Zwicker, on advice of counsel, declined to answer some questions, McCarthy savaged the decorated World War II combat veteran, saying he was "not fit to wear that uniform."

The abuse of Zwicker was the final straw for Eisenhower, who, though remaining behind the scenes, began scheming to break McCarthy's power. The president instructed the army to release internal records about a bizarre episode that reflected poorly on the senator.

Figure 2.4 A young mother watches the televised Army–McCarthy hearings, 1954. Source: Bettmann / Getty Images.

In late 1953, David Schine had been drafted into the army as a private. Over the ensuing weeks, with McCarthy's indulgence, Cohn relentlessly pressured the army to give Schine favorable treatment, such as relief from menial tasks and frequent leaves of absence. The army, seeking to placate the chief aide of a powerful senator investigating it, repeatedly bowed to Cohn's demands. (The revelations were almost as embarrassing to the army as they were to McCarthy, Cohn, and Schine, but Ike was willing to incur that collateral damage.) McCarthy countercharged that the army had treated Schine as a "hostage" to force the senator to abandon his investigation. To adjudicate the competing claims, in the spring of 1954 the Senate Subcommittee on Investigations held public hearings known as the Army–McCarthy hearings. McCarthy, who had temporarily recused himself as subcommittee chair but continued to participate as both a member and a witness, angrily sparred with army representatives and lawyers, as well as with fellow senators. The new medium of television broadcast the proceedings live; an estimated eighty million viewers saw at least part of the two-month spectacle.

The Army–McCarthy hearings proved deeply damaging to McCarthy, mostly because of the overbearing and reckless manner in which he conducted himself. Previously, television and newsreel viewers had seen only brief film sequences of McCarthy speaking at press conferences or orating from podiums. Now, they had an extended opportunity to watch him interrupting, berating, insulting, and threatening those who got in his way. The US Army's chief counsel, Joseph Welch, whose avuncular, grandfatherly demeanor concealed a shrewdly competitive legal mind, skillfully goaded the senator into revealing his full boorishness.

In one odd but significant respect, the Army–McCarthy hearings were a contest about mentors and protégés, about what cold war America owed to, and could demand of, its up-and-coming young men. McCarthy's and Cohn's cavalier attitude about Schine's army duties – a pattern the hearings vividly detailed – was a serious demerit for the McCarthy side. Behind the scenes, Cohn's own eligibility for military service was another matter of concern. Though young and apparently healthy, Cohn had somehow avoided conscription, causing observers to wonder if he had received favorable treatment. To keep this embarrassing topic out of the hearings, Cohn and McCarthy struck an informal bargain with Welch. If Welch stayed quiet about Cohn's draft status, Cohn and McCarthy would say nothing about the past associations of a young attorney working at Welch's Boston law firm. The lawyer, Frederick Fisher, had in his college days been a member of the National Lawyers Guild (NLG), a left-leaning organization suspected of communist ties. Initially, Welch had planned to include Fisher on the legal team representing the army. After learning of the young man's history, however, Welch had dropped Fisher from the team so as not to expose him to harmful scrutiny.

Each party to the informal agreement had pledged to exercise self-restraint, a quality McCarthy notoriously lacked. On June 9, Welch led Cohn through a deftly mocking cross-examination that left Cohn looking a bit foolish. Furious at seeing his aide humiliated, McCarthy made an impulsive and vicious lunge at Welch's own protectee. He revealed to the millions following the hearings that Welch "has in his law firm a young man named Fisher whom he recommended, incidentally, to do work on this committee, who has been for a number of years a member of an organization which was named … as the legal bulwark of the Communist Party." It was a stunning breach of the gentlemen's agreement, but Welch had anticipated it and was ready with a devastating riposte. Yes, he said, Fisher had told him about the NLG connection, and Welch had kept him off the Army–McCarthy case precisely to spare him this sort of damaging exposure. "Little did I dream," Welch told McCarthy, "you could be so reckless and so cruel as to do an injury to that lad.… I fear he shall always bear a scar needlessly inflicted by you."

McCarthy seemed oblivious to the import of Welch's statement, and he tried to resume his attack on Fisher. Welch broke in: "Let us not assassinate this lad further. You've done enough. Have you no sense of decency, sir, at long last? Have you left no sense of decency?" When Welch concluded his remarks a few minutes later, observers in the Senate gallery broke into rare applause. His question had crystallized their sentiments and those of millions watching and listening from home.

The Subcommittee on Investigations ultimately concluded that Cohn, though not McCarthy himself, had improperly intervened on Private Schine's behalf. It also faulted the army for obstructing McCarthy's investigation at Fort Monmouth. But, if the official verdict was mixed, the political fallout was more consistently damaging to McCarthy. Overall, the public spectacle accelerated a decline in McCarthy's standing that had begun in early 1954. In March, several weeks prior to the start of the hearings, CBS TV's highly regarded reporter Edward R. Murrow hosted a withering exposé of McCarthy's unscrupulous methods. By June, the month the proceedings ended, the senator's Gallup poll approval rating was at 34 percent, down from 50 percent in January. Journalists widely panned his performance in the hearings. More and more Senate Republicans found the courage to criticize their Wisconsin colleague.

In December 1954, the Senate censured McCarthy by a vote of sixty-seven to twenty-two. The rebuke was milder than it could have been. The charges had initially included the mishandling of classified materials and the abuse of witnesses. In the end, McCarthy was censured only for mistreating his Senate colleagues. Politically and personally, however, it was a blow from which McCarthy never recovered. Although he remained in the Senate, his influence rapidly dwindled. In 1957, at the age of forty-eight, he died of alcohol-related disease.

***

The censure of McCarthy encouraged a somewhat more restrained approach to combating alleged communist subversion in American domestic life. To be sure, anticommunism continued to suffuse public discourse, and the blacklists that had taken hold in Hollywood, broadcasting, the civil service, academia, trade unionism, and numerous other realms would remain in effect until the early 1960s in most cases. The FBI and HUAC would continue to target individuals and groups that they genuinely, or conveniently, suspected of communist ties. Anticommunism would be especially long-lived within segregationist politics. Jim Crow's defenders had long claimed that African American resistance to that oppressive order resulted from communist agitation rather than genuine discontent. As the civil rights movement gathered momentum after the mid-1950s, southern state governments used anticommunist legislation and law enforcement mechanisms to prosecute and harass African American individuals and organizations. The FBI, too, would employ anticommunism as a rationale for surveilling and harassing even mainstream civil rights activists until the late 1960s.

With all that, from the mid-fifties on anticommunism gradually became, on the whole, less pervasive and coercive in American public life. Domestically, the recent experience with McCarthy had shown that exaggerating the communist threat, or countering it too broadly, posed dangers of its own. In foreign affairs, Stalin's death and the Korean armistice had created space for a less relentlessly antagonistic relationship between the United States and the Soviet Union. The growing diplomatic prominence of Asian, Middle Eastern, and North African nations, moreover, complicated the international scene and further diminished the salience of crude cold war thinking. In a nation and world marked by greater dynamism and fluidity, Americans could think and act a bit more freely. As we shall see in the next two chapters, the 1950s featured considerable social conformity but also persistent undercurrents of skepticism and rebellion. Those latter qualities grew more prevalent as the pall of McCarthyism steadily lifted.

READING QUESTIONS

1. Consider the arguments made by those who, by early 1950, insisted that greater vigilance against domestic communist subversion had become necessary. Which of these arguments were the most persuasive, and which were the least? Why?

2. Many historians regard the outbreak of the Korean War in June 1950 as a pivotal event both in domestic US history and in the history of US foreign relations. What is the basis for this assessment in each area?
3. Why did so many Republicans consider Senator Joseph McCarthy a political asset? What risks did they ultimately run in encouraging his anticommunist efforts?
4. Are you more inclined to see Dwight Eisenhower (first as presidential candidate and then as president) as a cynical appeaser of Joe McCarthy or as a shrewd underminer of the Wisconsin senator? Was Eisenhower actually both of those things? Something in between?

SUGGESTIONS FOR FURTHER READING

Anderson, Carol. *Eyes Off the Prize: The United Nations and the African American Struggle for Human Rights, 1944–1955*. New York: Cambridge University Press, 2003.

Byrnes, Mark S. *The Truman Years, 1945–1953*. New York: Longman, 2000.

Dallek, Robert. *Harry S. Truman*. New York: Times Books, 2008.

Gallant, Gregory P. *Hope and Fear in Margaret Chase Smith's America: A Continuous Tangle*. Lanham, MD: Lexington Books, 2014.

Horne, Gerald. *Paul Robeson: The Artist as Revolutionary*. London: Pluto Press, 2016.

Johnson, David K. *The Lavender Scare: The Cold War Persecution of Gays and Lesbians in the Federal Government*. Chicago: University of Chicago Press, 2004.

Oshinsky, David M. *A Conspiracy So Immense: The World of Joe McCarthy*, 2nd edn. New York: Oxford University Press, 2005.

Plummer, Brenda Gayle. *Rising Wind: Black Americans and US Foreign Affairs, 1935–1960*. Chapel Hill, NC: University of North Carolina Press, 1996.

Schrecker, Ellen. *Many Are the Crimes: McCarthyism in America*. Princeton, NJ: Princeton University Press, 1998.

Sherman, Janann. *No Place for a Woman: A Life of Senator Margaret Chase Smith*. New Brunswick, NJ: Rutgers University Press, 1999.

Stueck, William. *The Korean War: An International History*. Princeton, NJ: Princeton University Press, 1995.

Theoharis, Athan G. *The FBI and American Democracy: A Brief Critical History*. Lawrence, KS: University Press of Kansas, 2004.

Whitfield, Stephen J. *The Culture of the Cold War*. Baltimore: Johns Hopkins University Press, 1991.

3 It's Like Turning Over a Rock

America in the Fifties

Introduction

It was the publishing sensation of the decade, a runaway success by a young, first-time author. Grace Metalious's novel, *Peyton Place*, was a lurid exposé of provincial hypocrisy, a sprawling saga of a small New England town that appeared serene on the surface but churned underneath with sexual intrigue, malicious gossip, class exploitation, and domestic violence. The novel was based, Metalious intimated, on real-life events in her own town of Gilmanton, New Hampshire. Places such as Gilmanton, she told an interviewer, might to an outsider "look as peaceful as a postcard picture. But if you go beneath that picture, it's like turning over a rock with your foot – all kinds of strange things crawl out."

Peyton Place soared to the top of the bestseller lists in the fall of 1956 and stayed there for many months, eventually becoming the top-selling American novel of the twentieth century. Fueling the phenomenon were new techniques of mass printing and marketing, and a new aggressiveness in exploiting multimedia tie-ins to create what a later generation would call "buzz." In a decade in which millions of Americans shared the same tastes in mayonnaise, deodorant, and television situation comedies, it seemed fitting that they should be reading the same paperbacks, too. The novel's 1957 movie adaptation, and its third incarnation as a television series from 1964 to 1969, further enshrined *Peyton Place* in the popular imagination.

That said, the disturbing content of *Peyton Place* – including an incest subplot – was light years from the bland sensibilities guiding most consumer culture in the 1950s. The novel's breakout success revealed a keen appetite for discordant themes on the part of the public, especially the book's largely female readership. Decades later, some scholars would detect quasifeminist elements in Metalious's work, most notably her flawed but gritty female characters, who struggle to carve out independent lives and regard many of the men in their midst with righteous fury or cool disdain. Metalious herself was a stubborn obstacle to publicists' attempts to package the thirty-two-year-old "authoress" as a glamorous, winking sharer of dishy secrets. She appeared in public in lumberjack shirts, jeans, sneakers, a ponytail, and no makeup. She made no effort to slim down or to hide the fact that she drank heavily and had extramarital affairs. "I think diets are stupid," she declared. "I don't wear nylon stockings or girdles. I don't waste any time shopping." The publicists made the best of it by dubbing Metalious "Pandora in blue jeans," but that was the closest they could get her to any marketable feminine archetype.

Even so, the consumer culture had formidable resources. The movie version of *Peyton Place* significantly softened the novel's content, turning biting commentary into frothy melodrama. "In leaning backwards not to offend," *Variety* quipped in its review, "producer and writer have gone acrobatic." Metalious wept after watching the film, telling her husband, "It's over … It's all over." Here was an object lesson in the dominant culture's capacity – displayed repeatedly throughout the decade, and beyond – to absorb and tame even the sharpest critiques. The TV series of the 1960s was blander still, though Metalious never saw it, for she died of alcohol-related liver disease several months before it started to air.

The tensions surrounding *Peyton Place* and its reception – between appearance and reality, between conformity and idiosyncrasy, between smooth acquiescence and prickly rebellion – provide a useful framework for apprehending American life in the 1950s. The decade is remembered, rightly, as a time of unprecedented prosperity and unusual societal cohesion, during which most Americans were more interested in living comfortably and fitting in than in posing difficult questions about their society. With the majority of the population now solidly middle-class, and with earlier ideological battles largely settled, stalemated, or paused, it was, for most, a time of respite and consolidation.

At the same time, it took little *Peyton*ian probing to find considerable dissatisfaction with the status quo and evidence that millions were not sharing in the American dream. Conformity may have been the reigning mood, but there was no shortage of doubters and dissenters. At the political margins, radical labor activists and immigrant rights advocates waged their battles, with little validation from the journalistic mainstream. Receiving much wider recognition were the prominent artists, writers, and social critics who raised penetrating questions about the established order but generally privileged individual autonomy over social action. In the second half of the decade, bolder challenges emanated from the Beat movement, from the creators and consumers of rhythm and blues and rock and roll, and from a diffuse set of cultural and political actors who sounded alarms about nuclear dangers. But the most consequential disrupter of business as usual was an ascendant civil rights movement whose campaigns, for the first time, received sustained national attention. All of these stirrings were a vital prelude to the much broader social, cultural, and political rebellions of the next decade.

A Thriving Economy – and Its Challenges

One of the most striking features of American life in the 1950s was the continuation and expansion of the economic prosperity that the nation had enjoyed since the end of World War II. Between 1945 and 1960, the gross national product (GNP) expanded by 250 percent, and per capita income increased by 35 percent. In 1945, 40 percent of American families had owned homes; by 1960, the figure was 60 percent. By the mid-1950s, 60 percent of families had achieved middle-class status, defined as receiving annual incomes between $3,000 and $10,000. During the Depression, the unemployment rate had risen as high as 25 percent. For most of the 1950s, it hovered at 5 percent or lower. Eighty-seven percent of households owned television sets in 1960, up from just 9 percent ten years earlier.

A major driver of postwar prosperity was the national government's involvement in the private economy. During World War II, the government had pumped billions of dollars into the private sector by means of war contracts; it enlisted private companies to furnish armaments and other products and services needed for the war effort. The resulting boom in productivity created millions of jobs, increasing the purchasing power of ordinary Americans and thus stimulating the economy. Federal spending during the war solved the conundrum of underconsumption; federal action in the postwar years kept it from recurring.

The latter phenomenon unfolded in a number of ways. Cold war tensions, and especially the Korean War, occasioned a new surge of contracting and production, creating, albeit on a smaller scale, the same sorts of jobs that had become available during World War II. Even after the Korean armistice, a massive and growing defense establishment remained. To sustain it, Washington invested billions in the emerging high-technology sector, subsidizing research and development in electronics, aerospace, fiber optics, laser technology, and chemicals. Although their primary motivation was military, these investments led to technological spin-offs – in aircraft design, medicine, computers, and other fields – that stimulated the civilian economy. Meanwhile, as noted in Chapter 1, Washington primed the economic pump with the GI Bill, which enabled returning veterans to receive university and vocational training, start businesses, and buy homes. Though distributed unequally (especially when it came to race), the program's benefits lifted millions of Americans into the middle class, allowing them to take part in, and fuel, the burgeoning consumer economy.

To ensure maximum consumer participation, corporations enlisted the services of advertising agencies, which formed a $12-billion-a-year industry by 1960. Employing sophisticated techniques of persuasion, ads appearing in magazines, on billboards, on radio, and especially on television stimulated new appetites among consumers, while assuring them that their purchasing choices enhanced their social status or gained them admission into a world of carefree adventure. Catchy slogans such as "See the USA in your Chevrolet" and "More bounce to the ounce" (for Pepsi Cola) lodged in people's consciousness and helped to knit a national consumer culture. Credit was another major lubricant of consumption. Installment buying had been around for some decades, but the appearance in 1950 of the modern credit card, which could be used for purchases from multiple vendors, vastly expanded consumers' ability to "buy now and pay later." Although the innovation, unsurprisingly, increased Americans' indebtedness, it placed both the necessities and luxuries of life within ever easier reach.

Still, the economic picture was not entirely sunny. A mild recession took place in 1953–1954, and a more severe one occurred in 1957–1958, when the unemployment rate reached 7.5 percent. The nation's wealth, moreover, was very unevenly distributed, with the bottom fifth of American families earning less than 5 percent of the national income and the top fifth taking in over 40 percent, a discrepancy that persisted throughout the decade. The nation's poorest tended to be clustered in inner cities and isolated rural areas. They were disproportionately people of color: urban African Americans and Latinos; Black sharecroppers in the South; Latino migrant laborers in the West and Southwest; Native Americans on reservations. Millions of whites also remained very poor, especially in rural areas. All of these forms of poverty were largely invisible to the wider society. Not until the following decade would they attract national attention or would comprehensive efforts be made to alleviate them. A major cause of such neglect in the 1950s was the robustness of the new middle class, which had become sufficiently broad-based to ensure a level of consumption that kept the general prosperity going. In the 1930s, the poor had been so numerous that their lack of purchasing power dragged the national economy down. Two decades later, the pockets of poverty were too small and isolated to do that, and so they could be safely ignored.

Throughout the 1950s, about a third of the US workforce belonged to unions. Although the period is often remembered as a time of relative harmony in labor relations, during which management achieved peace on the factory floor by offering workers generous terms, the reality was more complicated. Unions were, by and large, able to negotiate regular wage increases and continued benefits, and these gains raised the standards for much of nonunion labor as well. Median family incomes steadily rose during the decade, and millions of wage earners were able to buy homes, take paid vacations, and enjoy other benefits of middle-class life. Yet this was also a period of considerable labor conflict. An average of 352 major authorized strikes, and a comparable number of unauthorized ones, erupted each year in the 1950s. Most of these stoppages focused on wages, hours, and benefits rather than on the broader aspirations for shared management that trade unionists had harbored in the previous decade. In this respect, the strikes revealed the diminished clout of unions, and the narrowed scope in which they could operate, following the 1947 Taft–Hartley Act (see Chapter 1).

Moreover, corporate managers in the 1950s were pioneering strategies that, a generation later, would enable them to break unions' power. General Electric, the Ford Motor Company, the Radio Corporation of America, and numerous lesser-known companies moved some of their factories to southern states, where workers earned less and were almost entirely unorganized. (Fearing that unions would empower African Americans, the South's political and economic elite had long suppressed labor activism across the board, to the detriment of workers of all racial and ethnic backgrounds.) Executives were also perfecting their stiff-arm tactics. In a practice known as Boulwarism, named after General Electric's vice president for labor relations, Lemuel Ricketts Boulware, GE ceased holding genuine negotiations with union representatives. Instead, the company would go through the motions of bargaining and then unveil a take-it-or-leave-it offer. The purpose was to demonstrate that workers had nothing to gain by pressuring the company or, indeed, by organizing at all. Such antilabor practices grew somewhat more prevalent in the late 1950s, amid an economic recession that increased unemployment and thus reduced workers' bargaining power. Still, they remained a minor feature of the overall labor picture.

For those at the bottom of the labor scale, of course, life was much harder. Agricultural laborers and domestic servants, disproportionately people of color, worked in backbreaking or degrading conditions for paltry wages. Very few of them enjoyed union representation.

Many Latino farm laborers, and many Latinos generally, faced the added burden of threatened deportation. Since the early 1940s, economic dislocation in their home country and a demand for labor from US employers, especially in agriculture, had caused hundreds of thousands of Mexicans to enter the United States. Through the Bracero Program (1942–1964), the US and Mexican governments cooperated with each other to manage this migrant flow. With Mexico's approval, the United States granted Mexican workers temporary permits that obligated them to return home after completing their labor contracts. As US demand for seasonal labor increased, growing numbers of Mexicans entered or remained in the United States illegally. In response, Washington beefed up its southern Border Patrol, which apprehended unlawful border crossers and delivered them to Mexican authorities, who, to discourage further attempted crossings, transported them into Mexico's interior.

By the early 1950s, the US Border Patrol was conducting raids against settled Mexican communities in the United States, rounding up and deporting those deemed illegal. It was a massive effort; a single raid could entail scores of agents, thousands of deportees, fleets of buses for transport to the border, and even surveillance aircraft. In 1954, Herbert Brownell, President Eisenhower's attorney general, unveiled the deportation program with great fanfare, downplaying the fact that it had been going on for some years. He called it Operation Wetback, employing a derogatory word for Mexicans who illicitly entered the country by wading or swimming across the Rio Grande, the river bordering Mexico and Texas. ("Wetback" has always been pejorative, but it was far more accepted in the 1950s than it would be in later decades. A 1951 *Life* magazine article was titled "Wetbacks Swarm In," and even some Mexican American leaders used the term in public.)

Two aims of Brownell's publicity were to deter future attempts at illegal entry and to persuade undocumented Mexican migrants to choose to return to Mexico. Indeed, most of the approximately 500,000 repatriations occurring under the program were voluntary – a preferred option for many, as it preserved returnees' legal ability to apply to reenter the United States at some later date. Inevitably, people of Mexican origin who had lived in the United States for decades, some with credible claims to legal residency or even US citizenship, were compelled to leave. The policy also caused great hardship to deportees' family members who were themselves legal residents or citizens.

The intensification of the red scare in the early 1950s only deepened the vulnerability of Mexican immigrants and those close to them. The Internal Security Act of 1950 (see Chapter 2) increased the president's authority to exclude or deport foreigners classified as subversive. The Immigration and Naturalization Service (INS) began deploying these powers against Mexican immigrants with radical associations. Emblematic was the case of fifty-nine-year-old Elias Espinoza of Santa Ana, California, who had lived in the United States for forty-eight years and had eight US-born children. In the 1930s, Espinoza had been a member of the Workers' Alliance, a leftist organization with ties to the Communist Party. In 1951, federal authorities in southern California arrested Espinoza and three other Mexican men with radical pasts and subjected them to deportation proceedings. Immigrant rights activists furnished legal services to the detainees, and Mexican American community members sent letters and telegrams to the local immigration office on behalf of the "Santa

Ana Four." In his own letter to an INS official, Espinoza's nine-year-old son Joel pleaded that he and his seven siblings "need someone to make a living for us." The boy added: "My brother Danny and I are Cub Scouts and we need our father to take us on hikes and to Pack meetings." Although one of the Santa Ana Four was allowed to remain in the country, Espinoza and the two other defendants lost their cases and were deported to Mexico.

Suburbia

For growing numbers of Americans in the 1950s, talk of Cub Scout hikes and pack meetings evoked a far less troubled world, one of comfort and community in the nation's rapidly expanding suburbs. From 1950 to 1960, the suburban population increased by about seventeen million, and by decade's end 30 percent of Americans lived in suburbs. Whole communities sprang up nearly overnight, linked to workplaces by commuter trains and newly built highways. The Federal Highway Act of 1956 funded the construction of a 41,000-mile interstate highway system. Though partly designed to evacuate cities in case of nuclear war, the Act made travel between cities and suburbs much faster and easier. It became increasingly common for middle-class families to own more than one car – previously a luxury confined to the rich – so that homemakers (almost invariably wives) could run errands while breadwinners (almost invariably husbands) drove to paid employment.

Suburbanization was facilitated, of course, by loans provided to veterans under the GI Bill. Key, too, was a revolution in the construction and marketing of housing. The best-known figure in that transformation was a real estate developer named William Levitt. Levitt had built airfields for the Navy during World War II, whose exigencies forced him to perfect techniques for streamlining construction. Immediately after the war, there was a huge demand for housing, as veterans returned home and the marriage and birth rates spiked. In 1946, Levitt purchased a tract of land on Long Island, New York, on which he created the largest American housing development to date, eventually consisting of 17,000 homes, each selling for about $8,000. To accomplish this scale, Levitt applied to home construction some of the manufacturing techniques automakers had pioneered in the 1910s and 1920s. But there was this difference: in the auto industry, the workers had been stationary and the cars had glided by on conveyor belts; in Levitt's operation, the houses were stationary and the workers were mobile. Teams moved from house to house in rapid succession, each performing a specific task – drywalling, tiling, painting, window installing – that was repeated at every site.

The result was a simple, durable, and affordable dwelling that, though hardly luxurious, was considerably more spacious and comfortable than what most of Levitt's recently working-class customers were used to. The county built five public schools to serve the thousands of families forming the new community. Levitt named his housing development "Island Trees," but everyone called it "Levittown." The formula was immensely popular, and soon Levitt was building similar developments in upstate New York and Pennsylvania. Other developers imitated Levitt's approach. By 1955, three-quarters of all new housing starts were Levitt-style subdivisions.

Those moving to the suburbs often found themselves in an entirely new social world, with its own rules, norms, and expectations. Levitt-type developments usually imposed strict regulations on how residents were to mow and furnish their lawns. Residents were often barred from hanging laundry out to dry or raising chickens in their backyards. They also faced heavy social pressure to join neighborhood associations, put up Christmas tree lights, attend garage sales, hold bridge parties, and participate in countless other group activities. As Levitt himself famously boasted, "No man who owns his own house and lot can be a Communist. He has too much to do."

Ironically, then, an activity many considered the ultimate expression of American individualism – home buying – could be a profoundly collectivist act. Many suburbanites thrived on the cult of togetherness. Families carpooled and baby-sat for each other; they pitched in to fund the addition of playgrounds, landscaping, and other improvements to their subdivisions. For people no longer living in close proximity to extended family, the suburban community could be a source of comfort, support, and entertainment. But others found the social expectations stultifying. Those showing insufficient enthusiasm for neighborhood activities risked being branded antisocial and ostracized by the community. A faux pas could cast a household into social purgatory. From afar, social critics derided suburban developments as "fresh-air slums" and "treeless communal wasteland[s]" where bland and mindless uniformity prevailed.

There was, of course, considerably more diversity of outlook and habit in the 'burbs than such snobbery acknowledged. But in one respect the rigid homogeneity exceeded what mainstream commentators alleged. African Americans were barred from buying homes in any of Levitt's subdivisions, a restriction that lasted until the late 1960s and was replicated in other housing developments. Levitt insisted that he was powerless in the matter. "As a Jew I have no room in my mind or heart for racial prejudice," he said in 1954. "But ... if we sell one house to a Negro family, then 90 to 95 percent of our white customers will not buy into the community. That is their attitude, not ours.... As a company our position is simply this: we can solve a housing problem, or we can try to solve a racial problem. But we cannot combine the two."

Levitt told only part of the story. Racial exclusion wasn't just a reflection of popular white sentiment; it also grew out of national policy. Since the creation of the Federal Housing Authority in 1934, the federal government had guaranteed private bank loans to home buyers. This New Deal program, along with the subsequent GI Bill, had enabled lenders to offer long-term, low-interest mortgages to millions of Americans, fueling the massive growth of suburbs. Federal loan guarantees were generally unavailable, however, for home buying in racially mixed neighborhoods, on the ground that their lack of "stability" made them "actuarially unsound." Thus white homeowners, and the realtors who catered to them, had powerful financial incentives to ensure that all-white neighborhoods stayed that way. Residential segregation also drew sustenance from federal *inaction*. In the 1948 case *Shelley v. Kraemer*, the US Supreme Court ruled that racially restrictive covenants – clauses in real estate deeds forbidding homeowners from selling their property to racial minorities and Jews – were legally unenforceable. But the decision stated that private parties could voluntarily abide by such covenants, which remained ubiquitous in real estate contracts.

Figure 3.1 William and Daisy Myers, 1957. Source: Bettmann / Getty Images.

Opponents of segregation did try, with limited success, to breach the color line in suburban housing developments. In the early 1950s, Levitt opened a subdivision twenty miles out of Philadelphia. The American Friends Services Committee (AFSC), a Quaker organization concerned with peace and social justice, set out to integrate the new Levittown. It took some years for the AFSC to make the necessary arrangements, but in 1957 a Black family – William and Daisy Myers and their three young children – acquired a home from a willing white seller and moved into the development.

As the AFSC had taken pains to ensure, the Myerses bore all the markings of middle-class respectability. William was a World War II veteran, a college graduate, and a refrigeration technician; Daisy was a schoolteacher and a member of the county's recreation board. Yet these facts scarcely blunted the hostility of their white neighbors. For several weeks following the Myerses' arrival, white protesters gathered outside their home, displaying Confederate flags and shouting racial epithets. Vandals broke the Myerses' windows and spraypainted "KKK" (for Ku Klux Klan) on their house. Someone burned a cross on the lawn of a white AFSC activist assisting the Myerses. The white Levittowner who had sold his home to them was fired from his job. Although the overt resistance eventually subsided, the community continued to seethe, and the newcomers could never drop their guard. Tiring of the constant scrutiny and tension, the Myerses left Levittown in 1959. By then, a second Black family, also recruited by the AFSC, had moved into the development without sparking a violent revolt. But the Myerses' ordeal had been widely covered in the Black press, and few other African Americans, even if they could afford it, sought to undergo such an experience themselves.

Popular and Public Culture in the Fifties

Although social conflict of this sort sometimes broke through into mainstream news coverage, it was mostly absent from popular entertainment, which instead projected images of national harmony and homogeneity, usually drawn from white, middle-class archetypes. Television underwent explosive growth in this era. The technology had been pioneered in the 1920s but did not become commercially viable until the early postwar years. In 1946, just six TV stations existed nationwide; by 1956 there were 442, most of them affiliated with, and standardized by, the three main networks, ABC, CBS, and NBC. In the late 1940s and early 1950s, a handful of realistic, high-quality dramas aired on television, but they soon gave way to blander fare, which netted larger audiences and thus ampler advertising revenues. Family-centered shows such as *Ozzie and Harriet*, *Father Knows Best*, and *Leave it to Beaver*, the historian Paul Boyer writes, "peddled a standard image of middle-class family life and gender roles: supportive wives and mothers who never leave home or remove their aprons, benign fathers who materialize at dinnertime to resolve the petty crises of the day, wise-cracking kids who get into amusing scrapes and indulge in innocuous protest gestures but who ultimately recognize their parents' authority." *The Honeymooners* and *I Love Lucy* were somewhat more adventurous. While the former featured working-class characters whose bickering occasionally spoofed traditional gender roles, the latter centered on a marriage between a white American woman and a Cuban man. Lucy's ditziness, however, struck no blows for feminism.

Relentlessly, American habits conformed to the new medium. By the mid-1950s, surveys showed, the average household had the television set on for five hours a day. The invention of frozen TV dinners in 1954 encouraged families to watch during meals. That same year, city officials in Toledo, Ohio, noticed that water consumption spiked during the commercial breaks of popular TV shows, as thousands of city dwellers flushed as one. By 1956, average weekly movie attendance was half the size it had been a decade earlier. Television also enabled numerous nationwide fads. The popular children's show *Davy Crockett*, about the nineteenth-century frontiersman and politician, loosed a torrent of Crockett-themed commercial paraphernalia – knives, bow-and-arrow sets, sound recordings, and, especially, raccoon skin caps. The era's Hula-Hoop craze largely resulted from a TV advertising campaign mounted by Wham-O, a California toy company.

But fifties TV wasn't all commercialism and frivolity. Occasionally, television journalists aired hard-hitting reports that held the powerful to account and posed challenging questions to the wider society. In the spring of 1954 (admittedly, a bit late in the day), Edward R. Murrow used his popular CBS program *See It Now* to expose Senator Joseph McCarthy's recklessly dishonest methods. In 1960, Murrow hosted the CBS documentary *Harvest of Shame*, which laid bare the squalid and exploitative working conditions of mostly Black migrant farm laborers up and down the East Coast, provoking furious complaints from agribusiness. Religious programs, too, became a broadcasting staple. Millions tuned in to the televised sermons of Billy Graham, an evangelical Baptist minister, and Fulton J. Sheen, a Roman Catholic bishop.

Indeed, overt religiosity was a defining feature of the era. Between 1940 and 1960, Church membership nearly doubled (from 64 million to 114 million), while the nation's population increased by a bit more than a third (from 132 million to 180 million). A 1958 survey found that 98 percent of Americans professed a belief in God. Reflecting the public mood, in 1954 Congress voted to insert "under God" into the Pledge of Allegiance and engrave "In God We Trust" on American coins. No doubt, the religious turn grew out of genuine conviction, but it also appeared to answer a yearning for connection on the part of Americans recently separated from the tight-knit communities of their upbringing. Churches sprang up around the new suburban subdivisions and became centers of social activity. Spiritual devotion also, of course, distinguished the United States and its allies from the atheistic communist bloc. "Our religious faith gives us the answer to the false beliefs of communism," President Truman remarked in 1951. "Surely, we can follow that faith with the same devotion and determination the Communists give to their godless creed."

Opinion leaders often downplayed the theological content of Americans' beliefs and celebrated the fact that their fellow citizens believed in *something*. "Our form of government has no sense unless it is founded in a deeply felt religious faith," President-elect Eisenhower proclaimed in late 1952, "and I don't care what it is." The statement struck some commentators as vacuous, but it did signal a more accepting attitude toward Catholics and Jews, groups the Protestant-dominated society had historically regarded with suspicion or outright hostility. Cold war ideology reinforced such inclusiveness. The huge audience for Bishop Sheen's television program *Life Is Worth Living* contained large numbers of non-Catholics who appreciated, among other things, the host's staunch anticommunism. The era's most famous anticommunist, Joe McCarthy, was another Catholic whose appeal extended far beyond his denomination, especially in the decade's early years. In his 1953 testimony before the House Committee on Un-American Activities, the University of Chicago historian Daniel Boorstin insisted that he had fully repudiated his youthful infatuation with communism. Asked to demonstrate that this was so, Boorstin pleased his interrogators by citing his participation in Hillel, a Jewish campus organization.

Gender and Domesticity

As in previous eras, the Bible was the top-selling book in fifties America. Number two was Dr. Benjamin Spock's *Common Sense Book of Baby and Child Care*, first published in 1946. Spock urged mothers of young children to see parenting as their central calling. "If a mother realizes clearly how vital this kind of care is to a small child," he wrote, "it may make it easier for her to decide that the extra money she might earn, or the satisfaction she might receive from an outside job, is not so important after all." Spock joined a chorus of authority figures – doctors, psychologists, social scientists, advice columnists, clergy, and others – who insisted that a woman's true happiness resided in devoting herself to her husband and children and in making the home an island of comfort, nurture, harmony, and culinary excellence in an increasingly harsh and impersonal world. If a woman expressed misgivings about playing such a role, she could be labeled selfish, antisocial, neurotic, or "masculinized." If, on the other hand, she wholly surrendered to domesticity, she was assured that ultimate fulfillment, including sexual gratification, lay within reach.

The women at the center of these exhortations were middle-class and presumptively white; women lacking those characteristics were seldom the target of mainstream advice on marriage, childrearing, homemaking, and fashion. Even for the first group, however, significant discrepancies existed between ideology and reality. It is true that, by 1950, almost 60 percent of women between the ages of eighteen and twenty-four were married, in contrast with just 42 percent in 1940. The birth rate soared in the 1950s, and the US population grew by nearly thirty million. (Medical advances such as the wider distribution of antibiotics, developed in earlier decades, and the introduction of a polio vaccine in the mid-1950s helped to extend life expectancy, contributing to rapid population growth.) Yet employment figures from the era complicate the picture. Even as more and more women were marrying, moving to the suburbs, and having children, they were entering the job market in unprecedented numbers, though the typical woman doing those first three things often was a younger version of the woman doing the fourth.

For a few years after World War II, the percentage of women in paid employment declined. But that number started rising again in the late 1940s and continued to do so throughout the next decade. By 1960, more than a third of American women worked outside the home. Many women joining the workforce in the 1950s took clerical, secretarial, or other white-collar jobs, meeting the labor demands of an increasingly service-oriented and bureaucratized economy. The general profile of the female worker was shifting toward someone who was better educated and a bit older – say, a married mother with college education whose children were now in school. A major driver of this change was perceived economic necessity. All too often, a married couple couldn't achieve the middle-class standard of living to which it aspired unless the wife supplemented the husband's earnings. Thus the surge in female employment, writes the historian William Chafe, was "led by the same middle-class wives and mothers who allegedly had found new contentment in domesticity." These women earned only about sixty cents for every dollar that men earned for comparable work. After all, employers rationalized, the female hires were merely working for "pin money." Because so many of them worked part-time or for only a few years, they were poorly positioned to advocate for higher pay. Hardly any could build professionally satisfying careers.

Meanwhile, it was increasingly expected that young middle-class women would attend college, and hundreds of thousands did so in the 1950s. The purpose of such education was often unclear, however. Many female students, like their male counterparts, were promised that college would broaden their intellectual horizons and provide them with important professional skills. Yet many also got the message that the real reason to go to college was to find a suitable mate; they were discouraged from acting "too smart" and scaring away potential suitors. Forty percent of students surveyed at Barnard College, the women's auxiliary of Columbia University, reported that they "played dumb" on dates. College-educated women who became full-time homemakers sometimes struggled with the tedium of their new lives. "[T]he plunge," one of them observed, "from the strictly intellectual college life to the 24-hour a day domestic one is a terrible shock."

Clearly, there were significant contradictions in the expectations and experiences of middle-class women, some of whom were deeply conflicted. But few had the language to articulate their discontent, and so it tended to emerge indirectly. The same women's magazines that extolled the blessings of homemaking ran occasional stories on rising rates of divorce and alcoholism in the suburbs. A December 1956 *Life* magazine article captured a piece of the truth when it observed that stay-at-home wives were prone to "feel thwarted and somehow inferior, because society has given them underlying attitudes that make them believe that the full, rich life lies elsewhere." The article concluded, however, that such beliefs were mistaken and that housewives would find happiness once they realized that "the full, rich life" lay right under their noses. Several years later, drawing on impressions, research, and personal testimonies first gathered in this period, a part-time journalist and homemaker named Betty Friedan would incisively mine such contradictions in a bestselling book, *The Feminine Mystique* (see Chapters 5 and 8). Friedan's 1963 opus would help to launch a fundamental reimagining of relations between the sexes and of women's roles in a rapidly changing society.

The Eisenhower Presidency

In the realm of high politics – where presidents, cabinet members, congressional leaders, and foreign actors cooperated and clashed over America's fundamental domestic policies and position in the world – concerns such as Friedan's scarcely registered. For most of the decade, the dominant political figure was President Dwight D. Eisenhower, whose pair of terms lasted from January 1953 to January 1961. He scored landslide victories in 1952 and 1956, both times against the same Democratic opponent, the serving and then former governor of Illinois, Adlai E. Stevenson. Eisenhower, or "Ike," as he was known, had won international acclaim during the latter stages of World War II, when, as a US Army general, he had organized and overseen the landing of Allied forces in France and the subsequent defeat of Nazi Germany. After the war, Eisenhower served as army chief of staff, president of Columbia University, and supreme commander of NATO forces, before accepting the Republican presidential nomination in 1952.

Although nearly everyone revered Ike's military record, some observers underestimated his abilities as a civilian leader, seeing the president as an amiable but passive figure who relied too heavily on his advisers and played a bit too much golf for a man in his position. Eisenhower was sixty-two when he took office and seventy when he left it, an advanced age range by the standards of the day. A heart attack in 1955 and a mild stroke in 1957 noticeably slowed him down. His jumbled syntax at press conferences, gently lampooned by pundits and comedians, reinforced the impression of a man well past his prime. Years later, however, the declassification of Eisenhower's presidential papers revealed a leader considerably more in command of events than he seemed at the time, a shrewd executive content to govern behind the scenes and allow subordinates to take the credit – or blame – for his administration's actions. Whatever the merits of his performance in office, Eisenhower retained his popularity with the public, a reassuring presence to millions of Americans.

Mostly, Eisenhower governed as a moderate conservative. To the dismay of rightwing Republicans, he refused to seek the dismantling of key New Deal programs such as Social Security and federal subsidies for farmers. The president believed that the public now took these programs for granted and that trying to undo them would be political folly. "Should any political party attempt to abolish social security, unemployment insurance, and eliminate labor laws and farm programs," Eisenhower wrote his brother in 1954, "you would not hear of that party again in our political history. There is a tiny splinter group, of course, that believes you can do these things.... Their number is negligible and they are stupid." (The fact that Democrats controlled both houses of Congress for six of Ike's eight years in office, from 1955 to 1961, was a further inducement to moderation.) Eisenhower's acceptance of those New Deal programs was highly consequential; it made them bipartisan and thus entrenched them more deeply in American political culture.

Within the limits of this basic concession, however, Eisenhower was deferential to the private sector and sought to limit federal involvement in the economy. Several of his cabinet members were corporate executives. The chief exemplar of the type was Secretary of Defense Charles Wilson, the former head of General Motors, who famously declared at his confirmation hearing, "[F]or years I thought what was good for our country was good for General Motors, and vice versa." The "vice versa" gave liberals license to invert the quotation and make it sound a lot worse. To combat what he saw as excessive statism, Eisenhower encouraged Congress to pass legislation transferring $40 billion worth of oil-rich offshore lands from federal to state control, a boon to oil companies, which could now more easily exploit those areas. Eisenhower also cancelled a plan, developed by the Truman administration, for the federal government to build a major dam on Idaho's Snake River, instead authorizing private companies to dam that waterway.

In two areas of domestic life, Ike's record has come in for sharp criticism by historians. First, as noted in Chapter 2, Eisenhower remained silent for most of Joe McCarthy's anticommunist rampage; not until 1954 did he start working to thwart the senator, and even those efforts occurred mainly behind the scenes. Second, as we shall see later in this chapter, Eisenhower exerted hardly any leadership on one of the most pressing moral and political issues of the decade: the struggle of Black Americans for civic equality and dignity.

In foreign affairs, Eisenhower continued his predecessor's stance of vigorous cold war containment, with some modifications. Ike presided over a considerable expansion of the US arsenal, especially nuclear weapons. In part, the nuclear emphasis was an economic measure. It cost far less to achieve a given level of destructive power with nuclear weapons than it did by conventional means, all the more so after the nation's successful testing of a hydrogen bomb in November 1952. Nuclear weapons, it was said, yielded "more bang for the buck." They also were essential to the Eisenhower administration's favored strategy of cold war deterrence. Eisenhower and his secretary of state, John Foster Dulles, downplayed the Truman administration's policy of blocking communist nations with conventional forces wherever they tried to expand, as had occurred in Korea. They instead proclaimed a policy of "massive retaliation": the readiness of the United States to use nuclear weapons, in places of its own choosing, to answer aggressive or provocative behavior by the Soviet Union or its allies. In a further effort at cold war containment, the Eisenhower administration encouraged anticommunist nations in Southeast Asia and the Middle East to forge mutual defense pacts allied with the United States.

Behind closed doors, Eisenhower and Dulles relied heavily on covert action, a stance underscored by Eisenhower's appointment of Allen Dulles, brother of the secretary of state, to head the Central Intelligence Agency. Early in its tenure, the Eisenhower administration enjoyed two striking successes using covert methods, though both achievements would receive deservedly harsh criticism from future generations of Americans. In 1953, the CIA collaborated with British intelligence to orchestrate the overthrow of Mohammad Mossadeq, Iran's constitutional prime minister, and the restoration of the country's pro-Western monarch, Shah Mohammad Reza Pahlavi. Mossadeq had presided over the nationalization of Iran's British-run oil facilities and had intermittently cooperated with Iranian communists, causing US officials to fear for the stability of that oil-rich and pivotally located country. (Iran bordered both the Soviet Union and the strategically vital Persian Gulf.) Mossadeq's ouster, and the harsh rule the shah subsequently imposed on the country, aroused bitter resentment of the United States among the Iranian public, as later US policy-makers would learn to their chagrin.

In 1954, a CIA-sponsored coup d'état within the Guatemalan army caused the downfall of that country's democratically elected president, Jacobo Arbenz Guzman. Arbenz had promulgated land reforms that threatened the holdings of the Boston-based United Fruit Company, which dominated Guatemalan agriculture; he had antagonized Washington by including local communists in his cabinet. His overthrow restored United Fruit's privileged position (though the company's holdings later suffered for other reasons) and handed state power to a succession of military dictators, who over the next three decades brutally exploited Guatemala's impoverished, and largely indigenous, peasant population.

For all of Ike's efforts to combat communism abroad, US–Soviet relations improved during his presidency. The Korean armistice of 1953 removed a violent flashpoint in the two nations' relations (while doing little to lessen Sino-US animosity), and the death of Joseph Stalin that same year allowed somewhat more conciliatory impulses to start shaping Soviet foreign policy. In 1955, Eisenhower and Nikita Khrushchev, his new Soviet counterpart, held the first of three summit meetings to occur during Ike's presidency, and the two nations began expanding their cultural exchanges. Relations sharply deteriorated, though, in Eisenhower's final months in office (see Chapter 4).

In later decades, historians would praise Eisenhower for evading a trap that ensnared his successors – but also chide him for contributing to the trap's enlargement. Vietnam had been a French colony since the nineteenth century. Japan occupied it during World War II, and France reclaimed it after Japan's defeat. By now, however, an indigenous coalition called the Viet Minh, dominated by communists, was pressing for national independence. In 1946, the Viet Minh and the French began clashing openly. The Truman administration provided

France with logistical and diplomatic support. Initially, the administration cared less about the merits of the Vietnamese struggle than about the need to placate the French and secure their backing for US diplomatic initiatives in Europe. But the Chinese Revolution of 1949 and the outbreak of the Korean War in 1950 caused US officials to pay closer attention to Vietnam. They grew increasingly convinced that a victory for the Viet Minh would be a victory for communist China, which gave the insurgents advice and support. By the early 1950s, the United States was extending military aid to the French war effort in Vietnam, a policy Eisenhower continued after becoming president.

In the spring of 1954, the Viet Minh besieged a French military base near the city of Dien Bien Phu, in northwestern Vietnam, subjecting it to withering artillery fire from surrounding hills. Realizing the base was in danger of falling, the French government appealed to Washington for help. The Eisenhower administration approached congressional leaders about authorizing a US military intervention. Several of the latter were unwilling to grant such authorization unless other allies, especially Britain, joined in the effort. They feared a replay of the Korean War, in which the United States had supplied most of the nonindigenous troops constituting the United Nations force. Yet the British government, believing the cause already lost, wanted no part in a rescue operation. Some US officials proposed intervening unilaterally, but Eisenhower balked. Under such a scenario, he presciently warned, "we would in the eyes of many Asiatic peoples merely replace French colonialism with American colonialism." Ike also wondered how the American public would react to another military venture so soon after the Korean armistice. The United States declined to come to France's aid. In May 1954, the Dien Bien Phu base fell to the Viet Minh.

Already, the great powers and some East Asian nations had gathered in Geneva, Switzerland, for extended talks on Korea and Vietnam. The Vietnam sessions took place just after the Dien Bien Phu surrender and reflected France's newly weakened position. The conferees agreed that Vietnam would be temporarily divided at the 17th parallel, which bisects the country, with the Viet Minh exercising provisional sovereignty to the north of that line and the French regrouping to its south. The Geneva Accords further established that general elections throughout the whole country would take place within two years' time; the victorious party would form a national government. Not wishing to endorse a document that ceded territory to communists, Secretary Dulles refused to sign the Geneva Accords, though he issued a separate statement pledging that the United States would not interfere with them.

Shortly thereafter, France pulled out of Vietnam, and the United States stepped in as the chief Western power in the country. Washington assumed responsibility for ensuring that Vietnam's southern half, now constituted as the Republic of Vietnam (or, more colloquially, South Vietnam), remained anticommunist. The Viet Minh consolidated their position north of the 17th parallel, an area that became commonly known as North Vietnam. But its formal name was the Democratic Republic of Vietnam, a nation declared in 1945, and the northern government, led by the Viet Minh's founder, Ho Chi Minh, claimed to represent all of Vietnam. Washington threw its support behind South Vietnam's president, No Dinh Diem, and backed Diem's refusal to hold the promised national elections, which

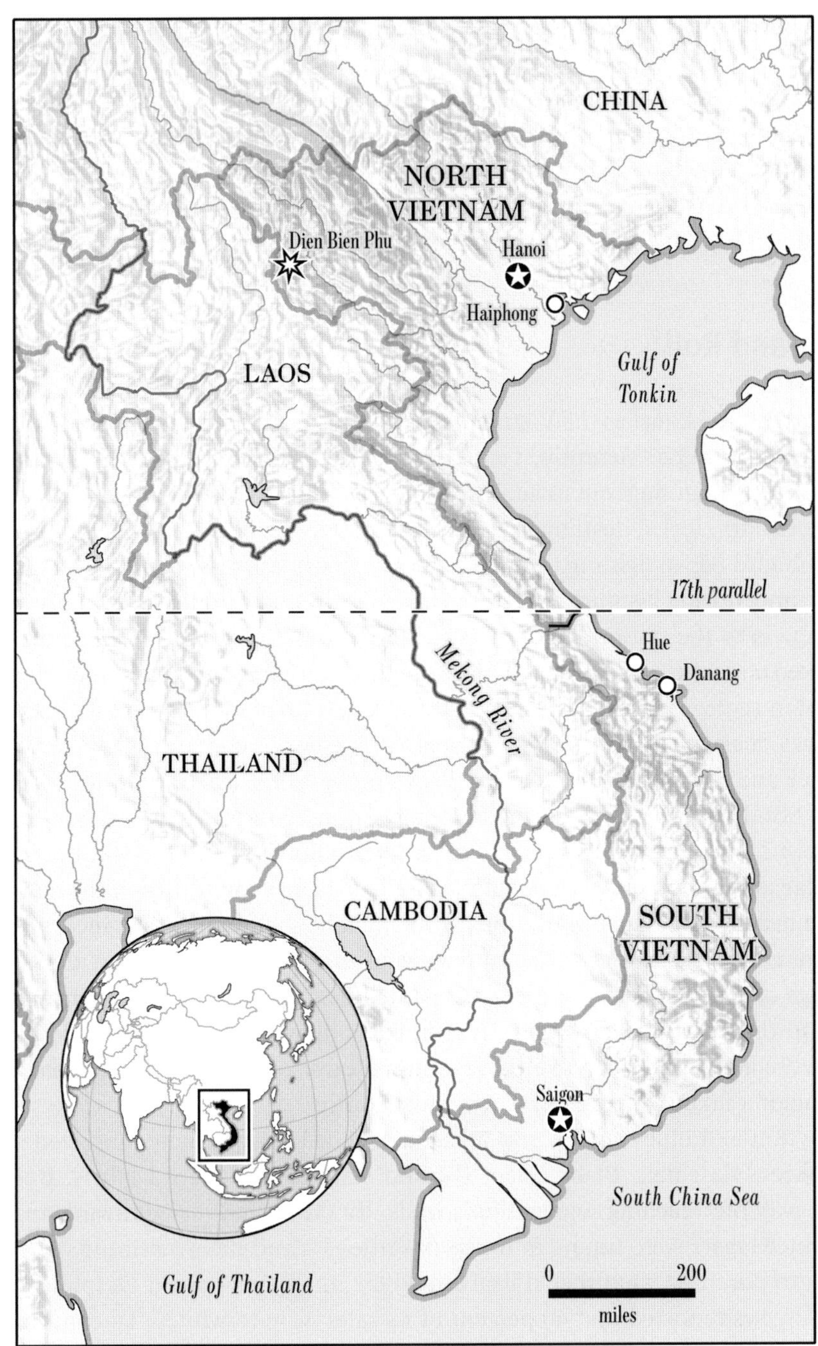

Map 3.1 Vietnam, 1955–1975. Source: Created by Joe LeMonnier.

Ho seemed certain to win. The political weakness of Diem went well beyond the fact that he was a Catholic trying to govern an overwhelmingly Buddhist population. The very idea of a separate South Vietnam aroused little evident enthusiasm among southern Vietnamese. Maintaining that nation would require ever greater investments of American treasure, arms, and, eventually, blood. The cost to the Vietnamese people, of course, would be far higher. Eisenhower avoided a sudden and drastic Americanization of the Vietnam conflict but set the stage for a slower version of that catastrophe.

Rock and Roll

On July 10, 1954, just as the Vietnam negotiations in Geneva entered their final phase, a disc jockey at WHBQ in Memphis, Tennessee, played a newly released single, recorded by a previously unknown singer in town. The song was "That's All Right (Mama)," a blues number with a country feel, a hustling beat, and a tremulous, echo-y vocal track. The radio station's switchboard began lighting up. At listeners' request, the disc jockey played the song several more times during his shift. He also arranged for the singer, nineteen-year-old Elvis Presley, to come in to the station later that night for an on-air interview. One of the first questions he asked was where Presley had gone to high school. Presley said Humes High, an all-white school in segregated Memphis. The DJ had coyly assured his white listeners that the rising star was one of their own.

Rock and roll was a vibrant mix of Black and white musical traditions, most of them rooted in the South. In the 1930s and 1940s, largely owing to the Great Migration of rural southern Blacks to cities throughout the country, blues idioms of rural origin became increasingly popular among urban African Americans. The genre evolved to suit the new surroundings. To be heard above the din of crowded nightclubs, blues musicians incorporated big-band instruments such as horns, saxophones, and drums and, sometimes, the exuberant vocal stylings of gospel choirs. They also exploited new techniques of amplification, most strikingly in their use of electric guitars. Amplifiers didn't just make things louder: played at a high volume, the notes of an electric guitar became distorted and sustained, mimicking the wailing of a saxophone or an excited human voice.

Rhythm and blues, as the new music was called, was initially marketed solely to Black audiences, via small, Black-oriented radio stations and record labels. But radio signals had a way of breaching segregation's walls. By the early 1950s, growing numbers of white urban teenagers were tuning in to Black stations – and then venturing out to R&B record stores to purchase what they'd heard. In 1952, the Black-owned Dolphin Record Store in Los Angeles reported that 40 percent of its sales were to whites. To capture this emerging white market, white disk jockeys and small record producers began adding R&B artists to their lineups. Then some major record companies swooped in, recruiting white musicians to record blander, and thus more saleable, versions of R&B songs. Pat Boone, the most successful of these "cover" performers, later insisted that he had helped the new genre gain wider acceptance. "R&B is a distinctive kind of music; it doesn't appeal to everybody," he

Figure 3.2 Elvis Presley, 1955. Source: Bettmann / Getty Images.

said. "So, if it hadn't been for the vanilla versions of the R&B songs in the '50s, you could certainly imagine that rock 'n' roll, as we think of it, would never have happened." There is surely some truth to this claim. Still, during the heyday of the "cover" era (roughly 1953 to 1955), many Black R&B artists were starved of radio exposure and record sales. Repeatedly, Boone and other white musicians scored hits with songs that had struggled to chart in their original Black-recorded versions. In the mid- to late 1950s, though, a handful of Black R&B performers, like Chuck Berry and Little Richard, did achieve major cross-racial success.

Meanwhile, in the early 1950s, white musicians in the South had created a brisk fusion of country music and bluegrass, with hints of the blues and R&B, known as rockabilly. The relative faintness of the Black influences was, to some, a beckoning opportunity. Sam Phillips, the white owner of Sun Records in Memphis, was on the lookout for "a white man who had the Negro sound and the Negro feel." He found him in Elvis Presley, a Mississippi-born singer steeped in country, blues, and gospel. In 1954, Sun released Presley's version of "That's All Right (Mama)," a song first recorded in 1946 by the Black bluesman Arthur Crudup. Unlike a typical Boone cover, Presley's rendition offered much of the spareness and raw energy of the original. The song sailed to the top of local country charts. (In an inversion of this pattern, Chuck Berry's first hit single, "Maybellene," released in 1955, had its origins in white country music. The owners of the Chicago studio where Berry recorded the song liked the novelty of a Black man singing a "hillbilly" tune. White teenagers attending Berry's early live appearances sometimes expressed surprise at the performer's race.)

The success of "That's All Right" enabled Presley and his sidemen to tour the white South, where audience members, especially teenage girls, reacted deliriously to the singer's flamboyant attire, defiant sneer, and gyrating and thrusting hips. A mostly regional sensation in 1954 and 1955, "Elvis the Pelvis" achieved wild national acclaim in 1956, thanks largely to several shrewdly planned appearances on network television. The Presley phenomenon – too vulgar to condone yet too huge and lucrative to resist – threw the nation's commercial tastemakers into a quandary. Ed Sullivan, host of the preeminent TV variety program, vowed never to showcase Presley, only to surrender weeks later and book him for three evenings. After two nights, the show's network, CBS, directed that Presley be filmed only from the waist up. Commentators scoffed that the idol was talentless. "Mr. Presley has no discernible singing ability," wrote *The New York Times*'s television critic. "His one specialty is an accented movement of the body that heretofore has been primarily identified with the repertoire of the blonde bombshells of the burlesque runway." Such carping failed to dampen, and in all likelihood further stoked, Elvis's phenomenal success. The singer not only sold millions of records but also licensed his image to appear on a vast array of commercial products – clothes, shoes, charm bracelets, board games – whose sale as of December 1957 had grossed some $55 million.

Adult disapproval of Presley applied, of course, to the entire rock and roll genre. Although much of the criticism was ordinary "kids these days" head-shaking, persistent undercurrents of anxiety, and occasional eruptions of hysteria, marked mainstream commentary on the new music. Throughout the 1950s, there were genuine and well-founded concerns about rising rates of "juvenile delinquency," as the problem was then called. In 1950, 3,424 New York City youths under the age of sixteen had been arrested for some infraction or crime; in 1959, that figure was 11,365. Earlier in the decade, politicians, clergy, psychologists, and other opinion leaders had linked the crisis to the coarsening influence of horror comic books (which *were* unusually graphic for the times).[1] In the mid- to late 1950s, rock and roll and its surrounding culture were ready-made culprits. "The gangster of tomorrow is the Elvis Presley type of today," a concerned parent wrote to a congressional committee investigating the causes of juvenile delinquency. Frank Sinatra, dethroned youth idol of yesteryear, called rock and roll "the martial music of every side-burned delinquent on the face of the earth."

Rock and roll's white critics also noted, accurately enough, that the music had deep roots in Black culture. A spokesman for the White Citizens Council of Birmingham, Alabama, claimed that "the basic, heavy beat music of the Negroes … brings out animalism and vulgarity" and constituted a "plot to mongrelize America." Northern white commentators generally avoided such crudeness, though Jack O'Brian, a critic for the New York *Journal-American*, was not above comparing Presley's gyrations to "an aborigine's mat-

[1] In the early 1950s, the comic book industry did not regulate its own content in the ways that film, radio, television, and other popular media did. In 1954, under pressure from parents' groups, clergy, civic organizations, and especially Congress, the industry established a Comics Code Authority that compelled comic book publishers to eliminate from their products imagery and storylines deemed excessively graphic or disturbing.

ing dance." Nor were national tastemakers immune to segregationist pressures from the South. In 1957, ABC TV cancelled a nationally broadcast rock and roll dance program after a Black teenage guest performer briefly danced with a white girl, sparking protests from ABC's southern affiliates.

Nonetheless, as was evident in the ubiquity of Elvis swag (and in the fact that ABC had such a dance show to begin with), rock and roll was big business. The youth market was huge and constantly growing; the oldest spawn of the "baby boom," which officially started in 1946, were on the cusp of adolescence. In 1958, teenagers bought 70 percent of all records in the country. Although few other rock and rollers achieved anything like Presley's commercial success, the genre as a whole afforded seemingly endless opportunities to cash in: selling records, concert tickets, and music magazines; placing and selling ads around rock-and-roll-themed TV shows; producing and distributing movies with rock and roll soundtracks; manufacturing and marketing fan paraphernalia for the biggest stars. Even as elite critics continued to wring their hands, rock and roll became embedded in the consumer economy. In the process, it lost some of its defiant edge. By decade's end (with Elvis briefly sidelined by his conscription into the US Army), a fresh cohort of white and Black performers – Frankie Avalon, Paul Anka, Connie Francis, the Drifters, the Platters, the Everly Brothers – dominated the charts with smoother sounds and presented a more wholesome face to the nation. In time, of course, new rebels would take the stage.

Artistic Dissent and Social Criticism

Rock and roll may have posed the most conspicuous challenge to the dominant culture's bland (and at times reactionary) sensibilities, but it was hardly the only dissenting genre. In literature, fine art, social commentary, film, and other forms of popular music, Americans pushed back against what they saw as the stultifying constraints of mainstream society. But this was a peculiar kind of rebellion, more concerned with matters of perception and psychology than with distributions of power and wealth.

Granted, some of the decade's major literary and artistic works did comment directly on political issues. Both Arthur Miller's 1953 play *The Crucible* (about the Salem witch trials) and Ray Bradbury's 1953 novel *Fahrenheit 451* (about a dystopian, book-burning society of the future) were unmistakable critiques of McCarthyism. Lorraine Hansberry's 1959 play *A Raisin in the Sun* addressed the exclusion of African Americans from white neighborhoods in the North. The visual artists Jack Levine, Charles White, and Ben Shahn criticized militarism, racism, and class oppression. But the most emblematic forms of artistic dissent tended to operate more obliquely. They expressed moods of introspection or alienation that challenged social conformism but existed at some remove from social and political engagement. From the swirling paint splatters of the abstract expressionist Jackson Pollack ("Jack the Dripper," detractors called him) to the edgy syncopation of bebop jazz musicians like Charlie Parker and Thelonious Monk, artists of the fifties evinced a freewheeling, individualistic, and idiosyncratic spirit.

A literary phenomenon known as the Beat movement was all those things, but more so. It grew out of a small coterie of white students and ex-students of New York's Columbia University in the mid- to late 1940s, chief among them Allen Ginsberg, Jack Kerouac, and Lucien Carr. Drawn to jazz, Zen Buddhism, sexual experimentation, illicit drug use, and urban street life (often in African American parts of town), they formed a bohemian subculture that rejected conventional strictures on sexuality and attire and disdained the emptiness and banality of America's postwar consumer society. They called themselves a "beat generation," ground down by dull and oppressive conformity. The Beats' literary work was experimental, anarchic, wildly expressive, often profane, some of it the result of drug-fueled free association. Most critics dismissed the work as lazy and standardless, but a handful took an interest in the Beats and publicized their material.

A turning point for the movement occurred in 1955, when Allen Ginsberg gave a public reading of his lengthy poem *Howl* at a San Francisco gallery. The poem's opening lines offered a hint of its incantatory, hallucinatory, hypnotic power: "I saw the best minds of my generation destroyed by madness, starving hysterical naked, dragging themselves through the negro streets at dawn looking for an angry fix, angelheaded hipsters burning for the ancient heavenly connection to the starry dynamo in the machinery of night...." Lawrence Ferlinghetti, the owner of San Francisco's Beat-friendly City Lights Bookstore, published the poem as a booklet, furnishing it a wider audience. In 1957, a ham-handed effort by California state authorities to suppress *Howl* as obscene (it contained curse words and sexually explicit passages) only drew more eyes to Ginsberg's work. That same year, Viking Press published Jack Kerouac's *On the Road*, a rambling, semiautobiographical account of a cross-country road trip the author had taken several years earlier with a shifting cast of Beat companions. The book sold half a million copies, and the Beats – or the "Beatniks," as the media derisively dubbed them – gained widespread notoriety. Mainstream news outlets parodied Beats as addled, incomprehensible, but basically harmless vagabonds. Much more preposterously, pulp novels and Hollywood movies depicted them as violent, overgrown juvenile delinquents. But the Beat sensibility stirred deep yearnings in the country and helped seed the ground for a far more robust counterculture in the following decade.

Social criticism of the 1950s, though much more conventional and restrained than Beat literature, was likewise concerned with the problem of preserving individuality, autonomy, and authenticity in an increasingly impersonal age. In his highly popular 1956 book *The Organization Man*, William Whyte argued that white-collar employees of large companies had become excessively risk-averse and conformist. Vance Packard's 1957 book *The Hidden Persuaders*, another bestseller, dissected the manipulative techniques of commercial advertisers and political campaign operatives. Unlike their counterparts in previous eras, who had been broadly preoccupied with issues of economic class and poverty, American social critics of the 1950s tended to focus on status and psychology. Rather than analyzing the deep structures of US capitalism, they explored how individual Americans (mainly in the middle class) could adjust to the disorientation and anxiety of living in a rapidly bureaucratizing society. In part, the change reflected the unprecedented prosperity Americans were

Figure 3.3 Allen Ginsberg, 1959. Source: *San Francisco Chronicle* / Hearst Newspapers via Getty Images.

enjoying by the 1950s; many observers genuinely believed that material want no longer posed a primary challenge to the nation. In part, the pervasive anticommunism of the era cast a cloud of suspicion over class-based analysis. Yet critics also responded to excesses from the right. The horrifying example of Nazi Germany, and to a lesser degree the disturbing experience with McCarthyism, stirred resistance to ideas hinting at mass mobilization or strident populism.

Of course, there were exceptions. The socialist writer Michael Harrington published articles on the persistence of severe poverty, work that would gain wide attention early in the following decade. More prominently at the time, C. Wright Mills, a non-Marxist leftist sociology professor at Columbia, fixed a withering gaze on the top echelons directing the nation's political, economic, and military affairs, a "power elite" adept at preserving its dominance despite the vagaries of popular elections. Academic critics grumbled that Mills oversimplified the case, but he had an engaging prose style that, along with his bracing ideas, won him a wide readership, especially among university students. Mill's unconventional attire – flannel shirts, khaki pants, and combat boots – and his habit of riding a motorcycle to campus enhanced his iconoclastic allure. The radical student movement coalescing in the early 1960s would be heavily indebted to Mills, though Mills himself would see little of that legacy, on account of his death in 1962 at the age of forty-five.

In popular cinema, too, themes of alienation and rebelliousness sometimes played out. In *The Man in the Gray Flannel Suit* (1956), adapted from Sloan Wilson's 1955 novel of the same name, a World War II veteran contends with the ennui and let-down of white-collar employment and suburban living. In *The Wild One* (1953), two rival motorcycle gangs wreak havoc on a placid California town. In *Rebel Without a Cause* (1955), affluent suburban teenagers act out against family dysfunction by indulging in reckless delinquency. Although all of these films supplied reassuring endings, they signaled the same disquiet that preoccupied more elite genres. The stars of the latter two movies, Marlon Brando and James Dean, respectively, became Hollywood's smoldering symbols of restless, defiant youth. Dean's death in a car crash at the age of twenty-four, just weeks before *Rebel*'s theatrical release, froze the actor for all time in his rebel incarnation. Movies such as these revealed Hollywood's ability to acknowledge, soften, and monetize challenges to the established order, much as the broader entertainment industry was doing with rock and roll.

One issue did push a wide cross-section of Americans toward a more concrete critique of the status quo and government policy: the threat posed by nuclear weapons. As we saw in Chapter 1, the atomic incineration of Hiroshima and Nagasaki had caused many Americans to dread the Bomb. The start of the cold war, ironically, helped to ease those fears, as much of the public came to see the US nuclear arsenal as a check on Soviet adventurism. Most Americans supported President Truman's 1950 decision to develop the hydrogen bomb. By mid-decade, however, antinuclear sentiments were again on the rise, now centering on the menace of nuclear fallout from bomb testing. In 1954, people across the globe were alarmed to learn that radiation from a US hydrogen bomb test in the South Pacific had contaminated a Japanese fishing vessel eighty miles away, gravely sickening the crew members, one of whom later died. Over the next several years, reported spikes in radiation levels in various American locales drew attention to government bomb tests in the Southwest. Scientists warned that nuclear fallout could cause bone cancer, leukemia, and horrifying birth defects. The Eisenhower administration insisted that such fears were overblown but was hard-pressed to quell them.

Across a wide swath of public expression – from comic books to rock music, to cinema, to fiction, to political advocacy – Americans gave voice to their society's morbid preoccupation with the nuclear peril. Some of this material made light of the threat. The 1954 rock and roll song "Thirteen Women (and Only One Man in Town)," by Bill Haley and the Comets, imagined a sexual cornucopia left in the wake of a hydrogen bomb attack. *Mad* magazine rhapsodized about postapocalyptic mutant lovers walking "arm in arm in arm." The decade's horror movies, in which the creatures' gruesome or freakishly magnified state was often attributed to nuclear testing gone awry, were ostensibly more serious, though their frenetic and overwrought quality surely amused many viewers at the time. In deadly earnest were novels like Mordecai Roshwald's *Level 7* (1959) and Walter Miller's *A Canticle for Leibowitz* (1960), sobering evocations of human ruin in the aftermath of nuclear war.

Against this troubled backdrop, nuclear testing became a potent political issue. In the 1956 presidential election, the Democratic nominee, Adlai Stevenson, proposed a ban on hydrogen bomb tests. Over the next couple of years, the Federation of American Scientists and the newly formed National Committee for a Sane Nuclear Policy issued the same cry more forcefully, sometimes in coordination with overseas organizations such as the European Federation Against Nuclear Arms and the (British) Committee for Nuclear Disarmament.

The German philanthropist Albert Schweitzer and the American chemist Linus Pauling, both Nobel laureates, endorsed a test ban. The idea polled extremely well with the US public, too. By the time the Soviet Union announced a unilateral moratorium on open-air nuclear testing, in March 1958, the public pressure on the Eisenhower administration was considerable. In October, Eisenhower declared a US moratorium, which continued until the end of his presidency. Skeptics noted, however, that each superpower waited to launch its moratorium until *after* it had befouled earth and air with a final round of bomb tests.

Challenges to the Racial Status Quo

As one movement challenged the excesses of US militarism, another sought to overturn the far older orthodoxy of white supremacy. Since 1945, civil rights activists had redoubled their efforts to advance voting rights in the South, combat legal segregation as it existed pervasively in the South and to a lesser degree elsewhere, and improve the economic circumstances of African Americans throughout the nation. In the mid-1950s, the desegregation of public schools became a key locus of the struggle, following the dramatic culmination of one strand of civil rights litigation.

In its 1896 decision *Plessy v. Ferguson*, the US Supreme Court had found that racial segregation in public institutions was constitutional as long as the separate facilities were of equal quality. The ruling had buttressed segregation in schools, employment, and public accommodations throughout the South, even though the facilities were often manifestly *un*equal. Starting in the 1930s, the National Association for the Advancement of Colored People had sued segregated southern school districts and universities for failing to treat Black students equally. A handful of cases reached the Supreme Court and yielded victories for the Black plaintiffs, without dislodging the core principle of *Plessy*. Fewer school segregation systems were passing constitutional muster, but segregation itself remained legal.

In the early 1950s, the NAACP, led by its doggedly resourceful chief counsel, Thurgood Marshall, decided to attack the "separate but equal" doctrine head-on. Marshall and his colleagues knew this was a risky course. A frontal approach might well prompt the Supreme Court to reaffirm the *Plessy* precedent, setting the cause of equality back for decades. Wouldn't it be wiser to keep picking away at *Plessy* indirectly? Rejecting the cautious option, and acting through local chapters, the NAACP sponsored five cases – in Delaware, Kansas, South Carolina, Virginia, and Washington, DC – in which Black parents had challenged the constitutionality of segregated public schools. After losing in lower courts, the parents appealed to the Supreme Court. The high court took up the cases, combining them in a single case called *Brown v. Board of Education* (named for a Black family in Topeka, Kansas).

At the Supreme Court, Marshall argued that segregation, by itself, placed a stamp of inferiority on Black children and thus was intrinsically unequal. He cited a study by Kenneth Clark, a prominent Black psychologist, showing that African American children reared in segregated settings harbored a negative self-image, a finding poignantly dramatized by the children's preference for white dolls over Black dolls. (Here, Marshall shrewdly invoked a more general concern of social critics of the era: an impersonal society's infliction of psychic harm on the individual.) Initially, the court seemed headed for a split decision. In the fall of 1953, however, Chief Justice Fred Vinson suddenly died and was replaced by Earl Warren, then serving as California's governor. Less attuned to legal intricacies than to broad issues of principle and policy, Warren quickly concluded that the court needed to overturn school segregation, and do so resoundingly. He patiently lobbied Robert Jackson and Stanley Reed, the two justices inclined to uphold segregation, eventually winning their support for a unanimous verdict on the opposite side. In May 1954, the court issued a nine-to-zero decision endorsing Marshall's argument: "To separate [Black children] from others of similar age and qualifications solely because of their race generates a feeling of inferiority as to their status in the community that may affect their hearts and minds in a way unlikely ever to be undone.... We conclude that in the field of public education the doctrine of 'separate but equal' has no place. Separate educational facilities are inherently unequal."

At first, it was widely expected that desegregation would proceed fairly quickly. Marshall predicted that all public schools would be integrated within five years. Although some southern politicians and newspapers vowed to resist the court's decision, many others seemed resigned to its implementation. "Arkansas will obey the law. It always has," said that state's governor, Francis Cherry. Southern school districts began contemplating the logistics of desegregation. But desegregation wasn't going to happen without constant pressure from the federal government, and it became increasingly evident that this would be lacking. In a second *Brown* decision, in May 1955, the Supreme Court called for the implementation of its desegregation decree "with all deliberate speed," an ambiguous phrase that sounded like something less than "full speed," imposing no deadline for this accomplishment. (To get his unanimous decision in 1954, Chief Justice Warren had had to promise that implementation would not be too rapid.)

More strikingly, the president stayed on the sidelines. Privately, Eisenhower opposed federally mandated desegregation, going so far as to tell Warren, at a White House dinner, that white southerners wanted nothing more than "to see that their sweet little girls are not required to sit in school alongside some big overgrown Negroes." Publicly, Ike pledged to abide by the *Brown* decision but refused to say whether he personally supported or opposed it. When asked by a reporter if he had any advice for southerners, he answered, "Not in the slightest." On another occasion, Eisenhower declared, "I don't believe you can change the hearts of men with laws or decisions." The statement aligned with his private conviction that southern whites were so committed to segregation that forcing them to abandon it would be futile and dangerous. Change, if it came, had to be cautious and gradual.

In all likelihood, had the Supreme Court issued a strict timetable for implementation, and had Eisenhower ringingly endorsed the *Brown* ruling and insisted that his administration would tolerate no obstruction of it, segregationists would have had fewer opportunities for resistance. Such firmness from above might have enabled them to claim, publicly, that their hands were tied and that they had no choice but to proceed with desegregation, however much they personally abhorred it. Instead, in the absence of federal leadership, southern white politicians felt compelled to vie with one another over who was upholding

Figure 3.4 The cartoonist Herblock (Herbert Block) ridicules President Dwight D. Eisenhower's passivity on civil rights, 1956. Source: © The Herb Block Foundation.

segregation most ardently. Resistance to the *Brown* ruling, and to other federal court decisions flowing from it, escalated. The legislatures of Alabama, Georgia, Mississippi, and Virginia passed resolutions declaring *Brown* null and void. In 1956, after rioting by angry whites, the University of Alabama expelled its first Black student, Autherine Lucy, whom a federal court had recently ordered the school to admit. That same year, Texas's governor dispatched state law enforcement to block the court-ordered desegregation of a high school in Mansfield, Texas. Eisenhower declined to intervene in these cases and resisted public pressure to speak out on the matter. "I don't know what another speech would do," he said at a February 1957 press conference, before leaving to vacation at Georgia's all-white Augusta National Golf Club.

On one occasion, though, segregationist resistance was so brazen that Eisenhower did have to act. In the fall of 1957 (in an incident discussed more fully in Chapter 4), Governor Orval Faubus of Arkansas obstructed the court-ordered integration of Central High School in Little Rock, creating a chaotic spectacle that conspicuously challenged Eisenhower's constitutional authority and America's image abroad. Reluctantly, the president sent the US Army into that city to enforce the desegregation decree. But Little Rock was the exception that proved the rule. Apart from overseeing the integration of schools in Washington, DC, Eisenhower did little else to desegregate public education.

Beyond education, the Eisenhower administration's principal civil rights achievement was sponsoring the Civil Rights Act of 1957, which Congress passed that summer. The Act established a Civil Rights Division within the Department of Justice, created a US Commission on Civil Rights to investigate attempted interference with the right to vote and recommend remedies, and granted the DOJ limited powers to enforce voting rights. This last feature was considerably weakened, however, when segregationist legislators inserted a provision guaranteeing jury trials for defendants in voting rights cases. Southern white officials running afoul of federal law could still count on the indulgence of all-white juries. The Civil Rights Act of 1957 did little to alter grim realities on the ground. Its chief significance lay in the fact that, for the first time since Reconstruction, Congress had passed any civil rights legislation at all.

A Burgeoning Civil Rights Movement

That a civil rights bill, albeit a modest one, could finally succeed in Congress was a sign that times were changing – and, more to the point, that Black Americans were pushing ever more relentlessly and resourcefully against the walls of racial oppression. The *Brown* decision, itself a product of civil rights activism and litigation, had shone a national spotlight on wide disparities in public education. In the ensuing months and years, activists drew that spotlight to other realms of racial injustice and, in so doing, developed strikingly effective techniques of political mobilization and public suasion.

In the summer of 1955, a brutal murder in Mississippi gained a measure of national notoriety that hundreds of previous lynchings in the Jim Crow South, and sometimes elsewhere, had failed to achieve. Emmett Till, a fourteen-year-old Black boy from Chicago, was visiting relatives in the Mississippi Delta. A white woman accused him of speaking lewdly to her, prompting her husband and his half-brother to abduct Till in full view of the boy's great-uncle. Days later, Till's body, savagely mutilated and shot in the head, was dredged from a nearby river. Till's connection to Chicago – a center of African American media, popular culture, and political and civic organization – ensured that his killing received wide coverage in the Black press, uniting the community in shock and outrage. Till's Chicago funeral was a four-day public event attended by hundreds; his mother insisted on an open casket. She allowed *Jet*, a popular African American magazine, to publish a photograph of her son's horribly disfigured head on its cover, an unforgettable image for Blacks across the country.

The scale and intensity of the African American response caught the attention of the white-dominated press. Many white readers, upon learning the details, became shocked as well. Till's was not the first racist murder in Mississippi following the *Brown* decision.

Earlier in that summer of 1955, in separate incidents, the Reverend George Lee, head of the NAACP's branch in Belzoni, and Lamar Smith, a Black farmer and activist, had been gunned down for registering Blacks to vote. But the notice these crimes received in the mainstream press paled in comparison with the coverage devoted to Till's killing. As the historian Darryl Mace writes, Till "was too young, too northern, too innocent, and too representative of the population *Brown* … was supposed to protect" for his murder to be brushed aside.

In the resulting publicity, authorities in Mississippi's Tallahatchie County were obliged to put Till's suspected killers, Roy Bryant and J. W. Milam, on trial. Here was another eye-opening event, vividly chronicled by an often startled national press corps. The prosecutor made a sincere effort to convict Bryant and Milam but was hampered by the fact that the county sheriff, charged with keeping order in the segregated courtroom and prone to do so with an iron hand, plainly sympathized with the defense team and testified on its behalf. One of the defense attorneys closed by telling the twelve white men of the jury, "I'm sure every last Anglo-Saxon one of you has the courage to free these men." The jury did so in sixty-seven minutes. It would have taken even less time, the jury foreman later said, had he and his fellow jurors not paused for a soda break. In early 1956, shielded from danger of re-prosecution by the double jeopardy clause of the Fifth Amendment, Bryant and Milam sold their story to *Look* magazine for $4,000. In it, they admitted that they had abducted and beaten Till and that Milam had shot him dead.

A few months after the Till trial, a small act of defiance in Montgomery, Alabama, sparked a year-long protest that captured the nation's attention. Like most southern cities, Montgomery required African Americans to sit in the back rows of public buses, leaving the front rows for whites. Between these two sections was an indeterminate row where Blacks could sit if no whites needed seats. Blacks had to vacate that area, however, whenever the white-only section overflowed. On December 1, 1955, Rosa Parks, a forty-two-year-old Black seamstress, was seated in an in-between row. When the bus driver instructed her to relinquish her seat to a white passenger, she refused and was arrested.

Black Montgomerians had long chafed under their city's demeaning system of bus segregation; the Montgomery NAACP and local activists (including Parks herself, no stranger to civil rights protests in the city) were eager to challenge it. In two recent, separate incidents, Black female passengers had been arrested for refusing to give up their seats. But distracting biographical information about both individuals – one was an unwed pregnant teenager, the other an impoverished daughter of an alcoholic – dissuaded Black community leaders from launching protests over those cases. Rosa Parks raised no respectability concerns. She was an esteemed member of her community, a married churchgoer who served as the secretary for the Montgomery NAACP. When E. D. Nixon, a union organizer who headed that NAACP chapter, arrived at the police station to bail Parks out on the night of her arrest, he was already convinced that her case furnished the long-awaited occasion for mounting a legal challenge. Over the objections of family members who feared for her safety, Parks agreed.

Also swinging into action that evening was Jo Ann Robinson, a college instructor and head of the Montgomery chapter of the Women's Political Council, a Black civic organization. Robinson and other WPC members stayed up till four in the morning mimeographing copies of a leaflet describing the incident: "Another Negro woman has been arrested and thrown in jail because she refused to get up out of her seat on the bus for a white person to sit down.... This has to be stopped." The statement urged Black Montgomerians to stay off the buses on December 5, three days later. By the afternoon of December 2, the women had delivered 50,000 leaflets to homes, schools, factories, barbershops, and other businesses. Nixon immediately endorsed the boycott idea and enlisted other Black community leaders in its support.

The one-day boycott was a stunning success; hardly any Black Montgomerians rode buses on December 5. That afternoon, Nixon convened a meeting of more than fifty Black community leaders at the Dexter Avenue Baptist Church. The attendees formed themselves into the Montgomery Improvement Association (MIA) and agreed to continue the protest, though they were momentarily undecided over how best to do so. Dexter's twenty-six-year-old pastor, Martin Luther King, Jr., was named president of the new group. Because he was young and fairly new in town, King was not deeply enmeshed in the politics and rivalries of Black Montgomery. He was someone nearly everyone could happily support. Later that evening, at a hugely attended mass meeting at a different church, King and other speakers rallied community members in support of the protest. By meeting's end, it was clear that the bus boycott would continue indefinitely.

A native of Atlanta, Georgia, where his father still led his own Baptist congregation, King had earned a doctorate in theology at Boston University. His influences included the Christian social gospel and the philosophy of nonviolent resistance championed by the Indian anticolonial leader Mohandas Gandhi. When King became pastor of the Dexter Avenue church in 1954, there was little sign that the civil rights struggle would dominate his ministry. He declined an invitation that year to run for president of the Montgomery NAACP chapter, choosing to focus on his new job, his family, and the completion of his doctorate. Although King was already admired as a skilled public speaker, the full dimensions of his oratorical mastery had yet to emerge.

Black Montgomerians pressed ahead with the open-ended boycott, hopeful that their numerical strength – three-quarters of the city's bus passengers were Black – would ultimately weigh in their favor. At first, the MIA held off on calling for an outright end to segregation on buses, demanding instead that the segregation be imposed more equitably and that Black passengers be treated with respect. The organization also called for the hiring of African American drivers on routes whose passengers were predominantly Black. The city leaders proved so intransigent, however, that the boycotters soon set aside their demands for fairer segregation and insisted on full integration. Meanwhile, the NAACP and local activists initiated a federal lawsuit challenging the constitutionality of segregated buses. The movement was done with half-measures.

To the amazement of white Montgomerians, the Black community persisted in its boycott for months on end, starving the bus system of revenue. People walked to work or participated in an intricate web of carpools organized by the MIA. Wealthier community members made their second cars available for others to drive. The MIA raised enough money to buy fifteen new station wagons. Some well-to-do white housewives, unwilling to dispense with domestic help, discreetly chauffeured their Black maids and cooks to and from work. To break the boycott, city authorities harassed and arrested Black carpoolers on trumped-up traffic charges. King himself was arrested and jailed for driving five miles over the speed limit. But a crowd of his supporters surrounded the jailhouse, and he was released after a few hours.

Days later, while King was attending a church meeting, someone dynamited his front porch. He rushed home, finding his wife and infant daughter unharmed. But about three hundred Black people, some carrying knives and guns, had gathered in front of the house and appeared on the verge of clashing with police. In a crystallizing moment for his emerging leadership, King calmed the crowd and persuaded it to disperse, averting an eruption that might well have destroyed the nascent movement. The pastor's words on that occasion blended clear-eyed realism with unshakable principle: "He who lives by the sword will perish by the sword. Remember that is what Jesus said. We are not advocating violence.... We must meet hate with love." Over the dozen years remaining to him, King would grow more radical in his politics and more audacious in his protest strategies, but he would never forsake his core commitment to nonviolence.

If the boycott drew strength from the resourcefulness and discipline of its leaders and rank-and-file members, it also benefited from a changing media environment. Montgomery's two major newspapers, the *Advertiser* and the *Alabama Journal*, were firmly ensconced in the segregationist power structure. A few years earlier, they could have stymied the boycott by depriving it of publicity. But new journalistic actors were on the scene. The city's first television station, the NBC-affiliated WSFA, had started broadcasting in 1954. Although it, too, was a product of the white South, the station was institutionally less committed to upholding segregation than to attracting viewers, and the boycott story was great television. Meanwhile, a national press corps freshly attuned to civil rights – first by the *Brown* decision and then by the Till trial – flocked to cover the drama in Montgomery. Not only did the national media outlets provide generally sympathetic coverage of the boycott; their presence made it harder for local authorities to use violence against the boycotters, enabling them to act more boldly.

In November 1956, the Supreme Court affirmed a lower court ruling that Montgomery's segregated bus system violated the Fourteenth Amendment's equal protection clause. The boycotters had won the battle. In late December, Montgomery's buses began operating on an integrated basis. The victory underscored the potential of mass mobilization to bring about change, especially on an issue of growing interest to the nation's news media. (The jubilation was blunted, however, by a frightening but thankfully brief spate of firebombings of Black homes and churches in Montgomery.) King soared to national prominence, his portrait appearing on the cover of *Time* in early 1957. At about this time, he joined with other Black community leaders in the South, most of them ministers, to form the Southern Christian Leadership Conference; King was named president of the Atlanta-based organization. The SCLC would strive to galvanize and coordinate further struggles against segregation. After all, despite the triumph in Montgomery, the work of implementing *Brown* and vindicating the principles it represented remained starkly, gallingly, incomplete.

***

In the spring of 1957, in recognition of his new prominence, King was invited to join a delegation of distinguished Black Americans – including the labor and civil rights leader A. Philip Randolph and the UN negotiator and Nobel laureate Ralph Bunche – on a visit to the West African nation of Ghana, formerly known as the Gold Coast. The visitors would participate in ceremonies marking Ghana's achievement of formal independence from Britain. King was enthusiastic about the trip. "I thought," he later recalled, "Ghana would become a symbol of hope for hundreds and thousands of oppressed peoples all over the world as they struggled for freedom," a drama unfolding in the United States as well. On the plane over the Atlantic, crew members recognized King from the recent *Time* cover. They invited him into the cockpit, where the pilot even gave him a brief turn at the controls. It was a changing world.

In Accra, the new nation's capital, King and hundreds of other international dignitaries gathered for a reception at the University College of Ghana. Vice President Richard M. Nixon was also in attendance, the highest-ranking representative of a government keen on persuading emerging nations to resist Soviet blandishments and align instead with the West. Nixon had failed to answer a recent telegram from King urging the Eisenhower administration to act against segregationist violence. In Africa, however, the politician dared not ignore the preacher. King shook the proffered hand, saying, "I'm very glad to meet you here. But I want you to come visit us down in Alabama where we are seeking the same kind of freedom the Gold Coast is celebrating." After an awkward pause, Nixon invited King to see him in Washington after both of them were stateside. Nixon said that he, too, had read and enjoyed the *Time* cover story on King.

"Having traveled halfway around the world to secure the audience that had eluded him at home," writes the historian Taylor Branch, "King did not miss the political lesson. The logic of diplomacy gave him a stature that he lacked as a political nonentity in the South." Over the coming years, King and likeminded advocates would vigorously pursue that logic, insisting that the drive to win nonwhite allies abroad was inseparable from the advancement of Black rights at home. The accelerating struggle for civil rights would be a key battleground in a rapidly evolving cold war.

READING QUESTIONS

1. In what ways was the dominant gender ideology of the 1950s at odds with what American middle-class women were actually doing? How did the resulting tension manifest itself?
2. Which of President Eisenhower's foreign policies reflected restraint, and which were more aggressive? Does the combination of those two features strike you as contradictory or as forming a coherent cold war strategy?
3. What features of mainstream American culture and ideology in the fifties did artistic, literary, and social critics challenge? In what ways were the critiques themselves manifestations of dominant outlooks?
4. How did the evolving media landscape of the 1950s provide leverage to civil rights advocates? In what ways did the advocates seize this opportunity?

SUGGESTIONS FOR FURTHER READING

Branch, Taylor. *Parting the Waters: America in the King Years, 1954–63*. New York: Simon & Schuster, 1988.

Friedlander, Paul. *Rock & Roll: A Social History*, 2nd edn. New York: Routledge, 2006.

Gleijeses, Piero. *Shattered Hope: The Guatemalan Revolution and the United States, 1944–1954*. Princeton, NJ: Princeton University Press, 1991.

Gunn, T. Jeremy. *Spiritual Weapons: The Cold War and the Forging of an American National Religion*. Westport, CT: Praeger Publishers, 2009.

Halberstam, David. *The Fifties*. New York: Villard Books, 1993.

Kinzer, Stephen. *All the Shah's Men: An American Coup and the Roots of Middle East Terror*. Hoboken, NJ: John Wiley & Sons, 2003.

Lichtenstein, Nelson. *State of the Union: A Century of American Labor*. Princeton, NJ: Princeton University Press, 2002.

Logevall, Fredrik. *Embers of War: The Fall of an Empire and the Making of America's Vietnam*. New York: Random House, 2012.

Mace, Darryl. *In Remembrance of Emmett Till: Regional Stories and Media Responses to the Black Freedom Struggle*. Lexington, KY: University Press of Kentucky, 2014.

Oliver, Susan. *Betty Friedan: The Personal Is Political*. New York: Pearson Longman, 2008.

Phillips-Fein, Kim. *Invisible Hands: The Businessmen's Crusade against the New Deal*. New York: W. W. Norton, 2010

Rosen, Ruth. *The World Split Open: How the Modern Women's Movement Changed America*. New York: Viking, 2000.

Sugrue, Thomas J. *Sweet Land of Liberty: The Forgotten Struggle for Civil Rights in the North*. New York: Random House, 2008.

Szatmary, David. *A Time to Rock: A Social History of Rock and Roll*. New York: Schirmer Books, 1996.

4 Listen, Yankee

The Transformation of America's Cold War, 1956–1963

Introduction

In November 1960, the McGraw-Hill Book Company published *Listen, Yankee*, a slim paperback by the iconoclastic American sociologist C. Wright Mills. A surprise bestseller, the book tackled the fraught subject of US relations with Cuba, which Fidel Castro had governed for nearly two years. Although Castro had proclaimed his anticommunism at the time he took power, his government thereafter moved steadily leftward, arousing Washington's hostility. As *Listen, Yankee* hit the bookstores, US–Cuban relations were rapidly deteriorating, and Cuba was drifting toward the Soviet bloc. Written in the voice of an imaginary Cuban defender of the new government in Havana, the book forcefully challenged the anti-Castroite critiques now so common in US discourse. The first sentence of the first chapter established the tone of the book: "We Cubans know that you believe we are all led by a bunch of Communists, that the Russians are soon going to set up a rocket base, or something like that, here in Cuba, aimed at you."

Mills was positing a wild misconception to debunk, but the passage was all too prescient. In October 1962, US spy agencies learned that the Soviet Union actually *was* installing nuclear missiles in Cuba aimed at the United States, a discovery that sparked the most dangerous international crisis of the postwar era. To be sure, those who shared Mills's outlook (though not Mills himself, who had died the previous March) could plausibly claim that the missiles were a response to US bullying of Cuba, the very activity Mills had condemned. In any event, by the fall of 1962 US–Cuban relations were wrecked beyond foreseeable repair.

The Mills passage and its foreshadowings underscored the contradictory nature of US cold war politics in the late 1950s and early 1960s. On the one hand, the superpower rivalry grew more fluid and complex in those years. The United States and the Soviet Union made genuine, and modestly successful, efforts to ease their mutual tensions, permitting, in turn, a steady loosening of anticommunist orthodoxies within the United States. American critics of cold war thinking, whether focusing on foreign or domestic affairs – Mills addressed both – found new and expanding audiences for their once heretical views. Meanwhile, the growing importance of countries in "the developing world" (which later generations would call "the Third World") further complicated the picture. Increasingly, for the US government, success in the cold war meant persuading those ascendant nations that the United States was worthy of their admiration. Yet an America conspicuously tainted by racial injustice was less and less likely to earn such esteem, a reality domestic civil rights activists turned to their advantage. Abroad and at home, older strictures were relaxing and fresh possibilities looming into view.

On the other hand, the technology of the superpower rivalry advanced extremely rapidly in this period, introducing a destabilizing new element that at times threatened to render all of the above developments moot. Spy planes, space vehicles, and especially nuclear missiles enabled the superpowers to menace – and occasionally terrify – one another as never before, causing those capabilities to become, in themselves, a central issue of the cold war. For the most part, each nation behaved in narrowly self-serving ways, showing anger and alarm over its adversary's provocative deployments while scarcely acknowledging the destabilizing impact of its own. But by 1963, following the traumatic Cuban Missile Crisis that *Listen, Yankee* inadvertently foretold, both superpowers were obliged to adopt a somewhat more empathetic approach to their deadly rivalry.

Khrushchev's Challenge

A central character in the cold war dramas of these years was Nikita Khrushchev, who by 1955 had emerged as the undisputed leader of the Soviet Union. (Officially, he was first secretary of the Communist Party of the Soviet Union from 1953 to 1964 and chairman of the Council of Ministers from 1958 to 1964.) Khrushchev held four summit meetings with Presidents Eisenhower and Kennedy and visited the United States twice, his squat, strutting figure a frequent presence on American television screens. His personal style was unpredictable: jovial and back-slapping at one moment, stern and hectoring at the next. Substantively, he oscillated between sincere attempts to improve East–West relations and tenacious, sometimes reckless efforts to press his nation's advantage.

Khrushchev's volatility stemmed partly from his personality, but it also reflected some deep dilemmas he faced. On the one hand, Khrushchev was determined to continue the easing of harsh repression at home (a process begun shortly after Joseph Stalin's death in 1953) and thereby unleash his country's full creative and productive potential. Khrushchev did preside over the widespread freeing of political prisoners and the relaxation of onerous censorship measures. On the other hand, a spirit of freedom in the Soviet Union could spread to Eastern Europe, encouraging people in those areas to try to exit the Soviet bloc. In that event, Khrushchev would feel duty-bound to use force to prevent the alliance from breaking apart, undermining his own commitment to liberalization.

The second dilemma concerned cold war tensions, which Khrushchev genuinely wished to reduce. The Soviet doctrine of the Stalinist era, proclaiming the inevitability of armed conflict between the communist and capitalist worlds, was ill suited to the nuclear age. Moreover, the scope for peaceful competition was widening. The accelerating pace of decolonization

Figure 4.1 Mao Zedong and Nikita Khrushchev, 1958. Source: Keystone France / Gamma-Rapho / Getty Images.

meant a proliferation of newly independent nations in Asia, Africa, and the Middle East, many with bitter (and very recent) memories of Western European domination; the Soviet Union could seek their friendship by diplomatic means. Working against this prospect, however, was Khrushchev's need to maintain his revolutionary credentials within the communist camp, and especially in the eyes of Mao Zedong of the People's Republic of China. Mao was a hardliner who looked increasingly askance at any conciliatory moves the Soviets might make toward the capitalist camp. Khrushchev often responded to this pressure by acting more stridently in his dealings with the West and in his quest for advantage in the decolonizing world.

A third, related dilemma touched on the US–Soviet arms race. Khrushchev desperately wanted the Soviet Union to be recognized as the military equal of the United States. Only that way, he believed, would Moscow's international positions be respected. But the Soviet Union was not America's military equal. It was encircled by US military bases and client states and faced a US bomber force far superior to its own. In the event of war, the United States and its allies could lay waste to Soviet territory, whereas the East bloc would be hard pressed to land a blow against the United States. Khrushchev's solution to this conundrum was, in essence, to bluff: to project the illusion that Soviet military capabilities were far greater than they actually were and to conduct himself with overbearing confidence and pugnacity. Such assertiveness, he hoped, would conceal Soviet military weakness and persuade Western adversaries that they crossed the Russian bear at their peril. (It could also address the second dilemma by reassuring Mao that the Soviet Union remained staunchly committed to the anticapitalist struggle.)

Two violent crises in the fall of 1956 – both culminating at almost exactly the same moment – showed the impact of these dilemmas on Khrushchev's international behavior. In Hungary, students emboldened by Khrushchev's domestic reforms revolted against the Soviet presence in their country. Hungary's communist regime collapsed, and a new, reformist government announced its withdrawal from the Warsaw Pact, the East bloc's counterpart to NATO. In early November, Soviet forces brutally crushed the rebellion, restoring the old regime along with Hungary's Warsaw Pact membership. Days earlier, Britain, France, and Israel militarily attacked Egypt following the latter's nationalization of the Suez Canal Company. The Soviet government, then grooming Egypt as a client state, publicly threatened to launch missiles against Britain and France, and shortly thereafter all three attackers desisted. This outcome had more to do with Eisenhower's own forceful opposition to the assault – Ike feared it would turn Arab, Muslim, and other developing nations against the West – but Khrushchev seemed to believe that Moscow's saber-rattling had done the trick. In both crises, he demonstrated that no commitment to internal liberalization or East–West coexistence could keep the Soviet Union from flexing its muscles when need be.

Suez and Hungary also revealed the growing complexity of cold war geopolitics. Over Suez, Washington sided with Moscow in opposing two NATO allies, while recoiling from the Soviet threat to fire missiles against them. On Hungary, the US government denounced the suppression of patriotic dissidents but made it clear it would not risk World War III by coming to their aid, thus tacitly recognizing Soviet domination of Eastern Europe. In both crises, the superpowers showed they cared deeply about the good opinion of small or developing nations. Moral ambiguity, scrambled coalitions, escalating danger, multiplying international voices – these were the features of the maturing cold war.

The Shock of the Sputniks

Though satisfied with the Soviet Union's performance during the Suez Crisis, Khrushchev remained concerned about its strategic inferiority vis-à-vis the United States. He had already decided to concede the US advantage in bomber aircraft and focus instead on mastering a new military technology: the intercontinental ballistic missile (ICBM), which could deliver a nuclear warhead to a target on the other side of the globe. The United States was working on an ICBM of its own, and Khrushchev urged the Soviet defense establishment to spare no effort in reaching this milestone first. In August 1957, from a base in the Kazakhstan desert, the Soviet Union successfully launched the first ICBM, whose nonlethal payload landed in the Pacific about 4,000 miles away.

Although the Soviets' ICBM test received little international attention, their next achievement was a stunner. In October 1957, a rocket launched from that same Kazakhstan base exited the atmosphere and put a beach-ball-sized metal sphere, weighing 184 pounds, into orbit around the earth. Sputnik (which means "traveling companion") circled the globe for three weeks before slipping back into the atmosphere and burning up. It transmitted radio signals that receivers on earth picked up as chirping sounds, furnishing rapid confirmation of Moscow's announcement of the feat. While the dawning of the satellite age thrilled American scientists and science enthusiasts, the fact that the Soviets had entered it first perturbed the broader US public. The ominous implications of the August ICBM test leapt into focus, all the more so as Khrushchev could not resist crowing about the Soviet achievements and claiming that the strategic balance had swung sharply in Moscow's favor. American pundits and politicians (especially Democrats sniffing partisan opportunity) lent credence to the boast. "Soon they will be dropping bombs on us from space," warned Senate Majority Leader Lyndon B. Johnson, "like kids dropping rocks onto cars from freeway overpasses."

The jolts kept coming. In November the Soviets launched Sputnik 2, a capsule large enough to carry a live passenger on its orbit, a dog named Laika (who died in the operation, there being no means of returning the satellite to earth intact). The following month, America's answer to the Sputniks, the Vanguard rocket – bearing a satellite weighing just three pounds – exploded on the launching pad. Newspaper headlines dubbed the failed US mission "Flopnik," "Kaputnik," "Goofnik," and "Stayputnik." John Foster Dulles, Eisenhower's secretary of state, privately complained that the United States had become "the laughing-stock of the whole Free World."

Eisenhower himself was having none of it. "Our satellite program has never been conducted as a race with other nations," he insisted in a speech days after the launch of Sputnik 1. Far from a disappointment, the US program was "well designed and properly scheduled to achieve the scientific purpose for which it was initiated." These sounded like the rationalizations of an also-ran, but Ike was genuinely untroubled by the Soviet achievement and baffled by the public hysteria over "one small ball in the air." He realized that Americans' fears centered on what the Sputniks portended, but he had no doubt that the United States would soon launch a satellite and an ICBM of its own. Sure enough, despite the Vanguard fiasco, both milestones were achieved in 1958.

Moreover, Eisenhower had it on good authority that Soviet military capabilities were rather less formidable than Khrushchev suggested. In 1955, Eisenhower had proposed that each superpower open its airspace to the other's surveillance aircraft, so that the military capabilities of both nations could be mutually disclosed. Khrushchev, fearful of revealing Soviet military weakness, rejected the proposal. Thus Eisenhower approved a top-secret program to conduct aerial reconnaissance over Soviet territory unilaterally. The plane designed for this purpose, the U-2, could fly at altitudes of up to 70,000 feet – so high that Soviet anti-aircraft missiles couldn't shoot them down – and yet take stunningly detailed photographs of Soviet military installations. (The spy flights were kept secret from the public, not Soviet leaders. The latter were well aware that U-2 planes were violating their airspace but embarrassed by their military's inability to shoot them down. So Moscow, too, kept quiet about the overflights.) By late 1957, U-2 flights had revealed that the Soviet bomber force was much smaller than previously estimated. The jury was still out on Soviet missile strength, but all indications were that Russia was not, as Khrushchev bragged, mass-producing ICBMs "like sausages." In case of war, it still would be much easier for the United States to devastate the Soviet Union than vice versa.

Unfortunately for Eisenhower, he couldn't *prove* this to the American public, and allay its anxiety about Soviet military strength, without publicizing the existence of the U-2 flights. All he could do was *assert* that the United States was militarily superior, hoping that his personal credibility on such matters sufficed to dispel the atmosphere of crisis at home. In this, he was only partly successful. When Congress, citing the national emergency, debated measures to increase defense spending, expand the federal role in higher education, and create a national agency for space exploration, Eisenhower reluctantly went along with these plans, though he persuaded Congress to spend less on defense and education than it would have otherwise. (All the same, the 1958 National Defense Education Act pumped hundreds of millions of dollars into higher education, especially for science programs and foreign language instruction.) The National Aeronautical and Space Administration (NASA) came into being in late 1958 and began planning manned space flights, an endeavor Eisenhower saw as a showy distraction from worthier efforts to develop reconnaissance, weather, and communications satellites. Ike slowed down the manned space program, but failed to stop it.

The Little Rock Crisis in World Politics

As Sputnik 1 orbited the earth, Radio Moscow took to announcing in its daily broadcasts the precise moment when the satellite would pass over various world cities. Cheekily included on the itinerary was Little Rock, Arkansas, whose very name signified a further cold war vulnerability for the United States. In early September 1957, nine African American teenagers had attempted to enroll at Little Rock's Central High School. Their effort was part of a broader campaign by the National Association for the Advancement of Colored People to begin desegregating all-white schools in the South and thereby implement the Supreme Court's 1954 *Brown v. the Board of Education* decision. A federal district court had ruled that Central High School must admit the "Little Rock Nine." But Arkansas Governor Orval Faubus, catering to the state's white segregationist majority, ordered the Arkansas National Guard to block the students' entry. Faubus's action made international news, along with photographs of a white mob harassing one of the students, fifteen-year-old Elizabeth Eckford, who had arrived at the school alone ahead of the others. For the next couple of weeks, the Black students stayed home as Faubus continued to defy the court order. Eisenhower met privately with the governor and urged him to comply with the order, which the federal court forcefully reissued on September 20.

In an abrupt tactical shift, Faubus withdrew the National Guard, ostensibly clearing the way for the students' enrollment, but he made no state-level provisions for their protection. Arriving at the school on the morning of September 23, the students were menaced by angry crowds that local police struggled to contain. The students managed to enter the school, but at midday the city authorities sent them home for their own protection, an escape accomplished via a harrowing car ride past throngs of jeering, rock-throwing whites.

The Little Rock crisis drew a chorus of international condemnation. In Britain, the Netherlands, Egypt, Tanganyika, India, Indonesia, and other countries, politicians and

Figure 4.2 White onlookers taunt Elizabeth Eckford as she arrives for her first day at Little Rock High School, Arkansas, 1957. Source: Bettmann / Getty Images.

editorialists decried the officially sanctioned racism and hooliganism on display at Central High School. "Troops Advance against Children!" headlined the Soviet youth newspaper *Komsomolskaya Pravda*. Such international criticism was hardly new. In recent years, the *Brown v. Board* decision, the Emmett Till murder, and the Montgomery bus boycott had all shone a global spotlight on American racism. But the scale and intensity of the denunciation over Little Rock set this case apart. So, too, did the fact that by 1957 the opinion of nonwhite nations counted a good deal more in world affairs than it had just a few years earlier. "The effect of this in Asia and Africa," Secretary of State Dulles privately lamented on September 24, "will be worse for us than Hungary was for the Russians."

That same day, Eisenhower sent hundreds of paratroopers from the Army's 101st Airborne Division into Little Rock to enforce the federal court order. Ike was no champion of desegregation and dispatched the troops only with great reluctance. But he feared an erosion of federal authority at home and a sullying of the nation's reputation abroad. As Eisenhower stated in a White House address explaining the intervention, "Our enemies are gloating over this incident and using it everywhere to misrepresent our whole nation."

Eisenhower's action produced a considerable easing of foreign criticism, though communist governments dismissed the intervention as window dressing, and even some friendly commentators cautioned that it was only a first step. The launching of Sputnik, ironically, brought a further reprieve. Although Moscow used the occasion to rub Americans' noses in their domestic shortcomings, the satellite actually chased Little Rock off the world's front pages. One US humiliation at a time, it seemed, was what the global traffic would bear.

Under the protection of federal troops, the Little Rock Nine remained at Central High for the 1957–1958 school year. But the victory was short-lived. Rather than continue the desegregation of Central High, Arkansas's government simply closed all public high schools in Little Rock for 1958–1959. When the schools reopened the following year, they refused general enrollment to African Americans. Instead, they admitted tiny numbers of Black students on the basis of elaborate criteria that, though colorblind on their face, were clearly designed to prevent large-scale desegregation. The US Supreme Court, which had upheld the district court's initial desegregation order, did not challenge this new procedure. Similarly (and not surprisingly), a world press that had condemned Arkansas's violent defense of the color line largely ignored the state's subtler measures to uphold it. Global denunciation of American racism, however, would resume in due course.

Liberal Dissent and *The Ugly American*

Even as foreign criticism of domestic American affairs somewhat abated, domestic criticism of US foreign policies was on the rise. To his Democratic and liberal opponents, Eisenhower's low-key reaction to Sputnik pointed to a more general deficiency of international leadership: not only was the Eisenhower administration losing the space race; it also was failing to reach out to developing countries, and thus forfeiting America's standing in the world. A host of Asian, Middle Eastern, and North African nations had recently shaken off the yoke of colonialism and were making their voices heard in the United Nations and other international bodies. In Latin America, countries formally independent since the nineteenth century were undergoing populist or leftist upheavals that challenged the authority of entrenched oligarchs, many with close ties to Washington. By the late 1950s, across a wide swath of such nations, the tenor of politics was increasingly critical of US global power. In May 1958, Vice President Richard Nixon made a goodwill tour of South America, where his visits were marred by hostile demonstrations. Protesters in Caracas, Venezuela, nearly dragged Nixon and his entourage out of their cars. Two months later, when US marines landed in Lebanon to bolster its pro-Western government, a wave of anti-US demonstrations swept the Arab world. The Soviet Union, by contrast, seemed to be making steady inroads into developing countries, dazzling them with superior rocketry and tantalizing them with offers of economic and military aid.

Why was the United States flailing in the developing world? The dominant liberal explanation highlighted American neglect, an attitude borne of complacency, laziness, and racial and cultural prejudice. Under Republican leadership, the argument went, the US diplomatic service had ignored the needs and aspirations of nonwhite nations, which were consequently turning away from the United States and growing ever more susceptible to communist appeals. Sharply voicing this critique was the 1958 novel *The Ugly American*, by William Lederer and Eugene Burdick. The book was an instant bestseller, widely read by members of the American political elite, especially Democrats. The novel unfolds in the imaginary Southeast Asian nation of Sarkhan, which is menaced by a communist insurgency backed by Russia and Red China. The insurgency makes rapid progress, largely because the American diplomats in the country are clueless dilettantes more interested in attending cocktail parties and shopping at the commissary than in learning about Sarkhan and its people. They cannot speak Sarkhanese and are disdainful of the nation's customs. US military advisers know nothing about communist guerrilla tactics under way in the Sarkhanese countryside. Soviet and Chinese diplomats and attachés display no such flaws and relentlessly draw Sarkhan into their sinister orbit.

The novel's message was clear: if the United States was to prevail in the cold war, it would have to become much more serious about winning over the nonwhite world. US diplomats and aid workers must roll up their sleeves, get out from behind their desks, and trek off to the countryside to work with native populations, not on grandiose projects such as suspension bridges and hydroelectric dams but in tiny village industries that made an immediate difference in people's lives. Americans abroad must learn local languages and willingly live among the natives as equals, not superiors. Counterinsurgency experts must inhabit the minds of their communist foes. *The Ugly American* was not high literature; its tone was preachy and its characters flat. But it expressed the dissatisfaction and malaise afflicting American liberalism in the late 1950s, a feeling that the United States had grown soft in its prosperity and must somehow recapture the spirit of mission and sacrifice that had made it a great nation in the first place.

Of course, a sterner diagnosis was conceivable: that the United States was resented not simply because it was neglectful or condescending but because it dealt with developing countries in domineering and exploitative ways, deliberately thwarting nationalist aspirations that impinged on its own strategic, economic, or ideological interests. Versions of this charge had circulated openly among American progressives earlier in the century, especially regarding repeated US military interventions in Latin America and the Caribbean in the 1910s and 1920s. With the onset of the cold war, such talk became harder to get away with in polite company; it sounded too similar to what Soviet diplomats were saying at the UN. But now, as the pall of McCarthyism slowly lifted, antiimperialist themes, or something approaching them, began creeping back into mainstream critiques of US foreign policy.

The Cuban Revolution

A drama unfolding on a Caribbean island nation brought the issue into sharper focus, inviting domestic US criticism both of the *Ugly American* variety and from points further left. Cuba had been a protectorate of the United States from 1903 to 1934, and under heavy US domination thereafter. By the late 1950s, sugar counted for 80 percent of Cuba's exports, over half of it destined for US markets; about three-quarters of Cuba's imports came from the United States. Ninety percent of the island's telephone and electrical services were controlled by US companies, and almost all of its mines and cattle ranches were North-American-owned. Cuba was a haven for American casino operators, many with ties to organized crime. Prostitution, largely catering to American male tourists, was rife on the island. And, for most of the previous quarter-century, a brutal and corrupt dictator named Fulgencio Batista had dominated Cuba with Washington's support.

By the second half of the 1950s, several Cuban political parties and paramilitary groups sought to unseat Batista. The most prominent of these was the 26th of July Movement (named for the date in 1953 when it launched a failed attack on a Cuban army facility), led by an energetic young lawyer named Fidel Castro. Ensconced in the Sierra Maestra mountains of southeastern Cuba, Castro and his band battled the Cuban army, gradually expanding their area of control. Cuban exiles in the United States backed the insurgency with cash, arms, and propaganda. The 26th of July Movement also benefited from extensive US media coverage, much of it sympathetic. Castro was charismatic, articulate, and, to reporters willing to make the arduous hike to his mountain headquarters, generous with his time. In lengthy interviews, he proclaimed his devotion to democracy, his contempt for Batista's authoritarianism and corruption, and his opposition to communism. (This last claim was plausible; Castro's relations with Cuba's communist party were frosty, and his public embrace of socialism lay a few years in the future.) The Batista regime's denunciations of Castro as a dangerous radical, while resonating in some quarters of the Eisenhower administration, had little influence on US media portrayals.

It was the Castroites, rather, who struck a chord with many Americans, especially in 1957 and 1958. Cold war liberals, embarrassed by their government's support for the hated Batista, celebrated Castro's brand of dynamic and popular anticommunism. Perhaps by aligning with such a force, they mused, the United States could recast itself as the champion of small and weak peoples. More diffusely, the specter of an insouciant, ragtag, rebel army in the hills, gallantly pinning down the superior forces of an oppressive regime, captured the spirit of restlessness and mild insubordination then taking hold in US culture. The mere fact that Castro had a beard, in this most clean-shaven of American decades, was appealingly transgressive. It was as if the reins of history had been seized by an armed hipster, or a younger, dark-whiskered Ernest Hemingway. (The original Hemingway famously resided on the island. Although he said little about Castro during the insurgency, he warmed up to him after he took power.) A steady stream of North American leftists, soldiers of fortune, and teenage runaways – small in number but ubiquitous in US news accounts – flowed into the ranks of the Sierra Maestra rebellion.

In late 1958, Batista's position disintegrated. An election to determine his successor, held amid escalating rebel attacks, rampant army desertions, and deepening civil unrest, drew few voters to the polls and was widely dismissed as fraudulent. There seemed little prospect that the pro-Batista victor could take office, or even that Batista could serve out his term, scheduled to expire in February 1959. The Eisenhower administration scrambled to find a "third force" to succeed the regime, untainted by ties to either Batista or Castro. The effort failed. Just hours into the New Year, Batista fled to the Dominican Republic. The army's resistance to the rebellion collapsed, and within days Castro's forces controlled the main state institutions. On January 7, the United States recognized the new government.

Once in power, Castro and his government moved to sever Cuba's ties of dependence to the United States. They shut down the American casinos, placed the country's telephone company, a US subsidiary, under government control, and launched an ambitious land reform program that resulted in the expropriation (with modest compensation) of numerous

US-owned properties, especially sugar farms held by the United Fruit Company. More controversially, the Castroites struck at the remnants of the old regime, executing hundreds of captured Batista officials after hasty trials. They also began cooperating with Cuban communists, whom they had previously shunned. Thousands of wealthy and middle-class Cubans fled to the United States, especially Miami, Florida, where a formidable anti-Castro exile movement took shape.

The Eisenhower administration tightened the economic screws on the Castro regime, reducing existing US aid programs to Cuba and pressuring international lending institutions to restrict its line of credit. The aim was to compel the Castro government to reconsider its radical course and return to the US-dominated fold. Instead, the Castroites hastened Cuba's exit from the US orbit and won the backing of a new patron. Early in 1960, Cuba concluded a barter agreement with the Soviet Union committing the latter to import Cuban sugar and provide crude oil in return. At Washington's urging, US oil companies in Cuba refused to refine the Soviet crude, prompting the Cuban government to nationalize them. The Eisenhower administration completely closed off the US market to Cuban sugar. By now, the CIA had begun secretly plotting Castro's overthrow. In July, Khrushchev proclaimed that "Soviet artillerymen can support the Cuban people with their rocket fire" in the event of an attack on Cuba, and the Cuban government publicly welcomed this offer of protection. In January 1961, as Eisenhower prepared to leave office, the United States severed diplomatic relations with Cuba.

US society as a whole was open to a wider array of opinions on Castro's Cuba. Yet here, too, the trend was one of growing disaffection. Until about mid-1959, press coverage and mainstream liberal commentary remained fairly sympathetic to the new government. In the months thereafter, though, both became increasingly critical of Havana's radical domestic programs, its dispensing of summary justice, its denunciations of the US government, and, eventually, its gravitation toward the Soviet bloc. Naturally, liberal critics saw to it that the Eisenhower administration received a share of the blame. In early 1960 Senator John F. Kennedy of Massachusetts, then seeking the Democratic Party's presidential nomination, wondered aloud "[w]hether Castro would have taken a more rational course after his victory had the United States Government not backed the dictator Batista so long and so uncritically, and had it given the fiery young rebel a warmer welcome in his hour of triumph."

As mainstream support receded, Castro's defenders dwindled to a more peripheral but still nationally visible cast of characters: left-wing Democrats, scholars specializing in Latin America, writers and public intellectuals, leaders of some Protestant denominations, and a handful of mainstream journalists now tolerated as eccentric gadflies at their newspapers and magazines. These figures pointed to the Cuban government's earnest efforts to eradicate poverty; to build schools, clinics, and housing; to block the restoration of Batista's vicious regime; to chart an independent and dignified course against the perilous headwinds of US hostility. The most organized propagator of such views was the Fair Play for Cuba Committee (FPCC), formed in early 1960 by left-liberal journalists, intellectuals, and activists. Claiming 7,000 members at its peak in early 1961, the FPCC staged rallies, placed display advertisements in newspapers, and sent delegations to Cuba to express solidarity with the revolution and gather favorable information about it. The organization was especially active on university campuses, appealing to an emerging cohort of students increasingly skeptical of received opinion, on matters both domestic and international. In the late 1950s, many of these young people had embraced C. Wright Mills's trenchant critiques of the nation's political and economic elites. The author's foray into Cuban affairs with the publication of *Listen, Yankee* amplified the FPCC's message among left-leaning youth.

In all of these pro-Castro efforts, African Americans were active participants. Their presence grew more noticeable as support for the Cuban revolution dwindled within US society at large. Cold war ideology had always had a more tenuous hold on the Black community, which, at best, enjoyed only limited access to the "American way of life" so vigorously touted abroad and, at worst, endured grinding poverty and brutal repression. Moreover, although Castro himself was light-skinned, his rhetoric was antiracist, his revolution simpatico with nonwhite liberation movements the world over, and the society he represented conspicuously marked by African lineage. These facts were widely publicized among African Americans, along with the welcome news that Castro's government had ended its predecessor's racial segregation of Cuban tourist facilities. True, some leading African Americans, such as the New York Congressman Adam Clayton Powell, Jr., and the baseball legend Jackie Robinson, had shed their initial admiration for Castro. But many Black Americans, elite and ordinary alike, remained friendly to the Cuban leader long after most whites had turned against him.

In September 1960, Castro came to New York City to address the UN General Assembly. The visit solidified his status within the African American community, while underscoring that community's own growing visibility on the world stage. Following a run-in with the management of their hotel in midtown Manhattan, Castro and his entourage decamped to the Hotel Theresa in the mostly Black neighborhood of Harlem. There, Castro hosted a procession of prominent Black well-wishers, including Nation of Islam minister Malcolm X. Several world leaders who were also in town for the General Assembly session – Gamal Abdel Nasser of Egypt, Jawaharlal Nehru of India, Kwame Nkrumah of Ghana, even a beaming Nikita Khrushchev – came to see Castro in Harlem and joined him in greeting the cheering crowds surrounding the hotel. "Why shouldn't we like [Castro]?" a Harlemite asked a reporter. "He ended racial discrimination in Cuba and that's more than the United States has done in this matter." A Black newspaperman observed that "Castro's move to the Theresa and Khrushchev's decision to visit him gave the Negroes of Harlem one of the biggest 'lifts' they have had in the cold racial war with the white man."

Dealing and Dueling with Khrushchev

By 1960, the specter of a Soviet leader walking the streets of an American city was far less outlandish than it would have been just a few years earlier, for Khrushchev was now a familiar, if often reviled, figure to the US public. His first meeting with Eisenhower, at a Geneva summit conference in 1955, had raised hopes for an East–West thaw. But subsequent developments, such as the Soviet crushing of the Hungarian uprising, the American alarm over Sputnik, and sharp disagreements over the status of Berlin, eroded that optimism. Still, the "spirit of Geneva" lived on in the US–Soviet cultural exchanges authorized at the summit. In July 1959, Vice President Nixon traveled to Moscow to help open the American National Exhibit, where US cultural and technological achievements were on lavish display. He and Khrushchev toured the exhibit together, the latter openly deriding American gadgets as frivolous and impractical, and American modern art as garish and degenerate. "Only a pederast would have done this," Khrushchev said, a bit oddly, of a female nude sculpture.

At several points during their exhibit tour, the two leaders publicly disputed the relative merits of capitalism and communism. Because one skirmish took place in a model American kitchen, featuring appliances billed as liberating American housewives from drudgery, the whole exchange was dubbed the "Kitchen Debate." But the most widely publicized moments occurred when Khrushchev and Nixon strolled into a model American television studio and resumed their argument before video cameras. Later aired in the United States, the encounter afforded American television audiences a fairly extended view of Khrushchev's diplomatic style: incessant, unyielding, gesticulating bluster, with flashes of impish humor. Nixon held his own, but protocol dictated that a vice president be less aggressive than a head of state. And, anyway, Nixon could speak from the quiet confidence that, Sputnik notwithstanding, his nation still held the strategic edge.

Two months later, Americans got an even closer look at Khrushchev when he visited the United States, the first Soviet leader to do so. He immediately embarked on a clamorous tour of the country, furnishing irresistible copy to the reporters in tow. At a huge banquet in Iowa hosted by a millionaire corn farmer, Khrushchev admitted that "the slaves of capitalism live very well," though he added that "the slaves of communism" did so, too. In Los Angeles, he attended a lunch at 20th Century Fox studios, mingling with Elizabeth Taylor, Marlon Brando, Marilyn Monroe, and other Hollywood stars. (The anticommunist actor Ronald Reagan boycotted the function.) When Khrushchev learned that security concerns ruled out a visit to Disneyland, his disappointment was palpable. "What is it?" he demanded. "Is there an epidemic of cholera there or something? Or have gangsters taken hold of the place that can destroy me?" If nothing else, the trip demonstrated that Khrushchev was human, and this in itself offered some reassurance. Although his meetings with Eisenhower yielded no substantive breakthroughs, the atmospherics were cordial. It was agreed that Eisenhower and Khrushchev would meet again in Paris in May 1960 and that Eisenhower would later visit the Soviet Union.

A subsequent diplomatic crisis, however, prevented Eisenhower from making the Soviet trip. Since 1956, U-2 planes had secretly overflown Soviet territory, photographing military installations. The Soviet government, aware of the flights but loath to admit its inability to shoot the planes down, had issued only private protests, which US officials brushed aside. Eisenhower knew he was risking an eventual public imbroglio over these violations of Soviet airspace, but the resulting intelligence was too valuable to pass up. (The first satellite images of Soviet territory would not be available until August 1960.) The U-2 photographs provided further assurance that Soviet military capabilities were far weaker than advertised, enabling Eisenhower to keep Khrushchev's bravado in perspective.

In early May 1960, however, a Soviet surface-to-air missile finally succeeded in shooting down a U-2. Believing the pilot must have perished, the Eisenhower administration issued a cover story: a NASA weather plane was missing; perhaps it had accidentally strayed into Soviet airspace. Triumphantly, Khrushchev revealed to the world that the pilot had survived, was in Soviet custody, and had obviously been flying a US spy mission. Washington was forced to recant its bogus story, acutely embarrassing Eisenhower. In mid-May he went to Paris for his summit meeting with Khrushchev, who demanded that Eisenhower publicly apologize for the U-2 fights. Eisenhower refused, and Khrushchev withdrew his invitation to visit the Soviet Union.[1] Cold war animosities resumed with a vengeance as the Eisenhower era drew to a close.

A Changing Cold War at Home

This was not, however, a simple return to the bad old days of the early 1950s. In some ways, the superpower standoff had become far deadlier, with each nation developing the capability, at least, to fire ICBMs at the other's territory and extend the arms race into space. Yet the preceding half-decade had also shown that gentler international approaches were possible, creating new expectations and norms for managing cold war tensions. Although many American politicians and pundits blasted Khrushchev's truculence over the U-2 incident and agreed that Eisenhower had nothing to apologize for, many others criticized the president's resort to aerial espionage as recklessly provocative. "Could it serve the purpose of peace and mutual trust," asked two-time Democratic presidential candidate Adlai Stevenson, "to send intelligence missions over the heart of the Soviet Union on the very eve of the long-awaited [Paris] summit conference?"

In American society writ large, cold war orthodoxies were becoming easier to challenge, or simply ignore. As we saw, many Americans continued to support Fidel Castro well after mainstream liberals had written him off. Within the African American community, pro-Castroism fit in with a broader inclination to cheer on the struggles of colonized peoples to win national independence and, thereafter, wield power in world politics. African developments were especially stirring. In 1960 alone, seventeen new nations appeared on the continent. It was hard not to connect that global drama to domestic racial politics, for 1960 was also the year that four African American college students in Greensboro, North Carolina, staged a sit-in to demand service at a segregated department store lunch counter, inspiring similar protests throughout the South and imparting a new urgency to the civil rights movement. "The events in Africa," the Black journalist Ethel Payne wrote that August, "... are making colored Americans more aware of international relations and the reciprocal effect

[1] Khrushchev visited New York City in September 1960 to attend a UN General Assembly session, but Eisenhower did not see him.

upon their own struggle for full citizenship." The fact that some of the ascendant African nationalists had socialist leanings or enjoyed cordial relations with communist nations was, for many Black Americans, quickly losing relevance.

In popular entertainment, a transformation in the marketing of American stand-up comedy drew a cohort of scruffy iconoclasts out of the obscurity of urban nightclubs and into the limelight of network television variety shows and major-label album releases. By 1958, wide swaths of the public could hear Mort Sahl jest, "For a while, every time the Russians threw an American in jail, the Un-American Activities Committee would retaliate by throwing an American in jail, too." (Sahl's use of the past tense was revealing.) A year later, and more daringly, Lenny Bruce portrayed Eisenhower as a smarmy but menacing mob boss who treated the machinery of diplomacy as a sort of Murder Incorporated for removing expendable members of his inner circle. In Bruce's imaginary White House, Ike urges Nixon to travel overseas, where he can be picked off at a distance: "Hello, Nick, sweetie. Siddown, baby . . . . I got the greatest idea for you. How'd you like to go to Lebanon? ... I don't know why you don't wanna go. You did great in Caracas."

The nation's nuclear weapons policies, too, had come in for their share of mainstream scrutiny and criticism, a development helped along by the well-founded suspicion that bomb tests in the American Southwest were poisoning the atmosphere with radiation. Calls for a halt to the nuclear arms race, voiced most prominently by the scientists, intellectuals, and religious leaders who formed the National Committee for a Sane Nuclear Policy (SANE), became increasingly audible in mainstream news coverage. In 1959, United Artists released *On the Beach*, a movie adaptation of Nevil Shute's 1957 novel of the same name. Produced and directed by Stanley Kramer, and starring Gregory Peck, Ava Gardner, and Fred Astaire, the film posits a numbingly bleak scenario in which most of humanity have perished in a nuclear holocaust and the surviving remnant choose suicide to escape the slow ravages of radiation sickness. Comedians brought a lighter touch to the issue. While *On the Beach* was still in production, Mort Sahl quipped that Kramer was making the film "in a hurry, before the world beats him to it." In his own sardonic ode to World War III, issued on vinyl in 1959, the musical satirist Tom Lehrer sang: "We will all go together when we go/ All suffused with an incandescent glow/No one will have the endurance/To collect on his insurance/Lloyds of London will be loaded when they go."

Liberals and leftists were not the only ones challenging the cold war status quo. Over the previous half-decade, an articulate, resourceful, and increasingly formidable conservative movement had castigated Eisenhower for his willingness to seek an accommodation with the Soviets. One of the most influential conservatives was William F. Buckley, Jr., the young founder and editor of the New-York-based journal *National Review*, which offered a synthesis of traditional conservatism, laissez-faire economics, vociferous anticommunism, and, to Buckley's later regret, overt white supremacy. In September 1959, as Khrushchev prepared to visit the country, Buckley threatened to mark the occasion by dyeing the Hudson River red, to signify the blood of communism's victims. Much further to Buckley's right was the John Birch Society, founded in 1958 by a wealthy Massachusetts candy manufacturer named Robert Welch. (John Birch had been a young Army captain and Baptist missionary killed by communists in China days after World War II ended.) Like the Buckleyites, the Birchers were outraged by Eisenhower's alleged softness on communism, but they viewed it in a far more sinister light. Welch even called Ike a "dedicated, conscious agent of the Communist conspiracy." This was too much for most mainstream conservatives, and Buckley later severed his ties to the Birch Society.

The 1960 Presidential Election

1960, of course, was a presidential election year. By late July, the two major-party candidates had emerged: Vice President Nixon for the Republicans and Senator John F. Kennedy for the Democrats. Although Nixon clearly benefited from his association with the popular Eisenhower, he also had to answer for the incumbent administration's perceived shortcomings, especially in foreign policy. Kennedy exploited this vulnerability, charging that Eisenhower and his team had been poor stewards of America's cold war interests. Channeling the authors of *The Ugly American* (a book the senator much admired), Kennedy claimed that the Eisenhower administration had shown paltry concern for the developing world and had failed to block communist gains there. Recent events in Cuba seemed to bolster the senator's critique. A decade earlier, Republicans had accused Democrats of "losing" China. Now, Kennedy could say that Republicans had "lost" Cuba.

Kennedy also assailed Eisenhower for letting down the nation's defenses. Soon after the Soviet ICBM test in 1957, the United States had begun deploying ICBMs of its own, but in the late 1950s some American commentators and congressional Democrats, citing selectively leaked US intelligence documents, started claiming that the Soviet Union was producing ICBMs at a much faster rate than the United States was – that a "missile gap" favoring Moscow had opened up and would soon grow much wider. Kennedy had echoed the "missile gap" charge as a senator, and he continued to sound the alarm during his presidential run. He also found a crafty way to pin the accusation of dereliction of duty on Nixon personally: by ridiculing his performance in the 1959 Kitchen Debate. "There are some instances where you may be ahead of us," Nixon had conceded to Khrushchev in Moscow, "for example in the development of the thrust of your rockets for the investigation of outer space. There may be some instances, for example color television, where we're ahead of you." Kennedy derided this statement as the height of decadence, revealing a scandalous willingness to trade hard strategic advantage for soft consumer luxury. With Spartan severity, the senator intoned, "I would rather take my television black and white and have the largest rockets in the world." Chiming in from a San Francisco nightclub, Mort Sahl said he hoped the Soviets would steal some American secrets – "then *they'll* be two years behind."

A clever line, but in this case Sahl was not speaking truth to power. By now Eisenhower and his top advisers, relying on U-2 photographs and other intelligence, had acquired a fairly detailed picture of Soviet military installations, and the emerging consensus was that Moscow had *not* embarked on a crash program to build ICBMs. A missile gap did exist, but it favored the United States, whose dozens of ICBMs vastly outnumbered the tiny handful

Figure 4.3 Mort Sahl, 1960. Source: CBS Photo Archive / Getty Images.

in the Soviets' arsenal. As in the past, however, the president was unwilling to reveal that he possessed this knowledge in any but the vaguest terms. True, the U-2 secret had been blown, but Eisenhower remained eager to preserve a tacit agreement that had arisen between him and his Soviet counterpart: Khrushchev would *pretend* that the Soviet Union was besting the United States in ICBM production, and Eisenhower would not sharply challenge that boast. As long as Khrushchev could be humored in this way, he was less likely to try to turn appearance into reality by drastically stepping up Soviet production of ICBMs.

At first glance, public warnings about a "missile gap" would seem to bolster this shared illusion, but in truth they posed an insidious threat to it. If enough Americans became truly convinced that the Soviets were about to gain an insurmountable lead in ICBMs, then the US government would be compelled to offer a detailed refutation of that view, destroying the tacit understanding. To get Kennedy to stop making the dangerous charge, Eisenhower arranged for him to receive an intelligence briefing from CIA director Allen Dulles. But Dulles's briefing was less conclusive than Eisenhower intended, and Kennedy felt free to persist in his alarmist rhetoric.

In November, Kennedy scored a narrow election victory, beating Nixon by about 112,000 votes nationwide. (The Electoral College result was, as usual, more lopsided, with Kennedy winning 303 electors to Nixon's 219.) At forty-three, Kennedy became the youngest elected president, the first one born in the twentieth century. He was also the first Roman Catholic to hold the office. Although Kennedy's Catholicism had been a prominent issue at various points in the campaign, it played little role in his presidential persona, which instead centered on his youth, handsomeness, glamour, wit, and curious combination of exhorting earnestness and ironic detachment.

JFK and the Cold War

Another hallmark of Kennedy's presidency was its preoccupation with foreign policy. That topic was the sole focus of his January 1961 Inaugural Address, which famously pledged that the United States would "pay any price, bear any burden, meet any hardship, support any friend, oppose any foe to ensure the survival and the success of liberty." Kennedy promised to seek improved relations with America's communist adversaries, but added: "We dare not tempt them with weakness. For only when our arms are sufficient beyond doubt can we be certain beyond doubt that they will never be employed." To newly independent nations, he gave "our word that one form of colonial control shall not have passed away merely to be replaced by a far more iron tyranny." Here, Kennedy acknowledged the undeniable force of the decolonization movement, then running at floodtide, while affirming the priority of the cold war struggle.

Taking office, Kennedy became privy to classified intelligence and was obliged to accept the reality he had resisted during the campaign: Soviet nuclear capabilities were indeed far weaker than his own "missile gap" rhetoric suggested. Yet Kennedy pressed ahead with a planned massive defense buildup, reasoning that such "overkill" would place America's global preeminence beyond question. Between 1961 and 1964, the US defense budget increased from $47.5 billion to $54.5 billion. The number of army divisions grew from eleven to sixteen; the nation's sixty-three ICBMs increased to 424. Days before Kennedy's inauguration, President Eisenhower had warned in his farewell address of the baneful influence of "the military-industrial complex" – the corrupting symbiosis between a bloated military establishment and an expanding arms industry bent on catering to it. The stodgy Eisenhower thus contributed a potent new phrase to the nation's political lexicon, one that progressive critics of US militarism would often repeat. His Democratic successor had other ideas.

In its relations with the developing world, the new administration would operate in two distinct registers, both keyed to *The Ugly American*'s cautionary message. On the one hand, Kennedy and his team cared deeply about America's standing among emerging nations and labored to woo the uncommitted ones to the side of the West. The administration spoke respectfully of their nationalist aspirations and offered them increased economic, technical, and sometimes military aid. In 1961, Kennedy launched the Peace Corps, which sent hundreds of idealistic young Americans to live and work in impoverished communities in Africa, Asia, and Latin America, helping local populations develop the skills and infrastructure to modernize their economies and raise their living standards.

On the other hand, the Kennedy administration was alarmed by the potential spread of communism in the developing world. Two weeks before the new president took office, Khrushchev proclaimed Moscow's support for "wars of national liberation." The statement was primarily aimed at appeasing Mao Zedong, who had grown increasingly critical

Figure 4.4 A Peace Corps teacher's aide speaks with a girl in Zamboanga, the Philippines, 1962. Source: Bettmann / Getty Images.

of Khrushchev's efforts to improve relations with the West. Kennedy, however, believed the Soviet leader was personally challenging him on the eve of his inauguration. Thereafter, whenever a local government or insurgent movement turned to Moscow or Beijing for help, Kennedy was liable to view that act as posing a severe international test. He took a particular interest in the counterinsurgency techniques that the US military had developed over the preceding decade. He saw the US Army Special Forces – informally known as the Green Berets – as key to his administration's efforts to wage the "brushfire wars" that Khrushchev and Mao seemed determined to foment.

In a way, the Peace Corps and the Green Berets represented two sides of the same coin. Within each organization, Americans abroad would adapt to the challenging environments of the Global South. Peace Corps volunteers would share the hardships and toils of indigenous populations, manifesting US solidarity and goodwill. The Green Berets would win the day through their mastery of jungle warfare, proving themselves the equals of local communist guerrillas. Seen from another angle, the two projects could be linked sequentially: "if the Peace Corps failed to do the job," writes the historian Patrick Hearden, "the Green Berets stood ready for action."

Vietnam, of course, became the chief testing ground for US counterinsurgency methods. In 1960, a communist-dominated insurgency called the National Liberation Front (NLF; *aka* the Vietcong) took up arms against the US-backed government in Saigon, South Vietnam's capital. The NLF received material support, and a large measure of direction, from the North Vietnamese regime. To help Saigon combat the NLF, Kennedy significantly enlarged the contingent of US military advisers that Eisenhower had stationed in South Vietnam; they numbered 16,000 by the time of Kennedy's assassination in November 1963.

Officially, the US military personnel were to refrain from direct combat and merely provide training and logistical support for the South Vietnamese army's own campaigns against the NLF. Secretly, they fought alongside South Vietnamese units and flew combat missions. None of this sufficed to end the insurgency or prevent the South Vietnamese regime's political position from deteriorating. Yet the full dimensions of the Vietnam debacle would not unfold until well after Kennedy's death.

US policy toward Cuba, by contrast, publicly unraveled with obliging promptness. Upon taking office, Kennedy learned that the CIA had prepared a plan for Castro's overthrow. The scheme was risky, but, considering the momentum it had so far acquired, and Kennedy's own campaign rhetoric on Cuba, canceling it would have been exceedingly difficult for the new president. He gave it the green light. The operation called for some 1,400 men, mostly Cuban exiles, to land at the Bay of Pigs, on Cuba's southern coast. Assisted by US air cover, the invaders would establish a beachhead. Word of the landing, planners hoped, would spark a successful domestic uprising against Castro's regime. Something not too different from this had occurred in Guatemala in 1954, when a rebel army, covertly supported by the United States, had crossed into the country from neighboring Honduras, as CIA-piloted planes buzzed Guatemala City; these actions panicked and immobilized Guatemala's left-leaning government, facilitating its ouster by the Guatemalan army.

The Bay of Pigs invasion, launched in April 1961, utterly failed to replicate the Guatemalan model. For one thing, the Cuban military was loyal to Castro. For another, precisely because the 1954 experience hovered in the background, Cuba's leaders were well prepared to defend their revolution. They fully mobilized Cuba's land and air forces to intercept the rebel landing, killing or capturing nearly all of the invaders. Kennedy authorized a single airstrike in support of the operation but barred additional strikes in a futile attempt to conceal US involvement. Within three days the effort had collapsed, a crushing defeat for the new president.

Abroad and at home, the public sphere rang with angry and defiant outcries. Moscow and Havana condemned the attempted invasion, and Castro announced for the first time that the Cuban revolution was socialist. Protesters besieged US embassies in Cairo, New Delhi, Tokyo, and Warsaw. They also marched in American cities, where Castro's defenders spoke out with unprecedented boldness. "I feel a desperate shame for my country ...," wrote C. Wright Mills. "Were I physically able to do so, I would at this moment be fighting alongside Fidel Castro." The FPCC pledged to "do all in our power to safeguard the integrity of the legitimate government of Cuba . . . . If this be treason, we stand condemned." Kennedy, too, was publicly unrepentant, telling a gathering of newspaper editors, "[W]e do not intend to be lectured on 'intervention' by those whose character was stamped for all time on the bloody streets of Budapest!"

Privately, Kennedy berated himself for authorizing such a foolhardy operation – and then redoubled his administration's campaign against Castro and his government. Operation Mongoose, as the initiative was called, entailed coordinating and stepping up previous US covert efforts to wreck the Cuban economy and target Castro personally. At the direction of the president's younger brother, Attorney General Robert F. Kennedy, CIA operatives and Cuban exiles infiltrated the island to mine harbors and destroy sugar fields. Other

US agents prepared pills, injections, and powders to kill or incapacitate Castro, though they never managed to administer the poisons. More openly, the United States imposed a trade embargo against Cuba and conducted military training exercises for an invasion of the country on Puerto Rico's Vieques Island.

Yet, if the Bay of Pigs disaster failed to dissuade President Kennedy from targeting Castro, it also emboldened Khrushchev to turn the heat up on Kennedy. The bungled invasion reinforced Khrushchev's impression that the new president was a callow and unsteady figure who could be pressured into giving ground on other international issues. And Washington's continued anti-Cuban measures, which even in their covert aspects were well known to Soviet officials, would draw Khrushchev to the defense of Cuba itself, especially now that Castro had declared for socialism. And yet, precisely because of his humiliation at the Bay of Pigs, Kennedy could ill afford to display further weakness in his dealings with Khrushchev. Consequently, 1961 and 1962 would be years of extraordinary tension in US–Soviet relations, in which the prospects of mutual annihilation were greater than they had ever been or would be for the remainder of the cold war.

The Berlin Crisis

In June 1961, at a grim summit meeting between the two leaders in Vienna, Khrushchev raised the anomalous status of Berlin. Although the city as a whole lay well within East German territory, its western half remained under US, British, and French occupation. The three Western nations enjoyed guaranteed access to West Berlin, an arrangement Moscow had failed to disrupt with its attempted blockade of the city in 1948–1949. The Western enclave in Berlin posed a serious challenge to both the Soviet and the East German governments. The Western powers had transformed it into a showcase of capitalist prosperity, making East Berlin look drab by comparison. Moreover, because no physical barrier then separated East and West Berlin, and because West Berlin had guaranteed contact with West Germany, West Berlin was the main channel through which East Germans relocated to the West. Since 1945, about a fifth of East Germany's population had moved from East to West Germany. There was no comparable migrant traffic in the opposite direction. This westward exodus not only humiliated East bloc governments but also caused an East German brain drain, for the migrants were disproportionately young, skilled, and well educated.

In Vienna, Khrushchev renewed an ultimatum he had issued in 1958 but allowed to lapse: the Soviet Union, the United States, Britain, and France should sign a treaty ending their occupation of Germany and recognizing the East German and West German states. Presumably, such an arrangement, by removing Western forces from West Berlin, would make the city as a whole more susceptible to East bloc control. If a multilateral treaty failed to materialize, Khrushchev continued, the Soviet Union would conclude a bilateral treaty with East Germany granting the latter control of the access routes into West Berlin. *That* step, no one doubted, would sharply restrict Western access to Berlin.

Kennedy replied that neither alternative was acceptable; the Western powers must remain in West Berlin. Were the United States to yield on the matter, all of its international pledges would be "mere scraps of paper." In a chilling close to the exchange, Khrushchev said the United States must decide "whether there will be war or peace." "Then, Mr. Chairman," Kennedy answered, "there will be war."

Back home, Kennedy spent several weeks deliberating with advisers over Khrushchev's ultimatum. In a televised speech in late July, he unveiled his administration's response. "We cannot and will not permit the Communists to drive us out of Berlin," he declared. "[W]e seek peace – but we shall not surrender." Kennedy asked Congress to appropriate $3.25 billion for additional defense and to expand the army from 875,000 to a million men. More ominously, he announced a crash program to build public fallout shelters so that more civilians could survive a nuclear attack; ordinary citizens were urged to build private shelters in their basements and backyards. Americans had heard such exhortations before, but not in the midst of a grave superpower standoff. Tens of thousands anxiously heeded the government's call, granting a summer bonanza to the installers of home fallout shelters. Kennedy had been assured that, in a nuclear war, shelters could reduce US deaths from 79 million to 50 million, a grotesque calculus if one held that such a war should have been unthinkable. But that was one of the purposes of these macabre appeals of the populace: to convince Moscow that Washington regarded a nuclear exchange as entirely thinkable. ("Crackpot realism" was C. Wright Mills's term for such brinkmanship.)

Many East Berliners fixated on a more localized danger: that their government might respond to the crisis by blocking their access to West Berlin. The east-to-west refugee traffic sharply increased. During one twenty-four-hour period in early August, nearly 2,000 East Berliners crossed to the other side. The fear was justified. On the morning of August 13, Berliners awoke to discover that East German authorities had erected barbed wire barricades between East and West Berlin. Over the coming days, the authorities replaced the barbed wire with a brick wall that completely surrounded West Berlin, separating it from East Berlin and other parts of East Germany (though still allowing US, British, and French forces access to West Berlin). East Berliners were no longer permitted to enter West Berlin. Those attempting to breach the barrier risked being shot dead by East German border guards. The wall was to divide the city for the next twenty-eight years.

American leaders denounced the Berlin Wall, saying it starkly encapsulated the evils of communism. It soon became apparent, however, that the wall might be a solution to Berlin's crisis. With East Berliners no longer fleeing in droves, the Soviet and East German governments found the situation more tolerable. In October Khrushchev quietly withdrew his ultimatum. The Western powers discovered that they, too, could live with the new status quo. They still had access and occupation rights in West Berlin, the retention of which had been their main objective. And both sides could heave a sigh of relief that a nuclear confrontation had been averted. The big losers were the people of Berlin, not just Easterners penned in behind the new barrier but also Westerners cut off from family members in the East. Yet even they would have been hard pressed to refute Kennedy's private assessment that "a wall is a hell of a lot better than a war."

Over the next few months, the Berlin crisis steadily eased, punctuated by brief periods of tension. The most dramatic was a sixteen-hour standoff in October between US and Soviet tanks at a border crossing along the wall known as "Checkpoint Charlie," triggered by East German guards' refusal to allow a US diplomat and his wife to enter East Berlin to attend the theater. Fortunately, both Kennedy and Khrushchev intervened to defuse the crisis.

That same month, Kennedy's deputy secretary of defense, Roswell Gilpatrick, delivered a public speech that spelled out, in stark detail, the extent of America's nuclear superiority over the Soviet Union. Gilpatrick noted that the United States possessed hundreds of bombers, dozens of ICBMs, and several submarines wielding scores of nuclear missiles. "[T]his nation has a retaliatory force of such lethal power," he said, "that an enemy move which brought it into play would be an act of self-destruction." Kennedy had authorized the statement in the hope of altering Khrushchev's behavior. Perhaps the Soviet leader would be less inclined to press his luck in places such as Berlin if he knew how confident the United States was in its own superiority. The danger, of course, was that Khrushchev might feel compelled to take vigorous, even desperate, steps to redress the imbalance. The Kennedy administration considered that risk but ultimately decided that calling Khrushchev's bluff would be safer than indulging it – a fateful miscalculation.

JFK, Civil Rights, and the Cold War

As jarring as all these international events were, they unfolded in an arena that Kennedy eagerly inhabited. The same could not be said of the great domestic drama of the day. Kennedy had spoken sympathetically of the civil rights movement during the 1960 campaign, but he gave it low priority after becoming president, fearful of alienating white segregationists in the Democratic Party and on Capitol Hill (see Chapter 5 for a fuller discussion of the civil rights movement in the early 1960s). To overcome his reluctance, civil rights activists often discussed the issue with Kennedy in global terms. In a February 1961 memorandum to the new president, Roy Wilkins and Arnold Aaronson of the Leadership Conference on Civil Rights wrote, "As the criterion by which our democratic professions are measured in many parts of the globe, civil rights is and will increasingly be an important aspect of our foreign relations."

Kennedy understood the problem: a conspicuous failure to live up to those "democratic professions" would imperil America's international standing. Thus his initial solution was to try to keep the failure *in*conspicuous. A recurring headache for his administration was the discriminatory treatment African diplomats endured when posted to the United States, and especially when driving along Maryland's Highway 40, which connected Washington and New York. African diplomats making the trip were frequently refused service at Maryland's roadside restaurants. Apprised of the problem, Kennedy proposed that the affronted envoys fly rather than drive.

Kennedy reacted similarly to the challenge posed by the Freedom Riders. In 1960, the Supreme Court had ruled that racial segregation in interstate public transportation was unlawful. Southern states continued, however, to segregate interstate bus passengers. In May 1961, Black and white activists from the Congress of Racial Equality and the Student Nonviolent Coordinating Committee sought to compel the federal government to enforce the court decision. They boarded Trailways and Greyhound buses and rode through the Deep South as integrated groups. On several occasions in Alabama, the activists encountered brutal resistance. One bus was firebombed and several Freedom Riders savagely beaten by white mobs, all while local police stood by. Kennedy was annoyed by the spectacle. A lurid display of segregationist violence was the last thing he needed as he prepared to fly to Vienna for his summit with Khrushchev. "Stop them!" the president instructed Harris Wofford, his special assistant on civil rights. "Get your friends off those buses!"

Kennedy's concern was well founded, for the Freedom Rides had captured the world's attention. A Pakistani newspaper noted that the segregationist mobs had "out-Little Rocked Little Rock." An East German newspaper claimed, opportunistically but not inaccurately, that Black Americans were growing "increasingly disillusioned" by Kennedy's "capitulation to race haters." The United States Information Agency (USIA), charged with attending to the nation's global reputation, warned that the attacks on the Freedom Riders were exerting "a highly detrimental influence on the views held abroad of the United States." It was indeed a replay of Little Rock, with the difference that, by 1961, questions of racial equality mattered even more to US global prestige than they had in 1957.

In fact, even as Kennedy vented to Wofford, administration officials (including most prominently Attorney General Robert Kennedy) were intervening to ensure the safety of Freedom Riders and other civil rights activists. At the height of the crisis, Martin Luther King, Jr., spoke in support of the riders at a large church gathering in Montgomery, Alabama. When a huge crowd of angry whites menaced the church building, the Department of Justice dispatched hundreds of federal marshals to prevent a violent assault. Meanwhile, the DOJ pressured the Alabama and Mississippi state governments to provide police protection for the Freedom Riders. When the activists reached Jackson, Mississippi, however, they were arrested and jailed on state charges of breaching the peace, without interference by federal authorities.

The Kennedy administration had compromised with segregationists, but to many foreign observers, including in nonwhite nations, its actions appeared broadly constructive; it had asserted national power on behalf of vulnerable Black citizens. Mixed in with the foreign criticism of American racism, therefore, was praise for the administration's moves to combat it. For President Kennedy, the political calculus was shifting: attacking segregation remained domestically risky, but the international compensations were growing more evident.

A civil rights showdown in September 1962 underscored the emerging pattern. The University of Mississippi had denied admission to James Meredith, a Mississippi resident, because he was African American. A federal appeals court had ruled the denial unconstitutional. To noisy acclaim from segregationists, Mississippi's governor, Ross Barnett, vowed to block

Meredith's enrollment with all his might. As in Little Rock, it was ultimately necessary to deploy the US Army to enforce the court's order. Kennedy found the experience distasteful, but he could take solace from his favorable reviews abroad. Reporting to the president a month later, a USIA official noted "a startling similarity" in foreign press coverage of the Meredith case. In Africa, Western Europe, Latin America, the Middle East, and Asia, commentators were baffled by the persistence of racial prejudice "in an advanced country like the US." Still, they appreciated the national government's "firmness and determination ... in enforcing law and order."

The Cuban Missile Crisis

By the time Kennedy received the USIA report, it is doubtful he was able to pay it much notice. In mid-October 1962, U-2 spy flights revealed that the Soviet Union had begun deploying dozens of medium- and intermediate-range ballistic missiles (MRBMs and IRBMs) in Cuba capable of striking US territory with nuclear payloads. The evidence indicated that the missiles were not yet operational but would become so within a week or two.

Khrushchev, with Castro's enthusiastic support, had aimed to complete the missiles' deployment in secret and then present Kennedy with a fait accompli. Local and global concerns alike drove the Soviet leader. He sought to deter the United States from escalating its attacks against Cuba and to redress the strategic imbalance that Roswell Gilpatrick had so gallingly publicized. How much difference the Cuban missiles would have made on the latter front is debatable. Soviet ICBMs were now capable of striking US soil, and Moscow was not only steadily augmenting those missiles but also preparing to supplement them with submarine-launched missiles targeting the United States. Materially, then, the missiles in Cuba promised little more than a modest acceleration in the development of Soviet ballistic capabilities. Psychologically, however, Khrushchev was issuing a potent challenge to the Americans' sense of geopolitical mastery, especially as the challenge emanated from an island that had recently escaped the US sphere of influence and had then so humiliatingly resisted recapture.

Kennedy, therefore, proceeded from the assumption that the Cuban missiles were intolerable and had to be removed. For the next thirteen days, he held lengthy, secret meetings with a group of high-ranking advisers known as the Executive Committee of the National Security Council, or ExComm, to determine how to achieve this goal. Initially, there was strong support within ExComm, including from the president himself, for an immediate assault on Cuba to destroy the missiles. But soon Kennedy and some ExComm members, among them his brother Bobby, began questioning an early military strike. Such a move would brand the United States an aggressor in world opinion; far worse, it could trigger a series of retaliations and counter-retaliations that quickly escalated to global thermonuclear war. Against powerful, and at times predominant, hawkish sentiment within ExComm, the president insisted on exploring diplomatic alternatives. Kennedy's relentless attacks on Cuba and ill-considered goading of Khrushchev had largely produced this appalling crisis. His lucidity, relative restraint, skill, and perseverance now helped to chart a course toward safety.

And so a more moderate US response took shape: the United States would impose a naval blockade around Cuba to prevent the Soviets from shipping additional missile components to the island; it would publicly demand that the existing missiles be immediately dismantled. If these measures were unavailing, the use of force was very much an option. Kennedy stated his government's position in a televised address on October 22, alerting the world to the terrifying standoff.

Khrushchev's initial response was defiant. Soviet military installations on Cuba were purely defensive, he said, and the United States had no right to intercept Soviet vessels. The world's eyes turned to the western Atlantic, where several Soviet cargo ships were nearing the perimeter of the US blockade. On October 24 the ships stopped or turned back, raising hopes that the crisis was heading for resolution. But the missiles remained in Cuba, and US intelligence analysts now worried that the Soviets could make them operational even without additional components shipped from abroad.

By now, American society was convulsed by the emergency. Although the vast majority of individuals and institutions kept to their routines, scenes of panic unfolded across the country. In Los Angeles, Miami, Austin, and Washington, DC, anxious supermarket shoppers stocked up on canned foods and bottled water. In Dallas, St. Petersburg, Florida, and Charlottesville, Virginia, residents ransacked sporting goods stores for handguns and rifles (less, it appears, to fend off invading communists than to deal with postapocalyptic breakdowns of social order). School administrators debated whether to keep children in school or send them home if war broke out. Where school fallout shelters were inadequate, they agonized over the criteria for deciding which students to accommodate and which to turn away. Some parents outfitted their children with dog tags so that their incinerated bodies could be later identified. Teenage boys made last-ditch efforts to lose their virginity. College officials warned female students not to succumb to doomsday pleas for sexual favors. In major cities and on some university campuses, members of the FPCC, SANE, and Women Strike for Peace protested the US blockade of Cuba, drawing boisterous counterdemonstrations from Cuban exiles, Young Americans for Freedom (a Buckleyite organization), and other anticommunist groups.

In a flurry of private and public messages on October 26 and 27, the Soviets proposed the elements of a deal: they would remove the missiles from Cuba if the United States pledged not to invade the island and agreed to dismantle its Jupiter missiles, IRBMs stationed in Turkey capable of striking Soviet territory. (The Soviets were making the point that they, too, felt threatened by nuclear missiles aimed from a nearby country.) The Kennedy administration had already decided that the Jupiter missiles were obsolete and should be removed, but it was loath to inject that issue into negotiations over the Cuban missiles, at least not openly. In a public reply, Kennedy repeated the demand for the removal of the Cuban missiles, pledging in return "to give assurances against an invasion of Cuba." The statement made no explicit reference to the Jupiter missiles. Privately, however, Kennedy

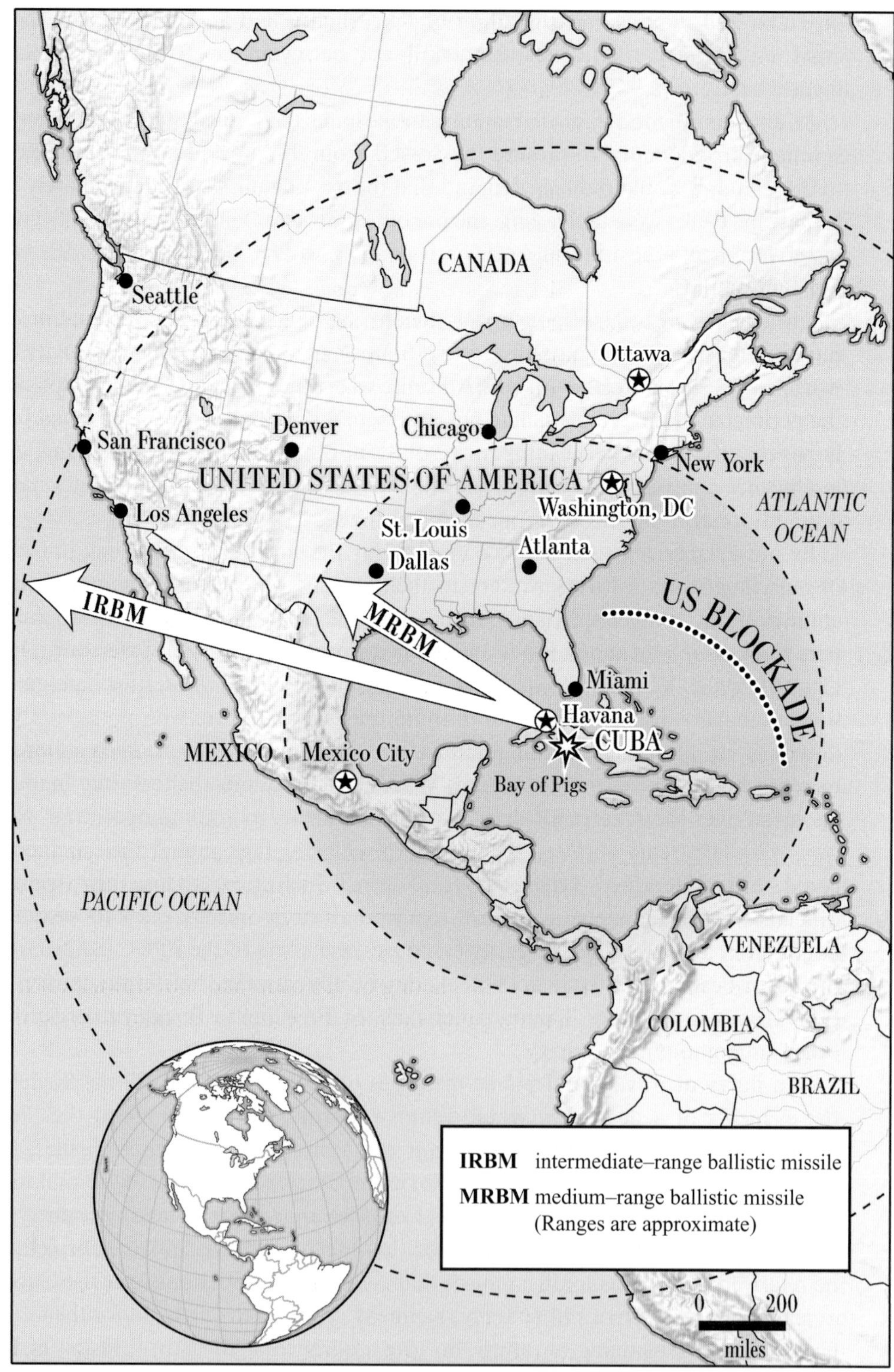

Map 4.1 Cuba, 1961–1962. Source: Created by Joe LeMonnier.

passed word to the Soviets that the Jupiters would eventually be dismantled, though this could not be part of any public deal. And, in case *that* gambit failed, Kennedy had a fallback plan. He prepared a statement to be given to U Thant, the secretary general of the United Nations, proposing that the Jupiter missiles and the missiles in Cuba be removed simultaneously. Only if Khrushchev insisted on a direct, public exchange of Turkish missiles for Cuban missiles was U Thant to receive Kennedy's statement.

Fortunately for Kennedy, it never came to that. On October 28, Khrushchev accepted Kennedy's public offer, stating that the Soviet Union would dismantle the Cuban missiles in exchange for Kennedy's pledge not to invade Cuba. Because the quid pro quo involving the Jupiter missiles remained secret – they were quietly dismantled months later – it appeared that Khrushchev had conceded far more than Kennedy had; the president emerged from the crisis with heightened stature. Not everyone was happy with the deal. Some of the Joint Chiefs of Staff privately denounced it as a sellout that tightened Castro's grip on Cuba. Castro was dismayed for the opposite reason. He saw Kennedy's no-invasion pledge as worthless and demanded, futilely, that Khrushchev keep the missiles in place to deter further US attacks (hardly a baseless concern, as US covert plotting against Castro would continue for the rest of Kennedy's presidency). Castro then tried to impede the agreement by preventing UN inspectors from verifying the Soviets' dismantling of the missiles. But the Kennedy administration certified the removal anyway and, on November 20, lifted its blockade.

As harrowing as it was for those who lived through it, the Cuban Missile Crisis was even more perilous than people realized at the time. Unbeknownst to US officials, Soviet forces on the island were already equipped with short-range nuclear missiles, and local Soviet commanders were authorized, in some circumstances, to launch them without specific permission from Moscow. Had the United States conducted an early assault on Cuba, the conflict might have escalated to global war much more rapidly than seemed likely during the standoff. Moreover, both Kennedy and Khrushchev had difficulty controlling their military establishments. On October 27, an American U-2 plane flying over Alaska accidentally strayed into Soviet airspace, briefly alarming Soviet air force commanders. Kennedy thought he had ordered a suspension of such flights. That same day, Khrushchev was shocked to learn that a Soviet military officer in Cuba, acting on his own, had shot down another U-2 with a surface-to-air missile, killing the pilot. Each of these incidents could have escalated disastrously. Thankfully, neither did.

Fallout from the Missile Crisis

The Cuban Missile Crisis had far-reaching consequences for US–Soviet relations. Publicly, Moscow appeared to have backed down, an outcome the Kremlin leadership attributed to Soviet military weakness. Thus, over the remainder of the decade, the Soviet Union launched a rapid buildup of ICBMs and other strategic weapons. The United States continued its own military expansion, but at a slower rate. By 1970, the Soviet Union had achieved rough nuclear parity with the United States. Khrushchev would not be around to take credit, however, for his Kremlin colleagues had removed him from office in 1964, partly because of his perceived mishandling of the Cuban crisis.

Still, even as they expanded their arsenals, the superpowers emerged from the standoff with a stronger determination to lessen the dangers of their nuclear rivalry. In August 1963, a direct Teletype line was installed between the White House and the Kremlin, enabling the US president and his Soviet counterpart to exchange typed messages within minutes and, hopefully, avoid fatal misunderstandings in future crises. (Under the previous system, a telegraphed message between Washington and Moscow had to be relayed across several countries, sometimes requiring hours for transmission.)

That same August, the United States, the Soviet Union, and Britain signed a treaty banning the testing of nuclear explosives in the atmosphere (though allowing such testing to continue underground). One purpose of the Limited Nuclear Test Ban Treaty was to slow the proliferation of nuclear arms technology to other countries. Another was to ameliorate the harmful effects of nuclear fallout in the atmosphere, a subject of growing international concern and protest. In a June 10, 1963, speech at the American University in Washington, DC, Kennedy invoked the new spirit of superpower cooperation and shared stewardship of the earth. While affirming his rejection of communism, he declared: "No government or social system is so evil that its people must be considered as lacking in virtue . . . . If we cannot now end our differences, at least we can help make the world safe for diversity. For, in the final analysis, our most basic common link is that we inhabit this small planet. We all breathe the same air. We all cherish our children's future. And we are all mortal." A few years later such sentiments would seem obvious, even banal, but in 1963 they were novel and challenging, especially when uttered by a serving US president.

Although their rivalry would continue for nearly three more decades, the United States and the Soviet Union grew more careful about provoking each other in areas of vital concern, such as Berlin and Cuba. In the main, cold war competition was relegated to peripheral areas, where skirmishes could be waged without immediate escalation to superpower conflict. More explicitly than before, though never as forthrightly as critics wished, both sides now acknowledged that nuclear war would be suicidal, resulting, in the aptly initialed expression of the day, in mutual assured destruction.

On the evening following his American University speech, Kennedy delivered another remarkable address, this one from the White House. Responding to a tumultuous civil rights campaign in Birmingham, Alabama, where acts of civil disobedience had provoked brutal repression from local authorities – eliciting protests across the country and another round of international condemnation of American racism – the president said he would ask Congress to outlaw racial segregation in public accommodations. Like Eisenhower at Little Rock, Kennedy expressed concern about America's global standing, but he also, for the first time, treated racial equality as a moral imperative: "We preach freedom around the world, and we mean it ..., but are we to say to the world, and much more importantly, to each other that this is the land of the free except for the Negroes ...?" As he had done the previous day, the president challenged Americans to search their consciences, and question old orthodoxies, on a vital human issue. Recounting both speeches, the left-leaning *Nation* magazine marveled that Kennedy "let two genii out of their respective bottles on successive days."

***

The next day, June 12, brought a third, more jolting departure from routine: photographs of a robed, bald Asian man, sitting cross-legged and impassive in a large city intersection, engulfed in flames. They appeared in newspapers throughout the world, and on the same Oval Office desk from which Kennedy had just spoken about civil rights. The day before, in Saigon, a Buddhist monk named Thich Quang Duc had burned himself to death to protest the South Vietnamese regime's crackdown on Buddhist religious displays. The act both symbolized and galvanized a growing civic uprising among South Vietnam's Buddhists, further endangering the regime's domestic position. The Kennedy administration was forced to pay heed, and months later it would take drastic, though ineffective, measures to salvage the situation. Thus an American government equipped with new insight, and even, perhaps, a touch of new wisdom, pressed on toward fresh disaster.

READING QUESTIONS

1. Why was President Eisenhower relatively unperturbed by the Soviet Union's launching of the first artificial satellite? How, for the rest of his presidency, did this attitude shape Eisenhower's public reaction to the technological challenges posed by the Soviet Union?
2. One could say that, from 1957 to 1960, Democrats attacked Eisenhower's conduct of foreign relations from both the left and the right. What examples bear out this statement?
3. In what ways, from 1957 to 1962, did US foreign relations and the American civil rights movement become enmeshed with one another?
4. President Kennedy's actions toward Cuba have inspired both condemnation and praise. What are the bases for each reaction?

SUGGESTIONS FOR FURTHER READING

Beschloss, Michael. *The Crisis Years: Kennedy and Khrushchev, 1960–1963*. New York: Edward Burlingame Books, 1991.

Curtis, James. *Last Man Standing: Mort Sahl and the Birth of Modern Comedy*. Jackson, MS: University Press of Mississippi, 2017.

Dudziak, Mary. *Cold War Civil Rights: Race and the Image of American Democracy*. Princeton, NJ: Princeton University Press, 2000.

George, Alice L. *Awaiting Armageddon: How Americans Faced the Cuban Missile Crisis*. Chapel Hill, NC: North Carolina University Press, 2003.

Gosse, Van. *Where the Boys Are: Cuba, Cold War America, and the Making of a New Left*. New York: Verso, 1993.

Hoffman, Elizabeth Cobbs. *All You Need Is Love: The Peace Corps and the Spirit of the 1960s*. Cambridge, MA: Harvard University Press, 1998.

Lederer, William, and Eugene Burdick. *The Ugly American*. New York: W. W. Norton, 1958.

McCray, W. Patrick. *Keep Watching the Skies! The Story of Operation Moonwatch and the Dawn of the Space Age*. Princeton, NJ: Princeton University Press, 2008.

Nachman, Gerald. *Seriously Funny: The Rebel Comedians of the 1950s and 1960s*. New York: Pantheon Books, 2003.

Naftali, Timothy, and Aleksandr Fursenko. *Khrushchev's Cold War: The Inside Story of an American Adversary*. New York: W. W. Norton, 2006.

Paterson, Thomas G. *Contesting Castro: The United States and the Triumph of the Cuban Revolution*. New York: Oxford University Press, 1995.

Plummer, Brenda Gayle. *Rising Wind: Black Americans and US Foreign Affairs, 1935–1960*. Chapel Hill, NC: University of North Carolina Press, 1996.

Rabe, Stephen G. *John F. Kennedy: World Leader*. Washington, DC: Potomac Books, 2010.

5 Is This America?

Civil Rights and the Liberal Moment, 1960–1965

Introduction

The attorney general had hoped for an evening of calm and searching dialogue, but things did not turn out that way. It was late May 1963, a moment of rising anger and confrontation in US race relations. Earlier that month, police in Birmingham, Alabama, had brutalized Black civil rights protesters, many of them children, with fire hoses and police dogs. African Americans everywhere were in an uproar over these attacks, staging indignant, and in some cases violent, demonstrations in cities across the country. In a Manhattan apartment, Robert F. Kennedy hosted an eclectic group of Black intellectuals, artists, and activists to hear their thoughts on the deepening crisis. The prominent Black author James Baldwin, at Kennedy's request, had hastily recruited the participants. Kennedy began the meeting by citing the many efforts he and his brother, President John F. Kennedy, had made to advance civil rights. Despite this unprecedented federal commitment, Bobby Kennedy said, Black criticism of the government was growing more and more audible. Why was this happening?

"You don't have no idea what trouble is," retorted one of Kennedy's guests. "Because I'm close to the moment where I'm ready to take up a gun." The speaker was Jerome Smith, a young civil rights worker whose nonviolent protests had earned him numerous beatings and jailings in the South. Smith added that the necessity of having to explain these realities to the nation's attorney general made him want to vomit. Kennedy was shocked by the comments and turned to the other guests, apparently expecting them to rebuke Smith. But Lorraine Hansberry, the acclaimed playwright, came to the activist's defense. "You've got a great many very, very accomplished people in this room, Mr. Attorney General," she said, "but the only man who should be listened to is that man over there." Hansberry stated that she, too, had entertained thoughts of killing white people. To Kennedy's chagrin, the remaining guests not only refused to disavow such talk but sharply criticized the administration's weak response to the crisis.

Most of the guests treated the violent rhetoric as a barometer of Black people's pain. Robert Kennedy took it literally and stayed angry for days. But the searing encounter got Bobby thinking and, according to many of his biographers, ultimately deepened his commitment to combating the scourge of American racism. Two summers later, Black frustration and rage erupted in six days of rioting in the Watts neighborhood of Los Angeles. When former president Dwight D. Eisenhower decried the disturbances and called for "greater respect for law," Kennedy, now a senator from New York, pushed back. "There is no point in telling Negroes to obey the law," he told a reporter. "To many Negroes, the law is the enemy. In Harlem, in Bedford-Stuyvesant [two predominantly Black neighborhoods in New York City], it has almost always been used against them." Kennedy's statement outraged many whites, much as Jerome Smith's remarks had once scandalized Kennedy.

Robert Kennedy's evolution was not America's in miniature – far from it – but the personal story did evoke patterns in the national one. Bobby was correct when he told his Black visitors that the Kennedy administration's commitment to civil rights was unprecedented. The administration approached the issue cautiously and reluctantly, and almost all of its civil rights actions responded to pressure generated by activists. By late May 1963, however, John Kennedy had addressed facets of the problem that no previous president had taken on, and he was about to embrace civil rights as a moral imperative. Lyndon B. Johnson, who became president upon Kennedy's assassination in November 1963, moved even more forcefully, securing federal legislation that outlawed nearly all remaining de jure racial discrimination in the country. Moreover, during his first two years in office, Johnson embedded civil rights in an extraordinary array of liberal reforms that extended the federal government's reach into virtually every area of domestic life. In August 1965, a *New York Times* reporter observed that the litany of new programs the president had coaxed out of Congress "reads better than the legislative achievements of most two-term presidents."

For all their ambitiousness, however, Johnson's reforms could not meet all the demands of their intended beneficiaries. By mid-decade, most civil rights activists were convinced that the dismantling of de jure discrimination in the South was insufficient; it was also necessary to address de facto discrimination across the country. Meanwhile, the ferocity of segregationist resistance had exacted a huge physical and psychic toll on activists, causing many of them to question their commitment to nonviolence and integration and to gravitate toward more militant or separatist approaches. Among the broader left, the liberal politics of the Kennedy and early Johnson years stimulated sharp critiques of the established order, touching on gender relations, the natural environment, the rights of the poor, and other issues. Relatively submerged in the first half of the decade, those challenges would burst to the surface of American life in the second half. A comparable delayed reaction unfolded on the right. Defenders of de jure segregation conspicuously lost their battle, and conservative Republicans suffered a humiliating defeat in the 1964 presidential election. Yet millions of Americans, in both major parties, increasingly felt that the federal government and its militant critics were pushing too far and too fast to enact social change. This sentiment, too, would be far more visible and consequential in the years to come.

An Accelerating Movement

The civil rights revolution of 1960–1965 occurred toward the end of the Second Great Migration. From 1940 to 1970, more than four million African Americans moved from mostly rural areas in the South to mostly urban areas in the rest of the country. This transformation created conditions that first aided, and then hindered, the struggle for racial equality. As Blacks congregated in cities, they found it easier to organize support for, and publicize, civil rights efforts in the South. They also became important constituents for big-city political machines and thus for the Democratic Party as a whole. Increasingly, the national party was willing to antagonize its segregationist wing in order to win and keep Black support. These patterns unfolded throughout the postwar period but came to a head in the early 1960s, as a steep upswing in civil rights protest in the South coincided with the arrival in Washington of a Democratic administration indebted to Black voters. The major civil rights legislation of the mid-1960s was the product of that historical nexus.

Yet white Americans responded to these transformations in ways that later blunted the momentum of civil rights reform, and ultimately weakened liberalism as a whole. Over the quarter-century following World War II, as national Democrats embraced civil rights, southern whites drifted away from the party, diminishing its national strength. Meanwhile, urban whites across the country relocated to suburbs, partly to enjoy a higher standard of living but partly to avoid living near African Americans. The exodus of these relatively well-off whites, which exceeded the influx of southern Blacks by a ratio of three to two, left cities with declining populations, shrunken tax bases, and diminished representation in state and national legislatures. Manufacturing jobs, too, moved from cities to suburbs, and sometimes to other regions of the country, increasing unemployment among urban African Americans. Consequently, in the 1950s and 1960s many inner-city Black communities grew poorer and more susceptible to poverty-related problems such as substance abuse, crime, and family breakdown. This urban crisis was broadly visible in the early 1960s but not central to mainstream civil rights activism until the middle of the decade. By then, it was increasingly doubtful that the American public would support truly effective measures to address the plight of the inner cities. Nor was it obvious how the national government could reconcile such an ambitious undertaking with its escalating involvement in Vietnam.

At the dawn of the decade, however, civil rights activists were focused on the South. Events such as the Montgomery bus boycott of 1955–1956 and the Little Rock crisis of 1957 had afforded the movement considerable momentum, along with national and even international attention, but concrete achievements were few. Across the South, only minuscule numbers of Black students had gained admission to all-white schools, public accommodations remained segregated by law, many jobs were off-limits for African Americans, and the vast majority of Black adults found it practically impossible to exercise their constitutionally recognized right to vote.

In southern cities, a particularly galling restriction was the denial of the right to dine at department store lunch counters. The department stores were perfectly happy to sell Black customers merchandise; they just wouldn't let them sit down for a bite to eat. In February 1960, four Black college freshmen in Greensboro, North Carolina, sat down at a Woolworth's lunch counter and ordered coffee. Told that the counter was for whites only, they refused to leave, remaining on their stools until closing time. Though not the first sit-in protest in the South, the Greensboro action struck a chord in the local Black student community, and beyond. When the "Greensboro Four" returned to Woolworth's the next day, twenty other students joined in, and reporters covered the story. In the coming days similar protests erupted in other southern cities, sometimes with sympathetic whites taking part.

Most sit-in protesters encountered no active resistance beyond the denial of service. Occasionally, however, hostile onlookers intervened, pouring ketchup on their heads, stubbing cigarettes out on their bare necks, and shouting racial epithets in their ears. The activists were prepared for such abuse (in some cases through rigorous prior training) and stoically endured it. Even when white toughs dragged them from their stools, threw them to the floor, and beat and kicked them, the protesters refused to fight back. When police arrested them, they often declined to make bail, putting pressure on the system by filling the jail cells.

As a political strategy, such nonviolent resistance was designed to dramatize the inhumanity of segregation. In their dignified refusal to retaliate when attacked, the activists posed the starkest possible contrast to their opponents, underscoring the justness of their cause. More profoundly, many civil rights activists, in the sit-in movement and in other early-1960s protests, saw nonviolence as a way of life, as an expression of redemptive love that could transform enemies into friends. For some, the philosophy of nonviolence derived from the Christian tradition of turning the other cheek. For others, the teachings of the Indian anticolonial leader Mohandas Gandhi provided the inspiration. (And some, following the example of Martin Luther King, Jr., drew on both wellsprings simultaneously.) In describing their nonviolent ethos, civil rights activists often spoke of the "Beloved Community," a term referring not only to the intense bonds of solidarity and affection they forged with one another but also to the just and loving society they hoped to create in the future.

Within two months, sit-ins had occurred in more than sixty cities in the South, typically buttressed by consumer boycotts in local Black communities. In the North, African Americans and some whites boycotted national chains, such as Woolworth's and Kress, whose stores in the South discriminated. The pressure was effective. In April 1960 department stores in Nashville, Tennessee – the site of one of the more extensive and widely publicized campaigns – agreed to open their lunch counters to Black customers. The breakthrough came on the heels of a 3,000-person protest march to the steps of city hall, where twenty-one-year-old Diane Nash, one of the Nashville movement's leaders, compelled Mayor Ben West, a moderate by the standards of white southern politics, to acknowledge that lunch counter segregation was wrong. Similar victories occurred in other cities, especially in the Upper South. Most lunch counters in the Deep South, however, remained barred to African Americans.

That same spring, 200 to 300 students from southern Black colleges and universities, many of them sit-in activists, gathered in Raleigh, North Carolina, to discuss new directions for the movement. The convener of the meeting was Ella Baker, executive director of the Southern Christian Leadership Conference (SCLC), which Martin Luther King, Jr., had helped found in 1957 and now led as president. With Baker's encouragement, the students formed the Temporary Student Nonviolent Coordinating Committee. Months later, the "Temporary" was dropped and the group became known by the initials SNCC (pronounced "Snick"). The idea was for SNCC to maintain its independence but work closely with the SCLC to combat racial discrimination in the South, and this expected cooperation largely came to pass. Yet in the coming years there would be considerable tension between the two organizations, and after 1966 the alliance disintegrated.

Some of the tension resulted from SNCC activists' perception that the SCLC was too dependent on King's charismatic leadership, too concerned about maintaining good relations with the federal government and white liberals, and too willing to compromise. SNCC, by contrast, favored radically democratized decision-making, sought to empower local communities, was prone to direct, spontaneous action, and, rather than seeking to balance a wide array of civil rights initiatives, pursued maximum justice in any given struggle. Over time, a deeper ideological difference emerged, deriving from the basic strategy that the two groups jointly pursued in the early to mid-1960s. The strategy was to compel the federal government to intervene in the South to end legal discrimination. This in turn was to be accomplished by dramatizing the evil of southern racism and convincing public opinion throughout the nation that federal action was necessary. To expose southern racism, SCLC and SNCC activists would seek confrontations with segregationists, contests in which the activists themselves remained nonviolent but in which their foes acted with predictable brutality. In short, for the strategy of nonviolence to succeed, there had to *be* violence, albeit the violence of segregationists.

The problem was not that the strategy failed but that it succeeded all too well. The violence elicited from segregationists was so appalling that it did, at key moments, force the necessary federal action. (Sometimes, the attacks provoked violence by African Americans who were not part of the organized movement, and the federal intervention occurred partly in response to *that*.) But segregationist brutality also caused African Americans across the country to question whether nonviolence was the only suitable response to vicious racism, whether white society would ever permit integration on a truly equal basis, and whether across-the-board integration was all that desirable anyway. The young activists in SNCC, many of whom bore the brunt of segregationist violence, increasingly shared this hardened outlook and began losing faith in the nonviolent and integrationist ideals to which King and the SCLC remained committed. Thus in the mid-1960s, just as it achieved some of its most far-reaching victories, the civil rights coalition started to crumble.

The Freedom Rides

John F. Kennedy, who took office in January 1961, was primarily concerned with foreign affairs. He tended to see domestic policy as a means of achieving the internal cohesion and stability necessary for waging the cold war, an outlook that positioned him near the political center domestically. Still, key elements of his governing coalition favored expanding the social safety net, enhancing labor's bargaining power, increasing federal aid to education, and other liberal measures. Kennedy did seek legislation to pursue many of these goals, albeit rather half-heartedly and with only modest success. On civil rights, the new president was similarly lukewarm, at least at first. He had expressed sympathy for the civil rights movement during the 1960 campaign and received 68 percent of the Black vote on Election Day. Once in office, however, Kennedy proceeded cautiously. He substantially increased the number of African Americans appointed to government positions and threatened to deny federal contracts to corporations guilty of racial discrimination. Yet he held off on seeking major civil rights legislation for fear of stirring up powerful opposition on Capitol Hill. (Although the Democratic Party had large majorities in both houses, a good portion of the Democratic caucus, including some powerful committee chairmen, were southern segregationists.)

Civil rights activists, however, were determined to compel federal action. A pressing issue was the persistence of segregation in interstate commercial bus travel. Legally, this area was subject to federal intervention, as the US Constitution empowers the national government to regulate interstate commerce. In 1960, the Supreme Court had overturned racial segregation in public transportation crossing state lines. But white southerners ignored the ruling, and interstate bus travel remained segregated in the South. Preoccupied with other challenges, the Kennedy administration initially took no action on the matter. To force its hand, in the spring of 1961 an organization called the Congress of Racial Equality (CORE) launched the Freedom Rides. In Washington, DC, an interracial group of CORE activists boarded two buses, one Greyhound and one Trailways, and headed toward the Deep South. Along the way, they challenged racial segregation in bus stations, with Blacks using white-only restrooms and waiting areas and whites using Black-only facilities. The Freedom Riders encountered little resistance in the border states but faced extreme violence further south, especially in Alabama. In Aniston, the Greyhound bus was firebombed, and at the Birmingham station a white mob viciously beat the Trailways passengers, with no interference by police. (The FBI, it turned out, had advance warning of the attacks but declined to share this information with the DOJ. FBI director J. Edgar Hoover saw civil rights activists as dangerous subversives and had little desire to protect them.)

The CORE activists were unprepared for such brutality, and most suspended their campaign in Alabama. Determined not to allow violence to thwart the movement, several SNCC activists hastened to Birmingham and met up with SNCC member (and Nashville sit-in leader) John Lewis, who had been on the CORE Freedom Rides and wished to continue. The newly constituted Freedom Riders proceeded to Montgomery, Alabama. The Kennedy administration, anxiously monitoring the situation but unwilling to intervene directly, extracted a pledge from Alabama authorities to protect the Freedom Riders from that point forward. When the Freedom Riders reached Montgomery, however, no police were in sight and attackers pummeled the Riders with baseball bats and lead pipes. Lewis received a concussion, and another activist suffered a broken back. Although some of the Freedom Riders were too injured to continue, the group as a whole vowed to press on to Mississippi.

Kennedy was chagrined by the violence, which had aroused international condemnation – hardly welcome news to a president preparing for a summit meeting with his Soviet

Figure 5.1 Freedom Riders John Lewis and James Zwerg after a violent attack by pro-segregationists in Montgomery, Alabama, 1961. Source: Bettmann / Getty Images.

counterpart and worrying about America's reputation among nonwhite nations. Unable to dissuade the Freedom Riders from continuing, the Kennedy administration stepped up its involvement. Attorney General Robert Kennedy sent hundreds of federal marshals into Montgomery to safeguard activists rallying in support of the Freedom Riders, and he increased the pressure on Alabama authorities, who belatedly furnished the Riders police protection. Meanwhile, Bobby Kennedy reached a deal with Mississippi's government: as the Freedom Riders arrived in Jackson, Mississippi, state authorities kept the mobs at bay; in return, the Kennedy administration made no objection when Mississippi arrested the activists, tried them on state charges, and jailed them in the notoriously inhumane Parchman Prison, in many cases for as long as two months. In the coming weeks, hundreds of additional Freedom Riders poured into Jackson, and they, too, were sent to Parchman.

In September 1961, at President Kennedy's behest, the Interstate Commerce Commission banned segregation in interstate transit facilities. The Freedom Riders had prevailed, but it was an extremely costly victory, showing how fiercely the white South would resist desegregation, and how reluctantly the federal government would promote it.

There was, moreover, no guarantee of future victories. From late 1961 to late 1962, the SCLC, SNCC, and the NAACP joined a local campaign in Albany, Georgia, to desegregate public accommodations – stores, theaters, restaurants, parks, and restrooms – and improve employment prospects for African Americans. The involvement of these organizations, and especially Martin Luther King's presence, made the Albany movement national news, but generating national outrage proved a much harder task. Intergroup tension hampered the effort; SNCC activists resented what they saw as the condescension of their elders in the SCLC and the NAACP. Worse still, Albany's leaders deftly avoided being cast in the villainous roles the activists had assigned to them. The city's police chief made a show of respect for protesters engaging in civil disobedience and instructed his officers to exercise restraint in public (keeping the beatings, kickings, arbitrary arrests, and squalid jail conditions safely off-camera). When King and his close adviser, Ralph Abernathy, got themselves arrested, Albany's mayor denied them martyrdom by secretly ordering their release. "I've been thrown out of lots of places in my day," said Abernathy, "but never before have I been thrown out of jail." After a year of frustration most of the outside campaigners left Albany, having done little to dramatize the ills of segregation to the nation. Local activists continued the struggle.

Broader Activist Stirrings

Briefly participating in the Albany movement was a twenty-two-year-old white activist named Tom Hayden. Hayden was a leading member of Students for a Democratic Society (SDS), a left-leaning organization, supported by labor unions, largely based at the University of Michigan in Ann Arbor. SDS members were part of a broader cohort of (mainly white) university students who, starting in the late 1950s, had challenged what they saw as a stultifying political and social atmosphere. Stimulated by critics such as the psychologist Erich Fromm and the sociologists David Riesman and C. Wright Mills, they had come to view the United States as an excessively acquisitive and conformist society, one whose citizens were discouraged from asking penetrating questions or from developing their full potential, one whose very existence (along with humanity's) was imperiled by an absurd nuclear arms race. More recently, many of these students had found inspiration and purpose in the burgeoning civil rights movement. Some, like Hayden, had gone south to take part in it.

Upon his return to Ann Arbor, Hayden, already known to his comrades as a prolific and thoughtful writer, received a daunting assignment from SDS: to draft "a political manifesto of the left." The result of Hayden's labors, to which many other SDS members contributed, was a 25,000-word document that the group approved at its June 1962 national meeting in Port Huron, Michigan. The Port Huron Statement charged that the nation's institutions – the government, political parties, corporations, labor unions, universities, and the like – had become so opaque, bureaucratic, and indifferent to human needs that millions of ordinary Americans were alienated from civic life. The institutions had also failed to solve concrete problems, such as the disfranchisement and impoverishment of African Americans, or to avert mounting dangers, like the threat of nuclear annihilation. The crisis was at once spiritual, material, and existential. Salvation, the Port Huron Statement proposed, lay in nurturing a system of "participatory democracy" that granted citizens direct control over the communities and institutions in which they lived, worked, studied, and played. Students themselves could catalyze the creation of such a system by working with sympathetic faculty to "wrest control" of universities and by then joining "with allies in labor, civil rights, and other liberal forces" to establish more humane priorities for the nation.

Precious little of the Port Huron vision would be realized, but the statement captured the imagination of young people throughout the country. Sixty thousand copies were published over the next four years, and, at least in a general way, the manifesto offered a template for a wide array of political and social protests throughout the decade. Membership in SDS ballooned from a few hundred to tens of thousands, though the group was almost always deeply divided over where to focus its energies.

As it happened, the Port Huron Statement was nearly thwarted at the outset, on account of its criticism of US cold war policies. The League for Industrial Democracy (LID), SDS's parent organization, was dominated by labor leaders who, though in some cases self-proclaimed socialists, detested the Soviet Union and believed the United States had to contain it aggressively. When SDS failed to revise the Port Huron Statement to LID's satisfaction, LID said it would fire SDS's top leaders and censor its materials. But LID eventually backed down and allowed the SDS statement to go forward. A few years later, the two organizations formally parted ways.

One of the loudest LID critics, lecturing Hayden late into the night in Port Huron, was a socialist intellectual named Michael Harrington, who by coincidence had recently issued a consequential statement of his own. In March 1962, Harrington's book *The Other America* appeared. It called attention to the fact that, despite the nation's unprecedented affluence, more than a fifth of the population – inner-city Blacks, Appalachian whites, Latino migrant farm workers, elderly Americans of all backgrounds – remained in poverty. They were kept in that state not by low incomes alone but by a host of interlocking disadvantages, such as poor health, inadequate education and housing, "low levels of aspiration and high levels of mental distress." Unless remedies could be found for this "web of disabilities," there was little hope of seriously addressing the problem.

The Other America received only modest attention until early 1963, when *The New Yorker* published a fifty-page review of it by the prominent social critic Dwight MacDonald. Thereafter, the book caught fire among liberal readers, who were startled to learn that poverty remained so stubborn and widespread. (The fact that Harrington made no mention of his socialist outlook and affiliations, omissions he later regretted, made it easier for the book to gain mainstream respectability.) Walter Heller, President Kennedy's chief economic adviser, passed the *New Yorker* review (or, in some accounts, the book itself) on to his boss. The Kennedy administration was already considering piecemeal measures to assist the poor; Harrington's findings helped persuade it to attack poverty comprehensively. On November 19, 1963, Kennedy told Heller he wanted to launch a major program in January. Three days later, the president was dead. Like the rest of his unfinished domestic agenda, the planned antipoverty effort now lay in Lyndon Johnson's hands.

The Other America was part of a distinct literary genre of the early 1960s: bestselling nonfiction that sounded the alarm about some hidden or neglected public crisis, setting the stage for later action by government agencies, an aroused citizenry, or both. In *Silent Spring* (1962), the biologist Rachel Carson warned that rampant use of chemical pesticides was distorting the earth's ecosystem in unintended ways. Not only were pesticides harming species of insects that hadn't been targeted for spraying, they were causing targeted species to develop immunities that would make them harder to control in the future. Carson also cautioned that some pesticides could cause deadly disease in human beings and other animal species. *Silent Spring* was partly responsible for prodding the federal government to start enacting major environmental legislation in the mid-1960s and for inspiring a broad-based movement at the popular level a few years after that.

Another bestseller, *The Feminine Mystique* (1963), revealed that many American housewives felt trapped in empty, lonely, and unfulfilling lives. The author, Betty Friedan, explored the profound let-down many middle-class women felt in their suburban existences, which bore so little resemblance to the intellectual adventures and broadened horizons of their college years. Of course, *The Feminine Mystique*'s concentration on stay-at-home wives who were middle-class, and presumptively white, captured only a narrow band of American female experience and outlook. (Friedan actually had a background in left-wing labor journalism and activism. Much as Harrington did with his socialism, however, she made no mention of that past, instead presenting herself to readers as a fellow housewife, which she partly was.) Still, the book's insights into what Friedan called "the problem that has no name" – and Friedan herself – would loom large in the feminist upheavals to come. As one observer archly noted at the time, having no way of knowing how right she was on both counts, Friedan had "done for women … what Rachel Carson did for the birds and trees." (See Chapter 8 for a fuller discussion of Friedan.)

Growing Civil Rights Militancy

Amid these portents of future activism, the civil rights movement continued to convulse the nation, despite the Albany setback. Indeed, Albany yielded lessons that prodded the movement's organizers to approach their next major action with greater shrewdness, unity, determination, and boldness. In the spring of 1963, King's SCLC went to Birmingham to augment and amplify a local campaign to desegregate commercial establishments and end employment discrimination. The SCLC had chosen the battlefield carefully. Birmingham was one of the most segregated cities in the nation; a civil rights victory there would make the cause seem unstoppable. Moreover, the defenders of the status quo in this case were perfect foils for the movement. Birmingham's police commissioner, Eugene "Bull" Connor, possessed a vicious streak that he was all too willing to display in public, in contrast with his savvier counterpart in Albany. Alabama's new governor, George Wallace, had gained notoriety by proclaiming in his inaugural speech "Segregation now, segregation tomorrow, segregation forever."

Even so, the Birmingham campaign faltered at first. The SCLC had hoped to clog the jails with local protesters, but few of Birmingham's Black adults volunteered to be arrested, as this could cause them to lose their jobs or, at best, require them to forfeit paid work hours. Throughout April, the campaign's success seemed in doubt. Then, in early May, the SCLC employed the brilliant yet controversial tactic of filling Birmingham's jails with minors – mostly teenagers and preteens, but in some cases children as young as seven or eight. The mass arrest of young people could stymie segregation's machinery of enforcement without depriving families of income. And the sight of white policemen hauling Black children off to jail would dramatize Jim Crow's evils as never before.

The Children's Crusade was almost too successful, goading Bull Connor into an overreaction so extreme that it threatened to plunge Birmingham, and other cities, into chaos. The young protesters quickly filled Birmingham's jails; authorities held some of them in outdoor pens at a nearby fairground. No longer seeking to arrest protesters, Connor used massive force to disperse them. In full view of television cameras, Birmingham's police blasted marchers of all ages with fire hoses – set at a pressure level to strip the bark off trees – and sicced police dogs on those who refused to turn back. Some protesters threw rocks and bottles at the police. This reaction alarmed King and other SCLC leaders, but it tended to serve their larger purpose. The violent confrontations brought commerce to a halt in Birmingham's downtown, making the local business community eager for a resolution. The Kennedy administration, worried as always about international appearances, stepped in to help broker an agreement. On May 10, Birmingham businesses pledged to desegregate their stores and hire more African Americans, in exchange for a halt to the protests.

Connor, Governor Wallace, the Ku Klux Klan, and other white supremacists immediately denounced the agreement. Bombs exploded at the Birmingham motel where King had recently stayed and at the home of his brother, Alfred Daniel King, a preacher in town. Infuriated by the attacks, Black Birminghamians clashed openly with city police and state troopers. Over fifty people were wounded in the melee. On May 12, President Kennedy sent 3,000 army troops to bases near Birmingham, and the violence abated. The Birmingham agreement slowly took effect, and the city's government started repealing its segregation laws.

But African Americans everywhere were aghast at what they had witnessed, and protests erupted throughout the nation. In Chicago, Philadelphia, Detroit, New York, and many other cities, Black residents confronted police and denounced racism, often in tones far more militant than those emanating from protest leaders in Birmingham. Although initially reacting to events in Alabama, northern protesters quickly shifted their focus to local grievances, such as police brutality and the failure of African Americans to get jobs on city construction projects. Many of these actions were purposely disruptive. In Newark and Trenton, New Jersey, protesters physically blockaded construction sites. In New York City, they held "sleep-ins" at the office of Governor Nelson Rockefeller, trying to force him to integrate building trade unions. In Chicago, Philadelphia, Elizabeth, New Jersey, and Cambridge, Maryland, demonstrators threw stones and bricks at police or engaged them in fistfights.

The moment was excruciating, but not without hope. The brutal Birmingham images that outraged Black Americans were also visible to whites, and the urgency of the crisis had started to break through on a broad scale. Prior to Birmingham, polls indicated that just 4 percent of Americans regarded civil rights as the most important national issue.

After Birmingham, 52 percent saw it that way. Doubtless, many whites were more disturbed by the nationwide eruption of Black militancy and violence than by the unjust conditions that had provoked this reaction. Either way, however, there was a growing feeling that the status quo had become untenable. Scores of other southern cities, hoping to avoid similar upheavals and presumably sensing the shift in the national mood, began quietly desegregating their commercial areas.

President Kennedy, too, detected the changing landscape of possibility, along with the danger of failing to act. In a televised address on June 11, he forcefully condemned racial discrimination and called civil rights "a moral issue." A century had passed since the emancipation of the slaves, he said, "yet their heirs, their grandsons, are not fully free. They are not yet freed from the bonds of injustice. They are not yet freed from social and economic oppression. And this Nation … will not be fully free until all its citizens are free." Days later, Kennedy asked Congress to pass a bill outlawing racial segregation in public accommodations and authorizing the federal government to sue public schools that remained segregated. The proposed bill faced rough going in Congress. It was one thing for southern civic leaders to agree to desegregate their own downtowns on a case-by-case basis, quite another for southern legislators to countenance an across-the-board mandate from the federal government. And the school desegregation provisions, of course, were sure to generate fierce opposition.

Most of the established civil rights leaders strongly supported Kennedy's bill, yet they differed with the president over how best to promote it. Plans were already afoot for a massive, interracial march on the nation's capital to demand economic and racial justice. Civil rights leaders now looked to the event as an excellent opportunity to rally support for the legislation, and to demand changes not mentioned in it. Kennedy feared that the march would inflame segregationists in Congress and tried to have it called off. When the organizers made it clear they would go forward, while also pledging there would be no civil disobedience, the president dropped his opposition. Held in August 1963, and drawing some 250,000 participants, the March on Washington was indeed a showcase of moderation, in which hardly any criticism of the Kennedy administration was heard from the rostrum. Its most memorable portion was King's stirring "I have a dream" speech, which imagined a day when "on the red hills of Georgia the sons of former slaves and the sons of former slaveowners will be able to sit down together at the table of brotherhood" – a pitch-perfect appeal for white liberal support.

All the same, the March on Washington forcefully challenged the racial status quo, and not just as it related to de jure discrimination in the South. The chief instigator of the march, A. Philip Randolph, founder and president of the Brotherhood of Sleeping Car Porters, was deeply embedded in the labor movement, and unions played key roles in organizing the event. Several platform speakers stressed the economic dimensions of racial injustice, especially rising Black unemployment in urban areas. Moreover, many rank-and-file attendees expressed militant sentiments that never made it over the loudspeakers. The New-York-based Freedom Now Party distributed handbills declaring "We have to *take* our freedom; no one will hand it to us." Another group of radicals carried signs demanding, "FREEDOM NOW – OR THE FIRE NEXT TIME." Some march participants were armed.

Even within the nonviolent movement, activists were growing increasingly angry over the impunity with which whites could attack African Americans. On the same evening that Kennedy spoke about civil rights, the NAACP's chief organizer in Mississippi, Medgar Evers, was murdered on his doorstep. Still more shockingly, in September 1963 a bomb exploded in Birmingham's Sixteenth Street Baptist Church, killing four Black girls, three of them aged fourteen and one just eleven. In both instances, white suspects were identified at the time, but they escaped conviction until prosecutors reopened the cases many years later. Outrages such as these placed enormous strain on activists' commitment to nonviolence.

Amid this darkening mood, a figure once seen as a sharp adversary of the nonviolent movement, even feared and reviled by some, began making modest inroads into it. Malcolm X (born Malcolm Little), a severe and imposing figure with a biting wit, was the public face of the Nation of Islam (NOI), then widely known as the Black Muslims. Based in Chicago and led by the reclusive Elijah Muhammad, the NOI propagated a racialized version of Islam, teaching that white people were devils (created in antiquity by an evil scientist named Yakub), that Black integration into white society was neither possible nor desirable, and that African Americans should build up their own communities and institutions in preparation for the establishment of a separate Black nation. The NOI also advocated personal discipline, self-help, thrift, and social uplift. In poor Black communities across the urban North, in cities and prisons alike, it seemed to offer a proven formula for redeeming lives of dereliction, drug abuse, crime, and despair. Malcolm Little himself had been a petty criminal in New York and Boston in the 1940s. While doing prison time in Massachusetts, he had converted to Islam and joined the NOI under the name Malcolm X. Paroled in 1952, Malcolm served as an NOI minister in Detroit, Boston, Philadelphia, and New York. By the late 1950s he was the organization's chief spokesman. In countless public appearances around the country, and sometimes abroad, Malcolm expounded the NOI's tenets, laying special emphasis on its bleak prognosis for Black–white coexistence. He derided the ethic of nonviolence as an affront to Black dignity and manhood.

Not surprisingly, Malcolm had long antagonized established civil rights leaders, who saw him as an embarrassment at best and, at worst, as a mortal threat to the political viability of their cause. By the early 1960s, however, some of the more militant members of SNCC and CORE found themselves drawn to Malcolm's bracing rhetoric and uncompromising persona. This affinity only deepened in the aftermath of Birmingham, in parallel with a surge in Malcolm's influence among Black people generally. When Malcolm scoffed that Kennedy's decision to seek civil rights legislation was a panicky reaction to Black violence, or that the March on Washington's organizers were displaying an unseemly eagerness to please white liberals, many battle-scarred civil rights workers nodded in agreement, and some openly applauded. Yet Malcolm was subtly moving in their direction, too. Even as he lambasted the mainstream civil rights movement, he increased his personal engagement with it, seeking opportunities to debate advocates of integration and nonviolence and forging cordial friendships with some of them. Clearly, Malcolm recognized that a momentous social and political transformation was under way within the civic mainstream, and he wanted, somehow, to play a bigger part in it.

The convergence continued in the months thereafter. As movement activists shed their faith in the Beloved Community, Malcolm grudgingly warmed up to the possibilities of interracial collaboration and to the prospect of effecting change in the political arena. In early 1964, he broke with the Nation of Islam, partly over the discovery of Elijah Muhammad's repeated marital infidelities, partly over the NOI's strict prohibition on involvement in the civil rights struggle. Freed of Muhammad's control, yet facing constant death threats from former NOI comrades, Malcolm spent much of 1964 traveling in Africa and the Middle East, meeting with heads of state and deepening his understanding of Sunni Islam, which he now embraced in place of Elijah Muhammad's creed. While in the United States, Malcolm urged Black Americans to fight for the right to vote and exercise it where they could, but to harbor no illusions about what the franchise alone could accomplish.

Over that same 1963–1964 period, J. Edgar Hoover stepped up his covert vendetta against Martin Luther King. Claiming that King was a communist sympathizer, Hoover pressed Robert Kennedy to authorize electronic surveillance of the minister (something the FBI had been doing for several years already). Bobby was skeptical of the accusation but in October 1963 authorized the surveillance, apparently concerned about the consequences of denying Hoover's request. Both Kennedys had reason to fear FBI leaks to the effect that they had ignored the Bureau's concerns about domestic communism. There was also the possibility that, should Hoover become sufficiently disgruntled, closely held evidence of President Kennedy's sexual indiscretions would mysteriously find its way into the public domain.

Armed with Bobby's permission, the FBI intensified its surveillance of King, supplementing it with harassment, threats, and attempted blackmail. King, too, had engaged in extramarital affairs, a datum Hoover seized on with malevolent glee. In November 1964, he arranged to have an incriminating tape recording of King mailed to SCLC headquarters, accompanied by a menacing anonymous letter. "Lend your sexually psychotic ear to the enclosure," it instructed King. "You will find yourself and in all your dirt, filth, evil and moronic talk exposed on the record for all time." The letter concluded with the words, "There is but one way out for you," which King interpreted as a command to commit suicide. (He immediately guessed, correctly, who had sent the package.) The FBI would hound King for the rest of his life.

Assassination in Dallas

By the fall of 1963, President Kennedy expected his pro-civil-rights stance to lose him some southern states in his 1964 reelection bid. He was all the more determined, therefore, to keep electoral-vote-rich Texas in his column. Political feuding among Texas Democrats threatened this prospect, so on November 21 Kennedy flew to the state to broker a truce. The next day, as he rode in a Dallas motorcade, bullets fired at long range struck the president in the neck and head. He was pronounced dead at a nearby hospital some thirty minutes later.

Kennedy's murder staggered the nation. The last presidential assassination had been William McKinley's in 1901, when communications media were far less vivid, instantaneous, and enveloping. Millions of Americans had grown intimately familiar with the youthful president and his appealing family; they now experienced his demise with brutal immediacy. Compounding the shock, two days later Kennedy's suspected killer, twenty-four-year-old Lee Harvey Oswald, was shot dead in a Dallas police station by a local nightclub owner. This second murder was broadcast live on television, a freakishly graphic viewing experience for 1963.

In a September 1964 report, a federal commission chaired by Chief Justice of the United States Earl Warren confirmed the Dallas police's early judgment that Oswald, acting alone, had killed Kennedy by firing from a building overlooking the motorcade route. This finding was almost certainly accurate. But the Warren Commission – prodded by Kennedy's successor, Lyndon B. Johnson, who hoped that a prompt report would inhibit the circulation of conspiracy theories – was hasty in its work, leaving too many loose ends for critics to pull on. In the coming years, a growing cadre of professional and amateur investigators would assail the Warren Commission report, insisting that Kennedy's murder had indeed been the work of a shadowy conspiracy, in which Oswald was knowingly complicit or for which he was unjustly blamed. The list of suspected culprits was endless, but the chief ones were the Soviet Union, Fidel Castro, anti-Castro Cubans, American organized crime, and top-secret US government agents alarmed by Kennedy's alleged determination to pull out of Vietnam. Oswald's brief involvement in the Fair Play for Cuba Committee was fodder for several competing theories, some implicating Castro or other communist actors, some fingering anticommunists using Oswald as a scapegoat. There were plenty of other suspicious circumstances connected to the Dallas tragedy, buttressing a still wider range of scenarios.

More diffusely, many Americans came to see Kennedy's assassination as a historical watershed, dividing a simpler, more wholesome time from an era of violence, failure, confusion, and moral ambiguity – a shift often captured by the phrase "loss of innocence." While even a cursory reading of pre-Dallas US history puts to rest any notion of innocence, Americans were indeed about to enter a more tumultuous period and become far less trusting of the government and other national institutions. Yet those transformations grew out of historical trajectories, mostly relating to disputes over race and the cold war, long under way by the time of Kennedy's assassination.

Lyndon B. Johnson

The tragedy thrust Vice President Lyndon B. Johnson, a Texan, into the presidency. Johnson had been in Washington for a quarter-century, serving as representative, senator, and eventually Senate majority leader before joining the Democratic national ticket in 1960. He had acquiesced in, and upheld, the brutal racial hierarchies of his region, while harboring a sympathy for the poor and downtrodden of all backgrounds. As vice president, Johnson was largely excluded from Kennedy's inner circle, a humiliating experience for a man accustomed to wielding great power (and for one subject to deep personal insecurities to boot). After the assassination, Johnson asked all of Kennedy's cabinet secretaries and top aides to stay in their posts, and most did, at least for a time. The new president then attacked his

Figure 5.2 Vice President Lyndon B. Johnson and President John F. Kennedy, 1963. Source: Corbis Historical / Getty Images.

duties with a curious display of deference and self-assertion. He presented himself as the grieving public servant who would champion the cause of the martyred Kennedy, but do so more skillfully and successfully than the martyr ever could.

Earthy and tactile, with a hulking physical presence, President Johnson had a remarkable ability to dominate those he met face to face and to bend them to his will. At times, especially during his first two years in office, he seemed to believe that he could do this to the nation at large; that, through the sheer force of his personality and the obvious benevolence of his policies, he could win the acclaim, even the love, of the vast majority of Americans, consigning dissenters to a ridiculed fringe. For several months spanning 1964 and 1965, Johnson appeared to do just that – and then political gravity kicked in with a vengeance.

Johnson's priority upon taking office was the passage of Kennedy's civil rights bill, which the new president believed essential to winning over liberals and African Americans (two groups that tended to distrust him) and to removing what he genuinely saw as a blight on his native South. By now, congressional liberals had strengthened the bill to include a ban on racial discrimination in private employment, but there was considerable doubt that the measure as a whole could withstand the opposition of segregationist legislators. Drawing on his deep familiarity with Congress's rules, traditions, and leading personalities, and on the enthusiastic support of civil rights, labor, and liberal groups, Johnson guided the bill through the House and Senate. A key early challenge was getting the bill out of the House Rules Committee and onto the House floor over the opposition of its segregationist chairman, Howard Smith of Virginia. A simple majority of House members could achieve this by signing a "discharge" petition, but many of the bill's backers initially hesitated to defy Smith in this way. A strong showing of public support for the bill eventually overcame that reluctance, producing the required majority. To avoid the humiliation of a discharge, Smith released the bill to the full House, which passed it in February 1964.[1]

In the Senate, the bill faced a segregationist filibuster, something no previous civil rights measure had survived. A vote to end it needed the approval of two-thirds of the Senate, a supermajority requiring substantial Republican support. Johnson's relentless wooing of the Senate's top Republican, Minority Leader Everett Dirksen, along with modest alterations of the bill to address Republican objections, mustered the necessary GOP votes. In mid-June, the Senate ended the filibuster and passed the bill. In early July, Johnson signed into law the Civil Rights Act of 1964. The Act banned discrimination in employment, federally funded programs, and public accommodations; authorized the attorney general to file lawsuits against school districts that failed to desegregate; and established an Equal Opportunity Employment Commission to monitor and enforce employers' compliance with the new law.

On the whole, the Civil Rights Act's measures regarding employment and public accommodations were less controversial than its provisions on school desegregation. That last issue, of course, had drawn bitter opposition from the white South since the Supreme Court's *Brown v. Board of Education* decision of 1954. After passage of the Civil Rights Act, white southerners proved less viscerally opposed to sharing public spaces and employment opportunities with African Americans than to letting their children attend school with them. Public schools throughout the South were glacially slow to desegregate; as they did so, many white families placed their children in all-white private or religious schools or moved to all-white neighborhoods or suburbs where desegregation policies did not apply. This issue would be revisited many times in the years ahead – and not just in the South.

Another Kennedy policy that Johnson now championed was an across-the-board reduction in individual and corporate taxes. Such a measure, his administration argued, would leave consumers and investors with more money to pump back into the economy, increasing its overall productivity. The House had passed a tax cut in September 1963, but in the Senate the bill faced opposition by fiscal conservatives of both parties, who warned of lost tax revenues and enlarged budget deficits. To overcome these objections, Johnson promised to keep the federal budget under $100 billion, down from the $108 billion his economic advisers urged. The pledge seemed at odds with Johnson's ambitious domestic policy agenda, but the president gambled that the tax cut would so stimulate the economy that, even with lower tax rates, federal revenues would expand. This outcome, combined with the enhanced popularity Johnson stood to reap from the growing prosperity, would enable him to request future budget increases. The Revenue Act of 1964, which lowered the top marginal rate from 91 percent to 77 percent, with corresponding reductions further down the tax scale, actually exceeded expectations. It not only generated more federal revenue but helped bring the unemployment rate down from 5.7 percent in 1963 to 4.5 percent in 1965, and then down under 4 percent for the rest of the decade.

[1] Ironically, Howard Smith took other action that strengthened the Civil Rights bill: adding a sex discrimination component. See Chapter 8 for this remarkable development.

Meanwhile, and more memorably, Johnson declared "unconditional war on poverty in America." Kennedy had made a general commitment to address the issue just before his death, and Johnson now placed his personal stamp on it. Despite the remarkable postwar prosperity, in 1962 between 20 and 25 percent of Americans remained in poverty, defined as living in families earning less than $3,000 per year (about $28,000 annually in 2022 dollars). As Michael Harrington and other commentators noted, many of these people had little hope of escaping their condition, for they lacked the education, training, and technological literacy to succeed in an increasingly automated and information-based economy. Although the problem was closely tied to race – 43 percent of Black families lived in poverty in 1965 – millions of whites, especially in the rural South, were shut out of the American dream. Indeed, one reason the issue appealed to Johnson was that it enabled him to "do something for" southern whites and thus, hopefully, blunt their opposition to federal desegregation policies.

The first salvo in Johnson's War on Poverty was passage of the Economic Opportunity Act in the summer of 1964. The Act provided job training programs for disadvantaged youth, grants for adult education, loans to impoverished rural families, and funds for preschool programs in underserved communities. It also created Volunteers in Service to America (VISTA), a sort of domestic Peace Corps, and authorized the formation of Community Action Programs (CAPs), local antipoverty efforts in which poor people themselves shared in the decision-making. The Food Stamp Act, passed that same summer, standardized a patchwork of existing programs to provide nutritious food to the poor. Johnson had more ambitious plans, but these would have to await the 1964 presidential election, which the president hoped would furnish him a mandate to govern in his own right, rather than merely serve out Kennedy's interrupted term.

Meanwhile, though, Johnson began folding his War on Poverty into a larger vision of what the nation could become over the next half-century. His term for that America was "the Great Society," a place where human creativity, having conquered material want, explored new frontiers of mind and spirit; a place, he proclaimed in a May 1964 speech, "where the city of man serves not only the needs of the body and the demands of commerce but the desire for beauty and the hunger for community." In practical terms, Johnson was proposing that the federal government continue to expand the social safety net while branching out to support public education, the arts, conservation, urban renewal, and other endeavors whose value was difficult to quantify. Given the remarkable prosperity over which he was presiding, and the impressive political momentum he had started to gain, this did not seem all that extravagant or presumptuous.

Freedom Summer and the 1964 Election

Implicit in Johnson's vision, however, were expectations of domestic harmony that real-life politics seldom bore out. In the summer of 1964, the president found his interests sharply at odds with those of many civil rights workers. Since 1961, SNCC had attempted to register

Black voters in Mississippi, whose Jim Crow system was more oppressive than any other found in the South. After three years of brutal resistance and scant progress, SNCC and some other groups launched a "Freedom Summer" campaign for 1964, recruiting hundreds of young volunteers, many of them white college students from the North, to assist with the Mississippi registration drive. Placing privileged whites in harm's way, the organizers grimly calculated, would draw the nation's eyes to the campaign as no other tactic could. Johnson feared that an outbreak of violence in Mississippi would disrupt party unity at the upcoming Democratic National Convention in Atlantic City, New Jersey, where he was to receive his party's nomination. Through emissaries, he cautioned the Freedom Summer organizers not to expect federal protection; the FBI could investigate, but not prevent, racially motivated crimes by white southerners. (Actually, Hoover's G-men were known to drag their feet in investigating such crimes, too.) With a combination of determination and dread, the organizers and volunteers pressed on.

In June, three young Freedom Summer volunteers – James Chaney, a Black Mississippian, and Richard Schwerner and Andrew Goodman, two white northerners – went missing in Mississippi. Amid the sudden flurry of national interest in Mississippi, Johnson ordered a reluctant FBI to assist state and local authorities in searching for the activists. The US Navy stepped in to dredge Mississippi's lakes and rivers. Weeks later, the bullet-ridden bodies of Chaney, Schwerner, and Goodman were found in an earthen dam. They had been kidnapped and murdered by Klansmen with the connivance of local police. Chaney's corpse bore evidence of torture. Undeterred, the Mississippi registration effort continued for the rest of the summer.

Freedom Summer activists made national news in another way, bringing their differences with Johnson more fully into view. One prong of the campaign was the formation of an alternative, racially integrated delegation to challenge the Mississippi Democratic Party's all-white delegation at the Democratic convention. The vehicle for the challenge was a new organization, the Mississippi Freedom Democratic Party (MFDP). In late August the MFDP delegates, four whites and sixty-four Blacks (many of the latter farmers, sharecroppers, and domestic workers), appeared at the Atlantic City convention and demanded to be seated, on the ground that they had been selected through an open process whereas the regular delegation was the product of Black disfranchisement.

The MFDP challenge placed Johnson in a bind. White southern delegates, and not just Mississippians, threatened to bolt the convention if the Democratic Party made any substantive concessions to the MFDP. A southern walkout would destroy the aura of consensus in which Johnson had enveloped his candidacy, and perhaps dim his electoral prospects. Yet the MFDP delegates were hard to ignore, especially after they made their case at a public hearing of the convention's credentials committee. Offering the most riveting testimony was a former sharecropper named Fannie Lou Hamer, who recounted the vicious reprisals she and other Black Mississippians had endured – eviction, imprisonment, beatings, even attempted murder – for trying to register to vote. "Is this America?" she asked. "The land of the free and the home of the brave? Where we have to sleep with our telephones off the hook, because our lives be threatened daily, because we want to

Figure 5.3 Mississippi Freedom Democratic Party delegate Fannie Lou Hamer with Anne and Nathan Schwerner, the parents of slain civil rights worker Michael Schwerner, at the Democratic National Convention in Atlantic City, New Jersey, 1964. Source: Robert Abbott Sengstacke / Archive Photos / Getty Images.

live as decent human beings, in America?" Hamer's words aired on national television, arousing widespread sympathy for the MFDP.

Recognizing that sentiment, yet loath to antagonize the Dixie delegates, Johnson rammed through a compromise: the MFDP would be offered sixty-six honorary nonvoting seats, two "at large" voting seats, and a pledge that future conventions would be conducted on a nondiscriminatory basis. Although Martin Luther King, NAACP executive director Roy Wilkins, and other civil rights leaders urged acceptance of the deal, the MFDP forcefully rejected it. "We didn't come all this way for no two seats," Hamer said. She and her comrades departed Johnson's coronation in disgust, having made a bigger point than they perhaps realized.

If the MFDP challenge shot holes in Johnson's cherished myth of consensus, other events kept it afloat for a while longer. At their own national convention in San Francisco, the Republicans greatly simplified the president's task by making Senator Barry Goldwater of Arizona their presidential nominee. Goldwater was a conservative ideologue whose every utterance allowed Johnson to claim to speak for a vast, sensible majority. The senator alarmed voters by complaining that Americans had an unhealthy fear of nuclear weapons and by urging an escalation of US military involvement in Vietnam. ("We are not about to send American boys nine or ten thousand miles away from home to do what Asian boys ought to be doing for themselves," Johnson tut-tutted in reply.) Goldwater's attacks on government assistance programs as "creeping socialism" raised the specter of a repeal of the New Deal. The senator also opposed the recently passed Civil Rights Act, less out of hostility to desegregation than out of a conviction that Washington had no business mandating such reforms. While accepting that Goldwater was "not himself a racist," King accused the Republican candidate of espousing "a philosophy which gives aid and comfort to the racist."

To the claim that his views were out of the mainstream, Goldwater made no objection. After all, he himself had declared in accepting his party's nomination that "extremism in the defense of liberty is no vice. And … moderation in the pursuit of justice is no virtue." There was something weirdly honorable in Goldwater's insistence on confining himself to the cramped margins and ceding all of the remaining political ground to his opponent. (The same went for his utter refusal to try to charm voters. In Georgia, Goldwater met a supporter who was promoting the Republican ticket by marketing a soft drink called "Gold Water." Offered a sip of the beverage, Goldwater spat it out and growled, "This tastes like piss!")

When Johnson went on to win the most lopsided presidential election victory to date, reaping 61 percent of the popular vote, he could be forgiven for imagining that he now embodied the national will. Commentators reinforced this view, treating the outcome as the triumph of simple reality over wild fantasy. The columnist Stewart Alsop wrote that Goldwater's brand of conservatism, far from offering "a coherent, rational alternative," was "hardly more than an angry cry of protest against things as they are." Other experts pronounced conservatism dead for a generation, if not longer.

And yet, for all its haplessness, the Goldwater campaign had accomplished two novel feats that boded ill for liberalism's own long-term prospects. First, the campaign had won five states in the Deep South: Alabama, Georgia, Louisiana, Mississippi, and South Carolina. Except for Louisiana in 1956, none of these states had voted Republican in a presidential election since Reconstruction. Goldwater's success in the region had everything to do with white southerners' rejection of Johnson's civil rights policies. In the years to come, racial politics and other issues would prompt a broad exodus of southern whites out of the Democratic Party and into the GOP (sometimes by way of third-party stepping stones). Second, the campaign had afforded a priceless opportunity for conservatives throughout the country, especially young people, to find each other, test strategies and themes, and identify future leaders. The experience showed that millions of voters hungered for sharp, unapologetic critiques of free-spending liberals in Congress, meddlesome bureaucrats in government agencies, smug pundits in the news media, timid diplomats at the State Department, angry picketers in the civil rights movement, and strident protesters on university campuses. One of Goldwater's most effective campaign surrogates was the former Hollywood actor Ronald Reagan, who in an oft-repeated speech skewered a number of those adversaries with humor and panache. Both of these developments, one demographic and the other mainly discursive, suggested that the liberal order was a good deal more vulnerable than observers generally realized.

The Great Society at Full Tide

For the moment, though, Lyndon Johnson and his politics were riding high. Finally, the president had a personal mandate from the voters, and a huge one at that. The Democrats had also substantially enlarged their majority in Congress. Upon his inauguration in early 1965, Johnson unleashed a frenzy of legislative activity, asking Congress to pass scores of bills touching on virtually every area of domestic life: education, employment, health care, urban affairs, rural development, consumer protection, cultural enrichment, and the natural environment. Johnson realized he had a precious, and likely fleeting, opportunity to act. "I want you guys to get off your asses," a cabinet secretary recalled him saying, "and do everything possible to get everything in my program passed as soon as possible, before the aura and the halo that surround me disappear. Don't waste a second." Johnson drove his legislative liaison staff to exhaustion. In his personal dealings with congressmembers, he used every technique at his command – flattery, intimidation, horse trading, blackmail, appeals to patriotism and to the demands of history – to force their acquiescence. Johnson won passage of almost all of his programs, causing commentators to shake their heads in wonder. "He's getting everything through the Congress but the abolition of the Republican Party," *New York Times* columnist James Reston wrote in August 1965, "and he hasn't tried that yet."

Among the most important achievements was passage of a pair of amendments to the Social Security Act of 1935. The first amendment established Medicare, a system of federally guaranteed health insurance for the elderly. The second created Medicaid, which insured low-income Americans of all ages. As with the 1964 civil rights bill, Johnson identified, and concentrated his fire on, the legislation's key congressional opponents. One of them was Harry Byrd of Virginia, chairman of the Senate Finance Committee. Fearing that Byrd would obstruct hearings on Medicare in his committee, the president invited him and several other members of Congress to a meeting at the White House. To the visitors' surprise, Johnson had arranged for the event to be televised. With the cameras rolling, he asked Byrd point-blank if there was anything preventing the Finance Committee from taking up the Medicare proposal. Byrd, who found it far easier to oppose Medicare behind closed doors than in the glare of publicity, mumbled that there was not. By these and similar means, the president swept aside obstacles to the far-reaching amendments, which Congress passed in the summer of 1965.

Also noteworthy were Johnson's environmental initiatives, representing a whole new focus for liberal reform. By mid-decade, the insights of Rachel Carson and other science writers had nurtured a wider appreciation of the fragility of the earth's ecosystems. News stories reported, and everyday experience increasingly confirmed, that car exhaust and factory emissions were choking the air with smog and that toxic waste was befouling the nation's rivers and lakes – a crisis distilled in the acid couplets of the musical satirist Tom Lehrer: "See the halibuts and the sturgeons/Being wiped out by detergents/ … Just go out for a breath of air/And you'll be ready for Medicare." In 1964 Congress had passed some wilderness preservation bills. In the following year, under Johnson's ceaseless prodding, it approved a host of measures to regulate industries' interaction with the environment, including the Water Quality Act, the Solid Waste Disposal Act, and a new Clean Air Act, updating a weaker 1963 version. The Highway Beautification Act, a special project of the president's wife, Lady Bird Johnson, regulated the placement of advertising billboards, junkyards, and other visual pollution along interstate highways.

Another reform enacted in 1965, receiving far less public attention than it merited, was an overhaul of the country's immigration laws. At the start of that year's legislative session, the old quota system from the 1920s, which privileged immigrants from Northern and Western Europe, remained substantially in place. Over the previous two decades, however, Congress had mandated exceptions that modestly eased restrictions on immigration from Eastern and Southern Europe, the Middle East, and East Asia. (East Asians were particularly in need of relief, as the original quota system excluded them almost entirely.) These revisions largely reflected a desire to present the United States as a beacon and haven of liberty in a world menaced by communist tyranny. It seemed especially imperative that America open its doors more widely to refugees from communist governments. By the early 1960s, much of the political establishment was convinced that the old quota system no longer suited US global responsibilities. Meanwhile, Americans of Eastern European and Asian ancestry, and racial egalitarians of all backgrounds, denounced the existing system as discriminatory and unjust.

Embracing both arguments, in 1963 President Kennedy sent Congress a bill that would abolish the national-origins quotas in favor of a new regime admitting immigrants from all countries who possessed valuable skills, were refugees, or sought to be reunited with family members in the United States. Enough support for the old system remained, however, to prevent Kennedy's bill from advancing. With the more liberal Congress in 1965, Johnson threw his support behind a new bill containing the same criteria for admission. Congress passed it in the late summer. At an October ceremony at the base of the Statue of Liberty, the president signed the Immigration and Nationality Act of 1965.

In the decades to come, the absence of national-origins quotas would permit a growing influx of non-European immigrants and a transformation in the nation's ethnic and racial makeup. Very few of the reform's advocates had expected those results. Most regarded the elimination of discriminatory quotas as largely symbolic. They assumed that the family reunification provision would tend to reinforce existing demographic patterns; they could not foresee the intricate ways in which that provision would create new pathways of entry into the United States. The point of the reform was not to open the floodgates of non-European immigration but to stop telling non-Europeans that they were unwelcome. At the signing ceremony, Johnson stated: "This … is not a revolutionary bill. It does not affect the lives of millions . . . . Yet it … does repair a very deep and painful flaw in the fabric of American justice." Though perhaps right about that second part, the president was, it turned out, quite wrong about the first.

The Selma Campaign and Voting Rights

In his January 1965 State of the Union Address, Johnson called for "the elimination of barriers to the right to vote." He was plainly alluding to the situation in the South, where a host of measures – poll taxes,[2] unequally applied literacy tests, threats of job loss and eviction, and violent attacks by police, the Ku Klux Klan, and other white supremacists – kept African Americans from the polls. The president was uncertain, however, that voting rights legislation could soon pass in the Congress. With so many other domestic initiatives under way, perhaps it would be wiser to postpone such an effort. Movement activists would not grant Johnson that respite. To spur federal action, in early 1965 King and the SCLC went to Selma, Alabama, to support an ongoing SNCC campaign to register Black voters. Like Birmingham, Selma was well chosen for the movement's needs. Fewer than 1 percent of Black adults in Dallas County, where Selma is located, were registered to vote, and James Clark, the Dallas County sheriff, was a crude sadist on the pattern of Bull Connor. In January and February, Black residents repeatedly marched on the county courthouse demanding to register. Clark and his deputies carted them off to jail, sometimes assaulting them with clubs and even electric cattle prods. As organizers had hoped, the campaign began attracting national attention.

In early February, a harried and exhausted Malcolm X appeared in Selma to address a church rally, in response to an invitation from SNCC. He praised the voter registration campaign but warned that Black people had "other ways to obtain their ends" if peaceful protests failed. Unable to see King, who was then in jail, Malcolm asked Coretta Scott King to assure her husband that "I didn't come to Selma to make his job difficult." Just the opposite: "If the white people realize what the alternative is, perhaps they will be more willing to hear Dr. King." Later that month, as he prepared to speak in a New York ballroom, Malcolm was shot dead by gunmen charging the stage; he was not yet forty. Three members of the Nation of Islam were convicted of the killing. Yet gnawing doubts would persist about the guilt of two of the accused, along with suspicions that the New York Police Department, and perhaps the FBI, had abetted the crime by disrupting Malcolm's security detail. Over the next several years, Malcolm X gained a stature he never possessed in life, offering a model of boundless racial pride and unflinching defiance of white oppression to an increasingly assertive Black freedom movement. On the other hand, despite considerable backing and filling and moments of outright contradiction, the clear trend of Malcolm's thinking during his final months had been toward greater interracial cooperation and engagement with electoral politics. The sheer unknowability of where this might have led became another part of his legacy.

On March 7, 1965, a date that would be remembered as "Bloody Sunday," about six hundred Selma activists began marching the fifty-four miles from Selma to Montgomery, Alabama's capital, to demand that Governor George Wallace protect Black registrants. To exit Selma, they crossed the Alabama River over the Edmund Pettus Bridge. On the other side, state troopers and Sheriff Clark's deputies, some of the latter on horseback, plowed into marchers, clubbing them, trampling them, and choking them with tear gas. Scores of marchers were injured. Widely covered in the press and on television, the assault outraged

[2] The Twenty-fourth Amendment to the Constitution, ratified in January 1965, outlawed the imposition of poll taxes in federal elections, but not in state elections. The 1966 Supreme Court decision *Harper v. Virginia State Board of Elections* banned poll taxes in state elections.

Americans as no other such event had. The SCLC announced plans to make another attempt to march on Montgomery, this one led by Martin Luther King, who had been preaching in Atlanta on Bloody Sunday. From across the country, activists, celebrities, and religious people of all races and denominations flocked to Selma to join the march.

Jolted by events in Selma, and prodded by civil rights picketers outside the White House, Johnson decisively entered the fray. He urged Wallace to protect the marchers, rather than obstructing and attacking them. On March 15 the president addressed Congress, announcing he would shortly request legislation to protect Black voting rights in the South. In a passage that brought tears to King's eyes, Johnson worked the words of the civil rights anthem into his speech: "Their cause must be our cause, too. Because it's not just Negroes, but really it's all of us who must overcome the crippling legacy of bigotry and injustice. And we shall overcome."

On March 21, about 8,000 marchers departed Selma for Montgomery. Wallace had pledged not to assault the protesters, but he sulkily insisted that his government lacked the funds to protect them. So Johnson federalized Alabama's National Guard, which provided security for the five-day trek. When the marchers reached Montgomery on March 25, their numbers had swelled to 25,000, an interracial pageant displaying the liberal coalition at its zenith. King addressed them from the steps of the state capitol. Painfully aware of the rising tides of anger and disillusionment among civil rights workers, he implored his movement allies not to lose heart, assuring them that, "however difficult the moment, however frustrating the hour," victory was now within reach.

That night, Viola Liuzzo, a white activist from Michigan, was returning to Montgomery after transporting some marchers back to Selma. Several Klansmen in a car pulled up alongside her and shot her to death. Two other people had lost their lives in altercations connected to the Selma movement: Jimmy Lee Jackson, a young Black man shot by a state trooper in a neighboring town in mid-February; and James Reeb, a white Unitarian Universalist minister severely beaten by white men in Selma shortly after Bloody Sunday, dying in a hospital two days later.

These tragedies underscored the enormous toll the struggle was taking on activists. In the vast majority of cases, the victims of violence were Black. Beyond direct physical harm, activists incurred extraordinary psychological costs. The strain of remaining calm in the face of relentless assaults, of pressing ahead despite gnawing fear, created inner turmoil that manifested itself in ulcers, headaches, nervous tension, and antisocial behavior. Protesters who had endured racist pummelings with Gandhian stoicism found themselves violently lashing out against those closest to them. Alvin Poussaint, a Black psychiatrist who treated movement activists around this time, recalled, "I frequently had to calm Negro civil-rights workers with large doses of tranquilizers for what I can describe clinically only as acute attacks of rage."

Over the spring and summer of 1965, Johnson's voting rights bill made its way through Congress, encountering fewer obstacles than the civil rights bill had the previous year. The new bill banned literacy tests in jurisdictions deemed guilty of voter discrimination and empowered the federal government, in some circumstances, to intervene in such jurisdictions to register voters itself. It did not ban the poll tax outright but stated that no one could be disfranchised for failure to pay it. Congress passed the bill in July, and Johnson signed it early the next month.

The Voting Rights Act markedly increased African American participation in southern electoral politics. Over the next four years, a million Black citizens were added to the region's voter rolls. (This occurred despite the fact that many rural Blacks continued to face severe retaliation, such as job loss, eviction, and physical violence, for registering to vote.) During that same period, in the six Deep South states primarily subject to the law, the number of Black elected office holders jumped from seventy to almost 400; by 1980, there were nearly twice that many. The new voters and office holders were overwhelmingly Democratic, but the movement of white southerners out of the Democratic column (coupled with the fact that white southerners became new voters at an even higher rate than Black southerners did) more than offset this gain for the Democrats. The gain for the nation, of course, was incalculable.

The Watts Riots and the Politics of Backlash

On August 11, five days after Johnson signed the Voting Rights Act, riots erupted in Watts, a low-income Black neighborhood of Los Angeles. The proximate cause was a scuffle resulting from white police officers' arrest of a Black motorist for drunk driving. Mistakenly believing an officer had struck a pregnant woman, onlookers threw rocks and chunks of concrete at the police. The violence quickly spread over forty-six square miles, continuing for six days and claiming thirty-four lives and $40 million in property damage. A relatively recent (and quintessentially Los Angelite) innovation called the "telecopter" – a helicopter outfitted with a television camera – beamed graphic scenes of burning, looting, and gunfire into homes across the nation.

After Watts, the tide of white sympathy for Black Americans' plight began to ebb. More and more whites took the view that the government had done all it reasonably could to remedy racial inequities and that African Americans should stop demanding further official redress. Johnson quickly sensed the shifting mood. Although he rushed $29 million in emergency economic aid to Watts and remained committed to pursuing both de facto and de jure equality for African Americans, he sharply reduced his public identification with the issue. He even ordered that the aid to Watts be kept secret, lest anyone accuse him of appeasing Black rioters.

Johnson's sudden reticence dismayed civil rights leaders, all the more so because it threatened to stymie a vital new presidential initiative. In a June 1965 speech, the president had said, "You do not take a person who, for years, has been hobbled by chains and liberate him, bring him up to the starting line of a race and then say, 'You are free to compete with all the others,' and still justly believe that you have been completely fair." Johnson's point was that the mere removal of formal discrimination would not suffice; it would be necessary, too, for the national government to take vigorous measures to address economic deprivation in Black communities throughout the country and to reverse the crippling effects of centuries of racial oppression. Nearly all civil rights leaders shared this view. But, whereas the Watts riots only deepened their conviction that a new federal commitment of this sort was needed, Watts pushed Johnson in the opposite direction.

In a related development, Johnson's War on Poverty, too, started running into trouble that summer. The Community Action Programs, which encouraged poor people themselves to help design and run antipoverty efforts, proved highly unpopular with big-city mayors, who chafed under the necessity of sharing decision-making – and federal dollars – with antipoverty activists they often viewed as hustlers or rabble rousers. Some claiming to represent the poor were indeed opportunists out for easy government money. Others were left-leaning idealists who saw the CAPs as a means of empowering the poor to fight oppressive conditions, including those imposed or tolerated by city hall. Among the latter was SDS's Tom Hayden, who, like many others in his organization, had sought in the years since Port Huron to awaken "participatory democracy" in impoverished urban communities. In 1964 he moved to Newark, New Jersey, and founded the Newark Community Union Project (NCUP). By the summer of 1965, NCUP was waging bitter turf battles with Newark's mayor, Hugh Addonizio, over the direction of the city's antipoverty programs. Similar skirmishes occurred in other major cities, whose mayors, typically well-connected Democrats, had little difficulty getting their version of events out to the media and members of Congress.

Also controversial was the War on Poverty's support for community art projects. Later that year, it was reported that a New York City CAP had sponsored plays by the militant Black playwright Leroi Jones (who later changed his name to Amiri Baraka). One of the plays, *J-E-L-L-O*, was a parody of TV's popular "Jack Benny Program" in which Rochester, Benny's Black valet, becomes radicalized and berates and robs his employer. A torrent of irate letters from citizens, protesting, as one put it, "*my* tax money being spent to produce plays of hate," descended on the White House. Here was another reason for Johnson to keep racial issues at arm's length.

Over the longer term, Johnson's War on Poverty would leave a mixed legacy. Its programs did help bring the national poverty rate down from around 20 percent in 1963 to around 12 percent at decade's end. Yet a good deal of that progress could also be attributed to a booming economy (itself partly stimulated by the Vietnam War, which Johnson escalated in the spring and summer of 1965). And, although the nation's share of poor people markedly diminished, those left in poverty, disproportionately people of color, faced ever more daunting challenges. Life was especially bleak in the inner cities, where crime, blight, joblessness, substance abuse, family breakdown, and similar problems all grew more acute and intractable. Retrospectively, the War on Poverty would draw criticism from multiple directions. Progressives and radicals faulted it for failing to attempt a thoroughgoing redistribution of the nation's wealth and power. Conservatives charged that its programs drew the poor into a web of dependence that destroyed their initiative and kept them in poverty. Even some of Johnson's liberal allies later rued that the effort had raised unrealistic expectations, had been pursued haphazardly, and had been underfunded on account of Johnson's growing preoccupation with Vietnam.

***

Figure 5.4 Conservative commentator William F. Buckley, Jr., running for mayor of New York, 1965. Source: Bettmann / Getty Images.

In the fall of 1965, shortly before the controversy over CAP and *J-E-L-L-O* erupted, New Yorkers were treated to another unusual spectacle, one that portended further trouble for American liberalism. William F. Buckley, Jr., the conservative publisher and polemicist, ran for mayor on New York's Conservative Party ticket. The Republican nominee was US Representative John V. Lindsay, a patrician liberal on a mission to cleanse his party of the Goldwater taint. To Buckley, there was little to distinguish Lindsay's politics from those of the Democratic nominee, city Comptroller Abraham Beame. Buckley knew he couldn't win the race. His aims, rather, were to air conservative ideas and to draw enough votes away from Lindsay to throw the election to Beame; Lindsay's defeat would hinder the effort to shift the Republican Party leftward. (True, this was only a mayor's race, but New York City was sufficiently important to exert a major influence on national politics.)

In the campaign, Buckley combined general reactionary stances (hostility to federal social programs, draconian measures for drug addicts and "chronic welfare cases," and a taunting dismissal of concerns about police brutality) with municipal proposals that resisted easy ideological classification (new ways to tax city services, installation of elevated bike lanes to ease congestion, and construction of a "Disneyland East" in Queens). Characteristically, he espoused all of these positions with a slashing eloquence that delighted many in the news media and the public. Less expectedly, Buckley's attacks on the liberal establishment struck a chord with lower-middle- and working-class whites – construction workers, cops, firefighters, shopkeepers, clerical workers, and others – who felt pinched by a declining quality of life in the Big Apple. Like other northeastern cities, New York had been hollowed out in the previous decade by an exodus of middle-class whites to the suburbs and of good manufacturing jobs to low-wage regions of the country. Municipal services were declining and crime was on the rise. Many of the less affluent whites who remained in the city believed that governing elites at all levels had failed to speak to their concerns, catering instead to racial minorities and the very poor. Some, no doubt, were also fed up with the increasingly assertive protests of civil rights activists and, more recently, opponents of US involvement in Vietnam. Buckley, a polysyllabic product of English boarding schools with the accent to prove it, was an unlikely tribune of this nascent blue-collar rebellion, but he voiced its grievances in ways that neither Lindsay nor Beame would.

On Election Day, Buckley received 13.4 percent of the vote, a respectable showing for a third-party effort but one that defeated his Machiavellian scheme. Many of Buckley's voters were lower-middle- and working-class white Democrats who would have gone for Beame in a two-candidate race. Deprived of their support, Beame lost to Lindsay. Yet the experience taught conservatives a valuable lesson: that many traditional Democrats were receptive to rightwing populist appeals and might support Republican candidates who made them. Buckley's losing candidacy, like Goldwater's the year before, honed the weapons for future assaults on liberalism.

Just months earlier, Lyndon Johnson's brand of consensus politics had seemed unbeatable. Now, sharp critiques of the status quo were gathering strength on both the left and the right. Into the second half of the decade, the challenge from each flank would grow ever more formidable, especially against the backdrop of Johnson's escalating war of choice in the jungles of Southeast Asia.

READING QUESTIONS

1. The author writes that the nonviolent strategy civil rights workers pursued from 1960 to 1965 "succeeded all too well." What does he mean by that, and what concrete examples does he probably have in mind? What were some of the broader implications of that overabundance of success?
2. Why did Malcolm X's message and persona have growing appeal to some nonviolent civil rights activists in the early to mid-1960s? How did Malcolm's own outlook change during this period?
3. What broad national circumstances help to explain the surge of domestic federal reform efforts in the middle years of the 1960s?
4. What political and social developments in the early to mid-1960s did conservative critics and activists find most objectionable? Why?

SUGGESTIONS FOR FURTHER READING

Branch, Taylor. *Pillar of Fire: America in the King Years, 1963–65*. New York: Simon & Schuster, 1998.

Parting the Waters: America in the King Years, 1954–63. New York: Simon & Schuster, 1988.

Dallek, Robert. *Flawed Giant: Lyndon Johnson and His Times, 1961–1973*. New York: Oxford University Press, 1998.

Farber, David. *The Age of Great Dreams: America in the 1960s*. New York: Hill & Wang, 1994.

Marable, Manning. *Malcolm X: A Life of Reinvention*. New York: Viking, 2011.

Matusow, Allen J. *The Unraveling of America: A History of Liberalism in the 1960s*. New York: Harper & Row, 1984.

McGuire, Danielle. *At the Dark End of the Street: Black Women, Rape, and Resistance – A New History of the Civil Rights Movement from Rosa Parks to Black Power*. New York: Knopf, 2010.

Miller, James. *"Democracy Is in the Streets": From Port Huron to the Siege of Chicago*. New York: Simon & Schuster, 1987.

Perlstein, Rick. *Before the Storm: Barry Goldwater and the Unmaking of the American Consensus*. New York: Hill & Wang, 2001.

Purdum, Todd S. *An Idea Whose Time Has Come: Two Presidents, Two Parties, and the Battle for the Civil Rights Act of 1964*. New York: Henry Holt & Company, 2014.

Schultz, Kevin M. *Buckley and Mailer: The Difficult Friendship that Shaped the Sixties*. New York: W. W. Norton, 2015.

Sugrue, Thomas J. *Sweet Land of Liberty: The Forgotten Struggle for Civil Rights in the North*. New York: Random House, 2008.

Unger, Debi, and Irwin Unger, *LBJ: A Life*. New York: John Wiley & Sons, 1999.

Wei, William. *The Asian-American Movement*. Philadelphia: Temple University Press, 1993.

Weisbrot, Robert. *Freedom Bound: A History of America's Civil Rights Movement*. New York: W. W. Norton, 1990.

Zelizer, Julian E. *The Fierce Urgency of Now: Lyndon Johnson, Congress, and the Battle for the Great Society*. New York: Penguin Books, 2015.

6 Berkeley Cong

Fighting Abroad and Unraveling at Home, 1963–1968

Introduction

In December 1966, Diane Nash and three other American women traveled to Hanoi, North Vietnam's capital, and began an eleven-day tour of that country. Opponents of US military involvement in Southeast Asia, the four were guests of the North Vietnamese government, which sought to draw the world's attention to the civilian carnage resulting from US aerial bombing attacks against North Vietnam. A twenty-eight-year-old African American, Nash had been a leader of the 1960 sit-in campaign in Nashville, Tennessee, and a key figure in subsequent civil rights protests. She saw her current antiwar activism as a logical extension of the struggle against racism. The three other travelers were two white activists and a Puerto Rican peace worker whose advocacy centered on her brother's refusal to fight in Vietnam.

Escorted by their North Vietnamese hosts, the four women toured parts of Hanoi and surrounding areas ravaged by US air raids. They visited hospitals where civilians struggled to recover from severe shrapnel wounds and neighborhoods whose residents told of devastating personal losses. A pregnant woman in Hanoi reported that, while she was paying a prenatal visit to a medical center just days earlier, bombs fell on her street and killed her seven-year-old son and two-and-a-half-year-old daughter. "My son's body was found under the rubble," she said. "My girl was blown to bits. The only part of her body we could find was a piece of her head and hair." In a town south of Hanoi, an air raid siren forced the American visitors to clamber into the one-person shelters, resembling manholes, that lined the street. The experience lent credence to the Vietnamese civilians' stories.

Upon their return home, Nash's traveling companions shared their impressions of North Vietnam widely in the US news media. Nash, however, insisted on speaking only to African American reporters. "I do not intend to have the white press interpret to black people what I have to say to them," she remarked at an all-Black news conference in Chicago; "… the white press has assumed far too much power in black affairs." Describing her trip, Nash recounted the devastation Washington had visited on North Vietnam, attributing this behavior to America's "interest in colonial acquisition" in Southeast Asia. "White Americans do not value [Asian] lives as they value white lives," she said. Thus "Negro Americans are going to have to decide whether they want to be the murderers of other colored people." She urged Black men to refuse to serve in the military, even if this meant going to jail. In her press conference, then, Nash endorsed some of the more assertive stances emanating from the protest politics of the day: African Americans' insistence on Black-only spaces and antiwar activists' portrayal of the Vietnam War as racist, colonial aggression and their defiance of military draft laws.

The mainstream press paid scant attention to Nash's observations on Vietnam, a consequence, it appears, of her shunning of white journalists. In a report published in March 1967, the House Committee on Un-American Activities did take note of Nash's "unauthorized trip to Hanoi," but that was incidental to an exposé of her husband, James Bevel, a top aide to Martin Luther King, Jr. of the Southern Christian Leadership Conference. King, who was stepping up his opposition to the Vietnam War, had tasked Bevel with organizing the SCLC's participation in major peace demonstrations planned for later that spring. These developments, the HUAC report darkly observed, "are evidence that the Communists have succeeded, at least partially, in implementing their strategy of fusing the Vietnam and civil rights issues," the better to undermine US policy in Vietnam. The report did not accuse King and Bevel of being communists but implied that they were dupes in the party's sinister schemes.

By 1967, however, charges of communist subversion retained little of their old political and cultural power, and Bevel easily dismissed the HUAC report. "We are against the mass murder of non-white people in Vietnam," he told a reporter. "You can't accuse us of being Communists for being against that." Nash had anticipated the same allegation at her press conference following her return from Hanoi: "I consider myself a loyal American whose loyalty would have been less had I not gone." Still, if classic red-baiting had lost vitality, the future of right-leaning politics was far from bleak. Across the country, millions of ordinary citizens, most but not all of them white, were bridling at the growing militancy of the Black freedom struggle and the antiwar movement. A conservative backlash was gathering momentum – ominous news for the liberal Democrats who dominated much of the national government.

The polemical interventions of Nash, Bevel, and HUAC punctuated a broader political drama coinciding with the presidency of Lyndon B. Johnson. Thrust into office in late 1963, and displaying an odd combination of recklessness and dread, Johnson vastly expanded the nation's military involvement in Vietnam. A stunningly destructive endeavor, Johnson's war not only failed to achieve US geopolitical aims but aroused keen discontent across the domestic political spectrum. The most audible protests came from the antiwar left, which increasingly channeled the spirit of an exuberant youth counterculture. Meanwhile, elements of the Black civil rights movement adopted a defiant mode of resistance, known as Black Power, that gave voice to the mounting frustration and anger of African Americans throughout the nation, not just in the South, over the persistence of racial injustice. These disruptive challenges to the status quo antagonized large swaths of the American public. More and more citizens turned away from the liberal policies that, in their view, enabled the disorder. The 1968 presidential election yielded a narrow victory for the Republican candidate, clouding the future of the Democratic coalition that for more than three decades had been a commanding presence in national politics.

Vietnam: JFK's Legacy

As we saw in Chapter 4, President John F. Kennedy significantly expanded US involvement in South Vietnam, raising the number of military "advisers" (who in truth did more than merely advise) to 16,000 by the fall of 1963. The Kennedy administration also continued to support South Vietnam's president, Ngo Dinh Diem, though US policy-makers worried about Diem's heavy-handed rule and the domestic resentment it increasingly aroused. The opposition was not confined to the National Liberation Front (also known as the Viet Cong). Buddhist orders chafed under the Saigon government's restrictions on their public activities and displays. It didn't help that Diem was a Catholic trying to govern a society that was, at least nominally, close to 80 percent Buddhist. The regime responded harshly to the Buddhists' protests, which grew larger and angrier in response. The self-immolation of a Buddhist monk in June 1963 ignited a much broader civic rebellion, as university and high school students, some of them Catholics, joined in mass protests that summer. Six more monks burned themselves to death.

Kennedy and his advisers blamed the unrest on the political inflexibility of Diem and his brother Ngo Dinh Nhu, who headed the secret police. The Americans telegraphed their displeasure to other elements of the regime and voiced no objection when South Vietnamese generals schemed to oust Diem and Nhu. The coup plotters struck on November 1, seizing military installations and communications facilities. Diem and Nhu were captured and shot. Although some US officials seemed unfazed by the murders, Kennedy was shaken. Three weeks later, he, too, was dead.

During his presidency, Kennedy had occasionally expressed skepticism about the long-term viability of an independent, noncommunist South Vietnam. Some historians have argued that, had Kennedy lived and been reelected in 1964, he likely would have found a face-saving exit from the commitment. This is conceivable. On the eve of his assassination, however, Kennedy had taken no concrete steps toward liquidating the venture, and he remained officially and publicly committed to South Vietnam's preservation. As the experience of the next president vividly showed, moreover, pessimism was no guarantee of prudence.

Vietnam: LBJ's Escalation

Lyndon B. Johnson inherited a grim situation in South Vietnam. The junta that overthrew Diem lasted just three months, and the one replacing it struggled to keep its footing. The massive demonstrations of summer had abated, but Saigon still seethed with unrest. The South Vietnamese regime enjoyed hardly any authority in the countryside, where the NLF was stepping up its attacks and expanding its sway. In the spring of 1964, Johnson's secretary of defense, Robert McNamara, privately estimated that up to 40 percent of South Vietnam was under NLF control. It grew increasingly clear that, if events continued on their current course, the Saigon regime would crumble.

A land war in Asia was not on Johnson's wish list. The new president yearned to devote himself to America's domestic needs – to defeat poverty, end racial discrimination, provide greater security to the elderly, support public education, and contribute in other ways to the nation's civic and cultural enrichment. He made remarkable progress toward these goals during his first two years in office. Still, Johnson believed he could not fail to act on behalf of South Vietnam. He was sure that Hanoi's efforts, via its NLF proxy, to reunify Vietnam under Northern control amounted to international aggression on behalf of world communism. To maintain its credibility as the leading nation in the anticommunist coalition, the United States simply had to block such a drive. Johnson also vividly recalled how the Chinese Revolution of 1949 had weakened the Truman administration domestically, allowing Republicans to accuse it of incompetence, cowardice, even disloyalty. "I am not going to be the president who saw Southeast Asia go the way China went," Johnson pledged just two days after taking office. The domestic concern was intraparty as well. Johnson had to wonder how Kennedy loyalists would react should he abandon the martyred president's pledge to preserve South Vietnam (an ironic fear, in light of the stance that the next carrier of the Kennedy torch would eventually take).

But openly escalating the war came with its own pair of international and domestic dangers. A military attack on the communist North could draw neighboring China into the fray, as had happened during the Korean War; perhaps even the Soviet Union would come to Hanoi's aid. Moreover, if Johnson conspicuously expanded the anticommunist effort in Vietnam, conservatives in Congress might claim that the United States now faced an international emergency and could no longer afford the president's ambitious domestic programs.

Thus Johnson followed what he saw as a moderate course: doing just enough to keep the South Vietnamese regime afloat, but not so much as to provoke unwanted responses from the communist superpowers or from Congressional conservatives. Yet the Saigon government was so dysfunctional that even the modest goal of maintaining its existence could not be achieved without drastically expanding the US role, producing the very escalation Johnson hoped to avoid. The president knew this. As early as May 1964, he told an adviser that "it looks like to me that we're getting into another Korea. It just worries the hell out of me . . . . I don't think it's worth fighting for, and I don't think we can get out. And it's just the biggest damn mess that I ever saw." Seeing no feasible way to avoid that "damn mess," Johnson embarked on his escalating middle course, hoping the outcome would not be quite as disastrous as he feared.

By the summer of 1964, some of Johnson's advisers wanted to turn up the pressure on North Vietnam. They recommended that the president seek a congressional resolution authorizing US airstrikes against some Northern targets. Other advisers warned that involving Congress would generate an unwelcome public debate about Vietnam policy. A set of murky naval events off the coast of North Vietnam soon altered the political calculus. On August 2, North Vietnamese gunboats in the Gulf of Tonkin fired on an American naval vessel called the USS *Maddox*, causing no damage. Two days later a second attempted North Vietnamese attack, on the *Maddox* and the USS *Turner Joy*, allegedly occurred. Johnson administration officials charged unprovoked aggression, but the reality was more complicated. The day before the first incident, South Vietnamese gunboats, at US direction, had attacked two North-Vietnamese-held islands in the gulf. The *Maddox* then sailed into the area to collect intelligence on the operation, a move North Vietnam saw as an extension of the South Vietnamese attack. The alleged second incident seems not to have occurred at all. Apparently, radar and sonar technicians aboard the US ships mistook stormy weather effects for indications of North Vietnamese torpedo launches and gunfire.

Johnson was ill served by his advisers, who made the evidence for North Vietnamese aggression sound much starker than it was. On the other hand, the president did not probe for a more nuanced account. Despite some initial hesitation, he now believed a forceful US response was called for. He ordered air attacks on military bases in North Vietnam and asked Congress for a resolution authorizing him to take whatever military action he deemed necessary to repel North Vietnamese attacks. In the resulting crisis atmosphere, Congress quickly passed the Gulf of Tonkin Resolution – unanimously in the House and by a vote of eighty-eight to two in the Senate. Johnson had achieved two objectives. First, he had secured Congress's blessing for the enlarged US role in Vietnam he feared would be necessary. Second, he had strengthened his own position in the 1964 presidential election campaign, which pitted him against Republican Senator Barry Goldwater of Arizona, a deeply anticommunist conservative. Johnson's handling of the crisis seemed firm but measured, and plainly in tune with public opinion. Goldwater's calls for sharper escalation sounded reckless by comparison. The contrast surely contributed to the president's landslide victory in November.

Over the next few years, versions of a joking lament would circulate in Republican ranks: "They told me if I voted for Goldwater we'd end up fighting in Vietnam. Well, I voted for Goldwater and that's what happened." Indeed, no sooner had Johnson won the election than he began rapidly expanding the US role in the conflict. This escalation had been planned months earlier, but its immediate catalyst was a series of lethal NLF attacks on South Vietnamese and US military bases in late 1964 and early 1965. Reinforcing the case for escalation was Hanoi's decision, in September 1964, to begin infiltrating units of the regular North Vietnamese Army (NVA) into the South. In March 1965, the United States launched a sustained aerial bombing campaign against North Vietnam called Operation Rolling Thunder; it would continue for the next three years. Meanwhile, Johnson increased the number of American troops stationed in South Vietnam, especially at the airbase at Da Nang, in northern South Vietnam, from which most Rolling Thunder raids originated. (In a self-perpetuating cycle, US bombing raids provoked NVA and NLF attacks on airbases, which now needed protection by US ground forces; attacks on ground forces, in turn, begot stepped-up US air raids.) By April 1965 over 30,000 US soldiers were in South Vietnam, and more were on the way. Their relaxed rules of engagement now permitted offensive operations against the enemy. The Johnson administration kept all of this activity as quiet as it could, hoping to avoid alarming Congress, the American public, or jumpy adversaries in Beijing and Moscow.

Despite these measures, the Saigon regime's position continued to deteriorate, and US officials increasingly feared an NVA/NLF victory. In June, the commander of US forces in South Vietnam, General William Westmoreland, requested that the 75,000 US troops then stationed in the South be immediately augmented to 125,000, with tens of thousands more deployed over the remainder of 1965. The following month, in a fateful decision, Johnson granted Westmoreland's request. The influx of so many US troops transformed the war, ensuring that the United States now bore the main responsibility for waging it.

The US aim was never to conquer North Vietnam. It was to compel it to stop supporting the NLF and to respect South Vietnam's sovereignty. From the perspective of Hanoi and the NLF, however, South Vietnam was not a separate nation enjoying sovereignty; it was a portion of Vietnam illegally occupied by a foreign power. Indeed, the 1954 Geneva Accords had stated that the 17th parallel was not an international border but merely a "provisional" military demarcation line. The United States had no legal basis for accusing North Vietnam of aggressing against the South.

Moreover, although Johnson's approach was a middle way of sorts, it was hardly free of brutality. The Americans refrained from invading the North, but they subjected it to relentless bombing, including in densely populated cities. They also massively bombed the South. By 1973, the United States had dropped over five million tons of explosives on both Vietnams. Chemical herbicides (used for clearing jungles in which enemy forces hid) destroyed crops and poisoned the soil; napalm melted human flesh. Hundreds of thousands of Vietnamese civilians would die over the next decade, tens of thousands of them in US bombing raids in which significant civilian casualties were the easily foreseeable, though not the officially intended, result.

In the South, the United States pursued a strategy extremely destructive to the fabric of village life. The main US objective was to eliminate the NVA's and the NLF's ability to fight the Saigon regime. One way to do that was simply to find and kill enemy combatants, and US officials were indeed obsessed with reaching the elusive "crossover point," when the rate at which enemy forces were removed from the battle exceeded the rate at which the NVA or the NLF could replenish them. But another way to defeat those adversaries was to destroy the local infrastructure on which they relied. When US commanders discovered that inhabitants of a village were harboring the NLF or storing food for it, a frequent response was to evacuate that village and destroy all of its dwellings and food stores. Such actions hardly endeared ordinary Vietnamese to the United States. True, the NLF committed vicious atrocities of its own against Vietnamese civilians, arousing local hostility to the insurgent cause. But such incidents also exposed the Saigon government's inability to protect its constituents and so, in that way, aided the insurgency.

The US military did not seek to hold and control all of South Vietnam's territory. The aim, rather, was to impose such heavy costs on the NVA and NLF that both forces abandoned their efforts to overrun the South. Repeatedly, US or South Vietnamese units would expel NVA or NLF fighters from a given area, only to withdraw from it days later and permit them to reoccupy it. No amount of US firepower or troop strength – and both increased markedly over the next three and a half years – could dissuade either adversary from fighting on. Although the US escalation seemed alarmingly rapid to antiwar critics at home, it was sufficiently gradual that both the North Vietnamese and the NLF had time to devise effective strategies for withstanding it. (Massive infusions of Soviet and Chinese military and logistical aid to North Vietnam also immensely benefited the NVA/NLF cause.) By early 1968, half a million US troops were in South Vietnam, with still no sign that the enemy's will was slackening.

Figure 6.1 A US marine watches residents of Lap Thuan, a village in South Vietnam, emerge from hiding, 1966. Source: Bettmann / Getty Images.

Domestic Criticism of LBJ's Vietnam Policies

For a few months after Johnson's mid-1965 decision to escalate the war, his Vietnam policy enjoyed a surge of popular support, as US military ventures typically do at first. Thereafter, public approval of the war steadily declined, and critics increasingly assailed it from all political directions. Among the earliest dissenters were young radicals, many of them university students. Since the start of the decade, a nascent, and predominantly white, left-liberal movement had flourished on college campuses, drawing major inspiration from the accelerating civil rights struggle, which revealed both the prevalence of injustice within dominant American institutions and the capacity of ordinary citizens to band together to fight back. Other major influences were the Ban the Bomb movement of the late 1950s and early 1960s, the Fair Play for Cuba Committee of the early 1960s, and Students for a Democratic Society, whose 1962 Port Huron Statement offered a sweeping, penetrating, though at times ponderous critique of American political, economic, industrial, technocratic, and educational institutions.

As early as the spring of 1965, young activists staged Vietnam "teach-ins" on a handful of university campuses. That April, an antiwar rally in Washington organized by SDS drew 25,000 people. Such events grew more numerous following the summer escalation, while still representing a tiny sliver of overall student opinion. Participants in the infant movement brought a wide range of ideological outlooks. Some were pacifists who opposed all wars; others, antiimperialists who saw the Vietnam venture as an attempt to dominate and exploit a weaker people. Still others remained in search of a satisfying analysis but were sure the war was wrong. By the standards of later antiwar activism, these protesters were orderly and respectful: clean-cut marchers carrying neatly printed signs displaying insistent but temperately worded slogans such as "GET OUT OF VIETNAM" and "OBSERVE GENEVA AGREEMENT." When events did get raucous, that was usually because hostile counterdemonstrators or enraged onlookers violently intervened. In the fall of 1965, the movement took a defiant turn as some young men started ritually burning their draft cards, an act Congress had recently made a federal offense punishable by up to five years in prison. (Even so, the first person prosecuted under the new law wore a suit for the public incineration of his card.)

Initially, mainstream reactions to this antiwar activism were extremely negative. Pundits denounced the movement as irresponsible. The Federal Bureau of Investigation, at Johnson's urging, launched a fruitless investigation to prove it was communist-controlled. By 1966, however, members of the political establishment were themselves criticizing Johnson's Vietnam policies, albeit on different grounds. In the parlance of the day, mainstream dissenters fell into two broad categories: "hawks" and "doves." Hawks, generally Republicans and conservative Democrats, strongly favored the preservation of an independent, anticommunist South Vietnam but opposed Johnson's means of pursuing that goal. They believed the war could not be won as long as Washington refused to wage it more aggressively, whether by intensifying the bombing of North Vietnam, by invading it outright, or by attacking the North's bases and supply trails in neighboring Laos and Cambodia. One prominent hawk was former Vice President Richard Nixon, who, though ostensibly retired from electoral politics, spoke out frequently on public affairs (in the service, it later turned out, of an improbable political comeback). Nixon favored stepped-up naval and air attacks against the North. Another vocal hardliner was retired Air Force General Curtis LeMay, a major architect of US bombing campaigns against Japan in World War II. In 1965, LeMay proposed telling the North Vietnamese to "stop their aggression, or we're going to bomb them back into the Stone Age." The conservative publisher and columnist William F. Buckley argued that the United States should be willing to use nuclear weapons in the conflict.

Politically, the escalation of the Vietnam War was a boon to conservative Republicans, who had suffered a crushing defeat in the 1964 election. They now had an issue around which to rally their bruised ranks and a handy club to use against liberals and leftists. Prior to 1965, a substantial number of American conservatives had been unenthusiastic about Vietnam. The general feeling on the right had been that the United States should either "win or get out," and, as it seemed unlikely that the Democrats in the White House would actually strive for victory, perhaps a pullout would be preferable to the grim and enervating status quo. But Johnson's escalation of the war in 1965 shifted the calculus; the nation had taken a stand against Hanoi and now dared not retreat. "Unpleasant as it may be," the newly formed American Conservative Union declared in the summer of 1965, "the battle line in Southeast Asia *is* Vietnam." Conservatives generally agreed and made steadfastness in Vietnam a litmus test of political virtue – a test Johnson was bound to fail as long as he declined to pulverize the North to the right's satisfaction.

Once radical antiwar protesters started taking to the streets, conservatives savaged them with undisguised relish. "I wonder," Buckley wrote in 1965 of some New York demonstrators, "how these self-conscious *boulevardiers* of protest would have fared if a platoon of American soldiers who have seen the gore in South Vietnam had parachuted down into their mincing ranks." In California in 1966, the former movie actor Ronald Reagan, a conservative Republican, ran to unseat Pat Brown, the Democratic governor. Reagan found antiwar protesters at the University of California (UC), Berkeley, whom he disparaged as "brats," "kooks," "freaks," and "the Berkeley Cong," invaluable foils in his political campaign. The point was not simply to attack the unruly students but also to castigate the liberal administrators of that public university – and, by extension, Governor Brown himself – for failing to maintain discipline on campus. In November, Reagan won by a landslide.

Doves had their own critiques of Johnson's handling of the war. Many agreed that preserving a noncommunist South Vietnam was a worthy aim but doubted it could be achieved at an acceptable cost. Continuing the war would cause too many American and Vietnamese casualties. Others argued that the Vietnamese conflict was essentially a civil war; the effort to carve out a separate South Vietnam violated the 1954 Geneva Accords, and was all the more repugnant considering the corruption and authoritarianism of the Saigon regime. Whatever their views on the war's underlying merits, virtually all doves recoiled from the growing ferocity of the US military effort – the massive bombing raids against densely populated cities, the use of napalm and chemical herbicides, the deliberate uprooting of villagers. The Johnson administration, many doves urged, should negotiate a face-saving exit from the war. Perhaps the United States could withdraw its forces from South Vietnam, leaving behind a coalition government that included the NLF. True, it would probably be only a matter of time before the South fell under Northern control, but even that would be preferable to the status quo. Prominent doves included Democratic senators Wayne Morse of Oregon and Ernest Gruening of Alaska (the two naysayers in the Gulf of Tonkin vote) and J. William Fulbright of Arkansas, chairman of the Senate Foreign Relations Committee. An initial supporter of Johnson's Vietnam policy, Fulbright turned against the war in 1966. Other war opponents were the esteemed writer and commentator Walter Lippmann and George Kennan of cold war "containment" fame.

In the civil rights community, the Americanization of the war reverberated with a special poignancy and menace. A wide swath of civil rights leaders and activists opposed Johnson's Vietnam policy on the merits, moved by the same pacifist, antiimperialist, humanitarian, and pragmatic concerns that drove other antiwar Americans. But there were particular racial dimensions to the war. The new enemies were nonwhite, and many critics detected an element of white supremacy in the ease with which US war planners sacrificed Vietnamese civilians to achieve military aims. In contrast with the traditional civil-rights-related objection to participation in America's foreign wars – why should African Americans fight for democracy abroad when denied it at home? – this more stringent critique posited a grim continuum between domestic and global racism. Moreover, it was clear that the Vietnam War would claim a huge share of the nation's treasure and attention, resources badly needed for addressing the plight of disadvantaged Americans. Finally, Black men were fighting in

Vietnam in disproportionate numbers, partly because they could not evade the draft as easily as middle-class whites could, partly because many of them had voluntarily enlisted for military service, seeing it as a rare means of escaping lives of poverty and despair. The path of opportunity now led to the killing fields.

Even so, civil rights advocates needed to tread carefully. The more established leaders, such as Martin Luther King, Roy Wilkins of the National Association for the Advancement of Colored People, and Whitney Young of the Urban League, had nurtured a fruitful alliance with President Johnson that had yielded extraordinary legislative achievements. The cooperation would surely end if they crossed him on Vietnam. A more basic danger, threatening the movement as a whole, was the potential accusation of disloyalty. For three decades, segregationists had denounced civil rights activists as procommunist subversives, a charge the FBI's J. Edgar Hoover had obsessively pursued behind the scenes. The dearth of persuasive evidence to support this claim had, by and large, kept it from becoming a potent issue in the national news media or on Capitol Hill. Would such forbearance continue if civil rights figures openly opposed the Vietnam War? And how, for that matter, would antiwar activism sit with the many African Americans who took pride in Black men's military service?

Throughout 1965 and 1966, civil rights leaders and activists tried to navigate this vexing dilemma. Wilkins and Young remained fully supportive of Johnson's policies, including the Vietnam escalation, but King abhorred the war and agonized over how to respond. In the spring and summer of 1965, he made a handful of public statements that, while avoiding criticism of Johnson himself, insisted that no military solution was possible. In August, King announced that he would write to the major powers embroiled in the conflict and urge them to settle their differences at an international conference. When, a month later, King added that the United States should recognize communist China, Johnson struck back. A torrent of criticism from the president's allies in Congress and the press, including the Black press, descended on King, instructing him to stick to civil rights and leave foreign policy to the experts. Wilkins and Young warned that antagonizing Johnson any further would be disastrous for the civil rights cause. Donors threatened to cut off support for the SCLC if the antiwar talk persisted. King was stunned by the reaction and privately admitted to aides, "I really don't have the strength to fight this issue [Vietnam] and keep my civil rights fight going." He abandoned his proposed letter-writing campaign and, for the time being, lowered the volume of his antiwar critiques.

The Student Nonviolent Coordinating Committee endured its own trial by fire over Vietnam. Throughout 1965, SNCC rank-and-file members pressed for an antiwar stance, but the national leadership hesitated to take a formal position. Though hardly shy about lambasting the US government on domestic issues, leaders feared that opposition to the war would expose the group to crippling red-baiting. In January 1966 SNCC overcame its reluctance, issuing a statement that not only denounced the war but also expressed "sympathy and support" for draft resisters. The statement provoked outrage from the mainstream media and members of Congress and stern rebukes from the NAACP and portions of the Black press. The controversy deepened when Julian Bond, SNCC's communications director, was dragged into the fray. At twenty-five, Bond had just been elected to Georgia's House of Representatives – an achievement made possible by the recently passed Voting Rights Act – and was preparing to take his seat. When a radio host asked if he endorsed SNCC's statement, Bond replied that he did. Georgia's entire political establishment loosed its fury against Bond. The lieutenant governor charged him with aiding the Kremlin; more consequentially, the Georgia House refused to seat him. The drama became a national story, and Bond, too, received a drubbing from mainstream critics, Black as well as white. King, however, forthrightly defended Bond, despite continuing pressure to steer clear of Vietnam. In December 1966, the US Supreme Court ruled that the Georgia House had violated Bond's First Amendment rights, and the young activist was finally able to take his seat.

A Transforming Civil Rights Movement

In 1966, the civil rights movement faced a more basic set of conundrums, touching on its core mission and identity. Regarding de jure discrimination in the South, the most glaring legislative needs had been met (although implementation of the new laws remained a challenge). There was broad agreement among civil rights groups that addressing de facto discrimination throughout the country had to be the next frontier. The scourges of structural unemployment, poor education, substandard housing, and police brutality clearly required immediate and sustained attention.

Still, there was no consensus over what strategies to follow, which allies to enlist, or even whom to regard as belonging to the movement. King and other established leaders remained committed to nonviolence and integration, and to preserving a productive relationship with the Johnson administration (now a tall order for anyone critical of the Vietnam War). SNCC and the Congress of Racial Equality were moving in very different directions. These two groups had been instrumental in winning the historic civil rights gains of the previous half-decade, but many of their members now found little to celebrate. The struggles for desegregation and voting rights had revealed a shocking capacity for brutality on the part of southern whites, and for indifference on the part of white Americans overall. SNCC and CORE veterans who had borne the brunt of those assaults were shedding their faith in nonviolence and integration. They were also questioning the wisdom of cultivating white allies. The Mississippi Freedom Democratic Party's painful sojourn at the 1964 Democratic Convention (see Chapter 5) was already an oft-told parable of white liberal perfidy – and even liberalism now seemed an ebbing force within the Johnson administration. Closer to home, many Black SNCC and CORE members had concluded that the presence of white activists in the movement impeded Black advancement. Coming largely from universities, the whites were more likely than their Black counterparts to possess the organizing, clerical, and communication skills needed for political work. Without necessarily intending to, they sometimes assumed an air of command or acted in ways that seemed patronizing.

There was also, among Black Americans more broadly, and especially within SNCC and CORE, a growing inclination to identify with Africa, with the African diaspora, and with other nonwhite peoples. Across the Third World, nations newly liberated from imperial domination or hoping to become so – Cuba, Algeria, Ghana, Vietnam – were challenging the global order in ways that thrilled many African Americans. During his last year of life, Malcolm X had conspicuously moved with these currents. As his stature soared in the months following his February 1965 assassination, an assertive global Black nationalism became an integral part of Malcolm's legacy. Also exerting a posthumous sway was the Caribbean anticolonial theorist Frantz Fanon, whose hugely influential book *The Wretched of the Earth*, published in 1961, the year of his death, portrayed revolutionary violence as both a geopolitical and a psychological necessity for oppressed people.

Some of these new sensibilities were showcased for the nation in a small Mississippi town in June 1966. James Meredith, who in 1962 had made national news by integrating the University of Mississippi, began a one-man march through the state to encourage voter registration. On the second day of the march, a white gunman (with unclear motives) shot and wounded Meredith, leaving him unable to continue. To show that violence could not stop the movement, King joined with Stokely Carmichael and Floyd McKissick, the heads of SNCC and CORE, respectively, to lead a new march along Meredith's intended route. In raw numbers, the James Meredith March Against Fear was a notable success. Along the way, participants registered about 4,000 Black Mississippians to vote. The marchers' ranks had swelled to 15,000 by the time they reached their destination, the capital city of Jackson. Yet the event also aired the movement's growing divisions. On the baking Mississippi highway, King openly vied with more militant activists over the direction of the movement. His calls for interracial brotherhood were met with chants of "Whitey's got to go" and "White blood will flow." When King and his followers sang "We shall overcome," SNCC members countered with their own version: "We shall overrun."

In Greenwood, Carmichael spoke before a local Black audience and took the opportunity to introduce a new rallying cry. "The only way we gonna stop them white men from whippin' us is to take over," he said. "We been saying freedom for six years and we ain't got nothin'. What we gonna start saying now is Black Power!'" Carmichael and another SNCC activist then led the crowd in a vigorous call-and-response: "What do you want?" "BLACK POWER!" "What do you want?" "BLACK POWER!"

An alarmed King persuaded Carmichael to stop using the "Black Power" slogan for the rest of the march. But the national media had picked up on the phrase, which immediately became a topic of discussion. The slogan did seem to capture the new mood of self-assertion taking hold in the Black community, but few could agree on what it meant or portended. It was a blank screen against which people of all colors and persuasions could project their fondest hopes or direst fears.

In its most positive sense, "Black Power" called on African Americans to cultivate their own strengths and value themselves for who they were. One legacy of centuries of racial domination was that many African Americans had internalized white standards of beauty and culture. Black women artificially straightened their hair, light-skinned Blacks enjoyed higher social status in the African American community, and Black Americans often dismissed Africa as backward. Black Power advocates frontally challenged such attitudes.

"It is time to stop being ashamed of being black – time to stop trying to be white," Stokely Carmichael told a Black audience in 1966. "When you see your daughter playing in the fields, with her nappy hair, her wide nose and her thick lips, tell her she is beautiful. *Tell your daughter she is beautiful.*" Embracing the slogan "Black is beautiful," more and more African Americans began expressing pride in their African features and heritage, growing out their hair in "Afro" styles, wearing dashikis and other African garments, sometimes taking African or Arabic names (in recognition of Africa's extensive Islamic heritage). Black Americans had done versions of these things for decades, but never in such large numbers or with such wide national visibility. The word "Negro" steadily fell out of favor, to be replaced by "black" or "Afro-American" (both of them older terms undergoing revival). Beyond symbolism, "Black Power" signified that African Americans would be much more insistent and resourceful in demanding their political and legal rights, building their communities, and confronting police brutality and other forms of white oppression.

On the negative side, "Black Power" alarmed many whites, including some who had sympathized with the civil rights struggle. Although the slogan was not inherently violent or chauvinistic, many heard it as both, and it was occasionally accompanied by explicit appeals to violence or antiwhite sentiment. H. Rap Brown, who succeeded Carmichael as SNCC chairman in May 1967, later that summer notoriously exhorted Black audience members, "Don't be trying to love the honkey to death. Shoot him to death." White liberal financial support for SNCC and CORE began drying up. Both organizations hastened the process by deciding, in 1966 and 1967, respectively, to expel white members from their ranks. As noted, there had been legitimate concern about disproportionate white influence within the movement, but expulsion was a drastic remedy that isolated SNCC and CORE from crucial sources of support.

More broadly, from about 1966 on there was a marked decline in northern white sympathy for the civil rights movement. This was partly a reaction to the perceived excesses of Black Power, but it also reflected the fact that the movement as a whole was shifting its attention to racial conditions outside the South, especially in impoverished and overcrowded inner cities. Northern whites who may have applauded the dismantling of formal segregation in the South, at no cost to themselves, were now being asked to address racial injustices in their own communities, and many balked at the suggestion. The decrease in white sympathy only confirmed Black militants' pessimistic view of white society, heightening the polarization.

The difficulty of taking the struggle North became clear in that same summer of 1966, when King and the SCLC stepped up a campaign, begun earlier that year, to force the city of Chicago to address squalid living conditions in its slums. But Chicago was not Birmingham, and Richard Daley, Chicago's mayor, was no Bull Connor. What protesters confronted in Chicago was not blatant discrimination enforced by fire hoses and police dogs but patterns of neglect that were hard to dramatize and for which there were few obvious human culprits. Instead of assaulting the protesters, Daley professed agreement with their goals, while offering only amorphous plans for achieving them. King and other sophisticated observers knew the mayor was conceding very little, but his show of reasonableness took much of the wind out of the campaign's sails. Moreover, Daley's political machine included a number of Black aldermen, business leaders, and clergymen who treated King as an outside rabble-rouser who didn't understand how things worked in Chicago.

King and the SCLC therefore focused on a different problem: the de facto exclusion of African Americans from many sections of the city. Black Chicagoans who could afford to buy homes in white middle-class neighborhoods faced enormous obstacles. Realtors refused to show houses in those areas; homeowners refused to sell; if a Black family did manage to purchase a home, it could be shunned, harassed, and even attacked by white neighbors. The injustice was replicated in cities across the country. To protest it, activists marched through all-white neighborhoods in southwest Chicago, provoking extremely hostile, and sometimes violent, reactions from residents. Many of these neighborhoods were home to working-class and lower-middle-class "white ethnics," people of Italian, Lithuanian, Polish, and other Eastern European backgrounds who decades earlier had themselves lived in urban poverty. Having relocated to more affluent settings, many feared that African Americans would bring the problems of the inner city into all-white neighborhoods or cause property values in those neighborhoods to decline. Some residents, greeting the marchers with racial epithets, Confederate flags, and even swastikas, were plainly moved by cruder impulses. "I think the people of Mississippi ought to come to Chicago to learn how to hate," King dryly remarked. Although the marches did vividly expose the problem of white hostility, they aroused little sympathy from northern whites, many of whom felt that King and his supporters were simply looking for trouble. Meanwhile, African Americans throughout the nation were outraged by what they had seen. Here was further evidence that whites would never treat them as equals.

Toward the end of the summer, the SCLC scaled back its campaign in exchange for a vague pledge by Daley to address the problems of Black Chicagoans. But the promise contained no timetable for implementation and was widely seen as offering little more than a face-saving exit for King. "Northern Jim Crow," writes the historian Thomas Sugrue, "… was more deeply entrenched and more difficult to uproot than King had ever imagined." The minister had lost a bit of his optimism, but not his determination to carry the struggle to all parts of the country.

As King's northern campaign faltered, other figures emerged to combat racial injustice in urban America. In the fall of 1966, Huey Newton and Bobby Seale, two community college students in Oakland, California, formed the Black Panther Party for Self-Defense (BPP). The Panthers boldly challenged excessive police violence. They followed the police as they cruised through Black neighborhoods and photographed them as they made arrests, often carrying guns themselves. Although BPP members did not initially fire their weapons, the specter of armed Black men fearlessly confronting white policemen deeply impressed African Americans victimized by police brutality, first in Oakland and later in cities across the country. Unlike some other Black Power groups, the BPP was not separatist. It professed solidarity with American radicals of other races and with liberation movements throughout the Third World. Black Americans themselves, the Panthers claimed, were a colonized people whom they would help to liberate, though precisely how they would do this remained unclear. The Panthers also provided social services to needy Black communities, most famously through a free breakfast program for poor children. It was their violent revolutionary rhetoric, however, that seemed most salient to local, state, and federal authorities. By 1967, law enforcement officers at all three levels were aggressively monitoring, infiltrating, and attempting to sabotage the BPP, setting the stage for later bloody confrontations.

Black anger was also taking less organized forms. In every summer from 1964 through 1968, violent riots erupted in American cities, usually growing out of Black residents' altercations with police. Two of the worst riots occurred in the summer of 1967 in Newark, New Jersey, and Detroit, Michigan. In the latter instance, forty-three people died, and President Johnson eventually sent the US Army's 82nd and 101st Airborne Divisions into Michigan to help quell the violence. (A decade earlier in Little Rock, Arkansas, the 101st Airborne had protected Black high school students from white mobs.) The riots angered and alarmed many white Americans, strengthening the conviction that the solution to America's race problem was not fuller justice for African Americans but greater respect for law and order.

Intensifying Protests and a Rising Counterculture

Through it all, Johnson kept escalating the war. By the summer of 1967, about 450,000 US troops were in Vietnam, and over 13,000 Americans had died there. The war's economic costs – around $21 billion in 1967 – were straining the federal budget. Partly to offset the military spending, and partly reflecting diminishing public support for government efforts to aid the poor, Congress had begun chipping away at the War on Poverty. Its 1967 appropriation for the Office of Economic Opportunity, the federal government's chief poverty-fighting agency, was $1.6 billion, less than half the $3.5 billion the OEO had requested. In August 1967, in a further effort to make budgetary ends meet, Johnson asked Congress to levy a 10 percent surcharge on individual and corporate taxes. Congress eventually granted the request, but only after imposing further cuts in social spending. In July 1967, a Gallup poll revealed for the first time that a majority of Americans, 52 percent, opposed Johnson's Vietnam policies. Behind the scenes, some liberal activists were trying to recruit a leading dove to challenge Johnson for the Democratic Party nomination in 1968. As of late summer, however, no Democrat of stature seemed willing to take on the president.

Radical antiwar protesters were growing much angrier and more confrontational, frustrated by their inability to alter Johnson's behavior. The urban riots that summer only compounded their sense of futility. Many white leftists viewed the disturbances as political uprisings; they longed to take part in them but didn't know how. "To be white and radical in America this summer," wrote the radical journalist Andrew Kopkind, "is to see horror and feel impotence. It is to watch the war and know no way to stop it, to understand the black rebellion and find no way to join it." Profanity had begun appearing on antiwar protesters' signs. A chant first heard in late 1965 – "Hey, hey, LBJ, how many kids did you kill today?" – was now a staple at rallies. Some demonstrators waved NLF flags, and it had become impossible for the president to speak on university campuses without being heckled. A hard core within the movement was turning toward violence. In October 1967 in

Figure 6.2 Antiwar demonstrators at the National Mall, Washington, DC, during the March on the Pentagon protest, October 1967. Source: Leif Skoogfors / Corbis Historical / Getty Images.

Washington, DC, tens of thousands of demonstrators congregated at the Lincoln Memorial and marched to the Pentagon building, headquarters of the Department of Defense (DOD). The vast majority were peaceful, but a small contingent physically clashed with soldiers and US marshals guarding the Pentagon. That same week in Oakland, throngs of militants battled with police and succeeded, for several hours, in closing down that city's military induction center. The purpose, a veteran of the Oakland action recalled, was "to make the cost of pursuing the war abroad the ungovernability of the society at home."

The antiwar movement had arisen alongside of, and was now increasingly enmeshed with, a much more basic societal and cultural rebellion. Since the previous decade, pockets of bohemianism had flourished in major cities, especially New York and San Francisco. The Beats had celebrated jazz, free-form poetry, Eastern religion, and recreational drug use. Though often apolitical in the narrow sense, they challenged the conventional work ethic and traditional strictures regarding sex, profanity, and personal grooming and deportment. Starting in the early 1960s, a host of historical circumstances allowed these sensibilities to coalesce, by mid-decade, into a much larger, bolder, and more visible counterculture. An accelerating civil rights movement frontally challenged deep-seated racial hierarchies and taboos. Horror at the nuclear arms race stirred alienation from the national government and mainstream political institutions. A liberalized federal judiciary overturned legislative bans on "indecency," permitting stronger profanity and franker depictions of sexuality, drug use, and other controversial topics to appear in print and on the screen. With the advent of the birth control pill, approved for general use in 1960 and gradually made more accessible over the next several years, heterosexual intercourse carried lower risk of unwanted pregnancy.

By the early 1960s, the baby boomers were entering their teen years. Coming of age in a time of unusual prosperity, they had higher expectations of attending college than any previous generation. Once there, they could be far more carefree and experimental. (True, these generalizations applied mainly to those who were at least middle-class, but an unprecedented share of the population, including many who were nonwhite, now enjoyed that status.) The boomers formed a huge audience and market for popular music, dance crazes, and other exuberant fads. More and more of them had televisions at home, and the other media they consumed were increasingly vivid and engaging. Records began appearing in stereo; magazines and movies were more likely to be in color. (Color television, though commercially available, did not become widespread until the early 1970s.) As never before, young people had the time, means, and inclination to postpone the responsibilities of breadwinning and seek experiences that were pleasurable, exciting, or otherwise personally fulfilling.

Enter LSD. Concocted in a Swiss laboratory in the late 1930s, and legal in the United States until 1966, lysergic acid diethylamide was the very definition of a mind-altering drug. In the words of the historian Alice Echols, it "opened up the mind to that flood of stimuli that the brain under normal functioning reduces to a manageable trickle." People ingesting the stuff sometimes felt as if they were comprehending all of creation in an instant. In a cosmic irony, LSD came to America through the portal of the national security state. Since the early 1950s, the CIA had explored the drug's potential as an interrogation tool, occasionally administering it to unwitting patients in federal prison hospitals. Meanwhile, the Agency awarded contracts to universities and research centers so that they, too, could test the substance's properties. In these cases, the human subjects were consenting, and many eagerly returned to be tested again … and again. Soon some of the researchers were joining in the fun. Small, knowing communities of the initiated sprang up on the placid campuses of fifties America.

In the early 1960s, a guru emerged on each coast to share the secret more widely. A Harvard clinical psychologist named Timothy Leary became such a single-minded evangelist for LSD that the university fired him for violating proper research and teaching practices. Leary founded a psychedelic commune in upstate New York and began touring the country with a sound-and-light show to propagate his mantra, "Turn on, tune in, drop out." In Palo Alto, California, a Stanford University graduate student named Ken Kesey got turned on when, to earn extra money, he volunteered for drug experiments at a local Veteran's Administration hospital. His consciousness forever altered, Kesey wrote *One Flew Over the Cuckoo's Nest* (1962), a bestselling novel set in a psychiatric hospital. In the summer of 1964, he and a group of friends calling themselves the Merry Pranksters daubed an old school bus in multicolored Day-Glo paint and embarked on a rambling, chemically enhanced journey across America, including the Deep South – time travelers from 1967 on a magical mystery tour through Goldwater Country. After returning to the Bay Area, Kesey and the Pranksters staged public viewings of home movies shot on their road trip. These events morphed into the Acid Tests, outdoor festivals whose zonked-out attendees gyrated to the accompaniment of swirling light shows and improvisational rock music, the latter courtesy of a local band called the Grateful Dead.

Partly nourished by the Acid Tests, in 1966 a distinct "hippie" scene took root in the Haight–Ashbury neighborhood of nearby San Francisco. Hippies resembled Beats but were hairier, druggier, and more visually striking. They wore army fatigues, mix-and-match period costumes, tie-dyed T-shirts, flowers, feathers, and beads. Local merchants in "the Haight" decorated their storefronts with vibrant pop-art posters and hawked records, incense, exotic fabrics, tarot cards, and books on astrology and Eastern philosophy. In the spring of 1967, the mainstream media discovered the San Francisco hippies, creating a nationwide buzz that spurred tens of thousands of curious young people, including teenage runaways, to flock to the city that summer. For some, the ballyhooed "Summer of Love" was indeed an ecstatic awakening. For many others, it became a dreary and squalid scene, as scores of uprooted youngsters fell prey to drug overdose, bad trips, sexual exploitation, street crime, pneumonia, hepatitis, venereal disease, and psychological distress. Hippiedom quickly lost most of its allure to San Franciscans, but it remained a captivating spectacle from afar. Elements of the new sensibility cropped up in communities around the country.

Of course, only a tiny share of American youth became fully immersed in the hippie lifestyle. Yet across the United States, especially but not only in urban and college settings, more and more young people adopted aspects of the counterculture. Their attire grew more casual, their hair longer and more unkempt; for young men, facial hair was increasingly common. Although systematic data on drug use did not become available until the late 1960s, some analysts estimate that, whereas just 4 percent of Americans aged eighteen-to-twenty-five had tried marijuana in 1962, 13 percent had done so by 1967. Two years later, a Gallup survey found that 22 percent of college students had smoked pot. LSD use was much rarer, though, registering only 4 percent in the 1969 survey. The experience of taking both drugs was introspective and observational; under their influence, once familiar words, thoughts, sights, sounds, and other sensations might be perceived as if for the first time. Rock musicians catered to the druggy sensibility and pushed it to new limits. Established bands such as the Beatles, the Rolling Stones, the Beach Boys, and the Who, along with newer acts like Jefferson Airplane, the Grateful Dead, the Mothers of Invention, and the Jimi Hendrix Experience, released experimental albums featuring aural tapestries that simulated hallucination and contained sly references to illicit drug use. (The Beatles' 1967 song "Lucy in the Sky with Diamonds" achieved the latter in its title – LSD, get it? – and the former in its intricate, surreal, and shimmery content.)

The counterculture carried a pervasive, if inchoate, political message: in favor of peace, togetherness, authenticity, irreverence, harmony with nature, and the pursuit of pleasure; opposed to a violent, wasteful, phony, mendacious, and self-destructive reigning order. In the popular music of the 1950s and early 1960s (with the important exception of religious genres), "love" had invariably referred only to romance – ostensibly of the chaste variety, though often with clear sexual overtones. By the second half of the sixties, the word continued to convey that meaning, but it could also evoke broader social bonds. "Come on, people, now," sang the Youngbloods in 1967, "smile on your brother/Everybody get together, try to love one another right now." The popular slogan "Make love not war" cleverly captured both the pleasure-seeking and the socially conscious prongs of the new philosophy.

Inevitably, the hippie ethos took hold in the radical antiwar movement, whose efforts were increasingly freewheeling and anarchic. In late 1966, at the end of a student antiwar organizing meeting at UC Berkeley, someone started to sing the old trade union standard "Solidarity forever" – and then everyone switched to the Beatles' "Yellow submarine." "Again, it's difficult to explain," a scraggly-bearded activist in a black Lone Ranger mask deadpanned to a baffled reporter. "It's a sort of – it's an understanding that we're banding together in a yellow submarine, and that it represents a new way of looking at life." In the lead-up to the Washington protest in October 1967, some organizers announced that a "flower power contingent" would perform a public "exorcism" of the Pentagon, causing the massive building to levitate three hundred feet in the air, and that other demonstrators would "fuck on the grass" of the city's parks and "piss, piss, piss" at the White House. If any of these events actually transpired, they went unrecorded. Yet flower power did reign in the form of a ubiquitous photograph of a mop-headed youth placing a carnation in the gun barrel of a Pentagon guard.

Meanwhile, in the antiwar movement's more sedate precincts, the "dump Johnson" Democrats had secretly recruited a standard bearer: Senator Eugene McCarthy of Minnesota, who in late November formally announced his candidacy for the party's presidential nomination. Initially, McCarthy's campaign failed to catch fire, largely because McCarthy himself was a cerebral and aloof figure who disdained emoting from the stump. The turbulent events of the New Year would dramatically transform the electoral contest – and much, much else.

The Tet Offensive and Johnson's Retreat

In late January 1968, the NVA and the NLF launched a major, coordinated offensive throughout South Vietnam. Because it coincided with the Vietnamese New Year, Tet, the campaign became known as the Tet Offensive. Over the next several weeks, NVA/NLF forces attacked over a hundred cities and towns, including Saigon and most of the provincial capitals, and even briefly occupied the grounds of the US embassy. Militarily, the Tet Offensive was a severe defeat for the NVA and NLF. They were eventually ousted from the strongholds they had seized and suffered enormous casualties. But the fact that the offensive occurred at all eroded morale within the US military and caused even more Americans back home to question the wisdom of the war. In the closing months of 1967, the Johnson administration had mounted a public relations drive to make the case that the war effort had turned a corner and was now heading toward victory. Tet demonstrated that, if kept on its current course, the conflict would drag on for years to come. The overall tenor of American news coverage, and the explicit content of commentary, became markedly more skeptical and pessimistic.

A series of striking vignettes from the Tet Offensive seemed to encapsulate the futility, brutality, and absurdity of the war: the sight of marines and armed embassy employees, the latter in civilian clothes, waging a fierce gun battle to take back the diplomatic compound; horrifying footage of Saigon's police chief raising his pistol to the temple of a captured NLF guerrilla and pulling the trigger; the remark of a US Army major following the brutal recapture of the South Vietnamese city of Ben Tre: "It became necessary to destroy the town to save it." (In popular renderings of the quotation, "town" was often changed to "village," perhaps to accentuate the power imbalance between the US military and Vietnamese civilians.) Five decades later, another chilling incident would come to light. In February 1968, to break the NVA's siege of a US Marine garrison near the South Vietnamese city of Khe Sanh (an engagement that started before the Tet Offensive and continued alongside it), General Westmoreland activated plans to transfer nuclear weapons to South Vietnam for possible use against the NVA. Johnson rescinded the move as soon as he learned of it.

Public dismay over the war energized Eugene McCarthy's lackluster presidential effort. As many as 3,000 college students flocked to his campaign, which was preparing to compete in New Hampshire's primary election. The scruffier among them trimmed their hair, shaved off their beards, and donned more conventional clothing – going "clean for Gene," the metamorphosis was called – before venturing out to knock on doors in the cities and towns of the Granite State. The primary took place on March 12. Although McCarthy did not win the election, he did far better than expected, receiving 42 percent of the vote to Johnson's 49 percent – a stunning moral defeat for the incumbent president. Not all of the McCarthy voters were doves; many thought the Vietnam War was being waged with insufficient vigor, and some may even have mistaken him for the late Joseph McCarthy, the anticommunist crusader of the previous decade. But the election results did show that Johnson was beatable, which was hopeful news for the war's opponents.

In mid-March Robert F. Kennedy – younger brother of President Kennedy, former attorney general, and now senator from New York – announced that he, too, would seek the Democratic nomination. An early supporter of the Vietnam War, Bobby Kennedy had recently swung sharply against it. Until the surprise in New Hampshire, however, he had assumed that Johnson was a shoo-in for renomination. If Kennedy's entry into the race annoyed the McCarthy camp, it caused deep consternation in the White House, whose chief occupant had long feared and hated Bobby. Sentiments aside, with his name, wealth, executive branch experience, and personal tenacity, Kennedy seemed a much stronger contender for Johnson's job than McCarthy. The president was feeling ever more besieged.

From South Vietnam, meanwhile, Westmoreland had asked for another 206,000 US troops, over and above the 535,000 already deployed. Such an infusion, he claimed, would enable the US military to exploit the disarray in the enemies' ranks following their failed offensive. Although some Johnson administration officials favored granting Westmoreland's request, many others argued that the current course was unsustainable, even with a massive troop surge. On March 22, Johnson formally rejected the request. A few days later, seeking broader guidance on the war, he met with a group of outside advisers (some of them officials from previous Democratic administrations) known as the Wise Men. Although they, too, were divided, the predominant view was that the preservation of a noncommunist South Vietnam was probably not achievable at an acceptable cost. Moreover, some Wise Men warned, the Johnson administration's preoccupation with Vietnam was raising doubts in the international community about the stability of US global leadership and even the soundness of the dollar. "[W]e must begin to take steps to disengage," urged former secretary of state Dean Acheson.

Johnson initially bridled at such pessimism, but he quickly concluded that there was little alternative to deescalation. In a televised address on March 31, he announced a partial bombing halt of North Vietnam and Washington's readiness for immediate negotiations with Hanoi. Johnson had by no means abandoned his goal of preserving a noncommunist South Vietnam, but he was ending the strategy of steady escalation. He now hoped that South Vietnamese forces could assume a larger share of the military burden, which the crushing of the Tet Offensive had rendered more manageable. The next president would call that policy "Vietnamization."

Johnson closed his speech with a stunning declaration. The quest for peace was far too important to be buffeted by partisan winds, he said. "Accordingly, I shall not seek, and I will not accept, the nomination of my party for another term as your president." Johnson's disavowal threw American politics into turmoil. The Democratic nomination was now truly up for grabs, along with the future direction of US Vietnam policy. (In another, smaller surprise, in early April North Vietnam accepted Johnson's offer to negotiate.) Antiwar activists of all stripes experienced a surge of euphoria. For many Americans who had recently despaired for their country's politics, the days following Johnson's March 31 speech – and really it would be just days – were a time of genuine hopefulness.

King in Winter

Watching the speech on television during a visit to Washington, DC, Martin Luther King shared in the rare optimism. Perhaps the nation finally could extricate itself from Johnson's disastrous war, which had become increasingly central to King's activism. A year earlier, after months of relatively muted protests, King had resumed his strong criticism of the war, calling it a moral abomination that precluded social justice at home while ravaging Vietnam. Indeed, his antiwar rhetoric by 1967 was far sterner than it had been 1965. The United States, he charged in an April 1967 speech, was "the greatest purveyor of violence in the world today." As in 1965, King's Vietnam stance drew sharp criticism from mainstream commentators and the civil rights "old guard." A livid Johnson made sure that liberal politicians saw salacious FBI reports of King's extramarital trysts. But by now, at least, a much larger antiwar movement existed to welcome and amplify the minister's calls for peace.

The racial politics of 1967–1968 were far bleaker for King. Most American whites, it seemed, wanted to wash their hands of the civil rights issue, whereas much of Black America was growing more militant. King's national popularity had significantly declined since its peak in 1964, most of the downturn attributable to growing white hostility. King himself was moving steadily leftward. He never lost faith in nonviolence and interracial solidarity. Just the opposite: he now called for a peaceful though radical reordering of the nation's priorities that lifted the downtrodden of all races out of poverty and hopelessness. This meant enormous federal investments in housing, education, job creation, and welfare, requiring a dramatic redistribution of the nation's wealth. King knew the "powers that be" had no interest in such a transformation. Change would come only through a massive civil disobedience campaign, far more relentless and coercive than anything previously tried. Of course, the effort had to be wholly nonviolent. Rather than rioting, King argued, protesters should seek "[t]o dislocate the functioning of a city without destroying it" (a fitting response, perhaps, to a system that would destroy a Vietnamese town in order to save it). Repeat that dislocation in a score of cities, and maybe the establishment would give some ground.

In this frame of mind, in late 1967 King and the SCLC began organizing the Poor People's Campaign. Starting in the spring of 1968, thousands of poor Americans of all races and ethnicities were to converge on Washington, DC, set up camp, and demand bolder federal action to address poverty. The plan called for a series of progressively coercive tactics – filling jails, disrupting government agencies, boycotting industries, physically occupying factories to prevent them from operating – until Congress and the president acceded to the campaign's demands.

In March 1968, in the midst of planning the Poor People's Campaign, King agreed to support a strike by mostly Black sanitation workers in Memphis, Tennessee. The garbage collectors, who labored under dangerous and miserable conditions for paltry wages, sought the city government's recognition of their union. They pleaded with the minister to lend publicity to their cause. So King went to Memphis, assuring his aides that this would be but a brief detour from preparations for the Poor People's Campaign (and in some ways a dry run for the Washington action). A protest rally he led in downtown Memphis on March 28 went disastrously wrong. Militants in the crowd smashed store windows and clashed with police, leading to a riot that left one dead and sixty injured. Mainstream critics, including some Black commentators, denounced King as a dangerous agitator who deliberately or heedlessly left chaos in his wake. When King was quoted after the debacle as saying that riots had become a fact of life in the United States, the African American columnist A. S. "Doc" Young accused him of shrugging off the tragedy. "What a terribly-horrible thing for the champion of non-violence to say!" Young wrote. "Did Mahatma Gandhi ever cop out like that?" In fact, King was distraught over the violence, and he vowed to return to Memphis to lead an entirely peaceful march. Everything seemed to ride on the fulfillment of that pledge: King's self-respect, the Poor People's Campaign, and the future of nonviolence as both a tactic and a way of life.

On April 4, 1968, while standing on the second-floor balcony of his Memphis hotel, King was shot dead by a sniper. He was just thirty-nine. The man later arrested for his murder was a white escaped convict named James Earl Ray, driven either by his own animus against King or by promises of money from others so motivated. Black Americans reacted with shock, grief, rage, and despair. Although some in the community had soured on King's leadership, no other figure in African American life commanded such widespread respect or had the ability to work productively with so many different factions. King had passionately disagreed with others in the struggle but had turned his back on none. A wave of violent riots swept the country, the worst of them in Washington, DC. Over forty people lost their lives nationwide. Federal troops were deployed in the nation's capital and in several other major cities.

In the wake of these upheavals, Congress hastily finalized passage of the Fair Housing Act, which prohibited racial discrimination in the sale or rental of real estate. The law benefited African Americans who could afford to move into middle-class white neighborhoods but did little for those in poverty. In a sign of the times, the act also made it a felony to cross state lines to encourage or participate in a riot. This was the last major civil rights legislation of the decade.

The 1968 Rebellion Abroad and at Home

In numerous countries in 1968, the established order came under sharp, often violent challenge by youthful rebellions. Some of these uprisings focused on the Vietnam War and other US policies; some reflected more local grievances. But the simultaneity of these events, and the fact that their participants could see and communicate with each other in real time – combined, as well, with the velocity, scale, and intensity of the cascading revolts – caused some to hope, and others to fear, that a worldwide revolution was at hand. Even when activists did not expect the outright overturning of the existing order, they were more inclined than ever before to see their protests as part of a global drama.

In April, hundreds of radical students and local Black Power activists occupied several buildings of New York's Columbia University and briefly held some administrators hostage, to protest the school's involvement in military research and its imperious relationship with adjacent Black neighborhoods. For a week, Columbia was both a laboratory and an international showcase of communal living and participatory democracy. The action inspired similar protests on campuses around the country and coincided with antiwar demonstrations in Paris, Rome, Venice, Prague, Tokyo, and other cities. The Paris events fed into a massive rebellion throughout France in May, as students and factory workers, revolting in tandem, nearly toppled the national government.

In Czechoslovakia, a sort of sanctioned uprising was under way. A reformist government, in power since January, had relaxed censorship and other forms of repression. The result was an outpouring of literary, artistic, and political criticism of official abuses under the pro-Soviet regime, along with an efflorescence of hippie-like youth culture. Western observers were fascinated; how much of this would Moscow tolerate? Not much, it turned out. In August, a Soviet invasion force stamped out the "Prague Spring," albeit with far less bloodshed than had been visited on the Hungarian uprising of 1956.

A much deadlier crackdown occurred in Mexico City. In early October, about 10,000 student-led demonstrators gathered in a public plaza to protest government repression. As if to prove the dissenters' point, military and police forces viciously attacked the assembly, killing as many as three hundred. The Mexican government concealed the extent of the massacre, anxious to avoid unfavorable publicity as it prepared to host the 1968 Olympic Games. Only decades later would a fuller picture emerge, and even today much remains unknown.

Back in the United States, the Black Panthers were no longer simply brandishing their weapons. A series of shootouts with the police, involving, most prominently, BPP cofounder Huey Newton in October 1967 and the group's minister of information Eldridge Cleaver in April 1968, had the paradoxical effects of crippling the party while transforming its leaders into heroes of the global left. Newton went to prison, and the demand for his release became an international *cause célèbre*. Cleaver avoided jail by fleeing to Cuba and then Algeria, acquiring the cachet of a political exile. For the remainder of the decade, both men enjoyed iconic status but were severely hampered in their efforts to lead the organization, all the more so because they bitterly disagreed over strategy. Whereas Cleaver advocated close, operational alliances with North Vietnam, North Korea, and other Marxist states, Newton preferred a looser form of Third World identification. Over the same period, ruthless police raids and deadly skirmishes with rival Black Power groups – or between feuding factions of the BPP – further weakened the party.

By 1968, members of other racial and ethnic minorities, often following the examples of the civil rights movement and Black Power, were mounting their own urgent protests. For decades, the struggle for Mexican American civil rights and economic advancement had been dominated by moderate, assimilationist organizations such as the League of United Latin American Citizens (LULAC). Established Mexican American leaders had touted the industriousness, civic-mindedness, and patriotism of their community, placing special emphasis on the military service of young Mexican American men. By the early 1960s, however, more assertive figures were coming to the fore. In California's Central Valley, César Chávez and Dolores Huerta formed the United Farm Workers of America (UFW) to represent harshly exploited Mexican American and Filipino American agricultural laborers. In 1965, the UFW joined an existing strike against California grape growers and soon became its main organizer; the effort continued until 1970, when the growers reluctantly recognized the union. Admirers of Mohandas Gandhi and Martin Luther King, Chávez and Huerta staged marches, hunger strikes, and other nonviolent protests to call attention to their cause. Often carrying banners of Our Lady of Guadalupe, a representation of the Virgin Mary historically associated with Mexican independence and with poor Mexicans' struggles for justice, the Mexican American strikers placed a distinct ethnic and cultural stamp on the movement. Robert Kennedy, a member of the Senate Subcommittee on Migratory Labor, strongly supported the UFW, considerably raising its national profile. In March 1968, just days before announcing his presidential run, Kennedy traveled to Delano, California, to celebrate mass with Chávez, his fellow devout Catholic, as the latter broke a twenty-five-day protest fast.

A week earlier, in an unrelated action, more than a thousand Mexican American students at Lincoln High School in East Los Angeles walked out of their classes. Inspired and organized by Sal Castro, a Mexican American teacher at the school, the students protested deficient facilities, overcrowded classrooms, low expectations by faculty and administrators, and

Figure 6.3 Senator Robert F. Kennedy with United Farm Workers of America leader César Chávez as the latter ends a twenty-five-day protest fast, Delano, California, 1968. Source: Bettmann / Getty Images.

a curriculum that barely acknowledged their Mexican background. Over the coming weeks, similar "blowouts," as they were called, occurred in other high schools in the Los Angeles area, and eventually across the American Southwest. "HOW CAN THEY EXPECT TO TEACH US IF THEY DO NOT KNOW US?" a group of LA students asked in a joint statement. Some college students in California staged walkouts of their own. The blowouts, which gained national attention, eventually yielded modest reforms in some LA public schools, which instituted bilingual programs, hired more Mexican American teachers, counselors, and administrators, and began better preparing Mexican American students for college. The protests also dovetailed with a broader transformation in ethnic and racial consciousness taking hold in the late 1960s, as more and more Mexican Americans, now calling themselves "Chicanos," rejected assimilation into the Anglo-dominated society, affirmed their Mexican heritage, and embraced their identity as dark-skinned descendants of indigenous people. Recently formed groups such as the LA-based Brown Berets, modeled after the Black Panthers, and the Texas-based Mexican American Youth Organization (MAYO) gave voice to the new Chicano sensibility, challenging the dominance of LULAC and other established organizations.

Although many Mexican Americans opposed the Vietnam War, that issue would not become central to Chicano activism until late 1969 and 1970. Pride in military service remained a powerful cultural force in the community, even within left-leaning groups.

Moreover, because Mexican Americans continued to serve in uniform at disproportionate levels, many Chicano activists had brothers or cousins deployed in South Vietnam. At a national Chicano conference held in San Antonio, Texas, in January 1968, officers of MAYO, the chief organizer of the event, physically ejected two participants who tried to push through a peace resolution. The conference proceedings noted that Mexican Americans' high casualty rates in Vietnam refuted "insensitive and stupid people who entertain any doubts as to our loyalty to citizenship and to our country." At this time, Chicano activists were mainly concerned with poverty, poor housing, substandard education, police brutality, the pervasiveness of Anglo supremacy, and the need to instill among Mexican Americans, and Americans generally, a greater appreciation of Chicano culture and achievements.

All the same, Chicanos did join with other activists of color to create a new, globally oriented mode of radical activism. By the second half of the 1960s, the celebration of Third World revolutionaries was a familiar feature of American leftist discourse. The notion that Americans themselves might be part of the Third World was less common, but the upheavals of 1968 gave it wider currency. Following the lead of the BPP and other Black Power groups, radical Chicano, Puerto Rican, Asian American, and Arab American organizations became more prone to identify their struggles with Third World liberation movements, especially those challenging the US-dominated world order.

In the fall of 1968, a multiracial Third World Liberation Front (TWLF) made national news by launching what turned into a months-long strike at San Francisco State College. The TWLF demanded the creation of an ethnic studies program, the implementation of stalled plans for a Black studies program, and increased enrollment for minority students. The most active groups within the coalition were the Black Student Union and a set of Asian American student groups whose members, rather like young Chicano activists, chafed against the accommodationism of their elders. (The name of one of the component groups, Free University for Chinatown Kids, Unincorporated, yielded an acronym well suited to the new mood.) The TWLF eventually won versions of its demands, but not before making a conservative hero out of the college's acting president, Samuel Ichiye ("S. I.") Hayakawa, who single-handedly shut down a TWLF rally by climbing onto a sound truck and yanking the wires from a loudspeaker, delighting members of the public fed up with noisy protesters of all backgrounds. (A Canadian-born Japanese American who had written a column for a Black newspaper and who famously sported a tam-o'-shanter, Hayakawa was himself an intriguing study in ethnicity. In the late 1970s and early 1980s, he would serve a single term as a Republican senator from California.)

The 1968 Presidential Election

Amid all this turmoil, Americans still needed to pick their next president. Throughout the spring of 1968, Gene McCarthy and Bobby Kennedy continued to seek the Democratic nomination, vying with each other and with Johnson's handpicked successor, Vice President Hubert Humphrey. McCarthy and Kennedy went head to head in a series of state primaries.

Humphrey, enjoying the support of the Democratic establishment, focused on nonprimary states, where party leaders could round up delegates on his behalf. Of the three candidates, Kennedy aroused the most excitement, attracting huge, adoring, and sometimes frenzied crowds to his rallies. Although many were simply reacting to the Kennedy name, the candidate himself had qualities of sincerity, empathy, intensity, and vulnerability that drew millions of voters to him. Since mid-decade, Kennedy had not only turned against the Vietnam War but also become passionately committed to combating racism and poverty, stances that won him strong support from African Americans and other minorities. At the same time, Kennedy retained his appeal among white blue-collar Democrats, many of whom had come to oppose federal policies on behalf of minorities and the poor. Here, then, was a candidate who seemed capable of bridging a widening, and damaging, divide in the Democratic coalition.

In early June, shortly after Kennedy won California's primary, a young Palestinian immigrant named Sirhan Sirhan shot and killed the victorious candidate in a Los Angeles hotel. Sirhan had been angered by Kennedy's calls for arming the state of Israel, whose creation had made him a refugee at the age of four, though the gunman also showed signs of mental disturbance. Coming just two months after King's assassination, the killing of Kennedy deepened the anguish and despair enveloping opponents of the Vietnam War. Much as King had done for the Black freedom movement, Kennedy had represented for many antiwar activists the last, best hope of achieving change by working within the system. For it was now clear that McCarthy lacked the personal qualities to draw Kennedy's supporters to his banner. He seemed merely to be going through the motions of running for president, and many wondered if he even wanted the job. Little stood in the way of Humphrey's nomination.

At the Democratic Convention in Chicago in August, Humphrey did receive the party's nod, but the event was a fiasco that damaged him for the general election. As delegates bitterly argued over Vietnam policy on the convention floor, Chicago police and antiwar demonstrators faced off in the city's streets and parks. Many activists had indeed come to foment violence, but the police made no effort to distinguish them from peaceful protesters and bystanders. Cops plowed through crowds, swinging billy clubs, firing tear gas, throwing people into paddy wagons and even through plate glass windows. A federal commission later concluded that such assaults amounted to a "police riot." Mayor Daley, whose authoritarian governance had more or less guaranteed this repressive spectacle, brooked no criticism of Chicago law enforcement. "The policeman isn't there to create disorder," he said at a press conference. "The policeman is there to *preserve* disorder." Pundits chortled at the malapropism, but things looked different to members of the public alarmed by rising crime rates, urban riots, and disruptive antiwar protests. In a Harris survey, 66 percent of respondents approved of Daley's use of the police during the Chicago disturbances, while only 14 percent thought the demonstrators' rights had been violated.

Earlier that August, the Republicans held their own convention in Miami Beach, Florida, and nominated former Vice President Nixon. It was a stunning comeback for the California politician. Pundits had written his political obituary back in 1962, when, following his defeat in the 1960 presidential election, he had run for governor of California and lost that race, too. But the Nixon of 1968 was a seasoned pro who had methodically studied and learned from his political failures. He assailed the Democrats' disastrous performance in Vietnam, pledging that, if elected, he would "end the war and win the peace." When asked to explain how he would do these things, Nixon begged off. Any such discussion, he said, would jeopardize the US–North Vietnamese negotiations, which had begun in Paris that May. Nixon had found a way to criticize Johnson's Vietnam policy while evading the obligation of proposing one of his own – and to appear statesmanlike in the process. (Some journalists reported that Nixon claimed to have a "secret plan" to end the war. The candidate never used that phrase, but he didn't dispute the quotation, either, probably because he liked the reassuring message it conveyed.) Nixon also charged that the Democrats had failed to uphold "law and order" at home, as evidenced by urban riots and angry antiwar protests (with events in Chicago furnishing a fresh exhibit for the case).

There was a third-party candidate that year: former Alabama Governor George Wallace. In the campaign's final weeks, the scrappy upstart with the slicked-back hair was a frequent presence on TV newscasts. Wallace had won fame earlier in the decade by violently resisting desegregation. But his appeal in 1968, especially outside the South, transcended the civil rights issue. Wallace tapped a general alienation among lower-middle- and working-class whites, stemming from the disorienting political, social, and cultural changes of the 1960s. In pungent populist terms, he lambasted Washington politicians, federal judges, government bureaucrats, university professors, and especially young protesters. These were Nixon's foils, too, but there was an important difference between the two candidates. Nixon spoke for middle-class respectability. Exploiting voters' yearning for a return to tranquility, he projected an air of mastery and calm. Wallace was the candidate of white blue-collar resentment. He channeled the impulse to lash out against the forces of change. Wallace's rallies typically attracted young hecklers, and the candidate loved to bait them from the podium. When they cursed him, he retorted, "You young people seem to know a lot of four-letter words. But I have two four-letter words you don't know: S-O-A-P and W-O-R-K." "Come up here after I've completed my speech," he would taunt, "and I'll autograph your sandals for you."

In late September Wallace was polling at 21 percent, an impressive feat for a third-party candidate. But soon thereafter his star faded, as voters wearied of the chaos surrounding his campaign, or simply concluded they would be better off supporting a major-party candidate with an actual shot at victory. Wallace also damaged his cause through his choice of running mate, the aforementioned uber-hawk General Curtis LeMay. At his first – and last – press conference as a vice-presidential candidate, LeMay confidently proclaimed, "I don't believe the world would end if we exploded a nuclear weapon" in Vietnam. The general then praised the impact of nuclear radiation on the natural environment of the South Pacific, where the United States had tested hydrogen bombs in the 1950s. Why, the rats on Bikini Atoll were "bigger, fatter, and healthier than they ever were before." Even for Wallace, this was too much, and he kept LeMay under wraps for the rest of the campaign. But the damage had been done, and the Alabaman's poll numbers continued to slide. On Election Day, he would receive 13.5 percent of the popular vote.

In the closing weeks of the campaign, then, the contest was essentially a two-man race between Humphrey and Nixon. As vice president, Humphrey was saddled with Johnson's

Figure 6.4 Former governor of Alabama George Wallace, 1968. Source: Bettmann / Getty Images.

Vietnam policy, which included the continued bombing of portions of North Vietnam. Humphrey's inability to separate himself from this activity kept doves from supporting his campaign, and the Democrat trailed in the polls. In late September, Humphrey finally broke with Johnson and called for a cessation of bombing throughout all of North Vietnam. Then, in late October, Johnson actually announced such a halt. Johnson hoped that this move would lead to a broadening of the peace talks to include not just the United States and North Vietnam but also South Vietnam and the NLF. That prospect faded, though, when South Vietnam refused to participate. Why did Saigon balk? Over the ensuing decades, journalists and historians pieced together an explanation, which in the 2010s was buttressed by convincing documentary evidence: candidate Nixon, already resorting to the dirty tricks that would mark his presidency, employed secret emissaries to persuade the South Vietnamese government to hold out for a better deal under a Republican administration. Despite this disappointment to Johnson, however, his and Humphrey's bombing halt statements made it easier for doves to back the Democratic ticket, and in the campaign's final days Humphrey's poll numbers surged.

It wasn't quite enough. In November, Nixon won by a margin of less than 1 percent of the popular vote, bringing an end to eight years of Democratic control of the executive branch. The Republicans gained seats in both the House and the Senate, but the Democrats kept their majority in each house.

***

The 1968 election results were a revealing snapshot of shifting electoral patterns. Thanks to the 1965 Voting Rights Act, over a million southern Blacks had registered to vote, and they were overwhelmingly Democratic. But this gain for the Democrats was more than offset by an exodus of southern whites from the party. In 1968, Nixon was not the sole beneficiary of this shift; Wallace won five states in the Deep South, while Nixon carried six. But the Democratic Party's hold on the region was broken, and its national power correspondingly diminished. In future presidential elections, when there would be no southern third-party candidates, Republican candidates would benefit much more than Nixon did in 1968.

And it wasn't just a southern phenomenon. Across the country, the Democratic Party was losing the support of working-class and lower-middle-class whites – the sort of people who protested so vigorously when Martin Luther King led marches through their Chicago neighborhoods in 1966. Although most of these Americans still voted Democratic in 1968, they were moving in the Republicans' direction, and in future elections they would be more firmly lodged in the GOP column. On a still broader plane, millions of voters of all backgrounds had come to see Lyndon Johnson's antipoverty programs as wasteful and counterproductive and to recoil from rising crime rates and reports of urban unrest. Many of these same voters were dismayed by the seeming futility of the military venture in Vietnam – and even more perturbed by the raucous and sometimes violent antiwar protests. All of these ills could, in some fashion, be laid at the door of the incumbent party in Washington, and it was now paying a political price. Just four years after its triumphant victory in 1964, the great Democratic coalition that Franklin Roosevelt had assembled in the 1930s was starting to come undone. By hook or by crook (with a strong preference for the latter), the new Republican president would strive to hasten that process.

READING QUESTIONS

1. What international and domestic dilemmas drove President Johnson to escalate the Vietnam War? What alternative courses of action could he have taken, and with what possible results in each case?
2. In what various ways did "hawks," "doves," radicals, and civil rights advocates criticize Johnson's Vietnam policies? Which of those criticisms do you find most persuasive, and why?
3. Why did "Black Power" sensibilities and approaches have growing appeal to African Americans in the mid- to late 1960s? What benefits resulted from the turn to Black Power? What costs may it have imposed on the broader civil rights movement?
4. How do you explain the triumph of conservative forces by the late 1960s, as exemplified by Richard M. Nixon's election in 1968?

SUGGESTIONS FOR FURTHER READING

Bloom, Joshua, and Waldo E. Martin. *Black against Empire: The History and Politics of the Black Panther Party*. Berkeley, CA: University of California Press, 2013.

Branch, Taylor. *At Canaan's Edge: America in the King Years, 1965–68*. New York: Simon & Schuster, 2006.

Cohen, Michael A. *American Maelstrom: The 1968 Election and the Politics of Division*. New York: Oxford University Press, 2016.

Dallek, Robert. *Flawed Giant: Lyndon Johnson and His Times, 1961–1973*. New York: Oxford University Press, 1998.

Farber, David. *The Age of Great Dreams: America in the 1960s*. New York: Hill & Wang, 1994.

Gitlin, Todd. *The Sixties: Years of Hope, Days of Rage*. New York: Bantam Books, 1987.

Herring, George. *America's Longest War: The United States and Vietnam, 1950–1975*, 5th edn. New York: McGraw-Hill, 2013.

Kurlansky, Mark. *1968: The Year that Rocked the World*. New York: Ballantine, 2004.

Lucks, Daniel S. *Selma to Saigon: The Civil Rights Movement and the Vietnam War*. Lexington, KY: University of Kentucky Press, 2014.

Malloy, Sean. *Out of Oakland: Black Panther Party Internationalism during the Cold War*. Ithaca, NY: Cornell University Press, 2017.

Marable, Manning. *Race, Reform, and Rebellion: The Second Reconstruction and Beyond in Black America*, 3rd edn. Jackson, MS: University Press of Mississippi, 2007.

Murch, Donna Jean. *Living for the City: Migration, Education, and the Rise of the Black Panther Party in Oakland, California*. Chapel Hill, NC: University of North Carolina, 2010.

Oropeza, Lorena. *¡Raza Si! ¡Guerra No! Chicano Protest and Patriotism during the Vietnam War Era*. Berkeley, CA: University of California Press, 2005.

Perlstein, Rick. *Nixonland: The Rise of a President and the Fracturing of America*. New York: Scribner, 2008.

Sitkoff, Harvard. *The Struggle for Black Equality*, 3rd edn. New York: Hill & Wang, 2008.

Stoll, Steven. *US Environmentalism since 1945: A Brief History with Documents*. New York: Palgrave Macmillan, 2007.

Unger, Debi, and Irwin Unger, *Turning Point, 1968*. New York: Scribner, 1988.

7 Expletive Deleted

The Presidency of Richard Nixon, 1969–1974

Introduction

This was one of the best perks of the job. In July 1969, President Richard M. Nixon flew to a remote island in the Pacific, rode an aircraft carrier out to the splashdown site, and stood on the flight deck as the first human beings to walk on the moon came aboard the naval vessel. The three Apollo 11 astronauts were loaded into a quarantine chamber, and the president bantered with them across a pane of glass. He asked if they had followed earthbound events from space. Did they know who won the major league baseball All-Star Game? Speaking more earnestly, Nixon lauded the astronauts for a feat that had mesmerized all of humankind, saying: "[A]s a result of what you have done, the world has never been closer together before."

During his Pacific trip, Nixon also visited the US territory of Guam. The United States had seized that island during the Spanish-American War of 1898 and used it as a headquarters for Pacific naval operations during the latter phases of World War II. Now preoccupied with another military venture, Nixon conferred in Guam with South Vietnam's president, Nguyen Van Thieu. Afterward, Nixon briefed reporters and outlined his views on the proper US posture toward the region. In the future, he said, "we must avoid the kind of policy that will make countries in Asia so dependent upon us that we are dragged into conflicts such as the one we have in Vietnam." America would honor its treaty commitments, he pledged, but, except for conflicts involving other nuclear powers, "the United States … has a right to expect that this problem will be handled by … the Asian nations themselves." Previous American presidents had voiced similar sentiments. Against the backdrop of the Vietnam debacle, however, Nixon's admonitory words caught the attention of pundits, who began calling his statement the "Guam Doctrine." Learning of this, Nixon launched a behind-the-scenes, and ultimately successful, campaign to get the name changed to "Nixon Doctrine." Clearly, the president wished to underscore the theme of restraint in US foreign relations and grant it his personal imprimatur. Over the next few years, the Nixon Doctrine came to signify a broader policy of lowering America's military profile and relying more heavily on local allies around the world.

Lunar travel and Asian security were not Nixon's only concerns during his Pacific trip. The president also had his eye on the coast of New England. Days earlier, Massachusetts's Democratic Senator Edward M. Kennedy, the youngest brother of President John F. Kennedy and, many believed, Nixon's likely challenger in the 1972 presidential election, had been involved in a deadly mishap. Leaving a late-night party on tiny Chappaquiddick Island, Massachusetts, Kennedy accidentally drove his car off a narrow bridge and into a pond. The senator freed himself from the submerged vehicle, but his passenger, a young campaign worker named Mary Jo Kopechne, drowned. In a lapse Kennedy himself now had difficulty explaining, he waited several hours before notifying authorities of the accident. Since well before this terrible event, Nixon had been obsessed with Ted Kennedy. The White House chief of staff, Harry Robbins ("H. R.") Haldeman, had been under general orders to maintain an around-the-clock surveillance of the senator, for the purpose of catching him in some disqualifying indiscretion. On July 25, the same day on which Nixon was to meet with Thieu in Guam, Kennedy planned to deliver a televised address on the tragedy. The president was dying to know what his rival would say, but there would be no television or radio coverage of the speech in Guam.

The ever-resourceful Haldeman, who was traveling with Nixon, devised a plan to slake his boss's curiosity. From Nimitz Hill, the naval headquarters where Nixon and his entourage were staying, Haldeman placed a long-distance call to the White House, where a staff member held his telephone receiver next to a television set as a somber Kennedy recounted the incident and threw himself on the mercy of Massachusetts's voters (whose verdict would be that he should stay in the Senate). The chief of staff took notes at his end and prepared a report for the president. "It was an odd feeling," Haldeman later recalled, "to sit in the house overlooking the Pacific from which Admiral Nimitz had directed much of the US operations in World War II and run through my notes on this rather bizarre subject on the eve of welcoming the first men back from the moon."[1]

The local, the national, the regional, the global, the extraterrestrial – a quarter-century into the post-World-War-II era, US governance extended into all these realms. The moon landing was a remarkable achievement for the United States, showcasing its unparalleled ability to marshal technology, organization, human dedication, and raw power in the pursuit of a barely attainable goal. And yet, at the summit of this endeavor, hard limits, more than the surpassing of them, seemed to define the national experience. After nearly four years of violent upheaval at home, over race and over a grinding, controversial war, a chest-thumping celebration of the planting of the nation's flag on the moon might have rung hollow to many Americans. It was fitting, then, that the president's marking of the occasion should be accompanied by a proclamation of partial retreat, issued from the westernmost reaches of the nation's formal empire.

[1] Admiral Chester Nimitz was commander in chief of the US Pacific fleet during World War II. Haldeman misremembered the chronology; Kennedy's speech and Nixon's meeting with Thieu both occurred the day after, not "on the eve of," the July 24, 1969, Apollo 11 splashdown.

If a certain irony was built into the historical situation, then the president's character and behavior added fresh layers of contradiction. Nixon read the plate tectonics of international affairs with uncommon shrewdness, but his brooding, conspiratorial nature rendered him almost powerless before the lure of petty and even vicious politics. He took office pledging an honorable exit from the Vietnam War yet continued to wage it for all of his first term, nearly matching the carnage of the previous four years. He promised an administration of "law and order," only to operate a sprawling criminal enterprise out of the White House. The controversies arising from his domestic misdeeds relegated him to the sidelines of his own intricate foreign policy. These events spelled a hard landing for the thirty-seventh president, and for Americans' confidence in their governing institutions.

Richard Nixon's Domestic Policies

The policies of Richard Nixon, who became president in January 1969, resist easy ideological classification. In both domestic and international affairs, he took many actions pleasing to conservatives and cold war hardliners, but many others that could be defended on progressive or peacemaking grounds. In large part, this contradiction reflected the circumstances in which Nixon operated. He now led the executive branch and wielded the levers of foreign policy, but Democrats remained in control of Congress, and US power had significantly declined relative to that of other nations. At home and abroad, Nixon tangled with adversaries when he could but often found it prudent to cede them ground. Another, frequently overlapping consideration was Nixon's unceasing drive to gain advantage over political rivals and to position himself for reelection in 1972. Some of the president's more puzzling moves become less so when examined in this starkly political light. As for Nixon's brazenly illegal domestic spying and sabotage activities – pursued despite his loudly professed fealty to the rule of law – they, too, reflected the president's obsessive preoccupation with 1972, as well as a desire to shield his Vietnam policies from scrutiny and criticism. All that said, there were times when Nixon simply did what he thought was right on the merits.

One domestic issue on which Nixon often, but not always, tacked right was race. To be comfortably reelected, he assumed he needed to win over most of the white southerners who had supported former Alabama Governor George Wallace's presidential run in 1968. Thus Nixon repeatedly signaled his sympathy for that sector, even if it meant backing some losing causes. When federal courts pushed southern school districts to implement desegregation plans, Nixon's Department of Justice petitioned the courts, unsuccessfully, to grant the districts more time. In 1969–1970, Nixon tried to put a white conservative from the Deep South on the Supreme Court. Two successive nominees failed to win confirmation. Senators' objections differed in each case, but Nixon publicly attributed both defeats to northerners' refusal to give a fair hearing to any "judge from the South who believes as I do in the strict construction of the Constitution" – a statement widely interpreted as supporting southern whites' efforts to impede desegregation.

In wooing this constituency, the president was most immediately concerned with his own electoral prospects, but he also had a longer-term project in mind: political realignment. The presidential campaign of Republican Senator Barry Goldwater of Arizona in 1964, and Wallace's run in 1968, had dislodged millions of white southerners from the Democratic Party. If those voters, and many more like them, could be persuaded to make the Republican Party their permanent home, then the party's national position would be vastly strengthened. Republicans would continue pursuing this "southern strategy" long after had Nixon left office.

And yet, even as he courted the white South, Nixon also supported racial affirmative action – the use of race-conscious remedies to redress generations of discrimination in employment, education, and other avenues of advancement. The most conspicuous arena for this surprising development was housing construction. In a 1969 initiative known as the Philadelphia Plan (because it began in that city before becoming the template for national policy), the Nixon administration mandated that construction firms receiving federal contracts produce "goals and timetables" for hiring African Americans and other minorities. Several motives drove this policy. Some administration officials feared a repetition of the urban riots that had marked Lyndon Johnson's presidency; opening job opportunities in Black communities might avert that danger. Officials also warned that the scarcity of skilled construction workers, and the slowness with which new ones were being hired and trained, could impede housing construction across the nation and, perhaps, contribute to general inflation. The aggressive recruitment of minorities could eliminate that bottleneck. Finally, the president saw an irresistible opportunity to sow further division in the Democratic coalition. For the new affirmative action requirements were imposed not just on companies but also on unions, some of which, especially in construction, had long histories of racial discrimination. When national labor leaders opposed the Philadelphia Plan as an unwarranted federal imposition, they found themselves at odds with their customary allies in the civil rights establishment.

Environmentalism was another issue on which Nixon took an unexpectedly progressive stance. The cause had gained powerful momentum in the late 1960s, fueled in part by the rise of the counterculture, which often decried the hubris, destructiveness, wastefulness, and "plastic" phoniness of industrial and consumer society. Days after Nixon's inauguration, a massive oil spill off the coast of Santa Barbara, California, produced a spike in nationwide concern about the environment. Months later, Americans reacted similarly to reports that a river in Cleveland, Ohio, had gotten so thick with oily sludge that it had caught fire. In April 1970, some twenty million Americans, and many millions more around the world, took part in the first Earth Day, holding demonstrations, teach-ins, celebrations, and other awareness-raising activities. Leaders in Congress were now championing the issue, chief among them Democratic Senator Edmund Muskie of Maine, the Democrats' vice-presidential nominee in 1968. Now that Ted Kennedy, tainted by Chappaquiddick, had bowed out of the next presidential election, Muskie was widely seen as Nixon's likely opponent in 1972. To Nixon, this was a parade to lead, not rain on. In December 1970, he issued an executive order creating the Environmental Protection Agency (EPA), which was to coordinate and enforce national environmental policies. The EPA became the central federal actor on the issue, not only implementing environmental legislation but sometimes promulgating policies of its own, such as the 1972 banning of the chemical pesticide dichlorodiphenyltrichloroethane (DDT, in human-speak).

On economics, too, Nixon showed that he was no doctrinaire conservative. In 1969, he proposed the Family Assistance Plan (FAP), whereby poor families would receive direct cash payments from the federal government. The annual minimum for a family of four would be $1,600, supplemented by food stamps amounting to at least $800 (about $12,600 and $6,300, respectively, in 2022 dollars). The originator of the FAP was Nixon's urban affairs adviser, Daniel Patrick Moynihan, a Harvard professor who had served in the Kennedy and Johnson administrations. (He was later elected to the US Senate as a Democrat from New York.) The ebullient Moynihan persuaded Nixon that the FAP would significantly improve on the existing federal welfare system, which conservatives derided as wasteful, meddlesome, and geared to foster habits of dependence among the poor. The new scheme would sweep aside that cumbersome bureaucracy and place resources directly in people's hands. "Cold cash!" Moynihan exhorted in a television interview. "It's a surprisingly good cure for a lot of social ills." FAP passed the House of Representatives but died in the Senate, attacked both by liberals who found the program too stingy and by conservatives who thought it would offer too much. Nixon's own waning enthusiasm helped to ensure FAP's demise. While it lasted, though, his championing of the program won uncharacteristic praise from liberals and leftists. The socialist author Michael Harrington, whose 1962 book *The Other America* helped to inspire Lyndon Johnson's War on Poverty, called FAP "the most radical idea since the New Deal."

Nixon acted against type on another economic matter. As he took office, the nation faced an unusual conundrum. Since the mid-1960s, federal social and military spending had markedly increased, yet federal taxation had not kept pace with these outlays. The resulting stimulation of the economy, without the dampening influence of high taxes, placed upward pressure on prices. Also fueling inflation were mounting labor costs, a consequence of successive wage increases negotiated by companies and unions. Meanwhile, the workforce was rapidly expanding – as baby boomers came of age and more and more women entered the labor market – yet the rate of job creation was not keeping up. Two indexes that traditionally existed in an inverse relation to one another, inflation and unemployment, were rising simultaneously; "stagflation" was commentators' term for this maddening problem. Business owners, possessing neither the bargaining power to hold wages down nor the desire to raise prices further during a slump, increasingly looked to Washington for a solution. Nixon at first resisted the pressure, but by 1971 he, too, was worried. After all, his reelection campaign was just around the corner. In an August executive order, the president imposed a ninety-day freeze on wages and prices, doing "what no Democratic liberal, much less a Republican, ever had come close to doing except in war," the journalist Tom Wicker later wrote. This bold move, combined with some tax adjustments, generally met Nixon's short-term goals, creating a more congenial economic climate for 1972. Soon thereafter, however, the curse of stagflation would return with vengeance.

Nixon, Henry Kissinger, and Vietnam

For all the intricacy of his domestic policies, Nixon was primarily interested in foreign affairs. He was determined to direct foreign policy from the White House, and he sought to accomplish this by appointing a secretive Harvard professor named Henry Kissinger to be his national security adviser. Kissinger was a German Jew who, as a boy in the 1930s, had fled with his family to the United States to escape Nazi persecution. He achieved prominence in the 1950s and 1960s as a political scientist and foreign policy analyst, serving as an occasional outside adviser to Presidents Kennedy and Johnson. Theoretically, Kissinger's role in Nixon's White House was to receive input from all the executive departments and agencies concerned with foreign affairs and then make recommendations to the president. In practice, the two men often ignored the incoming advice and formulated their own foreign policy opaquely. Indeed, the man Nixon appointed as his secretary of state, former Attorney General William P. Rogers, was selected partly because he knew little about foreign relations and was ill equipped to assert himself in this area.

Nixon and Kissinger were powerfully drawn to each other. As the journalist Seymour Hersh observed, "Nixon had a consuming need for flattery and Kissinger a consuming need to provide it." Each man thrived on intrigue and possessed a paranoid streak, though Nixon's was far more pronounced than Kissinger's. On the positive side, both thought in broad conceptual terms and were able to discern shifting patterns in global affairs. They realized that a new era in world politics had begun in which America's power relative to that of other nations had declined. Western Europe and Japan had fully recovered from the devastation of World War II and were now emerging as powerful economic rivals of the United States. Communist China had acquired the Bomb, and the Soviet Union was approaching rough nuclear parity with the United States. Most glaringly, the United States had failed to get its way in Vietnam, a development that both signified and accelerated Washington's loss of global stature.

Nixon and Kissinger knew they would have to adjust to these new realities, and to a considerable degree they did. Yet they were also determined to prevail in Vietnam; they truly believed they could succeed where their predecessors had failed. This latter conviction introduced a large measure of incoherence, waste, deception, and appalling human carnage to a foreign policy otherwise remembered, with *some* justification, for its realism and creativity.

As Lyndon Johnson had done at the start of his presidency, Nixon faced a basic dilemma over Vietnam. On the one hand, it was obvious that the present US involvement was unsustainable and had to be dramatically wound down, especially regarding troop levels. On the other hand, Nixon remained just as committed as his predecessors to the preservation of an independent, noncommunist South Vietnam. And he was absolutely determined, he told congressional leaders, not to "be the first president to lose a war." His solution was to deescalate the conflict in some ways and escalate it in others.

On the deescalation front, Nixon pursued a policy of "Vietnamization": withdrawing American troops from South Vietnam and progressively turning over the ground operations to the South Vietnamese army, which would continue to receive massive US material and logistical support. The troop withdrawal proceeded rapidly during Nixon's first term. At their peak level in the spring of 1969, US forces in South Vietnam numbered 543,000; by late 1970 they were down to 280,000; by late 1971, 140,000; by the spring of 1972, 70,000. The drawdown enabled Nixon to phase out the military draft and, with Congress, eliminate it altogether by January 1973 – popular moves, needless to say.

Meanwhile, however, the Nixon administration stepped up US air operations, supplementing existing activities inside South Vietnam with new raids against North Vietnamese Army positions in neighboring Cambodia and Laos. In time, US ground forces would operate in Cambodia, and US bombing raids would resume over North Vietnam. Within South Vietnam, the United States intensified an ongoing secret program to identify, capture, interrogate, and sometimes assassinate suspected National Liberation Front members. Operation Phoenix, as the effort was called, killed tens of thousands of Vietnamese (some of them civilians targeted indiscriminately) and was later revealed to entail torture, rape, beating, mutilation, and lengthy incarceration in squalid conditions. The purpose of all these escalatory moves was to disrupt the enemy's war-making ability in the South and to convince Hanoi that Washington would never abandon Saigon. Eventually, Nixon hoped, North Vietnam would see no alternative to a settlement that provided for South Vietnam's independence.

Indeed, the president went to inordinate, but ultimately futile, lengths to impress the North Vietnamese with his steely determination. In July 1969, through French and Soviet intermediaries, he secretly warned North Vietnam that, unless it softened its negotiating stance by November 1, the United States would subject it to devastating air attacks, possibly including the use of nuclear weapons. In October, Nixon ordered eighteen B-52 bomber aircraft carrying nuclear weapons to fly close to Soviet airspace, a mission Moscow was sure to detect. Apparently, the aim was to convince Soviet leaders that the US president was capable of extreme action and thus prompt them to pressure North Vietnam to be more flexible. But the Soviets failed to react to the flights, perhaps because they were confused by them, or perhaps because they realized the North Vietnamese were immovable. Sure enough, Hanoi ignored the US ultimatum, adhering to its long-held position that the war would continue until all US forces had left Vietnam and the Saigon regime had been dismantled. Nixon was enraged, but advisers persuaded him that carrying out his threat – even to the point of using nukes – would almost certainly fail to shake the North's resolve. The president backed down.

Instead, on November 3, Nixon delivered a televised address in which he called on "the great silent majority of my fellow Americans" to support him in helping South Vietnam resist Northern "aggression." "The more divided we are at home," he said, "the less likely the enemy is to negotiate at Paris . . . . North Vietnam cannot defeat or humiliate the United States; only Americans can do that." Thousands of ordinary citizens sent supportive telegrams and letters to the White House, and the president's public approval rating shot up to 67 percent. Nixon had shrewdly assessed public opinion, and done so against the grain of conventional wisdom. By late 1969, it was widely assumed that opposition to the war was now the dominant national sentiment. A couple of nationwide actions that fall known as the Vietnam Moratoriums, in which hundreds of thousands of presentable, middle-class Americans gathered in dignified protest, reinforced this impression. But Nixon grasped a countervailing reality: that millions of other Americans, while disturbed by the specter of US ground troops fighting and dying in a seemingly endless foreign war, still wanted to prevent a communist takeover of South Vietnam. They were eager for an exit from Vietnam but willing to give Nixon a chance to end the war in his own way.

Nixon also understood that many in the "silent majority" were fed up with disruptive antiwar protesters and with a liberal establishment that – so the characterization went – indulged the protesters' radicalism and offered snide and defeatist antiwar commentaries of its own. To cater to this sentiment, and to shore up his support on the Republican Party's right flank, Nixon encouraged his vice president, Spiro Agnew, to go on the attack. In late 1969 and 1970, Agnew obliged with a series of speeches that harshly assailed antiwar activists, university professors, liberal politicians, and members of the news media. Perhaps to dispel any notion that the vice president and his intended audience were unsophisticated, Agnew's speechwriters larded his addresses with high-sounding phrases and showy alliteration. Thus Agnew disparaged antiwar demonstrators as "ideological eunuchs" and called liberal intellectuals "an effete corps of impudent snobs." The Nixon administration's critics were "nattering nabobs of negativism" and "hopeless, hysterical hypochondriacs of history." "A paralyzing permissive philosophy pervades every policy they espouse," he pontificated. Liberals despised Agnew, but he gained a devoted following among conservative Republicans.

These domestic maneuverings did buy Nixon some time to seek a satisfactory exit from Vietnam. Unfortunately, he had no formula for ending the war anytime soon. After failing to get his way through threats, Nixon shifted his focus to North Vietnam's use of Cambodian territory as a staging area for raids into the South. In March 1969, his administration had begun an extensive bombing campaign against NVA bases in Cambodia. For the next fifteen months, the United States flew more than 3,600 bombing raids over that country, none of them publicly disclosed. The secrecy partly reflected a desire to avoid diplomatic complications with Cambodia's neutralist prime minister, Prince Norodom Sihanouk. In March 1970, a pro-US general overthrew Sihanouk's government, permitting the Nixon administration to act more openly. In late April, Nixon announced that US ground troops were entering Cambodia to attack NVA sanctuaries near the South Vietnamese border. During their two-month incursion, US forces killed about 2,000 enemy combatants and destroyed thousands of bunkers. These actions made little difference, however, as the NVA could quickly relocate to other parts of the country. The main result of the US intervention was to destabilize Cambodia and make it more susceptible to vastly greater upheavals in the future.

In the United States, the Cambodia operation shocked many observers, and angry protests erupted on hundreds of college campuses. At Ohio's Kent State University on May 4, state National Guardsmen opened fire on student demonstrators, killing four. On May 15, police killed two students at Jackson State College, a predominantly Black school in Mississippi. These fresh outrages (especially the Kent State tragedy, which happened earlier and whose victims were middle-class whites) only deepened the sense of crisis, and liberal commentators denounced Nixon for plunging the nation into chaos. But the president refused to give any ground to his critics, confident that the "silent majority" still supported him. Indeed, a Gallup poll revealed that 58 percent of respondents blamed the Kent State killings on the protesting students.

And so, despite powerful domestic sentiment in favor of exiting the war, direct US involvement in it would continue until the start of Nixon's second term. From 1969 to 1973, an additional 21,000 American soldiers lost their lives. Vietnamese deaths in that period came to over 600,000 combatants, North and South, and an untold number of Vietnamese civilians.

Continuing Protest at Home

The public's ungenerous view of antiwar demonstrators had a great deal to do with the raucousness of their protests. It also reflected the fact that some elements of the left had resorted to frightening violence. In the fall of 1969, the most prominent organization of the student left, Students for a Democratic Society, splintered into several mutually antagonistic factions. One of them, the Weather Underground, launched a campaign of clandestine violence designed to spark a domestic revolution. Over the next few years, Weather Underground members planted bombs in government buildings, banks, universities, and other places symbolizing authority. Most of these attacks targeted property rather than people, but in March 1970 three group members were killed in a Manhattan townhouse when the bomb they were making exploded prematurely. Numerous other, lesser-known underground organizations – championing causes ranging from revolutionary Marxism to Black Power to Puerto Rican liberation – set off bombs, robbed banks, and committed other violent crimes. According to (perhaps inflated) FBI statistics, during an eighteen-month period in 1971 and 1972 an average of nearly five bombings per day occurred in the United States. Yet in these instances, too, the primary aim was to air grievances rather than cause bodily harm. "Most bombings were followed by communiqués denouncing some aspect of the American condition," writes the popular historian Bryan Burrough; "bombs basically functioned as exploding press releases." This was scant solace, of course, to those in close proximity to the blasts.

By means fair and foul, the nation's law enforcers relentlessly pursued the left. A secret program within the FBI known as COINTELPRO (an abbreviation of counterintelligence program), launched in 1956 to thwart domestic communists, had since the late 1960s targeted New Left, Black Power, and other militant organizations. Under COINTELPRO's auspices, the FBI illegally surveilled these groups, sent anonymous letters to them to sow internal division, and, via infiltrators, goaded them into taking extreme actions that could justify official repression.

Unsurprisingly, nonwhite militants suffered the most egregious denials of due process, with Black Panther Party members receiving the harshest treatment. With their fractiousness, grandiosity, and lack of self-restraint, the Panthers were often their own worst enemies. From 1969 to 1971, however, the FBI and local law enforcement further crippled the BPP by staging deadly shootouts with its members and, sometimes, launching one-sided attacks on them. The most notorious of the latter occurred in December 1969, when Chicago police, furnished with intelligence and logistical help from the FBI, raided an apartment and killed twenty-one-year-old Fred Hampton, chair of the BPP's Illinois chapter, and twenty-two-year-old Mark Clark, a local BPP member, and wounded four of their associates. The Chicago police claimed that the Panthers had opened fire, but a later investigation revealed that the cops fired nearly a hundred bullets, while just one shot, fired at the ceiling, came from the BPP side. On other occasions, FBI or police infiltrators stirred up conflict between the BPP and other Black Power groups. In 1972, the BPP closed down all chapters outside its home base of Oakland, California, and devoted itself to electoral politics in that city. The party did eventually wield some municipal influence, but it was spent as a radical force. Much the same could be said of the rest of the far left.

Even so, potent antiwar activism continued. By the early 1970s, US military involvement in Vietnam had lasted long enough to produce hundreds of thousands of veterans, an appreciable minority of whom publicly opposed the war. In April 1971, an organization called Vietnam Veterans Against the War (VVAW) staged five days of demonstrations in Washington, DC, including an event at which several hundred veterans hurled their medals and ribbons onto the steps of the US Capitol. Many liberal congresspeople openly supported the protests, and VVAW's spokesman, John Kerry, was invited to testify before the Senate Foreign Relations Committee. The twenty-seven-year-old Navy veteran condemned the Vietnam venture as having accomplished little more than laying waste to Southeast Asia and brutalizing the young men sent to fight in America's name. (In 1984, Kerry would be elected to the Senate himself, as a Democrat from Massachusetts.)

One of the most effective antiwar salvos, launched just weeks after the VVAW protests, originated from within the US defense establishment. Back in 1967, Robert McNamara, Lyndon Johnson's secretary of defense, had asked his department to produce a study documenting how successive US administrations had been drawn into the Vietnam conflict. By now, McNamara had privately soured on the war, and he wanted to learn how such a massive blunder could have occurred. The study was completed in 1968 and filed away in the Pentagon's secret archives. In June 1971, a former Defense and State Department analyst named Daniel Ellsberg, an even sharper internal critic of the war, provided a copy of the study to *The New York Times*, which published it in installments. The "Pentagon Papers" were a huge story, for they revealed that the US policy-makers who had escalated the war were far more pessimistic about its chances of success than they publicly let on.

Although the Pentagon Papers said nothing about Nixon administration policies – they were compiled before the administration came into being – Nixon was agitated by the disclosure. It was only a matter of time, he believed, before dissenters began exposing his own private deliberations. Nixon's Department of Justice tried to get a court injunction against *The New York Times*, but the US Supreme Court upheld the newspaper's right to publish the Pentagon study. The DOJ then indicted Ellsberg for disseminating classified material. Behind the scenes, the affair goaded the White House into a frenzy of illegal activity. John Ehrlichman, Nixon's special adviser for domestic affairs, formed the White House Special Investigations Unit, informally known as the "plumbers" because the outfit's mission was to

Figure 7.1 Senator Edward Kennedy greeting Daniel Ellsberg at an antiwar meeting, 1971. Source: Bettmann / Getty Images.

prevent, or punish, leaks harmful to Nixon's interests. In September 1971, several plumbers broke into the Los Angeles office of Ellsberg's psychiatrist, in a futile attempt to obtain embarrassing information about Ellsberg. (The eventual disclosure of the break-in led to the dismissal of the government's legal case against Ellsberg.) The plumbers even considered firebombing the Brookings Institution, a liberal Washington think tank, to create a diversion that would permit operatives to sneak into the facility and seize sensitive documents that Brookings supposedly was harboring. Nothing, thankfully, came of this scheme.

The plumbers' antics quickly expanded into a much broader White House campaign to go after the administration's opponents by a host of illegal means. Nixon's minions planted wiretaps, burglarized offices, targeted political enemies for tax audits, forged letters accusing Democratic leaders of sexual indiscretions, and engaged in other "dirty tricks." Many of these activities were puerile and gratuitous, yielding no discernible advantage to Nixon's policy agenda or reelection prospects. But one shenanigan does appear to have made a real difference. In early 1972, the evident front-runner for the Democratic nomination was Senator Muskie, a mainstream Democrat widely seen as posing the most formidable threat to Nixon in the general election. As the New Hampshire primary election approached, a conservative paper in that state published an anonymous letter – later shown to have been forged by Nixon operatives – accusing Muskie of employing an ethnic slur against New Englanders of French Canadian background. At an outdoor event in snowy weather, Muskie angrily denounced the allegation. Some newspapers reported that the candidate wept as he spoke, though Muskie insisted that the apparent tears were streaks of melting snow on his face. The incident caused many in the public to question whether the candidate was "tough enough" to be president. Muskie won the New Hampshire primary, but by a smaller margin than expected, and diminishing support soon forced him to drop out of the race. As we shall see, the eventual Democratic nominee, Senator George McGovern of South Dakota, proved an exceedingly weak candidate against Nixon. In this case, at least, the White House's dirty trickery seems to have worked.

Nixon, Kissinger, and the Wider Cold War

It would take another year for the president's criminal conspiracy to start unraveling. Meanwhile, a quiet revolution was occurring in US relations with the communist world. Since taking office, Nixon and Kissinger had moved to improve relations with both the Soviet Union and the People's Republic of China. The Soviet initiative was rooted in precedent. Since the early 1960s, even as they continued to expand their strategic arsenals, Washington and Moscow had sought to exercise control over their nuclear rivalry, achieving modest successes with the Limited Test Ban Treaty of 1963 (see Chapter 4); the Outer Space Treaty of 1967, which banned the deployment of nuclear weapons in space; and the Nuclear Nonproliferation Treaty of 1968, in which the two superpowers joined with scores of other nations to establish protocols for regulating the spread of nuclear technology. To build on those achievements, in 1969 the Nixon administration began exploring with the Soviets further means of limiting the arms race.

Far less conventionally, and initially in deep secrecy, Nixon and Kissinger also moved to establish a dialogue with the PRC, which the United States had diplomatically shunned since 1949, and to use that new relationship to gain leverage against the Soviet Union. Making this latter scenario plausible was the fact that, in the spring of 1969, Sino-Soviet relations were at their lowest ebb. Those relations had steadily deteriorated since the late 1950s, when the PRC started publicly denouncing Soviet efforts to ease tensions with the West. A decade later, the two countries were behaving like mortal enemies. The Soviet Union amassed forces near Chinese territory, and the PRC encouraged its citizens to harass Soviet border guards on the Sino-Soviet frontier. In March 1969, the two nations engaged in armed clashes along the Ussuri River, which separates Manchuria from Russia. Full-scale war seemed a real possibility.

Moscow and Beijing pulled back from the brink, but their mutual hostility persisted, leaving Washington to contemplate ways of playing the two powers off against each other. Like the Sino-Soviet split itself, this scenario was not new. Occasionally in the 1960s, US officials had pondered how to exploit the rift. Almost invariably, though, such scenarios involved improving relations with the Soviet Union at China's expense. After all, Moscow was clearly the less hostile of the two adversaries. Moreover, bitter memories of 1949–1950, when Republicans had savaged the Truman administration for "losing" China, remained fresh in the minds of Kennedy and Johnson administration officials. Even if the PRC had expressed an interest in better relations with the United States, Democratic policy-makers would have had to think twice about reciprocating, lest they, too, be red-baited.

In a bold stroke, Nixon and Kissinger overturned these assumptions. Perhaps, they reasoned, their better option would be to improve relations with the PRC and use the prospect of a special Sino-US understanding to frighten the Soviets into granting diplomatic concessions. They also hoped that, in achieving such a rapprochement, they could persuade Beijing to reduce its support for Hanoi and thus facilitate a dignified US exit from Vietnam. The irony was exquisite. For a decade and a half, the United States had portrayed its military presence in Vietnam as a vital barrier to PRC expansion. Now, it was moving closer to the PRC in order to liquidate that military presence.

In 1969, Kissinger began secret negotiations in Warsaw, Poland, with PRC representatives, who were themselves interested in improving relations with the United States, which they hoped could serve as a counterweight to the Soviet Union. In July 1971, Kissinger secretly traveled to China, where he and Zhou Enlai, the PRC prime minister, agreed that Nixon himself would soon visit the country. The revelation of Kissinger's trip caused an international sensation, and Kissinger, who until now had worked in relative obscurity, became an instant celebrity. The notion that the leading figure in American foreign policy was a Harvard intellectual with a Central European accent, a dry wit, a flair for secret missions, and a passing resemblance to Dr. Strangelove (the antihero of Stanley Kubrick's eponymous 1964 film brutally satirizing the US–Soviet nuclear standoff) captured the imagination of many Americans. Even Kissinger's personal life became a subject of keen interest. Paparazzi followed his every move, and gossip columnists speculated about whom he was dating. The divorced Kissinger fed the fascination by appearing in public with a succession of Hollywood actresses on his arm. But this was merely for show; he already had a steady companion, whom he would marry a few years later. "The dirty little secret about Kissinger's relationship with women" a biographer writes, "was that there was no dirty little secret."

Nixon resented Kissinger's enjoyment of the limelight. Politically, however, the president benefited handsomely from the revelation of the secret trip, which confounded his liberal critics. Accustomed to blasting Nixon as too hawkish on foreign policy, liberals now had to respond to a White House peace initiative much bolder than anything they had dared to propose. Of course, Democrats were generally more vulnerable than Republicans to the accusation of being soft on communism, a charge Nixon himself had often made over the previous quarter-century. The president, by contrast, enjoyed the priceless advantage of being the only person on earth who didn't have to worry about what Dick Nixon would say if he cozied up to the communists in Beijing.

On US–Soviet relations, the China initiative seemed to have the desired effect. Perturbed by the new development, the Soviets grew more amenable to some US arms control positions, speeding progress toward a general agreement. Painfully aware that Nixon would be visiting China in early 1972, they invited him to come to Moscow a few months later. Thus Nixon would have two spectacular summit meetings in 1972, the same year in which he would later seek reelection.

The China visit took place in February. Trailed by the world's media, Nixon and his party toured the Forbidden City, attended the Chinese opera, and visited the Great Wall. Toasting Zhou Enlai at a state banquet, the president said, "Our two peoples tonight hold the future

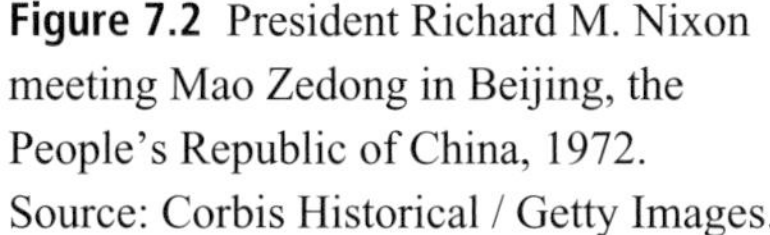

Figure 7.2 President Richard M. Nixon meeting Mao Zedong in Beijing, the People's Republic of China, 1972. Source: Corbis Historical / Getty Images.

of the world in our hands" – a statement calculated to play on Soviet anxieties. Behind the scenes, Nixon and Kissinger met with Zhou and an ailing Mao Zedong and agreed to ease restrictions on travel and trade. In 1973, the two countries would establish official liaison offices in each other's capitals.

In a crucial concession, the Nixon administration dropped its objection to the seating of the PRC at the United Nations, reversing over twenty years of US policy. The seat that Taiwan had previously occupied was now awarded to mainland China, meaning that the PRC not only acquired a vote in the General Assembly but also became a permanent member of the Security Council. The Taiwanese government and its (mostly Republican) American supporters bitterly fought this policy change but lacked the diplomatic or political clout to block it.

The Moscow summit was scheduled for the late spring of 1972. Several weeks earlier, North Vietnam launched a three-pronged offensive in the northern, central, and southern border areas of South Vietnam. Nixon responded by authorizing the first systematic bombing of North Vietnam since 1968. He also ordered US planes to drop mines in North Vietnam's Haiphong harbor, where Soviet ships happened to be anchored. Many US officials worried that the latter move would cause the Soviet government to cancel Nixon's planned visit. Nixon gambled that the Soviets were so desperate for a summit that they would not allow this provocation to derail it. He was right. Soviet leader Leonid Brezhnev denounced US aggression but did not withdraw his invitation to Nixon.

In late May, Nixon became the first US president to visit Moscow.[2] There, the superpowers concluded two major arms control agreements: the Strategic Arms Limitation Treaty

[2] In February 1945, President Franklin D. Roosevelt had met with his British and Soviet counterparts at Yalta, in the Soviet Crimea, but no president before Nixon had visited the Soviet capital while in office.

(SALT), which capped the number of intercontinental ballistic missiles that each side could deploy; and the Antiballistic Missile (ABM) Treaty, which limited each superpower's ability to deploy weapons capable of shooting down incoming ICBMs. (The case against ABMs was that they were inherently destabilizing. The more extensive ABM systems became, the more the superpowers would be tempted to expand their offensive arsenals to ensure they had the capability to overwhelm those defenses.) The two superpowers also agreed to liberalize their commerce. Between 1971 and 1973, US–Soviet trade levels jumped from about \$220 million to \$650 million per year. The arrangement was a boon to American farmers, as grain constituted a major share of US exports to the Soviet Union.

The Nixon administration's new modus vivendi with the Soviet Union and the PRC did not necessarily signal a more relaxed attitude toward socialist governments elsewhere. If anything, the further legitimation of communist spheres made the administration all the more zealous about policing areas subject to US influence and power. Hence Washington's rough dealings with the South American nation of Chile, where in September 1970 a socialist politician named Salvador Allende won a plurality in a three-way presidential election and stood poised to take office. Though not himself a communist, Allende was a vocal critic of capitalism and US cold war policies. He accepted support from Chile's communist party and was on friendly terms with Fidel Castro of Cuba. Nixon administration officials were alarmed by the prospect of another socialist government coming to power in the Western Hemisphere. Also perturbed was the American telecommunications firm International Telephone and Telegraph, which owned copper mines in Chile and a majority share of the country's main telephone company; IT&T feared the consequences of Allende's plans to nationalize those holdings.

The Nixon administration's first gambit was to try to prevent the Chilean Congress from confirming Allende as the winner of the presidential election. In October, the CIA secretly rushed arms to a group of Chilean officers who planned to detain General René Schneider, the commander-in-chief of the Chilean army. Schneider had declared his support for the Chilean constitution and his opposition to military interference in the nation's elections; temporarily, at least, he had to be sidelined. But the renegade officers bungled the operation, killing the general they were attempting to kidnap. Schneider's murder stirred outrage among the Chilean public, along with a wave of popular support for Allende. The Chilean Congress confirmed his election, and the Nixon administration could not stop him from taking office.

With Allende now in the presidency, Washington shifted to a new plan: destabilization. Over the next three years, the Nixon administration imposed economic sanctions against Chile, pressured international lending institutions to deny it loans, and funneled covert funds to Chilean opposition parties and to anti-Allende labor unions and business associations. Partly because of these tactics, and partly because of Allende's own mismanagement, the Chilean economy went into a tailspin, and the government lost significant popular support. In September 1973, another army commander-in-chief, General Augusto Pinochet, led a military coup that resulted in the death of Allende (apparently by suicide) and the overthrow of his government. Although no evidence of direct US involvement in the coup has surfaced, the Nixon administration clearly gave at least tacit encouragement to Pinochet and his officers. "[O]ur hand doesn't show on this one," Nixon told Kissinger in a private telephone call days later. Kissinger replied, "We didn't do it. I mean we helped them – created the conditions as great as possible." "That is right," Nixon said. "And that is the way it is going to be played." When Pinochet established a new regime with himself at the head, Washington warmly welcomed it, looking the other way as authorities arrested, tortured, and executed political dissidents and subjected the country to repressive rule. Chile was back in the US orbit, and that was what counted.

The Watergate Break-In, the 1972 Election, and the Vietnam Agreement

Just a couple of weeks after Nixon returned in triumph from the 1972 Moscow summit, the public got its first glimpse of the White House's seamy domestic underworld. In the early morning hours of June 17, police arrested five men attempting to break into the Democratic National Committee's headquarters in the Watergate apartment and office complex in Washington, DC. Notebooks and cash in the burglars' possession linked them to the Committee for the Reelection of the President (officially CRP, though critics could not resist calling it CREEP), a fundraising organization directed by Nixon's former attorney general, John Mitchell. Apparently, the intruders planned to replace defective listening devices they had previously planted in the Watergate offices, though the original purpose of the bugging remains unclear to this day. Despite news reports of the burglars' ties to Nixon's people – connections pursued most doggedly by two young *Washington Post* reporters, Bob Woodward and Carl Bernstein – the White House flatly denied any role in the affair. No evidence has come to light showing that Nixon himself knew about the break-in beforehand, but CREEP officials were complicit in it, and the president personally participated in efforts to cover up that fact. Woodward and Bernstein kept on the beat, writing numerous stories for the *Post* that pointedly challenged the official denials. Until well past the November election, however, most other news outlets ignored or downplayed the possibility of White House involvement.

Throughout that summer and into the fall, Nixon's reelection appeared all but assured. His opening to China and treaties with the Soviet Union lent credence to his claim to be leading the nation into a more cooperative international order. American troops remained in Vietnam, but on a greatly reduced basis. It was already known that superdiplomat Kissinger had negotiated secretly in Paris with North Vietnamese counterparts, in parallel with the publicly disclosed, lower-level talks held in the same city since 1968. Despite spasms of escalation over the previous few years, the Nixon administration did seem to be winding down the war. The Democrats, meanwhile, had nominated South Dakota Senator George McGovern, who advocated an immediate withdrawal from Vietnam, sharp reductions in military spending, a more generous welfare system, and legalized abortion. These stances pleased liberal

Democrats but alienated many of the party's centrists and conservatives, millions of whom gravitated toward Nixon. The president also benefited from the absence of a conservative third-party candidate who might have claimed many white southerners' votes.[3] In November, Nixon scored a landslide victory, winning forty-nine states and over 60 percent of the popular vote. As in every election since 1954, however, the Democrats prevailed in both the House and the Senate – a fateful vulnerability, it would turn out, for the triumphant president.

The election season and its aftermath coincided with a final flurry of US–North Vietnamese negotiations. For four years, the talks had been stalemated. Washington had insisted on the NVA's total withdrawal from the South; Hanoi had rejected this condition, calling instead for the dismantling of the South Vietnamese government. And then, in the late summer of 1972, the parties reached a tentative compromise: the NVA could stay in South Vietnam, the Saigon regime could remain in power, and the United States, on that basis, would withdraw its own forces from South Vietnam. The North Vietnamese softened their position partly because they had been weakened by the harsh US response to their spring offensive, but partly also because they were confident that, once the Americans departed, the South Vietnamese government would be doomed. Nixon and Kissinger more or less expected the same outcome. They hoped, however, to be able to furnish the South enough logistical and military support to delay its collapse for another two or three years. That way, Kissinger privately told Nixon in August, the final defeat would appear to be "the result of South Vietnamese incompetence" and not be blamed on *them*.

The Saigon regime, too, realized how precarious its position was. It refused to sign off on the agreement without significant changes, the main one being the establishment of a demilitarized zone to hamper further infiltrations of North Vietnamese soldiers and supplies into the South. When Kissinger conveyed this condition to the North Vietnamese, the latter were outraged. If alterations were permissible, Hanoi retorted, then it proposed to revive its old demand that the South Vietnamese regime be dismantled. Now it was Nixon's turn to lose his temper. In December 1972, he launched the so-called Christmas Bombing, a massive, twelve-day aerial campaign against North Vietnamese targets, including in Hanoi. Nixon's aims were to show the North Vietnamese he meant business and to assure the Saigon regime he was not about to abandon it. It was the most intensive bombing of the entire war. The United States dropped more than 36,000 tons of explosives and, despite efforts to avoid residential areas, killed over 1,600 civilians.

Early in the New Year, in an atmosphere thick with acrimony, the parties resumed negotiations. On January 27, they signed a peace agreement essentially the same as the one tentatively reached before the Christmas Bombing. American forces would exit South Vietnam, and both the NVA and the Saigon regime would remain in the South. The final agreement did mention a demilitarized zone, but it described it as "provisional" rather than permanent; Saigon's position had only marginally improved. So what had that final orgy of violence accomplished? "We bombed the North Vietnamese into accepting our concessions,"

[3] In the spring of 1972, George Wallace sought the Democratic presidential nomination. But an assassination attempt in May permanently paralyzed him and forced an end to his campaign.

an aide to Kissinger sardonically concluded. Some 58,000 Americans had lost their lives in the conflict. Vietnamese deaths were vastly greater: as many as three million, military and civilian, by the time the war finally ended in 1975.

The Intensification of Watergate

Outwardly, Nixon was in excellent political shape in the weeks following his second inauguration in January 1973. On the heels of a landslide reelection victory, he had finally engineered an exit from Vietnam, and nearly six hundred freed US prisoners of war, some captured as early as 1964, were coming home. Nixon's approval rating was at 67 percent in late January; the last time it had reached that high had been in the aftermath of his "silent majority" speech in November 1969.

As the president himself knew all too well, however, formidable political challenges lay ahead. Growing clusters of investigators – in Congress, in the courts, in the press, and within Nixon's own Department of Justice – were looking more closely at the attempted break-in at the Watergate complex, and at the broader cast of characters implicated in that act. The White House's legal exposure was considerable. Through pressure on the DOJ and the FBI, Nixon and his top aides had managed to slow down the federal investigation, but not quash it. DOJ attorneys had kept pursuing the case, working with a specially convened grand jury. Under questioning by the FBI or the grand jury, several CREEP and Nixon administration officials had lied to conceal the White House's involvement in the break-in. Nixon's chief of staff, H. R. Haldeman, was even arranging hush money payments to the Watergate burglars. In January 1973, the burglars were tried and quickly convicted in a federal district court. The judge in the case, John Sirica, keen on discovering who, ultimately, was behind this curious crime, threatened to give the defendants lengthy sentences unless they said all they knew. Congressional Democrats, meanwhile, had shaken off their despondency over McGovern's crushing defeat and were gearing up to investigate the matter. In February, the Senate formed a special Watergate Committee.

In those early months of 1973, Watergate remained a relatively minor item in the nation's public conversation. That changed in late March, when one of the Watergate burglars wrote a letter to Judge Sirica admitting that unnamed higher-ups had pressured the defendants "to plead guilty and remain silent." Sirica read the letter aloud in open court and called for further investigation. Watergate now became a major national story, as several prominent newspapers, not just *The Washington Post*, published leaks about the White House's connections to the burglary. Behind closed doors, Nixon, Haldeman, Ehrlichman, and other top aides scrambled to contain the damage. It was now undeniable that *someone* in the White House had broken the law; Nixon's best option, it appeared, was to pin the blame on some expendable official and insist that the conspiracy went no higher than that. As Nixon and his aides cast about for a suitable scapegoat – an effort that ultimately went nowhere – White House Counsel John Dean got the distinct impression that he was being set up as the fall guy. In early April, he began secretly cooperating with

Figure 7.3 Chair of Senate Watergate Committee Sam Ervin (center) sits with Senator Howard Baker (left, holding glasses) and Chief Counsel Sam Dash (right), 1973. Source: Wally McNamee / Corbis Historical / Getty Images.

DOJ and Senate Watergate investigators. Dean had been fully enmeshed in the Watergate cover-up and thus had quite a bit to say.

In May, the Senate Watergate Committee, chaired by Sam Ervin, a North Carolina Democrat, opened hearings on the affair. Continuing until early 1974, the televised proceedings were a national sensation. A survey found that 85 percent of American households tuned in to some portion of the hearings. The witnesses, many of them Nixon aides who had recently resigned their positions, gradually filled in a disturbing picture: the Watergate break-in was part of a much wider array of criminal acts – from wiretapping and burglary to witness tampering and perjury – committed on Nixon's behalf. But what about the president's own culpability? John Dean, himself now an ex-White-House official, appeared before the committee in June and publicly stated what he had already told investigators in private. Nixon, he said, had actively conspired with aides to cover up the White House's involvement in the Watergate burglary. Dean's allegations were not widely believed at first. After all, the accuser was an obscure thirty-four-year-old attorney, whereas the accused was an overwhelmingly reelected American president who, though now acknowledging that officials in his White House may have broken the law, adamantly denied any personal wrongdoing. In fact, Nixon said, he was just as eager as everyone else to get to the bottom of the Watergate mess. To prove it, he authorized his attorney general, Elliot Richardson, to appoint a special prosecutor to investigate the matter. Richardson chose Archibald Cox, a liberal Democrat who had served as solicitor general under Presidents Kennedy and Johnson.

In July came a key turning point: a White House aide testified to Ervin's committee that Nixon had installed a secret taping system in the White House; since 1971, thousands of hours of presidential conversations had been recorded on reel-to-reel audio tapes. Potentially, at least, a highly credible mechanism existed for settling the Nixon–Dean dispute and, more broadly, the question of Nixon's role in Watergate. Both the Senate Watergate Committee and Special Prosecutor Cox demanded that Nixon turn over the relevant tapes. Nixon refused, citing the doctrine of "executive privilege," which holds that presidents are entitled to keep certain information in confidence. The tussle over the White House tapes would be a central issue for the remainder of the Watergate controversy.

Kissinger, the Middle East, and Nixon's Diplomatic Eclipse

As the domestic scandal metastasized, the president became less and less able to concentrate on foreign affairs. National Security Adviser Henry Kissinger, who by the end of Nixon's first term was secretary of state in all but name, grew even more dominant in US foreign policy. In August 1973, Nixon made it official and nominated Kissinger to replace William Rogers as secretary of state. A month later, the Senate overwhelmingly confirmed him. The first major crisis Kissinger faced in that role, an eruption of violence in the Middle East, occasioned his nearly total eclipse of the president in the high-stakes game of Arab–Israeli diplomacy.

In the Arab–Israeli war of June 1967, Israel had won lopsided victories against its Arab neighbors, seizing the Sinai Peninsula and the Gaza Strip from Egypt, the Golan Heights from Syria, and the West Bank of the Jordan River (known simply as the West Bank) from Jordan. For years to come, Israel's occupation of those territories and the prospects for bringing it to an end would be a major diplomatic concern of the international community. Another consequence of the war was the rise of an independent Palestinian movement. Over the first couple of decades following Israel's creation in 1948, Palestinians displaced by this event had generally looked to the Arab countries to achieve the overthrow of the Zionist state and the "liberation" of Palestine. The 1967 debacle prompted Palestinians to take matters into their own hands. In 1969, the Palestine Liberation Organization (PLO), which the Arab League had created in 1964 to provide a harmless outlet for mounting Palestinian impatience, emerged as an independent force in Arab politics. For several years thereafter, the PLO proclaimed the objectives of dismantling Israel and establishing an independent Palestinian state in all of Palestine – that is, the territory comprising Israel, the West Bank, and the Gaza Strip. By the late 1970s, though, the PLO's dominant factions were signaling their readiness to settle for an independent Palestinian state in the West Bank and Gaza, whose Arab inhabitants now lived under Israeli occupation.

In later decades, the fate of the West Bank and Gaza would be the focus of Arab–Israeli diplomacy. In the early 1970s, however, the state-to-state standoff between Israel and its Arab neighbors, especially Egypt and Syria, took center stage in Middle East politics. By now, cold war rivalries were increasingly mapping themselves onto the Middle East dispute, as Washington became Israel's chief arms supplier and defender at the United Nations, and as Moscow continued to serve as the main military and diplomatic champion of Egypt and Syria. Any resumption of Arab–Israeli hostilities risked drawing in the superpowers.

As noted, Nixon's first secretary of state, Bill Rogers, wielded little overall authority in US foreign policy-making. One exception to this rule was the Middle East portfolio, which Nixon did place squarely in Rogers's hands – at least at first. From 1969 to 1971, Rogers promoted a diplomatic settlement entailing Israel's withdrawal from virtually all of the territories occupied in 1967 in exchange for the Arab states' formal recognition of Israel. Kissinger privately opposed the so-called Rogers Plan. He doubted the US government could persuade Israel to accept it. And, indeed, the Israeli government was harshly critical of the scheme, arguing that the pre-June-1967 borders were indefensible and that Israel should retain substantial portions of the occupied territories (or at least be free to seek such border changes in bilateral negotiations with individual Arab nations, rather than having to submit to a general US peace plan). Kissinger also believed that the status quo in the Middle East served US cold war interests. Why should the United States pressure its own ally to return territory to countries that had accepted Soviet support? The fact that many Arab governments, too, publicly criticized the Rogers Plan (while in some cases privately signaling that it could serve as a basis for further discussion) strengthened Kissinger's hand. By the end of 1971, Kissinger had persuaded Nixon that the Rogers Plan was unworkable and, along the way, had wrested control of Middle East policy from the hapless secretary of state.

Of course, stiff-arming aggrieved nations was a poor recipe for tranquility. In October 1973, Egypt and Syria launched major offensives against Israeli positions on the Sinai Peninsula and Golan Heights, respectively. Although the two Arab countries did surprisingly well at first, Israel soon gained the initiative and pushed them back to the 1967 ceasefire lines, and even behind them in places.

The three-week war deeply unsettled the international community. In response to a US arms airlift to Israel, several oil-producing Arab states cut off oil shipments to the United States and some other Western nations. Arab countries had long threatened to use the "oil weapon" against nations that supported Israel, but only now were they in a position to wield it effectively. Over the preceding decade, stepped-up industrial production had significantly increased global demand for oil, much of which originated in Arab countries. The oil embargo, which lasted until March 1974, caused panic buying, hoarding, and real and imagined gasoline shortages throughout the noncommunist industrialized world; these developments, in turn, severely dislocated an already troubled global economy. In the United States, motorists waited in long lines, sometimes stretching for blocks, to buy gas. Once it became readily available again, gas was far more expensive, around 55¢ per gallon in the spring of 1974 as opposed to 38¢ the previous summer (at a time when the median annual household income was about $11,000). The main instigator of the price hikes was the Organization of the Petroleum Exporting Countries (OPEC), which consisted of several Arab states along with non-Arab members such as Iran, Venezuela, and Nigeria. In December 1973, OPEC exploited spiking demand by raising its price from $5.11 per barrel to $11.65.

The conflict also briefly exacerbated superpower tensions – and in so doing became entangled with Watergate. Two weeks into the war, Kissinger, now serving as secretary of state, flew to Moscow to work out a superpower-sponsored ceasefire agreement. In the midst of these deliberations, Nixon's domestic crisis reached its most climactic moment. On the evening of October 20, in an event that became known as the "Saturday Night Massacre," Nixon ordered Attorney General Richardson to fire Special Prosecutor Cox, who had continued to demand the surrender of White House tapes. Richardson refused the dismissal order and resigned, as did Deputy Attorney General William Ruckelshaus. The third-ranking official at the Department of Justice, Solicitor General Robert Bork, carried out the dismissal. But the public outcry was intense, and days later Nixon turned over the subpoenaed tapes and allowed Bork to appoint a new special prosecutor, Leon Jaworski.

Undeterred by the chaos in Washington (in fact, Kissinger was relieved that Nixon was too distracted by his domestic woes to direct the diplomacy from afar), Kissinger and the Soviet leaders reached a ceasefire agreement, which the UN Security Council passed as a resolution on October 22, and which the US and Soviet governments then persuaded their respective proxies to accept. But Israel chafed under the agreement's terms, which required it to halt, in midcourse, an ongoing operation to encircle tens of thousands of Egyptian soldiers in the Sinai. Flouting the ceasefire it had just endorsed, Israel closed the trap, besieging the Egyptian soldiers and refusing to allow food, water, or medical supplies to reach them. In a panic, Egypt's president, Anwar Sadat, sent urgent messages to Moscow and Washington appealing for joint superpower intervention to force Israel to comply with the ceasefire. Although Sadat's message was intended to inspire US–Soviet cooperation, it inadvertently triggered a superpower showdown.

On the evening of October 24, the Soviet ambassador to the United States handed Kissinger a message from the Soviet government. It proposed that the United States and the Soviet Union grant Sadat's request and take joint military action to enforce the ceasefire; if Washington declined to act, Moscow would intervene unilaterally. Kissinger immediately convened a meeting with other top Nixon administration officials, including the secretary of defense, the CIA director, and the chairman of the Joint Chiefs of Staff, to decide how to respond to the Soviet message. Notably absent was the president, who had already turned in for the night. Kissinger had spoken to Nixon by telephone earlier that evening and had found him in a morbidly self-pitying mood. The furor over the Saturday Night Massacre was running at full steam, and prominent citizens were calling for his impeachment. Nixon moaned that domestic critics were motivated by a "desire to kill the president. And they may succeed. I may physically die." From this and other evidence, Kissinger and Alexander Haig, who had replaced Haldeman as White House chief of staff, concluded that Nixon probably was not in the best frame of mind to participate in a superpower showdown. The president slept on.

In their all-night meeting, Kissinger and his colleagues drafted a forceful reply to the Soviets to be sent in Nixon's name. Falsely denying that Israel had violated the ceasefire, they rejected the proposal for joint military action and warned that unilateral Soviet intervention "would produce incalculable consequences which would be in the interest of neither of our two countries." To underscore the message, the meeting participants arranged to have US troops and nuclear forces worldwide placed on heightened alert. Though not publicly announced, the alert was expected to generate extensive electronic signal traffic that the Soviets would detect, leaving them in no doubt about US resolve.

As it happened, news of the US alert leaked immediately and dominated news coverage on October 25. In a sign of the times, American journalists were openly suspicious that Nixon had manufactured the US–Soviet standoff to take the focus off Watergate. The superpower crisis was all too real, but, fortunately, it quickly eased. Sadat withdrew his request for US and Soviet intervention and called instead for the dispatching of an international peacekeeping force that excluded the superpowers. Washington and Moscow endorsed the proposal, and the UN Security Council passed another resolution, which reaffirmed the ceasefire, demanded that the warring parties return to the October 22 ceasefire lines, and authorized the deployment of a UN peacekeeping force that excluded permanent members of the UN Security Council. Military intervention by either superpower was thus off the table. Under pressure from Kissinger, who wanted Egypt weakened but not utterly humiliated, Israel ended its siege of the Egyptian soldiers, effectively bringing the war to a close.

Kissinger's approach to the Arab–Israeli conflict now entered a new phase. Acknowledging that he had underestimated the Arab countries' ability to threaten US interests on a global scale, the secretary of state threw himself into a sustained diplomatic effort to stabilize the regional situation and prevent the recurrence of another major Arab–Israeli war. Although Kissinger engaged with numerous Middle Eastern governments, his primary aim was to reach a bilateral understanding between Israel and Egypt – and thereby thwart rival diplomatic schemes. By late 1973, Israel faced growing international pressure, emanating not just from East bloc and Third World states but from many Western European governments as well, to withdraw to the pre-June-1967 lines. Kissinger, by contrast, still believed that Israel should be permitted to keep substantial portions of the occupied territories. To circumvent demands for total withdrawal, he capitalized on the attitude of Sadat, who was extremely eager to end his country's conflict with Israel and focus instead on Egypt's pressing economic needs. Sadat was so desperate for a deal that he was willing to drift away from the Soviet orbit and place his trust in Kissinger's mediation. Although Sadat insisted that any Egyptian-Israeli agreement be linked to a broader Arab–Israeli settlement, Kissinger suspected that the Egyptian president would, if necessary, accept the former without the latter. With Egyptian power thus removed from the military equation, the remaining Arab states would find it extremely difficult to resume major hostilities, and again galvanize world opinion, to achieve a full Israeli withdrawal.

And so, as Nixon sank further into the quicksand of Watergate, Kissinger brokered a series of bilateral negotiations whereby Egypt gradually reduced its state of belligerency against Israel in exchange for Israel's gradual withdrawal from portions of the Sinai. The culmination of Kissinger's Middle East diplomacy was the Sinai II Agreement of September 1975, in which Egypt regained a slice of territory in the western Sinai and pledged in return that it would never again use force to resolve its differences with Israel. The United States began furnishing Egypt military aid. Meanwhile, in a secret agreement with Israel, Kissinger promised

Figure 7.4 Henry Kissinger and Anwar Sadat, 1975. Source: Universal History Archive / Universal Images Group Editorial / Getty Images.

that the United States would not negotiate with the PLO as long as it refused to recognize Israel. This self-imposed restriction would prevent Washington from dealing with the Palestinians' chosen leadership until the late 1980s. Kissinger's scheme had not only stripped Moscow of a key Arab ally but also enabled Israel to retain most of the occupied territory and to avoid, for the foreseeable future, any serious reckoning with the Palestinian issue. It was a brilliantly executed recipe for an indefinite prolongation of the Arab–Israeli dispute.

Nixon's Fall

The destructive consequences of Kissinger's Middle East diplomacy would be clearer in retrospect. In the months following the 1973 war, American pundits hailed the secretary of state as a diplomatic miracle worker whose arcane formulas were dissolving ancient hatreds. Nixon tried to claim some vicarious glory, to little avail: whenever the focus shifted to him, Watergate was the sole topic of interest. (The chief exception to this rule was a Middle East trip Nixon took in June 1974. In Cairo, throngs of ordinary Egyptians, eager for peace and for a chance at US-assisted prosperity, gave the American president a hero's welcome. Kissinger later quipped that Nixon must have regretted "that Egyptians were not represented on the House Judiciary Committee," which by now was pursuing impeachment proceedings.)

The White House tapes Nixon had surrendered after the Saturday Night Massacre only whetted suspicions. A recording of a conversation occurring on June 20, 1972 – just three days after the Watergate break-in – contained an eighteen-and-a-half-minute gap. Nixon's secretary, Rose Mary Woods, told reporters that she had accidentally erased that section while trying to transcribe it as she was speaking on the phone. But the scenario Woods described was convoluted and implausible, and her later sworn testimony lent credence to the suspicion that the president had erased that section himself.

Meanwhile, Nixon faced a flurry of non-Watergate-related allegations: that he had underpaid his taxes, that the deed donating his vice-presidential papers to the National Archives contained falsified information, that his net worth had more than tripled during his presidency. "I am not a crook," Nixon insisted to a gathering of newspaper editors in November 1973, in a statement that could only delight his jeering detractors.

Another non-Watergate scandal made it easier to imagine Nixon's removal from office. In October 1973, ten days before the Saturday Night massacre, Vice President Agnew abruptly resigned as a consequence of federal bribery charges stemming from his prior tenure as Maryland's governor. Following procedures outlined in the Twenty-fifth Amendment, Nixon nominated House Minority Leader Gerald Ford, a Michigan Republican, to assume the vice presidency; the House and Senate approved the nomination in November and December, respectively. Wags had joked that Agnew was Nixon's "impeachment insurance" – that Democrats would never remove the president as long as the hated Agnew stood by to take his place. Ford was a very different proposition. Although some considered him a mediocrity, he carried none of Agnew's toxic baggage; Democrats would readily accept him as Nixon's replacement. The president had lost his impeachment insurance. (Nixon understood this but was in a bind: any vice-presidential nominee passing muster in Congress had to be someone the Democratic majorities could tolerate in the presidency.)

In February 1974, the House Judiciary Committee began investigating whether Nixon's misconduct warranted impeachment by the House. Along with the new special prosecutor, Leon Jaworski, the committee identified several additional White House tapes of interest and asked that they, too, be turned over. In April 1974, after Judge Sirica ordered Nixon to grant the request, the president partly complied by releasing edited transcripts of some of the conversations. Sold in paperback editions by *The New York Times* and *The Washington Post*, the transcripts were a public relations disaster for the president. It was later revealed that they omitted or mischaracterized several incriminating statements by Nixon. (In one instance, the transcripts quoted Nixon as expressing a desire "to get off the cover-up line." When congressional investigators subsequently listened to the tape themselves, they heard a president pushing "to get on with the cover-up plan.") But, even without such damaging evidence, the overall portrait the transcripts painted was of a president consumed by personal resentments and petty politics. In what proved to be a serious blunder, Nixon's staff had expunged the swear words and replaced them with the phrase "[expletive deleted]." Many of the excised terms were mildly profane words, such as "damn" and "hell," but the bracketed insertions invited readers to imagine the worst. Across the country, newspapers that had endorsed Nixon's reelection in 1972 castigated the president for creating such a tawdry atmosphere in the White House. Even Republican members of Congress expressed shock at what the transcripts seemed to reveal.

In March 1974, the Watergate grand jury indicted Haldeman, Ehrlichman, Mitchell, and other CREEP officials, charging them with bribery, wiretapping, destroying documents, and lying to investigators. Three months later, newspapers reported that a sealed addendum to the indictment had named Nixon an "unindicted co-conspirator" in a scheme to obstruct justice. The term joined "expletive deleted," "eighteen-and-a-half-minute gap," "I am not a crook," and other expressions in a growing store of Watergate catchphrases that Americans sardonically repeated to one another as the remarkable drama unfolded.

Nixon's "unindicted" status reflected the Department of Justice's view that a sitting president could not be criminally prosecuted. The ultimate check on Nixon would have to come from Capitol Hill, where the House Judiciary Committee was well launched on its impeachment investigation. Unsatisfied with the transcripts of the White House conversations, the committee continued to demand the release of actual tapes. Of special interest was a June 23, 1972, conversation between Nixon and Haldeman during which, surrounding circumstances suggested, the two men had likely discussed the Watergate break-in. Nixon, still citing executive privilege, refused to turn over this and other tapes. In late May 1974, Sirica ordered him to surrender a set of tapes that included the Nixon–Haldeman conversation. The president appealed to the Supreme Court, which on July 24 ruled unanimously that he had to furnish the recordings. Days later, in televised proceedings attracting tens of millions of viewers, the House Judiciary Committee approved three articles of impeachment, centering on Nixon's efforts to impede the investigation of Watergate and to violate "the constitutional rights of citizens." No one doubted that the full House would also vote for impeachment, necessitating a trial in the Senate.

On August 6, Nixon finally released the sought-after tapes, including the one containing the June 23, 1972, conversation. Here was the proverbial "smoking gun": clinching evidence that Nixon had indeed tried to obstruct the investigation of the Watergate break-in. The president could be heard approving a scheme (proposed, ironically, by his nemesis John Dean) to warn the FBI off the Watergate scent: the FBI should be told that the break-in was part of a US foreign intelligence operation from which domestic law enforcement ought to keep a patriotic distance. The CIA, Nixon told Haldeman, "should call the FBI in and say that we wish for the country, don't go any further into this case, period!" (The CIA declined to participate in the ruse, but Nixon's instruction revealed his criminal intent.)

Even before the release of the "smoking gun" tape, 66 percent of Americans had come to favor impeachment. Still, a hard core of conservative Republicans remained loyal to Nixon, giving him hope of surviving a Senate trial, in which a two-thirds supermajority would be needed for conviction and removal from office. The tape's release swiftly undermined the lingering Republican support. On August 7, a small delegation of Republican lawmakers, including Barry Goldwater, the conservative standard-bearer, told Nixon that he now lacked sufficient backing in the Senate to escape conviction. His options exhausted, on August 8 Nixon addressed the nation and announced that he would resign the presidency the following day, to be succeeded by Vice President Ford. Nixon admitted some errors of judgment but no legal or moral wrongdoing. On August 9, Ford took the oath of office and assured his fellow citizens that "our long national nightmare is over."

Interpretations of Watergate

Many of the top Nixon aides involved in Watergate – Mitchell, Haldeman, Ehrlichman, even Dean – were tried, convicted, and sentenced to brief prison terms. Nixon himself might well have shared this fate, but in September 1974 Ford pardoned his predecessor for any crimes he may have committed while in office. This decision infuriated millions of Americans and almost certainly contributed to Ford's failure to win the presidency in his own right in 1976. In subsequent years, however, many opinion leaders would come to see the pardon as a necessary and statesmanlike act that allowed the country to move on from its "long national nightmare." In 2001, the John F. Kennedy Presidential Library and Museum bestowed on former President Ford its Profile in Courage Award, specifically praising his pardon of Nixon. Not all later observers would be so admiring. In 2019, citing a train of presidential abuses occurring in the decades since Nixon's resignation, the historians Kevin Kruse and Julian Zelizer wrote, "The lessons are clear: If an administration commits crimes without being held accountable, the next commander in chief feels emboldened to keep skirting the rules and violating the public trust." Ultimately, the scholars warned, such officially sanctioned amnesia "does nothing to heal the nation," even when billed as doing precisely that.

The disagreement over the Ford pardon has dovetailed with a broader debate over the meaning of Watergate. The dominant interpretation has been to see the affair as demonstrating the resilience of the US political system. A corrupt president tried to subvert the Constitution to his own political ends, but the nation's institutions – Congress, the courts, the press, even other elements of the executive branch – exposed his criminality and forced it to stop. The crisis was resolved without the firing of a shot. The system worked.

Critics of this interpretation include not just those who, like Kruse and Zelizer, object that Nixon got off too easily. Commentators further to the left have argued that, yes, the system worked, but it worked in the ways it always has: for the privileged and the powerful. According to this view, Nixon's lawless behavior was not so different from that of his predecessors, or from his own conduct in other situations. Federal authorities had long used crudely unconstitutional methods to suppress domestic communists, antiwar protesters, Black Panther Party members, American Indian activists, and other radical dissenters. What made Watergate special was the state's choice of targets. In August 1973, while the scandal was still unfolding, the linguist and political analyst Noam Chomsky observed that Nixon's "gang of petty thieves … violated the rules of the game. They were attacking the political center" – that is, Democrats, mainstream journalists, and other members of the elite. "Such people are not fair game for persecution at the hands of the state." Unlike the radical targets, they had ample means to resist the Nixonian onslaught and, at the time of Chomsky's writing, were doing so with a vengeance.

For all the merits of the above critiques, the American civic polity of 1973–1974 was functional in at least one way that citizens took for granted at the time but would, decades later, recall with nostalgia. Throughout the Watergate imbroglio, most political actors and observers agreed on a *relatively* uniform set of standards for determining what had actually happened and where ethical boundaries lay. Once the major newspapers and television networks had reported that a tape recording existed of Nixon trying to interfere in an FBI investigation, a critical mass of his Republican allies saw no alternative to withdrawing their support. Future generations of politicians would not be bound in this manner. By the twenty-first century, alternative news sources and competing ethical standards would make it much harder to inculcate broadly shared perceptions of public reality or to enforce common codes of political conduct.

Whether, and in what ways, the system worked or did not, it was losing the confidence of millions of Americans. The debacle in Vietnam had already heightened the public's skepticism about the competence, veracity, and morality of governing institutions, especially at the national level. The Watergate scandal sharply accelerated this trend. In a 1964 survey, a mere 22 percent of respondents had agreed that "you cannot trust the government to do right most of the time." By 1974, 62 percent thought this was so. To be sure, other circumstances of the early to mid-1970s, such as a deepening economic crisis and spiking crime rates across the country, fed the public dissatisfaction. Yet Watergate, taken as a whole, was one of the largest single contributors.

***

This was a sea change in the nation's attitudes but by no means the only one to have occurred over the previous decade. By the mid-seventies, Americans were taking stock of another, equally profound transformation in societal outlooks, touching on matters of gender, sexuality, and family. In these realms, too – in ways exhilarating to some and dismaying or even frightening to others – the stable certainties of an earlier era were relentlessly coming undone.

READING QUESTIONS

1. Consider the range of foreign policy initiatives that President Nixon pursued. Do they come across as contradictory, or does a more coherent strategy emerge? Can elements of both assessments be true?
2. What motives drove Nixon to conduct, or encourage, the range of surreptitious activities that became known collectively as "Watergate"? Why, in your view, would a figure of such shrewdness and accomplishment behave in these ways?
3. Some historians give high marks to the Middle East diplomacy that Secretary of State Henry Kissinger conducted after the 1973 Arab–Israeli war. Yet the author calls it a "brilliantly executed recipe for an indefinite prolongation of the Arab–Israeli dispute." On what basis does he reach this conclusion?
4. The chapter closes by outlining some of the different interpretations of Watergate that commentators have offered over the years. Which of those interpretations do you find most persuasive, and why? Are there still other ways of understanding Watergate's meaning?

SUGGESTIONS FOR FURTHER READING

Bloom, Joshua, and Waldo E. Martin. *Black against Empire: The History and Politics of the Black Panther Party*. Berkeley, CA: University of California Press, 2013.

Burrough, Bryan. *Days of Rage: America's Radical Underground, the FBI, and the Forgotten Age of Revolutionary Violence*. New York: Penguin Books, 2015.

Flippen, J. Brooks. *Nixon and the Environment*. Albuquerque, NM: University of New Mexico Press, 2000.

Graff, Garrett M. *Watergate: A New History*. New York: Simon & Schuster, 2022.

Hanhimäki, Jussi. *Flawed Architect: Henry Kissinger and American Foreign Policy*. New York: Oxford University Press, 2004.

Herring, George. *America's Longest War: The United States and Vietnam, 1950–1975*, 5th edn. New York: McGraw-Hill, 2013.

Lassiter, Matthew D. *The Silent Majority: Conservative Politics in the Sunbelt South*. Princeton, NJ: Princeton University Press, 2013.

Matusow, Allen J. *Nixon's Economy: Booms, Busts, Dollars, and Votes*. Lawrence, KS: University of Kansas Press, 1998.

Perlstein, Rick. *Nixonland: The Rise of a President and the Fracturing of America*. New York: Scribner, 2008.

Qureshi, Lubna Z. *Nixon, Kissinger, and Allende: US Involvement in the 1973 Coup in Chile*. Lanham, MD: Lexington Books, 2009.

Rabe, Stephen G. *Kissinger and Latin America: Intervention, Human Rights, and Diplomacy*. Ithaca, NY: Cornell University Press, 2020.

Siniver, Asaf. *Nixon, Kissinger, and US Foreign Policy Making: The Machinery of Crisis*. New York: Cambridge University Press, 2011.

Stoll, Steven. *US Environmentalism since 1945: A Brief History with Documents*. New York: Palgrave Macmillan, 2007.

Yaqub, Salim. *Imperfect Strangers: Americans, Arabs, and US–Middle East Relations in the 1970s*. Ithaca, NY: Cornell University Press, 2016.

8 Great Blinding Lightbulb

Women's Rights, Gay and Lesbian Rights, and New Understandings of Gender, Sexuality, and Family, 1960–1975

Introduction

She was there to cover the protest, not get swept up in it, but events took a different turn. On a March evening in 1969, some three hundred women and a few men had gathered at New York City's Washington Square Methodist Church for a "speak-out" in favor of legalizing abortion, which was then prohibited in all fifty states. The event had been organized by Redstockings, a newly formed radical feminist group. Gloria Steinem, a journalist known for her friendly coverage of the protest movements of the day, was reporting on the gathering for *New York* magazine. She took notes as the featured speakers, twelve women who had had abortions – some by breaking the law, others by qualifying for the narrow exemptions granted in New York state – passed a microphone around and told their stories. One woman had threatened suicide to convince a psychiatric board that she was unfit to give birth. Another had submitted to "the scraping and scraping" of an illegal abortionist working without anesthetic.

As Steinem listened to the searing testimonies, her mind raced back a dozen years to her own secret abortion, which she had gotten in her early twenties. The memory switched on a "great blinding lightbulb," she later recalled. "Suddenly, I was no longer learning intellectually what was wrong. I knew. Why should each of us [who had had an abortion] be made to feel criminal and alone?" Steinem had already written sympathetically about women's protest actions, but this was different. She now embraced feminism wholeheartedly and made it her life's work.

One of Steinem's signature feminist achievements, facilitated by her journalistic and publishing connections, would be the launching of *Ms.*, a polished, mass-circulation magazine that made feminist ideas, figures, organizations, and causes accessible and appealing to tens of thousands of American women (and some men). The inaugural issue, published in early 1972, appeared to touch all the bases on a diverse and rapidly shifting field of political and cultural play. It featured contributions by mainstream and radical feminists, highlighting areas of agreement between two currents of women's activism often at odds with one another. It contained the essay "Welfare Is a Women's Issue," by Johnnie Tillmon, the

African American chairwoman of the National Welfare Rights Organization, who had herself been a single mother on public assistance. Emulating the helpful, instructional format of other women's magazines, it offered pointers on "How to Write Your Own Marriage Contract." Updating Redstocking's 1969 speak-out, it included a declaration, "We Have Had Abortions," signed by fifty-three prominent women, including the historian Barbara Tuchman, the writer Anaïs Nin, the tennis champion Billie Jean King – and *Ms.* coeditor Gloria Steinem.

There was also an interview with an anonymous woman who described a recent experience with same-sex intimacy. The editors prefaced it by noting that lesbians had received far less media attention than gay men, "a fact for which women might be grateful since interpretations of male homosexuality have often been inaccurate and prejudiced." True enough, but another article in that issue, "Down with Sexist Upbringing," suggested the editors' own lingering discomfort over the subject. The article reassured readers that letting boys play with dolls would not make them gay, citing a psychiatrist who asserted, "Boys become homosexual because of disturbed family relationships, not because their parents allowed them to do so-called feminine things."

In short, *Ms.*'s first issue provided a vivid and intricate snapshot of Americans' fast-changing understandings of gender, family, and sexuality in the early 1970s, understandings often inflected by the shifting politics of race and class. Though rooted in the evolving demographics of postwar America, the transformations had been spurred since the early 1960s by vigorous social movements. These included a mainstream feminist movement primarily concerned with gender discrimination in the public sphere; a radical feminist movement confronting male supremacy in private realms previously seen as beyond the reach of public policy; and varieties of Black women's activism that foregrounded injustices of race and class alongside those of sex. By the early 1970s, mainstream feminism – which *Ms.*, for all its edginess, exemplified – had accepted some of the positions of the other activist currents, especially the contention that private harms were a public concern. Over the same years, gay and lesbian activists transformed a set of scattered, cautious appeals for public toleration into a defiant national movement for liberation. All these struggles, along with the demographic changes that enabled them, disrupted a social order many had assumed was divinely or naturally ordained.

Gender, Family, and Same-Sex Intimacy in the Fifties

In the 1950s, American women of all racial, ethnic, and class backgrounds faced significant formal and informal discrimination, though of course those who were nonwhite, working-class, or poor suffered much greater disadvantages. The Nineteenth Amendment to the Constitution, ratified in 1920, barred any restriction of the right to vote on account of sex. In practice, however, millions of African American women throughout the South were, like Black men, prevented from voting. It was possible for women to hold public office, and a handful did so (often as the widows of male politicians who had died in office). A very small number of women, almost all of them white, were doctors, lawyers, professors, research scientists, or other advanced professionals. A combination of societal expectations and formal restrictions (many graduate programs and professional schools used quotas to limit the number of female applicants they admitted) discouraged even middle-class and affluent girls and women from aspiring to such careers. Across the economy, whole categories of jobs were deemed unsuitable for women, and employers were permitted, and indeed expected, to fill them only with men. Women could be barred from serving on juries or, if they were married, from opening bank accounts or obtaining credit cards without their husbands' permission. Abortion was illegal throughout the country, and in many states contraception was, too.

In no state was it specifically illegal for a man to rape his wife. In rape cases that did come to trial, it was standard practice for defense attorneys to interrogate alleged victims about their sexual pasts. The concept of "sexual harassment," as either a legally prohibited activity or a socially frowned-upon phenomenon, did not exist. (The closest the broader culture came to acknowledging such behavior was through the popular sight gag of a lecherous boss chasing his secretary around a desk.) For middle-class women attending college or employed in white-collar settings, unwanted sexual attention could be demeaning, psychologically distressing, and professionally crippling. Working-class, impoverished, or otherwise marginalized women faced much harsher sexual exploitation, including physical violence. Postwar civil rights activism, as we have seen, was partly a response to the impunity with which white men sexually assaulted Black women and girls.

We have also seen that, in the late 1940s and 1950s, educators, psychologists, clergy, advertisers, advice columnists, and other cultural arbiters urged middle-class women to view the tending of home and family as their highest calling. In some respects, women's (and men's) behavior seemed to fulfill this vision. In 1956, the median age at which American women entered into their first marriages reached an all-time low of 20.1 years. In 1957, the baby boom peaked at 4,332,000 births. A year later, the nation's divorce rate sank to a postwar low of 2.1 divorces per 1,000 people in the population. In other ways, however, the paeans to domesticity conflicted with what middle-class women were actually doing. By 1960, 35 percent of American women of working age were in paid employment, up from 31 percent in 1948. Middle-class married women accounted for a good portion of that increase. (Working-class women, of course, labored in paid employment at higher rates, but fewer opinion leaders expected them to stay home.) Between 1950 and 1960, the number of women attending college rose from 727,270 to 1,339,367, an increase from 31.6 of total enrollment to 37.1 percent. This gap between exhortation and experience, already the subject of some public commentary in the late 1950s, would become glaring in the next decade.

A smothering orthodoxy coexisting with portents of later challenge: a similar pattern marked the experience of gay men and lesbians in fifties America, albeit with a far heavier share of repression. Both legally and socially, the prohibitions against homosexuality were intense in these years. Every state in the union outlawed same-sex intimacy, and people suspected of it could be denied employment. The two forms of punishment often worked in tandem: gays and lesbians arrested for "lewd" or disorderly conduct in bars, parks, or public restrooms (and in private settings, too, though such arrests were rarer) gained criminal records that could cause them to lose their jobs. The postwar red scare was especially fertile ground for antigay sentiment. Many Americans believed that gays and lesbians could be blackmailed into aiding the communist enemy, or that same-sex attraction was inherently subversive. Reflecting such views, the federal government fired or forced out scores of employees suspected of homosexual conduct or orientation.

American gays and lesbians did organize on their own behalf in the 1950s, though they had to proceed cautiously. They formed what were known as "homophile" associations. The term was essentially a synonym for "homosexual," but it had a broader and presumably less threatening connotation. A derivation from Greek that meant "loving the same," it emphasized the range of human connections rather than just sex. The most prominent homophile organizations were the Mattachine Society, founded in Los Angeles in 1950 and purporting to represent both gay men and lesbians (though with the former predominating), and the Daughters of Bilitis (DOB), formed by lesbians in San Francisco in 1955.[1] The aims of both groups, which gradually acquired chapters in other cities, were to provide support for their members and encourage society to view gays and lesbians more sympathetically. They hosted semipublic events (at which participants often used aliases) to discuss the causes of homosexuality and strategies for lessening its stigma within society. Sometimes, they invited psychologists, physicians, legal analysts, and other professionals to deliver lectures. It was not uncommon for such "experts" to tell their listeners that same-sex attraction was a mental disorder susceptible to treatment, a liberal alternative to the view that it was a crime requiring punishment. Barbara Gittings, who formed a DOB chapter in New York, later said:

> It's amazing to people now that we put up with some of the nonsense that was parlayed in these lectures. And yet, we had to go through that because we really needed the recognition that we got from these people .... That was important – just their coming and recognizing our existence gave us a boost .... People ... talked about homosexuality being a sickness .... We'd sit there and listen and politely applaud and then go for the social hour afterward.

In 1961, legal problems and internal conflicts caused the national Mattachine Society to disband itself. Several local chapters of the society remained, however, and many new chapters would later emerge. The DOB, too, continued its work, along with a scattering of independent homophile groups, typically very small, in cities around the country.

Betty Friedan and *The Feminine Mystique*

In 1963, W. W. Norton published *The Feminine Mystique*, by the journalist and housewife Betty Friedan. The book's origins lay in a survey the author had conducted among her

[1] "Mattachine" was a term for male dancers in medieval France who mocked social conventions. "Daughters of Bilitis" referred to a collection of poems by the French author Pierre Louÿs (1870–1925). The obscure names allowed both groups to operate more discreetly.

former classmates at Smith College in 1957, fifteen years after their graduation. Friedan later interviewed many other middle-class and upper-middle-class women, sometimes in the privacy of their suburban homes, eliciting candid, and occasionally startling, self-reflections. To all appearances, these women were living the American dream, with gainfully employed husbands, thriving children, and comfortable households in safe middle-class neighborhoods. Yet, for reasons they had difficulty articulating, many were deeply dissatisfied, and few had any idea other women felt the same way. In *The Feminine Mystique*, Friedan did venture an explanation. In recent decades, she wrote, young women – at least those able to attend college – had received educations that broadened their horizons and encouraged them to dream big, yet society's sharply narrowed expectations of female adulthood offered hardly any outlet for such aspiration. Primed to appreciate art, literature, history, philosophy, political science, and, less often, mathematics and the physical sciences, women now found themselves enmeshed in the numbing routines of homemaking. "We can no longer ignore," Friedan wrote, "that voice within women that says: 'I want something more than my husband and my children and my home.'"

Although it received mixed reviews, *The Feminine Mystique* gained a wide and appreciative readership. It was excerpted in several women's magazines and quickly became a bestseller. Hundreds of women, most of them housewives, wrote to Friedan to tell her she had struck a chord. "I have been trying for years to tell my husband of my need to do something to find myself – to have a purpose," confided a mother of four in Florida. "All I've ever achieved was to end up feeling guilty about wanting to be more than a housewife and mother." A Wyoming woman wrote, "My secret scream as I stir the oatmeal, iron the blue jeans, and sell pop at the Little League baseball games is 'Stop the World, I want to get on Before it's too late!'"

Of course, by focusing on the experiences of economically comfortable (and presumptively white) women, Friedan had told only part of the story. Little in *The Feminine Mystique* addressed the challenges confronting poor and working-class women, who were disproportionately nonwhite. The author also neglected to mention that she had spent much of the 1940s and early 1950s writing for radical labor journals and imbibing the politics and social vision of the American left. By the mid-fifties, Friedan had mostly left that world behind and had settled into a suburban life of childrearing and homemaking, though she continued to write occasional stories for mainstream women's magazines. Only this later incarnation was visible to the readers of *The Feminine Mystique*. Apparently concerned about being redbaited, Friedan not only omitted her radical past but also shied away from discussing collective remedies for what she called "the problem that has no name." Instead, she urged individual women to achieve self-understanding (perhaps through psychological counseling) and to pursue the fulfilling careers that society had pressured them to forswear. The author, however, had yet another incarnation in her near future. Collective efforts were already under way to enable American women to thrive beyond the domestic sphere – efforts in which Friedan herself, recovering some of her old progressive leanings, would shortly play a leading role.

Mainstream Feminism in the 1960s

By the start of the 1960s, key segments of the US body politic were taking note of the growing presence of women in the workplace. Especially important were female labor activists, who had some influence within the Democratic Party and on the incoming administration of John F. Kennedy. At the same time, knowledgeable observers recognized that female Democratic operatives, by organizing numerous women's events during the 1960 election campaign, had helped Kennedy eke out his narrow victory against Vice President Richard M. Nixon. Democratic women were disappointed, therefore, when Kennedy failed to repay this debt by nominating a woman for his cabinet. Undaunted, Assistant Secretary of Labor Esther Peterson, who had long-standing ties to the union movement, organized a lobbying campaign to persuade the president to empanel a special commission to study the conditions of American women. In December 1961, Kennedy created the President's Commission on the Status of Women (PCSW), naming former First Lady Eleanor Roosevelt to chair it. Roosevelt died a year later, but the PCSW carried on with Peterson serving as its de facto head.

In October 1963, the PCSW issued its final report, which was an ambivalent statement. Although it reaffirmed the traditional view that women's primary place was in the home, it documented widespread discrimination against women in the workplace and their underrepresentation in higher education, the professions, and government. These findings received prominent coverage in the national news media. More consequentially, the PCSW's report inspired the creation of similar commissions at the state level; by 1967, each of the fifty states had one. The state commissions began participating in an annual national conference at which they shared the data they had gathered and discussed proposals for improving women's lives. Women from a wide array of organizations – labor unions, civil rights groups, women's clubs, businesses, schools, universities, churches, synagogues, and local chapters of the League of Women Voters – joined in these endeavors. The exchanges gave women of all racial, ethnic, and class backgrounds a clearer picture of the gender inequality pervading the nation's economic, educational, and civic life.

Also in 1963, in response to early pressures generated by the PCSW, Congress passed the Equal Pay Act, which mandated that women and men receive equal pay for the same work. The law did not affect most female employees, who labored in jobs defined as "women's work" (nursing, teaching, child care, secretarial duties, and so on) and thus subject to lower wage scales. But an important principle had been established, and over the next decade 171,000 women employees received back pay amounting to $84 million.

In 1964, advocates of gender equality scored another important victory, albeit in an odd way. As we saw in Chapter 5, the Civil Rights Act of that year outlawed racial segregation in employment and public accommodations. In both houses of Congress, southern segregationists waged a fierce but ultimately unsuccessful campaign to block the bill's passage. Democratic Representative Howard Smith of Virginia mounted one of the more creative sabotage efforts. He proposed adding the word "sex" to Title VII of the bill, so that the legislation would outlaw employment discrimination on the basis of "race, color, religion, sex, or national origin." Although Smith did genuinely seek greater employment opportunities for women (at least if they were white), he also hoped that his amendment would diminish the appeal of the whole civil rights bill, and perhaps cause his colleagues to vote it down. For that very reason, some of the bill's strongest supporters opposed Smith's amendment. But a number of congresswomen joined with segregationists to keep it in the bill. Many male legislators dismissed Smith's amendment as a frivolous measure that detracted from the bill's seriousness – much as Smith intended. Nonetheless, the legislation passed in both houses of Congress with the ban on sex discrimination included.

When President Lyndon B. Johnson signed the bill into law, no women took part in the ceremony, and news accounts generally ignored the fact that the Civil Rights Act contained a sex discrimination provision. If commentators did mention the Smith amendment, it was to dismiss it as a fluke that no one need take seriously. Wags predicted that the amendment would banish words such as "handyman" and "milkman" from ordinary speech and require Playboy clubs to hire male "bunnies." The act created a new federal agency, the Equal Employment Opportunity Commission (EEOC), which was charged with investigating allegations of employment discrimination on the basis of race, religion, national origin, and – thanks to Smith's amendment – sex. The EEOC was soon inundated with sex discrimination claims from female employees. Yet the commission refused to investigate most of them, arguing that the Civil Rights Act was not originally intended to address such frivolous complaints. Mainstream commentators agreed. As *The New Republic*, a liberal opinion journal, rhetorically asked in 1965, "Why should a mischievous joke perpetrated on the floor of the House of Representatives be treated by a responsible administration body with this kind of seriousness?"

This situation was extremely galling, of course, to the government officials, academics, labor activists, and other stakeholders, most of them women, who had taken part in the PCSW and its state-level counterparts. Betty Friedan, fueled by the success of *The Feminine Mystique*, had begun a journalistic investigation of the EEOC's handling of sex discrimination claims, and she, too, was disgusted by what she was learning. In the summer of 1966, at the third annual conference for state women's commissions in Washington, DC, some delegates proposed a resolution demanding that the EEOC enforce the sex discrimination ban. But conference officials, loath to antagonize the Johnson administration (which was sponsoring the event), refused to bring the item to a vote. In the conference's waning hours, the resolution's supporters – including Friedan, who was there on a guest pass – hastily agreed to reconvene that fall to create an independent organization capable of pressuring the government from the outside.

In October 1966, thirty-two activists, mostly women but including some men, and representing nearly three hundred charter members around the country who could not be present, met in Washington, DC, to form the National Organization for Women (NOW). Friedan was named president. Not only was she well known for *The Feminine Mystique*; she was highly skilled at both conceptualizing and articulating a broad political vision. Although her forceful personality rubbed some people the wrong way, it also enabled the fledgling organization to remain focused on its goals and fend off outside attacks and ridicule. Moreover,

Figure 8.1 National Organization for Women board chair Kathryn Clarenbach and NOW president Betty Friedan, 1967. Source: Bettmann / Getty Images.

Friedan was a charismatic public speaker whose appearances before college audiences and community groups spurred the expansion of NOW's membership and the founding of local chapters.

The organization's primary mission was to promote gender equality in the public sphere, especially in employment, education, and civic life. It was clear from the start, however, that this could not be accomplished without attending, in some measure, to the private sphere, too. Thus NOW argued that society as a whole should help women balance family and career responsibilities. There should be publicly supported daycare facilities, and jobs should be flexibly designed so that women could take time off to have children or care for family members. NOW also called for a reimagining of the marriage partnership so that husbands and wives bore equal, or nearly equal, responsibility for breadwinning and child rearing. The group endorsed the wide availability of contraceptives and, from 1967 on, the legalization of abortion.

Although its orientation was basically white and middle-class, NOW incorporated elements of a broader vision. African American women such as Aileen Hernandez and Pauli Murray, the former a labor organizer and civil rights activist, the latter a civil rights lawyer, were among the group's founders. In 1970, Hernandez became NOW's second president. Thanks partly to Murray's influence, NOW's original statement of purpose, which Friedan authored, located the struggle for gender equality within "the world-wide revolution of human rights now taking place within and beyond our national borders" and asserted "that women's problems are linked to many broader questions of social justice." The statement noted that African American women "are the victims of double discrimination of race and sex" and that "[a]bout two-thirds of Negro women workers are in the lowest paid service occupations." Murray soon grew disillusioned, however, over what she saw as NOW's failure to keep its promise to address poverty and racism head-on.

NOW enjoyed several early successes. One of its main grievances was the EEOC's ruling that newspapers could continue publishing separate job listings for men and women, with the result that whole categories of better-paying jobs remained off-limits for female applicants. In 1967, NOW staged nationwide demonstrations at which members dumped bundles of newspapers in front of local EEOC offices. By 1968, these and other actions had compelled the EEOC to ban sex-segregated "help wanted" ads. A year earlier, NOW persuaded President Johnson to add "sex" to an executive order denying federal contracts to companies that discriminated on the basis of race, color, religion, and national origin. NOW also took aim at commercial airlines' policy of forcing female flight attendants to quit their jobs once they had married or reached the ripe old age of thirty-two. This practice was highly lucrative for the airlines, as it allowed them to avoid paying pensions to employees or raises over a span of decades. (It also enabled them to indulge traveling businessmen by placing conventionally attractive young women at their beck and call.) But the negative publicity NOW generated, along with protests and lawsuits mounted by the flight attendants themselves, persuaded the EEOC to outlaw the policy in 1968.

Radical Women's Activism

By now, a younger and more radical wave of female activists, the champions of "women's liberation," had appeared on the scene. Whereas NOW concentrated on gender discrimination in the public sphere, these new activists foregrounded the oppression of women in more private realms. Women's liberation had its origins in sixties protest movements, especially the civil rights movement and the New Left. The key figures were young women, mostly but not entirely white, who came of age within these movements but later grew alienated from them because of the dismissive, uncomprehending, and sometimes cruel ways in which their male comrades treated them. Much of that harmful conduct occurred amid the rapidly shifting and often disorienting sexual politics of the era.

The early 1960s were a time of considerable flux in the behavior and attitudes of young American women, especially those who were middle-class and educated beyond high school. As more and more of them worked outside the home or attended college, they found new occasions for engaging in sexual relations outside marriage. This was especially true of young women moving to large cities to work as teachers, social workers, flight attendants, or office workers, usually with the intention of marrying and having children after a few years of relatively carefree single life. Helen Gurley Brown's 1962 bestseller *Sex and the Single Girl* – essentially a manual for young women seeking such urban adventures – validated the notion that single women could, at least for a time, enjoy premarital sex. In 1960, the US Food and Drug Administration (FDA) approved the use, with a doctor's prescription, of a new oral contraceptive for women. "The Pill" offered two key advantages over other methods: it was far more reliable, and its use was logistically separated from intercourse. "Many women," writes the historian Elizabeth Siegel Watkins, "found swallowing a small tablet once a day for twenty days each month to be more appealing than fumbling with a diaphragm and jelly or persuading their partners to wear a condom." Potentially, at least, the Pill afforded women considerable power over their sex lives. It quickly became exhibit A in commentators' claim that the nation was undergoing a "sexual revolution." The term was an exaggeration in the early 1960s but grew apter with the passage of time.

Indeed, it would be several years before the Pill became widely available. Until the 1965 Supreme Court decision *Griswold v. Connecticut*, which recognized the right of married couples to use birth control, some states continued to outlaw all contraception. Even after *Griswold*, states could prohibit doctors from prescribing the Pill to unmarried women. It took another Supreme Court ruling, *Eisenstadt v. Baird* in 1972, for single women throughout the country to gain legal access to the Pill. In the 1960s and early 1970s, married women were the oral contraceptive's main users. Nonetheless, the Pill did reach large numbers of young unmarried women in the 1960s, enabling them to engage in sexual activity with far less concern about unwanted pregnancy. A national study released at the end of the sixties found that the number of women engaging in premarital sexual intercourse had doubled during the previous decade.

Of course, even with contraception, sexually active women risked unwanted pregnancy. A pregnant woman unwilling or unable to bear a child could seek an illegal abortion. Under the best of circumstances, she might avail herself of an underground network of women's activists, doctors, and clergy who could arrange for her to have an abortion in Mexico or from a US-based doctor willing to hazard arrest. A woman lacking the requisite connections or funds could attempt a self-induced abortion (using various chemicals ingested orally or by douche) or seek the services of an illegal abortionist who might or might not possess any medical training. Such remedies, not surprisingly, were highly dangerous, and sometimes fatal. As more and more young people became sexually active in the 1960s, an awareness of these stark realities seeped into the consciousness of young women, especially those already attuned to social injustice.

During the first half of the 1960s, thousands of young women, white and Black, took part in the civil rights movement. The most concentrated phase of this involvement was the Freedom Summer campaign of 1964, when young northerners flocked to Mississippi to promote African American voter registration. Throughout that summer, Black and white activists of both sexes, some native to or familiar with the South and many new to it, lived and worked in close proximity, experiencing together the exhilaration, fear, frustration, anxiety, anger, uncertainty, camaraderie, and personal annoyance that arose from this dangerous and vital work. For all concerned, it was an enormously complex human situation, but one of its more vivid aspects was sexual. There were frequent sexual liaisons, some occurring across racial lines, and numerous other occasions when the possibility of physical intimacy hung in the air. Many white women, the historian Alice Echols writes, found themselves

> in a no-win situation . . . . If a white woman accepted a black man's sexual advance, she risked being ridiculed as loose; if she spurned him, she left herself vulnerable to the charge of racism. Of course, the interracial relationships that developed … often grew out of genuine caring and affection. But some black men used white women in an effort to reclaim their manhood and some white women used black men to prove their liberalism or to "expiate their guilt."

Some Black women, in turn, felt devalued by Black men's sexual interest in white women. And, to Black women and men alike, northern white activists of both sexes all too often came across as naïve adventurers whose blithe disregard of the region's white supremacist taboos exposed African Americans to severe reprisals that whites themselves almost always escaped.

Meanwhile, both Black and white women working in civil rights groups were relegated to stereotypically female tasks such as typing, mimeographing (a pre-photocopy form of duplication), making coffee and sandwiches, and other clerical or menial work. Although some women did play leadership roles, they seldom received formal recognition for them. The first to protest this situation was a group of Black women who staged a half-serious sit-in at the Atlanta offices of the Student Nonviolent Coordinating Committee in 1964. Later that year, two white women in SNCC, Mary King and Casey Hayden, anonymously wrote and circulated a paper that objected, in mild terms, to the subordination of women within the organization. The paper received little support from SNCC members; some women in the group, whether sincerely or for fear of ridicule, denied that sex discrimination was an issue for them. Stokely Carmichael, a charismatic and quick-witted SNCC activist who later headed the organization, delivered an infamous put-down of King's and Hayden's concerns. "What is the position of women in SNCC?" he wondered aloud. "The position of women in SNCC is prone!" Those within earshot of Carmichael's quip (a reference to the many sexual couplings during the recently concluded Freedom Summer) took no evident offense. King herself recalled that the comment sparked uproarious laughter and "drew us all close together, because, even in that moment, he was poking fun at his own attitudes." But Carmichael was a bit too pleased with his joke, which he repeated several times in the months and years ahead, to female listeners who were less amused.

Within the white-dominated New Left, women experienced similar frustrations and slights. The flagship New Left organization, Students for a Democratic Society, was strongly committed to the civil rights struggle, as well as to opposing the Vietnam War, which the Johnson administration began escalating in 1964–1965. Another, less well-publicized SDS cause was an effort to awaken an "interracial movement of the poor" that might compel the political and economic establishments to address poverty in a more thoroughgoing manner than seemed likely to occur under President Johnson's recently declared War on Poverty. Cadres of young activists, working within SDS's Economic Research and Action Project (ERAP), relocated to poor urban communities and tried to organize their residents.

Measured against its proclaimed ambitions, ERAP was a failure; no significant movement of the poor resulted from its exertions, at least not directly. (Some ERAP activists did help to launch local efforts that later became part of a national welfare rights movement, as discussed below.) Still, the activities undertaken in ERAP's name boosted the self-confidence of many of the women engaged in them. In general, SDS women proved more successful than their male counterparts in organizing the poor. The qualities such work required – patience, empathy, attentiveness, humility – were ones most SDS women had been encouraged to cultivate. They also benefited from a necessary course correction. Project planners had assumed that the principal endeavor would be organizing unemployed men to demand jobs. But a booming economy and a declining unemployment rate left an unexpectedly small pool of jobless men to work with. So ERAP's focus shifted to helping poor communities obtain better city services, such as street cleaning and garbage removal. The most effective way to do that was to work with female homemakers, whom SDS women could more easily approach. The limited successes ERAP did enjoy were due mainly to the efforts of SDS women.

In light of these accomplishments, SDS women were all the more dismayed to encounter the same denials of status and opportunity facing women in the civil rights movement – the same lack of representation in formal leadership positions, the same expectation that they would furnish the clerical and menial labor. In some ways, the problem of male domination was even more daunting in SDS. A product of universities, SDS was a charged arena of intellectual theorizing and debate, much of it fiercely competitive. Many women in the organization, raised to be accommodating and self-effacing, were intimidated by this atmosphere and preferred to remain silent in meetings. Those who did speak up were often ignored. One recalled that whenever a woman started talking "the men suddenly stretched, and chattered among themselves." A woman's contribution might be met with silence; when minutes later a man said more or less the same thing, voices would rise in keen engagement.

At the same time, the broader left (often called "the movement") was growing less hospitable to female activists. By 1966, it had become untenable for most whites to remain in SNCC or in other groups embracing Black Power. Meanwhile, ERAP was floundering. Stymied in those two areas, the white left redoubled its opposition to the Vietnam War, especially by supporting young men who refused conscription into the military. Draft resistance cast movement men in defiant, heroic roles, while relegating women to a supportive periphery. And "supportive" could have troubling undertones. A popular draft resistance slogan of the day, "Girls say yes to boys who say no," seemed playful on the surface, but it hinted at a coercive expectation taking hold within the left: that movement women would make themselves sexually available for "the cause." In ERAP work, some SDS men had pressured SDS women to sleep with the unemployed men they were trying to organize. In movement circles more broadly, recalled a female SDS member, "[w]omen were meant to put up a traveling SNCC leader, and what put up meant was to 'put out.'" Across the counterculture and the New Left, young men embraced the sexual revolution as an opportunity to enjoy multiple liaisons, often heedless of the fact that not all women felt the same way. Women seeking monogamous relationships or greater emotional connection with their partners were all too easily shamed as "uptight." Heightened sexual activity was also, of course, much riskier for women than for men. The Pill was increasingly available, but abortion remained against the law.

In the mid- to late 1960s, some activist women tried to raise the issue of sexism within left organizations. In late 1965, Mary King and Casey Hayden, who were in the process of leaving SNCC, wrote a fuller version of their 1964 paper and shared it in movement circles.

Although many SDS women were enthusiastic about the paper, it drew a tepid response from SDS men. In June 1967, at SDS's national convention in Ann Arbor, Michigan, a different set of feminists made their own bid for recognition. They issued a manifesto claiming that women's subordination to men, in the broader society and within SDS itself, was comparable to the relationship between colonized and colonizing nations. It was a sharp critique, yet the authors closed on a conciliatory note: "We recognize the difficulties our brothers will have in dealing with male chauvinism and we will assume our full responsibility in helping to resolve the contradiction. Freedom now! [W]e love you!" The SDS newspaper *New Left Notes* duly printed the manifesto, but an accompanying cartoon crudely parodied its message. It showed a young girl in a polkadot minidress with matching underwear, holding a sign that read, "We want our Rights & We want them NOW!"

The Feminist Exodus from the Left

For many radical women, this insult and others like it fueled a suddenly unstoppable drive for independence from the male-dominated left. In an October 1967 appeal "To the women of the left," a group of activists in Chicago wrote, "Women must not make the same mistake the blacks did at first of allowing others (whites in their case, men in ours) to define our issues, methods, and goals. Only we can and must define the terms of our struggle … [I]t is incumbent on us, as women, to organize a movement for women's liberation." This was already starting to happen. It would take the skills of an epidemiologist, writes the historian Ruth Rosen, to trace "the rapid transmission of the infectious enthusiasm for women's liberation that swept the country" from the fall of 1967 on. "Networks of New Left women, accustomed to traveling to national conferences and organizing local and national meetings, became the carriers of that enthusiasm." By the end of 1968, nearly every major American city boasted a women's liberation group.

Plenty of public activism would emanate from these gatherings. The most visible action of 1968 was a raucous protest against that year's Miss America pageant in Atlantic City, New Jersey, by a coalition of East Coast organizations that decried the pageant as a vulgar celebration of sexual exploitation, capitalist greed, white supremacy, and flag-waving imperialism. A more common activity of these new feminist groups, however, was a process of individual and collective self-discovery that became known as "consciousness-raising." In small meetings, women would share their personal experiences, reflecting on the choices that they had made – or that had been made for them – and on the ways in which their lives and society's expectations were tightly intertwined.

Repeatedly, women undertaking these personal excavations uncovered feelings of disappointment, loss, humiliation, and anger they had never fully acknowledged. They also learned that they were not alone. Individual struggles they had chalked up to their own maladjustment, they came to see, resulted from societal inequities suffered by countless other women. Therefore, collective solutions were needed. A slogan coined in 1968 by the former civil rights worker Carol Hanisch, "The personal is political," encapsulated that startling insight. “It was something that we had all been waiting for, for a long time,” ERAP veteran Mimi Feingold recalled of her San Francisco consciousness-raising group. “This was finally permission to look at our own lives and talk about how unhappy we were.” Nancy Hawley, another former SDS member, described what happened when she invited some friends over for dinner at her Boston home while her husband was away: “The flood broke loose gradually and then more swiftly. We talked about our families, our mothers, our fathers, our siblings; we talked about our men; … we talked about ‘the movement’ (which meant New Left men). For hours we talked and unburdened our souls and left high and planning to meet again the following week.”

A key tenet of consciousness-raising, whether openly stated or tacitly assumed, was that the emerging movement drew authority not from preexisting documents or traditions but, ultimately, from women’s own experiences with domineering male behavior. The manifesto of Redstockings, a New York group formed in early 1969, made this point explicitly: “We regard our personal experience, and our feelings about that experience, as the basis for an analysis of our common situation. We cannot rely on existing ideologies as they are all products of male supremacist culture. We question every generalization and accept none that are not confirmed by our experience.” In practice, many radical feminists continued to rely on received ideological or analytical frameworks, especially Marxism and its offshoots. Increasingly, though, such theories derived their power from their resonance with what women themselves had personally witnessed and felt. Many of the more painful experiences involved the men closest to them. The historian Sara Evans tells of a New Orleans activist who, at her women’s group, “mentioned casually that her boyfriend had made fun of her for going to a ‘women’s meeting.’ Suddenly everyone had a story about the negative response of the man she lived with. Some had been gently teased, others harshly ridiculed, but each felt that she had had to take a strong stand simply in order to come . . . . Their new collective consciousness transformed the group.”

Some radical feminists kept trying to engage the broader left, but many of the men who dominated it seemed deaf to their concerns. Both at home and abroad, 1968 was a year of youth rebellion, often taking the form of violent clashes between street protesters and police or other armed authorities. With global revolution at hand (or so many thought), some leftist men affected a macho swagger that was accompanied by casual, and at times even vicious, misogyny. In the lead-up to the Democratic Party’s national convention in Chicago, the Yippies – a countercultural protest group adept at political theater – presumptuously announced that “their” women would disrupt the event by posing as prostitutes and spiking delegates’ drinks with LSD. After the convention, Yippie leader Jerry Rubin disparaged “those old menopausal men who run this country.” In January 1969, movement groups staged a “counter-inaugural” in Washington, DC, to protest the inauguration of Richard Nixon. As the feminist activist Marilyn Webb spoke from the podium about women’s liberation, men in the crowd angrily tried to shout her down, with some even calling for Webb to be raped. The event’s male organizers made no attempt to silence the shocking outbursts. “Sisterhood was powerful,” former SDS leader Todd Gitlin later remarked, “partly because movement brotherhood was not.”

In the ensuing months, as the New Left splintered into mutually antagonistic factions – some of them eventually resorting to futile acts of armed rebellion against the US government – feminists hastened their angry departure from the male-dominated movement. In early 1970, a coalition of radical women seized control of the editorial office of *Rat*, an underground newspaper in New York, and published an all-women's issue. Its centerpiece was a blistering farewell penned by Robin Morgan: "Goodbye, goodbye forever, counterfeit Left . . . . Women are the real Left . . . . We are rising with a fury older and potentially greater than any force in history, and this time we will be free or no one will survive. *Power to all the people or to none.* All the way down, this time."

Black Women's Activism

Over the same years in which predominantly white feminist movements emerged, African American women created, or were major figures in, organizations devoted to addressing women's needs. Yet not all of these activists immediately, or ever, called themselves feminists. Outlooks varied from one individual or group to another. In general, though, the realities of racial and economic injustice were considered so pressing that any analysis failing to foreground them warranted, at the very least, deep skepticism. Most Black women concerned with gender inequities favored a blended perspective in which questions of race, and often class as well, remained squarely in view.

A case in point was the welfare rights movement, which emerged in the early 1960s in response to federal and state government measures to tighten eligibility requirements for public assistance. In cities around the country, welfare recipients, many of them Black women, formed community groups to pressure local welfare offices to treat them more respectfully and be more responsive to their families' needs. Often, these associations worked with local churches, civil rights organizations, or other activist groups. Boston's Mothers for Adequate Welfare (MAW), for example, was formed with the help of ERAP activists. In 1967, the disparate organizations coalesced to form the National Welfare Rights Organization (NWRO), headquartered in Washington, DC. The NWRO received financial support from churches and liberal foundations and by 1968 had acquired some 30,000 members, the vast majority of them African American women. Johnnie Tillmon, a Black welfare recipient who headed a group in Los Angeles, was named national chairwoman. Much of the actual decision-making, however, was in the hands of the executive director, George Wiley, an African American former chemistry professor, and a professional staff consisting mainly of middle-class white men. During the NWRO's early years, Tillmon and many other Black women in the organization proclaimed a vision of female welfare recipients' rights that increasingly placed them at odds with Wiley and the staff.

One of the NWRO's first public battles, in 1967, concerned Congress's consideration of the Work Incentive Program (WIN), a proposed reform of the Aid to Families with Dependent Children (AFDC) program. It would require mothers on AFDC with school-age children to take paid employment or enter job training programs; it would facilitate these transitions by funding the job training, along with child care for welfare recipients. WIN was a response to public criticisms that AFDC fostered dependence among the poor and created incentives for poor women to have more and more children at taxpayers' expense. The NWRO vigorously opposed WIN, arguing that it would deprive poor women of the ability to care for their children. The organization noted that middle-class mothers and homemakers, thanks to their husbands' ample paychecks, already received compensation for their domestic labor; why shouldn't poor mothers be compensated, too? In September 1967, Tillmon and other NWRO members testified before the Senate Finance Committee. As they spoke, senators filtered out of the hearing room until only two remained. To protest this disregard, the women staged an impromptu sit-in, refusing to leave until all the absent committee members returned. The committee's chairman, Russell Long of Louisiana, brought the proceedings to a close with such angry force that the head of his gavel broke off. (Long's disparaging reference to the NWRO as "Black Brood Mares, Inc." became notorious in welfare rights circles; a year later, Tillmon organized some protest actions called "Brood Mare Stampedes.") Despite its forceful opposition, the NWRO could not prevent WIN's passage.

Wiley and the NWRO's male-dominated staff had fought hard against WIN. Once it passed, however, they pivoted toward working within the new restrictions. In 1968, the NWRO applied for, and received, a $434,000 grant from the Department of Labor to enable welfare recipients to receive the mandated job training. "We are still opposed to forcing mothers to work," staff members explained in the NWRO newsletter, but, "since this law is on the books, we must see to it that the rights of recipients are protected." Many Black women in the organization believed that Wiley and the staff had surrendered too easily. Two community leaders in Philadelphia claimed that the NWRO was cooperating with "the most reactionary program in decades. It is designed to remove mothers from the home and place them into 'slave labor' jobs." The Pennsylvania NWRO chapter briefly threatened to pull out of the organization. Such dissent stirred little sympathy in the NWRO's Washington headquarters. A male staff member accused one of the Philadelphia leaders of "seeking ... to retain a secure position of local dominion to the detriment of the ideological goals of the movement."

According to the historian Premilla Nadasen, however, the female dissenters had their own coherent ideology, based not only on the recognition that parenting *is* work but, further, on their conviction that their role as mothers was essential to the thriving of their children and communities. "[T]he greatest thing that a woman can do is raise her own children," said Cassie Downer, head of a Milwaukee welfare rights organization, "and our society should recognize it as a job." This outlook conflicted with that of most NWRO staff members, who believed that welfare mothers generally preferred to work outside the home, provided the jobs they took offered dignity and decent pay. It also departed from the view of many white (and some Black) radical feminists of the era, who, while affirming that women had the right to opt for full-time motherhood, seldom portrayed that as an admirable or enviable choice. As Nadasen notes, however, "Few Black women had the 'luxury' of being fulltime mothers, and most worked outside the home out of necessity." Thus "the struggle to preserve their right to be mothers was viewed historically as a challenge to the subordination of African Americans," not as a capitulation to sexist norms.

Figure 8.2 National Welfare Rights Organization march in Boston, 1969. Source: *The Boston Globe* / Getty Images.

Another issue dividing the NWRO was that of single motherhood. Like many other liberals of the mid- to late 1960s (including some Black leaders of mainstream civil rights organizations), Wiley and the staff were concerned about the growing number of African American families headed by single women. This situation had arisen, they believed, because too many Black men lacked jobs or, worse, any real hope of future employment. Despairing of serving as breadwinners, they failed to take responsibility for the children they fathered, depriving them and their mothers of the economic and social stability needed to escape poverty. A key objective of federal social policy, then, had to be to afford Black men the robust employment prospects that would enable them to assume their family responsibilities. Many Black women in the NWRO rejected this logic, countering that single mothers could be successful heads of households if granted enough financial support. They resisted the notion that single welfare mothers should seize opportunities to marry and thereby make their families more traditional. Instead, these women should be free to enjoy extramarital relationships without losing their AFDC eligibility, as often happened when such relationships were discovered. A welfare rights handbook in West Virginia stated that a woman on public assistance "can have male visitors as often as she wants and go out on dates if she leaves her children in the care of a responsible person."

By the early 1970s, the NWRO's internal divisions had considerably widened, as declining membership, waning foundation support, and a more hostile political environment threatened the organization's viability. Wiley hoped to revive the NWRO by broadening its constituency to include unemployed fathers and the working poor. Most Black female leaders and members, by contrast, believed the focus should remain on the core constituency of welfare recipients. Meanwhile, the condescension emanating from the professional staff was getting harder to tolerate. An internal NWRO report observed that "[a]ttitudes of sexism on every level" prevented members from "participat[ing] in any meaningful way in their organization, and every time they attempt to participate they are ignored or regarded as emotional women." The documented remarks of a white male organizer at the Boston NWRO chapter – advising a student group not to hire a female organizer because "women in general are bad leaders. They have to take a week off to have emotions" – lent credence to the report's assessment.

Ultimately, Wiley and the professional staff lacked sufficient internal support to prevail. In 1972, Wiley resigned as executive director, and Johnnie Tillmon took his place. The NWRO reconstituted itself as a women's organization, and an avowedly feminist one at that. These changes failed, however, to stave off the challenges besetting the organization. In some cases, they made the challenges worse; outside funding dried up even more rapidly following Wiley's and other staff members' departure. The NWRO was forced to close its doors in 1975. Still, the organization and the broader movement it represented had ably served welfare recipients. Legal advocacy groups allied with the NWRO had won important Supreme Court cases, such as *King v. Smith* (1968), which ruled that single mothers could not be deprived of AFDC benefits for entering into new intimate relationships, and *Goldberg v. Kelly* (1970), which barred the cessation of benefits without due process. Here, the NWRO's principal role was to ensure, by vigilant monitoring and, if necessary, forceful protest, that local jurisdictions actually complied with the new rulings. One consequence of all these activities was a significant expansion of the population deemed eligible for public assistance. Nationwide, the number of AFDC recipients rose from 3.3 million in 1965 to 10.8 million in 1974. Less tangibly, writes the historian Ula Taylor, "NWRO members had expanded what counted as a woman's issue."

The same can be said of a strain of women's activism emerging from the Black Power movement. Like their white counterparts in SNCC and SDS, some Black women in SNCC, the Black Panther Party, and other Black Power groups increasingly chafed under the subordinate roles their male comrades had assigned to them. But more particular gender pressures were also at work. The valorization of defiant manhood sweeping the male left in the late 1960s was especially pronounced in Black Power circles. On one level, this was understandable. Militant Black men faced ever-present threats of lethal violence from law enforcement; they were not playacting at revolution in the ways that many white leftist men were. Still, the gender ideology emanating from some Black Power groups could be deeply retrograde. With Black men on the front lines, the exhortation went, Black women must unfailingly support their brothers from the sidelines. With the entire Black community facing "genocide" (a reference to an all too real practice of some welfare agencies to pressure poor, and especially nonwhite, women to become sterilized), it was Black women's "revolutionary duty" to bear as many children as possible. Of course, some Black Power women rejected these notions. When they did so, however, they usually addressed their male counterparts more gently than white radical feminists addressed theirs; after all, Black men continued to endure racist oppression. The dissenting Black Power women also tended to be critical of white feminists for failing to grapple sufficiently with questions of race and class.

In late 1968, Francis Beal, Gwen Patton, Mae Jackson, and other young activists established a women's caucus within SNCC's New York City chapter called the Black Women's Liberation Committee (BWLC). They did so partly in response to reports that poor Black and Puerto Rican women in the city had been coerced to undergo sterilization as a condition of continued welfare assistance. The BWLC discussed this matter, along with proposals to support Black men resisting the draft and to establish "liberation schools" for Black children, an idea the BPP later adopted. Thus the BWLC took up a mix of issues that concerned the Black Power movement in general and Black women in particular.

Over the ensuing months, however, the caucus developed a distinctly feminist approach to the questions it addressed. On Third World liberation, it cautioned that, "unless the woman in any oppressed nation is completely liberated, then a revolution cannot really be called a revolution." On the role of women in the Black freedom struggle, Gwen Patton agreed that "[t]he most beautiful thing that Black Power did was to get black brothers up there on the stages." But "[i]t doesn't make sense that in order for a man to be strong, I have to be weak." On reproductive issues, the BWLC denounced government efforts to sterilize poor women of color, yet it rejected the claim that family planning amounted to genocide. "Black people are always going to have children," a BWLC member said; "we don't have to get into hang-ups that if we use birth control we won't be able to build our nation." Instead, access to contraception "will free black women to participate in the revolution."

In 1970, the BWLC broke away from SNCC (which was on the verge of dissolution anyway) to become a standalone organization, the Black Women's Alliance (BWA). Soon thereafter, in recognition of the fact that some Puerto Rican activists had joined the group, the BWA renamed itself the Third World Women's Alliance (TWWA). In this instance, "Third World" encompassed actual Third World nations and the various nonwhite populations living in the United States, all of which, the activists believed, faced a common enemy in US imperialism. The TWWA maintained its predecessors' focus on the health and wellbeing of US women of color and on the roles that women were, or could be, playing in liberation struggles at home and abroad. The group also criticized the lack of adequate child care for working mothers and spoke out against inhumane prison conditions. To white feminists, it delivered a stringent and at times dismissive message: "[U]ntil you can deal with your own racism and until you can deal with your OWN poor white sisters, you will never be a liberation movement . . . . It is difficult for Third World women to address themselves to the petty problems of who is going to take out the garbage, when there isn't enough food in the house for anything to be thrown away."

Other Black female activists of the time combined the TWWA's liberationist sensibility with the NWRO's focus on poverty and family. In the Mount Vernon/New Rochelle area of New York, a shifting set of activists known variously as the Black Women's Liberation Group and Pat Robinson and Group (after one the founders, the psychotherapist and social worker Patricia Robinson) advocated for poor Black women and children, including welfare recipients. From an initial concern with teenage pregnancy, the Mount Vernon/New Rochelle activists became staunch advocates of contraception for women, countering Black Power's natalist ideology in more forceful terms than the BWLC or the TWWA typically employed. “Having too many babies stops us from supporting our children,” several Mount Vernon/New Rochelle activists wrote in 1967, “… and from fighting black men who still want to use and exploit us.” A 1968 statement situated childrearing in the context of global revolution: “Black women must ally themselves with the have-nots of the world and their revolutionary struggles and withdraw her [*sic*] children from male dominance and educate and support them herself.”

Feminism’s Breakthrough into National Awareness

In the late 1960s, all of these strands of women’s activism, especially those spearheaded by white women, attracted growing news coverage. But 1970 was the year in which the resurgence of feminism – or “Women’s lib,” as many glibly called it – became a major media preoccupation. The three main television networks aired more than twenty stories on the movement, including a half-hour documentary on ABC, a three-part series on CBS, and a six-part series on NBC. Newspapers provided extensive coverage, and national magazines published several cover stories. Media interest ran especially high during and shortly after the August 26 “Women’s Strike for Equality,” an event organized by NOW but involving women’s groups spanning the ideological and racial divides. The participants united behind three demands: legalized abortion, publicly funded child care, and equal opportunity in employment and education. Timed to mark the fiftieth anniversary of the Nineteenth Amendment’s ratification, the Women’s Strike consisted of rallies and demonstrations in cities and towns in forty-two states. The flagship event was a march along Manhattan’s Fifth Avenue that drew as many as 50,000 people, mostly women but including some men.

The Fifth Avenue march projected an image of expansive and exuberant sisterhood, but not all of the participants experienced it that way. Fran Beal and other TWWA members carried signs reading “Hands off Angela Davis.” Davis, a Black academic and activist, had just gone into hiding, suspected of involvement in an armed assault on a Northern California courtroom that left the attacker and three other people dead. Because the attack had been launched in the name of Black Power, many on the left saw Davis as a political fugitive. (She was later apprehended, tried, and acquitted.) Spotting the placards, an agitated NOW leader approached the TWWA marchers and said, “Angela Davis has nothing to do with women’s liberation.” “It has nothing to do with the kind of liberation you’re talking about,” Beal retorted, “but it has everything to do with the kind of liberation we’re talking about.”

The tense exchange signified a broader set of disagreements within feminist ranks. Not only were Black feminists rejecting approaches that failed to place race, and sometimes class, on a common footing with gender; white radical feminists were insisting that sexual oppression behind closed doors was at least as damaging as sex discrimination in the public sphere. Indeed, Betty Friedan had conceived of the Women’s Strike partly to show that women *could* unite around some core issues – and that, not incidentally, NOW and Friedan herself were second to none in channeling the rebellious spirit now sweeping women’s activism. But

Figure 8.3 Washington, DC, participants in the nationwide "Women's Strike for Equality," August 26, 1970. Source: Don Carl STEFFEN / Gamma-Rapho / Getty Images.

Friedan had a problem: although she could understand the need to show greater solidarity with Black women, she was baffled by radical feminists' preoccupation with private sexual relations, and alarmed by the claim, heard in some women's liberation circles, that all men were oppressors. The only feasible course, Friedan believed, was to push for full equality in the public sphere. Once that was achieved, women could renegotiate their relationships with men and thereby attain private fulfillment, too. "This is not a bedroom war," she declared at a rally after the Fifth Avenue march; "this is a political movement." (In her less generous moments, Friedan groused that the point of radical feminism seemed to be "to *make yourself ugly*, to stop shaving under your arms, to stop wearing makeup or pretty dresses—any skirts at all.")

Other NOW leaders, however, were more receptive to the new militant sensibility, which was taking hold among many NOW rank-and-file members. Into the early 1970s, NOW adopted some of the stylistic trappings of the radical groups. (In 1970, Friedan stepped down as NOW's president and became chair of its National Advisory Board, a position from which she wielded less influence than she had expected to.) Consciousness-raising meetings were a case in point. Friedan dismissed them as "naval-gazing rap sessions," yet as NOW's membership rapidly expanded – it grew by 50 percent in the months following the Women's Strike – organizers found that a looser, more conversational style was a useful way to orient new members, especially those unfamiliar with feminism or political activism.

Consciousness-raising, or at least a public version of it, also proved effective in the struggle to legalize abortion, a cause supported by mainstream and radical feminists alike.

By the late 1960s, several states had eased their abortion restrictions to permit the procedure under certain conditions, typically including a psychiatrist's finding that a pregnant woman lacked the mental capacity or emotional stability to bear a child. Not surprisingly, most feminists found this requirement insulting and demanded full legalization.[2] In March 1969, as the New York state legislature considered a further liberalization of its abortion laws, Redstockings held the abortion "speak-out" at which Gloria Steinem experienced her feminist epiphany. In the spring of 1970, New York decriminalized abortion. (Hawaii had done the same weeks earlier, but New York's decision was far more influential because of that state's national prominence.) Over the next few years, abortion rights advocates held speak-outs in other states. "The speak-out … turned out to be an incredible organizing tool," an activist recalled. "It brought abortion out of the closet where it had been hidden in secrecy and shame." In opinion polls, the percentage of Americans supporting a woman's right to abortion during the first trimester of pregnancy rose from 40 percent in December 1969 to 64 percent in June 1972.

In its 1973 decision *Roe v. Wade*, the US Supreme Court delighted abortion rights supporters by ruling that women had an unqualified right to abortion during the first trimester. In the second trimester, states could impose some regulations, and in the third trimester they could ban abortions altogether, on the ground that by this stage a fetus had a chance of surviving outside the womb. Abortion opponents, many of them conservative Catholics, immediately denounced the decision, though their ability to alter the new status quo seemed limited at first. By the second half of the decade, however, few would doubt the power and reach of antiabortion sentiment.

Another subject on which feminists made rapid progress in the early 1970s, albeit with little involvement by radical feminists, was the proposed Equal Rights Amendment (ERA) to the US Constitution. First broached in the 1920s, the ERA would prevent the federal government or any state from discriminating on the basis of sex. For decades, the ERA had split women's rights advocates. Supporters said it offered the surest route to first-class citizenship for women. Opponents, many of them in the labor movement, warned that its passage would outlaw "protective legislation" – laws shielding female employees from especially arduous or hazardous working conditions. Support for the ERA increased in the 1960s, as women both aspired to and enjoyed greater professional advancement. In 1967, NOW endorsed the ERA. The decision complicated NOW's relationship with organized labor, which continued to oppose the amendment. In 1970, however, the United Auto Workers came out in favor of the ERA, and three years later the American Federation of Labor and Congress of Industrial Organizations (AFL-CIO) did the same. The ERA became a key demand of mainstream feminists, and it polled well among the public and on Capitol Hill. By the spring of 1972, it had passed both houses of Congress, achieving the necessary

[2] Some feminists opposed taking on the abortion issue for fear that doing so would cost the movement public support. They were most prominently represented by the Women's Equity Action League (WEAL), which split off from NOW in 1968. WEAL pursued gender equality in education, employment, and tax law. In the early 1970s, however, WEAL itself came out in support of abortion rights.

two-thirds vote in each chamber, and had gone to the states for their ratification, which required a three-fourths supermajority. A year after the congressional vote, thirty of the needed thirty-eight states had ratified the amendment. As with the abortion ruling, however, an unexpectedly formidable conservative opposition would soon materialize, clouding the hopes of feminist reformers.

Still another issue on which views were rapidly shifting was the status of lesbianism within women's activism. The radical feminists surging to the fore in the late 1960s included vocal cohorts of declared lesbians who insisted that other feminists recognize and support them as such. Friedan adamantly resisted these demands. Acceding to them, she warned, would confirm the hostile stereotype that feminists were nothing but man-hating deviants. She called lesbianism a "lavender menace" that would fatally discredit mainstream feminism. Here again, however, the rest of NOW's leadership was more open to change. In 1971, the organization brushed aside Friedan's objections and declared that "a woman's right to her own person includes the right to define and express her own sexuality and to choose her own lifestyle; therefore, we acknowledge the oppression of lesbians as a legitimate concern of feminism." Not until the late 1970s would Friedan herself accept this position.

Gay and Lesbian Activism

In supporting lesbian rights, NOW responded not only to political pressures emanating from radical feminism but also to a broader transformation in Americans' social attitudes, unfolding over the previous decade, regarding the sexual orientation of both women and men. For a host of reasons, by the early 1960s the stark homophobia of the previous decade had started to dissipate. As domestic anticommunism eased, fewer Americans worried that blackmailed homosexuals might betray their country to communist foes, though of course this concern had not vanished. The Beat literature that had become prominent in the late 1950s, and remained influential into the next decade, dealt openly with gay themes, and leading Beat figures such as William Burroughs and Allen Ginsberg were unabashedly gay. President John F. Kennedy and First Lady Jacqueline Kennedy publicly embraced Hollywood, Broadway, and other institutions of the performing and visual arts, realms in which gays enjoyed unusual visibility and acceptance. The accelerating civil rights movement encouraged Americans to consider other areas in which harsh prejudice stymied the quest for freedom and understanding. Civil rights struggles also introduced an array of novel protest techniques, and, indeed, a whole new protest vocabulary, that could be placed in the service of other causes. The advent of the Pill was a reminder that not all sex had to be procreative. On its own, no single one of these changes could have significantly altered the course of homophile activism in the United States. Combined, they formed a new landscape of possibility.

In the San Francisco area, where many gay and lesbian veterans had settled after World War II, homophile activism exerted greater political and cultural influence than anywhere else in the country. In 1961, José Sarria, an activist and nightclub singer renowned for performing in drag, ran for the San Francisco Board of Supervisors, becoming the nation's first openly gay candidate for public office. Sarria did not win a seat, but the six thousand votes he received stunned political observers, who now had to consider the possible existence of a homophile political constituency. In 1964, DOB founders Phyllis Lyon and Del Martin joined with progressive clergy in the area to form the Council on Religion and the Homosexual (CRH), with a mission to assist gay and lesbian teenaged runaways and other marginalized homosexuals. When the CRH hosted a fundraising ball on New Year's Day 1965, the San Francisco Police Department (SFPD) stormed the premises and arrested some of the participants – only to find *itself* in the dock, at least as far as public opinion was concerned. Local newspapers criticized the raid as overkill, and the city's top legal talent lined up to defend the arrestees, until the judge in the case threw out the charges. A chastened SFPD pledged to show greater restraint in the future. Even so, sodomy remained illegal in California, as it was in all other states except Illinois.

In Washington, DC, an astronomer named Frank Kameny formed a Mattachine Society chapter in 1961. The Washington chapter was chiefly concerned with combating the federal government's discrimination against employees suspected of homosexuality. Kameny himself had lost his job at the US Army Map Service on account of a prior arrest for "lewd conduct," and his long, futile quest for reinstatement had equipped him with a vast knowledge of the federal bureaucracy. Kameny was also influenced by his occasional participation in the civil rights movement, from which he derived an unapologetic attitude about his own community's rights. He deplored the willingness of some homophile groups to debate the causes of homosexuality and to entertain the possibility that it could be reversed by treatment. "I do not see the NAACP [National Association for the Advancement of Colored People] or CORE [Congress of Racial Equality] worrying about which chromosome and gene produced a black skin," Kameny sarcastically noted, "or about the possibility of bleaching the Negro . . . . We are interested in obtaining rights ... AS HOMOSEXUALS."

In 1964–1965, the DC Mattachine Society joined with the American Civil Liberties Union to challenge a US Civil Service Commission (CSC) finding that a man named Bruce Scott was ineligible for federal employment on account of alleged homosexual conduct. The DC Court of Appeals ruled that the accusation against Scott was too vague to warrant his disqualification. Although the decision did not challenge outright the government's ability to exclude gays and lesbians, it narrowed the scope of permissible discrimination and thus was an important victory for Kameny's group.

In May 1965, the DC Mattachine Society staged a series of pickets in front of the CSC, the State Department, the Pentagon, and the White House to protest federal employment discrimination against gays and lesbians. These were the first public demonstrations in the nation's capital for gay and lesbian rights. The picketers, both men and women, wore conservative attire and quietly marched in single file, carrying neatly hand-lettered placards reading "SEXUAL PREFERENCE IS IRRELEVANT TO FEDERAL EMPLOYMENT" and "HOMOSEXUALS ARE AMERICAN CITIZENS, TOO." Kameny had insisted on such decorum. "If we want to be employed by the federal government," he said, "we have to look employable to the federal government." When a fellow activist questioned this preoccupation with respectability, Kameny doubled down: "Grubbiness has never, to

Figure 8.4 Gay and lesbian rights activists protest outside the White House, May 1965; Frank Kameny is second in line. Source: Bettmann / Getty Images.

my knowledge, been a stereotype of a homosexual. Do our pickets *your* way, and it will soon become so." The Washington action spawned a series of "Annual Reminder" pickets at Independence Hall in Philadelphia, organized by that city's Mattachine chapter. On every Fourth of July from 1965 to 1969, courteous activists carried signs and handed out leaflets to passersby, reminding them that gays and lesbians remained subject to harsh discrimination. Despite the picketers' nonthreatening demeanor, their mere existence could be stunning to onlookers. In 1967, CBS television aired a West Virginia sightseer's incredulous reaction to a Mattachine protest at the White House. "It's kind of weird!" the man exclaimed. "I think these people are a fit subject for a mental health program. These people need help!"

In the second half of the 1960s, homophile activism grew both more assertive and more widespread. The notion that homosexuality was a mental disorder, treatable or not, became discredited in homophile groups; self-affirmation was the new ethos. When, in 1966, gay activists in Los Angeles started an organization to combat police harassment and named it Personal Rights in Defense and Education (PRIDE), they struck upon an acronym that would resound through the decades. That same year, homophile groups met in Kansas City to form a national umbrella organization that became known as the North American Conference of Homophile Organizations (NACHO – admittedly, a less inspiring abbreviation). Two years later, NACHO adopted the motto "Gay is good," evoking the Black Power slogan "Black is beautiful." Between 1966 and 1969, the number of Mattachine Society chapters increased from fifteen to fifty.

What impact did all of this activism have on the lives of gays and lesbians around the country? Indirectly, it did make a positive difference, especially when it yielded significant legal victories or persuaded local governments to ease up on their "anti-vice" enforcement. Directly, however, homophile advocates' reach was limited. Their newsletters' circulations were tiny and press accounts of their actions sparse (though becoming steadily less so). A survey taken in the mid-1960s found that only 2 percent of American gays and lesbians even knew that homophile groups existed.

For ordinary gays and lesbians, a far more common way to assert a communal identity was to congregate in gay and lesbian bars in cities around the country. Doing so carried the risk of arrest (typically on charges of disorderly conduct), but that hazard was often mitigated by corrupt arrangements between municipal authorities and organized crime. In a given city, the Mafia or some other criminal syndicate would operate a gay bar and stave off police raids with bribes, creating, at least for a time, a relatively secure place for gays and lesbians to gather. All too often, though – perhaps because the Mob had fallen behind in its payments, or because the mayor hoped to gain popularity by ostentatiously "cleaning up" the city's red-light district – the police would raid the bar anyway, with potentially devastating consequences for the arrested patrons.

On the evening of June 27, 1969, New York City police raided the Stonewall Inn, a gay bar with a multiracial clientele. Unlike on countless previous occasions of this sort, the targets of the Stonewall raid fought back. The cops arrested a handful of patrons and staff and released the others, who formed an unruly throng outside the bar. As officers loaded the arrestees into paddy wagons, some in the crowd threw coins, and then bricks, at the police. The cops retreated into the bar and barricaded themselves against the crowd, which hurled rocks and improvised Molotov cocktails through the windows. A riot squad arrived and rescued the trapped policeman; it then scuffled and brawled with the protesters, some of whom taunted the cops by forming high-kicking chorus lines and belting out bawdy songs. By morning, thirteen people had been arrested; four policemen and an indeterminate number of rioters or onlookers had been injured. The unrest resumed the following evening, as protesters from the first night and many newcomers congregated at the Stonewall Inn to clash with police. Sporadic skirmishes continued for a couple of nights after that.

Leaders of New York's Mattachine chapter were distressed by the violence, fearing it would jeopardize ongoing efforts to wring concessions from city hall. But the prevailing sentiment among New York gay activists was to hail the altercations as a long-overdue call to arms. Cries of "Gay Power!" were in the air, and Mattachine leaders could not contain the wild energy. Martha Shelly, a young DOB member, spearheaded the formation of a committee within the New York Mattachine Society called the Gay Liberation Front (GLF). It quickly became an independent organization and, for gays and lesbians across the nation, the face of the movement's new militancy. One of the GLF's first acts was to distribute leaflets reading: "Do you think homosexuals are revolting? You bet your sweet ass we are." In cities and universities around the country, local GLFs sprang into existence, some forming spontaneously, others stirred to life by New York GLFers taking the cause on the road – not that the locals needed much prompting. It was "like a prairie fire," recalled Jim Fouratt, a GLF founder. "People were *ready*."

Back in New York, the GLF and other groups organized a flurry of events, culminating in a Gay Power parade in June 1970 to mark the first anniversary of the Stonewall uprising. As many as 10,000 people attended the procession. Frank Kameny, who had been a bit grumpy about the recent undisciplined turn in gay politics, came up to New York for the occasion. The veteran activist who had labored to recruit a dozen here, a score there, for lonely vigils outside the White House and Independence Hall now gazed at the thousands filling Manhattan's streets. In a piece published in a New York gay weekly, he and two Mattachine comrades confessed to being "awestruck by the vast throngs of confident humanity wending their way into a promised land of freedom-to-be."

Consisting largely of New Left veterans, the New York GLF embraced a host of other causes, such as the antiwar movement, Black Power, and, among lesbians, radical feminism. This lack of focus hampered the group, which lasted for only about two years. In late 1969, some GLFers split off to form the Gay Activist Alliance (GAA), a single-issue organization that in the coming years successfully challenged many of the city's discriminatory laws and policies. More broadly, both the GLF and the GAA drew nationwide attention to the cause of gay liberation, which by the early 1970s was the dominant paradigm for gay and lesbian activism. Hardly anyone was using the word "homophile" anymore. It evoked a time when gays and lesbians had beseeched society to grant them a measure of toleration, rather than demanding that it accept them for who they were. Mainstream journalists scrambled to make sense of the fast-moving situation. Early post-Stonewall feature stories remained wedded to the view that gays and lesbians were sick people deserving treatment, not punishment. But by 1971 and 1972 coverage was more positive, with less handwringing and a greater willingness to let the subjects of the stories speak for themselves.

A new fascination with gayness suffused the popular culture. Same-sex intimacy was portrayed much more explicitly, if still often stereotypically, in Hollywood films. Musicians such as Little Richard, Mick Jagger, David Bowie, and Elton John deliberately presented themselves in ways that invited speculation about their sexual orientation (though it would take another couple of decades before significant numbers of gay and lesbian celebrities openly declared themselves). David Susskind, Phil Donahue, and other television talk show hosts gave airtime to gay and lesbian activists. "The love that once dared not speak its name," joked *Boston Globe* columnist George Frazier, "now can't keep its mouth shut."

In 1973, responding to lobbying by Kameny, Barbara Gittings of the DOB, and other activists, as well as to dissent within the profession, the American Psychiatric Association stopped classifying homosexuality as a mental disorder. Meanwhile, a years-long campaign by activists to repeal laws against same-sex intimacy was yielding results. In 1971, Connecticut became the second state in the union, after Illinois nine years earlier, to decriminalize sodomy. A spate of state-level repeals ensued, and by 1979 twenty states had scrapped such laws. Of the states still banning sodomy, some had reduced the penalties. True, millions remained in criminal jeopardy, and the issue would not be resolved nationally for another generation. A series of arson attacks on gay institutions in 1973, including the torching of a New Orleans bar that left thirty-two dead, was a reminder that the struggle remained in its infancy. Still, the scope and velocity of change were remarkable. Gays and lesbians now formed a persistent and occasionally influential bloc within the Democratic Party, and more and more of them were seeking elective office (among them Kameny, who in 1971 ran unsuccessfully to be DC's nonvoting representative in Congress). In 1974, Elaine Noble was elected to the Massachusetts House of Representatives, becoming the nation's first openly gay state legislator. By 1976, twenty-nine cities and counties had outlawed discrimination on the basis of sexual orientation.

Feminist Achievements in the 1970s

Feminists, too, continued to extend their gains, scoring substantive and symbolic victories that, working together, transformed the character and texture of American life. The Equal Opportunity Credit Act (EOCA), passed by Congress in 1974, barred banks from denying credit to customers on the basis of gender or marital status; married women could now acquire credit cards in their own names. (Perhaps the most remarkable feature of the EOCA was the fact that it took this long to be enacted.) Two years earlier, Congress had passed Title IX of the Education Amendments, which denied federal funding to schools, colleges, and universities guilty of gender discrimination. To avoid potentially crippling losses of government support, these institutions had to demonstrate that their curricula and programs equitably served female students. The share of women receiving advanced degrees and professional training was already growing by the early 1970s, but Title IX greatly accelerated that process. In 1971, women earned 40 percent of master's degrees, 16 percent of doctoral degrees, and 6 percent of professional degrees (such as in law, medicine, dentistry, and pharmacology). By 1989, the respective figures were 52 percent, 36 percent, and, again, 36 percent. The legislation also gave a major boost to women's college athletics, transforming them from mere pastimes or afterthoughts into an integral and popular feature of the collegiate sports world. Title IX, quipped the historian Mary Jo Festle, was "the biggest thing to happen to sports since the whistle."

The career and activism of Billie Jean King, the world's top female tennis player in the early 1970s, exemplified the new prominence of women's athletics. In 1972, upon learning that her prize for winning the US Open was $15,000 smaller than the prize awarded to that year's male champion, King publicly refused to reenter the competition as long as the discrepancy continued. The US Open relented and, in 1973, became the first tournament to offer equal cash prizes to men and women. Soon thereafter, King cofounded the Women's Sports Foundation, with a mission to promote gender equity in sports, and persuaded the cigarette company Virginia Slims to sponsor a women's tennis tournament. King was best known, however, for competing in 1973's "Battle of the Sexes." The retired tennis champion Bobby Riggs had boasted that, even at age fifty-five, he could defeat any of the best female players. The twenty-nine-year-old King accepted the challenge and, in a massively publicized match at the Houston Astrodome, beat Riggs in three straight sets.

On network television, women were presented in more serious, diverse, and fully rounded ways. Until the early 1970s, only small numbers of female TV reporters, and hardly any female anchors, had appeared on the air. "[A]udiences are less prepared," opined NBC News president Reuven Frank in 1971, "to accept news from a woman's voice than from a man's." Over the next few years, however, it became much more common for women to serve as local news anchors. In 1976, ABC hired Barbara Walters to be the first female coanchor of a network evening news program, though no woman would solo-anchor such a show until well into the following decade. Entertainment television, meanwhile, offered several prime-time programs in which lead female characters occupied nontraditional roles or confronted controversial gender issues. *The Mary Tyler Moore Show* (1970–1977) featured a single woman working at a Minneapolis TV station. *One Day at a Time* (1975–1984) chronicled the travails of a divorced mother raising teenaged daughters. *Maude* (1972–1978) was about an outspoken feminist on her fourth marriage – she was widowed from her first husband and divorced from the next two – who in one episode opted to have an abortion.

These fictional representations of divorce reflected reality: in 1975, the divorce rate was more than twice what it had been in 1960. Conservatives were starting to blame this development on the subversive impact of "Women's lib." Many feminists had indeed argued that women should be freer to escape abusive, exploitative, or otherwise unhappy marriages, and they had sometimes done so in pungent terms. The radical feminist journalist Ellen Willis cracked that *The Ladies Home Journal*'s regular column "Can This Marriage Be Saved?" should be shortened to "Can This Marriage." But, although historians, sociologists, demographers, and other scholars have debated its precise causes, the surging divorce rate clearly resulted from broader attitudinal shifts (in which feminism did play a role) about sexuality, monogamy, religion, and other topics relating to matrimony. Overall, the marriage bond became less sacrosanct to Americans, and breaking it more socially acceptable. As the marriage counselor Esther Oshiver Fisher observed in 1974 (in language mirroring contemporaneous changes in discussion of homosexuality), "Time was when it was believed that those who divorced were 'sick' persons, misfits, hopeless neurotics . . . . These are certainly no longer valid assumptions."

Legal reforms both reflected and magnified the growing propensity toward divorce. In the late 1960s and early 1970s, many states enacted either "no-fault" or unilateral divorce laws. Instead of requiring proof that one party was guilty of adultery, abandonment, or other marital misconduct, a judge could grant a no-fault divorce if both parties demonstrated that their differences were irreconcilable; in a unilateral divorce, a marriage could be dissolved if one party strongly desired it. Feminists generally supported these changes, even as it became evident that divorce was often financially damaging to women. The appropriate response, most feminists agreed, was to preserve the new freedom to exit unhappy marriages and seek stronger legal and economic protections for divorced women.

In the first half of the 1970s, mainstream feminists tried, with mixed success, to respond to the concerns of feminists on the racial and political margins. NOW leaders recognized, of course, that racism and poverty oppressed millions of American women. In 1970, the organization announced an "immediate and continuing liaison with the National Welfare

Rights Organization," and in the coming years NOW endorsed some of the NWRO's initiatives in Congress. Still, cooperation was limited, largely because of the difficulty NOW had in mobilizing its mostly white, middle-class members to work on welfare issues. In 1971, Friedan and Bella Abzug, a Democratic House member from New York, cofounded the National Women's Political Caucus (NWPC) to promote female political candidates. The caucus's charter members included several prominent women of color, among them the Black civil rights leader Fannie Lou Hamer, the Chicana civil rights and labor activist Lupe Anguiano, and New York Congresswoman Shirley Chisholm, who in 1972 became the first African American woman to seek the presidential nomination of a major political party (the Democratic Party). The NWPC did make a serious and sustained effort to foreground matters of racial and economic injustice.

More consequentially, mainstream feminism absorbed several insights from radical feminism concerning a particular category of offenses against women: those occurring in realms previously regarded as private and thus beyond the reach of society or the law. Applying the consciousness-raising principle "The personal is political," feminist activists, writers, and legal analysts called attention to these harmful behaviors and, over time, persuaded the nation's public institutions to start treating them as unacceptable. Often, feminists publicized an issue by "naming" it: introducing a new phrase, such as "domestic violence," "sexual harassment," or "marital rape," to identify a social or legal concept that was itself novel. Although the initial activism over each issue typically occurred in the first half of the 1970s, the breakout into public awareness tended to happen in the second half.

Prior to the 1970s, police seldom interfered in cases of domestic violence, and women enduring it were often reluctant to report it. There was little public understanding of the social, economic, and psychological pressures – along with outright threats of violent reprisal – that might prevent a woman from leaving an abusive spouse or partner. Starting in 1974, feminists established battered women's shelters around the country and joined social workers and legal advocates in pushing governments at all levels to take the problem more seriously. In 1978, the US Department of Housing and Urban Development began offering grants to local women's shelters, and by decade's end fifteen states were providing them funding.

So it went with the issue of unwanted sexual attention in the workplace. In the early 1970s, female plaintiffs started suing employers for subjecting them to sexual coercion, occasionally prevailing in lower federal courts. In 1975, feminists in Ithaca, New York, named the practice by staging a "Speak-Out on Sexual Harassment." A flood of public testimonies ensued as women described the sexual pressures they had faced in universities, in corporate suites, in Hollywood casting offices, and on factory assembly lines. Numerous books on the subject appeared, the most formidable of them *The Sexual Harassment of Working Women* (1979) by the legal scholar Catharine MacKinnon. In 1980, the EEOC began including sexual harassment among the workplace grievances it considered. Six years later, the Supreme Court deemed sexual harassment a violation of Title VII of the 1964 Civil Rights Act.

Rape, of course, was already a crime, but in countless ways both the legal system and the surrounding culture had obscured and compounded its harms. With the important exception of cases in which Black men were accused of raping white women, legal jurisdictions had long placed daunting obstacles in the paths of women alleging rape. Complainants had to furnish corroborating witnesses, explain why they had not resisted the attacks with all their physical might, and endure defense lawyers' interrogations of their sexual histories. Even family members might chide them for inviting the assaults by dressing too provocatively. Popular entertainment made light of the subject, sometimes suggesting that rape victims enjoyed the sexual attention. The notion that a man could be guilty of raping his wife, when ventured at all, was often greeted with incomprehension. In the early 1970s, radical feminists protested these realities and established the nation's first rape crisis centers. Susan Brownmiller's 1975 bestseller *Against Our Will*, which portrayed rape as a transhistorical instrument of male domination, drew wide attention to the issue. In the late 1970s, under pressure from feminists, police departments and hospitals started training their personnel to treat traumatized rape victims with greater sensitivity and gather forensic evidence more systematically. States enacted "rape shield laws" that barred defense lawyers from questioning alleged rape victims about their sexual pasts. They also began to remove the exemptions from prosecution that rape statutes had granted to husbands and, in some cases, to classify "marital rape" as a distinct crime. These and similar reforms continued into the 1980s, and beyond.

***

By the mid-1970s, the striking social and cultural changes of the preceding decade and a half had touched virtually every facet of American life. Attitudes and behavior on matters of gender, sexuality, and family had shifted markedly in the direction of greater fluidity, openness, impermanence, and complexity. And, of course, further transformations were in the offing. Changes in the status of gays and lesbians (and others departing from heterosexual and, later, "cisnormative" expectations) would be especially dramatic in the decades ahead. Already, however, millions of Americans were alarmed by what they saw as an assault on "family values." In the second half of the 1970s, their discontent would fuel a powerful conservative movement, with profound implications for the nation's politics writ large.

READING QUESTIONS

1. Both the mainstream and the radical strands of white-dominated feminism in the 1960s traced some of their origins to the civil rights movement. How, in each case, did that legacy unfold?
2. In what ways did Black women's activism of the 1960s and early 1970s differ from white-dominated feminism of those years? How did these differences manifest themselves?
3. In examining gay and lesbian activism of the 1960s, consider the interplay between *seeking* and *demanding* acceptance from the broader society. Which forms of activism seemed more oriented toward the former mode, and which toward the latter? Were there instances in which the two modes were combined?

4. How, by the second half of the 1970s, had mainstream feminism begun to incorporate perspectives and insights from radical feminism and Black women's activism?

SUGGESTIONS FOR FURTHER READING

Bronski, Michael. *A Queer History of the United States*. Boston: Beacon Press, 2011.

Coleman, Marilyn, Lawrence Ganong, and Kelly Warzinik. *Family Life in 20th-Century America*. Westport, CT: Greenwood Press, 2007.

Dow, Bonnie J. *Watching Women's Liberation, 1970: Feminism's Pivotal Year on the Network News*. Urbana, IL: University of Illinois Press, 2014.

Duberman, Martin. *Stonewall*. New York: Dutton, 1993.

Echols, Alice. *Daring to Be Bad: Radical Feminism in America, 1967–1975*. Minneapolis: University of Minnesota Press, 1989.

Evans, Sara. *Personal Politics: The Roots of Women's Liberation in the Civil Rights Movement and the New Left*. New York: Knopf, 1979.

Faderman, Lillian. *Odd Girls and Twilight Lovers: A History of Lesbian Life in Twentieth-Century America*, 3rd edn. New York: Columbia University Press, 1991.

Ferree, Myra Marx, and Beth Hess. *Controversy and Coalition: The New Feminist Movement across Three Decades of Change*. New York: Routledge, 2000.

Hirshman, Linda. *Victory: The Triumphant Gay Revolution*. New York: Harpers, 2012.

Nadasen, Premilla. *Welfare Warriors: The Welfare Rights Movement in the United States*. New York: Routledge, 2005.

Oliver, Susan. *Betty Friedan: The Personal Is Political*. New York: Pearson Longman, 2008.

Rosen, Ruth. *The World Split Open: How the Modern Women's Movement Changed America*. New York: Viking, 2000.

Rosenberg, Rosalind. *Jane Crow: The Life of Pauli Murray*. New York: Oxford University Press, 2017.

Springer, Kimberly. *Living for the Revolution: Black Feminist Organizations, 1968–1980*. Durham, NC: Duke University Press, 2005.

9 Soylent Green Is People

America in the Seventies

Introduction

It was the ultimate disaster movie, a vision of the Apocalypse flickering in theaters across the land. Released in late 1977, and narrated by the legendary film director Orson Welles, *The Late Great Planet Earth* was a cinematic adaptation of Hal Lindsey's hugely popular book of the same title, first published in 1970. The book had argued that some recent historical events, such as the establishment of the state of Israel in 1948 and Israel's capture of East Jerusalem in 1967, fulfilled biblical prophecy. Such portents could only mean that the battle of Armageddon, Jesus Christ's return to earth, and the other momentous events foretold in the New Testament's Book of Revelation were shortly at hand.

The movie version was true to the core message of Lindsey's book, though it also paid homage to some of the countercultural sensibilities that had become mainstream in recent years, and to the real-world concerns that preoccupied many secular Americans in the 1970s. Lindsey himself was a frequent presence, standing amid windswept, ancient ruins as he spoke to the camera of upheavals to come. Wearing longish hair, a drooping mustache, bell-bottomed jeans, and a short-sleeved denim shirt with the top buttons unfastened to reveal a bare chest and a gaudy medallion, the forty-eight-year-old author looked less like the conservative evangelical figure he was than like a cool high school civics teacher staving off middle age. Lindsey's appearances were interspersed with harrowing news footage of wars, famines, hurricanes, oil spills, and other natural and manmade disasters; with scenes of cult members and adherents of Eastern religions chanting in exotic rituals; and with snippets of interviews with leading experts – demographers, biologists, ecologists, nuclear arms control advocates, and others – all bearing authoritative witness to the threatened extinction of the human species. Lindsey's own contention was that, while such truth seekers may have identified some of the major ills plaguing humankind, only the Scriptures could disclose their true meaning.

An eclectic barrage of data and images that stirred the viewer's darkest forebodings, and then offered salvation in the form of a conservative evangelical "end times" finale, *The Late Great Planet Earth* was a fitting relic of its day. On a more basic level, the film captured the contradictory and often disorienting nature of American public life in the 1970s. Politically and socially, the United States had become far more equitable and tolerant, and millions of Americans found new ways to connect with one another and expand the scope of personal freedom. Yet millions of others felt disconcerted, threatened, or disrespected by the pace of change. Across the political spectrum, there was a growing sense that natural resources were dwindling, that the quality of life was eroding, that national and global problems had become unmanageable, and that the nation's governing institutions had failed. The surge of political conservatism toward the end of the decade – a phenomenon including, but by no means confined to, the likes of Hal Lindsey – expressed a yearning to rescue imperiled assumptions, values, and feelings of national confidence.

Legacies of the Sixties

Both at the time and since, many Americans regarded the seventies as a sedate, uneventful sequel to the decade that preceded it, a time of escapism and retrenchment after years of upheaval. Although there is some truth to this assessment, the influences of the earlier period on the later one were both massive and intricate. The countercultural and antiauthoritarian modes of the 1960s continued into the following decade and, indeed, grew far more widespread. Casual attire and long hair (and facial hair in the case of males); the more or less open consumption of marijuana and other illegal drugs; the use of slang terms like "far out," "hang out," "uptight," and "bummer"; the free resort to profanity and frank discussion of sexuality; the indulgence in pre- and extramarital sex; the dispensing of formal titles such as "Mr." and "Mrs." in favor of first names; the appreciation of non-Western food, music, jewelry, fabrics, and spiritual homilies – all of these styles and behaviors became mainstream in the 1970s. Rock music, lucrative since the 1950s, was now a mammoth industry, as millionaire performers filled 70,000-seat sports arenas, staged elaborate light shows, and produced ambitious concept albums and rock operas that received respectful reviews in the mainstream press.

For most Americans, these countercultural pursuits were folded into their everyday lives, to be enjoyed, or paused, at will. But members of committed subcultures immersed themselves in religious or quasi-religious experiences such as Zen Buddhism, Transcendental Meditation, tarot card reading, astrology, and pagan witchcraft. Others embraced yoga, martial arts, jogging, organic farming, psychotherapy, tantric sex, alternative medicine, and countless varieties of massage. Often, the enthusiasts were veterans of sixties protests who saw their new passions as a continuation of the original project: to overturn and ultimately replace a destructive, wasteful, hierarchical, unjust, and spiritually empty prevailing order. Rather than frontally challenging the status quo, however, they now pursued its alternatives through self-improvement or the building of enlightened communities. Inevitably, critics mocked the new seekers as narcissistic navel-gazers. The journalist Tom Wolfe dubbed the 1970s the "Me decade," an era in which Americans underwent "lube jobs for the personality" and seized every chance to "wiggle their fannies" in front of their peers.

All the same, many Americans in the 1970s continued to engage in, or newly joined, collective efforts to remake society. They swelled the ranks of the environmental movement and ongoing struggles for racial justice. They became social workers, community organizers, consumer advocates, labor lawyers, public defenders, and physicians for the poor. Those of a more conservative bent, as we will see, waged vigorous campaigns against what they saw as liberal overreach. The fact that these efforts occurred "within the system" hardly suggested any lesser commitment. And some dissenters did openly defy the law. As noted in Chapter 7, a spate of bombings and other violent protests took place in the early 1970s, mounted by remnants of the New Left, by Black Power militants, and by activists professing solidarity with Third World liberation struggles. In 1973, members of the American Indian Movement and other Native American activists physically occupied the town of Wounded Knee, South Dakota, the site of an 1890 US Army massacre of hundreds of Lakota, to protest alleged corruption in tribal governance and the failure of the US government to abide by its treaty commitments. The militants held the town for seventy-one days, exchanging gunfire with federal authorities that resulted in the deaths of two Indian activists and the severe wounding of a US marshal.

For Black Americans, the most powerful legacy of the 1960s was the eradication of legal segregation in the South – and in the North, too, in the case of the 1968 outlawing of racial discrimination in housing sales. These measures, combined with the introduction of affirmative action programs in employment and higher education, enabled a significant expansion of the Black middle class. In 1960, 13 percent of Black families had annual incomes exceeding the equivalent of $10,000 in 1971 dollars (about $69,000 in 2022); by 1971, that figure was 31 percent. Over the ensuing decade, between 35 and 45 percent of African Americans were counted as middle-class. The number of Blacks enrolled in college grew from 227,000 in 1960 to twice that many by decade's end, and to 1.1 million in 1977. Rates of political representation told a similar story. In 1959, only four African Americans served in Congress, all of them in the House of Representatives. By 1977, there were sixteen Black congresspeople, including Republican Senator Edward Brooke of Massachusetts (and not including Walter Fauntroy, the nonvoting delegate from Washington, DC). The cities of Atlanta, Birmingham, Detroit, and Oakland elected Black mayors in the 1970s. Although such electoral gains were largely attributable to the greater enfranchisement and voter participation of Blacks, they also owed something to changing white attitudes. A 1958 survey found that only 37 percent of white respondents were willing to vote for a "generally well-qualified" Black candidate for president nominated by their political party. By 1981, 80 percent of whites said they would support a Black presidential candidate.

In seventies popular culture, Black performers were ubiquitous in sports, music, film, comedy, and television. One of the most popular TV situation comedies, CBS's *The Jeffersons*, featured an upwardly mobile Black couple integrating a luxury apartment building on New York's Upper East Side. Although some critics objected to the buffoonish portrayal of George Jefferson and to the unrealistic absence of racism in the Jeffersons' day-to-day lives, the positing of a fractious but racially benign social setting in which George suffered more from his own obnoxiousness than from white neighbors' intolerance was, in its way, groundbreaking. In stand-up comedy, the wild success of Richard Pryor showed that interracial audiences were ready for much sharper skewerings of American race relations. On the "squarer" side, the actress and Broadway singer Pearl Bailey gave several performances at the White House, including for visiting dignitaries such as President Anwar Sadat of Egypt and Shah Mohammad Reza Pahlavi of Iran.

Nonetheless, about 30 percent of African Americans remained in poverty, and in some respects their plight was getting harder to address. Since the early 1960s, companies had relocated their urban factories to suburbs and other parts of the country, causing spiking inner-city unemployment levels that disproportionately affected African Americans. Over the same period, some upwardly mobile Blacks managed to move from the inner city to integrated suburbs. Those left behind were in worse condition than before, for they had lost much of the material support, encouragement, and political advocacy that their more affluent Black neighbors had previously afforded them. In the abandoned and isolated inner city, rates of impoverishment, blight, substance abuse, crime, police brutality, school dropout, prostitution, out-of-wedlock childbirth, and child abandonment increased. In these ways, the creation of a robust Black middle class left those in the "underclass" less and less able to improve their lot.

Meanwhile, growing numbers of the Black poor were enmeshed in the welfare system, which all too often seemed designed to perpetuate poverty. The bureaucracy stigmatized and humiliated aid recipients, eroding their confidence in their ability to survive outside the welfare system – an outlook seemingly validated by the lack of available jobs. In many states, aid was withheld from households that included able-bodied men, creating an incentive for poor men to live apart from their children. Across the political spectrum, policy analysts, pundits, politicians, and ordinary citizens criticized the welfare system as perversely counterproductive, yet few could agree on how to address the problem.

Other nonwhite groups gained broad visibility in the 1970s. The Latino share of the US population grew from 4.5 percent in 1970 to 6.4 percent in 1980, an expansion powered mainly by Mexican immigration. In previous decades, the general thrust of Mexican American advocacy had been integrationist; after the late 1960s, nationalist voices grew more influential. A key figure in this shift was the Colorado-based activist and poet (and former boxer) Rodolfo "Corky" Gonzales, who left the Democratic Party to form a separate Mexican American political party and briefly considered appealing to the United Nations for support in gaining independence for Mexican Americans, or "Chicanos," as many in this community now called themselves. Gonzales's party soon faded from the scene, but in a more diffuse sense Chicanos' drive for recognition made impressive gains in the 1970s, with the establishment in universities of Chicano or ethnic studies programs and the proliferation of Chicano journals, publishing houses, and art galleries. In popular entertainment, the breakout success of the NBC sitcom *Chico and the Man* (though cut short by the suicide of its brilliant but troubled star, Freddie Prinze) was another sign that Chicanos had "arrived."

Meanwhile, the immigration reform of 1965, which went into effect in 1968, removed restrictions that had favored immigration from Western Europe, opening the country to arrivals from all parts of the Eastern Hemisphere. According to the 1970 census, 62 percent of the US foreign-born came from Europe. Ten years later, just 39 percent were European. Over that same decade, the Asian share of the foreign-born grew from 9 percent to 19 percent. The Asian American population itself was altered by the new patterns of immigration. In 1960, 90 percent of Asian Americans had been of Japanese, Chinese, or Filipino origin. By 1980, only 65 percent claimed ancestry from those three nations, with most of the remainder comprised of immigrants from Korea, Vietnam, and India. During the 1970s, Asian Americans grew more visible and assertive. As Asian American studies programs sprang up on university campuses, Japanese American activists pressured Washington to acknowledge and make amends for the internment of Japanese Americans and Japanese residents during World War II. In 1980, Congress appointed a special commission to examine the issue. The commission recommended that the government formally apologize for the internment and compensate survivors. Congress adopted the recommendations in 1988, and President Ronald Reagan signed the apology and restitution into law.

Portents of Disaster

Still, if American life in the 1970s reflected the exuberant, countercultural, and reformist spirit of the previous decade, it also displayed a much gloomier and more foreboding side. Over the last quarter-century, Americans had harbored plenty of dark premonitions, mostly relating to the threat of nuclear war. Those apprehensions continued into the seventies, though they now centered less on the prospects for US–Soviet conflict (this was, after all, a time of détente) than on the possibility that terrorist groups or extremist Third World governments might get their hands on nukes. Far more widespread were dire warnings about the ability of humankind to feed itself, find the fuel for its machines, or avoid destroying the planet it inhabited. Confined mainly to academic and activist circles in the early to mid-1960s, these anxious soundings gained broader appeal at the end of the decade, as reports of environmental disasters, economic dislocations, and looming energy shortages became more frequent in the news. By 1974, inflation, a biting recession, and aggravating gas shortages were impinging directly on Americans' day-to-day lives, lending the doomsday scenarios further credibility.

A series of bestsellers stoked the public alarm. *The Population Bomb* (1968), by the biologist Paul Ehrlich, argued that the world population was growing at a much faster rate than the planet's resources could sustain and that mass starvation was therefore inevitable. The best humans could do was mitigate the catastrophe by imposing drastic measures to discourage reproduction, including mass sterilization. *The Limits to Growth* (1972) was a report authored by a group of US-based scholars on behalf of the Club of Rome, an international association of scientists, economists, business leaders, and government officials concerned with global challenges. This book, too, warned that human consumption was rapidly outpacing available resources, especially when it came to fossil fuels. If current trends continued, world oil supplies would be exhausted in a few years' time. Critics objected that both works vastly underestimated the ability of new technologies to overcome projected shortages, and of course the bleak predictions failed to materialize. (Granted, some of those touted innovations, such as the improved pesticides that had already dramatically boosted agricultural yield around the world, caused other serious problems, but that was a separate debate.)

Popular entertainment echoed the forebodings. The 1973 movie *Soylent Green*, starring Charlton Heston, imagines a twenty-first-century society crippled by overpopulation and drought and dominated by ruthless overseers who nourish the masses with processed foods secretly derived from human corpses. (Heston's histrionic declaration in the final scene – "Soylent Green is *people*!" – would be mocked for decades to come.) In the 1977 novel *On the Brink*, by the father-and-son team Herbert and Benjamin Stein, OPEC drastically increases the price of oil. The US government responds by fecklessly printing money, producing hyperinflation so severe that it causes a collapse of public order.

Post-Watergate Doldrums

Compounding the pessimism was a growing lack of confidence in the nation's political institutions. The Watergate scandal, following so closely on the heels of the Vietnam debacle, convinced millions of Americans that the government, especially at the federal level, seldom acted in the best interests of the citizenry. Government failures to bring the economy or crime under control only deepened the disillusionment. In polls conducted in the early 1960s, about a quarter of respondents had agreed with the statement "I don't think public officials care much what people like me think." By 1976, over half endorsed the sentiment. In the 1950s and 1960s, about 60 percent of the voting-age population had voted in presidential elections. From 1976 through the end of the century, voter turnout would be stuck in the low fifties, or lower. "Don't vote," advised a 1976 bumper sticker; "it only encourages them."

The presidency of Gerald R. Ford, who succeeded the disgraced Richard Nixon in August 1974, was short and unhappy. Although Ford's friendly demeanor and reputation for personal integrity were a welcome relief from the Nixon years, the new president was hamstrung by his predecessor's legacy. A month after taking office, Ford issued a full pardon to Nixon for any crimes he may have committed while in office. This was an extremely unpopular move at the time. Many Americans suspected that Nixon had agreed to step down in exchange for Ford's promise to pardon him. No persuasive evidence points to such an unseemly deal. Ford was almost certainly telling the truth when he later claimed that his intention was to prevent a criminal trial of Nixon and thus avoid a distracting prolongation of the Watergate controversy at a time when his new administration faced daunting challenges. But the move backfired; the suspicion of a shady quid pro quo dogged Ford throughout his presidency and contributed to his electoral defeat in 1976. In November 1974, Ford and his party suffered another consequence of Watergate. In the congressional elections, Democrats exploited voters' disgust over the scandal and expanded their legislative majorities by forty-nine seats in the House and four in the Senate.

Ford also inherited an ailing economy. The Arab oil embargo of 1973–1974, combined with the OPEC price hikes of late 1973 (resulting in a near-quadrupling of the price of oil from October and December), had intensified a preexisting global economic crisis. Disruptions in oil markets wreaked quick havoc on industries directly reliant on petroleum – car manufacturing, transportation, trucking, shipping – and soon thereafter affected businesses at a further remove, causing job layoffs to ripple across the US economy. Soaring gas prices steepened an already troubling inflationary spike. Even after the embargo ended, crude oil remained at its newly elevated price, straining a US economy that, at the start of Ford's presidency, was getting 35 percent of its petroleum from abroad and becoming steadily more dependent on foreign oil. When Ford took office, the general inflation rate was 10 percent. Unemployment was at 5.4 percent and rapidly rising; it would exceed 9 percent in the spring of 1975. The US economy also suffered from foreign competition. Western Europe and Japan, now fully recovered from World War II, were producing goods that many Americans found preferable to US-made products, with baneful consequences for the nation's manufacturing. The problem was especially dire in the automobile industry. Now that gas was so expensive, small, fuel-efficient Japanese cars became increasingly desirable to US consumers. The auto manufacturers of Detroit, accustomed to churning out large, gas-guzzling sedans, failed to convert their production line quickly enough. They lost market share and laid off still more American workers.

President Ford floundered in his responses to the economic crises. With the country enduring simultaneous surges in inflation and unemployment – typically, one rose at the expense of the other – it was hard to know which problem to prioritize. Ford started with inflation, asking Congress to pass a 5 percent surtax on corporate and individual earnings – a measure designed to reduce consumer spending. The president also exhorted private businesses to "Whip inflation now" by restraining prices voluntarily; he urged ordinary citizens to support the effort by wearing red, white, and blue WIN lapel buttons. Congressional Democrats voted down the surtax, arguing that only the wealthy should be taxed. Some wore rival buttons displaying the acronym BATH – "Back again to Hoover," a reference to the president on whose watch the Great Depression began. His WIN campaign a flop, in early 1975 Ford switched to trying to stimulate the economy by asking Congress for a tax reduction. The resulting tax cut was bigger than Ford wanted, yielding a larger budget deficit than he thought prudent, but he signed it anyway. The intervention did help to ease the recession, and inflation started coming down, too. But the benefits were modest and did not really materialize until 1976, after many months of punishing "stagflation."

Ford also found himself holding the bag during the final, humiliating chapter of US involvement in Vietnam. In early 1973, Nixon had withdrawn US forces from South Vietnam, though the United States continued to give military and economic aid to the South Vietnamese regime, which North Vietnam remained determined to extinguish in its drive to reunite the country under its control. Still, Hanoi was taking it slow. It needed to recover from the heavy losses it had suffered in 1972, and it hoped to avoid provoking Washington into resuming air attacks. The South Vietnamese government, by contrast, overplayed its hand by launching military offensives against North Vietnamese Army units stationed in the

South. The NVA and National Liberation Front forces counterattacked, dealing Saigon a series of military defeats, a process spanning the transition from Nixon to Ford. Repeatedly, Ford and Secretary of State Henry Kissinger, who kept that position in the new administration, asked Congress to appropriate robust aid packages for Saigon. Repeatedly, Congress furnished far less than requested. With the US economy in the doldrums, and with the futility of maintaining the Saigon regime growing clearer by the day, legislators were increasingly anxious to liquidate the venture. It was time, argued Massachusetts's Democratic Senator Edward Kennedy, to cease "endless support for an endless war." The aid cutbacks sapped morale within the South Vietnamese army, which in 1974 lost 240,000 soldiers to desertion and by year's end was cracking under the NVA/NLF pressure.

In early 1975, the North Vietnamese launched what they expected would be a two-year offensive to complete the takeover of the South. To their surprise, South Vietnamese army resistance crumbled, and city after city succumbed to Northern forces. In mid-April, as the NVA closed in on Saigon, the Ford administration asked Congress for $722 million in emergency military aid; Congress turned down the request. On April 30, Saigon fell. Because the city's airport was under artillery attack, the last US civilians to leave South Vietnam had to be evacuated by helicopters from the US embassy and a US Department of Defense facility. Thousands of Vietnamese crowded into the embassy compound seeking spaces on the helicopters. Especially desperate were South Vietnamese officials and their families, and others associated with the US presence, who feared for their safety following a Northern takeover. Although many did manage to evacuate, many others were left behind.

That same spring, communist insurgencies seized power in neighboring Laos and Cambodia. Over the next four years, Cambodia's new rulers, the Khmer Rouge, subjected the country to an astonishingly brutal regime of forced collectivization and wholesale murder, leading to the deaths of more than a million and a half Cambodians. The scale of the Cambodian genocide did not become widely known until the late 1970s. When it did, Americans disagreed over the tragedy's meaning in ways that echoed earlier debates about Vietnam. To conservatives, the depravity of the Khmer Rouge showed that the United States had been right all along to oppose communism in Southeast Asia. Liberals countered that Nixon's extensive bombing of Cambodia from 1969 to 1973 had cruelly destabilized its society, creating fertile ground for political extremists. But most Americans, it appeared, just wanted to stop thinking about Southeast Asia altogether.

A related controversy focused on the secret activities of the US national security state. Both the Vietnam War and the Watergate scandal caused many Americans to wonder if the executive branch had gotten out of control. In 1975, a Senate committee chaired by Frank Church of Idaho and a House committee chaired by Otis Pike of New York, both Democrats, held separate hearings on CIA and FBI activities over the previous quarter-century. Using, or brandishing, their powers of subpoena, the committees compelled CIA and FBI officials to testify and provide documents. News outlets conducted their own investigations, sometimes publishing stories that the congressional committees preferred not to address publicly. The inquiries trained a harsh light on the CIA's attempts to assassinate Fidel Castro (including by seeking the help of a Mafia boss who shared a mistress with President John

F. Kennedy) and on the FBI's surveillance and harassment of Martin Luther King, Jr., Black Power and antiwar activists, and other domestic dissidents. The revelations stoked popular cynicism about government. In a 1975 poll, 69 percent of respondents agreed "that over the last ten years, this country's leaders have consistently lied to the people."

A more positive Nixon legacy that Ford inherited and built on was US–Soviet détente. In late 1974, Ford and Kissinger met with Soviet leaders in Vladivostok, on Russia's Pacific coast, and concurred on the outlines of a nuclear arms agreement to follow the Strategic Arms Limitations Treaty of 1972, though they did not finalize the new understanding. In the summer of 1975, the United States, the Soviet Union, and thirty-three European nations met in Helsinki, Finland, to resolve outstanding European issues. The conferees agreed to abide by the existing borders of Europe, a concession by Western nations, which had rejected the Soviet Union's annexation of the Baltic states of Estonia, Latvia, and Lithuania in 1940 and the legitimacy of East Germany's communist regime. In return, the Soviet and Eastern European governments pledged to allow the free movement of peoples across international frontiers and to respect civic freedoms within their borders. These commitments were honored more in the breach than in the observance. In the coming years, political dissidents in the East Bloc tested the promised freedoms by criticizing their governments, only to be beaten and jailed by authorities.

After the cold war ended, it became evident that some of these thwarted protests had planted seeds of rebellion in East bloc nations that bore fruit in the late 1980s. At the time, however, détente's critics charged that the West had been duped. Even before the Helsinki conference, Americans had attacked détente from both the right and the left. Conservatives alleged that US–Soviet arms control agreements weakened America's defenses. Liberals and conservatives accused Ford and Kissinger of ignoring the Soviet Union's mistreatment of dissidents, including those who wished to leave the country but were effectively barred from doing so, usually by prohibitive exit taxes. Soviet Jews were the most conspicuous victims of such policies. In 1974, Congress attached the Jackson–Vanik amendment to a trade bill. Named for its Democratic sponsors, Senator Henry Jackson of Washington and Representative Charles Vanik of Ohio, the amendment denied the Soviet Union most favored nation (MFN) trading status as long as it restricted emigration. (Although the term suggests otherwise, a nation enjoying MFN status is not granted special treatment but, rather, is permitted to trade with the United States on the same terms as most other countries. A nation denied MFN status is subject to trade penalties.) The Jackson–Vanik amendment infuriated the Soviet government and annoyed Ford and Kissinger, who saw superpower détente as too important a matter to be linked to such side issues.

The Politics of Race

For all the heat it generated among concerned parties, relatively few ordinary Americans closely followed the mid-seventies debate on détente. Attracting much greater public attention – and not in a good way – were festering racial controversies, especially disputes over court-ordered busing. In the previous decade, the federal government, prodded by civil rights activists, had ended legal desegregation in public schools. It was no longer possible for public schools to bar Black children outright. Still, white communities and parents across the country had found ways to avoid meaningful integration. Some white-dominated schools admitted token numbers of Black students and declared themselves integrated. Many white parents enrolled their children in all-white private or religious schools or moved to all-white neighborhoods or suburbs where desegregation decrees did not apply. The persistence (and in some areas the expansion) of residential segregation was a stubborn obstacle to school integration. As long as children attended school in the same neighborhoods in which they lived, huge sectors of public education would stay segregated.

As we saw in Chapter 3, federal agencies had in previous decades been instrumental in creating and maintaining racially segregated neighborhoods. But, even if government bore heavy responsibility for the existence of residential segregation, there was no real prospect of deploying government to undo it. A more feasible remedy was to sever the exclusive bond between school and neighborhood: to arrange for children from Black neighborhoods to attend schools in white neighborhoods, and vice versa. In the early 1970s, a series of Supreme Court decisions ordered local communities to do just that. *Swann v. Charlotte–Mecklenburg Board of Education* (1971) decreed that school systems that had previously practiced purposeful segregation had to take active measures to desegregate, noting that this could be accomplished by busing children between neighborhoods. *Keyes v. Denver School District no. 1* (1973) eased the standard for determining that purposeful segregation had once existed, in effect extending the *Swann* decision beyond the South to all parts of the country. But a third decision, *Millikan v. Bradley* (1974), limited the scope of busing by stating that cities and suburbs should not be conjoined for the purpose of desegregation. Urban Black children and suburban white children would not be bused to each other's schools. The real action would occur within city limits – often pitting low-income whites and Blacks against each other.

On the basis of this guidance, federal district courts issued busing decrees to school systems throughout the country. Although most communities complied with the court orders, some angrily opposed them. One of the bitterest fights erupted in Boston in the fall of 1974, after a federal judge ordered citywide busing to desegregate public schools. Residents of the white neighborhood of South Boston were infuriated to learn that their children would be bused across town to attend school in Roxbury, a Black neighborhood. To a considerable degree, racism fueled the reaction. This became obvious when throngs of white residents shouted racial epithets and hurled rocks and bottles at Roxbury students as they stepped off the buses at South Boston's public schools. But class divisions also came into play. South Boston's working-class and largely Irish American residents deeply resented that some of the white liberal judges and politicians who championed busing, in Boston and elsewhere, sent their own children to private schools or lived in suburbs exempted from the policy. Tragically, however, most of this anger was taken out on Black schoolchildren, rather than on privileged officials. (Still, the latter did receive some abuse. When Senator Edward Kennedy, a supporter of busing, tried to speak at an antibusing rally in Boston in

Figure 9.1 Black students arrive at predominantly white South Boston High School, September 1974. Source: Bettmann / Getty Images.

September 1974, he was jeered and chased from the podium. He retreated into the city's John F. Kennedy Federal Building; a crowd followed him there and smashed the plate glass entrance.)

For months thereafter, the schools of South Boston and Roxbury were battle zones, marked by daily racial scuffles and occasional outbursts of severe violence directed at Blacks and whites alike. Both in Boston and across the country (the standoff attracted massive media attention) the experience caused white opposition to busing, powerful to begin with, to intensify. Over the next two years, a third of the white students left the Boston public schools, either because their families moved out of Boston proper or because their parents enrolled them in private schools. Boston was not unique in this respect. Between 1972 and 1976, the number of white students in the public schools of Denver and San Francisco, two other cities subject to court-ordered busing, dropped by 31.6 percent and 42.6 percent, respectively. By the late 1970s, all three cities enrolled nonwhite majorities in their public schools. Whites were voting against busing with their feet.

Black opinion had long been divided on the issue. A 1972 Harris survey found that 52 percent of African Americans supported busing to achieve integration, with 34 percent opposed. The fierce busing fights of the mid-1970s bolstered the "antis." After all, most of busing's Black proponents had favored integration less for its own sake than as a means of improving Black children's education. "We decided," recalled Ruth Batson, a Boston desegregation activist, "that where there were a large number of white students, … that's where the money went. So therefore our theory was: move our kids into that school where they're putting all of the resources, so that they can get a better education." But, if doing so exposed Black children to psychic and even physical harm, perhaps the costs of integration exceeded its benefits. Another Black Bostonian remembered telling her school-aged daughters during the busing crisis, "You're going to be spat at, maybe pushed around some . . . . It's something we have to go through – something *you* have to go through – if this city is ever going to get integrated." Later the mother lay in bed crying. What, she asked herself, could her daughters "learn at a school like that, except how to hate?" In early 1981, a Gallup poll revealed that, whereas 40 percent of African Americans still favored busing, 50 percent agreed that it "has caused more difficulties than it is worth."

Meanwhile, controversy swirled around another race-conscious response to racial discrimination: affirmative action. In 1969, as we have seen, the Nixon administration made the Philadelphia Plan a template for a national affirmative action policy. All construction firms – and later all companies – receiving substantial federal contracts had to develop "goals and timetables" for hiring African Americans and other minorities. The new rules also applied to unions working with such companies. The initiative provoked strong opposition from labor leaders, especially those representing craft unions. They charged that Washington was forcing unions to admit unqualified minorities. "There seems to be a belief," AFL-CIO president George Meany said at a 1970 press conference, "that anybody can be a plumber, anybody can be a sheet metal worker, anybody can be an electrician with very little preparation or training." In the summer and fall of 1969, as the Nixon administration rolled out the new policy, white union members staged noisy demonstrations around the country. When Assistant Secretary of Labor Arthur Fletcher, an African American, held a hearing in Chicago on discrimination in the building trades, five hundred construction workers crowded into the meeting room and boisterously obstructed the proceedings. Outside, workers attacked Black protesters and clashed with Chicago police, sending four of them and one of their own to the hospital. "I had to wait my turn getting my apprenticeship," a union man told a reporter. "Why should these guys be given special consideration just because they happen to be black?"

Ultimately, however, white unionists couldn't block the Philadelphia Plan, which passed the Congress in late 1969 and survived legal challenges over the next couple of years. (In 1971, the Supreme Court settled the matter by declining to consider a lower court decision upholding the Philadelphia Plan's legality.) With varying degrees of enthusiasm, the white-dominated labor leadership made its peace with affirmative action. Thereafter, unions generally supported minority workers who charged their employers with discrimination.

Higher education was another major arena of affirmative action controversy. Starting in the early 1970s, American universities revised their admissions procedures to give preference to minority and female applicants. In 1973 and again in 1974, a white man named Allan Bakke was denied admission to the medical school at the University of California, Davis. After learning that the program had admitted minority applicants with lower grades and test scores than his, Bakke sued the University of California. The case eventually reached the US Supreme Court, which in June 1978 issued a five-to-four ruling that the UC Davis Medical School had violated the 1964 Civil Rights Act and had to admit Bakke. But the court also threw affirmative action a lifeline. One member of the majority, Justice Lewis Powell, stated in a separate opinion that, although the medical school had erred in using race as the sole basis for rejecting Bakke, race or ethnicity could be one of several "pertinent elements of diversity" in an applicant's profile that a university considered. Overtly, the Bakke decision only modestly affected affirmative action programs in higher education. Most of them continued as before, albeit buttressed by a new rationale: the "diversity" that minority applicants could bring to campus. Many observers, then and later, lamented that the new emphasis on diversity tended to obscure the injustice of past and continuing discrimination.

But if, as the critics alleged, American society writ large was shying away from hard truths about modern US racism, at least it was willing to confront the brutal history of American slavery. Or was it? In November 1976, the top entry in *The New York Times*'s fiction bestseller list was *Roots: The Saga of an American Family*, by the veteran Black journalist Alex Haley. The 729-page book was a fictionalized, panoramic recounting of seven generations of African American family history, starting with the life of Kunta Kinte, an eighteenth-century West African villager abducted as young man and shipped to slavery in the US South, and continuing through the lives of Kinte's American descendants, the last of whom was Haley himself. *Roots* received admiring reviews, won a Pulitzer Prize, and sold more than 1.5 million copies in its first eighteen months of publication. In January 1977, ABC TV aired a dramatization of the book; 130 million viewers, exceeding half the US population, watched all or part of the eight-day miniseries. It was the broadest exposure to the history of slavery that the American public had ever received, and portions of the account, especially the book version, were shattering in their horror.

Few white Americans, however, appeared to regard *Roots* as an invitation to learn more about US slavery or ponder its legacy. Instead, writes the historian Matthew Frye Jacobson, "Haley's narrative was quickly appropriated as a moveable template for considering *anyone's* familial origins in *any* distant village. In the wake of the broadcast … hundreds of thousands of white Americans descended on local libraries and archives in search of information, not about slavery or black history, but about themselves and their own ethnic past." The post-*Roots* genealogy craze, which in some ways still continues, was an offshoot of a phenomenon that had begun several years earlier: the celebration of white ethnicity. Americans of Eastern and Southern European origin, typically of Catholic or Orthodox faith, grew increasingly assertive in foregrounding their ethnic heritage and in resisting assimilation into Protestant, Anglo-Saxon cultural norms. (In some ways, American Jews were part of this story, though the separate historical experiences of Jews in Christian-dominated societies, especially the searing legacies of anti-Semitism and the Nazi Holocaust, often fostered a distinct identity.) "White ethnics" founded or reinvigorated organizations such as the Italian American Civil Rights League (which challenged media portrayals linking Italian Americans to organized crime) and the Polish American Congress (whose mission included combating Polish jokes, which, in the decade's more relaxed broadcasting climate, had started airing on television). The writers among them authored books with titles like *Blood of My Blood*, *The Decline of the WASP*, and *The Rise of the Unmeltable Ethnics*. Increasingly suspect was the notion of an American "melting pot" that inexorably dissolved the immigrant's culture. The approved metaphor was that of a "salad bowl," whose ingredients never lost their crunchy distinctiveness.

Although some "white ethnic" opinion leaders were to the left of center, the archetypal member of this community was a lower-middle-class Democrat increasingly at odds with liberal policies and outlooks: a resident of a white urban neighborhood whose children were bused across town; a union member resentful of promotion practices that favored racial minorities; a child of Eastern European immigrants affronted by strident antiwar protests and dismayed by US policies that legitimated communist dictatorship in the Old Country. While Republicans were implicated in some of these offenses, Democrats seemed far more culpable, and "white ethnics" broke heavily for Nixon in the 1972 election. Solidifying this tentative realignment became a key Republican objective, in parallel with the "southern strategy" of drawing white southerners into the GOP column. Democrats were equally eager to woo the ethnics back.

The 1976 Presidential Election

Even so, it was possible to take the ethnicity talk too far. Campaigning for the Democratic presidential nomination in the spring of 1976, former Governor of Georgia Jimmy Carter faltered when he said that Americans were justified in seeking to preserve the "ethnic purity" of their neighborhoods. The remark drew wide criticism, and Carter apologized, insisting he would "never condone any sort of discrimination" in housing. On "Weekend Update," the mock news segment of NBC's daring new comedy show *Saturday Night Live*, Chevy Chase announced that Carter was firing his speechwriter, "Bernie Goebbels."

It was a rare stumble during an extraordinary come-from-nowhere triumph. In a matter of months, the candidate transformed himself from "Jimmy who?" into the nominee of the party heavily favored to retake the White House. Touting his personal honesty, his small-town upbringing, his Southern Baptist faith, and his status as a political outsider obviously blameless for the nation's ills, Carter vanquished a phalanx of better-known Democratic rivals to claim the prize at his party's convention in New York City that July. Another ingredient in the Georgian's success, one that drove his opponents batty, was a studied vagueness on the issues. Carter intuited that millions of Americans yearned less for policy detail than for the ability to trust, once again, in a national leader. They were flattered by his call for "a government that is as good and honest and decent and competent and compassionate and as filled with love as are the American people" and by his rhetorical question, "You don't plot murder and I don't plot murder, so why should our government plot murder against some foreign leader?" These were potent appeals to an electorate shaken by Vietnam, Watergate, and more recent revelations of government skulduggery at home and abroad.

President Ford, who was completing Nixon's interrupted term, now sought election in his own right. His hopes for an easy nomination ran afoul of a surprisingly formidable primary challenge by former California Governor Ronald Reagan, who accused Ford of conceding too much to the Soviets and of overseeing a profligate welfare state. The president only barely defeated Reagan's insurgency and seemed in poor shape to face his Democratic opponent. Even after the polling bounce Ford received from the Republican convention in Kansas City, he trailed Carter by fifteen points.

In the ensuing general election campaign, Ford steadily closed the gap. The political magic Carter had wielded during the primaries evaporated after the conventions, as he committed a series of damaging gaffes and some Democrats seemed to experience buyer's remorse. Ford made his own missteps. The most spectacular was his claim, during a nationally televised debate, that "there is no Soviet domination of Eastern Europe, and there never will be under the Ford administration." The president meant that the people of Eastern Europe were indomitable and that his administration stood with them against their communist puppet governments, but he appeared to be denying plain reality. Carter responded that he "would like to see Mr. Ford convince the Polish-Americans and the Czech-Americans and the Hungarian-Americans" that their countries of origin were free of Moscow's grip. (Now, *that* was a blow for "white ethnics" that landed.) In November, Carter prevailed by a two percentage point margin in the popular vote and a 297–240 vote in the Electoral College. Both houses of Congress stayed Democratic, with hardly any change in the party balance.

Jimmy Carter in the White House

Carter began his presidency on a refreshingly humble note, making his inaugural journey from Capitol Hill to the White House on foot, smiling and waving to the crowds as he walked alongside his wife Rosalynn and young daughter Amy. Yet the very qualities that made Carter an appealing candidate – his outsider status, his air of moral rectitude – ill served him in the presidency. He failed to work effectively with Congress, even though it was under Democratic control. Once he had arrived at a given policy position, he resisted modifying it through the process of give and take. After all, he had examined the issue in all of its aspects and had determined the correct solution. Why should politics now come into play? Nor was Carter keen on cajoling legislators to support positions that logic or morality already dictated they espouse. "It's the damnedest thing," confessed his press secretary Jody Powell. "He went all over the country for two years asking everybody he saw to vote for him for President, but he doesn't like to call up a Congressman and ask for his support." Not surprisingly, members of Congress chafed against such self-righteousness and grew less and less willing to go the extra mile for the president. It didn't help that Congress itself was more fractious, having recently adopted internal, post-Watergate reforms that "democratized" the institution and made it harder for committee chairs to impose party discipline.

Carter, moreover, proved deeply unlucky. He confronted the same economic challenges that had bedeviled Nixon and Ford – stagflation and an inability to meet the nation's growing energy needs – though in Carter's case they struck with even greater force, especially in the second half of his presidential term. Those final two years were also marked by vexing foreign crises that tended to exacerbate the domestic woes. None of these problems could be addressed in the moralistic terms Carter had employed in seeking the office. "Poor bastard," the chairman of his reelection campaign remarked in 1980. "He used up all his luck getting here."

In his efforts to tackle economic problems, Carter repeatedly clashed with the liberal wing of his own party. Often, he would pledge overall support for liberal initiatives but at less generous levels than liberals wished. When they called for an increase in the federal minimum wage from $2.30 to $3 per hour, he proposed that it go up to just $2.50. Another example was the Humphrey–Hawkins bill, sponsored by Minnesota Senator (and former Vice President) Hubert Humphrey and California Representative Gus Hawkins, a member of the Congressional Black Caucus. As originally proposed, Humphrey–Hawkins required the federal government to guarantee "full employment" by holding the unemployment rate down to 4 percent and by hiring those who couldn't find jobs in the private sector. Carter supported, and Congress passed in 1978, a weaker version of the bill that changed the full employment "commitment" to a "goal" and no longer envisioned the federal government as the employer of last resort. In these ways, the historian Laura Kalman observes, "even the victories liberals achieved during Carter's presidency with his help seemed like defeats." Increasingly, moreover, Carter pursued measures to combat inflation and reduce the budget deficit, at the expense of policies to boost employment or public welfare. In early 1979, when Carter submitted a budget to Congress reflecting these priorities, liberals cried foul. Senator Edward Kennedy said that Carter "asks the poor, the black, the sick, the young, the cities and the unemployed to bear a disproportionate share" of austerity's costs. By now, some liberals were urging Kennedy to challenge Carter for the Democratic nomination in 1980.

The energy crisis was another major preoccupation for Carter. By early 1977, half of the oil Americans consumed came from abroad, and each barrel of foreign oil cost twice as much as it had in the fall of 1973. An unusually cold winter in 1976–1977 accentuated the dangerous dependence. In this instance, Carter was the one to venture out boldly, only to be frustrated by Congress. Three months after taking office, a stern-faced president proclaimed in a nationally televised address that the quest for energy independence was "the moral equivalent of war." (Critics mocked the phrase by reducing it to its acronym: MEOW.) The solution, Carter believed, lay in lessening the nation's dependence on fossil fuels, and this could be done in two ways: increasing fuel efficiency and seeking alternative sources of energy. In 1977 and 1978, Carter pushed Congress to pass legislation that promoted both of these remedies, by imposing stiffer tax penalties on gas-guzzling cars, by providing tax relief and subsidies to companies developing alternative energy sources, and by lowering price controls on oil and gas (on the theory that higher prices would reduce wasteful consumption). Carter's approach provoked stiff opposition from car-manufacturing companies, which objected to higher fuel efficiency standards, and from the oil and gas industry, which liked the reduced price controls but balked at higher taxes. Oil and gas lobbyists argued that salvation lay in exploiting untapped energy reserves in the United States, not conservation. Reflecting these influences, Congress either ignored Carter's initiatives or passed them in gutted form.

Foreign Relations under Carter

In foreign affairs, too, Carter aimed to act boldly – indeed, to recast America's role in the world. The debacle in Vietnam, along with recent revelations of US covert meddling abroad, convinced Carter that the nation had become dangerously overextended abroad and had lost its way morally. He could see that Third World countries were now much more vocal in world affairs and that issues such as global poverty, racial inequality, environmental degradation, and nuclear proliferation had come to the fore. Carter believed the United States should set aside its "inordinate fear of Communism" and instead address these issues of common concern. His administration would work to reduce tensions with cold war adversaries, lower America's domineering profile, seek resolutions of festering international disputes, and promote human rights abroad.

Carter appeared to make considerable headway in advancing this agenda. He elevated human rights as a foreign policy concern, pressuring governments throughout the world, especially in Latin America, to release political prisoners and allow greater civic freedom. In 1977, his administration concluded two treaties with the government of Panama to permit the latter to exercise sovereignty over the Panama Canal, which the United States had controlled for more than six decades. (Carter inherited the Panama initiative from Ford but quickly made it his own.) In 1978, at the presidential retreat at Camp David, Carter brokered a stunning agreement between Egypt and Israel in which those two nations pledged to end three decades of war. In early 1979, the United States and the People's Republic of China – again, after thirty years of mutual estrangement – established full diplomatic relations, consummating a process begun during Richard Nixon's presidency. Months later, Carter and his Soviet counterpart, Leonid Brezhnev, signed a second SALT treaty in Vienna, Austria, imposing caps on the two nations' stockpiles of nuclear weapons. Meanwhile, the Carter administration forthrightly opposed white minority rule in southern Africa, aiding Rhodesia's transition to majority rule (and change of name to Zimbabwe) in 1979–1980. The administration hardly ever considered military intervention in global trouble spots, and no US soldier died in combat on Carter's watch.

But several of these achievements contained less than met the eye or acquired a significance at odds with Carter's original intentions. Many governments guilty of human rights abuses escaped US criticism or punishment, because relations with them raised other, overriding foreign policy considerations. The Carter administration imposed no sanctions on the PRC, so as not to jeopardize the normalization of relations. Similarly, it sought no new sanctions against the Soviet Union, over and above those already contained in the Jackson–Vanik amendment, on the ground that US–Soviet arms control should take priority. (After all, preventing the nuclear incineration of the planet was not entirely divorced from the pursuit of human rights.) The authoritarian, pro-Western government of Iran, an oil-rich nation strategically situated between the Soviet Union and the Persian Gulf, also got a pass – a brief one, it turned out – on its human rights abuses.

Similarly, the Egyptian–Israeli agreement at Camp David, though widely regarded as Carter's greatest foreign policy achievement, was actually a disappointment to the president.

He had spent most of 1977 trying to broker a comprehensive settlement between Israel and all of its Arab neighbors, including the Palestinians. But both Israel and Egypt preferred a bilateral peace process unencumbered by the participation of other Arab actors, a formula Kissinger had pursued after the 1973 Arab–Israeli war (see Chapter 7). Carter was obliged, therefore, to embrace a diplomatic approach he had previously rejected as too narrow. Because the resulting Camp David Accords left Israel in control of Palestinian, Syrian, and Lebanese territory (only the Egyptians recovered occupied land), they intensified anti-US sentiment throughout the Arab world.

So it went for America's relations with its main communist adversaries. Carter had pursued rapprochement with China as a way of easing cold war tensions across the board. The PRC and the Soviet Union were deeply hostile toward one another, and Carter hoped to follow a balanced policy of improving relations with both nations simultaneously. Instead, Zbigniew Brzezinski, Carter's strongly anti-Soviet national security adviser, deliberately exploited the closer Sino-US ties to ratchet up anxieties in Moscow, much as Nixon had done in the early 1970s. In 1979, China launched a brief but extremely bloody war against Soviet-aligned Vietnam, drawing only pro forma criticism from the Carter administration. Not surprisingly, these developments placed serious strain on US–Soviet relations. SALT II, meanwhile, fell short of Carter's initial aspirations. The president had favored deep cuts in the US and Soviet nuclear arsenals. The Soviets, however, insisted on implementing the far more modest blueprint they had negotiated with the Ford administration in Vladivostok, and Carter had to go along.

In these approaches to the Arab–Israeli conflict, the PRC, and the Soviet Union, the legacy of previous US realpolitik prevented Carter from achieving a more hopeful vision. In a fourth policy area, US–Iranian relations, the weight of the past would be even more destructive and would impair the president's hold on political power. One reason that events in Iran, to which we will shortly return, proved so damaging to Carter was that they compounded an ongoing domestic economic crisis. Another was that they occurred at a time when several distinct, though at times loosely coordinated, conservative rebellions were already throwing Carter and other Democrats on the defensive.

The Rise of Conservatism

The nation's rightward turn preceded Carter's presidency and transcended his governing agenda. It dated back to the mid-1960s, when politically decisive coalitions began forming in reaction to the perceived excesses and failures of both radicals and liberals. The pattern grew more prevalent in the 1970s, bringing conservative sensibilities, critiques, protests, and policy recommendations into more and more areas of American life.

We've already seen how race-conscious measures such as busing and affirmative action aroused strong, and occasionally bitter, opposition. Crime policy, which was often inflected with racial controversy, was another arena in which conservative approaches were ascendant. Between 1961 and 1972, property crime rates had doubled in the nation, and rates of violent crime had increased two and a half times. Over that same period, the federal judiciary had shown greater deference to the rights of criminal defendants, most conspicuously through such landmark Supreme Court rulings as *Gideon v. Wainwright* (1963), which required states to provide free legal representation to indigent defendants, and *Miranda v. Arizona* (1966), which held that arrestees must be informed of their rights to remain silent and to seek legal counsel; any statements police extracted from suspects without first "reading them their rights" were inadmissible at trial. In 1972, the Supreme Court ruled that the death penalty, as currently administered, violated the Eighth Amendment's ban on cruel and unusual punishment. The specter of such official leniency against a backdrop of escalating crime rates caused more and more Americans to feel that the system was "coddling" criminals and slighting their victims. Popular movies like *Dirty Harry* (1971) and *Death Wish* (1974) gave vivid expression to such sentiments. In both films, avenging heroes – a maverick cop in the first case, the husband of a murdered woman in the second – hunt down violent criminals whom police authorities are too hamstrung to pursue.

For a host of often interlocking reasons, African Americans were disproportionately enmeshed in the criminal justice system. They were more likely to live in impoverished circumstances that encouraged criminal behavior; the militant protests of the late 1960s and early 1970s had fostered defiant attitudes toward law enforcement; they were policed more aggressively and punished much more harshly than middle-class whites. Thus debates about crime closely mapped onto debates about race, revealing a significant overlap between those who believed that the dominant order had grown "soft on crime" and those who felt that the government should limit itself to combating overt discrimination and abandon race-conscious remedies.

By the second half of the 1970s, the strict approach to crime was clearly prevailing. In 1976, the Supreme Court reversed its death penalty decision; the first post-reinstatement execution took place in Utah six months later. Across the country, state legislatures mandated stiffer penalties for various offenses and limited judges' discretion in imposing sentences. Although Republicans and conservatives were usually at the forefront of these reforms, plenty of liberal Democrats supported them, too, subject to what the historian Julilly Kohler-Hausmann calls "a near-compulsive political imperative to appear tough on crime." The nation's prison population, which had modestly decreased in the previous decade, had begun rising again in the early 1970s. Between 1975 and 1980, it surged from 240,593 to 315,974. (The increase seemed dramatic at the time, but it would be dwarfed by the massive, successive spikes in the prison population occurring over the quarter-century after 1980.)

Many Americans also wanted to crack down on welfare recipients. As we saw in Chapter 8, the welfare rights movement of the 1960s and early 1970s had pressured the federal and state governments to be more generous in dispensing aid and less intrusive in policing aid recipients' behavior. The results were a considerable easing of the Aid to Families with Dependent Children program's eligibility requirements and a dramatic expansion of its rolls, from 3.1 million recipients in 1960 to 10.8 million in 1974. Although welfare rights activists welcomed these changes and wanted to push them further, conservative critics decried what they saw as a bloated, out-of-control system that abetted recipients' slothful, fraudulent, or pathological behavior. Some conservatives did offer cogent analyses of ill-designed incentive structures and unintended consequences. Others shared lurid stories about (presumptively Black) "welfare queens" who lived lives of luxury on the public's dime. Many of these anecdotes were false or distorted; some were true but wildly unrepresentative.

On the economic front, the hard times of the 1970s gave conservative economists and politicians an opportunity to champion new approaches. A common claim among conservatives was that the government taxed too much at all levels, though there was disagreement over what could be accomplished by slashing tax rates. The standard view was that starving the government of revenue would force it to reduce wasteful spending, especially on social programs that, in most conservatives' eyes, encouraged an unhealthy dependence on government. A more novel theory, promoted by a young economist named Arthur Laffer, held that lowering tax rates would not necessarily require cuts in government spending. With a reduced tax burden, Laffer argued, private economic actors would become much more productive, enlarging the economy to such an extent that the government, even though taxing at lower percentages, would ultimately reap more revenue. Although Laffer's theory gained some traction among congressional Republicans in the second half of the 1970s, it remained a minority perspective (and in some cases a ridiculed one) within the party. In any event, Democratic control of the White House and both houses of Congress precluded, for the moment, the enactment of radical tax-cutting schemes in Washington.

At the state level, though, conservative activists had a freer hand. In the decade's closing years, several "tax revolts" occurred in which citizens passed ballot initiatives to block state legislatures from levying certain kinds of taxes. In the most prominent case, a retired California businessman named Howard Jarvis led a successful drive to pass Proposition 13, which sharply curtailed property taxes in that state. Prior to Proposition 13's passage in 1978, California's property taxes were pegged to housing prices, which had soared in recent years. In Los Angeles, the average price of a single-family home rose from $37,800 in 1974 to $83,200 in 1978. Because salaries were not increasing at comparable rates, homeowners struggled to pay their mounting property taxes. For those on fixed incomes, the burden could be crippling. Jarvis brilliantly exploited public unhappiness with the status quo, sharing heartrending accounts of senior citizens eating pet food to save money for property taxes and pooh-poohing warnings that the revenue shortfall would imperil essential public services. "[I]f a library here and there has to close Wednesday mornings from 9 to 11," he said, "life will go on. Who the hell goes to the library in the morning, anyway?" Jarvis's rumpled appearance, irascible demeanor, and ubiquitous media presence created an appealing persona of a tireless citizen-servant giving his all for the common taxpayer. Less evident to the average voter were the benefits Proposition 13 disproportionately conferred on the big fish in the pond, especially individual and corporate owners of large apartment complexes.

Foreign policy was another topic on which rightwing voices grew louder. Conservatives who had been willing to challenge Nixon's and Ford's détente policies felt even freer to attack Carter's moves in this area, especially as Carter sometimes questioned the assumption that anticommunism should be the main driver of US diplomacy. Hawkish think tanks such as the Committee on the Present Danger, the American Enterprise Institute, and the Heritage

Foundation churned out reams of congressional testimony and op/ed pieces lambasting Carter's nuclear arms control initiatives. At the 1979 signing ceremony for SALT II in Vienna, Carter was obliged to reciprocate Leonid Brezhnev's physical embrace. The conservative magazine *Human Events* asked whether the president would have "hugged Hitler."

In 1978, during the Senate debate over ratification of the Panama Canal treaties, conservative politicians, analysts, commentators, and activists waged a noisy campaign against the treaties, which, they insisted, would liquidate a vital US position in the Western Hemisphere and proclaim America's susceptibility to extortion by small nations. (In previous years, popular Panamanian demonstrations against US control of the Canal Zone had sometimes turned violent; Panama's strongman, General Omar Torrijos Herrera, was now warning that public disorder would resume if the status quo persisted.) The conservative onslaught against the treaties – in which Ronald Reagan, eyeing another run for the White House in 1980, played a conspicuous role – was highly effective. Although the Carter administration eked out a narrow Senate victory for ratification (by a margin of one vote for each treaty), the achievement proved costly. Twenty senators who voted for the treaties were up for reelection in November 1978. Six of them decided to retire; seven ran and lost their seats. For the rest of his term, Carter's supporters in the Senate would be fewer in number and less eager to stick their necks out for the president.

Social Conservatism

On social issues, too, conservative forces were growing more visible and powerful. The feminist movement came under sharp challenge in the second half of the 1970s, a counterattack often spearheaded by women. In 1972, Congress had finally passed the Equal Rights Amendment to the Constitution, which would prohibit discrimination on account of sex by the federal government or any state. The amendment now required ratification by thirty-eight states, or three-quarters of the total. This seemed eminently doable. The margins in the House and Senate had been overwhelming, and a solid majority of the public supported the amendment. Within just a year of the congressional milestone, thirty states had ratified the ERA. But then a remarkably formidable obstacle emerged, in the guise of a conservative women's organization called the Eagle Forum, which at its height boasted 50,000 members. Phyllis Schlafly, the head of the group, believed that the ERA threatened to deprive women of traditional privileges: financial support from husbands, exemption from military duty, and status as the keeper of family morality. If the ERA passed, Schlafly and other Eagle Forum activists warned, women would serve in combat, gay and lesbian marriages would be legalized, and unisex bathrooms would proliferate. (Critics dismissed these predictions as hysterical, yet decades later each of them would come to pass in some manner, though not as a result of any constitutional amendment.) The Eagle Forum inundated state legislatures with anti-ERA literature, a campaign that yielded impressive dividends. Although the deadline for ratification was extended from 1979 until 1982, the amendment failed to clear the thirty-eight-state threshold and remains unratified today.

Figure 9.2 Phyllis Schlafly, 1978. Source: Bettmann / Getty Images.

Another feminist cause to arouse powerful conservative opposition was abortion rights. In its 1973 decision *Roe v. Wade*, the Supreme Court had established that women had an unfettered right to terminate their pregnancies during the first trimester of gestation and a qualified right to do so in the second and third trimesters. Over the next few years, a broad-based antiabortion movement, initially led by Catholics but soon prominently featuring evangelical Protestants, Orthodox Jews, and others, emerged. Its core tenet was that the unborn are persons entitled to life. Here, too, women activists, including Schlafly, were highly visible. Although the Right to Life movement failed to get abortion outlawed again, it did persuade Congress in 1976 to pass the Hyde Amendment, a rider to a funding bill named for Republican Representative Henry Hyde of Illinois. By barring the use of federal funds to pay for abortion (except in cases of rape, incest, or health conditions threatening the life of the pregnant woman), the Hyde Amendment made it much harder for poor women to avail themselves of the procedure.

Many of these same activists opposed the movement for gay and lesbian rights, another cause that had gained powerful momentum in the early 1970s. In January 1977, Florida's Dade County (now Miami-Dade County) passed an ordinance banning discrimination on the basis of sexual orientation. Anita Bryant, a gospel singer and spokeswoman for the Florida Citrus Association, launched a campaign to repeal the ordinance by referendum. Warning that the new law would permit homosexuals to teach in public schools and "recruit" children to their "perverted, unnatural, and ungodly lifestyle," she formed an organization called Save Our Children, which became a vehicle for raising funds and generating publicity across the country. Stunningly, in November 1977 Bryant's repeal initiative prevailed by a two-to-one margin. As supporters of gay rights recoiled in horror at the vote (and retaliated by boycotting orange juice), Bryant became a conservative hero. A poll conducted by *Good Housekeeping* revealed her to be the most admired woman of 1978, 1979, and 1980.

Inspired by Bryant's success, John Briggs, a Republican California state assemblyman, introduced a statewide ballot measure that would bar gays and lesbians from teaching in California's public schools. In November 1978, the Briggs initiative was decisively defeated, a casualty of the state's more liberal social climate and of the fact that its two leading conservatives, former Governor Reagan and the newly famous Howard Jarvis, publicly opposed the measure as going too far. Still, the experience of mounting a campaign in such a large and diverse state afforded excellent political training for conservative activists eager to wield influence at the national level.

In each of these movements to maintain traditional understandings of gender and sexuality, conservative Protestant evangelicals, especially from the white South, were a growing presence. Evangelicalism holds that all people can achieve salvation by accepting Christ as their savior, an experience often described as being "born again." At a time when mainline Protestant denominations were losing members, evangelical branches were rapidly expanding. Between 1965 and 1975, the Southern Baptist Convention gained nearly two million members, and by 1980 it was the largest Protestant denomination in the country. In a 1976 Gallup poll, about a third of adult Americans described themselves as born-again Christians. It was increasingly common for evangelicals to attend churches with huge memberships – 2,000 congregants or more – known as megachurches. Evangelicals were more prosperous and better educated than ever before. In 1960, only 7 percent of them had received college education; by the mid-1970s, 23 percent had done so. Much of that education was self-administered, via a widening network of Christian colleges and seminaries.

Evangelicals' cultural offerings were gaining national visibility. The top-selling nonfiction book of the decade was Hal Lindsey's *The Late Great Planet Earth*, which, as noted, also became a movie. Other prominent evangelicals – Billy Graham, James Dobson, Francis Schaeffer, Tim and Beverly LaHaye – authored their own highly popular books. By the late 1970s, evangelicals operated three national television networks and aired scores of religious shows on other networks, enabling twenty million Americans to tune in regularly to evangelical programming. About a thousand "Jesus rock" bands played in churches, concert halls, and alcohol-free Christian nightclubs.

Several high-profile Americans were "born again" during the decade: former Black Panther Party leader Eldridge Cleaver, who renounced political radicalism in favor of conservative Christianity; Nixon White House counsel Charles Colson, who after doing time for his involvement in Watergate devoted his life to prison ministries; and singer-songwriter Bob Dylan, who released a Christian-themed album in 1979 and professed the faith for a couple of years thereafter. The most improbable conversion was that of Larry Flynt, publisher of the pornographic magazine *Hustler*, following a meeting with Ruth Carter Stapleton, President Carter's evangelist sister. In Flynt's case, the effect wore off after just a few months.

In previous decades, evangelicals had largely steered clear of politics. Yet in the early 1970s, in response to what they saw as an assault on traditional values by an arrogant liberal elite, they began publicly espousing conservative social causes such as banning abortion, outlawing homosexuality, and opposing the ERA. At first, many evangelicals were excited about the candidacy of Jimmy Carter, a Southern Baptist. But their enthusiasm dimmed as it became clear, over the course of 1976, that Carter's positions on social issues fell within the Democratic mainstream. Although the candidate said he personally opposed abortion and "the homosexual lifestyle," he did not favor recriminalizing them. The election took place before evangelicals' reservations could coalesce into firm opposition: Carter won 56 percent of the white Baptist vote; the televangelist Pat Robertson, a severe social conservative, cast his ballot for the Georgia Democrat. But just a few months into the new president's term, as his campaign positions assumed policy form, conservative evangelicals moved into open opposition. Even so, in 1977 and 1978 most of their energies were funneled into single-issue campaigns in various parts of the country, such as the antigay ballot initiatives in Florida and California. By 1979, however, evangelicals were ready for a broad-based intervention in national electoral politics.

Here, a key figure was the televangelist Jerry Falwell, who headed a Southern Baptist megachurch and college in Lynchburg, Virginia, and hosted a television show that aired on 373 stations nationwide. Falwell represented evangelicalism's fundamentalist tendency, which insists on the literal truth of Scripture. In early 1979, he joined forces with a loose cohort of young conservatives (some with no ties to evangelicalism) whom the media called the New Right. These activists had pioneered new methods of outreach – such as direct-mail fundraising campaigns aided by computer-generated address lists – to drum up support for a range of conservative causes. Applying New Right techniques to the task of mobilizing his followers for overtly electoral purposes, Falwell founded the Moral Majority, a political lobbying organization. Officially, the Moral Majority was open to all faiths, but most of its members were evangelical Christians. Although it prioritized abortion, homosexuality, pornography, and other social issues, it also weighed in on foreign policy, joining, for example, the conservative campaigns against the Panama Canal treaties and SALT II. By the time of the 1980 election, the Moral Majority had registered some two million new voters, the vast majority of them, presumably, buttressing the Republican Party's conservative wing.

The Iranian Revolution and the Energy Crisis

The coalescing of domestic conservative forces politically weakened Carter, hampering his ability to contend with foreign policy challenges, especially the cascade of crises and dislocations resulting from upheaval in Iran. Since the 1950s, the United States had staunchly backed that country's monarch, Shah Mohammad Reza Pahlavi, despite his atrocious human rights record. Relations had become especially close under President Nixon, who provided extensive military aid to Iran to enable it to guard Western interests in the Persian Gulf. By the mid-1970s, thousands of Iranian dissidents had been detained and tortured, and hundreds killed, in the shah's notorious prisons. Ordinary Iranians' hatred of the monarch finally overflowed during Carter's presidency. Starting in early 1978, anti-government demonstrations and strikes spread throughout the country. The regime's efforts to quell the disturbances, though in some cases remarkably violent, were ineffectual, and by fall the entire country was in revolutionary upheaval. Initially, the rebellion drew in leaders and activists from across the political spectrum, but soon conservative Shia elements gained ascendancy within the movement – much to the surprise of Iranian and US officials, who had been preoccupied with the regime's enemies on the secular, communist left. In early 1979, the shah fled the country, and his government collapsed. Ayatollah Ruhollah Khomeini, a seventy-six-year-old Shia cleric who had lived in exile since the mid-1960s, returned to preside over a new, theocratic government.

The shah's ouster was a major strategic setback for the United States. Nonetheless, the Carter administration thought it could establish tolerable relations with the new regime, which was staunchly anti-Soviet and included some moderate figures. So it formally recognized the Islamist government and kept the massive US embassy in Tehran open, albeit with a reduced staff, whose dependent family members were withdrawn from the country. American diplomats and military attachés explored avenues of potential cooperation with Iran's new leaders.

But the Iranian Revolution created other problems, chief among them a months-long cessation of that country's oil exports. Although the resulting shortfall did not, in itself, constitute a large percentage of world oil supply, it triggered disruptions in international markets that produced major spikes in oil prices and gasoline shortages in much of the industrialized world. By May 1979, Americans were languishing in gas lines, as they had done after the 1973 Arab–Israeli war. The inflation rate soared to 12 percent.

Energy was already much in the news that spring. Apart from concerns about Middle Eastern oil, controversy raged over the viability of nuclear power as an alternative to fossil fuels. Environmentalists had long criticized this option, warning that catastrophic nuclear accidents could occur and that there was no safe way to dispose of nuclear waste. Carter, who as a young naval officer had trained to serve on a nuclear-powered submarine (but was honorably discharged before he could do so), considered such fears overblown. But then a frightening mishap seemed to vindicate the environmentalists' warnings. In March 1979, at the Three Mile Island nuclear power plant near Harrisburg, Pennsylvania, a series of malfunctions led

Figure 9.3 Film actor Jane Fonda with her husband, former Students for a Democratic Society president Tom Hayden, at the Three Mile Island nuclear power plant, 1979. Source: Bettmann / Getty Images.

to the release of some radioactive gases into the atmosphere, prompting the state government to conduct a partial evacuation of the area. The actual health impacts were minimal, but the ordeal terrified those in the vicinity of the plant. By an amazing happenstance, this near-disaster coincided almost exactly with the release of *The China Syndrome*, a movie starring Jane Fonda and Jack Lemmon, which portrayed a nuclear power plant accident similar to the one at Three Mile Island. The two events amplified each other, a connection underscored when Fonda, who had famously protested the Vietnam War, addressed about 70,000 demonstrators at a "No Nukes" rally in Washington, DC, the largest of many antinuclear protests occurring around the country that spring. The federal process for approving the construction of new nuclear power plants drastically slowed. It would take more than thirty years for the next plant to receive the go-ahead.

In July 1979 – with the Iranian Revolution now exacerbating US energy woes, with Congress still resisting Carter's favored remedies for the problem, and with pundits panning his performance on a range of issues at home and abroad – the president spoke to the nation from the Oval Office. The extraordinary address became known as the "malaise" speech, though Carter never uttered that word. The nation's ills, he said, were ultimately rooted in something much deeper than the energy issue: "a moral and spiritual crisis" striking "at the very heart and soul and spirit of our national will . . . . In a nation that was proud of hard work, strong families, close-knit communities, and our faith in God, too many of us now tend to worship self-indulgence and consumption. Human identity is no longer defined by what one does, but by what one owns." Carter urged his fellow Americans to shun empty materialism and choose "the path of common purpose and the restoration of American values."

Initially, Carter's speech polled well with the public and impressed many news commentators. But days later the president squandered the goodwill by dismissing several cabinet members, a move that appeared vindictive and created an impression of instability at the top. The shakeup received harsh criticism in the press, compounded by the fact that some of the ousted cabinet secretaries had vocal supporters in Congress and the media. For the rest of that summer and into the fall, Carter's approval ratings were stuck in the low thirties.

The Iran Hostage Crisis

In Iran, things were about to get much worse. For months, the shah, who was exiled in Mexico, had requested via emissaries that he be granted asylum in the United States. Carter resisted the pressure, fearing that succumbing to it would enrage the new Iranian government and endanger the US diplomats still in Iran. "Fuck the shah," Carter retorted after aides conveyed to him yet another appeal. "I'm not going to welcome him here when he has other places to go where he'll be safe." The president bristled at the thought of the shah "here playing tennis while Americans in Tehran were being kidnapped or even killed." Carter subsequently learned, however, that the shah was gravely ill with cancer and needed advanced medical treatment available only in the United States. So, in October 1979, the president relented and agreed to admit the shah, though he still worried about reactions in Tehran. The concern was well founded. News of the decision infuriated and alarmed a group of militant Iranian students who saw themselves as guardians of the revolution. They were sure the story about the shah's illness was a sham, concocted to get the hated ex-monarch into the United States, where he could huddle with his CIA sponsors and plot his return to Iran. To expose and disrupt this unfolding scheme, they prepared a spectacular protest.

On November 4, 1979, during a massive demonstration outside the US embassy in Tehran, about 150 students peeled off from the crowd and executed a separate, secret plan. Using bolt cutters to sever the chains securing the outer gates, they entered the embassy grounds, disarmed the marine guards (who were under orders not to use force in such an eventuality), seized control of the compound, and took physical custody of more than sixty Americans in the embassy's employ.

At first, nearly everyone, including the students themselves, expected the embassy takeover to end soon. Surely, Iranian authorities – perhaps after allowing the students to parade the American detainees around for a while and deliver some fiery speeches – would step in to tell the impetuous youths that they had made their point and it was time to go home. Instead, Ayatollah Khomeini publicly blessed their action, seeing it as a rallying point around which

Figure 9.4 William Gallegos and Rodney Sickmann, marine guards held hostage at the US embassy in Tehran, reading Christmas cards, December 1979. Source: Bettmann / Getty Images.

to consolidate popular support for the revolution. With official Iranian government sponsorship, the students continued to hold the detainees, refusing to release them until the US government returned the shah to Iran so he could face trial – a demand Washington rejected out of hand. The students did make one conciliatory gesture. A couple of weeks after the embassy takeover, at Khomeini's urging, they released thirteen hostages who were Black or female, on the grounds that African Americans were themselves victims of US oppression and that "Islam reserves special rights for women." Fifty-two Americans, all but two of them male, remained in custody.

The seizure of the embassy drew an emotional response from the US public. Televised images of blindfolded hostages being trotted out before news cameras, and of strident Iranian demonstrators chanting "Death to America," left millions of Americans feeling helpless and angry. Although most found peaceful ways to express their outrage, some violently lashed out against Iranians, or those believed to be Iranians, living in the United States. Scapegoating tends to be an inexact science, so plenty of Arabs, South Asians, Latin Americans, and others faced nativist hostility. (With their beards, turbans, and long tunics, Coptic clergyman and Sikhs were especially vulnerable.) But the public outpouring could be generous, too. Americans attended prayer vigils, rang church bells, tied yellow ribbons around trees and lampposts, and wrote letters appealing for the hostages' release to Iran's embassy in Washington and its UN delegation in New York. These responses, argues the historian David Farber, challenge the common impression of the 1970s as a narcissistic "Me decade."

Carter threw himself into the task of addressing the crisis – consoling hostages' families; lining up diplomatic support from other governments; exploring legal options in the event Tehran made good on its threat to try the hostages as spies; and devising means, short of military action, to pressure Iran to release the Americans. In mid-November, the Carter administration froze billions of dollars in Iranian government assets deposited in US banks. These efforts, combined with the "rally around the flag" effect that often accompanies foreign crises, produced a spike in Carter's public approval ratings. As the president himself understood all too well, however, such support was sure to wane if the hostages' captivity dragged on much longer.

Late in December 1979 another upheaval shook Central Asia. Tens of thousands of Soviet troops invaded Afghanistan, a neighbor of both the Soviet Union and Iran, to prevent Afghanistan's Marxist government from being overthrown by Islamist rebels. The Soviets had blundered into a quagmire that in the coming decade would severely diminish their international, and even their domestic, power. At the time, however, Moscow appeared to have seized the initiative from a weakened and demoralized West. Iran's turmoil only heightened these fears. Having moved south to occupy Afghanistan, might not the Soviets be tempted to veer westward into chaotic and ill-defended Iran and thereby gain a foothold on the vital Persian Gulf?

Carter responded harshly to the Soviet move. In his January 1980 State of the Union Address, he declared that intervention in the Gulf area by an outside power "will be repelled by any means necessary, including military force," a statement pundits called the Carter Doctrine. The president asked Congress for a substantial increase in military spending and for the authority to require young men to register for military service; withdrew SALT II from consideration by the Senate (the treaty would never be ratified); and successfully pressured the US Olympic Committee to boycott the 1980 Olympic Games scheduled to take place in Moscow. Cold war tensions scarily escalated. To a significant degree, the sharp anti-Soviet policies associated with President Ronald Reagan got their start in the final year of his predecessor's term. These were a far cry from the conciliatory stances with which Carter had begun his presidency.

As if all this were not enough, anxiety over spiking oil prices and the upheavals in Iran and Afghanistan caused a run on gold. The world price of that metal skyrocketed from about $450 per ounce in mid-December 1979 to $850 per ounce a month later.

And still Iran held onto the hostages. By the spring of 1980, the surge in public approval Carter had enjoyed following the embassy seizure had vanished, and the president faced growing pressure to bring the crisis to an end. In April, he authorized a military operation to rescue the hostages. Starting from an aircraft carrier in the Gulf of Oman, a special tactics team would be helicoptered to a secret base outside Tehran that, somehow, remained under US control. They would be driven in trucks to the US embassy compound, forcibly rescue the hostages, and return them to safety. The sheer preposterousness of the plan was an argument in its favor; it was so far-fetched that the Iranians could not possibly prepare for it. But Carter aborted the operation in an early phase when, at a staging area in the Iranian desert, some of the aircraft encountered technical difficulties. During the ensuing evacuation, a helicopter collided with a transport plane, killing eight servicemen. A downcast Carter appeared on national television to disclose the tragedy and take full responsibility for it. *Time* magazine captured the public fallout at home: "While most of Carter's political foes tactfully withheld criticism, his image as inept has been renewed."

The 1980 Presidential Election

One of those political foes was Ted Kennedy, who, heeding the call of his liberal supporters, and accusing Carter of purveying "Republican economics," had decided to run for the Democratic nomination. Yet the insurgent campaign suffered from poor timing. Kennedy launched his candidacy in November 1979, just days after the embassy takeover. The "rally around the flag" phenomenon enabled Carter to defeat Kennedy in nearly all of the early primaries. Carter's subsequent loss of popularity, especially following the failed rescue effort, afforded Kennedy some important primary wins later in the spring. But it was too little, too late, and Carter's renomination was assured. Still, Kennedy politically weakened the president by continuing his candidacy until the Democratic Party's August convention in New York and, even after conceding, offering Carter only a tepid endorsement. A month earlier, the Republicans met in Detroit and nominated Ronald Reagan for president. It was a dramatic comeback for the party's conservative wing, whose political obituary pundits (and some moderate Republicans) had written after Senator Barry Goldwater's crushing defeat in 1964.

Heading into the general election season, the nation was in severe economic pain. Back in October 1979, Federal Reserve Chairman Paul Volcker, seeking to break the back of inflation, had instituted measures that effectively restricted the growth of the money supply and caused interest rates to soar. Inevitably, the unemployment rate shot up, too, hitting 7.8 percent in July 1980. Americans reeled under the twin blows of job layoffs and steep home mortgage rates. To protest the destructive impact of high mortgages on the home-building industry, the bricklayers' union dumped truckloads of bricks at the entrance of the Federal Reserve building. But Volcker stayed the course, insisting that only a drastic economic slowdown could vanquish inflation. The inflation rate would eventually come down, from an annual average of 13.5 percent in 1980 to 10.3 percent in the following year, and then to 6.1 percent in 1982. But Carter had to face the electorate before this improvement occurred, and during a time of induced recession.

The hard times of 1979–1980 posed special challenges for organized labor, whose bargaining power, which had been slipping for years, now took a plunge. Amid rampant layoffs, workers were obliged to make painful concessions just to keep their jobs. This was at least partly what Volcker had intended. After all, it was widely recognized that labor's success at the bargaining table in the 1960s and early 1970s had contributed to the high inflation. Diminishing unions' leverage was thus essential to controlling the cost of living. Carter, who had appointed Volcker to his position in August 1979, may not have shared the Fed chair's antilabor agenda, but he did want to subdue inflation. So he went along with the shock treatment, gambling that the voters would forgive him in the end. As for the unions, their present weakness would, in a few years' time, give way to collapse.

On the campaign trail, Reagan blasted Carter for failing to stand up to either the Iranians or the Soviets and for undercutting America's allies in his misguided promotion of human rights. The Republican also hammered away at the dismal state of the economy, delighting supporters with the maxim "A recession is when your neighbor loses his job; a depression is when you lose yours; and recovery is when Jimmy Carter loses his." Carter countered that Reagan's conservative stances on social issues were extreme and that his hawkish leanings were downright dangerous in the nuclear age. But Reagan's avuncular performance in the two candidates' single televised debate neutralized these charges. His rhetorical questions to viewers – "Are you better off than you were four years ago? Is it easier for you to go and buy things in the stores than it was four years ago? … Is America as respected throughout the world as it was?" – crisply stated the case for change.

Election Day brought disaster for Carter and the Democrats. Reagan decisively won the presidency, receiving 50.8 percent of the popular vote to Carter's 41.0 percent. The Electoral College result was a crushing 489 to 49. Except for his native Georgia, Carter won not a single southern state; he had swept that entire region in 1976. (A third-party candidate, former Republican Representative John Anderson of Illinois, who had run in the Republican primaries but then launched an independent campaign after Reagan's nomination, won 6.6 percent of the popular vote and no Electoral College votes.) The Republicans also took back the Senate, which they had not held since 1955. Several highly prominent Democratic senators, including George McGovern, the presidential nominee in 1972, and Frank Church, chair of the Senate committee that had investigated the CIA and the FBI, lost their seats. Only the House remained in Democratic hands. The victory thrilled conservatives, especially evangelical Christians, 56 percent of whom had abandoned their coreligionist to support the Presbyterian Reagan. "There's no question that Moral Majority and other religious right organizations turned out millions of voters who otherwise would not have been at the polls," Jerry Falwell exulted. The result was a "national avalanche" in favor of Reagan and other conservatives.

***

Now a lame duck, Carter spent his final weeks in office tirelessly negotiating with Iran, via third parties, over the fate of the hostages, determined to secure their freedom while he was still president. Recent events had improved the prospects for a deal. Shortly after the embassy takeover, Carter had asked the shah to leave the United States. The ex-monarch settled in Egypt, where his death in July 1980 eliminated the possibility of his repatriation to face trial, an Iranian demand the US government was never going to accept. In September, war broke out between Iran and neighboring Iraq; the conflict would last eight years and cost over a million lives on both sides. Suddenly facing an existential threat, the Iranians had a strong incentive to settle the hostage issue. By the end of Carter's term, the essentials of an agreement were in place: Washington would release about $8 billion in frozen Iranian assets and pledge not to interfere in Iran's internal affairs; Tehran would let the hostages go. In a final effort to humiliate Carter, however, Iran delayed releasing the Americans until around half an hour after Reagan took the oath of office on January 20, 1981. Superficially, it appeared as if the arrival of the "new sheriff in town" had cowed Iran into instant conciliation, an impression Reagan's partisans would nurture for years. Unquestionably, though, the diplomatic achievement belonged to the defeated president.

The conservative currents that swept Reagan and other Republicans into power had been swelling since the mid-1960s, when significant segments of the electorate began challenging liberal policies on race, crime, foreign relations, and other issues. In the late 1960s and early 1970s, Republicans benefited from this rising antiliberalism. For a few years in the mid-seventies, however, public dismay over Watergate halted their advance, at least at the national level. Now the Republicans were roaring into Washington, granted a better opportunity to set the national agenda than any they had enjoyed in nearly thirty years. The economic crisis that had largely given them this chance remained very much in force and seemed likely to deepen in the months ahead; it was far from assured that the GOP would govern effectively. But the broad Democratic coalition that Franklin Roosevelt had forged in the 1930s had sustained a crushing, and arguably a fatal, blow.

READING QUESTIONS

1. In what ways – positive, negative, or not necessarily either – did the legacies of the 1960s shape the lives of African Americans in the following decade?
2. By 1976, millions of Americans had come to doubt the virtue, honesty, competence, or effectiveness of the nation's governing institutions. How do you explain this loss of confidence?
3. In what ways did President Jimmy Carter hope to recast US foreign relations? What obstacles prevented him from doing so as thoroughly as he wished?
4. In seeking to explain the political triumph of conservatism in 1980, it is helpful to think in two distinct time frames: the decade and a half from 1965 to 1980, and the closing years of the 1970s. How did events within that briefer period, combined with developments over the longer one, create a climate ultimately conducive to conservative electoral victories?

SUGGESTIONS FOR FURTHER READING

Alter, Jonathan. *His Very Best: Jimmy Carter, a Life*. New York: Simon & Schuster, 2020.

Anderson, Terry. *The Pursuit of Fairness: A History of Affirmative Action*. New York: Oxford University Press, 2004.

Carroll, Peter N. *It Seemed Like Nothing Happened: America in the 1970s*. New Brunswick, NJ: Rutgers University Press, 1990.

Deslippe, Dennis. *Protesting Affirmative Action: The Struggle over Equality after the Civil Rights Revolution*. Baltimore: Johns Hopkins University Press, 2012.

Farber, David. *Taken Hostage: The Iran Hostage Crisis and America's First Encounter with Radical Islam*. Princeton, NJ: Princeton University Press, 2005.

FitzGerald, Francis. *The Evangelicals: The Struggle to Shape America*. New York: Simon & Schuster, 2017.
Formisano, Ronald P. *Boston against Busing: Race, Class, and Ethnicity in the 1960s and 1970s*. Chapel, NC: University of North Carolina Press, 2004.
Frum, David, *How We Got Here: The 70s, the Decade that Brought you Modern Life (for Better or Worse)*. New York: Basic Books, 2000.
Jacobson, Matthew Frye. *Roots Too: White Ethnic Revival in Post-Civil Rights America*. Cambridge, MA: Harvard University Press, 2006.
Kalman, Laura. *Right Star Rising: A New Politics, 1974–1980*. New York: W. W. Norton, 2010.
Kohler-Hausmann, Julilly. *Getting Tough: Welfare and Imprisonment in 1970s America*. Princeton, NJ: Princeton University Press, 2017.
Lichtenstein, Nelson. *State of the Union: A Century of American Labor*. Princeton, NJ: Princeton University Press, 2002.
Phillips-Fein, Kim. *Invisible Hands: The Businessmen's Crusade against the New Deal*. New York: W. W. Norton, 2010.
Schulman, Bruce. *The Seventies: The Great Shift in American Culture, Society, and Politics*. New York: Free Press, 2001.
Sugrue, Thomas J. *Sweet Land of Liberty: The Forgotten Struggle for Civil Rights in the North*. New York: Random House, 2008.
Williams, Daniel K. *God's Own Party: The Making of the Christian Right*. New York: Oxford University Press, 2010.

10 The Picture Always Overrides

America in the Reagan Years, 1981–1989

Introduction

Hands Across America – that was the stirring vision, and concrete plan, of Ken Kragen, a commercial music manager who had recently branched out to producing high-profile charity events. On May 25, 1986, at 3:00 p.m. Eastern Daylight Time – noon on the West Coast – millions of Americans would link hands, forming a human chain stretching from New York City to Los Angeles. For fifteen minutes, they would all sing the same songs, piped in simultaneously by hundreds of radio stations and public address systems, and savor the moment of national unity. Each participant would pay at least $10 for a place in the line, and corporations would sponsor stretches along the route. Scores of A-list celebrities would shine their star power on the event. In these ways, Hands Across America (HAA) would generate awareness about hunger and homelessness in the United States, problems that had grown acute in recent years, and raise tens of millions of dollars for their alleviation. "In order to make a difference," Kragen told *The New York Times*, "you have to do something major that captures the attention. This is just impossible enough to be possible."

The logistical challenges were immense: arranging human coverage along each of the route's 4,152 miles; maintaining a database of participants' names, addresses, credit card numbers, and route assignments; keeping track of corporate sponsorships; securing permits from local jurisdictions; coordinating among the thousands of event facilitators on the ground; ensuring adequate water supplies, medical facilities, and portable toilets. To manage the undertaking, HAA organizers employed a network of computers, telephone lines, radio connections, closed-circuit televisions, and satellite linkups. Desk workers at far-flung regional offices instantly communicated with one another via a newfangled "electronic mail" system made available by the telecommunications giant MCI. "Three or four years ago this event could not have been done," said Fred Droz, HAA's national project director. "Computers, TV, telephones, teleconferencing – the technology has come together."

Politically, though, HAA afforded occasions for pulling apart. As the big day approached, skeptics dismissed HAA as a feel-good event that would allow corporate sponsors and ordinary citizens alike to congratulate themselves for an effort that, ultimately, could

Figure 10.1 Hands Across America participants, Buckeye, Arizona, 1986. Source: Bettmann / Getty Images.

make little material difference. Criticism intensified when, at the last minute, President Ronald Reagan and First Lady Nancy Reagan decided to join the human chain, whose route passed in front of the White House. They stood at the entrance, linked hands with White House staffers and their children, and did their best to sing along with the HAA anthem. Homeless rights advocates were disgusted by the participation of the president, who had repeatedly persuaded Congress to slash antipoverty programs. They staged a protest demonstration at neighboring Lafayette Park. The Reverend Jesse Jackson, the African American civil rights leader who two years earlier had run unsuccessfully for president, agreed with the dissenters. Reagan's inclusion was "obscene," Jackson said. "He should not be in the line. His policies created the line." But one of Jackson's protégés felt differently. Twenty-six-year-old Donna Brazile, a veteran of Jackson's 1984 campaign, now served as the HAA director for Washington, DC. Immersed in the logistics of the event, Brazile was dismayed by the naysayers at Lafayette Park, whose protest, she thought, "ruined the spirit of the day." Despite her own strong disagreement with Reagan's poverty policies, Brazile welcomed his participation in HAA. "His home was clearly on the route," she told a reporter, "and he paid his money."

When it was over, organizers claimed a smashing success. True, there had been gaps in the chain, especially in desert regions. In some cities, harried facilitators had allowed people to join the line without paying their fees. But an estimated five million souls turned out, and local television news shows across the land aired stirring footage of exuberant citizens clasping hands in song. There were heartwarming stories of marriages, baptisms, and bar mitzvahs occurring on the line. It later emerged that HAA had netted only about $15 million for charity, well short of the hoped-for $50 million – and a mere pittance, critics noted, compared with the billions Washington could have, but had not, devoted to poverty programs. Yet Kragen was upbeat. "Far more significant than the money we have collected," he said, "is the idea of making solutions to these problems a national priority." He had a point. In the coming months and years, the national news media did run more features on poverty and hunger. In 1987, Congress passed its first major legislation to address the homeless crisis, though homeless advocates considered it inadequate. Kragen touted another, less tangible accomplishment: HAA "made Americans feel good about themselves." It was an assessment well in tune with the spirit of the decade.

Indeed, the whole HAA experience was emblematic of the political, cultural, economic, and technological transformations overtaking the nation in the 1980s. Politically, this was a time of ascendant conservatism, when the private sector, not the national government, was widely celebrated as the main engine of American progress. After a rocky start in 1981–1982, Ronald Reagan's business-friendly policies had helped to fuel a dramatic economic recovery, and in 1984 voters resoundingly returned the president to office, rewarding him not just for his policy accomplishments but also for the optimism he inspired in their ranks. Still, the "Reagan Revolution" left millions behind, a reality glaringly evident in the deepening poverty and rising homelessness that HAA's organizers sought to address. Even the broad swath of middle-class Americans who escaped economic calamity tasted little of the wild prosperity so conspicuously enjoyed by those at the top. There was no shortage of dissatisfaction with the prevailing order, yet Reagan's liberal and progressive opponents struggled to muster effective means of resistance. Their efforts showed considerable resourcefulness and creativity but yielded little electoral success. Meanwhile, striking technological innovations, especially in the area of computers, fundamentally altered how Americans worked, studied, entertained themselves, managed their private affairs, and, like the stagers of HAA, tried to make a difference in the world.

President Ronald Reagan

More than any other president of the post-World-War-II period, Ronald Reagan placed his stamp on the era in which he governed. In modern times more broadly, the closest parallel was Franklin D. Roosevelt, who indelibly marked the years 1933 to 1945. Each of these leaders embodied a paradigm shift in US politics. Roosevelt led the country into a new era in which the federal government took much greater responsibility for the national economy and evinced an active and humane concern for those occupying its lower rungs. The resulting New Deal order prevailed for a generation after Roosevelt's death in 1945 but faltered in the late 1960s and 1970s, as the Democratic coalition FDR had forged began coming apart. The election of Reagan in 1980 augured a new national paradigm, persisting long after *he* left office, in which government efforts to regulate the economy and combat poverty were discredited and the values of the private sector exalted. Roosevelt and Reagan were also similar in that they each became president at a time when Americans had suffered a crippling loss of confidence (though the crisis was far worse in FDR's day), and each played a significant role in restoring that confidence. Both were cheerful and charismatic figures whose breezy optimism proved infectious.

A major difference between the two, apart from their opposing political stances, was that, whereas Roosevelt was pragmatic and experimental, Reagan adhered to a small number of fixed ideological principles: that government was too big (except where military spending was concerned), that Washington's role in the private economy had become too intrusive, and that communism was evil and must be vigorously combated. Once he had laid out these general precepts, Reagan was not too concerned about the precise means of their implementation. That was for his advisers and handlers to work out.

Reagan is a puzzling figure, a politician with both striking weaknesses and astonishing strengths. Among the weaknesses were an often rudimentary understanding of the issues of American politics and a lack of interest in becoming better informed. The president had starkly defined views on numerous topics, positions he buttressed with a motley store of anecdotes and statistics, many of them dubiously sourced and some preposterous on their face. He sprinkled these factoids into his speeches and casual remarks, untroubled when journalists exposed their falsehood. During the 1980 campaign, Reagan said that trees and vegetation were responsible for most air pollution. As president, he defended his opposition to abortion by asserting that three-month-old fetuses could survive outside the womb. In 1985, he said that South Africa's apartheid government had already "eliminated the segregation that we once had in our own country," a claim refuted by even a cursory glance at newspaper headlines of the time.

A related quality was Reagan's ability to tune out painful or inconvenient realities. Sometimes, the implications of this trait were purely personal. After having a cancerous polyp removed from his colon in 1985, Reagan told a reporter, "I didn't have cancer. I had something inside me that had cancer in it, and it was removed." But all too often the denial had serious public consequences. Throughout his presidency, Reagan seemed largely oblivious to rising rates of poverty and homelessness and to the fact that a frightening new disease, acquired immune deficiency syndrome (AIDS), was ravaging the lives of more and more Americans. These crises challenged the image of a prosperous and happy nation, and so Reagan mostly ignored them, hampering his own ability to offer solutions.

Among Reagan's strengths, however, was an uncanny ability to connect with the American electorate. Through his speeches and gestures, the president instilled in the public a powerful sense of reassurance and confidence; for this, he was known as the "Great Communicator." Undoubtedly, Reagan's acting background helped him in this respect. In his former profession, Reagan's task had been to project himself onto his audiences, to make *them* feel the range of emotions he was called upon to express. Reagan proved a master at evoking the desired reactions in his political performances, too. To millions of Americans, especially those watching him on television, the president was a highly appealing figure, with a folksy demeanor, a warm smile, a reassuring voice, and a trim, powerful physique for a man of his age. (He turned seventy a couple of weeks after his first inauguration.) Reagan was blessed, too, with a stable of talented speechwriters whose work he regularly improved in delivery. Shortly before Reagan left office, a journalist asked him if acting had been good preparation for the presidency. "There have been times in this office," came the reply, "when I've wondered how you could do the job if you hadn't been an actor."

Reagan's White House staff appreciated the performative nature of his role, and they shrewdly placed the president in settings that maximized his emotional impact. In 1984, the television reporter Leslie Stahl narrated a story on CBS News that contrasted Reagan's ceremonial attendance of the Handicapped Olympics with his efforts to cut aid programs for the disabled. Soon afterward, a White House aide thanked Stahl for the "great piece." "Didn't you hear what I said?" Stahl asked. "Nobody heard what you said," the aide replied. "They just saw the five minutes of beautiful pictures of Ronald Reagan. They saw the balloons, they saw the flags, they saw the red, white and blue. Haven't you people figured out yet that the picture always overrides what you say?"

Reagan's advisers also understood that their boss worked best when his surroundings resembled a film production. James Baker, Reagan's first chief of staff, admiringly recounted a series of phone calls the president made to members of Congress to seek their support for his economic agenda. "We would give him a script for each of these congressional calls," Baker said, "and he never, he never missed it." Lou Cannon, a Reagan biographer, relates a vignette in which "Secretary of State George P. Shultz, huddling with Reagan in the secure vault of the American ambassador's residence in Moscow during the 1988 summit, coached him for his meeting with Soviet leader Mikhail Gorbachev by telling him what to do 'in this scene.' Shultz proceeded through a series of precise directions in stage terminology, telling Reagan where to stand and what to say." Indeed, Reagan was the face of a disciplined and coordinated publicity machine devoted to standardizing his administration's message and thereby generating public support. Each morning, the White House staff issued a "line of the day," a phrase that the president and all other administration spokespeople were to stress in that day's public events. Reporters rolled their eyes at the numbing repetition, but the technique enabled the administration to dominate Washington's policy discussion and, usually, get its way.

From a personal standpoint, Reagan had arrived at an approach to the presidency that, for the most part, served him extremely well. He worked moderate hours, took regular naps, and spent a substantial amount of his time on vacation. These habits left him looking fresh and relaxed for the cameras, enhancing his reassuring persona. President Carter, although half a generation younger than his successor, had sometimes appeared alarmingly haggard in public on account of his punishing work schedule. Similarly, by focusing on broad themes and leaving implementation to subordinates, Reagan himself repeatedly escaped criticism, or at least got off lightly, when his policies faltered or failed altogether. Patricia Schroeder, a Democratic congresswoman from Colorado, called Reagan the "Teflon president," because nothing seemed to stick to him. A bemused press corps adopted the expression, acting as if the Teflon were some mysterious external force, rather than a protective coating that they themselves liberally applied in their inability, or reluctance, to challenge a popular president.

Reaganomics

In its early months in office, the Reagan administration focused on its economic program, contained in a series of bills proposed to Congress. The main elements were a slashing of individual and corporate taxes by 30 percent over three years, a measure that would benefit everyone but especially favor the wealthy; and a $41 billion reduction in domestic federal spending, accomplished by eliminating or shrinking many welfare programs. The program aroused vigorous opposition among the public and on Capitol Hill, and initially there was some doubt that it could be enacted. But a pair of defining events in that first year boosted Reagan's political standing, to the benefit of most of his governing initiatives. In March 1981, as Reagan exited a Washington hotel, a mentally disturbed young man fired several handgun rounds at the president and his entourage. Reagan was struck near the heart, and his press secretary, James Brady, suffered a head wound that left him permanently disabled. Although Reagan's own injury was much graver than the public realized at the time – his lung had been punctured and his blood pressure precipitously fell – the president faced the crisis in style, joking to doctors as they prepared to operate on him, "I hope you're all Republicans." "Today, Mr. President, we're all Republicans," the chief surgeon replied. Reagan went on to make a rapid recovery (though close observers noticed some loss of vigor thereafter), and his popularity soared.

In the summer of 1981, Reagan's first budget, with its large social spending cuts, passed both houses of Congress; so did his tax cuts. For many Democrats in Congress, it had become too politically dangerous to oppose the resilient and cheerful president. National news outlets, swept up in the drama of Reagan's triumphant return to public life, powerfully, if unwittingly, aided his legislative agenda. As the journalist Mark Hertsgaard later wrote, "News coverage, especially on television, focused primarily on Ronald Reagan as an unstoppable political phenomenon and all but ignored what it was he was actually winning and what it meant to the country." The story "was not Rich vs. Poor but Gipper sweeps Congress." ("The Gipper" was an affectionate nickname for Reagan drawn from one of his movie roles.)

The second defining event occurred that same summer, when the Professional Air Traffic Controllers Union (PATCO), whose members were federal employees, went on strike. The work stoppage was illegal, and Reagan ordered the nearly 12,000 strikers to return to work. When they refused, he summarily fired them. The action shocked PATCO members, who had endorsed Reagan in the 1980 election and scarcely imagined he would follow through on his threat. Although other labor unions condemned the firing, it played well with the public, which saw PATCO's position as unreasonable. The dispute both symbolized and hastened organized labor's decline in the Reagan era. Finding much greater federal sympathy for their antilabor outlooks than in recent years, private employers stepped up their union-busting activities, which had started gathering momentum in the late 1970s. Between 1980 and 1987, the percentage of American workers belonging to unions would drop from 23 percent to just 17 percent. The PATCO incident also burnished Reagan's reputation as a tough leader who would unflinchingly carry out his threats, further strengthening his bargaining position on Capitol Hill.

So Reagan pressed ahead with his early legislative agenda, whose three main planks were tax cuts, reductions in social spending, and a dramatic expansion of the defense budget (see Chapter 11 for a fuller discussion of Reagan's defense and foreign policies). Reagan presented all of these measures as part of an integrated plan to restore fiscal sanity to the federal government – that is, to bring down the budget deficit, which had climbed to nearly $80 billion per year during Carter's presidency, and slow the growth of the government's accumulated debt, which passed the $1 trillion mark in 1981. The problem, of course, was that two of the three planks, cutting taxes and increasing defense spending, seemed guaranteed to enlarge both the deficit and the national debt. But Reagan believed he could square the circle, through the near-miraculous powers of the "supply side" theory most prominently championed by the conservative economist Arthur Laffer. As Laffer saw it, the government should do everything possible to put money in the pockets of those who *supplied* the goods and services in the national economy, or, more precisely, those who invested in businesses that supplied the goods and services. If wealthy individuals and corporations received generous tax cuts, Laffer argued, they would invest the extra money in the private economy, making it more productive. The resulting increase in prosperity would be so phenomenal that the federal government, even though taxing at much lower rates, would reap huge tax revenues. The government could increase defense spending and reduce the budget deficit simultaneously.

Although the president himself was sold on this theory, not all of his economic advisers were. David Stockman, Reagan's young budget director, later admitted that he had never embraced supply-side economics. Rather, he championed substantial tax cuts as a way of starving the federal government of funds and thus forcing Congress to cut domestic spending even more deeply than Reagan advocated. Stockman wanted Congress to slash not just welfare programs for the poor but also middle-class entitlements such as Social Security and Medicare, two programs that, on their own, accounted for 48 percent of the federal budget in 1982. He believed Congress might actually cut middle-class entitlements if it was confronted with an alarming shortfall in federal tax revenue.

But both predictions – of the supply-side theory and of Stockman's Machiavellian scheme – turned out to be wrong. Although the tax cuts did encourage greater investment in the private economy, the increase was far smaller than the supply-siders projected. Tax revenues grew, but nowhere nearly enough to cover the increased defense spending. Meanwhile, Stockman's gambit backfired. Precious few members of Congress could vote to cut middle-class entitlements and hope to keep their seats. So the entitlements remained intact, the defense budget expanded, tax revenues failed to keep pace, and both the budget deficit and the national debt ballooned. The former ranged from $128 billion to over $200 billion per year for the rest of Reagan's presidency. The latter stood at nearly $2.7 trillion by 1989.

On the whole, Reagan's economic policies favored the well off and penalized those at the lower ends of the economic scale. The tax cuts, which totaled $750 billion between 1981 and 1986, were applied across the board. This meant that the wealthy, whose marginal tax rates had been set at higher percentages, benefited disproportionately. Meanwhile, although middle-class entitlements continued to receive robust support, Congress agreed, at Reagan's behest, to scale back programs for the poor, many of them rooted in Lyndon Johnson's War on Poverty. Congress reduced food stamp benefits, eliminated 300,000 jobs from federal poverty programs, cut the welfare rolls by 10 percent, and lowered the benefits of 300,000 families still receiving welfare. Much of the burden of caring for the poor shifted to the states, which had to raise their own revenues, so even the vaunted federal tax cuts amounted to less than met the eye. Over the course of the 1980s, the average family income of the poorest fifth of the population dropped by 5.2 percent, while the income of the wealthiest fifth rose by 32.5 percent. The top 1 percent fared even better, enjoying an 81 percent increase in salaries alone and a 112 percent spike in taxable income from investments. The earning power of people in the middle strata remained largely unchanged.

Rates of poverty increased markedly during Reagan's presidency, especially during his first term, with women and children particularly hard hit. The share of Americans living below the poverty line surged from 11.6 percent in 1979 to 15.2 percent in 1983, declining slowly in the years thereafter. By 1990, 13.5 percent of Americans were officially poor. In 1987, nearly half of US households headed by single mothers lived in poverty, and 20.6 percent of all American children were poor, up from 15.9 percent in 1978. People of color, not surprisingly, were disproportionately represented in these statistics. In the late 1980s, some three-fifths of Black and Latina single mothers were impoverished, as compared with a bit under two-fifths of white single mothers. 45 percent of Black and 39 percent of Latino children, regardless of parental situation, lived in poverty.

A related crisis was the increasingly visible problem of urban homelessness. Like poverty in general, homelessness was exacerbated by the loss of inner-city jobs (an issue many years in the making, as we saw in Chapters 6 and 9) and the weakening of the government safety net. Other factors were a decreasing supply of affordable housing; diminishing public support for programs to assist people suffering from substance abuse and mental illness; and urban renewal policies that, by destroying skid rows and cheap residential hotels, pushed impoverished, addicted, and mentally ill people into central urban spaces, where they were more conspicuous. Reagan was by no means solely responsible for the homeless crisis, but he showed little interest in addressing it or even in granting it much public notice.

Other Conservative Initiatives

Apart from these core economic agenda items, Reagan attempted, with somewhat lesser fervor, to advance conservative policies on a range of other public issues. With respect to race, he pushed to eliminate or curtail affirmative action programs, on the ground that they subverted the principle of meritocracy. Reagan's stance departed from that of the two most recent Republican presidents, Richard Nixon and Gerald Ford, who had generally supported affirmative action. Reagan instructed his attorney general to challenge affirmative action programs in the federal courts and placed opponents of such remedies in executive agencies charged with combating racial discrimination and segregation. His team identified Black conservatives who could spearhead the effort, chief among them the "two Clarences":

Clarence Pendleton, chair of the US Commission on Civil Rights; and Clarence Thomas, Reagan's pick to oversee civil rights issues within the Department of Education and then to head the Equal Employment Opportunity Commission. In 1991, Thomas joined the Supreme Court.

Although Reagan's opposition to affirmative action could be defended in high-minded, "colorblind" terms, some of his other actions on race harkened back to the cruder "white backlash" politics he had practiced before becoming president. Reagan had opposed most of the civil rights acts of the 1960s, and during the 1980 campaign he infamously championed "states' rights," the rallying cry of segregationists, while speaking in the same Mississippi county in which three Freedom Summer activists had been abducted and murdered in 1964 (see Chapter 5). When Congress voted in 1983 to create a federal holiday honoring Martin Luther King, Jr., Reagan resisted signing the legislation, saying the civil rights leader's heroic reputation was "based on an image, not reality," and darkly hinting that King had communist sympathies. The statements caused an uproar, and Reagan retreated and signed the bill into law. Earlier in his presidency, the president had tried to get Congress to water down the 1965 Voting Rights Act. After Congress refused, his Department of Justice quietly subverted the act by declining to look into many allegations of interference with African Americans' voting rights, in favor of investigating possible fraud in voter registration drives on behalf of Black citizens.

Reagan also took aim at the environmental movement, which he saw as an obstacle to economic growth and the rights of business. His first secretary of the interior, James Watt, zealously opposed environmental regulation. Asked during his confirmation hearing whether he wished to preserve the environment for future generations, Watt replied, "I don't know how many generations we can count on before the Lord returns," though he pledged to be a good steward in the meantime. Once in office, Watt relaxed federal controls over public lands and opened many of them to private exploitation, especially by oil and gas companies. A close ally of Watt was Anne Gorsuch, Reagan's choice to head the Environmental Protection Agency (EPA). Gorsuch (the mother of future Supreme Court justice Neil Gorsuch) asked Congress to cut her budget and worked to ease enforcement of environmental laws. The EPA's assistant administrator, Rita Lavelle, glaringly mismanaged the task of cleaning up toxic waste dumps. Many suspected that she did so deliberately for partisan reasons – that, for example, she delayed the cleanup of a California dump in order to make Jerry Brown, California's Democratic governor and a candidate for the Senate in 1982, seem ineffectual. In 1983, the public outcry forced both Gorsuch and Lavelle out of their jobs, and Lavelle was later jailed for lying to Congress. By then, the outspoken Watt had been compelled to resign, too, after declaring (in an attempt to demonstrate his commitment to diversity) that he had convened an advisory panel with "every kind of mix you can have. I have a black, I have a woman, two Jews, and a cripple."

Another prong of Reagan's domestic agenda was a series of initiatives favored by social conservatives, especially members of the Christian right: banning abortion, restoring prayer in public schools, combating the feminist and gay rights movements, cracking down on pornography, and similar measures. Reagan had less success in promoting these causes, partly because he was not as committed to them as he was to his economic policies, and partly because they had highly motivated and resourceful opponents. Reagan did not spearhead much social conservative legislation. Instead, he appointed federal judges – not just to the Supreme Court but to the lower courts as well – who seemed likely to uphold social conservative policies. Reagan also relied on executive orders, such as his 1988 ban on federal funding for family planning clinics that discussed abortion as an option. Finally, he endorsed calls for constitutional amendments to ban abortion and bring back school prayer, even though he realized they had no foreseeable chance of passage. Reagan chronicler Lou Cannon writes that such statements were "never more than throwaway lines intended to comfort the Religious Right or some other element of the conservative constituency."

From Recession to Resurgence

Reagan took office amid a severe economic crisis, which got much worse early in his presidency. Paul Volcker, who continued as chair of the Federal Reserve, persisted in his efforts to control inflation by restricting the money supply, a policy Reagan endorsed, albeit only privately. The Fed's measures did bring the inflation rate down from 13.5 percent in 1980 to just over 3 percent in 1983, but the achievement came at the cost of punishingly high unemployment. Hovering at around 7.5 percent for most of 1981, the unemployment rate began climbing at the end of the year, peaking at 10.8 percent in November 1982. By then, more than 11.5 million Americans were out of work, and perhaps ten million more had been forced to take lower-paying jobs. Not since the Great Depression had the economic picture been so bleak.

Americans grown accustomed to comfortable circumstances suddenly found themselves confronting painful new realities. "It is not a pleasant experience," a laid-off schoolteacher near Flint, Michigan, wrote to the *Detroit Free Press*, "to be out of work and standing in an unemployment line, thinking about how you may lose your house, health insurance and car in the near future." "I mailed off 80 resumes, I'd guess," said Julie Arenkiel, an out-of-work restaurant manager in Minnetonka, Minnesota, "and I've gone to lots of places. They're just not hiring. I used to make a substantial salary, but now my bank account is falling short and checks are bouncing. That never happened before." Allan Kerbe, who lost his job at a General Motors auto plant in Baltimore, struggled with the double bind that many laid-off union workers faced. No one would give him a lower-paying job for fear that he would quit once his old position returned. "As soon as you put GM down [on a job application]," he told a reporter, "that's an automatic no." And yet economists were warning that many of the old union jobs had vanished for good, as companies permanently closed their plants or moved them to countries where workers earned less. "I feel like a walking doormat," Kerbe said. "My hope's kind of dying out." In January 1983, 20,000 people lined up in subfreezing weather to apply for two hundred jobs at a Milwaukee auto frame plant.

Reagan's public approval ratings plunged in tandem with the economy, from 60 percent in the summer of 1981 to 41 percent a year later, then to just 35 percent in January 1983.

Figure 10.2 Seven hundred people crowd inside an unemployment office to avoid waiting outside in freezing weather, Detroit, 1983. Source: Bettmann / Getty Images.

In mid-1982, advocates for the homeless erected "tent cities" outside the White House and in fourteen other cities. They called the encampments "Reagan ranches," an allusion to the "Hooverville" shantytowns of the early Depression years. In the 1982 midterm elections, the Democrats failed to take back the Senate, but they gained one seat in that body and enlarged their majority in the House by twenty-six seats. Reagan's own reelection seemed very much in doubt; some wondered if the septuagenarian would even run again.

In 1983, however, the economy rebounded. The unemployment rate started coming down, sinking to 5.5 percent in 1988, with inflation averaging a manageable 4.4 percent that year. Eighteen million new jobs were created between 1983 and 1989, and stocks tripled in value. The recovery had several causes. Volcker had begun relaxing monetary restrictions in the summer of 1982, and Reagan's tax cuts, while failing to produce the fiscal miracle predicted by the supply-siders, did stimulate the economy. Other contributors to prosperity were a decline in the price of imported oil; the expansion of the military budget, which created thousands of defense-related jobs; and the deregulation of major industries, accomplished both by congressional legislation and by the Reagan administration's behind-the-scenes obstruction of regulations that remained on the books, the shenanigans at the EPA being just one example of this practice.

Of course, many of these developments proved costly in the long run. The tax cuts and the increased military spending exploded the deficit and the national debt, and the defanging of the EPA hastened the degradation of the environment. Weakened financial and banking regulations would, as we shall see, enable major abuses in those areas. Nor was the rapid job creation all it was cracked up to be. High-paying industrial jobs continued to disappear, and the jobs that replaced them were concentrated in low-wage service industries. Half of the jobs created in the 1980s furnished salaries too low to keep a family of four above the official poverty line. Despite these shortcomings, the overall impression was one of triumphant regeneration. Reagan's approval numbers turned around and began a steady climb, approaching 60 percent by the fall of 1984.

Politically, of course, the timing was exquisite, for Reagan had decided to seek a second term. Proclaiming a new "Morning in America" in which the economy was bouncing back, the US military standing tall, and the American citizenry unabashedly celebrating its patriotism once again, the president sailed to easy reelection in 1984, trouncing Walter Mondale, his Democratic opponent. Mondale had served ably as a senator from Minnesota and as Jimmy Carter's vice president, and few questioned his sincerity and integrity. But he inspired little public excitement and was vulnerable to the charge of being too solicitous of the "special interest" groups forming the Democratic base: African Americans, feminists, labor leaders, environmentalists, and others. Meanwhile, in a pattern reminiscent of the 1972 election, millions of the sorts of voters who a generation earlier had swelled the Democratic coalition – mainly working-class and lower-middle-class whites – voted Republican. These "Reagan Democrats" thrilled to the president's buoyant invocation of flag, family, neighborhood, and church. Reagan received 58.8 percent of the popular vote and swept forty-nine states. Mondale got just 40.6 percent of the popular vote and won only his native Minnesota and Washington, DC. In the lead-up to the widely anticipated blowout, *Saturday Night Live* aired an ungenerous skit in which a delegation from the Reagan campaign petitioned Mondale to vote for the president rather than himself on Election Day. That way, the result would be unanimous.

A Mixed Balance Sheet for Women

One of the Mondale campaign's few electric moments occurred when the candidate asked Geraldine Ferraro, a Democratic House member from New York, to be his running mate. Once the Democratic National Convention affirmed the choice, Ferraro became the first female vice-presidential nominee of a major American political party. She was one of several "first women" in the 1980s, a group that included Sandra Day O'Connor, the first woman to serve on the US Supreme Court, nominated by President Reagan in 1981; Sally Ride, the first American woman to travel into space, on a Space Shuttle flight in 1983; and Lynne Russell, who in that same year became the first woman to solo-anchor a prime-time newscast, on the recently launched Cable News Network (CNN). Ferraro's nomination caused a surge of excitement across the country, especially among liberal women. It was a much-needed tonic to Mondale's anemic campaign.

Or so it seemed. Within days, Ferraro's candidacy was engulfed in controversy, as reporters aggressively probed the questionable financial dealings of her husband, John Zaccaro, a wealthy New York City real estate investor. It was not unreasonable for journalists to raise the issue; on some financial disclosure forms, the congresswoman had listed herself as Zaccaro's business associate. Still, the ease with which Ferraro's own qualifications were eclipsed by the alleged misdeeds of her husband dismayed advocates of gender equality. Would such a feeding frenzy have occurred if the sexes were reversed? True, it was hard to think of many politicians' *wives* who were high rollers in the business world, but that was just another way of describing the asymmetry. The questions eventually subsided, but Ferraro's momentum was stalled. Whatever enthusiasm her addition to the ticket may have generated was not enough to prevent its crushing defeat in November, or even draw New York state into the Democratic column. Fewer women than men voted for Reagan in 1984, but the "gender gap" was smaller than in the previous presidential election (4 percent as opposed to 8 percent in 1980), and a decisive majority of the female electorate, 58 percent, supported Reagan's reelection.

Ferraro's was obviously a very special case, but it hinted at the mixed balance sheet for American women in the 1980s, a time of encouraging advances toward, but persistent obstacles to, equality of opportunity and status between the sexes. It was more expected than ever before (and also more economically necessary) that women work outside the home. The share of women in paid employment grew from 47.7 percent in 1980 to 54.3 percent in 1990. Female labor participation expanded across the board – in domestic work, the service industry, the building trades, and white-collar professions. As of 1991, women earned only 74¢ for every dollar men earned, but that was up from 60¢ in 1979. The percentage of employees in managerial or executive positions who were women rose from 32 percent in 1983 to 41 percent in 1991. More and more, female experts appeared as "talking heads" on TV news programs, consulted not just on "women's issues" but on traditionally male-dominated topics such as the economy, electoral politics, and foreign affairs. Interviewers respectfully addressed them as "Doctor," "Professor," or "Ms." It was increasingly common for married women to keep their original surnames, as Ferraro (an early adopter of the practice) had done after marrying Zaccaro in 1960. Public speakers got in the habit of extolling the "men and women" of America's armed forces. Starting with the designation of Hurricane Bob in 1979, the National Weather Service gave hurricanes both male and female names – a roundabout way of acknowledging that men, too, could be tempestuous.

Popular culture affirmed women's growing presence in the professional world, while sometimes suggesting that this participation came at a cost. Popular television programs such as *Hill Street Blues* (1981–1987, a police show), *St. Elsewhere* (1982–1988, about an urban teaching hospital), and *LA Law* (1986–1994, about a private law firm) featured intelligent female characters performing successfully in challenging professions. Much more than their male counterparts, however, these protagonists found their work lives enmeshed with their romantic and family lives, with mental health concerns, and with other personal challenges. "The women characters' problems are distinctive," writes the communications scholar Bonnie J. Dow of such shows, "… in that they stem from an implicit (but sometimes explicitly stated) conflict between careerism and personal health and happiness." The Hollywood films *Private Benjamin* (1980), *Legal Eagles* (1986), and *Gorillas in the Mist* (1988) showcased women boldly navigating male-dominated realms. By contrast, the neurotic and predatory career woman in *Fatal Attraction* (1987), who upends the life of the married man who assumes he can have a brief fling with her and move on, painted a less admiring portrait of women in the professions.

And many women, of course, were denied the privilege of being resented for their professional status. Women, and especially single mothers, were disproportionately poor, a reality captured by a common phrase of the decade, "the feminization of poverty." Although many struggling women had been poor all along, a substantial number slid into that condition as a consequence of divorce, rates of which more than doubled between 1965 and 1980. "Judges," write the sociologists Myra Marx Ferree and Beth B. Hess, "had been quick to turn the feminist claim that women should be economically dependent into a myth that women actually were financially self-sufficient," and thus failed to order adequate alimony and child support.

With social conservatives in the ascendancy, abortion was a flashpoint throughout the decade, especially its second half. In the mid-1980s, the tactics of antiabortion activists became more confrontational. Operation Rescue and similar groups staged protests at abortion clinics, either physically blocking women from entering the facilities to receive abortions or, when court injunctions kept activists at a distance, seeking to dissuade women from entering by shouting antiabortion slogans and waving signs graphically depicting aborted fetuses. Clinic protesters insisted that these tactics were justified by dire necessity. "If you were about to be murdered," Operation Rescue founder Randall Terry wrote in 1990, "I'm sure you would want me to do more than write your congressman!" Abortion rights advocates viewed clinic protests as harassment and intimidation, an assessment endorsed by many federal and state judges, as well as by more moderate opponents of abortion. Further out on the fringes, extremist groups such as the Army of God torched and bombed abortion clinics. In the 1980s, such attacks generally targeted property rather than persons, but they took a lethal turn early in the next decade, with the murders of several doctors and staff members employed by abortion clinics.

Meanwhile, antiabortion litigation wended its way through lower federal courts, creating opportunities for the Supreme Court, shortly after Reagan left office, to chip away at the broad right to abortion staked out in the 1973 *Roe v. Wade* decision. In *Webster v. Reproductive Health Services* (1989) and *Planned Parenthood v. Casey* (1992), the court reaffirmed *Roe* but upheld states' authority to enact certain restrictions on abortion, such as prohibiting the use of public funds for abortions, imposing a 24-hour waiting period between the request for an abortion and its performance, and requiring pregnant minors to gain parental consent before availing themselves of the procedure. In both Supreme Court decisions, all of Reagan's appointees were in the majority; all would remain on the court until well into the twenty-first century.[1]

[1] Ronald Reagan's Supreme Court appointees were Sandra Day O'Connor (who joined the court in 1981 and retired in 2006), Antonin Scalia (who was appointed in 1986 and died in 2016), and Anthony Kennedy (who was appointed in 1988 and retired in 2018). In 1986, Reagan proposed and the Senate approved the elevation of Associate Justice William Rehnquist, who had joined the court in 1972, to the position of chief justice. Rehnquist served in that role until his death in 2005.

A New Gospel of Wealth

Morally severe in one realm, the White House's influence could be indulgent and carefree in another, as the president and first lady established a new benchmark of conspicuous extravagance. The first inaugural celebration, costing upward of $12 million, featured two nights of show-business entertainment, nine inaugural balls, and an $800,000 fireworks display at the Lincoln Memorial. With private donations, Nancy Reagan oversaw a redecoration of the White House's family quarters costing another $800,000 and spent over $200,000 on a new set of gilt-edged china. Her immediate predecessor, Rosalynn Carter, had failed to use up the $50,000 in public funds earmarked for such purposes, and President Carter had famously forsaken expensive suits for cardigan sweaters. Commentators criticized the Reagans' comportment as gauche and insensitive, especially when so many Americans were struggling economically, but it set the tone for similar (and even greater) excesses in the private sector. "We are all living and entertaining more lavishly now," remarked the society columnist and celebrity event planner Patricia Montandon in 1981. "The Reagans are setting a lifestyle so different from the hide-it-under-a-bushel attitude of the Carters. The feeling now is that if you have it, why not enjoy it?"

Far more consequential, of course, were the Reagan administration's and Congress's concrete actions regarding private wealth. The relaxation of financial regulations unleashed a frenzy of activity on Wall Street, geared less toward producing valuable goods and services than toward enriching small numbers of shrewdly situated individuals. It became much easier for one company to purchase another. In the most predatory form of the practice, the managers of a stronger firm would gain control of a more vulnerable one, dismantle it, sell off its assets, fire its employees, and reap hefty rewards for themselves and the cadres of brokers, lawyers, and consultants engineering the takeover. The top players in this game of "mergers and acquisitions," figures such as Ivan Boesky, Carl Icahn, and T. Boone Pickens, gained something approaching heroic stature, their aggressive exploits keenly admired in the business world, and beyond. "Greed is all right," Boesky told an audience at the University of California at Berkeley School of Business Administration in 1985. "You can be greedy and still feel good about yourself." On the campus where a decade and half earlier protesters had battled Governor Reagan's state troopers, aspiring titans of finance laughed and applauded. In 1986, Boesky was arrested and charged with using confidential information in stock trading, eventually spending a couple of years in jail.

One form of deregulation produced a much broader calamity. For decades, savings and loan institutions (S&Ls) had provided long-term, fixed-rate mortgages to homebuyers, funding these transactions by allowing depositors to open savings accounts at low rates of interest. A federal agency from the New Deal era insured the deposits and limited the interest S&Ls could both charge and pay out. The system worked well until the late 1970s, when spiking inflation caused depositors to shun S&Ls in favor of unregulated money markets offering higher interest. Starved of capital, S&Ls offered fewer mortgages, to the detriment of the real estate market and thus the broader economy. In 1980, Congress increased the level at which S&L depositors were federally insured, a measure that provided only limited relief. In 1982, the Reagan administration worked with Congress to pass legislation that comprehensively deregulated the industry, freeing S&Ls to invest much more widely and offer dramatically higher interest to their depositors. At the signing ceremony, Reagan extolled the new law as a historic initiative to revitalize the nation's financial system. "All in all," he said, "I think we hit the jackpot."

For opportunists, the president's statement proved all too accurate. In previous years, S&Ls had been mostly confined to offering low-profit mortgages on single-family homes. Now, they could use federally insured deposits to invest in raw land, apartment complexes, office towers, shopping malls, and numerous other ventures with no connection to real estate. The new law also made it much easier to acquire or create S&Ls. Speculators flocked to this newly lucrative market, turning S&Ls into vehicles for pushing the limits on high-risk, high-reward investment, confident that Uncle Sam would ultimately recoup any losses. Some S&L owners gambled on corporate mergers and "junk bonds," risky stocks carrying the potential for handsome return. Inevitably, many of these investments failed, and by decade's end hundreds of S&Ls had gone bankrupt, with several S&L officers (who could not resist flattening even the minimal guardrails that remained) facing criminal indictment. To honor the federal guarantee to depositors, the American taxpayers were stuck with a bill that eventually exceeded $120 billion.

Many of the foot soldiers in this financial revolution – the stock traders, accountants, lawyers, and analysts – were members of the baby boom generation now moving squarely into adulthood. The quintessential baby boomer occupying the higher echelons of white-collar employment was the "yuppie," or young urban professional. According to the stereotype, yuppies disdained the sorts of social and political causes that had stirred young people in the 1960s and early 1970s, and for which some of the older yuppies themselves had fought. Instead, they focused on advancing their careers and enjoying the material and social perquisites of affluence: expensive cars, swanky apartments, well-cut "power suits," exclusive gym memberships, and the like. The popular portrait was overdrawn (and sometimes descended to outright caricature), but a significant shift in the outlooks of young, middle-class, well-educated Americans does seem to have occurred between the 1960s and the 1980s. In a survey conducted at the University of California at Los Angeles, when freshmen in the late 1960s were asked to state their personal goals, about 82 percent said they wished "to develop a meaningful philosophy of life," and about 43 percent listed "being well off financially." By 1986, the priorities were roughly reversed, with just under 44 percent citing a meaningful life philosophy and over 70 percent hoping for financial success. Politically, yuppies tended to be conservative on economic matters and liberal on social issues such as abortion, gender equality, and gay rights.

Popular entertainment catered to the public's fascination with excessive wealth. Yuppie-themed movies like *Wall Street* (1987) and *Bright Lights, Big City* (1988) were ostensibly cautionary tales about the wages of avarice and self-indulgence, but they vividly conveyed the allure of life "in the fast lane." (*Wall Street*'s villain, Gordon Gekko, was partly inspired by Ivan Boesky, whose downfall occurred during the film's production. "Greed … is good," Gekko proclaims in a shareholders' meeting. "Greed is right. Greed works.") On television, the primetime soap operas *Dallas* and *Dynasty* depicted fabulously wealthy families whose members schemed and feuded over money, power, status, and sex. *Lifestyles of the Rich and Famous* offered glimpses of the opulent mansions and expensive pastimes of entertainers, athletes, tycoons, and occasional royalty. Those of a more literary bent could relish the skewering of Wall Street's movers and shakers in Tom Wolfe's novel *The Bonfire of the Vanities* (1987), or devour the rapidly proliferating businessmen's how-to books, such as Stephen Covey's *The 7 Habits of Highly Effective People* (1989) and *The Art of the Deal* (1987), credited to a brash New York real estate developer named Donald Trump (though actually penned by his cowriter, Tony Schwartz, who decades later expressed remorse for helping to make Trump a household name).

A Changing Media Landscape

When it came to mass media, mergers and acquisitions did not just appear on the page and screen; they transformed the conditions under which popular content was produced. Media companies consolidated rapidly in the 1980s. In 1983, fifty corporations controlled the majority of American media outlets; by 1990, only twenty-three did so. At decade's end, a single corporation, Advance Publications, owned twenty-seven newspapers, the magazines *Vogue*, *Vanity Fair*, *House & Garden*, and the *New Yorker*, and the massive publishing company Random House with its several imprints, including Knopf, Pantheon, and Vintage. By the late 1980s, twelve newspaper chains controlled nearly half of the nation's daily papers. Concentration occurred across different media. In 1989, the magazine company Time Inc. bought Warner Communications, which was already a massive conglomerate of film, magazine, and cable television companies. Federal deregulation expanded the number of local television stations that large newspapers like *The Washington Post* could own.

Ironically, as media producers consolidated, the audiences they targeted grew more and more segmented. A major driver of this trend was the increasing availability of cable television, a consequence of both technological and licensing changes. At the start of the 1980s, fewer than 20 percent of American homes received cable TV; by decade's end, that figure exceeded 54 percent. Cable stations provided specialized programming – news, sports, weather, movies, religion, popular music, Spanish-language content, African American culture and concerns, and so on – to viewers willing to pay for it. Increasingly, these stations formed into national cable networks, which grew in number from twenty-eight in 1980 to seventy-nine in 1990. The original three broadcast networks, ABC, CBS, and NBC, which in earlier decades had enjoyed a near-monopoly on viewership, saw their audience share shrink to 61 percent by 1989.

Similar "narrowcasting" proliferated in commercial radio, which, like television, had once been dominated by a relatively small number of programs that attracted mass followings. By the 1980s, radio stations were targeting "niche" audiences in much the same way that cable TV stations were. Especially consequential was the emergence of political talk radio, which by the late 1980s was a bastion of hardline conservatism. In the coming decades, hosts like Rush Limbaugh and Sean Hannity would help push the Republican base, and with it the party's leadership, further to the right.

Figure 10.3 Children using a computer at school, New York City, 1984. Source: Barbara Alper / Archive Photos / Getty Images.

Technological innovation brought new physical devices into Americans' homes and offices, altering the pace and texture of everyday life. Videocassette recorders (VCRs) allowed people to watch content of their choosing (usually commercially marketed recordings of Hollywood movies) on their TVs, further eroding the three broadcast networks' market share. In the space of a few years, digital compact discs (CDs) replaced vinyl records as the chief medium of commercial music. The number of Americans owning personal computers jumped from two million in 1981 to forty-five million by 1988. With computers, writers could edit their prose and shift bodies of text around much more easily than in the typewriter era. Data analysts could "crunch numbers" with far greater speed, complexity, and precision than had been possible with slide rules or pocket calculators. In the 1980s, a small number of people connected to research universities or employed by the US Department of Defense or some large telecommunications companies had access to sparse networks of linked computers, though the commercial internet would not emerge until the early to mid-1990s.

In the 1950s, social critics had warned that mass media were creating a homogenized and blandly conformist culture. By the end of the 1980s, commentators were waxing nostalgic about that bygone era. As *Wall Street Journal* publisher Peter Kann observed in 1991:

> Once upon a time, before cable channels, VCRs and the myriad choices we now have on those boxes in our bedrooms, the networks did create a national TV culture. When our family gathered in the living room to watch "Mr. Peepers," "The Ed Sullivan Show," "Gunsmoke" or "The $64,000 question," we could be almost certain our neighbors were watching it too. I'm not sure we've traded up today, with one child watching the Disney Channel, another a Dumbo video and another MTV, while we parents flick from C-SPAN to ESPN.

In 1988, a book reviewer for *The New York Times* voiced a similar concern: "As new forms of television change broadcasting into 'narrowcasting,' what will happen to social cohesiveness?"

African American Challenges and Achievements

Whether one focused on the 1950s or the 1980s, any notion of "social cohesiveness" grew harder to sustain once racial disparities entered the picture. In the 1980s, as we have seen, African Americans were disproportionately numbered among the poor. The processes that had immiserated the inner city in the 1960s and 1970s – the exodus of jobs, capital, and upwardly mobile residents and the deepening isolation of those left behind – persisted in the 1980s and were now supplemented by the fraying of the social safety net. By 1990, about a third of the Black population lived in poverty, up from approximately 30 percent in the 1970s. The Black infant mortality rate of 18.6 deaths per 1,000 births was more than twice the national rate and higher than that of Bulgaria or Costa Rica. African Americans were disproportionately enmeshed in the criminal justice system, as both the victims and the accused perpetrators of property and violent crime.

Indeed, in many urban Black communities, the crime rate increased significantly during the decade, especially its second half, largely because of the growing prevalence of crack cocaine. Crack was created by combining powder cocaine with baking soda, cooking the mixture, and breaking it into small pieces, called "rocks," that were smoked in a pipe. The substance was much cheaper than powder cocaine and delivered a more intense high; it was also extremely addictive. These qualities made for a high-demand, high-velocity, and violent drug market. Crack dealers sold small quantities to desperate customers who smoked the rocks quickly, sometimes returning a few hours later to buy more. Addicts were so driven to get crack that they depleted their earnings or welfare payments, sold their possessions, resorted to prostitution, and stole from those around them. A former resident of a crack-ravaged neighborhood later recalled, "Fiends were breaking into cars for stereos, breaking into neighbors' cribs [apartments] for television and VCRs, stealing their mom's jewelry, their kids' record player, anything they could trade for crack." On the supply side, the crack business was so lucrative that dealers, and the gangs they formed, waged lethal turf battles for control of the market. New York City suffered 2,245 homicides in 1990, as compared with 1,821 in 1980. Authorities attributed much of the increase to crack-related violence.

Even as Black poverty and the crises surrounding it remained intractable, African Americans at the higher ends of the socioeconomic scale became more visible and accepted. The share of the Black population qualifying as middle-class hovered at roughly 40 percent in the 1980s, about the same as in the previous decade. But African Americans continued to break into domains that had recently been off-limits, or nearly so. The Black suburban population grew by 34 percent over the decade; by 1986, more than seven million Black families lived in suburbs. African American TV news anchors such as Bryant Gumbel, Bernard Shaw, and Charlayne Hunter-Gault (who in the early 1960s, as Charlayne Hunter, had made national news by integrating the University of Georgia) became familiar figures to millions of viewers of all backgrounds. In 1989, Douglas Wilder became the first African American governor since Reconstruction, after Virginia's voters elected him chief executive of their state. One area undergoing little change, at least in numerical terms, was higher education. After a dramatic expansion in the 1960s and 1970s, the percentage of college students who were Black remained at around 9 percent throughout the decade. About 80 percent of Black college students attended predominantly white institutions, a rate that held steady throughout the 1980s.

The decade's most popular TV situation comedy was NBC's *The Cosby Show*, starring the standup comedian Bill Cosby. It featured an upper-middle-class Black family – the father was an obstetrician and the mother a lawyer – living in a comfortable brownstone in Brooklyn Heights, New York. Although the show seldom addressed racial themes overtly, it quietly affirmed African American culture by showcasing the work of Black musicians and visual artists and presenting historically Black colleges and universities in a favorable light. Mostly, it was a lighthearted show about the challenges and foibles of appealing American family members who happened to be Black. Some commentators faulted the program for failing to tackle racism head-on, but others applauded it for defying societal expectations that a Black show focus on Black issues. As Cosby himself said of his critics, "Why do they want to deny me the pleasure of being an American and just enjoying life? … I'm a human being and I want to have fun. I want to show the happiness within our people. I want to show that we have the same kinds of wants and needs as other American families." Decades later, it was credibly alleged that Cosby, over the course of his career, had sexually assaulted numerous women and threatened reprisals against them to ensure their silence. He was convicted and imprisoned in Pennsylvania for some of those offenses (and then freed after the Pennsylvania Supreme Court found that a prosecutor had violated his due process rights). During the heyday of his eponymous sitcom, however, Cosby was celebrated as "America's dad," and some observers found hope in the casting of a Black man in that role.

In the realm of Black politics, the 1980s were a time of considerable ferment and self-assertion. For most politically engaged African Americans, Reagan's stances on race – his hostility to affirmative action, his moves to cut social programs on which Blacks especially relied, and his history of opposing much of the civil rights movement – were alarming. (Because African Americans generally had left-of-center views, the president's other policies tended to antagonize them, too. A small number of influential Black conservatives, such as the economist and columnist Thomas Sowell and the aforementioned Clarence Pendleton and Clarence Thomas, forcefully challenged this inclination.) "Well, we'd better fasten our seatbelts," said Southern Christian Leadership Conference (SCLC) president Joseph Lowery as Reagan prepared to take office. "There's going to be some turbulence ahead."

Some early turbulence occurred over the 1965 Voting Rights Act, which was scheduled to expire in 1982. When the Reagan administration proposed that the act be renewed in weakened form, the SCLC, the National Association for the Advancement of Colored People, and other civil rights groups joined with the Congressional Black Caucus to demand a robust renewal (containing additional provisions to overcome recent adverse rulings of the

Supreme Court). In mid-1982, after a vigorous public campaign that included a 5,000-person march across the Edmund Pettus Bridge in Selma, Alabama, where in 1965 state troopers had bloodied Black voting rights activists, Congress overwhelmingly passed a renewal bill very close to the one favored by the civil rights community. Reagan signed the legislation, though, as noted, his administration later worked to subvert it. During this same period, civil rights activists lobbied hard for the establishment of a federal holiday honoring Martin Luther King, a measure Congress passed, and Reagan reluctantly signed, in the fall of 1983.

At about this time, forty-two-year-old Jesse Jackson, a Chicago-based Black minister and civil rights leader, launched his candidacy for the Democratic Party nomination in 1984. This was the first of two presidential campaigns by Jackson, the second taking place in 1988. Both times, he ran well to the left of the other Democratic contenders, all of them white men. In neither year could Jackson realistically hope to win the nomination, though he exceeded expectations in 1988. His aims, rather, were to champion policy positions that mainstream Democrats shied away from, supported only tepidly, or actively opposed (such as a much more generous safety net, a reduction in military spending, and greater sympathy for the Palestinian people); to enhance the leverage of Black voters and office holders within the Democratic Party; and to encourage African Americans and other minorities to register to vote, further boosting their intraparty leverage and strengthening Democrats overall. In both 1984 and 1988, Jackson ran in the name of the "Rainbow Coalition," a diverse ingathering of citizens whom the dominant society had historically disadvantaged, ignored, or brutally oppressed: African Americans, working-class whites, Latinos, Asian Americans, Middle Eastern Americans, Native Americans, women, gays and lesbians, disabled people, and others. Binding the whole effort were Jackson's commanding stage presence and mesmerizing oratory, his ability to distill messages in poetic cadences – "Get dope out of our veins and hope into our brains"; "Choose the human race over the nuclear race"; "Dream of priests and preachers … who will mold prophesy and not profiteer" – and work them seamlessly into his campaign rhetoric, even when speaking off the cuff.

Jackson's campaigns were partly successful. They did raise the profile, and possibly the popularity, of some progressive causes. They also highlighted the importance of Black voters to the Democratic Party, though sometimes this had the counterproductive effect of prompting white Democratic politicians to distance themselves from Black-identified issues to show they were not beholden to "special interests." During the 1984 campaign, *The Washington Post* reported that Jackson had referred to Jews as "Hymies" and to New York City as "Hymietown." Jackson initially denied he had made those remarks but later acknowledged and apologized for them. The incident, combined with Jackson's friendly association with Nation of Islam leader Louis Farrakhan, who had himself made anti-Semitic statements, caused many Jews to view the candidate with suspicion (and muddied his pro-Palestinian advocacy). In both campaigns, Jackson received overwhelming Black support, but his record of transracial and multiethnic outreach was mixed. Non-Black participation in the Rainbow Coalition was highly visible in both campaigns, and it markedly increased between 1984 and the 1988. Still, with the exception of Puerto Ricans in New York in 1988 and, possibly, Arab Americans in either or both of the two campaign years, no non-Black group gave Jackson majority support. The Rainbow Coalition remained, by and large, an African American movement. Taking the long view, though, one could argue that Jackson's campaigns provided a loose organizing model for Barack Obama's far more successful, though also more politically conventional, presidential runs in 2008 and 2012.

Where Jackson was most immediately successful was in expanding and diversifying his party's voter rolls. During Jackson's two races, his campaign registered nearly four million Americans of all backgrounds. In 1984, over a million of those new voters were southern Blacks. In the 1986 midterm elections, Democrats took back the Senate, and analysts partly attributed the victory to the enlarged Democratic electorate. For several newly elected white Democratic senators in the South, Jackson-registered Democrats appeared to have supplied the margin of victory. Some of this political debt was repaid in 1987, after President Reagan nominated Robert Bork, an outspokenly conservative appellate judge, to a vacancy on the Supreme Court. By a vote of fifty-eight to forty-two, the Senate rejected the nomination. Senators opposing Bork repeatedly cited his hostility to what most saw as settled civil rights law – a concern it was now politically wise to acknowledge. "One after another," wrote the journalist Andrew Kopkind, "Southern Democrats, who wouldn't have dreamed of supporting Northern liberals in a straight ideological struggle ten or twenty years ago, now joined in the vote against Bork . . . . The difference, this time, was Jackson."

There were limits, however, to Democrats' ability to benefit from the heightened salience of the race issue. As often as not, Republicans turned that salience to their own political advantage. The Republicans' presidential nominee in 1988 was George H. W. Bush, nearing the end of two terms as Reagan's vice president. The Democratic nominee, to whom Jackson had placed a distant but dogged second, was the governor of Massachusetts, Michael Dukakis. Presenting himself as a technocratic problem solver, Dukakis insisted that the election "isn't about ideology; it's about competence." Bush's strategy was to *make* the contest about ideology and paint his rival as too liberal for the US electorate. The Bush campaign called attention to a Massachusetts program, begun by a Republican predecessor but continued under Governor Dukakis, to grant weekend furloughs to inmates in state prisons. William Horton, a Black convicted murderer, had escaped while out on furlough; he raped a white woman and pistol-whipped and stabbed her white fiancé. In his own public comments on the "Willie" Horton case – the name was altered in an apparent attempt to make the perpetrator seem even more transgressive – Bush did not mention Horton's race. But Bush's campaign manager, Lee Atwater, crudely raised it in an address to a Republican gathering. Alluding to reports that Dukakis was considering Jesse Jackson as his running mate (Dukakis later picked Senator Lloyd Bentsen of Texas), Atwater quipped that maybe the Democratic nominee "will put this Willie Horton on the ticket after all is said and done."

Far more conspicuously, an independent conservative political action committee ran an anti-Dukakis advertisement on cable television that briefly narrated the Horton incident and displayed a grainy, menacing photograph of the criminal. The Bush campaign denied any involvement in the incendiary ad and even publicly denounced it. Critics noted, however, that the condemnation occurred only after the ad had aired for some weeks and had almost completed its scheduled cable run. James Baker, now serving as George Bush's campaign chairman, later acknowledged that many suspected the "Bush team of coordinating with a not-so-independent political action group to produce the inflammatory ad, so we could then repudiate it and enjoy the best of two worlds." Baker added that "as far as I know" no such collusion occurred – though he revealed a keen understanding of how a canny operator *would* play that double game were he so inclined. Hammering away at the Horton case and other "hot-button" issues (such as Dukakis's opposition to the death penalty and his vetoing, on First Amendment grounds, of legislation requiring Massachusetts public school students to pledge allegiance to the American flag), Bush successfully portrayed his opponent as a "Massachusetts liberal" out of touch with the broad American public. In November, he decisively defeated Dukakis, winning 53.4 percent of the popular vote to Dukakis's 45.7 percent and 426 electoral votes to the governor's 111.

On one level, Bush's exploitation of the Horton case was a continuation of the "southern strategy," whereby Republican politicians invoked racially charged issues to win the votes of previously Democratic white southerners. This was an effort to which Lee Atwater had devoted much of his career as a political operative, and it succeeded handsomely in 1988, when the vice president won every southern state, including Texas, the home state of Dukakis's running mate. Yet Bush was also moving beyond the southern strategy to tap into a genuine concern, felt by voters of all backgrounds and in every part of the country, about the growing prevalence of violent and property crime, a wave that had swelled over the previous quarter-century and would crest in the early to mid-1990s. President Reagan had worked with Congress to pass legislation increasing the penalties for certain offenses (especially involving drugs), eliminating the federal parole, and empowering the federal government to punish offenses previously penalized only at the state level. Both the first President Bush and his Democratic successor, Bill Clinton, would embrace this "tough on crime" approach, which clearly enjoyed wide public support.

Immigration and Shifting Patterns of Ethnicity

All the while, a substantial influx of immigrants continued to transform the nation's ethnic makeup. Nearly six and a half million people legally emigrated to the United States in the 1980s, more than four-fifths of them from Asia or Latin America. There was also considerable immigration from Middle Eastern countries, especially Iran. In 1980, the immigrant population was about fourteen million; ten years later it approached twenty million, over 8 percent of the total US population. In some cities, such as New York and Los Angeles, as many as a third of the residents were foreign-born. Overwhelmingly, these massive influxes unfolded peaceably. Native-born and immigrant populations adjusted to one another, all of them transformed in some measure, with immigrants and their children naturally changing the most. As had happened eight, nine, and ten decades earlier, some native-born Americans complained that the fresh immigrants were unassimilable. Yet the vast majority of the newcomers did assimilate (even though "assimilation" was becoming a dirty word to some immigration activists and scholars, who feared it promoted the erasure of the immigrants' home cultures).

Still, there were flashpoints, moments when economic or political grievance blended with nativism to produce acts of shocking violence. As in the 1970s, Japanese cars and other manufactured goods competed extremely successfully against their US counterparts. Many laid-off American factory workers grew bitterly resentful of Japan. Labor activists, and members of Congress with constituencies facing stiff Japanese competition, sometimes staged protests in which they ritually smashed Japanese consumer products. In 1982, two white auto workers in the Detroit area, one of them recently laid off, accosted Vincent Chin, a young Chinese American they assumed to be Japanese, and beat him to death. Middle Eastern conflicts, too, roiled the domestic American sphere. In the mid-1980s, some Palestinian and Lebanese organizations launched terrorist attacks that victimized American civilians, and the Reagan administration repeatedly clashed with the Libyan government, which it accused of bankrolling terrorist groups. These events provoked a sharp domestic backlash against Arab Americans, occasionally taking the form of hate crimes. In 1985, a bomb planted in the Los Angeles office of the American Arab Anti-Discrimination Committee killed Alex Odeh, the organization's West Coast regional director. The three far right Zionists suspected of the murder fled to Israel and remained at large. For years thereafter, American commentators would warn that the Middle East's turmoil might soon spawn terrorist attacks on US soil – failing to note that this had already happened.

Meanwhile, somewhere between 100,000 and 300,000 people entered the country illegally each year, the vast majority by crossing the US–Mexican border. Most were Mexican nationals, though a substantial number were refugees from war-torn Central American countries, whose turmoil US policies exacerbated (see Chapter 11). In 1980, there were perhaps two million undocumented immigrants in the United States; by 1986, there were an estimated 3.2 million. The situation aroused bitter controversy, especially in California, where about half of the undocumented population resided. Some charged that undocumented immigrants took jobs away from those legally in the country, drove down wages through their willingness to work for low pay, and were a drain on public services. Others countered that the undocumented bolstered the economy by working in arduous or unpleasant jobs that few US citizens would take, especially in seasonal agriculture. A more general objection, applying to legal and illegal immigration alike, was that the new arrivals were subverting the dominant culture, especially in their perceived inability or refusal to learn English. In 1986, California voters overwhelmingly approved a ballot initiative declaring English the state's official language. Although the measure was largely symbolic, critics objected that its passage worsened an already hostile environment in the state by granting nativists implicit license to harass the foreign-born. Thirteen other states enacted English-only statutes or constitutional amendments in the 1980s.

Also in 1986, Congress passed the Immigration Reform and Control Act (IRCA), which outlawed the hiring of undocumented workers while granting amnesty to undocumented immigrants who had lived continuously in the United States since January 1982. It also exempted certain categories of agricultural employment from immigration restrictions, a boon to US agribusiness, which profited from low-wage undocumented labor. The new law failed, however, to stem the influx of unauthorized migrants into the country. The employer sanctions were weakly enforced and evaded by extensive fraud on the part of employers and workers alike. Moreover, once immigrants received amnesty, family members in their home countries were eager to join them in the United States. They applied for legal entry, found themselves placed at the end of daunting waiting lists, and, in many cases, dispensed with the formal process and entered the country illegally. Consequently, although 2.7 million people received amnesty under IRCA, the overall number of undocumented immigrants soon returned to the 1986 level and kept on rising, reaching five million in 1996 and eleven million by 2006. In retrospect, the immigration controversies of the 1980s would pale in comparison with the fierce battles of later decades.

The HIV/AIDS Crisis

One provision of IRCA, not prominently featured in debates preceding the law's passage, barred entry to immigrants testing positive for the human immunodeficiency virus (HIV). The exclusion responded to the recent emergence of a disease that, though still confined to a minuscule share of the US population, was horrifying in its details and appeared to kill nearly everyone who caught it. The crisis had crept up gradually on the nation. In 1981, medical experts began compiling reports of an odd set of maladies afflicting young men, especially in New York City, San Francisco, and Los Angeles. The two diseases were pneumocystis pneumonia (PCP) and Kaposi sarcoma (KS), a rare cancer found mainly among the elderly. By August, over a hundred men had contracted one or both of the diseases, and nearly half had died. Doctors puzzled over the situation. All of the patients were gay, and many reported that they'd had multiple sexual partners, so it seemed likely that the infections were transmitted though gay sex. Yet doctors could not rule out other explanations. Perhaps the diseases spread through more superficial human contact, or were related to the drugs some gay men took to enhance sexual pleasure. Whatever its cause, the syndrome was spreading quickly, with the number of victims doubling every six months.

In many instances, moreover, patients' symptoms went well beyond those of PCP and KS to include numerous other maladies. "I found myself bedridden with a cold that wouldn't go away," a patient wrote, "viral bronchitis, fever, diarrhea, loss of appetite, and extreme fatigue." "Weight loss – *massive* weight loss: fifty pounds!" recorded another. "Pain, unexplained pain in my limbs, headaches, nausea, and unexplained diarrhea for seven months." A doctor in New York remarked of the early cases, "It's the worst way I've ever seen anyone go. I've seen young people die of cancer. But this is total body rot. It's merciless." By October 1982, 634 cases had been reported, and 260 people had died.

Whatever afflicted these young men was crippling their immune systems, leaving them gravely vulnerable to all manner of infections. Doctors initially called the syndrome GRID, for gay-related immunodeficiency. But the deficiency was also prevalent among some other populations, such as intravenous drug users and people who, for medical reasons, received regular blood transfusions. So the name was soon changed to AIDS, for acquired immune deficiency syndrome. It became increasingly clear that AIDS was caused by a blood-borne virus that could be transmitted sexually, presumably via infected semen during anal sex. Young gay men were especially susceptible because of their relatively high rate of sexual activity and because of the ease with which the anal membrane could tear, providing pathways for the virus into the bloodstream. By mid-decade, rival teams of US and French researchers – whose competition sometimes spurred, and sometimes hindered, their shared progress – had identified the AIDS virus as HIV and developed rudimentary means of testing for its presence in the blood.

Meanwhile, the plague kept spreading. In June 1983, the Atlanta-based Centers for Disease Control and Prevention (CDC) reported 1,676 AIDS cases and 750 deaths. A year later, the CDC reported 5,000 cases and nearly 2,300 deaths. By June 1985, the respective figures were 11,010 and 5,441. With mounting alarm, public health officials and some gay community leaders devised a range of measures to contain the infection. They urged gay men to reduce the number of their sexual partners, wear condoms during anal intercourse, and engage in other "safe sex" practices. They further recommended that municipal authorities in New York, San Francisco, and other cities close down the bathhouses in which gay men congregated to have sex, often with multiple partners. To one degree or another, all of these measures provoked resistance. For many gay men, the freedom to seek sexual gratification was a central achievement of the gay liberation movement. Submitting to external restrictions on that freedom felt like a dangerous retreat, one that would embolden the forces of repression that gays and lesbians had successfully resisted over the last two decades. The proposal to close bathhouses was especially controversial, for it evoked an all-too-recent past when police routinely raided gay establishments and arrested people for engaging in homosexual acts. "[I]nstitutions that have fought against sexual repression for years," warned the San Francisco activist Konstantin Berlandt, "are being attacked under the guise of medical strategy." Critics also argued that bathhouses were potential venues for sharing information about safe sex. Closing them would make gay men harder to reach.

Ultimately, the imperative of saving lives prevailed. By the end of 1985, New York, San Francisco, and most other cities had shut down their bathhouses, drawing fewer protests from the gay community than closure proponents had feared. Gay men also substantially altered their sexual behavior, reducing the number of their partners and using condoms far more readily. Annual US condom sales rose from $182 million to $338 million over the first half of the decade. More gay men pursued monogamous relationships, and some abstained from sex altogether. "Basically, I make love to my VCR a lot," one wryly remarked. All of these measures caused the rate of new HIV infection among gays to level off in the mid-1980s and start declining in 1987, though the virus's long incubation period ensured that thousands of people infected earlier in the decade would develop AIDS in the years ahead. Increasingly, the focus shifted to other vulnerable populations, especially intravenous drug users (among whom HIV spread through the sharing of needles) and their sexual partners. These AIDS sufferers were disproportionately poor and nonwhite. Some city governments began furnishing clean needles to intravenous drug users, along with information about their hygienic use, despite criticism that these actions subverted drug laws. Recipients of blood transfusions were also vulnerable, but the danger to them decreased after blood banks began screening their blood supplies for HIV in 1986.

In the first half of the decade, AIDS remained on the periphery of the nation's public awareness. This dramatically changed in July 1985, when it was revealed that fifty-nine-year-old Rock Hudson, a movie star celebrated for his confidence, charm, and masculine good looks, was gravely ill with AIDS. The actor, a closeted gay man, died months later. Although Hudson's tragedy helped to humanize people with AIDS, it also aroused deep and irrational fears among Americans, who all too often ignored experts' assurances that the virus could not spread through casual contact. During the 1985–1986 school year, Ryan White, a Kokomo, Indiana, teenager who had contracted AIDS via blood transfusion, fought a lengthy and ultimately successful legal battle against his public middle school, which barred him from campus after parents and faculty learned of his condition. White and his family also endured severe ostracism in their broader community. The publicity generated by White's case eventually helped to lessen the stigma surrounding the disease, but only after revealing the stigma's enormous potency. (White died in 1990 at the age of eighteen.) Meanwhile, social conservatives increasingly invoked AIDS in their battle against public acceptance of gays. "Homosexuals and the pro-homosexual politicians," Moral Majority founder Jerry Falwell declared in 1987, "have joined together with the liberal, gay influenced media to cover up the facts concerning AIDS." A year earlier, the conservative writer and commentator William F. Buckley called for the tattooing of people with AIDS. Conservatives in Congress proposed, but failed to pass, legislation mandating compulsory AIDS testing and barring people with AIDS from certain kinds of employment.

Both at the time and later, critics charged that the Reagan administration essentially ignored the AIDS epidemic and allowed it to rage unchecked for years on end. It is true that Reagan himself was slow to take outward notice of the crisis. He did not publicly mention AIDS until 1985 and remained personally indifferent to it even after it became big news. But key figures and agencies under Reagan's authority did take AIDS seriously, and his administration devoted considerable resources to combating it, though this often required sharp prodding from Congress. In 1983, Secretary of Health and Human Services Margaret Heckler called AIDS her "top priority." At a time when almost all people with AIDS were gay men, she appeared at the bedside of a hospitalized AIDS patient. "We ought to be comforting the sick rather than inflicting them and making them a class of outcasts," Heckler said. By 1987, the federal government was spending several hundred million dollars annually on AIDS research, distributing the funds among the CDC, the National Institutes of Health, the Food and Drug Administration, and other agencies. Washington devoted more resources per AIDS patient than for any other infectious disease.

Nonetheless, the Reagan administration was an arena of clashing ideological responses to the crisis. In early 1986, the president asked his surgeon general, C. Everett Koop, to produce a report on AIDS that stressed prevention. Koop, described by one journalist as "a stern-visaged evangelical Christian with a Dutch sea captain's beard," had won applause from the right for his harsh denunciations of abortion. It was thus startling when the resulting report, issued in October, boldly departed from social conservative positions on AIDS. Yes, Koop said, abstinence was the surest guarantee of safety, and lifelong monogamy the runner-up. But for the millions of Americans who chose neither, scrupulous condom use was imperative, pending a vaccine or more effective treatment. The surgeon general further argued that mandatory AIDS testing would scare away people most in need of medical attention; testing must be voluntary and strictly confidential. Finally, Koop called for public education about AIDS "at the earliest grade possible."

Koop's report outraged social conservatives. Phyllis Schlafly of the Eagle Forum accused the surgeon general of seeking to teach "safe sodomy" to schoolchildren. Within the Reagan administration, Undersecretary of Education Gary Bauer said that AIDS education for early teens would be "clinically correct but morally empty," because it would make sexual activity seem acceptable. Bauer's immediate superior, Secretary of Education William Bennett, echoed this critique. Still, although Reagan offered no ringing endorsement of Koop, he did not repudiate or silence him, either. The surgeon general made several media appearances, and his frank message broke through to a public unaccustomed to hearing high-ranking government officials use words like "condom" and "gay." As the pioneering AIDS journalist Randy Shilts wrote of Koop's impact: "It took a square-jawed, heterosexually perceived actor like Rock Hudson to make AIDS something people could talk about. It took an ultra-conservative fundamentalist who looked like an Old Testament prophet to credibly call for all of America to take the epidemic seriously at last."

By the second half of the 1980s, pharmaceutical researchers were testing and refining a number of drugs to treat AIDS-related symptoms. The first FDA-approved AIDS drug was azidothymidine (AZT), which worked only for some patients, caused serious side effects, and was extremely expensive. Other drugs seemed more promising but had not yet received FDA approval. Fearful of repeating nightmares of earlier decades in which poorly vetted drugs had caused widespread death or disability, the FDA insisted on following rigorous, years-long screening procedures – an untenable proposition for desperately ill AIDS patients. A New-York-based organization called AIDS Coalition to Unleash Power (ACT UP) conducted boisterous and theatrical protests to demand that AZT's manufacturer, Burroughs Wellcome Co., lower the price of its product and that the federal government speed up approval of other AIDS drugs. Fueled by the slogan "Silence = Death," ACT UP members staged "die-ins" outside FDA offices, hanged the FDA commissioner in effigy, occupied Burroughs Wellcome's North Carolina headquarters, and stormed the floor of the New York Stock Exchange. They publicly berated Anthony Fauci, director of the National Institute of Allergy and Infectious Diseases (NIAID), a brilliant and dedicated immunologist whose by-the-book adherence to protocol abetted the FDA's slowness and enraged AIDS activists.

Soon, however, Dr. Fauci started to bend, acknowledging that some of the drug-approval safeguards were unnecessarily rigid. "The gay groups said we were killing people with red tape," he later recalled. "When the smoke cleared we realized that much of their criticism was absolutely valid." While still maintaining his basic caution, Fauci began pressuring the

Figure 10.4 ACT UP protesters at the headquarters of the Food and Drug Administration, Rockville, Maryland, 1988. Source: Catherine McGann / Getty Images Archive.

FDA to streamline its processes. Under his prodding, in 1989 the FDA approved for commercial use a drug called ganciclovir, which practical experience had shown could prevent blindness in AIDS patients, even though formal testing data were lacking.

The following decade brought a major breakthrough. Researchers discovered that a category of drugs known as protease inhibitors could, when combined with AZT (or other drugs like it), prevent the HIV virus from replicating itself within the body. In 1995 and 1996, clinical trials yielded stunning cases of gravely ill people rising from their hospital beds and resuming normal lives. Doctors called it "the Lazarus effect." The drug combinations did not cure people of AIDS, but in many instances they brought the viral load down so low that symptoms almost entirely vanished – as long as patients strictly followed the expensive drug regimens. The chief beneficiaries were middle-class or affluent people afflicted with the disease. For them, AIDS became a chronic and treatable condition instead of a death sentence. Poor and working-class AIDS sufferers, who were disproportionately people of color, had much more limited access to the new drugs. Even so, the overall impact was dramatic. In 1995, 50,877 people died of AIDS in the United States; in 2001, the American death toll was 15,603. For some people with AIDS, the windfall of life was both exhilarating and strangely unsettling. As one of them remarked, "I'm going to live, but now I've got to figure out how to feed myself or pay the mortgage. It's mind-boggling to have these dilemmas. But I'm as grateful as I can be to be struggling with this one."

Globally, the Lazarus effect was largely confined to industrialized nations. In parts of the Third World, especially sub-Saharan Africa, the disease continued to ravage vulnerable populations (and would, as we shall see in Chapter 13, later become an important focus of US humanitarian policy).

***

The onset of the AIDS epidemic had, by happenstance, roughly coincided with the start of Reagan's presidency. Another frightening development of the early 1980s, a sharp escalation in tensions between the United States and the Soviet Union, was much more meaningfully connected to the attitudes and behavior of the White House's new occupant. The dramatic intensification of this long-standing rivalry and its equally dramatic easing in the decade's closing years constitute one of the most extraordinary episodes in post-1945 US foreign relations history. We turn our attention to it in the next chapter.

READING QUESTIONS

1. Throughout President Reagan's first term, critics accurately noted the inequitable features of his economic policies. Nonetheless, Reagan was overwhelmingly reelected in 1984. How do you explain this outcome?
2. What sorts of gains did American women make in the 1980s? What obstacles, both concrete and intangible, continued to block their progress or became even more daunting?
3. Of the changes in media technology and organization occurring in the 1980s, which seem to have been the most enduring? How have they shaped the media landscape of today?
4. What ethical dilemmas arose in the efforts to contain the spread of acquired immune deficiency syndrome and develop treatments for AIDS patients? In what different ways did public health professionals, gay community leaders, AIDS activists, and others respond to those dilemmas?

SUGGESTIONS FOR FURTHER READING

Cannon, Lou. *President Reagan: The Role of a Lifetime*. New York: Public Affairs, 2000.

Dow, Bonnie J. *Prime-Time Feminism: Television, Media Culture, and the Women's Movement since 1970*. Philadelphia: University of Pennsylvania Press, 1996.

Engel, Jonathan. *The Epidemic: A Global History of AIDS*. New York: Smithsonian Books, 2006.

Farber, David. *Crack: Rock Cocaine, Street Capitalism, and the Decade of Greed*. New York: Cambridge University Press, 2019.

Ferree, Myra Marx, and Beth Hess. *Controversy and Coalition: The New Feminist Movement across Three Decades of Change*. New York: Routledge, 2000.

France, David. *How to Survive a Plague: The Story of How Activists and Scientists Tamed AIDS*. New York: Vintage Books, 2017.

McCartin, Joseph A. *Collision Course: Ronald Reagan, the Air Traffic Controllers, and the Strike that Changed America*. New York: Oxford University Press, 2011.

Morgan, Iwan. *Reagan: American Icon*. London: I. B. Tauris, 2016.

Minian, Ana Raquel. *Undocumented Lives: The Untold Story of Mexican Migration*. Cambridge, MA: Harvard University Press, 2018.

Rosen, Ruth. *The World Split Open: How the Modern Women's Movement Changed America*. New York: Viking, 2000.

Rossinow, Doug. *The Reagan Era: A History of the 1980s*. New York: Columbia University Press, 2015.

Schaller, Michael. *Reckoning with Reagan: America and Its President in the 1980s*. New York: Oxford University Press, 1992.

Shilts, Randy. *And the Band Played On: Politics, People, and the AIDS Epidemic*. New York: Penguin Books, 1988.

Smith, Robert. *We Have No Leaders: African Americans in the Post-Civil Rights Era*. Albany, NY: State University of New York Press, 1996.

11 To Look Over the Horizon

From New Cold War to New World Order, 1981–1991

Introduction

It was not in itself a momentous decision, merely a question of which route to take home. Secretary of State James Baker was visiting Mongolia in early August 1990 when a dismaying bulletin arrived from the Persian Gulf. An earlier, tentative report was confirmed: Iraq had indeed violently invaded neighboring Kuwait. Clearly, Baker would have to cut short his trip and hasten home for consultations with President George H. W. Bush. But the traveling distance from Mongolia to Washington, DC, was roughly similar whether one flew westward over the Atlantic Ocean or eastward over the Pacific. Astutely, Baker chose the first course, as that would enable a quick stopover in Moscow and an attempt, perhaps, at some early coalition building.

In a hastily arranged meeting at a Moscow airport, Baker sounded out Soviet Foreign Minister Eduard Shevardnadze on his government's attitude toward the transgression by Iraq, until now a large recipient of Soviet military aid. The American diplomat well knew that the Soviet government, in order to focus on economic reforms at home, had recently scaled back many of its overseas activities and distanced itself from erstwhile allies. So Baker was not shocked when Shevardnadze agreed to share in a joint statement, issued on the spot, condemning Iraq's invasion of Kuwait and calling for an international arms embargo against the aggressor. It was, nonetheless, an extraordinary development. "The remarkable scene at Moscow's Vnukovo Airport," wrote a foreign policy analyst at *The Washington Post*, "... would have been inconceivable just a few months ago." As Baker himself later observed, "[I]t was certainly clear that day that the Cold War was over."

The Baker–Shevardnadze encounter highlighted two prominent themes in international politics at the start of the 1990s: a dramatic thawing of cold war hostility; and a resumption of violent upheaval in the Persian Gulf region. The event also suggested that the two themes were linked, with the former enabling the United States to attend more closely to – and at times exacerbate – the latter. In a broad sense, this linkage had marked US foreign relations for much of the preceding decade, and it would continue to do so until December 1991, when the Soviet Union's outright demise banished any lingering doubt that the cold war had ended. Taking office in 1981, President Ronald Reagan had significantly hardened the nation's stance toward the Soviet Union, presiding over a vast US military buildup and seeking to thwart Soviet power and influence across the globe. Few at the time could have predicted, therefore, that East–West tensions would markedly ease in the second half of that decade and come to a stunning end early in the next. Even less foreseeably, the manner in which the United States waged the last phases of the cold war, and positioned itself for the post-cold-war world, stimulated new challenges to US global power, many of them emanating from the Persian Gulf region. As one adversary faded into history, the United States turned its attention to new foes, setting the stage for turbulent ventures to come.

Reagan versus the "Evil Empire"

Ronald Reagan came to the presidency bearing a stark message: that Moscow had been getting away with murder internationally and that this would no longer be tolerated. "Let's not delude ourselves," he said during the 1980 election campaign. "The Soviet Union underlies all the unrest that is going on. If they weren't engaged in this game of dominoes, there wouldn't be any hot spots in the world." At his first press conference as president, Reagan charged that the Soviets "reserve unto themselves the right to commit any crime, to lie, to cheat," in their quest for world domination. In an address to the National Association of Evangelicals in the spring of 1983, he called the Soviet Union an "evil empire" and "the focus of evil in the modern world."

To combat this "evil empire," Reagan oversaw a massive buildup in conventional and nuclear forces. The annual defense budget grew from $134 billion in 1980 to $253 billion in 1985. Reagan began implementing programs to expand the nation's arsenal of intercontinental ballistic missiles, enlarge and modernize its fleet of bomber aircraft, and update its nuclear forces in Europe (initiatives actually planned during the latter phase of Jimmy Carter's administration). The new president also resisted growing international pressure to engage the Soviets in serious arms control negotiations.

Officially, the Reagan administration did have proposals for limiting nuclear arsenals, but few observers expected them to go anywhere. According to one plan, known as the "zero option," the United States would forgo deploying new classes of intermediate-range missiles in Western Europe (called cruise and Pershing II missiles) that would be capable of striking targets in Eastern Europe and parts of the Soviet Union; in exchange, the Soviet Union would remove intermediate-range SS-20 missiles, targeted at Western Europe, that it had recently deployed in Eastern Europe. Of course, this proposal was heavily lopsided in favor of the Americans, who would be relinquishing mere blueprints while the Soviets would have to dismantle actual weapons systems that they had spent billions of rubles producing and deploying. On ICBMs, Reagan called for dramatic cuts on both sides, with the Soviets relinquishing a disproportionately large share, on the theory that they were already ahead in key categories. Not surprisingly, Moscow rejected both US proposals. This suited the Reagan administration, which could now continue with its planned weapons buildup while claiming it had tried to reach an understanding with the Soviets.

As the buildup proceeded, Reagan and other administration officials sometimes spoke about nuclear war in ways that alarmed the public. In October 1981, the president told a group of newspaper editors that he could imagine an "exchange of tactical weapons against troops in the field without it bringing either one of the major powers to pushing the button" to launch World War III. More notoriously, in early 1982 a mid-level DOD official named Thomas K. Jones insisted to a reporter that Americans could survive a nuclear attack by digging fallout shelters: "Everybody's going to make it if there are enough shovels to go around." Evidently, the purpose of such rhetoric was to bolster deterrence. If the Soviets truly believed that the United States was prepared to wage nuclear war, perhaps they would be more cautious about pushing their luck. The effect, however, was to make Reagan and his team appear cavalier regarding this terrifying matter.

The new US stridency provoked massive protests in the Western world. An anti-nuclear-weapons movement that had started gathering force in 1979 (in conjunction with the movement against civilian nuclear power following the Three Mile Island incident) expanded rapidly during Reagan's first two years in office. In the spring of 1982, huge protest marches, each one turning out hundreds of thousands of people, took place in Amsterdam, Athens, Bonn, Brussels, London, and Madrid. In June, nearly a million protested in New York's Central Park, the largest peace demonstration in US history. Most American activists united under the banner of the nuclear "Freeze," a demand that the superpowers immediately halt the production and deployment of all nuclear weapons and then negotiate their arsenals down. In the fall of 1982, voters passed Freeze initiatives in nine states and thirty-four cities and counties. In five polls conducted in 1983, an average of 72 percent of respondents supported the Freeze. That same year, a Freeze resolution passed in the House of Representatives while a similar one failed in the Senate (an unsurprising outcome, given that Democrats controlled the first body and Republicans the second). In 1984, the Democratic Party included a pro-Freeze plank in its presidential campaign platform.

Reagan denounced the Freeze movement as ill informed and misguided, even alleging in 1982 that it was under the sway of Soviet agents. Pressed to substantiate the claim, Reagan cited two *Reader's Digest* articles and a House Intelligence Committee report, none of which, upon inspection, furnished vindication. As he so often did, the president blithely ignored the fact checkers and persisted in his charge.

Privately, however, Reagan had his own deep reservations about the nuclear status quo. He strongly opposed the doctrine of mutual assured destruction (MAD), the notion that a shared fear of annihilation was all that kept the superpowers from waging war against each other. It is possible, as some of his advisers have suggested, that Reagan worried that deterrence might fail – that an American president might be presented with an appalling bulletin that Soviet ICBMs were on their way and have to decide, within minutes, whether or not to respond in kind. Yet Reagan also was drawn to nuclear strategists who rejected MAD less out of visceral fear than because the doctrine assumed indefinite parity between

Figure 11.1 Nuclear Freeze demonstration, New York City, June 1982. Source: Authenticated News / Archive Photos / Getty Images.

the superpowers. These analysts argued that the United States could, and must, regain the position of nuclear superiority it had enjoyed in the first couple of decades of the cold war.

Whatever his motivation, Reagan was keen on discovering an alternative to MAD. He found it in the Strategic Defense Initiative (SDI), a visionary scheme to destroy incoming enemy ICBMs before they could strike their targets. As we saw in Chapter 7, both superpowers had developed antiballistic missile systems in the 1960s, only to agree a few years later that missile defense was inherently destabilizing (because it undermined MAD's deterrent logic) and to conclude a treaty in 1972 strictly curtailing each other's ability to deploy ABM systems. Reagan chafed under this limitation, and he responded enthusiastically when an informal group of scientific advisers told him that missile defense was not only strategically sound but achievable on far more ambitious terms. Instead of relying on ground-based ABM projectiles, the United States could launch lasers or other weapons systems into earth orbit and then use them, if necessary, to zap incoming ICBMs from above. It was a highly speculative concept, but Reagan embraced it wholeheartedly, envisioning SDI as a virtual shield against which the enemy's assaults would futilely bounce off. He unveiled the scheme in a March 1983 speech, saying it held the promise of "rendering … nuclear weapons impotent and obsolete."

Few senior Reagan administration officials appear to have shared the president's boundless faith in SDI's technological feasibility. Still, they recognized its value as a pressure point on Moscow. For it was clear that SDI terrified the Soviets, less because *they* thought it would work as advertised than for what it seemed to say about US intentions. To Soviet strategists, SDI made no sense as a purely defensive system. An SDI-equipped United States would still be fatally vulnerable to a Soviet first strike, as there would be far too many incoming ICBMs to shoot down. But the Americans *could* launch a first strike of their own that destroyed most Soviet ICBMs in their silos; they could then use SDI to intercept the small number of ICBMs that their stricken adversaries managed to launch in retaliation. Thus Moscow could scarcely shrug SDI off as a wasteful delusion but, rather, had to try to match any US efforts to implement it. Soviet leaders realized, however, that they would be hard pressed to muster the economic and technological resources for such a feat. Their best bet was to try to block SDI diplomatically.

Within the United States, SDI aroused fierce controversy. Democrats scoffed that it was a pipe dream that would accomplish little beyond depleting the Treasury and further exacerbating US–Soviet tensions. To show their disdain, they called the program "Star Wars," after George Lucas's hugely popular movie series. Although some prominent scientists backed SDI, most expressed skepticism about its efficacy and alarm at the notion of extending the arms race into space. Vigorously supporting SDI was the advocacy group High Frontier, led by Daniel Graham, a retired army officer and former deputy director of the CIA. High Frontier blitzed the news media with pro-SDI materials, including a TV documentary film hosted by Lorne Greene, star of the long-running television program *Bonanza* (and, perhaps more relevantly, of the shorter-lived TV show *Battlestar Galactica*). These efforts, along with Reagan's own paeans to SDI, helped to place a more benign cast on US nuclear policies. Who could object to protecting America? The Freeze campaign would rapidly lose momentum from early 1984 on, and there is some evidence that SDI contributed to that result.

Meanwhile, though, US–Soviet tensions continued to escalate, reaching a peak in the late summer and fall of 1983. A horrifying air incident in the North Pacific ratcheted up global anxieties. By now, the United States had taken to equipping large Boeing planes (which from a distance resembled commercial jetliners) with electronic surveillance equipment and sending them on intelligence missions close to Soviet territory. On September 1, Korean Air Lines flight 007, a passenger plane flying from Anchorage, Alaska, to Seoul, South Korea, accidentally strayed into Soviet airspace. Believing KAL 007 to be a US spy plane, and receiving no response to its warnings from the KAL pilot, the Soviet air force shot the plane down, killing all 269 people on board, including House of Representatives member Lawrence McDonald, a conservative Democrat from Georgia. A wave of revulsion swept the globe, and the Reagan administration accused Moscow of "wanton, calculated, deliberate murder." Soviet leaders realized they had made a terrible blunder but were loath to admit it. Brazening it out, they insisted that KAL 007 was indeed a US spy plane and that Washington was to blame for the tragedy.

Over the next few months, cold war fears intensified. The United States proceeded with the planned deployment of cruise and Pershing II missiles in Western Europe. The Soviets responded by walking out of mid-level disarmament talks in Geneva. In November, ABC TV aired *The Day After*, a fictional portrayal of the aftermath of a nuclear exchange between NATO and Warsaw Pact forces. In excruciating detail, the two-hour film portrayed the slow impact of that cataclysm on the residents of Lawrence, Kansas. A major cultural event, the broadcast of *The Day After* was widely and nervously anticipated. Churches and civic organizations arranged for members to watch the film in small groups and discuss it afterward. ABC and its local affiliates set up telephone hotlines for distressed viewers to call. School boards mailed letters to parents urging them not to allow young children to watch the program. On the night of the broadcast, about a hundred million people tuned in, the largest audience an American made-for-TV movie has ever attracted. Afterward, ABC aired an interview with Secretary of State George Shultz and a panel discussion featuring, among others, former Secretary of State Henry Kissinger, astronomer Carl Sagan, and author and Holocaust expert (and survivor) Elie Wiesel. "I'm scared," Wiesel confessed to the studio audience. "I'm scared because … I know that the impossible is possible." As few other media events have done, *The Day After* drew the attention and emotional engagement of millions of Americans at all levels of society.

Unbeknownst to those anxious multitudes, an exceptionally dangerous incident occurred a couple weeks prior to the broadcast. In early November 1983, NATO staged a week-long military exercise called Able Archer. Designed to test NATO's readiness for war, the exercise simulated computerized procedures for launching nuclear weapons across Western Europe. Detecting this activity, Soviet high command grew fearful that the Western powers were preparing an actual attack and placed its own forces on heightened alert. Able Archer ended without incident, and the Soviets' immediate alarm subsided, though Moscow remained extremely apprehensive about Western intentions.

Over the ensuing weeks, US intelligence received word that Soviet leaders genuinely feared a NATO strike. "I don't see how they could believe that," a perturbed Reagan remarked to his national security adviser, Robert "Bud" McFarlane, " – but it's something to think about." Reagan's pollster, Richard Wirthlin, was already warning that the president's hawkishness on US–Soviet relations could be a liability in his upcoming bid for reelection. So Reagan moved to calm the waters. In a January 1984 address, broadcast live to American and Western European viewers, he declared that "a year of opportunities for peace" had begun and pledged his readiness for "compromise" with the Soviets. In the speech's most memorable passage, he invited his audiences to "suppose … that an Ivan and Anya could find themselves, say, in a waiting room or sharing a shelter from the rain with Jim and Sally, and there was no language barrier to keep them from getting acquainted. Would they then debate the differences between their respective governments? Or would they find themselves comparing notes about their children and what each other did for a living?" Reagan's point, as welcome as it was obvious, was that the American and Soviet people shared a common humanity and must spare no effort to bridge their misunderstandings. It was a significant tonal shift, one that the Soviets, in time, would more than reciprocate (though not before sneering that Jim and Sally should worry about being placed under FBI surveillance for daring to associate with Russians). Substantively, however, Reagan was giving no ground on arms control.

Reagan's Cold War in Central America

Nor was the president ready for conciliation when it came to upheaval in Central America, a problem he inherited and made much worse. By the late 1970s, the region was in turmoil. Decades of impoverishment and political repression, enforced by rightwing (and often US-backed) authoritarian regimes, had spawned leftist revolts in Nicaragua, El Salvador, and Guatemala. In 1979, the Sandinistas, a group of Marxist insurgents named after Augusto Sandino, a Nicaraguan rebel leader of the 1920s and 1930s, seized power in Nicaragua, ousting the US-supported dictator Anastasio Somoza Debayle. President Carter hoped for cordial relations with the new Sandinista government, but his slowness in persuading Congress to appropriate aid for Nicaragua, which was in a desperate condition after years of Somoza's plundering and a civil conflict that had claimed 50,000 lives, alienated the Sandinistas, who turned increasingly to leftist Cuba for material and diplomatic support (while also receiving substantial assistance from Canada, Japan, and some Western European nations). Not surprisingly, the ascendancy of the staunchly anticommunist Reagan brought a further deterioration in US–Nicaraguan relations. The Reagan administration charged that Nicaragua had joined Cuba's long-standing campaign to foment revolution throughout Central America, pointing specifically to alleged, but never substantiated, Nicaraguan arms transfers to leftist insurgents in El Salvador. In secret bases in Honduras, the CIA began training the Contras, an exile army built around a nucleus of former National Guard officers of the deposed Somoza regime. Their mission was to overthrow, or, failing that, harass and weaken, the Sandinista government.

Meanwhile, in El Salvador and Guatemala, Marxist-led revolts were in full swing. The new Reagan administration made Central America a showcase of its determination to confront communist influence throughout the world. It stepped up its support for the rightwing governments of El Salvador and Guatemala and launched a heavy-handed publicity campaign to persuade the US public that the Soviets, working through their Cuban proxies, were menacing the Western Hemisphere. (Cuba was indeed backing the insurgencies, but the Soviet government considered them futile and offered little encouragement.) A key challenge the Reagan administration faced was the fact that the Salvadoran and Guatemalan regimes were brutally repressive, something difficult to conceal from Congress and the American people. El Salvador's case was especially glaring, as paramilitary "death squads" allied with the government had unleashed a reign of terror not just against suspected rebels but also against villagers accused of harboring them and against peaceful political dissidents, including clergymen and -women. Another problem was that the Reagan administration's own activities in El Salvador were disturbingly reminiscent of US involvement in South Vietnam in the early 1960s. Once again, teams of US military "advisers" were working with the army of a war-torn country to suppress a jungle rebellion. To many Americans, it seemed only a matter of time before US troops joined in the fighting themselves. By the spring of 1981, antiwar demonstrations had erupted across the United States, and members of Congress were loudly criticizing US policy.

Figure 11.2 Members of a local human rights commission view the exhumed body of a person presumably killed by a government-affiliated death squad, San Salvador, El Salvador, 1984. Source: Robert Nickelsberg / Archive Photos / Getty Images.

Though initially taken aback by the opposition, the Reagan administration eventually cobbled together a formula that enabled it to continue supporting the Salvadoran regime. It facilitated an electoral process that conferred formal power on a centrist political party (which, once in office, wielded little authority over the military). It systematically concealed the close linkages between the death squads and the regular Salvadoran army, shielding the latter from blame for the ongoing atrocities. Finally, seeing that their simplistic "good versus evil" framing lacked credibility, US officials fashioned a more sophisticated, but still misleading, political narrative of a courageous moderate government laboring, with US help, to combat extremists of both left and right. On this basis, Congress kept the aid flowing. Between 1981 and 1992, when the Salvadoran civil war finally ended, the regime received \$4.7 billion in US assistance. Over that same period, around 70,000 Salvadorans were killed, most of them by death squads or the military, and more than a million fled the country.

About half of those refugees entered the United States, and many remained there without documentation. Their applications for asylum status, on the grounds of past or feared political persecution, were routinely denied by the Reagan administration, which realized that granting such claims could jeopardize congressional support for the Salvadoran government. The administration meted out similar treatment to the smaller number of Guatemalan refugees residing in the United States. A largely church-based "Sanctuary" movement emerged to protect Central American refugees from deportation, furnish them legal services, and in other ways enable them to remain in the country. Eventually, some five hundred American congregations and towns declared themselves sanctuaries. Launched mainly on humanitarian grounds, the sanctuary movement soon became a vehicle for mobilizing political opposition to US policies in Central America. "This was a tremendous organizing tool," a sanctuary activist recalled. "After hearing refugees tell their stories, these mainstream church people were more than willing to transport and house refugees, donate money, whatever. They also became very skeptical, at the very least, of the White House line about what was going on in Central America."

Over its Nicaraguan policy, the Reagan administration faced powerful resistance not just from activists but from Congress, too. At first, the administration hid its support for the Honduras-based Contra army, which, from 1982 on, conducted nearly daily raids into Nicaragua to destroy bridges and other infrastructure, attack the Sandinista army, and terrorize civilians. The Contras posed little threat to the Nicaraguan military, but they caused considerable economic damage and by 1985 had killed some 13,000 Nicaraguans. The Reagan administration's role in the attacks quickly became public knowledge, and Congress tried to stop them. From 1982 to 1984, it attached three riders to defense appropriations bills known as the Boland amendments, named for their sponsor, Democratic Representative Edward Boland of Massachusetts. The third and most restrictive amendment prohibited any government agency involved in intelligence matters from assisting the Contras. Reagan's anti-Sandinista campaign seemed to have encountered a major obstacle.

In fact, the president was not so easily deterred. He privately instructed National Security Adviser McFarlane to "do whatever you have to do to help [the Contras] keep body and soul together," a lawless directive that set in motion an intricate and bizarre foreign policy scandal. McFarlane and other White House aides solicited donations from wealthy American conservatives and from the governments of Brunei, Israel, Saudi Arabia, South Africa, South Korea, and Taiwan. Oliver North, a marine lieutenant colonel then working in obscurity in the National Security Council (NSC), placed the donated funds in Swiss bank accounts earmarked for the Nicaraguan rebels. Sometimes, a foreign contribution came directly from a country's US assistance package and thus constituted a roundabout transfer from the US Treasury to the Contras. Through strained reasoning, Reagan and his team may have persuaded themselves that they were following the letter of the law, but they knew their actions were politically explosive. If any of these efforts should become public, Reagan quipped in a 1984 meeting with his top aides, "we'll all be hanging by our thumbs in front of the White House."

Arms for Hostages, Arms for Contras

Over time, Reagan's pro-Contra campaign grew more and more elaborate, so much so that comprehending it requires a brief excursion into US Middle East policy. In the summer of 1982, Israel invaded Lebanon, its northern neighbor, as part of its ongoing conflict with the

Palestine Liberation Organization, which was based in that country. The Israeli invasion profoundly destabilized Lebanon, which was already in the throes of civil war. To help calm the situation, Reagan dispatched US marines to occupy the country. American opinion leaders tended to portray the marine deployment as a neutral and constructive endeavor, but many Middle Easterners viewed it in a more sinister light. For one thing, the United States was Israel's strongest supporter; it had supplied the arms with which Israel conducted the invasion. Israel's action had reduced much of Lebanon to rubble and killed thousands of Lebanese and Palestinian civilians. Lebanese Shia communities were especially hard hit – and thus ill disposed toward the United States. For another thing, the US marines were now in Lebanon to support that country's government, which was locked in conflict with several Lebanese factions, including Shia organizations that received support from revolutionary Iran and were allied with neighboring Syria, a staunch geopolitical adversary of the United States. The marines had entered a situation in which they were bound to encounter violent resistance.

In October 1983, a suicide bomber – apparently a Lebanese Shia supported by Syria – drove a truck laden with explosives into the US marine barracks in Beirut, Lebanon's capital, killing 241 American serviceman. It was a devastating blow to the United States, and Americans across the political spectrum called on Reagan to bring the troops home. The president did so in early 1984, but this was hardly the last of America's troubles in Lebanon. Scores of US citizens continued to live in the country, and they were vulnerable to anti-US reprisals. In the mid-1980s, Lebanese Shia militant groups kidnapped several American residents, some of whom would remain in captivity for several years and three of whom would be killed by their captors. The Reagan administration faced constant pressure from the hostages' families to secure the release of their loved ones by making a deal with the hostage takers, whose most frequently heard demand was for the freeing of militant comrades imprisoned in Kuwait. Some family members were highly resourceful in generating media coverage and support from members of Congress. Publicly, the Reagan administration insisted that negotiating with the kidnappers was out of the question; doing so would only encourage the taking of more hostages.

Behind closed doors, however, different motivations were at work. Reagan, who always approached policy matters in highly personal terms, was distressed by the plight of the hostages and eager to free them. Meanwhile, some members of his administration, especially Bud McFarlane and CIA director William Casey, hoped to explore prospects for improved relations with Iran, whose size, oil wealth, and strategic location lent it, as always, great significance in American eyes. Through private emissaries, these US officials secretly established contact with the Iranian government. (McFarlane himself, accompanied by Ollie North, paid a clandestine and somewhat farcical visit to Tehran.) In the course of those exchanges, a general understanding emerged whereby the United States would sell Iran shipments of arms (ultimately amounting to more than two thousand antitank missiles and over two hundred spare parts for antiaircraft missiles); in return, the Iranians would pressure the hostage takers in Lebanon, with whom they were allied, to free the American captives. In 1985 and 1986, three American hostages were released through this quid pro quo.

If the arms-for-hostages deal violated the Reagan administration's proclaimed opposition to negotiating with hostage takers, it also subverted its basic approach to the geopolitics of the Persian Gulf region. Since 1980, Iran and Iraq had waged a brutal war against one another. Officially, the United States was neutral on the conflict; unofficially, it tilted toward Iraq, which, though a harsh dictatorship with close ties to Moscow, seemed the lesser evil. Moreover, several Arab nations with which the United States was allied, such as Saudi Arabia, Kuwait, Jordan, and Egypt, strongly backed the Iraqi war effort. One way the Reagan administration manifested its partiality was through Operation Staunch, a diplomatic campaign to dissuade other countries from selling arms to Iran. Obviously, the secret US understanding with Iran made a hash of that policy. Citing this objection, along with the impropriety of trading arms for hostages, both Secretary of State George Shultz and Secretary of Defense Caspar Weinberger privately opposed the Iran initiative. But Reagan, vaguely endorsing the concept of improved relations with Iran, and fervently wishing to bring the hostages home, gave the initiative his blessing.

At the time of the hostages' release, the American public had no inkling of the strange machinations that had produced the happy result. Yet those machinations became even stranger. Someone in the Reagan administration, possibly CIA director Casey (who died before investigators could question him on the matter), hatched a bold scheme to kill two birds with one stone. The Iranians had been overcharged for the US weapons they had purchased. So why not take some of the resulting profits and divert them, too, to the Nicaraguan Contras? Again, Ollie North handled the money transfers, which in this case amounted to at least $3.6 million.

Ironically, after a two-year frenzy of unorthodox measures to sustain the Contras, the Reagan administration achieved its greatest success on the issue by more traditional means. In June 1986, it finally persuaded Congress to repeal the Boland amendment and appropriate $100 million for the Contras. The vote came on the heels of an extended White House public relations campaign in which Reagan hailed the Nicaraguan rebels as "the moral equal of our Founding Fathers" (outraging liberals not yet in the habit of foregrounding the Founders' sins as slaveholders). The Contra appropriation was a major political victory for the administration, tempered by the knowledge, on the part of a select few, that US officials had acted and were continuing to act with reckless zeal. For the moment, though, the secret held.

A New Soviet Leader

On the US–Soviet front, fascinating changes were afoot, in ways few could have predicted a couple of years earlier. In early 1984, Reagan had softened his anti-Soviet rhetoric. Over the ensuing months, however, the two superpowers took little concrete action to improve their relations. In part, the president was preoccupied with his own reelection, which he overwhelmingly secured that November. Mostly, though, Moscow was in no shape for vigorous diplomacy. Yuri Andropov, who at age sixty-eight had taken the helm of Soviet leadership after Leonid Brezhnev's death in November 1982, was shortly stricken with poor health and died in February 1984. His successor, seventy-two-year-old Konstantin Chernenko, was in frail condition himself and lasted only until March 1985. "How am I supposed to get anyplace with the Russians," Reagan recalled asking First Lady Nancy Reagan upon learning of Chernenko's demise, "if they keep dying on me?"

The next Soviet leader broke the mold. Just fifty-four, Mikhail Gorbachev was energetic, outgoing, and open in his manner. He seemed comfortable mingling with ordinary Soviet citizens, willing to listen to their opinions and even their complaints. These qualities enabled Gorbachev to start addressing some of the Soviet Union's long-term problems. By the mid-1980s, the Soviet economy was plagued by shortages, low productivity, and galling waste, conditions exacerbated by the diversion of resources toward the massive military buildups of the 1960s and 1970s. The nation had fallen far behind in the high-technology race, as it lacked the traditions of openness and innovation necessary for advancement in this area (hence Moscow's alarm over SDI). Rates of alcoholism, drug abuse, crime, and worker absenteeism were on the rise. Soviet citizens increasingly resented the drabness of their lives, the lack of civic and political freedom, and the necessity of waiting in long lines to buy basic household goods. The malaise impaired worker productivity, aggravating the economic crisis and further feeding the malaise. "They pretend to pay us, and we pretend to work," Soviet employees wryly joked.

Gorbachev – or "Gorby," as he became known in the West – realized that the Soviet economy was in need of major overhaul. The term he used for the task was *perestroika*, or restructuring. Key features of his program were a campaign to combat alcoholism, a crackdown on corruption, a phasing out of wasteful projects, and increased investment in heavy industry. *Perestroika* later entailed efforts to introduce market mechanisms. But it was also clear that economic reform would be impossible without significant changes in Soviet domestic affairs and foreign policy. At home, the lack of transparency crippled economic performance. Across the system, bureaucrats and provincial leaders were cooking the books, fearful of suffering reprisals if they honestly reported difficulties in their areas of responsibility. Such opacity made it impossible to identify problems until they had become too acute to ignore, by which time they were often close to insoluble. So *perestroika* became linked to another word in Gorbachev's lexicon: *glasnost*, or openness. Soviet officials, journalists, and citizens had to be free to discuss problems candidly, without risk of punishment. During his first few years in power, Gorbachev made impressive gains in dispelling the climate of fear and obfuscation that had pervaded Soviet society for decades.

Perestroika also required changes in Soviet foreign policy. By the mid-1980s, the Soviet Union was spending about 15 percent of its gross national product on the military, whereas the United States devoted just 7 percent of GNP for that purpose. (The discrepancy had less to do with a higher absolute level of Soviet military spending than with the fact that Soviet GNP was much smaller than its US counterpart.) The only way to jumpstart the Soviet economy was to spend less on arms, and this in turn necessitated an easing of international tensions. Soon after taking office, therefore, Gorbachev began calling for renewed efforts at

US–Soviet arms control, issuing a series of dramatic public proposals for mutual freezes or cuts in various classes of nuclear weapons.

Reagan responded cautiously. He shared the widespread suspicion among his advisers, and among conservatives generally, that Gorbachev's diplomatic offensive was insincere. Following a June 1985 meeting with Armand Hammer, a prominent American industrialist with extensive business dealings in the Soviet Union, Reagan wrote in his diary, "He's convinced 'Gorby' is a different type than past Soviet leaders & that we can get along. I'm too cynical to believe that." Still, Reagan saw the value of testing Gorbachev's bona fides, and in November 1985 he traveled to Geneva to meet with his Soviet counterpart. The two leaders sparred vigorously over the relevant issues and reached no significant agreements, but their personal chemistry was better than expected. "You could almost get to like the guy," Reagan admitted to aides. The fact that US and Soviet heads of state were talking again generated some international optimism, as did their joint declaration that "a nuclear war cannot be won and must never be fought."

Less than a year later, in October 1986, Reagan and Gorbachev met again in Reykjavik, Iceland. Unexpectedly, Gorbachev and his negotiators called for the elimination of all intermediate-range nuclear missiles in Europe and a 50 percent reduction in each superpower's arsenal of ICBMs. In response, Reagan and his team proposed to dismantle all ballistic missiles, regardless of range. The Soviets moved to top *that* suggestion, and soon both sides were discussing the elimination of all nuclear weapons, of any delivery method or range, in ten years' time. At moments during the exchange, feelings of euphoria overtook the negotiators. An end to the forty-year-old US–Soviet arms race seemed tantalizingly close.

It was, alas, too good to be true. For Gorbachev attached a condition to any disarmament agreement: that neither side be permitted to deploy a missile defense system. Reagan refused to countenance limitations on his cherished SDI, insisting it was a purely harmless endeavor. Why, once the technology was perfected, Washington would gladly share it with Moscow! Gorbachev ridiculed this notion, retorting that the Americans had not even been willing to share milking machines with the Soviets. Unable to bridge the impasse, the two leaders grimly parted ways. The failure at Reykjavik came as a relief to several NATO governments, which had not been consulted about abolishing the nuclear deterrent on which they believed their security rested. In the United States, by contrast, Democrats expressed dismay that Reagan's stubborn attachment to Star Wars had sabotaged such a precious diplomatic opportunity.

Although initially despondent over the summit's results, Reagan and his top aides quickly took a more favorable view of the event. The exchanges had covered extraordinary ground, revealing vast areas of potential accord. "The significance of that meeting at Reykjavik is not that we didn't sign agreements in the end," the president told US disarmament officials upon his return home; "the significance is that we got as close as we did." Gorbachev, too, was stressing the positive, remarking at a post-summit news conference that the parties had "traveled a long road" and "reached agreement on many things." Far from a failure, Reykjavik was "a breakthrough, which allowed us for the first time to look over the horizon."

The Iran–Contra Scandal

Reagan, however, faced serious trouble in the here and now. In the November 1986 midterm elections, Democrats held onto the House of Representatives and took back the Senate, ending six years of Republican control of the latter body. The president had stumped heavily for GOP candidates, and many pundits interpreted the outcome as a sign that his influence was waning. Things were about to get much worse for him. The day before the elections, a Beirut magazine reported that the United States had sold arms to Iran to secure the release of American hostages in Lebanon. Within days, the story was all over the American media. It was explosive news, suggesting a stark contradiction between the Reagan administration's public refusal to negotiate with hostage takers and its secret willingness to do just that.

Over the ensuing weeks, Reagan acknowledged, in dribs and drabs, that US arms sales to Iran had contributed to the release of kidnapped Americans. The president insisted, however, that his administration's overriding goal had been to cultivate Iranian "moderates," with a view to exploring prospects for improved relations with that country. The furnishing of arms and the freeing of hostages, he suggested, were mere confidence-building gestures in the pursuit of that goal, and they certainly didn't amount to a quid pro quo. Yet neither Reagan nor any other administration official could say who those Iranian moderates were. Years later, figures meriting that label would hold leadership positions in Tehran, but in the 1980s they had yet to emerge. Meanwhile, cascading revelations about the activities of McFarlane, North, and a growing cast of shady operatives relentlessly undermined Reagan's version of events. In a March 1987 televised address, the president finally offered a tortured mea culpa: "A few months ago I told the American people that I did not trade arms for hostages. My heart and my best intentions still tell me that is true, but the facts and evidence tell me it is not."

Well before that admission, the Central American half of the imbroglio had come to light, too. In late November 1986, the Reagan administration itself, trying to get ahead of the story, revealed that proceeds from the Iranian arms sales had been redirected to the Nicaraguan Contras. What journalists had started to call "Irangate" now became the "Iran–Contra affair." Reagan repeatedly maintained that he had known nothing about the diversion to the Contras while it was happening and learned of it only because his attorney general, Edwin Meese, conducted an internal investigation after the Iran initiative became public. No evidence emerged to contradict Reagan's claim, which was consistent with the testimony of John Poindexter, McFarlane's successor as national security adviser, who said he had authorized the diversion without telling his boss. Of course, Reagan's original "body and soul" directive underlay all of the extralegal initiatives to fund the Contras, including efforts unrelated to Iran that the president clearly did know about, such as the solicitation of contributions from Saudi Arabia, Taiwan, and other countries.

Whatever the state of his awareness, Reagan now had a true scandal on his hands. He had presided over an ocean of misconduct – behavior that defied Congress, broke the law, deceived the American people, subverted US policy, and undermined the authority of the secretary of state. When Reagan had not himself actively violated the public trust, he had passively or obliviously allowed underlings to do so. In a *New York Times*/CBS poll, the president's public approval rating plunged from 67 percent in early November 1986 to 46 percent a month later. The "I word" – impeachment – was in the air, drawing potency from the realization that Democrats were about to take charge of the Senate. Even if, following a hypothetical impeachment decision in the House, Senate Democrats failed to persuade enough Republicans to join them in a supermajority for conviction and removal from office, they would still set the rules of a Senate trial and could conduct it in ways deeply damaging to the president.

Reagan weathered the storm. In late 1986, he named former Senator John Tower, a Texas Republican, to head a special commission to examine the Reagan administration's conduct in the Iran–Contra affair. The Tower Commission report, released in February 1987, deplored the administration's internal procedures but soft-pedaled its criticism of Reagan himself. Meanwhile, Lawrence Walsh, a former federal judge whom Attorney General Meese appointed independent counsel, embarked on what became a six-year investigation into possible criminal behavior relating to Iran–Contra, an inquiry focusing on figures other than Reagan. The House did not impeach the president. Instead, in the summer of 1987, it held joint hearings with the Senate into the affair. The televised proceedings brought a parade of colorful witnesses into American living rooms: administration officials, Contra leaders, arms merchants, financiers, and wealthy donors to the Contra cause. Offering the most dramatic testimony was a uniformed and conspicuously bemedaled Oliver North, who unapologetically owned up to his deceptive activities, insisting they were necessary to nurture the hope of freedom in Nicaragua. Although many congressional committee members, including some Republicans, recoiled from the authoritarian tenor of North's defense, his charismatic testimony stirred a groundswell of conservative support across the country, launching the officer (once his legal troubles were resolved)[1] on a long, lucrative career in rightwing media and political advocacy.

Paradoxically, the very scale of the scandal probably benefited Reagan. Had the controversy remained confined to Iran, public indignation over the hypocrisy of the arms-for-hostages deal, which Reagan had unquestionably approved, might well have caused him even greater political harm. Once Central America became part of the mix, however, attention shifted to the one misdeed for which the president could credibly deny culpability, the diversion of funds to the Contras. And anyway, as the reaction to North's testimony showed, many Americans would have applauded if Reagan *had* authorized the diversion. For most of 1987, Reagan's public approval rating hovered at around 50 percent. This was a significant comedown from previous levels, but at least he was no longer hemorrhaging support.

[1] In 1989, Oliver North was convicted of obstructing Congress, destroying documents, and accepting an illegal gift; he was fined and sentenced to community service. In 1990, however, a federal appeals court overturned the conviction on the ground that Independent Counsel Lawrence Walsh had, in his prosecution, used congressional testimony by North for which the latter had been granted immunity.

Portentous Moves in the Persian Gulf – and Points East

The damage, however, was not confined to the domestic sphere. The Iranian part of the scandal had undermined America's diplomatic position in the Persian Gulf region, and the Reagan administration now scrambled to restore it. The Iraqis, still at war with Iran, were furious to learn of the US arms sales to their mortal enemies, a sentiment shared by other Arab governments on the Gulf. A formidable Iranian offensive in early 1987 only sharpened the sense, among Gulf Arabs and many in the Reagan administration, that quick action was needed to repair the harm and shore up Iraq. Defense Secretary Caspar Weinberger, who had opposed the Iran initiative and was thus in an "I told you so" mood, said in a January NSC meeting, "We should not only be supportive of Iraq, but should be seen as supportive. This is an opportunity to recoup some of our standing in the region and regain credibility with the Arab states." This time, Weinberger's position prevailed. In 1987 and 1988, the Reagan administration stepped up the aid it had extended to the Iraqi war effort since the early 1980s: agricultural credits that enabled Iraq to purchase US farm products (thus freeing up Iraqi funds to buy arms elsewhere); licenses to buy US civilian equipment that could be put to, or upgraded for, military use; and US satellite and aerial intelligence information on the location and size of Iranian troop formations. The administration also quietly encouraged France and Italy to sell arms to Iraq.

There was another way that the United States helped Iraq: by tolerating its war crimes. In March 1988, the Iraqi government used chemical weapons (CWs) against Iraqi Kurdish villages and towns in which Iranian-supported Kurdish resistance units were active. As many as 5,000 people, most of them civilians, died horribly. It was the largest CW attack in history against a civilian population. Although the Reagan administration criticized the atrocity (as it had done in 1984, when Iraq used chemical weapons against Iranian soldiers), the rebuke was mild, and US support and encouragement of Iraq continued. "Praising with faint damnation" would be an apt characterization of Washington's stance.

By now, moreover, the United States was engaged in an undeclared naval war against Iran in the Persian Gulf. In the course of their brutal conflict, Iran and Iraq had taken to attacking each other's merchant fleets, paying particular attention to oil shipments. Starting in late 1986, in response to Iraq's escalation of the shipping war, Iran targeted the maritime oil exports of Arab countries that supported Iraq, especially Kuwait, and acted in ways that threatened to close the narrow Strait of Hormuz, the Persian Gulf's maritime outlet to the rest of the world. Preventing any obstruction of the strait, through which, each day, about eight million barrels of oil were shipped to world markets, was a vital US interest. In the summer of 1987, the Reagan administration began providing naval escorts to Kuwaiti oil tankers transiting the Gulf and permitting them to fly the American flag. As part of the escorts, the US Navy destroyed Iranian mine-laying boats, along with oil platforms that Iran used for intelligence gathering. When Iranian gunboats interfered with these operations, the US Navy sank them. The strait stayed open for the rest of the war, which finally ended in August 1988, when Iran and Iraq concluded a truce on terms that delivered victory to neither side.

Although US responses to the Iran–Iraq war observed a certain geopolitical logic, many Americans found them difficult to follow. The whole business of tanker "reflagging" – whereby international shipping companies opted, for legal, financial, or security reasons, to alter the national flags under which they sailed – seemed especially arcane. Was this the stirring cause for which America would fight its next major war? Former Governor of Arizona Bruce Babbitt, mounting an ultimately failed bid for the Democratic Party presidential nomination in 1988, drew nervous laughter from an audience with this topsy-turvy description of Reagan's actions in the Persian Gulf: "He heard that the Kuwaitis were on the run, so he put American flags on Kuwaiti ships carrying Kuwaiti oil to Japan – in a gulf where American-owned tankers are flying Panamanian flags carrying Iranian oil to Japan. Now who is on first?" Comprehensible or not, security interests in the Gulf were claiming an ever larger share of US policy-makers' attention. Millions of ordinary Americans would soon have to consider them, too.

Further to the east lay another time bomb for the United States, albeit one set on a longer delay. Into the second half of the 1980s, Soviet forces remained bogged down in Afghanistan, Iran's eastern neighbor, waging a vicious though ineffectual campaign to suppress a coalition of indigenous resistance forces. These insurgents, called the Mujahidin, were devout Muslims determined to oust the Soviets, whose atheistic ideology made their occupation of Afghanistan all the more galling. To Washington, the Mujahidin were a handy weapon to deploy against Moscow. Since the start of the Soviet invasion in December 1979, both the Carter and the Reagan administrations had extended modest logistical and military assistance to the Mujahidin. The government of Pakistan, which lies to Afghanistan's southeast, served as the main conduit of US aid.

In 1986, the Reagan administration stepped up its involvement. It began supplying the Mujahidin with Stinger missiles, shoulder-fired antiaircraft weapons that were lethally effective in shooting down Soviet helicopter gunships. It also started to bankroll an ongoing Pakistani government program to enlist young men from across the Muslim world to come to Pakistan, receive weapons and training, and cross into Afghanistan to fight alongside the Mujahidin. Between 1982 and 1992, about 35,000 recruits from the Middle East, North and East Africa, and Central, South, and East Asia responded to the call, joining what for many Muslims had become a transnational cause célèbre. One of those recruits was a lanky youth named Osama bin Laden, the scion of an extremely wealthy and well-connected Saudi family. Bin Laden's social prominence made him more than a regular foot soldier; he functioned mainly as a financier and emissary, sent by the Saudi royal family to signal its commitment to the Mujahidin cause. Indirectly, then, the Americans were allied with a figure who would later orchestrate deadly terrorist attacks against the United States. Bin Laden was not, as some have imagined, on the CIA payroll, but he and the Americans moved in parallel against a shared enemy.

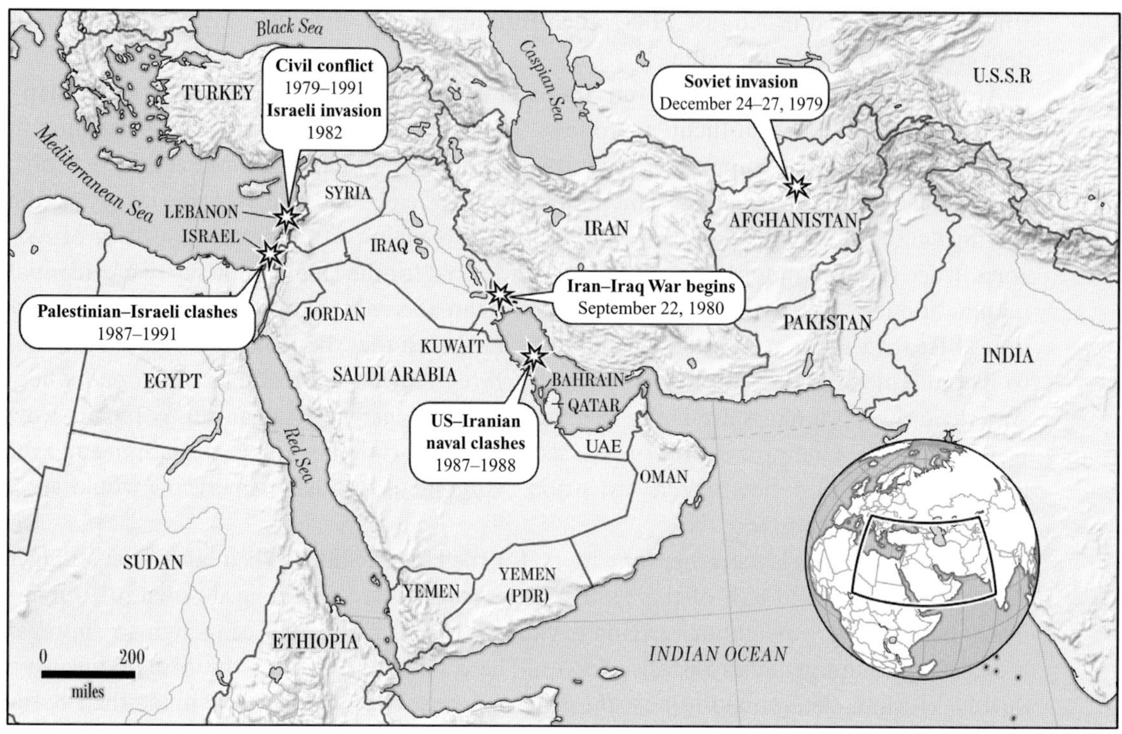

Map 11.1 The Middle East and Central Asia, 1979–1989. Source: Created by Joe LeMonnier.

A Rapid Thaw in the Cold War

One reason the Iran–Contra affair inflicted less political damage on Reagan than pundits predicted, apart from the scandal's breadth and complexity, was a sudden renewal of prospects for superpower arms control. In the spring of 1987, Gorbachev unexpectedly called for an agreement on intermediate-range nuclear weapons in Europe. A European weapons ban had been part of the package deal discussed at Reykjavik. Gorbachev now proposed that it be "singled out" from the other matters and pursued in a stand-alone treaty. Though still adamantly opposed to SDI, he no longer treated it as an obstacle to further diplomatic progress – a frank acknowledgement of Reagan's immobility on the issue. The Reagan administration, eager to change the subject from the dispiriting Iran–Contra affair, publicly welcomed Gorbachev's initiative. "In an ironic twist," wrote the syndicated columnist James McCartney, "Soviet leader Mikhail Gorbachev may wind up being Ronald Reagan's best friend in his hour of need." In the coming months, US and Soviet negotiators worked out the terms of an intermediate-range nuclear forces (INF) agreement. Reagan invited Gorbachev to visit Washington in December to sign the treaty. Meanwhile, though, the president kept up the political pressure on his Soviet counterpart. During a June 1987 trip to West Germany, Reagan delivered a speech in front of the

Berlin Wall, which continued to divide the city between east and west. "Mr. Gorbachev," he cried, "tear down this wall!"

Gorbachev's December 1987 visit to the US capital was one of the more memorable events of the late cold war. According to the Gallup polling company, Gorbachev was now the eighth most admired man among Americans, right behind Ollie North. (Reagan was number one.) Millions of American television viewers, and millions of others across the globe, followed the Soviet leader on his Washington rounds with fascination and gratitude. In their public appearances, Reagan and Gorbachev displayed an easy, bantering rapport that delighted onlookers and threw a convivial cast over the whole event. At a White House ceremony, Reagan and Gorbachev signed the INF Treaty, which committed the superpowers to destroy all of their intermediate-range nuclear missiles in Western and Eastern Europe, 846 weapons on the US side and 1,846 on the Soviet side. These constituted just 4 percent of the total US and Soviet nuclear arsenals, but for the first time an entire class of weapons was being scrapped. Some American conservatives denounced the INF Treaty as a shameful surrender that would leave Western Europe defenseless against the East bloc's larger conventional forces. Howard Phillips of the Conservative Caucus, a policy advocacy group, even called Reagan "a useful idiot for Soviet propaganda." But such criticism detracted little from the visit and, if anything, reassured those who had worried about Reagan's hawkishness.

Indeed, Washington seemed gripped by what one columnist called "Gorby fever." On the last day of the summit, as Gorbachev was en route from the Soviet embassy to the White House, he instructed the limousine driver to stop, bounded out of the car, and shook hands with and waved to awestruck Washingtonians. "That guy is a PR genius!" exclaimed a young woman in the crowd. Asked if he felt upstaged by Gorbachev, Reagan replied, "I don't resent his popularity. Good Lord, I co-starred with Errol Flynn once."

During Reagan's last year in office, his administration negotiated with the Soviets over reductions in strategic, or long-range, nuclear missiles, but the parties were unable to reach an agreement before the expiration of his term. Nonetheless, in May–June 1988 Reagan reciprocated Gorbachev's visit with his own trip to Moscow. Although substantive talks did occur, the event was dominated by symbolic and ceremonial occasions. As the two leaders toured the Kremlin grounds, a journalist asked Reagan if he believed he was in "an evil empire." No, Reagan said, he had been "talking about another time, another era," when he used that harsh term a mere five years earlier.

George H. W. Bush and Upheaval in the Communist World

By now, Vice President George H. W. Bush was the presumptive Republican nominee in that year's presidential election, a status formalized at the party's national convention in New Orleans in August. Bush went on to win a dramatic come-from-behind victory against his Democratic rival, Massachusetts Governor Michael Dukakis, though the Democrats retained control of both the Senate and the House. Bush came to the presidency with extensive foreign policy experience. After serving as a Texas congressman in the 1960s, he had

Figure 11.3 Soviet leader Mikhail Gorbachev with US President Ronald Reagan and Vice President George H. W. Bush, 1988. Source: *New York Daily News* Archive / *The New York Daily News* / Getty Images.

been Richard Nixon's ambassador to the United Nations, Gerald Ford's special envoy to China, and Ford's CIA director. As vice president, he had been broadly consulted on foreign policy and had executed some sensitive diplomatic assignments. Although Bush loyally supported Reagan's cold war policies, he privately believed that Reagan had embraced Gorbachev too hastily. Even granting the Soviet leader's sincerity in seeking to end the cold war, there was no guarantee that his ambitious reforms would succeed, and failure could prompt a resumption of old cold war thinking in Moscow. Upon taking office, therefore, Bush and his foreign policy advisers slowed the pace of US–Soviet rapprochement. They spent the first few months of 1989 conducting a comprehensive review of foreign policy, forgoing in the meantime any new initiatives.

Yet events would not await Bush's leisurely study. Gorbachev was now racing to end the cold war, so that he could convert military resources to domestic needs and, he hoped, gain Western help in revitalizing an increasingly desperate Soviet economy. In December 1988, as Bush prepared to assume the presidency, Gorbachev announced a unilateral reduction in Soviet armed forces by 500,000 troops (around 10 percent of the total) and the withdrawal of 50,000 Soviet troops from Eastern Europe, where they had been stationed under the terms of the Warsaw Pact. Earlier that same year, he had begun pulling Soviet troops out of Afghanistan, recognizing the futility of seeking to subdue the Mujahidin, especially now that those insurgents enjoyed generous US support. The Soviet withdrawal was completed in February 1989. Much as the United States had done sixteen years earlier in South Vietnam, the Soviets left behind, and continued to prop up, a client regime whose ability to withstand ongoing insurgent attacks seemed doubtful without the direct involvement of its superpower patron.

At around this time, Gorbachev also ended military support for Nicaragua's Sandinista government. The Iran–Contra scandal had already forced an end to US military aid to the Contras. Making a virtue of necessity, both Washington and Moscow agreed to support a peace plan sponsored by Costa Rica: a ceasefire within Nicaragua, to be followed by internationally monitored elections. (When the elections took place a year later, the heavily favored Sandinistas lost to an anticommunist party that had received covert CIA support and whose election, the Bush administration had publicly promised, would end a crippling US trade embargo imposed on Nicaragua since 1985.)

Prodded by Gorbachev's increasingly obvious desire to end the East–West standoff, Bush completed his policy review and, in a series of speeches in May 1989, announced his government's determination "to move beyond containment" and "seek the integration of the Soviet Union into the community of nations." As a first step, he proposed substantial reductions in NATO's and the Warsaw Pact's conventional forces in Europe. Bush's initiative won favorable reviews at home and abroad, but it was soon overshadowed by a host of upheavals in the communist world that would mark 1989 as one of the most extraordinary years in modern history.

The first of these events occurred in the People's Republic of China. By the late 1980s, in tandem with its growing diplomatic engagement with the West, the PRC had dramatically opened its economy to trade with and investment from the capitalist world, and politically it was far less repressive than it had been a couple of decades earlier. Domestic reformers attempted to push this evolution much further; in doing so, they collided with a conservative and brutally determined ruling establishment. In the spring of 1989, hundreds of thousands of Chinese students, many inspired by Gorbachev's policies, began camping out in Beijing's massive Tiananmen Square, calling for democracy. For weeks, they occupied the square, earnestly debating the future of their country and staging dramatic demonstrations, including the unveiling of a huge foam and papier-mâché replica of the Statue of Liberty. Initially, Chinese authorities hesitated. In June, however, PRC soldiers moved in on the square and ruthlessly crushed the rebellion, killing hundreds and perhaps thousands of people.

The Tiananmen Square massacre was harshly condemned throughout the world and across the US political spectrum. Angry demonstrations occurred in Los Angeles, San Francisco, New York, Philadelphia, and Washington, DC, staged mainly by Chinese students attending American universities. Bush, too, deplored the crackdown, and he ended the sale of some US military and high-tech items to China. Pundits and politicians left and right demanded a stronger response, but the president declined to go further, fearful of reversing the PRC's nearly two-decades-long opening to the West. "Now is the time to look beyond the moment," he said at a news conference, "to important and enduring aspects of this vital relationship for the United States."

In Eastern Europe, another, ultimately more successful mass rebellion was under way. In public statements in the spring and summer of 1989, Gorbachev and other Soviet officials suggested that Eastern European nations should be free to choose their own systems of government. Privately, Gorbachev urged Eastern European leaders to permit greater political openness. He evidently gambled that Eastern European citizens, if granted a choice, would freely opt for socialism and continued association with Moscow, especially now that a more humane and democratic version of socialism was taking hold in the Soviet Union. But ordinary Eastern Europeans were as dissatisfied with the status quo as Soviet citizens had been – perhaps even more so, for they also suffered the indignity of foreign domination. In the coming months, in one country after another, popular movements swept communist regimes from power.

The upheavals followed different patterns. The governments of Poland and Hungary, under heavy domestic pressure, agreed to hold national elections, confident that their control of the news media and state institutions would ensure their victory. Unexpectedly, in both cases the government parties lost the elections. In another pattern, antigovernment street demonstrations grew so large and formidable that state authorities, realizing that Gorbachev would not support violent repression, bent to the popular will. In November 1989, up to half a million people protested in Prague, Czechoslovakia's capital, demanding free elections and the resignation of the communist regime. Days later, the government did resign and allowed an interim government led by Václav Havel, a dissident playwright, to take power. A later election formalized Havel's elevation to the presidency. Meanwhile, demonstrations erupted in several East German cities. Authorities initially tried to crush the dissent, but the protests only grew. The government relented and agreed to institute reforms, including an end to restrictions on travel from East to West Berlin. On November 9, in a stirring spectacle seen by millions around the world, border guards opened the crossing barriers at the Berlin Wall, allowing East Berliners, for the first time in twenty-eight years, to pass freely to the western side of the city. In early 1990, East Germany's governing party was voted out of office, paving the way for the reunification of Germany later that year.

Throughout these momentous events, the horrifying example of Tiananmen Square hovered in the background. Even though most East European governments ultimately shrank from using maximum force to retain power, no one could confidently predict that outcome. Dissidents' willingness to press ahead in the face of such uncertainty was one of the aspects of the drama that made it so riveting. One Eastern European government did attempt a PRC-style solution: the Romanian regime of Nicolae Ceaușescu, the most brutal of all Eastern European leaders. In December 1989, thousands of Romanians staged antigovernment demonstrations in the city of Timișoara. The army opened fire, killing about seventy people. This violent repression (and rumors of a much larger death toll) provoked protests and riots elsewhere in the country, including in Bucharest, the nation's capital. Ceaușescu ordered a wholesale crackdown, but elements of the army turned against the government, sided with the protesters, and captured and summarily executed Ceaușescu and his wife. The dissident army faction gained control over the country and established an interim regime, which held elections in 1990. In this case, officials of the old communist regime, by forming a new party that won the elections, managed to stay in power. Still, the new government had made a relatively clean break with the past.

Bush navigated these perilous transitions with shrewdness and patience, ably assisted by Secretary of State James Baker, a Washington insider possessing limited foreign policy experience but impressive skills as a negotiator and bureaucratic tactician. The most delicate European issue they faced concerned the fate of Germany, whose division had lain at the heart of the East–West standoff. The matter boiled down to two questions: should the two Germanys reunify; and, if so, on what terms? The first question increasingly answered itself. The West German government was pushing hard for reunification, and so, too, was public opinion in East Germany, whose economy was in deep crisis and whose governing authorities had lost nearly all credibility. Neither the doomed communist regime nor the noncommunist government that replaced it in March 1990 saw any alternative to absorption into the prosperous West. Officially, the four nations that had occupied Germany since 1945 – the United States, Britain, France, and the Soviet Union – were the arbiters of German security arrangements. Realistically, though, any attempt on their part to block an indigenous drive for reunification risked throwing Europe into chaos.

If, then, a reunified Germany was inevitable, should it be a member of NATO, as West Germany had been since 1955? Yes, Bush insisted; a NATO without Germany would be dangerously weakened, and, as events in the first half of the twentieth century had shown, a Germany unmoored from larger security structures was unlikely to be a force for stability in Europe. Not surprisingly, Gorbachev vehemently resisted the US position. If Moscow accepted it, he said, the domestic backlash would drive him from power and destroy his reforms. "[T]hen you are going to have the destabilization of the Soviet Union," he warned Baker. Some Western governments questioned the wisdom of pushing for NATO membership in the face of such fierce Soviet opposition. Over several months, however, Bush and Baker met repeatedly with NATO allies, gradually persuading them that the US position on Germany was diplomatically viable. Meanwhile, the Soviet economy steadily deteriorated, making Gorbachev ever more desperate for outside help. Meeting with Bush at the White House in May–June 1990, Gorbachev overruled his appalled advisers and struck an informal bargain: Washington would relax immigration-related trade sanctions it had imposed since the 1970s (see Chapter 9), and Moscow would drop its objections to a reunified Germany's membership in NATO. (West Germany later sweetened the deal by covering most of the costs of repatriating Soviet soldiers stationed in East Germany.) Gorbachev had been right to predict that a Soviet cave-in on Germany would provoke sharp opposition at home, but he now felt he had no choice but to pay that price. By October 1990, Germany was reunified.

The US Invasion of Panama

As cold war tensions wound down in 1989 and 1990, many Americans spoke eagerly of a "peace dividend," a hoped-for reallocation of budgetary resources from the military sector to pressing domestic needs. There was no shortage of potential uses for such a windfall – from paying down the national debt (well over $3 trillion by 1990), to revitalizing decaying inner cities, to reversing decades of environmental degradation. The Bush administration agreed that the defense budget could come down by a couple of percentage points, adjusted for inflation; military spending had already started leveling off in 1986. But the administration successfully resisted substantial defunding of the Pentagon, arguing that stability in a post-cold-war world required a robust US military presence, in Europe and elsewhere. The benefits of such continuing stability would be, in themselves, a handsome return on the investment. "The peace dividend," said Secretary of Defense Richard Cheney, "is peace."

Another Pentagon argument, running somewhat counter to Cheney's formulation, was that the United States had many active uses for its military unrelated to communist threats. A US intervention in Panama in late 1989 was a case in point. That nation's authoritarian leader, Manuel Noriega, had been Washington's ally in the early to mid-1980s, making Panamanian airfields available for covert US arms shipments to the Nicaraguan Contras. The Reagan administration rewarded the strongman by secretly bankrolling him – unlike Osama bin Laden, Noriega actually *was* on the CIA payroll – and overlooking his involvement in cocaine trafficking. In the second half of the decade, however, Noriega's drug activities became too flagrant to ignore, and he alienated the Reagan administration by supporting a regional diplomatic initiative at odds with US efforts to overthrow the Sandinistas. So the administration turned against Noriega, imposing economic sanctions on Panama and authorizing a federal prosecutor in Miami to indict the dictator on drug-trafficking charges, a move that seemed mostly symbolic at the time. During Bush's first year in office, US–Panamanian relations deteriorated further. Noriega brazenly nullified a presidential election when it became clear that his US-backed opponent would win. The Panama Canal Zone (which, under the terms of the second 1977 Panama Canal treaty, US forces were entitled to occupy through 1999) became a site of escalating physical altercations between US and Panamanian soldiers.

In December 1989, after a pair of incidents resulted in the death of a US marine and the abusive treatment of a US Navy lieutenant and his wife, Bush launched a military invasion of Panama. Within days, US forces had defeated the Panamanian military and sent Noriega on the run. He took refuge in the Vatican embassy in Panama City, eventually surrendering to the US military, which whisked him to Miami to face the suddenly all-too-real drug charges. Noriega was convicted and given a lengthy jail sentence. Twenty-three American soldiers and several hundred Panamanian soldiers and civilians had been killed, and some 20,000 Panamanian civilians displaced. In publicly justifying the invasion, Bush cited Noriega's drug trafficking, his antidemocratic behavior, the need to protect the 13,000 US troops in the canal zone, and the necessity of safeguarding the canal itself. The first two claims were accurate enough, though skeptics noted that the United States had tolerated such behavior in other parts of the hemisphere and even in Panama earlier in the decade. They also questioned whether Panamanian forces had truly threatened US troops or the canal and whether violent regime change was an appropriate remedy even if they had. These were potent critiques. Bush's real motivations appear to have been to make an example of a leader who had so conspicuously challenged US hegemony in the region and to silence US media criticism of his earlier indecisiveness on the matter.

Crisis in the Persian Gulf

The invasion of Panama afforded Pentagon officials and military leaders some opportunity to show off their impressive new weapons and thus make the case for generous defense appropriations in the future. The next major US military venture, conducted in the arid expanses of the Persian Gulf region, would provide a more extended occasion for such display. The Gulf War of 1991 shared another attribute with the Panama intervention: here, too, Washington found itself disciplining a former client. In Iraq, as in Panama, the United States in the 1980s had cooperated with an unsavory leader in order to advance its own geopolitical interests. As in Panama, the leader subsequently pursued an independent course that sharply conflicted with US policy, bringing America's wrath down upon his head.

The Iraqi leader was Saddam Hussein, a cruel and ruthless figure who had been the nation's president since 1979 and its de facto ruler for some years before that. Hussein emerged from the Iran–Iraq War, which ended in 1988, bitterly resentful of the "conspiring bastards" in Washington, whose arms sales to Iran wiped out whatever goodwill they had earned through their informal support of the Iraqi war effort. Exacerbating Hussein's foul mood was Iraq's dismal condition in the war's aftermath: 300,000 dead, a million wounded, a ravaged infrastructure, and huge war debts to other Arab countries. The debt issue degenerated into a nasty diplomatic dispute. Although most of Iraq's Arab creditors wholly or partially forgave its debts, Kuwait, Iraq's tiny, oil-rich neighbor to the southeast, insisted on full repayment of the money it was owed. Hussein was outraged. Iraq had paid in blood to defend Kuwait and other Arab states from the Iranian menace; Kuwait's refusal to waive a mere monetary debt was ungrateful in the extreme. Hussein also accused Kuwait of selling too much oil, thereby depressing petroleum prices to the detriment of Iraq's own oil revenues, and of stealing Iraqi oil outright via "slant drilling" along the Kuwaiti–Iraqi border.

In August 1990, Iraqi troops stormed into Kuwait, quickly overwhelming its defenses and sending its ruling family into exile. Iraq's occupation forces behaved with extreme crudeness and brutality, looting and defacing Kuwaiti property, arresting Kuwaiti officials and anyone resisting the invasion, torturing and killing hundreds in captivity. Hussein proclaimed that Kuwait was now the "nineteenth province of Iraq."

Bush and his advisers were shocked by the Iraqi move, but few of them, at first, favored drastic action to counter it. "Does anybody really care about Kuwait?" asked Chairman of the Joint Chiefs of Staff Colin Powell. The blunt answer was: no, not really. American officials were mainly interested in the uninterrupted export of Persian Gulf oil, and it seemed likely that Kuwaiti crude would keep flowing regardless of who governed that nation. Over the next couple of days, however, Bush adopted the view, pressed by some of his advisers, that the issue transcended Kuwait. Tolerating Hussein's transgression would set a terrible international precedent, especially now that the waning of cold war tensions had raised expectations of more elevated conduct among nations. Vigorously enforcing those expectations, conversely, would further cement America's claim to shape and dominate a "new world order" in which international law, not brute force, governed states' interactions. (Critics would rightly object that the United States had often tolerated aggressive behavior by its allies and even acted aggressively itself. The strongest counterargument was that Iraq's abrupt and wholesale extinguishing of Kuwaiti sovereignty was a significant escalation over past practices.) Three days into the Iraqi invasion, Bush told reporters on the White House lawn, "This will not stand. This will not stand, this aggression against Kuwait."

Skillfully, Bush laid the diplomatic and military basis for reversing Iraq's action. He persuaded the king of Saudi Arabia to permit the stationing of US troops on his nation's territory. Officially, the deployment aimed to deter Iraq from continuing its invasion into Saudi Arabia. But the rapid expansion of the US force, which numbered 250,000 troops by early November, suggested a more ambitious mission. Meanwhile, the Bush administration worked with the United Nations Security Council to pass a series of resolutions condemning the Iraqi invasion, demanding an immediate withdrawal from Kuwait, and imposing stringent economic sanctions against the aggressor. These resolutions were possible because Moscow declined to veto them, as it almost certainly would have done a few years earlier. Iraq had been a close ally of the Soviet Union, but by now Gorbachev was far more interested in continuing his rapprochement with the United States, and thus securing Western help for the gasping Soviet economy, than in shielding Hussein from the consequences of his misbehavior. With Secretary of State Baker's help, Bush enlisted a diverse coalition of over thirty countries, including several Arab states, that opposed the Iraqi invasion and were willing to reverse it by force if necessary. Like the coalition that had rallied to South Korea's defense in 1950, this new group would shortly operate under a formal UN mandate but be dominated by the United States, which contributed the bulk of the troops and furnished an army general, Norman Schwarzkopf, Jr., to command the coalition.

In November 1990, Bush announced a doubling of the US troop presence in Saudi Arabia to half a million, nearly as many soldiers as had been deployed at the peak of the Vietnam War. Later that month, the UN Security Council passed a new resolution demanding that Iraq withdraw from Kuwait by January 15, 1991, authorizing the use of force against Iraq should it fail to comply. The prospect of US military intervention sparked enormous anxiety within the United States. Large antiwar demonstrations occurred throughout the country, especially in major cities. Many protesters alleged that Bush's purpose was not to thwart aggression but merely to ensure Western access to Persian Gulf oil, a view captured in the slogan "No blood for oil." Demonstrators also warned that, if war came, thousands of Americans might return home in body bags, as had happened during the Vietnam War. Indeed, it could be worse than Vietnam. Hussein had already used poison gas against Iranian soldiers and Iraqi Kurdish civilians. Why would he hesitate to turn that horrific weapon against invading US troops? Bush's war preparations also aroused criticism in the American news media, in Congress, and within the US foreign policy and military establishments. From these more mainstream sectors, the principal message was that the UN-imposed economic sanctions should be given a chance to work. "Who can doubt," asked former Secretary of Defense Robert McNamara, a chastened architect of the Vietnam debacle, "that a year of blockade would be cheaper than one week of war?"

Even some active-duty military leaders fretted about the consequences of resorting to force. Chairman Powell of the Joint Chiefs was himself haunted by the drawn-out failure in

Vietnam, where he had served as a young army officer. He extracted a promise from Bush that, if war with Iraq proved unavoidable, the military would have all the resources and political backing it needed for a swift, decisive, and overwhelming victory.

In early January 1991, Congress debated whether to authorize the president to use force against Iraq. The opponents of authorization, most of them Democrats, argued that the economic sanctions would eventually compel Iraq to leave Kuwait. Those favoring authorization, who were mainly Republicans but also included a substantial number of Democrats, insisted that only force could achieve liberation. Bush said he would welcome a congressional authorization, while making it clear that a negative vote would not tie his hands. On January 12, both houses approved the use of force, the Senate by a vote of 52 to 47, the House by a 250–183 vote.

The Gulf War

The January 15 deadline came and went with no Iraqi withdrawal from Kuwait. Throughout the crisis, Hussein appears to have believed that the US-led coalition arrayed against Iraq would, in the end, shrink from using force; or that, if it did attack, the Iraqi military would bloody it in ways that eroded its will to continue the campaign. What Hussein failed to appreciate were the technological and organizational sophistication of the US military and his own army's unwillingness to fight. On January 17, the United States and its coalition partners commenced massive air attacks against Iraqi positions in Kuwait and Iraq, striking military targets in both countries. The coalition also targeted Iraqi communications and transportation systems – bridges, roads, railways, telephone lines, radio stations – along with industrial targets. The aim was not just to destroy Iraq's fighting ability but to cripple its civilian infrastructure as well.

Even more than the Panama operation, the Gulf War's air campaign publicly showcased the Pentagon's dazzling new equipment: global positioning systems, stealth aircraft, heat-seeking missiles, laser-guided munitions, and other high-tech devices. General Schwarzkopf and fellow military officers often used video monitors in their news briefings, and the clips they played of "smart bombs" striking targets with pinpoint accuracy were genuinely impressive, especially to American audiences just a few years into the digital age. Even so, some of the military's claims proved to have been exaggerated. At the time, the US Army maintained that its Patriot surface-to-air missiles successfully intercepted a high percentage of the Soviet-designed but Iraqi-made Scud missiles that Iraq fired at Saudi Arabia and Israel, an assertion buttressed by dramatic footage of Scuds exploding in midflight. Only later was it revealed that the shoddily welded Iraqi missiles had often disintegrated on their own. Moreover, although smart bombs did, in general, enable US commanders to isolate military targets and minimize civilian casualties, precision targeting was only as good as the human intelligence behind it. In mid-February, the US Air Force bombed what it thought was a military facility in Baghdad. It turned out to be a public air raid shelter; over four hundred Iraqi civilians were killed, many of them burned alive.

Figure 11.4 Iraqi soldiers surrendering to coalition forces, February 1991. Source: Patrick Durand / Sygma / Getty Images.

Despite the ferocity of the air attacks, Iraq refused to withdraw from Kuwait. So on February 24 the coalition forces launched a ground campaign, sending tens of thousands of troops and thousands of tanks and armored vehicles into Kuwait and parts of Iraq. Although some Iraqi troops offered heavy resistance, thousands of others surrendered after little or no fighting, plainly uncommitted to the cause in which their government had conscripted them. Just four days into the ground operations, Bush announced the liberation of Kuwait. Somewhere between 25,000 and 50,000 Iraqi soldiers had been killed, with civilian deaths ranging from 2,500 to 4,000; many thousands more would shortly succumb to infectious diseases and malnutrition resulting from the destruction of Iraq's infrastructure. On the coalition side, fewer than four hundred died, all of them military personnel and nearly half of them killed in nonhostile incidents.

Americans wildly applauded the victory, and Bush's approval rating soared to 89 percent. The antiwar movement was discredited in many Americans' eyes. Its spokespeople had often downplayed moral arguments against going to war in favor of predicting a deadly quagmire for US troops, on the assumption that "body bag" appeals were more likely to reach the broad American public. Bush and his advisers had made a similar calculation. Fearing that public opinion would turn against the war if it dragged on too long and killed too many Americans, they had mustered overwhelming power to ensure a swift victory that cost relatively few US lives. In the glow of this achievement, Bush voiced confidence that his fellow citizens would be less gun-shy in the future. "By God," he exclaimed in a March 1 address to state legislators, "we've kicked the Vietnam syndrome once and for all."

In Iraq, however, the chaos continued. With the Baghdad regime now in disarray, two separate Iraqi rebellions, among Shia in the south and Kurds in the north, erupted. For some weeks, it seemed possible that one or both of those regions would break free of Hussein's control, but by early April his government had regrouped and mercilessly crushed the uprisings. Some Americans called on the Bush administration to rescue the rebels, but the administration declined, on the grounds that the UN mandate had been confined to liberating Kuwait and that an American intervention in Iraq itself would likely lead to grief. "[I]f we had gone in there," Defense Secretary Cheney remarked in 1992, "I would still have forces in Baghdad today. We'd be running the country. And … I don't think you could have done all of that without significant additional US casualties." Bush had been right, Cheney said, to avoid getting "bogged down in the problems of trying to take over and govern Iraq." A decade later, Vice President Cheney would have little time for such prudence.

As it happened, the Bush administration did intervene in parts of Iraq. The suppression of the two rebellions caused an acute humanitarian crisis, especially for the Kurds, a million and a half of whom became internal refugees or crossed into neighboring Turkey and Iran, suffering terrible material deprivation. In northern Iraq, the US military set up refugee camps for displaced Kurds. To keep Baghdad authorities from attacking Kurds with helicopters, it declared a "no-fly zone" in the north over which Iraqi military aircraft were forbidden to operate. Another no-fly zone, to prevent government attacks on Iraqi Shia, was later declared in the south. In the coming years, US and British aircraft would patrol both no-fly zones, occasionally skirmishing with Iraqi antiaircraft positions.

American naval vessels in the Persian Gulf would also remain active, policing Iraqi compliance with the UN economic sanctions, which continued after the war. It turned out that Iraq not only had acquired (and used) chemical weapons but had launched programs to develop biological and nuclear capabilities as well. Thus the UN Security Council refused to lift the sanctions until Iraq dismantled all its programs for weapons of mass destruction (WMDs). To prevent Iraq from importing items banned by the sanctions, the US Navy aggressively patrolled Gulf waters, inspecting and sometimes interdicting maritime cargoes headed for Iraqi ports.

After the war, the United States withdrew nearly all of the 500,000 troops it had deployed in the Gulf region. Yet several thousand remained stationed in Saudi Arabia, to signal US support for the kingdom and deter renewed Iraqi adventurism. The presence of non-Muslim soldiers on the soil of Saudi Arabia, which contains Islam's two holiest cities, Mecca and Medina, angered some ultraconservative Muslims. The Saudi government's hosting of the Americans, they charged, violated a saying attributed to the prophet Muhammad, "Let there be no two religions in Arabia." Among those most violently affronted was the former anti-Soviet warrior Osama bin Laden, who had returned home in triumph following Moscow's retreat from Afghanistan. Bin Laden's denunciations were so vociferous that in 1992 the Saudi government expelled the prosperous upstart. With a group of militant supporters forming an organization called al-Qa'ida (Arabic for "the Base"), bin Laden relocated to the northeast African nation of Sudan, his sights set on new foes.

Gorbachev and the Demise of the Soviet Union

As Washington grew ever bolder on the world stage, Moscow's authority dwindled at home. Gorbachev had enjoyed marked success in reforming the political system, but he was unable to arrest the economy's steep downward slide. "Perestroika had become radical enough to destroy the old command economy," writes the historian Hal Brands, "but not radical enough to force a decisive shift to a functioning market system." Soviet GNP in 1990 shrank by a shocking 12 percent. Shortages of consumer goods grew more frequent and acute, and the standard of living for ordinary Soviet citizens sharply declined. At the very time that people gained greater freedom to complain, they had more and more to complain about, and Gorbachev's popularity plummeted. Meanwhile, several Soviet republics, inspired by events in Eastern Europe, agitated for independence from the Soviet Union. Gorbachev was determined to keep the republics inside the union but agonized over how much force to use to oppose secessionism. If he used too little force, the republics would secede, precipitating the Soviet Union's disintegration. If he used too much, he would lose even more popular support and also alienate the Western nations, reviving the very cold war tensions he had worked so hard to end. So in 1990 and 1991 Gorbachev vacillated between a soft line and a hard line, which pleased no one and further diminished his domestic position.

Within the Soviet government, Gorbachev faced growing opposition from a group of hardliners who believed he was courting the union's demise. His chief liberal rival was Boris Yeltsin, a former member of the Soviet parliament who had left the Communist Party and in June 1991 was elected president of the Russian Republic. Yeltsin attacked Gorbachev's timidity in adopting market economics and in allowing greater autonomy in the republics.

Bush and his main advisers now trusted Gorbachev and very much wanted him to survive, but the old doubts about his political viability had returned. Consequently, although the Bush administration extended some economic assistance to the Soviet Union, it never aided it at the levels Gorbachev requested. Brent Scowcroft, Bush's national security adviser, warned against "schemes that simply pour money down a rathole." The administration was keener on reaching arms control agreements with Gorbachev while he remained in power. At a July 1991 summit in Moscow, the parties signed the Strategic Arms Reduction Treaty (START), which committed each side to deploying no more than 6,000 strategic warheads, roughly halving the two nations' strategic arsenals.

And then – a heart stopper. For three days in August 1991, the world anxiously watched as Soviet hardliners attempted to depose Gorbachev and establish martial law. But the coup leaders were both bungling and irresolute, and their bid for power almost immediately began to unravel. With Gorbachev under house arrest for the duration, Boris Yeltsin stepped forward to denounce the coup attempt and rally public support for the principle of constitutional government. After the Soviet military refused the coup plotters' orders to use deadly force against protesters, the plotters were forced to admit defeat. Throughout the frightening power struggle, whose stakes included control of a massive nuclear arsenal, Bush acted cautiously. He moderated his public criticism of the coup leaders in the early hours of the crisis but ratcheted it up as their failure grew increasingly likely. "Here was a clear example," the historian Jeffrey Engel observes, "of Bush's ability to succeed merely by avoiding doing the wrong thing."

In the aftermath of the abortive coup, Gorbachev acted as if he could resume his duties as usual, but the Soviet Union was now a completely different place. Yeltsin had won enormous prestige for resisting the attempted putsch, and he was the one calling the shots. As president of Russia, he issued decrees that directly challenged the Communist Party, declaring, for example, that the party was to blame for the coup attempt and suspending its activities inside Russia. The other Soviet republics banned or suspended the party in their jurisdictions, too. Seeing that the Communist Party was doomed, Gorbachev resigned as the party's general secretary and banned its activities within the Soviet government, while retaining his position as Soviet president.

In September 1991, desperately trying to keep the Soviet Union together, Gorbachev granted independence to the Baltic republics of Estonia, Latvia, and Lithuania, where secessionist sentiment ran especially high. He urged the remaining republics to reaffirm their membership in the Soviet Union via a new union treaty. Instead, several other republics followed the Baltic states' example and declared independence. In early December, Yeltsin met with the leaders of Ukraine and Belarus to establish a new political entity, the Commonwealth of Independent States. Two weeks later, eight other republics joined the commonwealth. In late December, recognizing that the Soviet Union had been effectively abolished, Gorbachev resigned as Soviet president and transferred control of the Soviet nuclear arsenal to Yeltsin. The upper chamber of the Supreme Soviet, the union's chief legislative body, then voted to dissolve both itself and the Soviet Union.

What Did It All Mean?

From about 1989 on, after it became clear that the cold war truly was coming to an end, American opinion leaders, intellectuals, and ordinary citizens debated the causes and meaning of this extraordinary transformation. Was it a triumph for the United States, as many politicians and pundits claimed? If so, who, or what, deserved credit for the achievement? Or were there other ways of understanding this epochal event? Among those arguing for a US victory, some gave Ronald Reagan high marks for placing overwhelming pressure on the Soviets to change their ways and responding favorably once they did so. Reagan, argued the historian John Lewis Gaddis in 1992, "combined militancy with a surprising degree of operational pragmatism and a shrewd sense of timing." Others agreed that the United States had prevailed but spread the credit more widely. Victory, wrote the journalist R. C. Longworth that same year, "belongs to generations of leaders, Republican and Democratic, who fought the Cold War with … bipartisan steadiness." For more than four decades, this argument went, successive US administrations had followed a calm but firm strategy of matching the Soviets' military expenditures and blocking their attempted expansion at key points across the globe. Washington also saw to it that the West was prosperous and democratic, in stark contrast with the dingy and repressive Soviet sphere. This containment policy frustrated and demoralized Soviet leaders and eventually forced them to look inward to address the contradictions at the heart of their system.

Still other commentators scoffed at the idea that the United States had won the cold war. The nation, they said, had spent hundreds of billions of dollars waging a global struggle that either had been wholly unnecessary or had become pointless many years earlier (say, in the wake of the 1962 Cuban missile crisis, or with the rise of détente in the early 1970s). Meanwhile, neglected domestic problems such as industrial decline, poverty, drug abuse, crime, AIDS, environmental degradation, and failing public schools had become almost unmanageable. The increasingly acute and visible crisis of urban homelessness appeared frequently in this line of argument. "[T]rust the evidence of your senses," the radical columnist Alexander Cockburn wrote in 1989. "Look at … the bodies bundled in niches on New York's streets and lodged amid the bushes under the Los Angeles freeways. This is victory?"

A final argument held that the end of the cold war had very little to do with the United States at all. As the columnist and former diplomat Leslie Gelb summed it up: "The Soviets lost the cold war because of the rot of the Communist system far more than we won it by the policy of containing Soviet power."

***

Whichever interpretation, or interpretations, proved most persuasive, one consequence of the cold war's demise was that the United States now enjoyed much greater freedom to exert its power abroad. The interventions in Panama and especially the Persian Gulf had made this plain even before the Soviet Union sank into oblivion. Although the geopolitical and military implications of the new reality did make their appearance over the ensuing decade, they would not fully unfold until the early years of the twenty-first century. In the interim, domestic pursuits pushed to the forefront of the nation's public life.

READING QUESTIONS

1. What varying motives drove the Reagan administration to embrace the Strategic Defense Initiative? Why did US officials see value in SDI apart from its technological feasibility?
2. What do the terms *perestroika* and *glasnost* mean, and how were those two concepts linked in the thinking of Soviet leader Mikhail Gorbachev?
3. How did the fact that the cold war was ending aid President George H. W. Bush's efforts to spearhead an international campaign to oust Iraqi forces from Kuwait?
4. The chapter closes by outlining a number of competing interpretations of the end of the cold war. Which of them do you find most persuasive, and why?

SUGGESTIONS FOR FURTHER READING

Brands, Hal. *Making the Unipolar Moment: US Foreign Policy and the Rise of the Post-Cold War Order*. Ithaca, NY: Cornell University Press, 2016.

Buckley, Kevin. *Panama: The Whole Story*. New York: Simon & Schuster, 1991.

Byrne, Malcolm. *Iran–Contra: Reagan's Scandal and the Unchecked Abuse of Presidential Power*. Lawrence, KS: University Press of Kansas, 2017.

Cannon, Lou. *President Reagan: The Role of a Lifetime*. New York: Public Affairs, 2000.

Crandall, Russell. *The Salvador Option: The United States in El Salvador, 1977–1992*. New York: Cambridge University Press, 2016.

Engels, Jeffrey. *When the World Seemed New: George H. W. Bush and the End of the Cold War*. New York: Houghton Mifflin, 2017.

Fischer, Beth. *The Reagan Reversal: Foreign Policy and the End of the Cold War*. Columbia, MO: University of Missouri Press, 1997.

Gordon, Michael R., and Bernard E. Trainor. *The Generals' War: The Inside Story of the Conflict in the Gulf*. Boston: Little, Brown, 1995.

LeoGrande, William. *Our Own Backyard: The United States in Central America, 1977–1992*. Chapel Hill, NC: University of North Carolina Press, 1998.

Maar, Henry Richard, III. *Freeze! The Grassroots Movement to Halt the Arms Race and End the Cold War*. Ithaca, NY: Cornell University Press, 2022.

Maynard, Christopher. *Out of the Shadow: George H. W. Bush and the End of the Cold War*. College Station, TX: Texas A & M University Press, 2008.

Meacham, Jon. *Destiny and Power: The American Odyssey of George Herbert Walker Bush*. New York: Random House, 2015.

Oberdorfer, Don. *From the Cold War to a New Era: The United States and the Soviet Union, 1983–1991*. Baltimore: Johns Hopkins University Press, 1998.

Rhodes, Richard. *Arsenals of Folly: The Making of the Nuclear Arms Race*. New York: Knopf, 2007.

Smith, Christian. *Resisting Reagan: The US Central America Peace Movement*. Chicago: University of Chicago Press, 1996.

Wilson, James Graham, *The Triumph of Improvisation: Gorbachev's Adaptability, Reagan's Engagement, and the End of the Cold War*. Ithaca, NY: Cornell University Press, 2014.

12 Triangulation

The Nineties and Bill Clinton

Introduction

On December 19, 1998, the House of Representatives impeached William Jefferson Clinton, making him only the second US president to suffer that fate. The House charged him with lying and witness tampering in legal proceedings involving his own illicit sexual activity. As House members deliberated over the president's conduct, US cruise missiles and bombers pounded Iraq, in retaliation for the Iraqi government's failure to account for weapons of mass destruction it allegedly possessed. The Republican House members driving the impeachment process generally supported the military action, but some bluntly accused the president of exploiting the foreign crisis to derail impeachment. It was all but assured that Clinton would not be removed from office. That would require a supermajority of two-thirds of the Senate, and the votes were not there. Nor was that likely to change, for Clinton's job approval rating had just climbed to 73 percent in public opinion polls. Yet the House Republicans pressed ahead, determined to record for posterity that the president's dissembling about his sexual behavior amounted to "high crimes and misdemeanors." The proceedings were at once grave and farcical – "[a] disaster movie scripted by the Marx Brothers," as Democratic Representative Barney Frank of Massachusetts observed.

Compounding the incongruity were the nation's robust fundamentals. The cold war was over, the Soviet Union had disappeared, and the US military enjoyed unprecedented freedom of action across the globe. The economy was booming, the federal budget was in balance, and numerous other economic and social indicators seemed headed in the right direction. Immediately following the impeachment vote, a *Washington Post* writer wondered if the event would be remembered as "a bizarre burst of unhappiness in a sea of prosperity, military strength, vanquished enemies, falling crime rates, rising employment and personal optimism." The projection was not far from the mark. To be sure, Americans in the 1990s experienced no shortage of turmoil, tragedy, misery, anxiety, and disappointment. But years later that decade, especially its second half, would stand out as a time of relative security, prosperity, expansion, and hope. Remarkably, most of those conditions took hold during a time of divided national government and in an atmosphere of poisonous partisanship – indeed, amid a chorus of public lamentation over Washington's dysfunction. But some global and domestic trends were too large and autonomous for the US government to alter. And, where they *could* make a difference, Democrats and Republicans often did cooperate productively, despite their sharp mutual antagonism. On occasion, their collaboration took the form of ignoring, or unwittingly exacerbating, problems that were not fully understood at the time but would emerge as acute crises in the new century.

The Culture Wars

In the very early 1990s, the outlook was rather less sunny than it became later in the decade. True, the cold war was ending on terms highly favorable to the United States, and Americans widely cheered the outcome of the Gulf War. But the nation's economy was in a slump, with unemployment topping 7 percent by late 1991 (and cresting at 7.8 percent in mid-1992). Less tangibly, many Americans were engaged in what commentators called the "culture wars," a set of simmering disputes over the nation's identity and values. What did it mean to be American? On what basis could outsiders be drawn into the fold? Into which new areas, if any, should the struggle for equality, dignity, and social acceptance be extended? Such questions had long stirred the public sphere, but they acquired a special salience at this moment, as Americans sought to come to terms with, or address the practical implications of, more basic transformations from the 1960s and 1970s. Although the culture wars were waged on a seemingly endless number of fronts, the most conspicuous disputes touched on ethnicity, race, and relations between the sexes.

When Congress passed the Immigration and Nationality Act of 1965, few expected the legislation to have far-reaching consequences. A quarter-century later, however, it was clear that the reform, by eliminating the quotas favoring European immigration, had made it much easier for people of all nationalities to come to the United States. The result was a markedly more diverse population. In 1950, nearly 90 percent of Americans had been of European origin. In 1990, that figure was under 84 percent, and it was projected to dip below 73 percent by 2050. (If one counted only non-Hispanic whites, the numbers were significantly lower: 73 percent in 1990 and under 53 percent projected for 2050.) Hispanics of all races, comprising 4.9 percent of the population in 1970, had grown to 9 percent in 1990 and were expected to exceed 24 percent by the middle of the next century. Asian/Pacific Islanders, just 3 percent of the population in 1990, were projected to account for 9 percent in 2050. African Americans comprised 12.3 percent in 1990 and were expected to increase to 15 percent by 2050. Significant to begin with, these changes were sometimes exaggerated in the public rhetoric of the early 1990s. It was not uncommon for polemicists to claim, whether anxiously or triumphantly, that whites were just a few decades away from outright minority status.

One product of these demographic transformations (whether they were accurately perceived or not) was a contentious debate over the merits and drawbacks of "multiculturalism."

Proponents of multiculturalism, generally on the left, extolled America's ethnic and racial diversity and looked askance at attempts to treat the Anglo-Protestant heritage as normative. Multiculturalists also tended to take a highly critical view of American history, stressing the complicity of the dominant Anglo culture in racism, genocide, dispossession, slavery, and oppression. Multiculturalism's critics, who were mostly conservative, warned that too much multiculturalism would obscure the original meaning of America and that disparaging the nation's past would inspire cynicism and self-doubt. Though not necessarily opposed to accepting new immigrants or celebrating ethnic diversity, the critics insisted that such inclusiveness occur within an overarching Americanism. Outsiders were welcome as long as they immigrated legally, learned English, and adopted traditional American customs; if they refused to do those things, their presence threatened national cohesion. Such an outlook bore little resemblance to the view of multiculturalists, who sympathized with uprooted foreigners desperate enough to break immigration laws and were open to the notion that American values themselves might change, along with the country's ethnic makeup.

In the first half of the 1990s, restrictionists stepped up their efforts to halt illegal immigration and ensure that legal immigration did not disrupt the dominant culture. Such measures included a spate of "English-only" campaigns, which sought to make English the official language of the nation or of individual states. In 1994, California's voters passed Proposition 187, which denied public services to illegal immigrants and required the state's police officers to help enforce federal immigration laws. The measure was obviously aimed at the hundreds of thousands of Mexicans and other Latin Americans residing in California without documentation. (Latino and civil liberties groups later succeeded, however, in defeating Proposition 187 in the federal courts.)

Black–white controversies in the early 1990s followed a more familiar pattern – with a new twist furnished by advances in media technology. In March 1991, Los Angeles police officers attempted to pull over a young Black man named Rodney King for speeding. After a lengthy chase, they forced his car to a stop. When King seemed to resist arrest, the cops relentlessly tased, clubbed, and kicked him, causing multiple bruises and lacerations and even some broken bones. An onlooker's video footage of the beating aired on television and caused a national outcry. For many African Americans, this was an all-too-common experience with law enforcement, finally captured on film for the rest of the country to see. Four white police officers went on trial for the assault, their conviction widely expected. In April 1992, however, the mostly white jury acquitted them, swayed by the defense lawyers' claims that the officers genuinely felt threatened by King. Immediately following the verdict, the largely African American South Central LA erupted in riots, which lasted six days and resulted in sixty-three deaths and over two thousand injuries. As so often in the past, the disturbances trained a harsh light on the persistent, and heavily racialized, poverty and oppression plaguing American cities.

In fact, the King beating and LA riots occurred at a time when Black urban sensibilities, art forms, and concerns were already receiving greater attention in white-dominated society. Spike Lee's 1989 independent film *Do the Right Thing*, which explored simmering

Figure 12.1 South Central Los Angeles in the aftermath of the 1992 riots. Source: Ted Soqui / Corbis Premium Historical / Getty Images.

tensions between residents of a Black neighborhood in Brooklyn, New York, and Italian American shopkeepers (and which culminated in a riot), was a critical and commercial success that sparked debate about racism and police violence. Several prominent record labels, along with the popular music television channel MTV, had recently signed contracts with rap musicians, exposing white suburban teenagers to a genre until then mostly confined to African American audiences. The breakout success of the television sketch comedy show *In Living Color* (1990–1994) further popularized rap and the broader hip-hop culture from which it emerged. Many commercial rap acts, like the duo DJ Jazzy Jeff & the Fresh Prince, were soft-edged and relatively "family-friendly." (One of the two, Will Smith, starred in a popular TV sitcom, *The Fresh Prince of Bel-Air* [1990–1996]; Jazzy Jeff played a supporting role.) But other rappers enjoying crossover success, such as Ice-T, Sister Souljah, and N.W.A. (Niggaz with Attitude), offered violent and profanity-laced depictions of drug use, gang warfare, and police brutality – at times shading over into exhortations to kill cops – that outraged conservative commentators. Some of this material featured misogynistic lyrics and images that liberals, including many African Americans, found offensive as well. Still, "gangsta rap" was but one part of a vast rap genre operating in countless registers and moods.

For feminists, the early 1990s were a tumultuous, frustrating, but ultimately productive time, as important legal concepts previously unfamiliar to most Americans surged to the forefront of public consciousness. In 1991, President George H. W. Bush nominated Clarence Thomas, a conservative African American appellate judge and former chair of the Equal Employment Opportunity Commission, to the Supreme Court. During the Senate

Figure 12.2 Anita Hill testifying before the Senate Judiciary Committee, October 1991. Source: *The Washington Post* / Getty Images.

confirmation hearing, a lawyer named Anita Hill claimed that Thomas had subjected her to crude sexual harassment while supervising her at the Department of Education and the EEOC, an accusation Thomas angrily denied. Hill's televised testimony before the Senate Judiciary Committee was graphic and searing, and feminists across the country, including several female members of the House of Representatives, rallied to her support. African Americans were divided. Once again, many believed, a Black man was facing wild accusations of sexual misconduct – "a high-tech lynching," as Thomas himself bitterly charged. But the fact that Hill, too, was Black complicated the picture. And many African Americans, like many Americans generally, found her believable. The Senate ultimately confirmed Thomas, but the spectacle made "sexual harassment" a household term, something feminist activists and legal scholars had labored to do, with limited success, since the mid-1970s.

Also in 1991, William Kennedy Smith, a nephew of President John F. Kennedy, was tried in Florida for raping a woman named Patricia Bowman. The two had met in a Palm Beach bar and then gone to the Kennedy family's nearby estate. They had a sexual encounter, which Smith claimed was consensual and Bowman insisted was not. Like the Thomas-Hill hearing, the Smith trial was nationally televised and drew millions of viewers. Smith was acquitted, but this event, too, brought widespread attention to a sexual offense – in this case acquaintance rape – that feminists had identified half a generation earlier but that, until now, had remained relatively obscure.

The 1992 Presidential Election

Amid these and other smoldering controversies, the 1992 presidential contest got under way. Coasting on his Gulf War triumph, in the spring and summer of 1991 President Bush seemed a shoo-in for reelection. Several top-tier Democrats, including House Majority Leader Richard Gephardt and New York Governor Mario Cuomo, opted not to seek their party's nomination, leaving the field to lesser-known figures. Among them was Arkansas Governor Bill Clinton, still in his mid-forties. Despite early stumbles on account of embarrassing revelations from his past (more on those below), Clinton trounced his primary election rivals, former Massachusetts Senator Paul Tsongas and former California Governor Jerry Brown.

By the time Clinton received the Democratic nomination in July 1992, Bush's poll numbers had plunged, a consequence of the economic downturn, for which the president seemed to have few solutions. (Appearances were deceiving, however, for Bush had already taken beneficial, though politically damaging, action on the economy. In 1990, he agreed with congressional Democrats to raise federal taxes, despite his signature 1988 campaign pledge, "Read my lips: no new taxes." The move outraged conservative Republicans and allowed Democrats to paint Bush as a hypocrite. But it also imposed some control over the massive budget deficit, laying a basis for renewed fiscal health later in the decade.) Meanwhile, a fabulously wealthy, and erratic, Texas businessman named H. Ross Perot was mounting a surprisingly effective third-party candidacy. Lacking clear ideological leanings, Perot presented himself as an apolitical problem solver who would break the gridlock in Washington and restore sanity to government, especially by shrinking the deficit. Perot drew support from Republicans and Democrats alike, but from midsummer till Election Day Clinton held a consistent lead over both rivals. In November he was elected with 43 percent of the vote. Bush received a little over 37 percent and Perot 19 percent, the strongest showing by a third-party presidential candidate in eighty years. Democrats retained control of both congressional houses.

A politician of surpassing skill – albeit one whose smoothness sometimes got the better of him – Clinton was the first US president of the sixties generation. Though never a flaming radical, he had partaken of some of the countercultural expressions of the era. He smoked marijuana (though he later insisted he didn't inhale), wore long hair and a beard, and protested the Vietnam War. He attended law school at Yale University, where he met his future wife, Hillary Rodham, and he worked as an organizer for George McGovern's failed 1972 presidential campaign. He returned to Arkansas and in 1974 ran unsuccessfully for congress. In 1976 was he was elected Arkansas attorney general. Two years later, at age thirty-two, he became the state's second-youngest governor. Turned out of office in 1980, he won back the governorship in 1982 and held on to it until elected president a decade later.

To be electable in Arkansas, Clinton was obliged to shed much of his liberal baggage and remake himself as a centrist "New Democrat" – friendly to business, in favor of the death penalty, hawkish on foreign policy, and respectful of white evangelicals. In the 1980s, he was a leading figure in the Democratic Leadership Council (DLC), a group of centrist and conservative Democrats who hoped to move their party away from the liberal positions it

Figure 12.3 Hillary and Bill Clinton, 1992. Source: Andrew Lichtenstein / Corbis Historical / Getty Images.

had espoused since the early 1970s. Clinton and the DLC warned that the Democratic Party would keep losing national elections as long as voters considered it beholden to labor unions, peace activists, racial minorities, feminists, environmentalists, and other "special interests."

Early in the 1992 primary election season, two issues from Clinton's past nearly ended his campaign. Evidence surfaced that, in 1969, twenty-three-year-old Clinton had gamed the system to avoid military service in Vietnam. Thousands of other young men in that era had found legal ways of escaping the draft, but Clinton's efforts were more sophisticated – and so, to many, more calculated and cynical – than usual. The other issue was marital infidelity. A lounge singer and former Arkansas state employee named Gennifer Flowers claimed that she had had a twelve-year affair with Clinton. She produced tape recordings of her telephone conversations with the governor that suggested, at the very least, an intimate friendship. Clinton artfully finessed these crises. He portrayed his Vietnam-era actions as the struggles of an idealistic yet conflicted young man, and he confessed to "causing pain in my marriage" while insisting, with Hillary Clinton's emphatic agreement, that the couple had worked through their difficulties and come out stronger on the other side.

From the moment he appeared on the national scene, Clinton came under harsh attack from Republicans, who portrayed him as a doctrinaire liberal. In conventional political terms, the characterization made little sense. As a New Democrat, Clinton was trying to move his party rightward on key issues (while loyally affirming some stances, such as support for abortion rights, that were now bedrock positions within the party). So how to explain Republicans' antipathy? Partly, it reflected the intensification of partisan sentiment within the GOP over the dozen years since a Democrat had last occupied the White House. Partly, it reflected the *cultural* nature of Clinton's political identity. Clinton had drifted away from, but not repudiated, his hippie-like persona of the late 1960s. Moreover, he was married to a feminist careerwoman whose public statements sometimes rankled more traditionally minded Americans. When aspects of her legal career came under scrutiny during the campaign, Hillary Clinton sarcastically remarked to reporters, "I suppose I could have stayed home, baked cookies, and had teas, but what I decided to do was fulfill my profession." The comment offended many women who were fulltime homemakers. Finally, the very fact that Bill Clinton was stealing the Republicans' clothes – that he was coopting some conservative positions and thereby luring voters away from the GOP column – was a novel, and maddening, challenge to Republicans.

Clinton in the White House

Clinton had promised a dramatic departure from the Reagan/Bush era, and in some areas he was able to deliver. Very early in his presidency, he issued an executive order rescinding a Reagan-era policy forbidding employees of federally funded family planning clinics to counsel abortion. He also signed the Family and Medical Leave Act, which Bush had vetoed a few months earlier. The legislation required employers of a certain size to grant employees unpaid time off from work to attend to health or family needs. Feminists had long pushed for more flexible leave policies, as the lack of such flexibility disproportionately burdened female employees. Both by signing the bill and by lifting the abortion "gag order," Clinton handed early victories to this constituency.

Other progressive goals proved more elusive. During the campaign, Clinton had promised to end the policy of barring gays and lesbians from serving openly in the military. When he tried to fulfill that pledge as president, however, he faced united opposition from the top military commanders and key congressional leaders of both parties, all of whom argued that lifting the ban would erode morale and discipline within the armed forces. Given his personal history with the draft, Clinton was poorly positioned to force the issue. Nor did it help that his main opponent in the controversy was the chairman of the Joint Chiefs of Staff, Colin Powell, who stayed in his post for most of 1993. As the highest-ranking African American, and as one of the most widely admired figures in American public life, Powell could powerfully counter any suggestion that homophobia was comparable to racism. If Clinton tried to end the ban via executive order, Congress, supported by Powell and the Joint Chiefs, would likely pass veto-proof legislation to reinstate the ban. Antigay restrictions could become even more deeply entrenched.

Clinton and the military eventually compromised. In a policy informally known as "Don't ask, don't tell," gays and lesbians could serve as long as they did not publicize their sexual orientation. The military would not inquire about enlistees' status but retained the right to expel members for any homosexual activity it discovered. Gay rights advocates cried betrayal, but this was as far as the military would bend.

On some issues, Clinton showed his "New Democrat" colors by continuing Republican policies. A case in point was the North American Free Trade Agreement (NAFTA), which Bush had signed with the leaders of Canada and Mexico in December 1992, to establish a mostly tariff-free trading zone among the three nations. The agreement still required congressional approval when Clinton took office. American labor unions and some environmental groups vigorously opposed NAFTA, the former warning of a loss of American manufacturing jobs to low-wage Mexico, the latter arguing that Mexico's lax environmental regulations would tempt American corporations to build high-polluting factories south of the border, befouling Mexico and parts of the United States. But the Clinton administration strongly supported NAFTA. It insisted that the greater prosperity resulting from free trade would be a net gain for American workers, and that NAFTA would pull Mexico up toward American labor and environmental standards, rather than the reverse. In November 1993, Congress approved NAFTA with more Republican than Democratic votes. (The debate over NAFTA's merits would continue in the years to come. The agreement's consequences were sufficiently complex that both its advocates and its opponents could claim vindication.)

"The economy, stupid" had been an informal slogan of Clinton's 1992 campaign (though it would be slightly misremembered as "*It's* the economy, stupid"). The candidate had promised ambitious public investments and tax cuts for the middle class. Once in office, however, he had to face the reality that a middle-class tax cut would deprive the government of revenue and enlarge an already bloated budget deficit. So Clinton reluctantly dropped that feature from his economic program, which now consisted of a short-term economic stimulus package, some trimming of the federal bureaucracy, and significant tax increases for corporations and the wealthy. Despite the bows to fiscal conservatism, the Republicans fiercely opposed Clinton's plan. In April 1993, Senate Republicans killed the stimulus package via a filibuster, and in August they almost defeated the president's first budget, which contained the tax hikes. The White House just barely got the budget through Congress – by a two-vote margin in the House and a fifty-fifty tie in the Senate, which Vice President Al Gore broke in favor of passage. In the coming years, the tax increases (building on the foundation laid by Bush and congressional Democrats in 1990) would go a long way toward improving the nation's fiscal health and thus toward bolstering Clinton's popularity. In 1993, however, the budget's near-death on Capitol Hill created a vivid impression of presidential weakness, especially after Clinton's previous compromises and defeats.

On crime policy, it was the reverse pattern: a legislative success at the time, remembered far less fondly years later. In the summer of 1994, partly at Clinton's behest, Congress passed the massive, multi-section Violent Crime Control and Law Enforcement Act. Some of the act's provisions advanced conciliatory approaches to combating crime, such as "community policing" measures (to improve relations between crime-ridden neighborhoods and the cops who patrolled them) and "midnight basketball" programs (to offer inner-city youths constructive alternatives to drug use and crime). But the act's most consequential features were punitive: more federal dollars for coercive police methods, the denial of federal grants to felons, an expanded federal death penalty, and stricter sentences for federal crimes, especially drug-related offenses. These changes rippled out beyond the federal system, encouraging legislators, prosecutors, and judges in state and local jurisdictions to impose stiffer penalties. Emblematic of the new outlook, at both the federal and the state levels, was the proliferation of "three strikes" laws, which mandated life sentences for defendants convicted of three offenses, if at least one of them had been a violent felony. All too often, judges were required to mete out that crushing penalty to defendants they otherwise would have sentenced far more leniently.

The 1994 crime act and its emanations would impose heavy costs on African American and other minority communities. People of color were already disproportionately enmeshed in the criminal justice system, and some of the new laws were sociologically biased. For example, crack cocaine, which was more prevalent among inner-city Blacks, carried harsher penalties than powder cocaine, a favored drug among middle-class and affluent whites. The cumulative effect was to accelerate an ongoing expansion of the US prison population. Some 315,000 Americans had been incarcerated in 1980; about a million were in 1994; that figure reached 2.3 million in 2008 and slightly declined thereafter. In the 1990s and 2000s, African Americans accounted for about 45 percent of the nation's prisoners, despite constituting just over 12 percent of the population. Millions of other Black citizens were on probation or parole.

After peaking in 1993, rates of violent crime in the United States would dramatically decline over the next quarter-century. Although social scientists attributed some of this change to punitive law enforcement, they also cited the aging of the population, the revitalization of urban areas previously abandoned as slums, and some of the "soft" anticrime measures, such as community policing and after-hours recreational programs, that had emerged alongside the "hard" approaches. By the late 2010s, some earlier proponents of the "tough on crime" stance were publicly reconsidering, and a bipartisan coalition in favor of sentencing reform was gaining influence in Congress (see Epilogue). But in the early to mid-1990s, when the scourge of violent crime seemed most oppressive, there was strong public support for more draconian measures, including among African Americans, who, after all, tended to bear the brunt of the crisis.

Clinton deftly illustrated that last point in a November 1993 address at the Mason Temple Church of God in Christ in Memphis, Tennessee, where Martin Luther King, Jr., had spoken the night before his assassination. Adopting the cadence of a southern preacher (white or Black), Clinton invited his African American audience to imagine how King would react to the spiking crime rates in Black communities in the years since his death. "[W]hat would he say?" the president asked. "He would say, 'I fought to stop white people from being so filled with hate that they would wreak violence on black people. I did not fight for the right of black people to murder other black people with reckless abandon.'" Uttered by any other white politician then on the national stage, such a statement would have seemed wildly presumptuous. Coming from Clinton, it sounded authentic. Throughout his address, which contained several other passages in that vein, audience members nodded in somber agreement, called out in keen affirmation, and erupted in bouts of warm applause. It was a message of "tough love" many had heard, or delivered, at their own church services and community events.

To be sure, plenty of African Americans deplored the punitive thrust of Clinton's anti-crime policies. Such sentiment within the Congressional Black Caucus (CBC) briefly blocked passage of the 1994 crime bill. Ultimately, though, most CBC members supported the bill, fearing that any alternative would be much worse. Overall, the Black community was more divided on the issue than it would be in later years, a reality Clinton shrewdly exploited.

Clinton showed similar skill in navigating the politics of race-based affirmative action. When he took office, affirmative action programs faced mounting criticism, not just from conservative Republicans alleging "reverse discrimination" but also from centrist Democrats. Many of the latter argued that an alternative system of preferences, based on class rather than race, could win back blue-collar whites who had drifted away from the Democratic Party, while still benefiting the many racial minorities who were economically disadvantaged. Defenders of racial affirmative action forcefully resisted this challenge to a program they deemed essential to the pursuit of elementary justice. Clinton addressed the issue in a July 1995 speech at the National Archives. While insisting that race-conscious remedies remained vitally necessary, he acknowledged flaws in the design and execution of some programs. He promised that all federal affirmative action programs would contain no quotas, be available only to qualified individuals, and be "retired" once they had fulfilled their purpose. "Mend it, but don't end it" was his message on affirmative action. Meanwhile, in a nod to proponents of class-based remedies, Clinton pledged greater federal attention to depressed regions of the country where whites predominated. Although conservatives remained sharply critical of racial affirmative action, Clinton's nuanced presentation helped to quiet Democratic dissension over the issue.

The O. J. Simpson Trial

As the nation's body politic debated these racially inflected issues, the broader public was engrossed in a sensational legal drama in which race always was the subtext – and at key moments became the main text, too. In June 1994 in Los Angeles, the former football star Orenthal James ("O. J.") Simpson was arrested for the grisly stabbing deaths of his ex-wife Nicole Brown Simpson and her friend Ron Goldman. O. J. Simpson was African American; the two victims were white. The forensic and circumstantial evidence linking O. J. to the crimes was overwhelming, and the suspect had an incontrovertible record of battering, stalking, and threatening his ex-wife. But the LA police were sloppy in their handling of some of the physical evidence, and it turned out that the main police detective handling the case had a history of disparaging African Americans, a fact he had lied about under oath. In the ensuing murder trial, which transfixed the nation for several months, Simpson's high-powered defense team relentlessly bore down on these vulnerabilities in the prosecution's case, arguing that a racist system was trying to frame a Black defendant. In October 1995, the mostly African American jury acquitted Simpson of both murders.

If the verdict was startling, then so, too, were the public's reactions. Whereas whites generally greeted the result with shock and disgust, African Americans openly cheered it. Many Blacks flatly proclaimed Simpson's innocence; many others assumed his culpability while still seeing the police's behavior as lawless and oppressive. "They framed a guilty man," a Black barber in LA later concluded. Like a lightning bolt illuminating a landscape only dimly perceived beforehand, the verdict exposed a stark divide: between a white America blithely confident in the basic fairness of the criminal justice system, and a Black America taking a far more jaundiced view of it – an outlook grounded in authentic and bitter experience. The Simpson case was hardly the best illustration of the problem, but there could be no doubt about the system's failure to dispense equal justice, not in the past and not in the 1990s, either.

The broader public's demand for a different legal outcome received some outlet a year later, when the families of Nicole Brown Simpson and Ron Goldman filed wrongful death lawsuits against O. J. Simpson in civil court. Facing a lesser burden of proof, the plaintiffs prevailed, and O. J. was ordered to pay them $33.5 million. Like the murder trial, the civil trial received incessant media coverage, especially on television. When the verdict was announced in February 1997, the networks broadcast the event live on a split screen with Clinton's State of the Union Address, which was airing at the same time.

First-Term Stumbles

That Clinton would even be there in early 1997, addressing the Congress after a triumphant inauguration to a second term, was something few pundits would have bet on a couple of years earlier. Clinton had faltered badly during his first term, suffering a historic defeat that handed the initiative to his Republican adversaries and even threatened him with political oblivion.

A major source of his difficulties was health care policy, on which the new president had been determined to make his mark. By the early 1990s, health care costs were spiking and millions of Americans found it impossible to afford effective insurance. The need to address the crisis was a centerpiece of Clinton's presidential campaign. Once in office, Clinton appointed Hillary Clinton to lead a task force to develop a health care overhaul plan that could be presented to Congress. The First Lady was extremely well versed in the issue, and she approached the challenge with thoroughness and tenacity. But she also acted imperiously, holding secretive meetings and failing to grant congressional leaders a meaningful role in shaping the proposal prior to its submission to Capitol Hill. To the dismay of left-leaning Democrats, her task force rejected a "single-payer" system (whereby the national government uses tax revenues to insure everyone) in favor of an intricate public–private scheme known as "managed competition." Under that system, most Americans would purchase health coverage through regional cooperatives, which would contract with private insurers to provide plans that observed federally mandated quality standards and price ceilings. Employers would be required to help cover the costs of workers' plans.

Delivered to Capitol Hill, "Hillarycare" suffered a humiliating demise. Private interests attacked its provisions, with insurance companies blasting the cost control measures and business advocates decrying the employer mandate. Republicans condemned the plan as an attempted government takeover of health care. Democrats, whose unified support the Clintons had failed to enlist, were hopelessly divided. While some supported the proposal, others busied themselves crafting alternatives. The sheer complexity of the White House plan was a major vulnerability. Because few ordinary Americans understood how it would work, its backers struggled to rally popular support for it. Conservative opponents had a simpler message, hammered home in skillfully produced TV advertisements: you may not be crazy about your current insurance policy, but the Clintons' plan will make things much, much worse. Especially memorable were the "Harry and Louise" ads, a series of spots produced by the Health Insurance Association of America, featuring a white, middle-class, suburban married couple lamenting the inflexibility and stinginess of the White House plan. A March 1994 poll found that more Americans opposed than supported Hillarycare. A summer blitz by congressional Democratic leaders failed to rescue the program. In September, they pronounced it dead.

By now, the 1994 midterm elections were approaching, and the Democratic president was in sorry political shape. It wasn't just the health care debacle. The battle over the crime bill, while ultimately yielding a White House victory, had been strenuous and bitter, fraying Clinton's relations with the CBC. The economy was starting to revive, but few Americans felt it yet. And already the young administration was mired in alleged scandals. The most prominent of these was Whitewater, named for a patch of Arkansas real estate that the Clintons and some business partners had purchased back in the late 1970s, when Bill Clinton was state attorney general. The buyers lost money on the deal, but one of the Clintons' partners owned a savings and loan company that later ran afoul of federal banking laws; suspicions arose that some of the S&L's tainted funds had fueled Bill Clinton's 1984 gubernatorial campaign. In a further wrinkle, the S&L had hired the services of a Little Rock law firm where Hillary Clinton was a partner. It was never established that either Clinton acted improperly, but others involved in these dealings were convicted of lawbreaking.

Questions about Whitewater surfaced briefly during the 1992 campaign and returned with a vengeance several months into Clinton's presidency. Congressional Republicans naturally played up the controversy, and a startling tragedy aided their efforts. In July 1993, Deputy White House Counsel Vincent Foster was found shot to death in a Virginia park outside Washington; police ruled it a suicide. Foster had been a partner at Hillary's Arkansas law firm, and it soon emerged that, two days after his death, White House Counsel Bernard Nussbaum had removed Whitewater-related files from Foster's office. Nussbaum may have acted in good faith (if foolishly), but the revelation loosed a frenzy of speculation. Mainstream journalists wondered if Foster had become so fearful of being exposed for Whitewater malfeasance that he decided to end it all. On the right, there were dark accusations of foul play: clearly, the man knew too much and had to be silenced. Even some Republican congressmen echoed this talk.

In early 1994, President Clinton bowed to public pressure and agreed to the appointment of a special counsel to investigate Whitewater and other alleged wrongdoing by him and his wife. Robert Fiske, the moderate Republican entrusted with the task, toiled away for several months and seemed on the verge of clearing the First Couple. In August, however, the three-judge panel charged with overseeing the investigation decided that Fiske lacked sufficient independence (he had been appointed by Clinton's attorney general) and replaced him with former Solicitor General Kenneth Starr. Starr's reputation as a staunch conservative alarmed the Clintons, but they knew they couldn't object without being accused of obstructing justice – the charge that had felled Richard Nixon. Starr took up Fiske's investigations, clearly in no hurry to complete them anytime soon.

President Clinton's political difficulties were all the more daunting because they arose at a time of intensifying partisanship, especially from Republicans. A key driver of this evolution was House minority whip Newt Gingrich of Georgia, the second-ranking Republican in that body. Since joining Congress in 1979 at the age of thirty-five, Gingrich had challenged what he saw as a defeatist attitude among House Republicans, who he believed had grown too comfortable in their minority status. (Republicans had not controlled the House since 1955.) Over the ensuing decade, Gingrich staged a series of showy battles and stunts designed to demonstrate that his party had more to gain by confronting the Democratic majority than cooperating with it. Gingrich's combativeness perturbed some moderates and institutionalists within the House GOP, but it had growing appeal in the broader Republican caucus, which was already moving rightward on substance. The young firebrand started to gain a following. Although most of his antics were symbolic, Gingrich scored a stunning concrete victory in 1989, when his exposure of nest-feathering by the Democratic Speaker of the House, James Wright of Texas, prompted the latter to resign both his speakership and his seat. That same year, Gingrich was elected minority whip, a position from which he frequently opposed President Bush's efforts to cut deals with congressional Democrats, chief among them the 1990 agreement to raise taxes. Gingrich later insisted that such compromises had muddied the Republican message and had ensured Bush's defeat in the 1992 election.

Fortified in his hyperpartisanship, Gingrich set out to make life miserable for the new administration. He was at the forefront of the hostile politics that proved so damaging to Bill and Hillary Clinton, such as the savaging of the White House health care plan and the relentless probing into Whitewater. As the 1994 midterm elections loomed, Gingrich sensed a historic opportunity. Everyone expected the Republicans to pick up seats; the "outs" almost always do so in midterms, and by the summer of 1994 the "ins" were especially vulnerable, with their standard-bearer's poll numbers slumping into the low forties. But Gingrich saw something more tantalizing: a chance for House Republicans to shed their minority status and regain outright control of that chamber. The key was to nationalize the midterms: to persuade voters across the country to express their disappointment in Clinton by voting Republican in the congressional races. With the national GOP's encouragement – and employing a new digital technique – Republican candidates ran TV ads "morphing" photographs of their Democratic opponents into pictures of Clinton. Meanwhile, to standardize the party's message, Gingrich and his allies drew up a list of simple, appealing, poll-tested pledges for Republican candidates to run on. The ten items, which included calls for tax cuts, term limits, increased defense spending, and balanced budgets, were known collectively as the Contract with America. Liberals sneered about a contract *on* America, but the idea took hold among Republican congressional candidates, most of whom signed and ran on the Contract.

Many Republican candidates benefited from an eleventh issue, one not formally included in the Contract. As part of the 1994 crime bill, Congress had passed a ten-year ban on the civilian manufacture, sale, and possession of semiautomatic firearms often known as assault weapons. The legislation had been spurred by some recent mass shootings, most prominently a 1993 killing spree in San Francisco that left nine dead and six wounded. Incensed by the ban, the National Rifle Association (NRA) mobilized to unseat lawmakers who had supported it, a list consisting mostly of Democrats. So began a newly aggressive phase of the NRA's legislative lobbying, one that continued well into the next century.

On Election Day, nineteen of the twenty-four Democrats whom the NRA had prioritized for defeat lost their seats. It was part of a much larger bloodbath, in which Republicans won control of both congressional houses. Republicans had held the Senate as recently as 1987, but the victory ended a forty-year reign for House Democrats. Even Speaker of the House Thomas Foley, who had replaced Jim Wright in 1989, went down to defeat in his Washington state district. (He had been on the NRA hit list.) And now the man who had ousted Jim Wright from the speakership, and arguably helped do the same to Foley, was poised to take the office himself. House Minority Leader Robert Michel was leaving the House, clearing the way for his second-in-command. When the House reconvened in January 1995, the new Republican majority elected Newt Gingrich Speaker of the House.

Clinton was on the ropes. It was impossible to interpret the election results as anything but a wholesale repudiation of his leadership. Everyone, it seemed – reporters, pundits, members of both major parties – attributed the rout to his shortcomings. Worse still, people acted as if Clinton no longer mattered. His pleas to the contrary at an April 1995 press conference sounded almost pathetic: "The president is relevant . . . . The Constitution gives me relevance." True enough, but the fact that two of the three major TV networks declined to broadcast the press conference was not altogether encouraging.

A Post-Cold-War Foreign Policy

An unquestioned area of Clinton's constitutional relevance was foreign policy. This was a realm on which the partisan politics of the 1990s had comparatively little direct bearing. For a president who had gained office partly by disparaging his predecessor's overseas preoccupations, Clinton displayed remarkable military and diplomatic activism. While in the White House, he ordered military action in Somalia, Haiti, Bosnia, Kosovo, Iraq, Sudan, and Afghanistan. He became personally involved in peace negotiations over the Middle East and Northern Ireland, and in the diplomacy to expand the North Atlantic Treaty Organization and to prevent North Korea from acquiring nuclear weapons.

This was an ironic development, but hardly a mysterious one. Clinton was the first US president whose entire tenure in office occurred after the cold war had ended – that is, the first president to enjoy the full benefit of America's new status as the sole remaining superpower. He could intervene in foreign trouble spots without worrying about Soviet reactions, for the simple reason that the Soviet Union no longer existed. Arguably, Clinton was the first president *ever* who, throughout his administration, could take significant military action abroad untroubled by the prospect of interference by major powers. Moreover, Clinton served at a time of considerable humanitarian upheaval across the globe, some of it resulting from forces unleashed by the end of the cold war, some of it following separate historical trajectories. Whenever one of those crises became sufficiently destabilizing or glaring, Clinton faced powerful international or domestic pressure to address it, including by force. On a more optimistic plane, the cold war's demise created fresh opportunities for resolving some long-festering international disputes. Many foreign policy actors and observers, at home and abroad, believed the United States was uniquely positioned to lead such diplomatic efforts.

To be sure, there were still plenty of constraints on an activist US foreign policy: the fear of incurring American casualties; the threat of being drawn into a quagmire with no exit strategy; the potential loss of US prestige following a conspicuous international failure; the prospect of offending particular domestic constituencies or of losing overall public support. These concerns – or the confidence that they were manageable – strongly conditioned Clinton's willingness to act boldly overseas.

The tension between caution and self-assurance was especially evident in decisions for and against the use of armed force – choices repeatedly presenting themselves during Clinton's first term. Clinton inherited his first military intervention from his predecessor. In December 1992, George Bush, now a lame duck, sent US troops into Somalia, on the Horn of Africa. A civil war had engulfed that country, disrupting agricultural production and causing starvation in some areas. International relief organizations sent food to Somalia, but rival factions blocked food shipments into each other's territory, deepening the humanitarian crisis. Heartbreaking images of emaciated children were broadcast around the world, spurring demands for international action. The troops Bush dispatched operated as part of a United Nations task force, which undertook to secure supply routes so that food could reach starving people. The international action succeeded in easing the blockades and substantially reducing the starvation. President Clinton pledged to continue supporting the effort.

Over the course of 1993, however, the mission soured. With UN encouragement, the warring factions concluded a ceasefire, but one group, the Somali National Alliance (SNA), resisted the agreement's terms. When UN forces tried to disarm the SNA, it fought back. Clinton expanded the US contingent in Somalia and ordered it to pursue the SNA. In October 1993, a massive firefight in Mogadishu, Somalia's capital, resulted in the downing of two US helicopters and the death of eighteen US soldiers. The Americans killed hundreds of SNA fighters and Somali civilians. American television cameras filmed Somalis dragging the bodies of slain US servicemen through the streets. The carnage caused deep dismay in Congress and the US public, and within months Clinton had withdrawn the US troops, leaving it to the UN and the Somalis themselves to sort out that country's troubles.

But, if heedless interventionism had its drawbacks, an exaggerated reluctance to use force could impose an even higher price. In the spring of 1994, appalling violence erupted in the Central African nation of Rwanda, where two ethnic groups, the Hutus and the Tutsis, had long vied for power (their rivalry stoked by decades of European colonial domination, which formally ended in 1962). In April, Hutu hardliners seized the government and exhorted their followers to kill Tutsis and moderate Hutus en masse. Over the next three months, some 800,000 people were massacred, many hacked to death with machetes. Far from quelling the violence, the international community essentially fled the scene. With US support, the UN Security Council withdrew most of the peacekeepers already stationed in the country. Clinton never convened his national security team to discuss the crisis, and his State Department refused to utter the word "genocide," for fear of triggering a legal obligation to act. Recent difficulties elsewhere on the continent clearly contributed to the administration's inertia. "I would think, especially in the wake of Somalia," recalled Clinton's national security adviser Anthony Lake, "that there was no chance that the Congress would ever have authorized funds to send American troops into Rwanda." Such an intervention "was almost literally inconceivable." The killing subsided only when a rebel coalition, dominated by Tutsis but including some Hutus, overthrew the genocidal regime. At that point, the United States did send some logistical and humanitarian assistance to address the tragedy's aftermath.

Another reason for inaction in Rwanda was the fact that the Clinton administration was considering another intervention much closer to home. In 1991, Jean-Bertrand Aristide, Haiti's democratically elected president, had been ousted in a rightwing coup. The new regime imposed a reign of terror on that impoverished Caribbean nation, causing tens of thousands of Haitians to flee in makeshift boats, many attempting to land in Florida. Both the Bush and the Clinton administrations ordered the US Coast Guard to intercept the refugees and return them to Haiti. Each administration insisted that it was trying to dissuade Haitians from attempting life-threatening sea voyages and that, ultimately, the solution lay in a resolution of Haiti's political crisis. These claims probably masked a less noble motive: to prevent an unpopular influx of impoverished, dark-skinned migrants into electoral-vote-rich Florida.

Even so, President Clinton was serious about seeking a Haitian political solution, which he equated with Aristide's restoration to the presidency. Many African Americans, especially in the CBC, shared this view. Throughout 1993 and into 1994, the Clinton administration tried to dislodge the Haitian junta by means of economic sanctions, but the regime dug in. When threats of military intervention proved unavailing, Clinton set the real thing in motion: in September 1994, US naval forces and airborne paratroopers began closing in on Haiti. To forestall this imminent hostile invasion, the junta stepped down, allowing US troops peacefully to occupy the country and oversee Aristide's return to office. Though pleasing to the CBC, Clinton's military measures on behalf of the left-leaning Aristide found little support in the broader US public, and Republicans accused the president of deploying the armed forces for an unworthy cause. But Clinton believed he had ameliorated a crisis that, if left unattended, would have caused worse trouble down the road. He also took perverse satisfaction in defying popular opinion – and thus countering his public image as a poll-driven politician incapable of acting on principle. "Taking a lonely stand on a tough issue like Haiti," Clinton's communications director George Stephanopolous later wrote, "was the best way for Clinton to demonstrate presidential character."

All of the above crises, while immensely tragic for the peoples concerned, were fairly peripheral to US geopolitical interests as defined by the Washington foreign policy establishment. The political disintegration of the Balkans was a different matter, for it implicated America's closest European allies, as well as posing stark humanitarian dilemmas of its own. Yugoslavia had been a confederation of disparate ethnic groups: Serbs, Croats, Bosniaks (Bosnian Muslims), and others. For decades, the communist central government had suppressed ethnic nationalism in favor of promoting a broader Yugoslav identity. As the cold war ended, however, areas dominated by the different ethnicities proclaimed their independence, sparking political disputes that quickly descended into interethnic violence. The ensuing tragedy was multilayered and intricate, but its most lethal element was a series of aggressive wars waged by Slobodan Milošević, the Serbian president of the remnant Yugoslav federation (now consisting only of Serbia and Montenegro), to annex portions of the breakaway states that contained ethnic Serbs. Newly independent Bosnia suffered the worst of this campaign. With Milošević's support, Serb militants expelled Bosniaks and ethnic Croats from Serb enclaves in Bosnia. This "ethnic cleansing" often entailed brutal methods – murder, rape, looting, forced deportation – that revived memories of the Nazi era. (Milošević and his allies were hardly the sole perpetrators of such atrocities, but they engaged in them more systematically and extensively than other Balkan actors did.)

The Balkan wars began during Bush's presidency and raged on into the Clinton years. Initially, Clinton tried to limit US involvement, urging NATO's European members to take the lead in seeking a resolution. As the carve-up of Bosnia continued, however, Clinton grew more active. In 1994 and 1995, he ordered the US Air Force to participate in NATO airstrikes against Bosnian Serb positions.[1] These measures, combined with battlefield gains by a coalition of Bosniak–Croat militias, weakened the Bosnian Serbs and made them more amenable to compromise. In late 1995, Clinton invited Milošević and the presidents of Bosnia and Croatia to come to Dayton, Ohio, to work out a settlement. The Dayton Agreement established a federal system whereby 51 percent of Bosnia became a Bosniak–Croat federation and the remaining 49 percent a Bosnian Serb republic. Twenty thousand US troops were stationed in the country as part of a NATO peacekeeping force. Critics objected that the Dayton Agreement rewarded Serbian aggression, but it ended a vicious war that had killed some 100,000 people.

The Persian Gulf region was yet another arena of military intervention during Clinton's first term. As noted in the previous chapter, an extensive US military presence remained in the area following the Gulf War: American warplanes policed the no-fly zones over southern

[1] The Western powers did not fully involve the United Nations Security Council because Russia, a permanent Security Council member, opposed taking forceful action against Serbia, with which it was allied. NATO loosely justified its military actions on the basis of UN Security Council resolutions, passed in 1992 and 1993, that established a no-fly zone over Bosnia and authorized member states to enforce it.

and northern Iraq; US naval vessels patrolled Gulf waters to prevent Iraq from importing items banned by international sanctions. About five thousand US troops remained stationed in Saudi Arabia, and the US Air Force operated bases in the kingdom. In June 1993, Clinton authorized a cruise missile strike against an Iraqi intelligence facility in Baghdad, in retaliation for an alleged (and unsuccessful) Iraqi attempt to assassinate former President Bush during a visit to Kuwait two months earlier. In 1996, the CIA encouraged Iraqi officers to mount a coup against President Saddam Hussein, but forces loyal to Hussein thwarted the scheme.

Meanwhile, controversy raged over the international economic sanctions, which remained in effect despite the end of the Gulf War. The UN Security Council, mainly at US and British insistence, refused to lift the sanctions until Iraq demonstrated it no longer possessed weapons of mass destruction. In conjunction with the sanctions regime, UN weapons inspectors circulated through Iraq, identifying WMD-related facilities and compelling the Iraqi government to destroy them. In retrospect, it appears that virtually all of Iraq's WMD capabilities were thus eliminated in the 1990s. But because the inspectors were unable to certify that accomplishment, and because Saddam Hussein himself was evidently reluctant to publicize his forfeiture of the WMD deterrent (mainly for fear of emboldening Iran, Iraq's long-standing adversary), the UN sanctions continued. Officially, the sanctions barred Iraq from importing any items that could be put to military use. The UN Sanctions Committee interpreted this provision expansively, blocking all manner of items – computers, electronics, machines, chemicals – with conceivable military applications. The denial of such imports hampered the post-Gulf-War recovery of Iraq's economy and infrastructure, causing widespread malnutrition and outbreaks of preventable disease. By some estimates, hundreds of thousands of Iraqi children died as a result. This humanitarian calamity provoked outrage throughout the world, especially in Arab and Muslim countries. The US and British governments insisted that the Iraqi government was to blame: it had failed to come clean on WMDs and was preventing a humane allocation of resources within Iraq. True enough, critics countered, but shouldn't Washington and London have factored Baghdad's likely obstinacy into their sanctions strategy?

Clinton's other main Middle East endeavor was, at least outwardly, conciliatory rather than coercive. Yet it, too, failed to win many Arab or Muslim friends. During his first year in office, Clinton learned that Israel and its archenemy, the Palestine Liberation Organization, were secretly negotiating in Oslo, Norway. In September 1993, he hosted a ceremony on the White House lawn at which the Israeli prime minister, Yitzhak Rabin, and the PLO chairman, Yasser Arafat, unveiled an interim agreement: Israel would pull back its occupying forces from portions of the Gaza Strip and the West Bank, allowing Palestinians to exercise autonomy in those areas; the parties would negotiate over the rest of the occupied Palestinian territories. Talks did continue on this basis, with the Clinton administration, and sometimes Clinton personally, serving as chief mediator. Yet the "Oslo process" was fatally flawed. Even as they negotiated with the Palestinians, the Israelis kept expanding Jewish settlements in the West Bank and building up the infrastructure of the occupation – acts that violated international law. Increasingly, ordinary Palestinians saw Oslo as a subterfuge for Israel's creeping annexation of Palestinian land, a perception widely shared in Arab and Muslim opinion. Some Palestinian militants sought to derail the negotiations by staging deadly attacks on Israeli civilians, convincing many Israelis that Palestinians as a whole opposed coexistence. Massively disproportionate reprisals by Israeli forces bred still more Palestinian terrorism. The peace process limped along for the remainder of Clinton's presidency, finally collapsing under the weight of its contradictions in late 2000.

Clinton's Political Comeback

It was back home, however, that Clinton won for himself the privilege of incurring foreign policy setbacks in a second term. Over the two years following the 1994 midterm debacle, the president cannily resuscitated his political fortunes. Some of this simply came down to allowing his adversaries to overreach. Flush with victory, Gingrich and the congressional Republicans raced to enact their agenda, a key feature of which was moving toward a balanced budget. To achieve the necessary savings, the Republicans proposed budgets containing reduced spending on Medicare, an unpopular move with an electorate drawn to fiscal conservatism in theory but less enamored of it when middle-class entitlements were at stake. On those occasions, Clinton and the Democrats could pose as the protectors of that sacred program against the depredations of heartless Republicans.

A shocking terrorist attack also aided Clinton's comeback. In April 1995, a massive explosion tore through the federal building in Oklahoma City, killing 168 people, nineteen of them children. The perpetrator was a white, homegrown Gulf War veteran with links to rightwing militia groups. Clinton became consoler in chief, a role he performed with sensitivity and skill. He traveled to Oklahoma City to assure grieving community members that the nation stood with them, a Democratic president bringing solace to a mostly Republican state. Overtly, Clinton's rhetoric in the tragedy's aftermath stressed national healing and unity, but it was framed in ways that subtly served his partisan interests. Clinton claimed that the attack had arisen from a paranoid climate created by "loud and angry voices" that "spread hate" throughout the land. "It is time we all stood up and spoke against that kind of reckless speech and behavior." Clinton named no names, but he seemed to be referring to the vociferous radio commentators agitating the Republican Party's right flank – a supposition reinforced when Rush Limbaugh, the most prominent talk show host on conservative radio, indignantly accused the president of trying to silence him. Conservatives were on the defensive; Clinton occupied the responsible, grieving, compassionate center.

Yet Clinton's political revival also relied on the appropriation of some Republican issues. Shortly after the 1994 defeat, Clinton asked an outside political consultant named Dick Morris, who had worked with him on campaigns in Arkansas, to come to the White House to help the administration regain its footing. An adviser to Democrats and Republicans alike, Morris struck Clinton's liberal advisers as a shameless political mercenary; why on earth was the president listening to *him*? Morris promoted a strategy he called "triangulation": Clinton should position himself at a point roughly equidistant from, and above, congressional

Democrats and Republicans, embracing the most popular ideas from each side and discarding the unpopular ones. New Democrat that he was, Clinton was doing some of this already, but Morris proposed a more brazen version of the straddle. In the debate over affirmative action described above, he was among those urging Clinton to scrap race-based remedies altogether. Morris also wanted the president to join Republicans in dismantling parts of the social safety net. Clinton rejected the first recommendation but proved somewhat amenable to the second; on a range of other issues, he selectively adopted Morris's suggestions. In short, Clinton triangulated between his liberal advisers and the champion of triangulation.

Morris's influence was most evident when it came to issues that were symbolic or somewhat peripheral. In his January 1996 State of the Union address, Clinton dismayed liberals by proclaiming: "The era of big government is over." He went on to outline ways his administration was promoting stronger values among the young: encouraging public schools to require curfews and uniforms; combating the marketing of cigarettes to minors; calling for the installation of "V chips" in televisions to enable parents to screen out inappropriate content. Critics belittled these "small-bore" initiatives, but they polled favorably with the public and showed that Morris did have some political acumen.

Viewed another way, Clinton's verbal interment of "big government" was a magnanimous flourish in the aftermath of a key Democratic victory. Throughout 1995, the Republicans had pushed a multiyear deficit reduction plan entailing significant reductions in Medicare spending, a course Clinton abhorred. In November and December, they passed bills containing those cuts and dared the president to veto them, a move that would halt all nonessential government operations. On both occasions, Clinton surprised the Republicans by vetoing the legislation. The Republicans were even more surprised to find themselves receiving the lion's share of blame for the resulting government shutdowns. Democratic denunciations of "the Gingrich who stole Christmas" struck a chord with the public. Each time, the Republicans had to abandon their maximum position, and Clinton scored a big political win. Still, in the preceding budget negotiations, the president had been obliged to produce a deficit reduction plan of his own (albeit with smaller hits to Medicare), an outcome for which Republicans could take some credit. Together, the parties were addressing the fiscal crisis.

During the shutdowns, when many paid White House staffers were barred from working, unpaid interns normally assigned to the nearby Executive Office Building came to the West Wing to answer phones. One of them was a twenty-two-year-old Californian named Monica Lewinsky. She and the president struck up a flirtation that quickly became intimate. In late 1995 and early 1996, they arranged several secret trysts in rooms adjoining the Oval Office. They engaged in oral sex but did not have intercourse, a distinction Clinton was later at pains to underscore. In April 1996, a suspicious White House deputy had Lewinsky transferred to a paid staff position at the Pentagon, ending the secret meetings until the spring of 1997, when they briefly resumed. In May, Clinton broke off the intimate relationship.

Clinton's behavior with Lewinsky was extraordinarily reckless, in striking contrast with his cautious, calculated politicking to win a second term. In the summer of 1996, Clinton performed his most consequential act of Morris-style triangulation, when he signed legislation ending welfare as a federal entitlement. Washington instead would provide block grants to the states, which would place welfare recipients on temporary assistance and facilitate their entry into the workforce. Under the new system, a person could receive no more than five years of assistance over a lifetime, though individual states could, and many did, impose briefer limits. In negotiations with congressional Republicans, Clinton had urged that the termination of the federal entitlement be accompanied by generous national investments in job training and child care, to enable welfare recipients to get and keep decent jobs. But the Republicans rejected this proposal in favor of the measlier block grants, which the states could use largely as they pleased. Against fierce opposition from most of his liberal advisers, some of whom quit in protest, Clinton signed the Personal Responsibility and Work Opportunity Act into law. The legislation was popular, and the 1996 election was rapidly approaching. Back in 1992, Clinton had pledged to "end welfare as we know it," arguing that the existing system harmed the poor by instilling in them crippling habits of dependence. He could now return to the electorate having kept an ambitious promise.

If the purpose of the 1996 reform was simply to remove people from the welfare rolls, the measure resoundingly succeeded. When it passed in 1996, about three-quarters of poor families were on federal public assistance. Two decades later, just 23 percent were receiving such aid, now administered by the states. If the goal was to lift people out of poverty, however, then the record was more discouraging. In 1996, 13.7 percent of the US population officially lived in poverty; in 2016, that figure was 12.7 percent. (The poverty rate varied more widely in the intervening years, reaching a high of over 15 percent and a low of slightly over 11 percent.) Only a handful of states used their block grants to develop robust programs to help people transition from welfare to work. Although some welfare recipients did move into paid employment, many others remained jobless and poor, relying on family, private charity, or nonfederal public assistance.

By the fall of 1996, Clinton's reelection was a virtual certainty. The economic recovery was now clear to all. The unemployment rate had fallen to 5.2 percent, the stock market was surging, and the budget was moving toward balance. Clinton's rhetoric of community, personal responsibility, moderation, technological innovation, and harmonious multiculturalism appealed to much of the electorate. The Republican nominee, seventy-three-year-old Robert Dole, until very recently the Senate majority leader, was a respected Washington insider with a sardonic wit and a record of heroism in World War II. But he seemed behind the times, and he struggled to find suitable ground from which to attack the president. Ross Perot had launched another third-party bid but was far less formidable than in 1992. On Election Day, Clinton decisively prevailed with 49.2 percent of the vote; Dole received 40.7 percent and Perot just 8.4 percent. Republicans kept control of Congress.

The fates seemed to smile on Clinton, and on the nation generally, as he began his second term in January 1997. His job approval rating exceeded 60 percent, and the economy was doing even better than in the fall. A major impetus for the boom was the explosion of the "dot.com" sector. Back in the 1960s, computer scientists at American universities and military research labs had begun to establish remote linkages with one another. These networking technologies became commercially available in the late 1980s and started proliferating rapidly with the development of powerful search engines in the early 1990s. In 1994, an estimated three million people worldwide were connected to the internet. By 1997, that figure approached seventy million. What at the start of the decade had been a curiosity at the margins of everyday American life – the province of computer programmers and other hi-tech geeks – was by the second half of the 1990s a basic tool of commerce, as Amazon.com and other online vendors empowered consumers to order books, compact disks, and other consumer items with a few keystrokes on a computer. Companies such as TravelWeb and Travelocity were transforming the ways in which Americans purchased airfare. By 1996, Congress was already trying, vainly, to regulate online pornography. Internet startups were springing up everywhere, creating jobs and investment opportunities unimagined at the start of the decade.

Politically, Clinton now enjoyed a bit of the honeymoon he never got in 1993. A temporarily mellowed Speaker Gingrich, joined by Senate Majority Leader Trent Lott, was negotiating productively with the president over the budget; there was no more talk of government shutdowns. Kenneth Starr, the independent counsel,[2] had so little to show for his years of investigation that in February 1997 he tried to quit that job to become dean of a law school in Southern California. A conservative outcry forced Starr to set aside those plans and stay on as independent counsel. Democrats rolled their eyes and settled in for another round of pointless snooping by Starr. Little did they know what he would soon find.

Clinton's Scandal

The Clinton impeachment imbroglio resulted, of course, from the discovery of specific sexual indiscretions. But it also can be understood in broader societal terms. The president's personal conduct became a national concern because it collided with two trends that had recently gathered force in American public life: the intensification of partisan rancor (especially Republicans' consuming disdain for Clinton); and efforts by feminists to place firmer limits on predatory male behavior.

As we saw, Anita Hill's 1991 accusations against Clarence Thomas had shone a national spotlight on the issue of sexual harassment. Efforts to address the problem were shortly under way in Congress. In 1994, as part of that year's omnibus crime bill, Congress passed the Violence Against Women Act (VAWA). One of VAWA's provisions required defendants in federal sexual misconduct lawsuits to provide information about any unwanted sexual contact they had had with people other than the plaintiffs. Such information would make it easier for plaintiffs to demonstrate a "pattern of misconduct" on the part of the accused. Clinton enthusiastically supported this provision, which, ironically, would later allow his enemies to make a public issue of his private behavior. Although VAWA specified *unwelcome* sexual advances, in practice it acquired a broader application. Realizing that

[2] Whereas Robert Fiske had held the title of special counsel, Kenneth Starr served as independent counsel. The change was pursuant to the 1994 Independent Counsel Reauthorization Act, which granted the position greater independence from the president.

defendants were likely to regard their own sexual activity as entirely consensual, judges took to requiring them to disclose all such activity, leaving it to the legal process to determine whether any of it formed a relevant "pattern of misconduct."

Also in 1994, a young woman named Paula Jones filed a sexual harassment suit against Clinton in an Arkansas federal court. Jones claimed that at a public function in a Little Rock hotel in 1991, when Clinton was governor and Jones a low-ranking state employee, Clinton summoned her to his hotel room, exposed himself, and asked her to perform oral sex on him, a request she refused. Clinton's lawyer argued that a sitting president could not be sued for a private matter of this sort. The issue eventually reached the US Supreme Court, which, in a May 1997 decision that many observers came to see as stunningly naïve, ruled that Jones's lawsuit would not unduly interfere with Clinton's public duties. "As for the case at hand," the unanimous opinion breezily observed, "it appears to us highly unlikely to occupy any substantial amount of [the president's] time." Events would soon make a mockery of that prediction.

Invoking their rights under VAWA, Jones's lawyers obtained permission from a federal district judge to interview Clinton about all of his extramarital sexual activities during his years in public life. By now, Jones's lawyers knew about Clinton's illicit encounters with Monica Lewinsky. Lewinsky had discussed the affair with Linda Tripp, a coworker at the Pentagon office to which Lewinsky had been transferred after her White House stint; Tripp, in turn, had tipped off Jones's lawyers. In their January 1998 deposition of the president, the lawyers asked Clinton if he had had sexual relations with Lewinsky. Clinton said he had not.

Jones's lawyers were also in contact with Starr's lawyers. Both legal teams consisted largely of conservative attorneys who fiercely opposed the president (and were being furtively egged on by a wider assemblage of rightwing lawyers, polemicists, funders, and activists). When Starr learned about Clinton's testimony to Jones's lawyers, he expanded his investigation to include the relationship with Lewinsky, on the ground that the president's lie constituted an obstruction of justice. Starr further suspected, but could never prove, that Clinton had urged Lewinsky, too, to lie under oath about their relationship. (In an affidavit submitted to Jones's lawyers, Lewinsky had denied the affair, but she later insisted that no one had coached her in that false testimony.)

Later that January, the public learned, through leaks, that Starr was investigating an alleged affair between Clinton and Lewinsky. For all the next year, the country was consumed by the controversy. Starr continued to probe the matter, interviewing witnesses and participants (eventually including Clinton and Lewinsky themselves) and preparing a report for Congress. The president continued to deny that he had had sexual relations with the intern. Hillary Clinton, ignorant of the truth, called the allegation the product of a "vast right-wing conspiracy." Commentators ridiculed the claim, but the first lady was not entirely wrong. For several years, a substantial (if not quite vast) network of conservative lawyers, politicians, activists, writers, and radio personalities had worked overtime to bring President Clinton down. His personal recklessness now handed them a golden opportunity.

Monicagate unfolded in a rapidly transforming media climate. It was the first major American scandal of the internet age. Indeed, the first public mention of the story occurred on "The Drudge Report," a right-leaning website specializing in political gossip. Just a couple of years earlier, two new national cable stations, the conservative Fox News and the then centrist MSNBC, had begun competing with the established Cable News Network (CNN) to provide around-the-clock television news coverage. Thus more and more reporters and commentators had both the incentive and the ability to fill the airwaves and nascent blogosphere with titillating reports, rumors, speculations, and predictions, not all of them well founded. "All Monica, all the time," media critics harrumphed about this latest degradation of the public square – while inescapably contributing to it.

Confronting al-Qa'ida

Throughout the frenzy, Clinton sought refuge in his official duties, especially foreign policy, which was further removed from the scandal than domestic affairs were – or so he assumed. Publicly ignoring the controversy, he forged ahead in pursuing peace settlements in Israel/Palestine and Northern Ireland, in keeping the pressure on Saddam Hussein, and in contending with the emergence of Osama bin Laden's al-Qa'ida network. Critics scoffed that Clinton was trying to distract the public from his embarrassing predicament. Some even joked that he might foment a war for that purpose. With eerie prescience, a satirical movie released some weeks before the scandal broke – *Wag the Dog*, produced and directed by Barry Levinson – posited a scenario strikingly similar to the one now transfixing the nation: a presidency imperiled by revelations of extramarital shenanigans in the Oval Office. The fictional president diverts attention from the scandal by enlisting Hollywood studio wizards to stage a simulated war against Albania. ("Why Albania?" asks a White House aide. "What have they done to us?" "What have they done *for* us?" the project's mastermind retorts.) In real life, the phrase "Wag the dog" became a winking reference to Clinton's own presumed eagerness to change the subject.

There is no evidence that Clinton ever treated foreign policy in this manner, and in at least one area he confronted a genuine, and gathering, threat to the nation. As we saw in Chapter 11, in the early 1990s Osama bin Laden and his al-Qa'ida followers had been expelled from Saudi Arabia, in retaliation for their agitation against the kingdom. They then set up camp in Sudan, guests of a simpatico Islamist government. From there, al-Qa'ida provided inspiration and training to a loose network of Islamist paramilitary groups, some of which staged terrorist attacks in the Middle East and elsewhere. Bin Laden's name began flashing on the radar screen of US intelligence. In 1996, bin Laden and his group returned to Afghanistan, where the Taliban, a fanatical Islamist party, were then taking power. Taliban rule was extraordinarily repressive, banning everything from soccer to kite-flying to music to television. Girls were forbidden to attend school; women were forced to cover every inch of their bodies, including their faces, in public; men were required to grow long beards.

The Taliban even outlawed paper bags, on the off chance they were made from recycled pages of the Koran. Although the Taliban leaders were more concerned with policing fellow Afghans than with combating foreign foes, they had no ideological objection to bin Laden's use of their country as a staging area for increasingly audacious attacks on his enemies abroad.

In the summer of 1996, soon after arriving in Afghanistan, bin Laden issued a call for *jihad* against the United States, which he accused of trespassing on the sacred soil of Islam, a reference to the continuing deployment of US troops in Saudi Arabia. In early 1998 he renewed the call, this time urging followers "to kill and fight Americans and their allies, whether civilians or military." Along with the US troop presence in Saudi Arabia, bin Laden cited Israel's mistreatment of Palestinians in the occupied territories and the humanitarian crisis resulting from international sanctions against Iraq. These were issues of deep concern to people throughout the Arab and Muslim worlds, including those of a more secular bent. Indeed, they moved people the world over. Clearly, bin Laden was seeking to broaden his appeal.

In retrospect, bin Laden's violent exhortations were chilling, and Clinton did take them seriously at the time. But the US news media were far more interested in the president's sex scandal, which erupted shortly before Laden issued his second call for *jihad*. It so happened, moreover, that Clinton's moment of military confrontation with al-Qa'ida occurred just as the scandal reached one of its crescendos, making "Wag the dog" speculation even harder to resist. On August 7, 1998, two suicide bombers, acting minutes apart, detonated massive explosions at the US embassies in Nairobi, Kenya, and Dar es Salaam, Tanzania, killing 224 people in total. Evidence quickly pointed to al-Qa'ida's culpability. Later that month, Clinton ordered the US Navy to launch cruise missiles against al-Qa'ida training camps in Afghanistan and against a pharmaceutical plant in Khartoum, Sudan, that US officials claimed was complicit in producing chemical weapons for al-Qa'ida.

Bin Laden was a personal target of the Afghanistan attack, but he and his top lieutenants escaped unharmed; al-Qa'ida's activities were scarcely disrupted. The attack on the Khartoum pharmaceutical plant was worse than ineffectual. The Sudanese government furiously denied Washington's CW accusation, convincingly portraying the demolition of the plant, the sole manufacturer of medicines in that impoverished nation, as cruelly destructive. The Clinton administration's failure to substantiate its claim fueled suspicions, at home and abroad, that other motives must have been at work. It escaped no one's notice that the cruise missile launches occurred just three days after Clinton finally admitted, in public, to having had an inappropriate relationship with Lewinsky, who had provided Starr with testimony and physical evidence (including, to Clinton's humiliation, a semen-stained dress) substantiating the affair. Maybe this really was a wild effort to distract. The angry protesters on the streets of Khartoum, waving signs reading "Wag the dog" and "No war for Monika," seemed to think so. The evidence suggests that US officials genuinely believed that the Khartoum plant was involved in producing CWs, but they were either unable or unwilling to furnish proof of the charge. Their mishandling of the matter undermined the broader case for taking the al-Qa'ida threat seriously.

Figure 12.4 Sudanese women protesting a US missile attack on a Sudanese pharmaceutical factory, 1998. Source: Maher Attar / Sygma / Getty Images.

Impeachment

Meanwhile, the machinery of scandal churned away. In September 1998, Starr submitted his report to the House of Representatives, recommending that it consider impeaching Clinton. The Starr Report, which the House immediately made public, was excruciatingly detailed. To refute the charge that he had lied to Jones's lawyers in denying a sexual relationship with Lewinsky, Clinton had posited an absurdly hairsplitting definition of sex. To refute Clinton's refutation, Starr now offered an exhaustive recitation of the president's sessions with the intern. Over the several days following its release, the report was the main subject of national conversation, as people everywhere recounted its salacious passages in tones of astonishment, disgust, amusement, or gleeful *schadenfreude*. Many pundits treated Clinton's resignation as inevitable. The report's contents were so graphic and tawdry, they said, that it would be impossible for Clinton to retain the dignity and respect necessary for credible governance. The Republican-controlled House began preparing for impeachment hearings.

The broader public saw things quite differently, however. Opinion polls showed that ordinary Americans felt sympathy for Clinton and anger at Starr and the House Republicans for making, quite literally, a federal case out of private philandering. Republicans maintained that the issue was perjury, not sex, but few in the public seemed to believe them. (During the controversy, some House Republicans were themselves revealed to have engaged in extramarital affairs, making Republicans all the more insistent that it really, really was not about sex.) In the 1998 midterm elections, the Democrats gained several House seats, shrinking the Republicans' majority; the balance in the Senate remained unchanged at fifty-five Republicans to forty-five Democrats. Given that the GOP had expected to make major gains that year, the results were widely interpreted as disastrous for the party – so disastrous that Gingrich was obliged to emulate Jim Wright, his former adversary, and relinquish both the speakership and his House seat. ("It would ill become me to gloat," Wright observed from retirement, but Gingrich "reminds me of an arsonist who sets fire to his building without stopping to realize the flames are going to consume his own apartment.")

Despite the rebuke from the electorate, the conservative Republicans who still dominated the House pressed ahead with impeachment, whether out of sincere abhorrence of Clinton's actions or to appease conservative constituents calling for his head. In December 1998, against the backdrop of US airstrikes in Iraq – another military spectacle inviting "Wag the dog" commentary and ridicule – the House impeached Clinton on two counts: perjury and obstruction of justice. The case proceeded to the Senate, where a two-thirds supermajority was necessary to convict the president and thereby remove him from office. It was virtually certain that no conviction would occur. Even if all fifty-five Republican Senators voted to convict, at least twelve Democrats would have to join them for either count to prevail. When the Senate voted in February 1999, the inverse occurred: all forty-five Senate Democrats voted to acquit on both counts, and varying numbers of Republicans peeled off to do the same. The final tallies were fifty-five to forty-five for conviction on perjury and fifty to fifty for conviction on obstruction of justice. Battered, shamed, yet grimly defiant, the president clung to power.

Throughout the scandal, Clinton received strong backing from mainstream feminists, a response that was both ironic and understandable. Feminists had to acknowledge that Clinton's legal troubles had started with a sexual harassment case – and also that there was something creepy about a middle-aged chief executive cavorting with an intern in her early twenties. But ultimately, they argued, Lewinsky was a consenting adult who eagerly sought a relationship with Clinton. "Welcome sexual behavior," the feminist leader Gloria Steinem wrote in a 1998 *New York Times* op/ed piece, "is about as relevant to sexual harassment as borrowing a car is to stealing one." Moreover, Steinem noted, Clinton staunchly supported abortion rights and thus was "vital … to preserving reproductive freedom." Feminists should unapologetically fight to keep such a leader in office.

The case of Paula Jones raised more troubling questions. If her accusation was truthful, then Clinton's conduct had bordered on sexual assault. The fact that Jones was now surrounding herself with conservative ideologues, however, made it easier for many feminists to question her veracity – even after Clinton agreed, in late 1998, to settle the case by paying

Jones $850,000. Another allegation from Clinton's past was far more disturbing. During the Lewinsky scandal, an Arkansas nursing home administrator named Juanita Broaddrick, a generation older than Jones and Lewinsky, charged that Clinton had raped her in 1978, an accusation Clinton denied through his lawyer. Adjudicating the claim twenty years later was no easy task. As recently as early 1998, Broaddrick herself had denied the rape allegation in a sworn affidavit, which she now recanted. These circumstances, combined with the fact that Broaddrick's case, too, had become a conservative *cause célèbre*, kept most feminists from crediting her story.

Years later, some feminist commentators would express regret that Jones and Broaddrick had not received fuller hearings at the time. Some also wished they had more forcefully challenged the relentless public shaming of Lewinsky, who was plunged into a deep and at times nearly suicidal depression, a grossly disproportionate penalty for such a youthful, and human, misstep. Indeed, the notion that Lewinsky had been fully consenting aroused considerable skepticism a couple of decades after the event. In 2018, in a warmly received article for *Vanity Fair*, Lewinsky herself wrote, "Now, at 44, I'm beginning (just beginning) to consider the implications of the power differentials that were so vast between a president and a White House intern." In light of such disparity, "the idea of consent might well be rendered moot."

Winding Down the Clinton Presidency

The impeachment crisis cast only a partial shadow over Clinton's remaining two years in office, and on many days its memory seemed absent from public awareness. The president's approval rating mostly stayed above 60 percent, buoyed by continuing prosperity. Clinton found he could still work with Republican lawmakers, especially on legislation that advanced their market-friendly preferences. In November 1999, he signed the Gramm–Leach–Bliley Act. Named for its three Republican cosponsors (Senator Phil Gramm of Texas, Representative James Leach of Iowa, and Representative Thomas J. Bliley of Virginia), the act repealed the 1933 Glass–Steagall Act, a New-Deal-era law that had prohibited commercial banks from engaging in speculative investment. Elements of Glass–Steagall had been chipped away at in recent years, but Gramm–Leach–Bliley completed that process, freeing banks to affiliate with investment firms and insurance companies and thereby enter speculative markets. Proponents of the new law argued that it would "modernize" the financial system, making American financial institutions more globally competitive and enabling customers to satisfy all of their banking and investment needs in one place. A decade later, however, after an implosion of the nation's financial institutions had sent the economy into a tailspin (see Chapter 13), critics would cite the 1999 law as one of a series of deregulatory measures, enacted in the eighties, nineties, and aughts by Republicans and Democrats alike, that made such a disaster more likely.

Clinton also continued to act boldly on the world stage. When the Balkans again erupted, he confidently waded into the crisis, practically daring pundits to suggest that impeachment had in any way impaired his legitimacy or effectiveness. Kosovo was an autonomous province of Serbia, populated mostly by Muslim ethnic Albanians. Slobodan Milošević's recent efforts to turn the province into a Serb-dominated area had provoked violent resistance from the Kosovo Liberation Army (KLA). The Serbian leader set out to crush the KLA. In March 1999, after Milošević rejected a NATO-imposed settlement, NATO forces launched a massive bombing campaign against Serb targets in Kosovo and in Serbia itself. To minimize their own casualties, the NATO countries relied solely on air power. Both indirectly and directly, the air attacks for a time exacerbated Kosovo's humanitarian crisis. Serbian forces accelerated their ethnic cleansing of the province, and NATO bombs unintentionally killed many Kosovar civilians (along with civilians in Serbia). In the United States, critics insisted that the war could not be won from the air; if Clinton was unwilling to deploy ground troops, he should abandon the effort altogether. In June 1999, however, Milošević agreed to withdraw his forces from Kosovo and permit the entry of NATO-led peacekeepers, enabling Clinton to claim victory. (The fact that he had acted on behalf of ethnic *Albanians*, moreover, was a nifty rebuke to the "Wag the dog" smart alecks.)

Clinton was less visibly forceful in confronting the continuing threat posed by al-Qa'ida. In December 1999, an Algerian man was arrested at the border between Canada and Washington state with materials for explosives in his car. It later emerged that he had received al-Qa'ida training in Afghanistan and planned to bomb Los Angeles International Airport. Off the coast of Yemen in October 2000, a boat packed with explosives rammed the warship USS *Cole*, blowing a massive hole in the ship and killing seventeen American sailors. Months after Clinton left office, bin Laden took credit for the attack. In both cases, US officials immediately suspected al-Qa'ida involvement, and the Clinton administration quietly stepped up its antiterrorism measures. It urged the Pakistani government to use its presumed influence with the Taliban to persuade them to expel bin Laden. American intelligence forged ties with the Northern Alliance, a coalition of anti-Taliban Afghan factions, which offered to assist in tracking bin Laden. Nothing valuable came of these measures.

The impeachment experience did hinder Clinton's efforts to keep the White House in Democratic hands. In the fall of 2000, Vice President Al Gore was the party's presidential nominee, opposing Texas Governor George W. Bush, son of the former president. Ordinarily, a vice president after the top job would embrace an incumbent president doing so well in the polls and overseeing such a strong economy. But Gore feared the taint of the Lewinsky scandal and kept Clinton at arm's length, limiting him to just a few campaign appearances. When he did speak, the silver-tongued president invariably made a much stronger case for Gore's election than the charisma-challenged nominee could himself, leaving observers to wonder what might have happened had Clinton's talents been fully deployed. As it was, Gore ran behind for most of the campaign.

The 2000 election was one of the closest in US history, and it took several weeks to settle the outcome. Although Gore won half a million more popular votes than Bush did, the electoral college result hinged on the fate of Florida, and that in turn came down to a margin of fewer than 600 ballots out of nearly six million cast in the state. Florida's secretary of state certified Bush as the winner of the state, but numerous irregularities came to light, and

Gore called for hand recounts in several counties. The Florida Supreme Court mandated a statewide recount, heartening the Gore forces. In mid-December, however, a divided US Supreme Court ordered a halt to the recount, effectively declaring Bush the next president. Democrats were outraged by what they saw as a nakedly partisan ruling by the court's conservative majority, but Gore graciously conceded defeat.

The congressional races left Republicans with a narrow majority in the House and produced a fifty-fifty split in the Senate, meaning that the incoming vice president, Richard Cheney, could break any tie in the Republicans' favor. Also noteworthy was the election of Hillary Clinton, who had gained considerable public sympathy on account of her husband's caddishness, to a Senate seat from her newly adopted state of New York.

The fundamentals remained strong as the Clintons made way for the White House's new occupants. True, a fresh controversy was raging over the outgoing president's cavalier use of the pardon power.[3] But unemployment had dipped below 4 percent, and the last three federal budgets had actually yielded surpluses. Still, some discordant notes were growing more audible, and others would shortly sound. The dot.com bubble that had formed in the mid-1990s burst in the year 2000, causing many internet ventures to fail. The impact on the broader economy was modest as yet, but the reversal pointed to a more basic feature of American economic behavior: a penchant for incautious investment that, unless contained by sturdy guardrails, could mean real trouble. The recent passage of the Gramm–Leach–Bliley Act, which discarded New-Deal-era financial regulations, was a case in point. Those regulations were more than six decades old and, according to experts of both parties, ill suited to a modern economy. Weren't financial institutions better off without all that red tape? The drawbacks to such thinking would become painfully evident several years into the next decade.

Other rumblings were closer, at least to those with relevant security clearances. As 2001 got under way, US intelligence officials kept picking up signs that al-Qa'ida operatives planned further attacks. Unfortunately, American foreign and domestic intelligence gathering was poorly coordinated, and the new administration was far less worried about bin Laden than its predecessor had been. The consequences of *that* complacency would soon rock the nation, and the world.

READING QUESTIONS

1. What basic issues or questions animated the "culture wars" of the early 1990s? Why, in your estimation, did such controversies surge to the fore at this historical moment?
2. How did President Clinton's domestic policies blend traditional Democratic stances with more conservative ideas?

[3] Shortly before leaving office, Clinton pardoned Marc Rich, a wealthy American businessman who had fled to Switzerland to avoid imprisonment for tax evasion, wire fraud, and other crimes. Rich's ex-wife was a major donor to Clinton's political campaigns. The pardon stirred a loud public outcry and led to congressional and Department of Justice inquiries, which found improprieties but no illegal behavior on Clinton's part.

3. Why, despite his concessions to conservatism, did Clinton elicit such intense Republican opposition? In what ways did he make himself more vulnerable to partisan challenges?
4. How did the scandal resulting in Clinton's impeachment reflect evolving attitudes about gender and sexuality?

SUGGESTIONS FOR FURTHER READING

Bergen, Peter L., *Holy War, Inc.: Inside the Secret World of Osama bin Laden*. New York: Free Press, 2001.

Berman, William. *From the Center to the Edge: The Politics and Policies of the Clinton Presidency*. Lanham, MD: Rowman & Littlefield, 2001.

Boys, James D. *Clinton's Grand Strategy: US Foreign Policy in a Post-Cold War World*. London: Bloomsbury, 2015.

Cannon, Lou. *Official Negligence: How Rodney King and the Riots Shaped Los Angeles and the LAPD*. New York: Random House, 1998.

Carter, Daryl. *Brother Bill: President Clinton and the Politics of Race and Class*. Fayetteville, AR: University of Arkansas Press, 2016.

Chafe, William H. *Bill and Hillary: The Politics of the Personal*. New York: Farrar, Straus and Giroux, 2012.

Coll, Steve. *Ghost Wars: The Secret History of the CIA, Afghanistan, and bin Laden, from the Soviet Invasion to September 10, 2011*. New York: Penguin Books, 2004.

Gitlin, Todd. *The Twilight of Common Dreams: Why America Is Wracked by Culture Wars*. New York: Henry Holt & Company, 1995.

Kornacki, Steve, *The Red and the Blue: The 1990s and the Birth of Political Tribalism*. New York: HarperCollins, 2019.

Stephanopoulos, George. *All Too Human: A Political Education*. Boston: Little, Brown, 1999.

Tomasky, Michael. *Bill Clinton*. New York: Henry Holt & Company, 2017.

Toobin, Jeffrey. *A Vast Conspiracy: The Real Story of the Sex Scandal that Nearly Brought Down a President*. New York: Random House, 2000

Wright, Lawrence. *The Looming Tower: Al-Qaeda and the Road to 9/11*. New York: Knopf, 2006.

13 Freedom Fries

George W. Bush, 9/11, and the Iraq War, 2001–2008

Introduction

In June 2004, President George W. Bush joined Senator John McCain of Arizona, a fellow Republican, in addressing 6,000 US soldiers rallying at Fort Lewis, a military base near Spokane, Washington. Officially, the president was there to honor those troops, many of whom had just returned from, or would soon be sent to, the ongoing conflict in Iraq. Yet Bush also had an eye on his bid for reelection the following November, and on the need to lock in the support of the unpredictable Senator McCain, who had unsuccessfully challenged Bush for the Republican nomination in 2000 and, more recently, toyed with joining the presidential ticket of Democratic Senator John Kerry of Massachusetts, Bush's expected opponent in the 2004 election. A US Navy veteran who had spent five and a half years as a prisoner of war in North Vietnam, McCain would surely appreciate the opportunity to share the stage with the president at a military event.

Addressing the troops, each leader offered a full-throated defense of Bush's decision to invade Iraq fifteen months earlier. Both insisted that the removal of the Iraqi dictator Saddam Hussein, now in US military custody, had struck a blow for US security and the cause of human freedom. Still, each man's remarks contained hints that the Iraqi venture was going less than swimmingly. "[Y]ou took the fight to Iraq with the tyrant Saddam," McCain told the assembled soldiers, "whether he possessed the terrible weapons that would've turned this war into a fight for survival or not" – an allusion to the failure of US authorities to find Iraq's weapons of mass destruction, whose proclaimed existence had been the main justification for war. Bush noted that some of the soldiers at Fort Lewis "are preparing to head out for a second tour" in Iraq, a consequence of the Department of Defense's recently implemented "stop-loss" program, which sought to address a shortage of available troops by requiring some of them to remain enlisted even after their initial tours of duty had ended. Thus both Bush and McCain obliquely acknowledged issues and critiques fueling the growing antiwar sentiment at home.

The rally completed, Bush proceeded to his next event, one that foregrounded the war's costs far more vividly and poignantly. For two and half hours, he met privately with the family members of twenty-eight slain soldiers. Such encounters were a frequent occurrence during his presidency but were little known to the public. While in office, Bush met with about 550 "families of the fallen." At Fort Lewis, most of the grieving relatives were cordial to the president, but a woman whose son had died in Iraq angrily lashed out. "You are as big a terrorist as Osama bin Laden," she said. "There wasn't much to say in response," Bush later recalled.

The US-led invasion of Iraq in March 2003, which Bush portrayed as an appropriate and necessary response to the devastating terrorist attacks of September 11, 2001, rightly stands as the most ill-considered act of his presidency. Launched on highly dubious grounds, it led to the deaths of thousands of Americans and tens of thousands of Iraqis, further destabilized an already volatile Middle East, and sharply eroded America's international standing. Though enjoying prominent Democratic support at the outset, the war intensified the partisan rancor that had suffused American politics at the start of the decade but had briefly abated in the aftermath of 9/11. Within the confines of this disastrous policy, Bush did display a certain dogged fortitude, never turning away from the tragic human consequences of his war (at least insofar as they afflicted fellow Americans) and never flagging in his efforts to stabilize the Middle Eastern nation he had thrown into chaos. Toward the end of his presidency, he landed on a military/political strategy that, at least partly, achieved the latter objective. But the shadow of Bush's colossal 2003 blunder would extend far beyond his own time in office.

A terrifying economic downturn during Bush's final months only strengthened the public impression of a failed presidency. Here, too, Bush managed to stanch the worst hemorrhaging, but he bequeathed another appalling crisis to his successor.

The George W. Bush Administration

The highly unusual circumstances of the 2000 presidential election – in which Bush emerged victorious despite narrowly losing the popular vote and only after the intervention of a conservative majority on the Supreme Court – shaped public expectations about his presidency. Many pundits agreed that, if Bush hoped for any governing success, he would need to tack to the political center and seek common ground with Democrats. Bush's people had other ideas. They privately circulated survey data showing that the American electorate was now polarized between two large, immovable blocs and that the percentage of voters open to shifting their allegiances from one major party to the other had sharply declined. Rather than chasing the rapidly vanishing "swing voter," Bush's political strategists advised, the president should govern in ways that shored up and motivated the Republican base. Such analysis was music to the ears of administration officials already inclined toward hardline conservatism, most notably Vice President Richard Cheney, whose soft-spoken manner and lack of personal ambition (he clearly had no interest in becoming president himself) concealed an iron determination to shift national policy rightward on most issues. Indeed, across the administration, the notion that Bush had failed to win a sufficient "mandate" for moving in bold new directions drew snorts of derision. Capture of the White House was mandate enough, especially with a congress under Republican control.

At first, the rightward trend was most pronounced in domestic affairs, as Bush reached back beyond the moderate conservatism of his own father's administration to revive, and in some cases exceed, hardline stances from the Reagan years. Soon after taking office, Bush proposed a \$1.6 trillion tax cut (trimmed to \$1.3 trillion when Congress passed it in June 2001) that lowered rates for people at all income levels but provided the greatest benefit to those in the top brackets. The tax cut also starved the government of revenue, quickly erasing the budget surplus left by Bill Clinton and the Republican-controlled congresses of the late 1990s. By Bush's second year in office, the federal government was running a deficit of \$157 billion, which significantly grew in subsequent years. In environmental policy, Bush rescinded the executive orders his predecessor had signed aimed at controlling arsenic levels in water supplies and restricting logging in Western forests. He pulled the United States out of the Kyoto Protocol, a 1997 international agreement to limit the proliferation of "greenhouse gases" such as carbon dioxide, methane, and nitrous oxide, which trap heat within the atmosphere and alter the earth's climate. As Reagan had done two decades earlier, Bush strove to dismantle the Environmental Protection Agency's regulatory functions. To fortify all of these policies against possible legal challenge, he seeded the federal judiciary with conservative judges.

A partial exception to the rule was Bush's education policy, which resisted simple ideological classification. Working with congressional Democrats, chief among them Senator Edward Kennedy of Massachusetts, Bush secured passage of the No Child Left Behind Act of 2001. The act strengthened federal support for "K through 12" (kindergarten to twelfth grade) public education, while requiring that school districts receiving federal aid induce their students to meet rigorous testing standards in core subjects such as math and English. No Child Left Behind reduced the power of teachers' unions, key players in Democratic politics, and antagonized those, generally on the left, who saw a preoccupation with test scores as bad pedagogy. At the same time, the reaffirmation of the federal government's role in education dismayed many conservatives, some of whom had long called for abolishing the Department of Education.

Education policy notwithstanding, the Bush administration's rightward march was sufficiently headlong that it provoked a small but consequential revolt within the Republican Party. In May 2001, Senator James Jeffords of Vermont, a moderate Republican, left the GOP to caucus with the Democrats, lamenting the administration's refusal to "go beyond the conservative Republican base." Heretofore, Senate Republicans had enjoyed an effective majority: a fifty-fifty tie that Vice President Cheney could break in their favor. Overnight, that advantage disappeared.

Bush's foreign policy in his first year displayed a distinct unilateralist bent, a desire to extricate the United States from encumbering obligations and tiresome negotiations. Bush withdrew from the Antiballistic Missile Treaty, concluded by the United States and the Soviet Union in 1972, so as to gain a freer hand to develop missile defense systems. He jettisoned a US initiative, pursued by President Clinton, to promote rapprochement between

South Korea and North Korea and persuade the latter not to acquire nuclear weapons. He abandoned Clinton's Israeli–Palestinian peace efforts (admittedly, already on life support), allowing Israel to do more or less as it pleased in the occupied territories. Yet Bush also showed he could be conciliatory when necessary. In March 2001, a US spy plane collided with a Chinese jet fighter over the South China Sea and made an emergency landing on Chinese soil; Beijing authorities detained the twenty-four crew members. The Chinese pilot did not survive the crash, and his government demanded an apology from Washington. To secure the release of the American crew, Bush authorized his ambassador in Beijing to issue a statement of regret over the loss of life. The Chinese government publicly characterized the statement as an apology, though US officials insisted it fell short of that. Hawkish Republicans, Cheney among them, believed that Bush had conceded too much, but the president prided himself on having defused a potentially explosive dispute.

During the presidential transition, outgoing Clinton officials warned their Bush counterparts of the danger posed by Osama bin Laden's al-Qa'ida network. Richard Clarke, the chief civil servant in the Bush White House charged with counterterrorism, who had held the same job under Clinton, loudly repeated these alarms as the new administration got under way. But Bush's people generally dismissed the al-Qa'ida threat. Fretting over a band of militants in the Afghan mountains was a Clintonian obsession; the new president and his team had more pressing national security concerns. Many high-ranking Bush administration officials, reflecting a view shared more broadly by hawkish members of the US foreign policy establishment, considered the Iraqi regime of Saddam Hussein a far bigger problem for the United States. Hussein's Iraq was a galling outlier, the only Arab country on the Persian Gulf that was hostile to the United States. Although it had taken a terrible beating in the Gulf War of 1991 and remained subject to stringent international economic sanctions, Baghdad continued to thumb its nose at the United States and its allies, employing various subterfuges to evade the sanctions and refusing to provide adequate assurances that it had abandoned its drive to acquire chemical, biological, or nuclear weapons.

Within the new Bush administration, the figure most nakedly determined to rid the world of Hussein's regime was Deputy Secretary of Defense Paul Wolfowitz. His boss, Secretary of Defense Donald Rumsfeld, and Vice President Cheney clearly sympathized with this position but espoused it more circumspectly during the early months of the administration. Taking a contrary view was Secretary of State Colin Powell, the former chairman of the Joint Chiefs of Staff who had engineered the 1991 victory against Iraq. Despite that résumé – actually, in keeping with it – Powell had little interest in the bellicose talk on Iraq. He realized there was a world of difference between pushing an aggressor nation back behind its borders and overthrowing an established regime in a conflict-ridden region. The former was the occasional duty of the sole remaining superpower, ideally in coalition with much of the international community; the latter, a likely prelude to a quagmire. More broadly, Powell was waging a losing internal battle against the Bush administration's rapid retreat from international obligations and diplomatic engagement. His efforts to thwart the Iraq hawks would fare no better.

Meanwhile, counterterrorism chief Dick Clarke was growing increasingly agitated about the Bush administration's blasé attitude toward al-Qa'ida. Sometimes, administration officials directly disputed the warnings, as when Wolfowitz told Clarke in an April 2001 meeting, "You give bin Laden too much credit," and changed the subject to Iraq. More often, officials acknowledged that Clarke had a point, without displaying the sense of urgency he thought necessary. It did not help Clarke's case that information was so sketchy. Over the spring and into summer, US intelligence picked up signs that al-Qa'ida was preparing a major attack in the United States. The CIA got word that the network's operatives had entered the country. The FBI learned that suspiciously behaving Middle Eastern men were enrolling in flight training programs in the United States. But coordination between the two agencies was poor, and analysts failed to assemble the scattered reports into a coherent narrative of an unfolding plot.

Since January, Clarke had urged the convening of a "Principals Committee" meeting, involving cabinet secretaries and agency directors, to address the al-Qa'ida threat; it finally took place on September 4, 2001. The principals discussed a diplomatic strategy to induce Afghanistan's Taliban government to stop providing sanctuary to al-Qa'ida, but there was no plan for funding or implementing the scheme. The meeting ended inconclusively.

The 9/11 Attacks and US Intervention in Afghanistan

One week later, nineteen al-Qa'ida operatives, all of them Arab men, boarded four American commercial airliners departing from East Coast cities for various domestic destinations. Armed with box cutters and knives, they overpowered the flight crews, killed the pilots, and took over the planes' controls. They flew two planes to New York City and, in kamikaze fashion, slammed each of them into one of the twin towers of the World Trade Center, among the tallest buildings in the world. They crashed the third plane into the Pentagon, the massive building outside Washington, DC, housing the US Department of Defense. The hijackers of the fourth plane also headed toward Washington, apparently intending to strike the White House or the Capitol building. Passengers on board, learning of the other collisions by cellphone, battled the hijackers for control of the plane, which crashed in a Pennsylvania field. In New York, as huge fires raged on the skyscrapers' upper floors, firefighters and police raced to evacuate the buildings. Well before they could be emptied, however, both towers collapsed, their steel girders buckling in the intense heat. All of this took place within the space of three hours. Nearly three thousand people were killed.

The attacks of 9/11 constituted the largest terrorist event to occur on American soil. The experience was unprecedented in its vividness and immediacy. Millions of television viewers, at home and around the world, saw the twin towers burn and crumble in real time. Before each building collapsed, they saw desperate people jump to their deaths from the upper floors. Some saw live footage of the second plane crashing into the South Tower, and everyone else saw video replays of that shocking moment broadcast repeatedly throughout

Figure 13.1 Pedestrians crossing the Brooklyn Bridge as the twin towers of the World Trade Center burn behind them, September 11, 2001. Source: Henry Ray Abrams / Stringer / AFP / Getty Images.

the day. (Footage of the first collision was much rarer. Because that event was completely unexpected, it was filmed only by accident by a tiny number of onlookers.) Recordings of bewildered, frantic, or valedictory cellphone messages, left by people trapped in burning buildings or on planes hurtling toward destruction, aired on TV and radio. In almost all previous large-scale terrorist attacks, the rawest and most horrifying moments had been shrouded from view, available to the public only as testimony by survivors and witnesses. This time, far less was left to the imagination.

In the days immediately following 9/11, a sense of togetherness defined the national mood. Americans generally set aside their political differences and concentrated on what united them: shock and grief over the staggering loss of life; admiration for the first responders who ran toward danger; appreciation of the courage, selflessness, and familial devotion shown by ordinary people caught up in the tragedy; gratitude for an "American way of life" that seemed to have come under foreign assault. Bush's approval rating shot up to 90 percent, and Democratic grumbling about his political illegitimacy briefly abated. CBS News anchor Dan Rather, to many conservatives a notorious exemplar of "liberal media bias," proclaimed that Bush "is my commander in chief. All he has to do is tell me where to line up and I'll do it." Of course, fury over the attacks was also a common reaction. From offstage came reports of violent hate crimes against Muslims or those mistaken for them (including an Indian-born Sikh murdered in Mesa, Arizona, apparently targeted because of his turban and beard). Most American opinion leaders forcefully condemned anti-Muslim scapegoating; such exhortations were often incorporated into the pageant of national unity. Bush himself set the tone by visiting the Islamic Center in Washington, DC, and publicly insisting that the September 11 attacks "violate the fundamental tenets of the Islamic faith." But the position of Muslims in America had, overnight, grown much more complicated and precarious.

For some hours after the attacks, Bush was thrown back on his heels, but he quickly regained his footing and mustered a response that conveyed confidence and resolve. He publicly identified al-Qa'ida as the culprit and vowed to spare no effort to eradicate it as a threat. The attacks of 9/11 "were more than acts of terror," Bush declared. "They were acts of war," and the United States would respond accordingly. Upon his request, Congress passed, with near-unanimity, a resolution authorizing the president to use "all necessary and appropriate force against those nations, organizations, or persons he determines planned, authorized, committed, or aided the terrorist attacks that occurred on September 11, 2001, or harbored such organizations or persons." The "harbored" clause put Afghanistan in the crosshairs. Bush demanded that the Taliban turn bin Laden and other al-Qa'ida members over to the United States or "suffer the consequences."

Behind closed doors, there was talk of taking the battle to Iraq as well. On the afternoon of 9/11, Secretary of Defense Rumsfeld asked his aides, according to meeting notes, whether intelligence about the attacks was "good enough [to] hit S.H. [Saddam Hussein] @ same time—not only U.B.L. [Usama bin Laden]" The next day, Wolfowitz argued in a National Security Council meeting that al-Qa'ida lacked the sophistication to stage such an elaborate operation on its own; Iraq must have provided crucial assistance. Secretary of State Powell dismissed this notion, insisting the focus needed to stay on al-Qa'ida. Bush agreed, but only for the time being. "Start with bin Laden, which Americans expect," he said, adding, "If we succeed we've struck a huge blow and can move forward." Later that evening, Bush pulled Dick Clarke aside and instructed him to "go back over everything, everything. See if Saddam did this." When a flabbergasted Clarke protested that al-Qa'ida was the obvious perpetrator, Bush said, "I know, I know, but … see if Saddam was involved. Just look. I want to know any shred."

But Afghanistan was the immediate priority. The Taliban rejected Bush's ultimatum, saying they could not rescind the sanctuary they had granted bin Laden. Thus on October 7, 2001, the president dispatched the US military to defeat al-Qa'ida and Taliban forces in Afghanistan. Key to the success of "Operation Enduring Freedom" was the assistance of the Northern Alliance, a coalition of anti-Taliban Afghan militias that Washington had intermittently cultivated over the previous couple of years. To solidify that relationship, US Special Forces and CIA operatives entered northeastern Afghanistan and dispensed generous bribes to Northern Alliance leaders, who agreed to aid the US effort. The Northern Alliance conducted the main ground operations against the Taliban and al-Qa'ida. It also furnished vital intelligence about the location of enemy positions, enabling the US Air Force to strike those targets with lethal precision. Neither the Taliban nor al-Qa'ida had adequate defenses against the combined Northern Alliance and US assaults. By December 2001, the Taliban had been ousted from Afghanistan's capital, Kabul, and other major cities; al-Qa'ida's forces were scattered and on the run. The Bush administration had won an early battle in what it now called the "Global War on Terror."

Even so, the US victory was qualified. A large number of Afghan civilians had been killed in the fighting, with estimates ranging from 1,000 to 3,600. Moreover, although the Taliban had been forced to abandon the seat of government, they were not permanently defeated. They retreated to the countryside, mostly in southern and eastern Afghanistan, and in the coming years would mount a potent insurgency against the new pro-US government installed in Kabul. To prevent that government's collapse, and to keep Afghanistan from again becoming a haven for terrorists with global reach, US troops would have to remain in the country indefinitely. (The military occupation ultimately lasted for nearly twenty years.) Finally, US and Northern Alliance forces had missed an opportunity to decapitate al-Qa'ida. Briefly in December, bin Laden and about a thousand al-Qa'ida militants were trapped in Tora Bora, an Afghan cave complex near the eastern border with Pakistan. Lacking sufficient forces on the ground to capture or kill bin Laden itself, the US military entrusted the task to the Northern Alliance, which failed to prevent the al-Qa'ida leader from slipping into western Pakistan. There, bin Laden found effective sanctuary, made possible by Pakistan's ambiguous geopolitical position. Although the Pakistani government officially supported the US-led War on Terror, the country's military and intelligence service were honeycombed with officers sympathetic to al-Qa'ida.

Casting Off Restraints

The Afghan venture also created a situation that, in short order, raised a host of deeply troubling legal, political, and moral issues. During the operation, the US military gained custody of hundreds of suspected al-Qa'ida and Taliban combatants. The Bush administration insisted that these detainees could not be treated as ordinary prisoners of war. Many of them had committed heinous acts of terrorism for which they had to be punished; many would likely kill again if set free; and some surely possessed valuable information about plans for future attacks. So the administration improvised a set of procedures designed to maximize its own freedom of action on the detainee question.

In November 2001, Bush signed an executive order authorizing the US military to detain people it considered "enemy combatants" and try them in military tribunals. "Enemy combatants" would enjoy few of the protections afforded to defendants in civilian or standard military courts, and the tribunals would not be subject to judicial review. To house and interrogate the detainees, the administration established secret prisons known as "black sites" in Asian, Middle Eastern, and Eastern European countries. It also held detainees at the US naval base at Guantánamo Bay, Cuba, which the United States maintained against the wishes of Cuba's government. Rumsfeld claimed that the United States was imprisoning "the worst of the worst." Although this description did arguably apply to a handful of detainees, among them the Pakistani militant Khalid Sheikh Mohammad, the alleged mastermind of the 9/11 attacks, it was dubious as a broader characterization. Many of the detainees had been delivered to US authorities by Afghans who received cash bounties as a reward. It strained credulity to suppose that all, or even most, of the captured individuals were hardened terrorists. Indeed, it later emerged that the captives included teenaged boys, some as young as fourteen.

If arbitrary prisons were disturbing, then so, too, was what occurred within their walls. To extract every conceivable morsel of actionable intelligence from detainees, US officials cast aside previous restraints on cruel and harmful treatment. Partly, they did this by outsourcing the abuse. In a policy known as "extraordinary rendition," they handed certain detainees over to foreign governments, like those of Egypt, Jordan, Morocco, Syria, Thailand, and Uzbekistan, that were willing to employ harsh interrogation methods, including torture. Months later, the Bush administration made it easier for Americans themselves to engage in such conduct. In a secret opinion in August 2002, the DOJ defined torture so restrictively that a wide range of abusive interrogation techniques no longer reached that forbidden threshold. Armed with such legal reasoning, US interrogators subjected terror suspects to slapping, sleep deprivation, forced standing, extended confinement in extremely cramped spaces (including boxes as small as 21 inches wide, 30 inches long, and 30 inches high), and waterboarding, which involved pouring water onto a cloth wrapped around a detainee's face, simulating the sensation of drowning. Cheney and Rumsfeld swore by these "enhanced interrogation techniques," but it now appears that the information extracted by such means had already been obtained through more traditional interrogation methods. There was another problem, one with fateful implications for the integrity of US intelligence gathering: after a certain point, a tortured detainee would do *anything* to make the agony stop, including supplying a bogus story if that was what the torturer seemed to want.

The Bush administration's domestic response to September 11 placed similar, if somewhat less severe, strains on legal and moral norms. Administration officials were shaken by their failure to uncover the hijacking plot and terrified at the thought that other al-Qa'ida operatives were already in the country planning future attacks. Those fears only intensified when, about ten days after 9/11, anonymously mailed envelopes containing anthrax, a deadly biological agent, began arriving at the offices of several national media outlets. Similar letters were later sent to two Democratic lawmakers, Senate Majority Leader Tom Daschle of South Dakota and Senator Patrick Leahy of Vermont. Five people, none of them prominent, died as a result of exposure to the substance. The anthrax mailings proved to be unrelated to Middle Eastern terrorist groups, but they alarmed an already jittery public and underscored the nation's vulnerability to novel forms of attack. Under such circumstances, the administration argued, existing methods of crime detection and law enforcement – and long-standing safeguards against federal authorities' overzealous performance of those functions – had to be rethought. Americans questioning this reasoning were hardly silent, but they had little sway in the news media or on Capitol Hill.

In October 2001, at the administration's urging, Congress overwhelmingly passed the Uniting and Strengthening America by Providing Appropriate Tools Required to Intercept and Obstruct Terrorism Act. The purpose of that torrent of words became obvious when the title was reduced to its acronym: the USA PATRIOT Act. The act empowered the government to monitor email, business, and library records; to conduct "roving wiretaps" on individuals who used multiple phones (rather than having to seek a separate warrant for each phone); to impose harsher measures against undocumented immigrants; and to detain foreigners suspected of terrorist involvement. Secretly, Bush exceeded even this expansive writ, authorizing the National Security Agency (NSA), without judicial warrant, to engage in the high-tech monitoring of phone and email communications between people in the United States (citizens and noncitizens alike) and individuals abroad.

In the domestic realm, as overseas, the government's expanded powers fell most heavily on Muslims. In the weeks after 9/11, federal authorities detained at least 1,200 noncitizens, nearly all of them young men from Muslim-majority countries in North Africa, the Middle East, and South Asia. They were held on suspicion of terrorist involvement or associations, but hardly any were ultimately convicted of terrorism-related offenses. Those who did face legal charges were mostly accused of visa violations. Many were detained for several months; some were deported. (Official statistics are sparse, so much of this story has to be told in estimates.) These detainees were not forced to endure the harsh interrogation measures visited on prisoners held abroad. After all, the Bush administration did not really suspect the stateside detainees of active involvement in terrorism. Rather, it lacked definite proof that they were *not* so involved and sought to hold them until they could be cleared or deported. In the chaotic detention centers, however, guards occasionally subjected their charges to low-level cruelty or neglect that caused significant harm. One detainee was slammed against a wall with such force that his teeth were loosened. Another later recalled, "I developed a kidney stone because we weren't allowed to have cups, not even plastic ones, and I had to sip water from the tap in the cell. I couldn't drink enough water this way, and living thirsty for eight months affected my kidneys."

Though aimed at foreigners, the government dragnet, combined with the intense anti-Muslim sentiment now circulating among the public, cast a pall of suspicion over the roughly 2.5 million Muslims who were US citizens. Some Muslim Americans had noncitizen family members enmeshed in the machinery of detention. Most others lacked such direct kinship ties but were tarred in the public mind by association with the 9/11 attacks. In countless ways, Muslim Americans got the message that they were unwelcome. They received stepped-up scrutiny at airports (and were sometimes removed from planes when other passengers complained). They encountered harassment and other forms of discrimination in the workplace. They endured taunts and menacing looks when they appeared in public. They suffered through media coverage and commentary that caricatured their religion and countries of origin. Their community centers were vandalized and immobilized by bomb threats, their private property and even their persons subject to violent attack. The FBI reported 481 anti-Muslim hate crimes in 2001, most of them in the final quarter of the year, up from twenty-eight in 2000. For the next three years, that figure hovered at around 150 hate crimes annually.

Of course, there were other sides to the story: the many non-Muslims who, in the days after September 11, formed protective cordons around beleaguered mosques and Muslim community centers; the thousands of churches, synagogues, grade schools, and clubs that invited Muslim community leaders or Middle East experts to address their members, feeding a hunger for knowledge about the Islamic world taking hold in the American public in the post-9/11 months; the spike in enrollment in Middle Eastern language courses in colleges and universities across the country. Many Muslim Americans themselves sought to learn more about Islam, out of simple curiosity or a desire to defend their religious heritage more effectively. It is difficult to generalize about a population so ethnically, racially, and sociologically diverse, but the searing aftermath of 9/11 appears to have made Muslim Americans, on the whole, more conscious of their Muslim-ness and more prone to place it at the center of their identity. Often, they did so by participating more fully in Muslim rituals such as prayer and fasting or, if they were female, by wearing headscarves in public. Many others outwardly conformed to mainstream American culture but saw themselves as standing apart from dominant political currents, especially when it came to US policy toward the Middle East.

The Pivot to Iraq

And, in *that* realm, the Bush administration and its domestic allies were certainly pushing the envelope. By early 2002, the president, his advisers, and a host of outside commentators had conspicuously pivoted from Afghanistan to Iraq, portraying a "regime change" in the latter country as a logical and necessary response to the September 11 attacks. There were a couple of different ways – one crude and preposterous, the other subtler but still deeply flawed – in which US opinion leaders sought to link 9/11 to Saddam Hussein. The first was to insist that Hussein's regime had been directly involved in the attacks, a claim supported by no credible evidence. This charge emanated primarily from hawkish analysts and pundits in the private sector. One of the most energetic was a political scientist named Laurie Mylroie, who, having already published a book accusing Iraq of complicity in an earlier, less deadly attack on the World Trade Center, now insisted that Baghdad had masterminded the towers' destruction.

A handful of prominent US officials, such as Cheney, Rumsfeld, and, of course, Wolfowitz, did publicly endorse some of Mylroie's claims, but the Bush administration generally avoided this direct accusation. It instead argued that, in a post-9/11 world, a "rogue regime" like Hussein's was no longer tolerable. The Iraqi government was deeply hostile to the United States; it was known to harbor nuclear ambitions; it had actually used chemical weapons against Iraqi Kurdish civilians in 1988. True, Iraq had been obliged under international pressure to dismantle some of its weapon of mass destruction facilities in the 1990s. But who could say that it had completely disarmed itself, or that it was not currently replenishing its forfeited stockpiles? True again, a WMD-equipped Iraq was unlikely to be so rash as to launch a direct assault against the United States. But it *could* surreptitiously share its WMD capabilities with terrorist groups such as al-Qa'ida that were fanatically eager to attack America. On a single morning in September 2001, nineteen hijackers armed with box cutters and knives had murdered thousands of people. One shuddered to imagine what they might have done with even the crudest chemical, biological, or nuclear weapon. Critics noted that Baghdad and al-Qa'ida despised each other; why would the Iraqis arm their enemies with WMDs? In the fraught post-9/11 mood, however, such skepticism gained little traction.

Key to the Bush administration's anti-Iraq campaign was the claim that Baghdad actually was reconstituting its WMD programs, and doing so at an alarming rate. The administration further insisted that Iraq and al-Qa'ida were already collaborating. To make these cases, administration officials scoured the available intelligence, highlighting evidence that supported the most alarming assessments and downplaying reports painting a murkier picture. A British intelligence official visiting Washington in the summer of 2002 reported home that "Bush wanted to remove Saddam" and that "the intelligence and facts were being fixed around the policy."

Some of the evidence the administration touted was highly questionable. An Iraqi defector named Rafid Ahmed Alwan (aka "Curveball") had told German intelligence officials that Iraq was secretly developing mobile biological weapons laboratories. The Germans concluded that Curveball was "crazy" and "out of control," and they shared this assessment with the US government. But the Bush administration seized on the allegation and included it in the overall case for regime change. Even more disturbingly, a captured Libyan al-Qa'ida operative named Ibn al-Shaykh al-Libi had told Egyptian interrogators, *under torture*, that Iraq was training al-Qa'ida in the use of chemical and biological weapons. The circumstances of al-Libi's interrogation should have raised immediate and overpowering doubts about the veracity of his testimony, but it, too, became part of Washington's bill of particulars against Baghdad. Indeed, in a high-profile presentation to the UN General Assembly in February 2003 – an address widely praised in the US media for its seeming gravitas and credibility – Secretary Powell specifically cited Curveball's and al-Libi's WMD claims. He said nothing about the allegations' troubling backstories, about which he himself was not yet fully informed. Powell later charged that members of the intelligence community misled him. Critics countered that he was too easily misled.

Powell, as noted, had initially questioned the wisdom of attacking Iraq, warning Bush that the United States could find itself in a quagmire. But, as it became clear over the course of 2002 that Bush was hell-bent on dislodging Hussein, Powell adopted a fall-back position: the inevitable war should have some measure of international sanction and participation. Cheney wanted to proceed unilaterally, but Bush agreed that Powell had a point. In September 2002, the president addressed the UN General Assembly and called for action to curb Iraq's alleged WMD programs. Bush's speech got a stony reception, but the UN Security Council agreed to take up the matter.

As the Security Council deliberated, the administration encouraged Congress to weigh in as well. Bush's position was similar to his father's during the lead-up to the first Gulf War a dozen years earlier: the president would welcome a congressional resolution supporting the use of force but not be bound by a negative vote. To aid Congress's deliberation, Bush instructed CIA director George Tenet to oversee the production of a National Intelligence Estimate (NIE) on Iraq's alleged WMD programs – a synthesis of US intelligence agencies' recent reports on the subject. Typically, an NIE on a topic of such magnitude would take months to create; the intelligence community was to produce this one in the space of a couple of weeks. During that interval, Cheney and other administration officials paid several visits to CIA headquarters to assess the analysts' progress. Without explicitly demanding a particular result, they made it unmistakably clear – both in private meetings with analysts and in public statements on TV news programs – what they expected to hear. The CIA analyst Paul Pillar, who oversaw the NIE's production, later said that he and his colleagues "felt a strong wind consistently blowing in one direction. The desire to bend with such a wind is natural and strong, even if unconscious." The administration's media statements were also, of course, intended to sway congressional and public opinion.

On October 1, the CIA submitted the NIE to Congress. It was withheld from the broader public and available only for lawmakers' private viewing in a secure room on Capitol Hill. In what Tenet later conceded was a "flawed analysis," the NIE concluded that Iraq still possessed biological and chemical weapons and was "reconstituting its nuclear weapons program." If Baghdad imported sufficient fissile material, "it could make a nuclear weapon within several months to a year." A close reading of the full NIE, especially the footnotes, reveals that the evidence supporting its claims was tentative and ambiguous. But few congresspeople read the document in the secure room; most relied on the alarming topline conclusions, which the administration immediately publicized in a slickly produced "White Paper" that made the case for war even more starkly and tendentiously. On October 10, the House voted 296 to 133 to approve the force authorization bill. Just after midnight that evening, the Senate did the same by a vote of 77 to 23. Senate yea-sayers included such prominent Democrats as Majority Leader Daschle, Joseph Biden of Delaware, John Kerry of Massachusetts, and Hillary Clinton of New York.

Doubtless, memories of the first Gulf War weighed heavily on would-be critics of current Iraq policy. In 1991, most Democratic congressmembers had voted against the authorization for war, with many warning that thousands of American soldiers might come home in body bags – only to lose credibility when the war effort succeeded quickly with unexpectedly low US casualties. Few Democrats in 2002 wished to make that "mistake" again. The Bush administration compounded Democrats' political vulnerability by insisting on holding the war authorization vote prior to that year's midterm elections. Many Democrats voted "Yes" simply to save their seats. Their party did poorly anyway. On Election Day, the Republicans beat the odds by taking back the Senate and expanding their House majority by six seats. The party holding the White House almost always loses seats in midterm elections, but these were extraordinary times. The Bush administration had gotten the best of both worlds: authorization for war and a resumption of full GOP control on Capitol Hill.

On November 8, the UN Security Council unanimously passed Resolution 1441, which found Iraq in "material breach" of previous WMD resolutions and gave it "a final opportunity to comply with its disarmament obligations." Iraq would face "serious consequences" if it failed to do so. The resolution mandated the return to Iraq of UN inspectors (there had been none in the country since December 1998) to certify that Baghdad was accounting for, and eliminating, all of its WMD programs. By December 2002, the inspectors were at work.

Resolution 1441 did not specify what "serious consequences" meant. It merely stated that, once the weapons inspectors had reported their findings, the Security Council would reconvene to consider whether Iraq had met its obligations and decide what to do if it had not. The Bush administration, however, treated the resolution as a virtual international authorization for war, matching the domestic authorization just secured from Congress. By January 2003, Bush had already decided to launch the operation in March. A rapid buildup of US troops, soon to exceed 250,000, was under way in the region.

Opponents of the war, too, were mobilizing in impressive numbers. In late October 2002, between 100,000 and 200,000 protesters marched on the National Mall in Washington, DC. In the coming weeks, protests erupted in thirty-seven states, and thirty-three city governments passed antiwar resolutions. Arab and Muslim Americans were visible participants in the movement, especially in large cities (even as a small contingent of Iraqi Americans, Muslim and Christian, publicly welcomed the prospect of removing Hussein's dictatorial regime). Antiwar dissent was not confined to the United States. London, Paris, Berlin, Florence, and Madrid were the sites of massive street protests, some numbering in the hundreds of thousands. Smaller demonstrations took place in cities across the globe. The outcry reached a crescendo on the weekend of February 15–16, when more than eight million people marched against war worldwide.

Still, in late 2002 and early 2003, opinion surveys revealed that a solid majority of Americans – always somewhere between 52 and 64 percent in the Gallup polls – favored military action in Iraq. In view of the surrounding climate, this is not surprising. Most national politicians spoke approvingly of the use of force. Although national news outlets gave antiwar dissenters generally respectful coverage, mainstream commentary was heavily skewed in favor of war, and skeptical media voices enjoyed little institutional support. MSNBC TV canceled a nightly talk show hosted by Phil Donahue, a liberal who frequently interviewed antiwar guests. Poor ratings were the public justification, but a network executive admitted in a private memorandum that "Donahue represents a difficult public face for NBC in a time of war," especially when "our competitors are waving the flag at every opportunity." Conservative outlets openly disseminated unfounded claims about Iraq's complicity in 9/11, drawing sustenance from Bush's own repeated description of Saddam Hussein as "an ally of al-Qaeda."

Meanwhile, in Iraq, the weapons inspectors methodically searched for evidence of lingering WMD programs. In successive statements in early 2003, they reported that they had found no indication of such programs but needed more time to complete their work. Bush administration officials were openly dismissive of the inspections regime. The case for Iraqi WMDs was so airtight, they insisted, that any failure to find them was further evidence of Iraqi perfidy. If the inspectors came up short, Rumsfeld declared, "it would prove that the inspections process had been successfully defeated by the Iraqis." "The dictator is not disarming," Bush said in his January 2003 State of the Union address. "To the contrary, he is deceiving." Bush's people also let it be known that the inspections' leisurely pace was upsetting their war plans. A successful operation had to be launched no later than spring; otherwise, it would drag on into the sweltering summer months.

The administration's impatience for war caused a sharp rift in the Western alliance. Britain's prime minister, Tony Blair, steadfastly supported the US position on Iraq, even as he urged Bush, futilely, to seek a second UN Security Council resolution before going to war. The French and German governments, however, vocally opposed a military solution.

France, a permanent member of the Security Council, infuriated the Bush administration by announcing it would veto any UN resolution authorizing the use of force. Not since the 1956 Suez crisis had the US government been so openly at odds with fellow NATO members. Hearkening back to a still earlier era – when Americans inflamed by their nation's entry into World War I expunged all references to Germany from the names of popular food – House Republicans changed "French fries" to "freedom fries" on the US Capitol cafeteria menu.

The Iraq War

On March 17, Bush declared that Saddam Hussein had forty-eight hours to relinquish power and leave Iraq; otherwise, he and his regime would be dislodged by force. Hussein shrugged off the ultimatum. On the 19th, Bush launched Operation Iraqi Freedom, a hostile invasion spearheaded by the United States and Britain and supported by a coalition of lesser powers whose contribution was largely symbolic. The attackers enjoyed overwhelming strategic and technological advantages, and within three weeks the Iraqi army was vanquished and the Baghdad regime dissolved. Hussein went into hiding, only to be captured several months later and executed by the successor Iraqi government a few years after that. Briefly in that spring of 2003, ordinary Iraqis joyously celebrated the dictator's ouster, seemingly vindicating Cheney's prediction that American soldiers would "be greeted as liberators." On the deck of an aircraft carrier off the California coast, with a banner bearing the words "MISSION ACCOMPLISHED" draped on the carrier's bridge behind him, Bush proclaimed an end to "major combat operations in Iraq . . . . [T]he United States and our allies have prevailed."

The nightmare, in fact, was only just beginning. The administration had woefully underestimated the chaos that would follow the collapse of Hussein's regime. Coalition forces failed to contain the looting, violence, and extrajudicial score-settling that suddenly engulfed the country. Especially hard hit was Iraq's National Museum, which lost priceless historical artifacts to theft and vandalism. In a pair of fateful decisions, the US-led Coalition Provisional Authority, the first post-invasion government of Iraq, dissolved the Iraqi army and the Iraqi Ba'th Party, the only sanctioned political organization under Hussein's rule. Both institutions, the argument went, were so thoroughly enmeshed with the old regime as to be beyond salvaging. This was a valid concern, but the dissolution decrees meant that hundreds of thousands of Iraqis, many of them armed, were suddenly thrown out of work and told they had no place in a post-Hussein Iraq. These "POIs" – "pissed-off Iraqis" – as the US military called them, swelled the ranks of the violent Iraqi insurgency that broke out in the summer of 2003 and bedeviled American troops for years thereafter.

Moreover, despite months of scouring by US authorities, no WMD stores could be found in the country. Evidently, UN weapons inspectors had successfully eliminated Iraq's WMD programs in the 1990s, and Saddam Hussein, to avoid appearing vulnerable to Iraq's strategic rival Iran, had done his best to obscure that fact. Bush's central justification for invading Iraq was nullified. So the president began stressing a different rationale, one that had not

Figure 13.2 Iraqis flee Baghdad as it descends into looting and lawlessness in the aftermath of the US-led intervention, April 2003. Source: Eric Feferberg / AFP / Getty Images.

figured prominently in the administration's case for war prior to March 2003: the need to democratize Iraq and transform it into a model for other Middle Eastern countries to follow. By 2005, under US guidance, Iraq had acquired a new, pluralistic constitution and had held at least a semblance of free and fair elections. But Sunni Muslims (who felt disempowered by the removal of the Sunni-dominated Hussein regime) widely boycotted those elections, depriving them of full legitimacy. In 2006, Iraq descended into massive sectarian violence, even as insurgent attacks continued. Few Middle Easterners saw anything worth emulating.

Nor was the setback to US policy confined to Iraq itself. In ousting the Baghdad regime, the United States had removed a significant check on Iranian power and influence, all the more so because Iraq's new Shia-dominated government generally sympathized with Tehran. The Bush administration had rid itself of one adversary only to find it had bolstered another. It was also benefiting a third enemy: with Iraq now in chaos, al-Qa'ida-affiliated terrorist groups had little difficulty infiltrating the country and establishing bases there. Bush's fanciful tale of a menacing Iraq–al-Qa'ida nexus was, through his own actions, finally coming true. Moreover, the Iraq War caused a steep decline in international esteem for the United States, as measured in opinion surveys conducted overseas. The loss of standing occurred not just in Middle Eastern and Third World nations but also in Western European countries with extremely close political and cultural ties to the United States.

Through it all, tens of thousands of US troops remained deployed in Iraq, battling insurgents and trying to contain the metastasizing civil war. In April 2004, CBS News aired photographs of US soldiers horribly abusing Iraqi detainees at Abu Ghraib prison near Baghdad, further antagonizing international opinion, especially in the Middle East. Inside Iraq, outraged insurgents intensified their attacks on US troops.

All of these circumstances significantly eroded Americans' support for the Iraq venture. At the start of the invasion, a Gallup survey revealed that 23 percent of respondents believed the war was a mistake. From mid-2005 till the end of Bush's presidency in January 2009, nearly every Gallup poll showed a majority taking that position.

Fighting AIDS in Africa

Even as he counted down to his catastrophic war, Bush launched the most constructive overseas initiative of his presidency. In his January 2003 State of the Union address, he called on Congress to join him in a massive effort to combat the acquired immune deficiency syndrome epidemic in Africa. At the time he spoke, nearly thirty million Africans had been afflicted with the disease, and in some countries the infection rate exceeded 30 percent. In the industrialized world, new treatments and drugs had dramatically extended the lives of people with AIDS, and aggressive public health measures were blunting the spread of the virus. These advances had scarcely affected the African continent, where an AIDS diagnosis still essentially amounted to a death sentence and where the epidemic raged largely unchecked.

At the start of Bush's presidency, the United States was spending about $500 million annually to combat AIDS worldwide, in a largely uncoordinated effort. Over the next two years, Bush modestly stepped up these contributions, but the scale and severity of the crisis in Africa persuaded him that much more was needed. "He wanted to do something game-changing," recalled the then White House deputy chief of staff, Josh Bolten; "something that ... might actually change the trajectory of this disease, which, from the reports we were getting, was headed to destroy a whole continent." At Bush's direction, Bolten convened a team of experts, led by National Institute of Allergy and Infectious Diseases director Dr. Anthony Fauci, to develop a plan for Africa. Fauci's group proposed an ambitious program, costing $15 billion over five years, to deliver antiretroviral drugs and other care to millions of people and to develop far-reaching prevention measures. Some of Bush's advisers balked at the price tag or questioned the program's likely effectiveness. But the president forged ahead, goaded by the stark admonition of his speechwriter, Michael Gerson: "If we can do this and don't, it will be a source of shame." In the spring of 2003, Congress overwhelmingly passed the President's Emergency Plan for AIDS Relief (PEPFAR), the largest US government effort to date to combat a single disease.

By all accounts, PEPFAR, which Congress bolstered with another $39 billion in 2008, was a ringing success. During Bush's presidency, the program saved millions of lives and reversed a precipitous decline in life expectancy that had occurred in several African countries in the 1990s. PEPFAR was not without flaws. For moral reasons, the Bush administration insisted that some of the funding go to programs promoting sexual abstinence and marital fidelity, even though the effectiveness of such advocacy (as compared with, say, the encouragement of condom use, which PEPFAR also promoted) had not been empirically demonstrated. Still, the initiative was an extraordinary achievement. "[I]f Africa is gaining ground against AIDS," *Washington Post* columnist Eugene Robinson, ordinarily a stringent critic of the forty-third president, wrote in 2012, "history will note that it was Bush, more than any other individual, who turned the tide."

Reelection and a Faltering Second Term

In 2003 and 2004, however, the unraveling situation in the Middle East seemed far more newsworthy than the president's humanitarian ambitions in Africa. Indeed, the growing public perception that Bush had blundered in Iraq clouded his reelection prospects. The Democratic presidential nominee in 2004, Senator John Kerry of Massachusetts, was a recognized expert in foreign policy who as a young navy officer had served with valor in Vietnam, before returning home to become an eloquent and photogenic leader in the antiwar movement. Here was a Democratic challenger who had shown the courage to both wage and resist war. But two decades in the Senate had blunted Kerry's dissident edge; in 2002 he voted to authorize the use of force against Hussein's regime. By 2004 Kerry was again a forceful antiwar critic – struggling to explain an apparent flip-flop on Iraq. He never did find a pithy way to make his evolving stance seem coherent or principled. Bush scorned his opponent as muddled-headed and irresolute. Meanwhile, a pro-Bush political action committee (PAC) ran stunningly dishonest television spots charging Kerry with falsifying his military record in Vietnam. Bush's reelection campaign denied any involvement in the scurrilous ads, but critics noted that their modus operandi – attacking an opponent where he seemed most unassailable, rather than where he was weakest – came right out of the playbook of Karl Rove, Bush's chief political strategist. A toss-up at the end, the contest yielded a narrow victory for the president. Both the Senate and the House remained in Republican hands.

Reelection was sweet vindication for Bush, but thereafter his political fortunes steadily declined, reflecting the cumulative impact of his Iraq decision and the public's reaction to fresh missteps. At the start of his second term, Bush launched a drive to reform the Social Security system. Taxpayers, he argued, should be permitted to invest portions of their payroll taxes in stocks, bonds, or mutual funds and thus gain greater control over their finances in old age. The proposal would fundamentally transform a sacred federal program, but Bush believed the 2004 election had granted him a mandate to enact his market-friendly vision. "I've got political capital," he told congressional Republicans in early 2005, "and now I'm going to spend it." He then embarked on a "60 cities in 60 days" speaking tour to drum up public support.

The plan went nowhere. Bush himself heard few objections from the handpicked "ordinary citizens" sharing the stage with him at his choreographed events. But Republican congressmembers holding their own town hall meetings, which were far less controlled, got an earful from alarmed constituents. Were Republicans really talking about throwing vulnerable seniors on the mercy of cutthroat markets? A host of advocacy groups – labor

Figure 13.3 A married couple navigating the flooded streets of New Orleans following Hurricane Katrina, 2005. Source: Mark Wilson / Getty Images News / Getty Images.

unions, liberal PACs, and especially the American Association of Retired Persons (AARP), which had thirty-five million members – mobilized to thwart Bush's "privatization" scheme. Smelling blood, Democratic leaders in Congress snapped out of their post-election funk and pressured rank-and-file Democrats to oppose the reform as a unified bloc. Congressional Republicans, few of whom had sought this fight in the first place, offered at best tepid support of the plan. By the fall of 2005 it was dead and buried.

Vastly more damaging to Bush's reputation was his administration's sluggish response to Hurricane Katrina, which battered the Florida and Louisiana coasts in late August 2005. New Orleans bore the brunt of the disaster, especially after surging flood tides breached the levees holding back the waters of Lake Pontchartrain, submerging much of the city. Louisiana authorities had ordered an evacuation of New Orleans, but tens of thousands lacking the means to leave, most of them people of color, were trapped in a bog of misery and desperation, deprived of shelter, sanitation, food, drinking water, and other vital necessities. More than 1,800 people lost their lives during the storm and its immediate aftermath.

Government rescue and relief efforts were maddeningly slow. For days on end, stranded New Orleaners pleaded with journalists to publicize their plight and displayed makeshift signs proclaiming their distress to television news helicopters circling overhead – to hardly any avail. Officials at the municipal, state, and federal levels coordinated poorly with one another and were at times shockingly ill informed about the unfolding crisis. Bush's people offloaded as much blame as they could onto New Orleans Mayor Ray Nagin and Louisiana Governor Kathleen Blanco, both of them Democrats. Nagin and Blanco made plenty of missteps, but a catastrophe this immense demanded a national culprit. So the news media zeroed in on Bush's own numerous failings, which included the appointment of political cronies to run the Federal Emergency Management Agency (FEMA) and the recent countenancing of a government reorganization that diminished FEMA's stature and independence. It did not help that the Bush administration's top disaster management officials distrusted each other, or that Secretary of Defense Rumsfeld dragged his feet about deploying federal troops to help reestablish order and dispense relief. Some critics charged that Bush bungled the disaster response out of indifference to the suffering of Black and brown people. It would be more accurate to say that generations of racial oppression and discrimination – the amelioration of which was not exactly a priority of his administration – had placed minority communities on the Gulf Coast in a deeply vulnerable position. In any case, the president never recovered the public standing he lost during this natural and human debacle.

Bush suffered a further setback in the fall of 2005 after he nominated his White House counsel, Harriet Miers, to replace retiring Supreme Court justice Sandra Day O'Connor. Miers was a respected member of Bush's inner circle who had served as a Dallas City Council member and as the first female president of the Texas State Bar Association. But she had little grounding in constitutional law, and several conservative pundits immediately pronounced her unqualified, a verdict echoed by some Republican senators whose votes were needed for confirmation. Administration officials coaching Miers for her Senate confirmation hearings were alarmed by her unfamiliarity with basic concepts of jurisprudence; they feared a humiliating fiasco if the process went forward. At Bush's pained but firm urging, Miers withdrew her name from consideration. The president then nominated Samuel Alito, a conservative appellate judge with more conventional qualifications, whom the Republican-dominated Senate confirmed in January 2006. Alito would be a reliable pro-administration vote on the court, and his replacing of the moderate O'Connor shifted the entire bench rightward.[1] Clearly, however, Bush's personal clout among conservatives and Republicans was on the wane.

Meanwhile, the president's handling of the War on Terror was taking fire from several directions. In late 2005, Congress passed an amendment to a defense spending bill barring US personnel from engaging in torture and other forms of cruel and inhumane treatment. The amendment's author was Senator John McCain, who had endured torture as a prisoner of war in North Vietnam. Bush was incensed by the legislation, but the majorities supporting it were veto-proof, and he reluctantly signed it into law. As he did so, however, he announced he would construe the torture ban "in a manner consistent with the constitutional authority of the President … as Commander in Chief" responsible for "protecting the American people from further terrorist attacks" – thus implying that the new restrictions

[1] Weeks earlier, Bush nominated and the Senate confirmed another appellate judge, John Roberts, to be the new chief justice of the United States, in place of William Rehnquist, who had died in office. In this instance, one conservative replaced another, but the ascension of the fifty-year-old Roberts (Rehnquist had been eighty) gave conservatism on the high court a new lease on life.

would not fully bind him. It was one of many "signing statements" Bush issued during his presidency to grant himself exemptions from unwanted congressional mandates. Still, by 2006 the Bush administration had ended its harshest interrogation practices, partly because of the public controversy surrounding such techniques and partly because of growing internal doubts about their legality or effectiveness.

The press, too, was becoming more assertive. In November 2005, *The Washington Post* revealed the existence of the overseas "black site" prisons, where the Bush administration was detaining and interrogating terror suspects in secret, beyond the reach of judicial oversight. The resulting uproar threw the administration on the defensive. A month later, *The New York Times* exposed the warrantless surveillance program, under which the NSA surreptitiously monitored thousands of Americans' international telephone calls and email messages without legal authorization. The *Times* had learned of the surveillance in late 2004 but had heeded the administration's warnings that disclosure would gravely imperil national security. A year later, mainstream journalists were in a more skeptical mood, and not even the personal intervention of President Bush – who summoned the *Times*'s publisher and top editors to the Oval Office and charged that they would have "blood on [their] hands" if any terrorism occurred following the program's exposure – could keep the paper from publishing its long-withheld scoop.

Just around this time, the US Supreme Court agreed to hear the case of Salim Ahmed Hamdan, a Yemeni national who had served as Osama bin Laden's bodyguard and driver. He had been apprehended in Afghanistan in late 2001 and held in the US detention facility at Guantánamo Bay, eventually charged with conspiracy to commit acts of terrorism. Through his lawyers, Hamdan argued that his incarceration was unlawful, a claim affirmed by a US district court in Washington, DC, and then rejected by the DC Court of Appeals. In *Hamdan v. Rumsfeld*, announced in June 2006, the Supreme Court ruled that the imprisonment of Hamdan – and by extension scores of other "enemy combatants" held at Guantánamo and overseas black sites – violated the Geneva Convention and the US Uniform Code of Military Justice. Civil libertarians hailed this reassertion of judicial oversight after nearly five years of post-9/11 deference to the executive branch. For the rest of the summer, acrimonious debate over the issue raged in Congress, within the executive, and among the public. In September, the Bush administration secured legislation that enabled it to continue holding terror suspects (including Hamdan, whom a military court later convicted of providing material assistance to al-Qa'ida) in conditions not much different from those that had previously existed. But the *Hamdan* decision limited the administration's ability to decide the fate of "enemy combatants" without regard to the other two federal branches.

Debacle in Iraq

The administration's biggest problem, however, was the spiraling crisis in Iraq, where US, British, and other occupying forces struggled vainly to keep control. By the fall of 2005, some 2,000 US troops had been killed in the country. Iraqi deaths, always difficult to tabulate, ran in the tens of thousands. The US military combated an array of foes: a massive Sunni-dominated insurgency, Shia militia staging sporadic revolts, and al-Qa'ida-affiliated militants who had set up camp in the country. There were no front lines in this war; US soldiers could be attacked anywhere. Their adversaries shot at them from apartment windows, lobbed shells into their barracks, fired rockets at their helicopters, drove explosives-laden cars into their checkpoints. One of the most lethal weapons Americans faced was the improvised explosive device (IED), a roadside bomb detonated by remote control as US soldiers drove or walked by. Terrifying in their randomness, IEDs exacted a huge physical and psychological toll on US troops, especially in the occupation's early phase, before their vehicles were better armored.

As word of such grim realities spread, enlistment in the US armed forces plummeted. Yet the military now needed more troops than ever, not just to arrest the unraveling of Iraq but to contend with a resurgence of Taliban militancy in Afghanistan. Rumsfeld had instituted a "stop-loss" program, which forced many troops to remain enlisted even after their tours of duty ended. American soldiers were increasingly exhausted and demoralized, prone to rising rates of depression, drug abuse, domestic violence, divorce, and suicide. True, the fact that military service was voluntary (at least at the point of initial enlistment) meant that a mere sliver of the population directly experienced these torments. As of late 2006, only about one in 230 Americans had served in uniform in Iraq or Afghanistan. Increasingly, however, the anguish of military families gained national attention, further eroding political support for the war and, in some cases, fueling public dissent. In the summer of 2005, Cindy Sheehan of California, whose son had been killed in Iraq the previous year, launched a one-woman protest against the war. She camped out near Bush's vacation home in Crawford, Texas, demanding that the president meet with her. Bush refused, not out of an unwillingness to meet with families bereaved by the Iraq War; he did so frequently during his presidency, sometimes silently absorbing their rage against his war policies. Rather, he believed that acceding to Sheehan's demand would be tantamount to rewarding a publicity campaign – her Crawford encampment had attracted considerable media attention – and thus encourage similar protests.

And then, things in Iraq got even worse. In February 2006 in the city of Samarra, a huge explosion destroyed the dome of the al-Askari Mosque, one of the holiest sites in Shia Islam, presumably the work of Sunni extremists. There were no casualties, but the attack set off months of massive sectarian violence. Sunni and Shia fighters turned on each other's communities with unprecedented ferocity, employing car bombings, suicide attacks, kidnappings, targeted killings, and grisly acts of torture. By June, an average of 100 civilians were being killed each day. In large cities, thousands of families left mixed neighborhoods to seek safety among their coreligionists; Iraq's population was regrouping along sectarian lines. By fall, over 100,000 Iraqis were fleeing the country every month, straining the resources of neighboring states. American troops were practically impotent in such circumstances. "Honestly," a soldier told a reporter, "it feels like we're driving around waiting to get blown up."

Back home, public opinion swung even more sharply against the president and his policies. A poll conducted in late 2006 indicated that 70 percent of Americans disapproved of

Bush's handling of Iraq. Mainstream pundits, including some conservatives, pronounced the war a debacle. The 2006 midterm elections were a rout for the Republicans, with the Democrats taking back both houses of Congress. Of course, many factors contributed to this "thumpin'," as Bush called it. Voters responded positively to Democrats' pledges to raise the minimum wage, improve access to health care, and protect Social Security. The GOP, meanwhile, was tainted by a host of embarrassing scandals, including one in which a Florida House Republican was revealed to have sent sexually explicit emails and instant messages to underage Capitol Hill pages. To a considerable degree, though, the contest was a referendum on Bush's Iraq policy, and the public's verdict was unmistakable.

Immigration Reform Efforts

On one issue, however, the president saw opportunity in the election results. Republicans campaigning against the scourge of illegal immigration had, overall, failed to make political hay of the issue; some of the staunchest restrictionists had even lost their seats. Perhaps Bush could now work with the victorious Democrats to fashion a moderate solution to what virtually all observers agreed was an untenable situation.

By the mid-2000s, about eleven million undocumented immigrants, most of them from Mexico and elsewhere in Latin America, lived in the United States. As we saw in Chapters 10 and 12, since the 1980s a powerful immigration restrictionist movement had emerged, and it was especially active in the Republican Party. In some cases, Republican opposition to illegal immigration shaded over into efforts to curtail legal immigration, too. President Bush resisted these tendencies. He had genuine sympathy, rooted partly in friendships forged in Texas, for those seeking a better life in the United States for themselves and their families. On pro-business grounds, he wanted to make it easier for large employers, particularly in agriculture, to hire immigrants willing to do arduous work for low pay. Finally, he believed the GOP could significantly expand its share of the Hispanic vote by adopting an immigrant-friendly stance, as he himself had demonstrated while governing Texas in the 1990s.

During his first presidential term, Bush had given low priority to immigration, preoccupied with the War on Terror and Iraq. Following his reelection, he urged Congress to authorize a guest worker program that would grant temporary legal residency to undocumented immigrants if they found employment in certain industries. Bush was willing to couple this program with enhanced measures to prevent illegal entry into the country. But congressional Republicans, under pressure from restrictionists in their base – including vigilante groups such as the "Minutemen Project," which ostentatiously patrolled the US–Mexico border – shunned compromise. In December 2005, the House of Representatives passed House Resolution (HR) 4437, an "enforcement only" bill. If enacted, it would extend the border wall, impose stricter penalties on employers hiring undocumented workers, make it easier to deport certain illegal immigrants (such as those convicted of drunk driving), and impose criminal penalties on third parties providing transportation and other assistance to illegal immigrants. Most strikingly, HR 4437 would make "unlawful presence" in the

United States a felony in and of itself, jeopardizing the future immigration status of anyone convicted of the offense. The House bill was a rebuke to Bush, but he publicly endorsed it, hoping the Senate version would include a guest worker program.

In the spring of 2006, as senators debated rival immigration bills, immigrant communities and their supporters erupted in protest against HR 4437. As many as 300,000 people demonstrated in Chicago on March 10, and half a million took to the streets in Los Angeles two weeks later. In a National Day of Action for Immigrant Justice called for April 10, protests occurred in cities across the country, including another 500,000-person march in Dallas. All told, some five million people participated in over 300 events, an unusually large outpouring for a constituency including so many foreign-born and undocumented members. The protests signaled a new assertiveness by Latin American immigrants and their supporters, a mood captured by the slogan "Today we march, tomorrow we vote." In 2017, the political scientist Tom K. Wong wrote that "HR 4437 crystallized the contemporary immigrant rights movement." The protests' more immediate impact is difficult to gauge. A handful of Republican lawmakers were caught off-guard by the outcry and slightly softened their stances. But some protest tactics – such as the chanting of Spanish slogans and the waving of Mexican flags – provoked an angry backlash among the public that prompted other congressional Republicans to double down on their restrictionism.

In May, the Senate passed a comprehensive bill consisting of much of HR 4437, a guest worker program, and provisions enabling undocumented immigrants, over a period of years, to gain permanent legal residency. To induce House Republicans to support the new package, Bush tightened up border enforcement through executive action (including the deportation of some undocumented immigrants) and supported passage of a separate, narrower bill to extend the border wall. But House GOP members were unmoved by these gestures and refused to take up the Senate bill in conference, effectively killing the legislation.

After the Republican defeat in the 2006 midterms, Bush resumed his quest for comprehensive immigration reform, now working with the new, Democratically controlled Congress. The main action was in the Senate, where the chief negotiators were Democrat Edward Kennedy and Jon Kyl of Arizona, a Republican with strong restrictionist leanings. Anxious to keep Kyl engaged in the talks, Kennedy and his allies gave considerable ground. The Kennedy–Kyl bill that emerged in the spring of 2007 was similar to the Senate bill of the previous year, but with an important new provision: a "point system" that privileged immigrants with advanced degrees or specialized work skills. As comparatively few Latin American migrants possessed such qualifications, the point system was a major concession to those determined to limit immigration from south of the border. Nonetheless, Kennedy–Kyl aroused intense restrictionist opposition. Already, several Republican politicians were running hard for their party's presidential nomination in 2008, vying with one another over who was toughest on illegal immigration. Meanwhile, a host of restrictionist groups inundated senators with phone calls and email messages opposing the bill, and conservative talk show hosts condemned the proposed granting of "amnesty" to "illegal aliens." Immigrant rights organizations, seeing a historic opportunity to put millions of undocumented immigrants on a path to legalization, generally supported Kennedy–Kyl. But the bill's point system dampened their enthusiasm. They were also disheartened by the Bush administration's deportation measures, which the president had intensified to placate the right. Passion and energy lay on the restrictionist side.

Heeding the pressure, Senate Republicans offered amendment after amendment to weaken the bill's generous features and strengthen its draconian ones. Pro-liberalization senators proposed amendments of their own but had less success in altering the bill. The only hope of preserving the original reform was a vote to end Senate debate before Kennedy–Kyl had been amended out of existence. But a series of cloture motions in June 2007 failed to reach the sixty-vote threshold, and the bill's supporters had to admit defeat. Hopes for bipartisan, comprehensive immigration reform were dead for the foreseeable future.

A New Strategy in Iraq

Amid all this contention, Bush still had to address the spiraling calamity in Iraq. In January 2007 he embarked on a major course correction, albeit one that ran counter to popular American sentiment and to the recommendations of some of his foreign policy advisers. The new approach, commonly known as the "troop surge," entailed sending 21,500 additional US troops to Iraq (the number later would later rise to 30,000) to halt the slide into anarchy. The surge was part of a broader military/political strategy promoted by US Army General David Petraeus, whom Bush now placed in command of military operations in Iraq. The idea was to work simultaneously toward providing greater security for the Iraqi population and toward forging cooperative relationships with local leaders and militias, especially in Sunni areas that had become strongholds of the insurgency and havens for al-Qa'ida-affiliated groups. In many of those areas, Petraeus and other surge advocates argued, Sunni militants and extremists had worn out their welcome, and ordinary Iraqis were desperate for a measure of tranquility. By ensuring the safety of civilian residents and treating their local leaders with respect, the US military could gain the cooperation of Iraqi actors who had, until now, seemed implacably hostile.

The troop surge was deeply unpopular at home. Opinion surveys revealed strong opposition to the move, and liberal commentators blasted it as a depraved effort to thwart the popular will and deny plain reality. In April 2007, the new Democratic majorities in Congress passed legislation requiring the president to start withdrawing troops from Iraq on October 1 of that year. Bush vetoed the bill, and Congress lacked the votes to override him. Thereafter, congressional Democrats did not significantly impede Bush's Iraq policies and, indeed, voted to fund the troop surge. "George Bush is still the commander in chief," observed the new Senate Majority Leader, Harry Reid of Nevada, "and this is his war." In short, Democrats would allow Bush to bear the onus of his catastrophic blunder and concentrate on winning the White House in 2008.

Initially, the troop surge made the situation in Iraq even worse. Stepped-up US military operations provoked a sharp response from America's adversaries in Iraq. The violence erupting that spring and summer would make 2007 the deadliest year of the Iraq War, with

904 US combat deaths. As usual, Iraqi civilians bore the brunt of the carnage. From mid-June to mid-July, nearly 600 unidentified bodies turned up in Baghdad. In the second half of 2007, however, the broader strategy started bearing fruit. In Baghdad, insurgent attacks on US troops significantly declined, as did incidents of car bombings and intercommunal attacks on civilians. A semblance of civic life began returning to the capital. The partial pacification of Baghdad enabled US and Iraqi forces to fan out to other parts of the country. Paying special attention to Sunni-dominated areas, most notably Anbar Province, the largest in Iraq, US military commanders worked on winning over local leaders. The Baghdad government, which was Shia-dominated and thus suspect to many Iraqi Sunnis, did its part by agreeing to fund some Sunni militias and to permit some Sunni former Ba'th Party members to take government jobs. These efforts were slow and halting and punctuated by appalling violence, but Iraq was gradually becoming more habitable.

Not all of this progress could be attributed to the new US strategy. For reasons of its own, in the summer of 2007 Iran brokered an agreement between the Iraqi government and Iraqi Shia militias, prompting the latter to halt their attacks on the US forces backing the Baghdad regime. Moreover, the sectarian partition of Iraq's cities, especially the capital, was by now virtually complete, making it easier for US and Iraqi forces to restore order. The first phase of the US troop surge had, by chance, coincided with a crescendo of sectarian violence that probably would have subsided anyway. But, whatever the mix of shrewdness and happenstance, the new US strategy got results that few observers expected. In July 2008, Bush called a halt to the surge and began withdrawing the additional troops. In December, he signed the Status of Forces Agreement with Iraqi President Nouri al-Maliki, establishing that all US forces would leave the country by December 2011. At the time of the agreement, some 4,200 US soldiers and perhaps as many as 100,000 Iraqi combatants and civilians had been killed.

A Presidential Election amid Economic Calamity

The final troop withdrawal was, of course, scheduled to occur on the watch of Bush's successor. The process of selecting that person proved to be an extraordinary drama that consumed almost all of 2008. In the Republican primaries, John McCain (whose presidential campaign had nearly collapsed the previous summer) quickly emerged as the front-runner and by early March had clinched his party's nomination. On the Democratic side, New York Senator and former First Lady Hillary Clinton began the year heavily favored to become the first woman to head a major-party ticket. But in January a fellow senator named Barack Obama, a forty-six-year-old Black Illinoisan, defeated Clinton in the Iowa caucuses, instantly banishing the aura of inevitability surrounding her candidacy. For several months, the two senators waged a series of contentious primary battles to determine which of them would make history as their party's nominee. By June Obama had prevailed, thanks to a shrewder electoral strategy (focusing less on winning primary races outright than on racking up delegates, even from states he lost) and a superior campaign organization on the ground.

The challenger's background was nothing if not unusual. The son of a Kenyan father and a white American mother, Obama had been born in Hawaii and spent part of his childhood in Indonesia. He worked as a community organizer in Chicago, received a law degree from Harvard University, served in the Illinois state Senate while simultaneously teaching constitutional law at the University of Chicago, and then was elected to the US Senate. Obama moved comfortably in both white and Black American circles (though he gained the latter familiarity mostly as a teenager and young adult) and had insight into how foreigners regarded the United States. To some extent, that "feel" extended to the Islamic world. While himself a Christian, Obama had Muslim heritage on his Kenyan side, and his middle name was Hussein; Indonesia is a Muslim-majority nation. Xenophobes would vastly overstate this element of his identity, as well as falsely claim that Obama had been born outside the United States and thus was ineligible for the presidency. But to many other voters, mostly but not exclusively to the left of center, Obama's exoticism was part of his appeal. After two terms under a swaggering white Texan with a shoot-first-and-ask-questions-later foreign policy, millions of Americans were ready for a biracial intellectual whose very biography was a reminder that the United States belonged to a family of nations. Unlike Hillary Clinton, Obama had publicly opposed going to war in Iraq. By 2008, that distinction was an unmixed political asset.

On the issues, Obama was a conventional liberal, but he lamented the polarization of American politics and insisted that Democrats and Republicans could, and must, work together again. During the primaries, Clinton mocked this stance as hopelessly naïve, but it had wide political appeal. Obama's multicultural background, while seldom an explicit theme of his campaign rhetoric, subliminally reinforced his message of reconciliation. Throughout his life, Obama had bridged yawning international, cultural, and racial divides. If anyone could bring the country together, perhaps it was the intriguing young senator from Illinois.

McCain, of course, had a compelling story of his own: a courageous and selfless captivity in Hanoi; a dogged, and partly successful, legislative crusade in the 1990s and early 2000s to limit the corrupting influence of money on political campaigns;[2] a more recent drive, fueled by searing personal experience, to stop his government from torturing. Nonetheless, McCain's choice of running mate, Alaska Governor Sarah Palin, cast doubt on his political judgment. Palin was a charismatic politician whose scrappy "hockey mom" persona appealed to many voters, especially lower-middle-class white women. But she was startlingly ill informed about public affairs and delivered demagogic speeches about Obama's supposed ties to terrorism. (The flimsy basis for this charge was Obama's acquaintanceship with a former member of the Weather Underground who had renounced violence decades earlier, and with a Palestinian American historian who criticized US Middle East policies.) McCain himself steered clear of such attacks but had no good explanation for his running

[2] In the late 1990s, McCain joined with Senator Russell Feingold, a Wisconsin Democrat, to sponsor legislation closing loopholes in existing campaign finance law that enabled private donors (by contributing to political parties rather than to candidates) to funnel unlimited amounts of money into political campaigns. In 2002, Congress passed and President Bush signed a version of that legislation. In 2010, however, the US Supreme Court invalidated parts of the law.

mate's resort to them. Obama's own vice-presidential pick, Senator Joe Biden of Delaware, was a chronic sufferer of foot-in-mouth disease, but he seemed a model of dignified restraint compared with his Republican counterpart.

In the fall campaign, Obama and McCain addressed the standard mix of domestic and foreign policy issues. Although each candidate's political "brand" required a rejection of the prevailing hyperpartisanship, their stances tended to be the conventional ones within their respective parties. Starting in mid-September, however, a terrifying economic crisis dominated the campaign. It resulted from a real estate boom earlier in the decade, abetted in turn by a long-term trend of financial deregulation.

In the early to mid-2000s, banks offered extremely enticing terms to homebuyers, enabling people who ordinarily would not qualify for loans to enter the real estate market. The loans were highly risky, but lenders extended them because they could now more easily escape the consequences of default. Since the 1980s, Congress and the executive branch had eased laws and regulations, some dating back to the New Deal, preventing commercial banks from engaging in certain kinds of investment. By the start of the new millennium, banks were using this greater freedom to convert home mortgages into units of value that could be publicly traded. From the banks' perspective, it mattered less whether homebuyers were able to pay off their loans than that these "mortgage-backed securities" could be sold to traders on Wall Street. And the traders purchased the securities not out of any confidence in the soundness of the underlying mortgages but because the securities could be passed on, at a profit, to other Wall Street traders. Mortgage-backed securities were so lucrative that investment banks began trafficking in them en masse. Insurance companies sold policies to those banks, promising to cover their losses if the securities' value plummeted. In these ways, the whole financial system became dangerously dependent on something to which few participants in the system gave any thought: the ability of homebuyers to keep up with their mortgage payments.

In 2007, the house of cards started to collapse. Across the country, and especially in certain states such as Nevada and Florida, homeowners defaulted on their loans, prompting banks to foreclose on the properties. This was a devastating experience for hundreds of thousands of families, but the tragedy did not end there. Financial institutions that had loaded up on mortgage-based assets now faced bankruptcy. Some of those firms were enormous, and their failure could imperil the entire economy. Realizing this, in March 2008 the federal government stepped in to prevent the massive investment bank Bear Stearns from going under. The following September, another huge firm, Lehman Brothers, appealed for government help. This time, Treasury Secretary Henry Paulson refused to intervene, fearful of establishing a pattern of endless federal bailouts. On September 15, Lehman Brothers declared bankruptcy, triggering, to Paulson's shock, a system-wide panic. Over the next month, the Dow Jones Industrial Average lost more than a quarter of its value. Credit markets froze as potential lenders lost either the funds to invest or the confidence that they would be repaid. Companies laid off workers, causing the national unemployment rate to spike from just over 6 percent in September 2008 to 10 percent in October 2009. The worst economic slump since the Great Depression had begun.

Figure 13.4
A Las Vegas real estate agent facing the foreclosure of her own home, 2008. Source: Orjan F. Ellingvag / Corbis Historical / Getty Images.

It could have been much worse. In the days after Lehman Brothers' failure, Paulson and Ben Bernanke, chair of the Federal Reserve, feared a wholesale collapse of the US economy, an event that would not be nationally contained. "If we don't act," Bernanke warned the president, "we could be facing another Great Depression – this one worldwide." Swallowing its free-market dogmas, the Bush administration rushed to Congress and got it to authorize a $700 billion federal loan to key financial institutions, so that credit could start circulating again. Like its military precursor in Iraq, this financial "surge" staved off the worst-case scenario. Even so, the specter of Washington bailing out Wall Street caused millions of Americans to turn away in disgust, convinced, in the words of the journalist Tim Alberta, "that the economy was rigged against them; that professional politicians had sold them out." Such sentiments spanned the political spectrum but would, in the years ahead, find expression in ever more venomous partisanship.

Meanwhile, of course, Americans still had to pick their next president. The financial crisis had moved to the center of the campaign, and it strongly redounded to Obama's benefit. The fact that it had erupted on a Republican president's watch automatically boosted the Democratic candidate. Moreover, McCain himself had championed the deregulatory policies that underlay the meltdown, and he now seemed devoid of ideas for addressing it. Obama, by contrast, discussed the crisis in a manner that appeared both responsible and surefooted. He unhesitatingly supported Bush's federal rescue package while chiding Republicans for their deregulatory excesses (and downplaying Democrats' own complicity in dismantling New-Deal-era safeguards). The Iraq War was another strike against McCain, both generically as a Republican and personally as an early and vocal cheerleader of the venture. Obama was one of the few national leaders of either party unsullied by that fiasco.

A Democratic victory was widely expected. It was nevertheless stunning when, on November 4, 2008, Americans decisively elected the nation's first Black president. Obama received 52.9 percent of the popular vote to McCain's 45.7 percent and more than twice as many electoral votes as his Republican opponent. The Democrats retained both the House and the Senate. "This is a historic election," McCain noted in a gracious concession speech. "I recognize the special significance it has for African Americans and for the special pride that must be theirs tonight." Following Obama's own stirring victory speech in Chicago's Grant Park, TV cameras panning the crowd caught the tear-streaked face of the Reverend Jesse Jackson, who in the 1980s had made two unsuccessful but path-breaking bids for the presidency.

***

The incoming president faced daunting trials. Although the $700 billion rescue package had prevented a wholesale economic collapse, the crisis was deepening by the day. Whatever further measures the new administration and Congress might devise, conditions were bound to get a lot worse before they could start to improve. Obama was also, of course, about to assume command of two draining overseas wars. Still another, far less anticipated, challenge would be ethnocultural. The 2008 election inspired some commentators to rhapsodize that America was entering a "postracial" era in which divisions of color and caste, while by no means entirely banished, would have less and less political and societal relevance. In fact, Obama's recent African lineage was drawing submerged currents of racism and nativism to the surface, introducing an ugliness to American politics not seen in decades, at least not so openly. Governor Palin's xenophobic populism had received scathing media reviews and probably repelled more voters than it attracted. But it also revealed the latent strength of a constituency – mostly white Republicans lacking college education – who delighted in audacious, even vulgar attacks on public norms, especially concerning discussion of race and ethnicity. This was a newly visible force in American politics, one that, in more capable and ruthless hands, possessed the power to upend the nation's civic life.

READING QUESTIONS

1. Why did the administration of George W. Bush, along with the permanent bureaucracies concerned with national security and law enforcement, not respond more effectively to intelligence reports of the gathering threat posed by al-Qaʻida?
2. Why, despite the absence of evidence of Iraq's involvement in the attacks of September 11, 2001, did the Bush administration insist that "regime change" in Iraq was an appropriate response to 9/11? How did the administration use the analysis of intelligence to make this case?
3. In 1986, a Republican president (Ronald Reagan) and a divided Congress (a Republican-controlled Senate and a Democratic-controlled House of Representatives) cooperated to enact immigration reform that legalized the status of many undocumented immigrants.

In 2007, another Republican president and another divided Congress (a Democratic Senate and a Republican House) proved unable to enact legislation that, again, would have furnished legal pathways to some of the undocumented. What, in your estimation, accounts for this difference in outcome? How had circumstances changed over the intervening two decades?

4. By what chain of events could transformations in the US real estate market ultimately contribute to the unraveling of the national, and even the international, economy? What policy changes helped to create that chain of events?

SUGGESTIONS FOR FURTHER READING

Anderson, Terry H. *Bush's Wars*. New York: Oxford University Press, 2011.

Baker, Peter. *Days of Fire: Bush and Cheney in the White House*. New York: Doubleday, 2013.

Brill, Steven. *After: The Rebuilding and Defending of America in the September 12 Era*. New York: Simon & Schuster, 2003.

Caldwell, Dan. *Vortex of Conflict: US Policy toward Afghanistan, Pakistan, and Iraq*. Stanford, CA: Stanford University Press, 2011.

Cainkar, Louise A. *Homeland Insecurity: The Arab American and Muslim American Experience after 9/11*. New York: Russell Sage Foundation, 2009.

Clarke, Richard A. *Against All Enemies: Inside America's War on Terror*. New York: Free Press, 2004.

DeSipio, Louis, and Rodolfo O. de la Garza. *US Immigration in the Twenty-First Century: Making Americans, Remaking America*. Boulder, CO: Westview Press, 2015.

Draper, Robert. *Dead Certain: The Presidency of George W. Bush*. New York: Free Press, 2007.

Graham, John D. *Bush on the Home Front: Domestic Policy Triumphs and Setbacks*. Bloomington, IN: Indiana University Press, 2010.

Little, Douglas. *Us versus Them: The United States, Radical Islam, and the Rise of the Green Threat*. Chapel Hill, NC: University of North Carolina Press, 2016.

Peek, Lori. *Behind the Backlash: Muslim Americans after 9/11*. Philadelphia: Temple University Press, 2010.

Shiekh, Irum. *Detained without Cause: Muslims' Stories of Detention and Deportation in America after 9/11*. London: Palgrave Macmillan, 2011.

Smith, Jean Edward. *Bush*. New York: Simon & Schuster, 2016.

Wong, Tom K. *The Politics of Immigration: Partisanship, Demographic Change, and American National Identity*. New York: Oxford University Press, 2017.

14 Yes We Can't

American Politics, 2009–2015

Introduction

It was for the good of the public, New Jersey authorities insisted. That was why thirty-three-year-old Kaci Hickox had been whisked away from Newark Airport, outfitted in paper scrubs, and confined in a plastic tent on the grounds of a nearby hospital. Hickox, a nurse working for the international humanitarian organization Doctors Without Borders, had just returned from Sierra Leone, where she had treated patients suffering from Ebola, the wasting, deadly, contagious disease ravaging parts of West Africa during that fall of 2014. Speaking to reporters on her cellphone (her sole means of communicating with the outside world), Hickox angrily protested her forced quarantine. After all, she exhibited no symptoms of Ebola and would very soon test negative for it. Medical experts had determined, moreover, that the disease could be spread only through physical contact with a symptomatic patient. Federal health officials, including Dr. Anthony Fauci, the acclaimed expert on infectious diseases, sided with Hickox. But Chris Christie, New Jersey's combative Republican governor, declared that his state would confine the nurse for the next twenty-one days. "We need to protect the public safety of the folks in the most densely populated area in the country," he told reporters. Cynics suspected Christie was engaging in political grandstanding, to position himself more favorably for a presidential run in 2016. If so, the gambit fizzled, for the governor soon relented under public pressure and allowed Hickox to return to her home in Maine.

But other Republicans were more effective in exploiting the crisis, something the imminent midterm elections of 2014 gave them every incentive to do. When Democratic President Barack Obama, following the advice of Fauci, the Centers for Disease Control and Prevention, and other federal health authorities, resisted panicky calls to ban flights from West Africa, Republican Senator Ted Cruz of Texas scoffed that "the doctors making this argument are working for the administration." Senator Rand Paul, a Kentucky Republican, accused the public health community as a whole of "not really making sound, rational, scientific decisions." "President Obama – close down the flights from Ebola infected areas right now, before it is too late!" tweeted Donald Trump, the wealthy New York real estate developer and television reality show host. "What the hell is wrong with you?" Other Republicans recommended sealing the US–Mexican border to keep Ebola sufferers from entering the country by that route. And if interdiction failed, opined Todd Kincannon, former director of South Carolina's Republican Party, "people with Ebola in the US need to be humanely put down immediately." As so often happened during Obama's presidency, currents of racism and xenophobia swirled together in a toxic political swamp. The suggestion that Obama was somehow reluctant to contain a virus emanating from the continent of his father's birth – preposterous when voiced aloud – hovered unspoken in the partisan air. The right-wing talk show host Michael Savage came close to making it explicit when he dubbed the chief executive "President Ebola."

Few mainstream journalists credited such talk, but their anxious coverage reinforced a more diffuse critique that something truly perilous was afoot that Obama was underplaying. Consequently, the Ebola outbreak was one of several international and domestic crises in 2014 that politically damaged the president and his party. In the November midterms, the Republicans enlarged their majority in the House of Representatives and gained control of the Senate. Only in the weeks after the election, as Ebola receded as a threat to the United States (while continuing for some months to ravage West Africa, ultimately killing more than 11,000 people), did media outlets generally acknowledge that Obama's strategy of calm but vigilant monitoring and testing, combined with the dispatching of medical teams to help West African nations stamp out the virus, had been effective. In the end, there were four Ebola cases in the United States, only one of them fatal. The Republicans dropped the issue almost immediately after their electoral triumph.

The Ebola crisis and its political fallout illustrated some basic ironies of the Obama era: the irony of a cerebral, pragmatic, and imperturbable president governing in an age of poisonous partisanship; that of a record of notable achievement harshly punished at the polls. As an individual candidate, Obama was an immensely appealing figure whom the voters powerfully validated each time he faced their judgment. As their president, he returned the favor by helping to avert a second Great Depression and offering intricate and often workable formulas to address the atrophying of the nation's health insurance system, the warming of the planet, and other seemingly intractable problems. Seldom, however, could Obama transfer his political magic to the party he headed. Both in Congress and within the states, Democratic power shriveled on his watch. Perhaps no Democratic president could have done much better at withstanding the driven, win-at-all-costs ethos overtaking the Republican Party at all levels in the 2010s. But there can be no question that *this* president, for reasons of lineage and pigmentation, activated latent forces of bigotry in American life, blamelessly compounding his own political predicament. Increasingly, it was the nation's predicament, too.

Reviving a Stricken Economy

At the start of his administration, Obama's most urgent challenge was rescuing the economy. In December 2008, as the president-elect prepared to take office, advisers told him that the situation was far worse than he had realized. The crisis in the financial sector had brought lending to a near-halt, and values on Wall Street were plummeting. Across the country, businesses were laying off hundreds of thousands of employees, and banks were foreclosing on tens of thousands of homes. The automobile industry seemed about to go under. If current trends continued, experts predicted, the US economy would lose $2 trillion in value over the next two years, and the unemployment rate would climb to 9 percent. (Reality proved even direr than that: unemployment would peak at 10 percent in late 2009.) When Obama had launched his presidential bid in early 2007, he had scarcely imagined that he would face such a calamity if elected. "Is it too late to ask for a recount?" he now wryly wondered to his aides.

Following his inauguration in January 2009, Obama asked Congress to appropriate $800 billion to provide relief to struggling Americans and stimulate the economy. Some economists urged a much larger package, but the president hoped to blunt criticism from fiscal conservatives by keeping the cost well under a trillion dollars. The economic plan consisted of expanded unemployment benefits, a middle-class tax cut, and a host of federal contracts, grants, and loans extended to businesses, organizations, and state governments, which in turn launched public works projects and other pursuits that employed idle workers. In February, Congress approved the stimulus plan without a single Republican vote in the House of Representatives and only three Republican votes in the Senate. Later that spring, Obama authorized a federal rescue of the auto industry, which was hemorrhaging sales and jobs and verging on collapse. The US government assumed temporary control of General Motors and pushed Chrysler into a merger with the Italian car company Fiat. Both GM and Chrysler went into planned bankruptcy, during which they restructured their operations with the help of federal loans. (The third of the "big three" auto companies, Ford, was in less desperate shape, but it, too, got government help.) By summer, the auto industry was on the road to recovery. The companies eventually repaid most of the $80 billion they received from Washington. Although the auto bailout won the support of some GOP congresspeople from the Midwest – a region directly dependent on car making – most Republicans opposed the action as government overreach.

Given the severity of the economic crisis, and the fact that Obama's recovery plan included tax cuts, favors to businesses, and other traditionally Republican-friendly measures, one might have expected to see more support from across the political aisle. But the Republican opposition was entering a hyper-partisan phase, one that made the last time a Democratic president squared off against GOP lawmakers – the 1990s – seem like an era of good feelings. In Newt Gingrich's day, Republicans in Congress had despised President Bill Clinton but cooperated with him when he pursued conservative initiatives, such as welfare reform and banking deregulation. This time, Republicans were hellbent on denying the Democratic president any achievements at all, regardless of content.

In part, the Republicans' obstreperousness reflected a sense of vulnerability. Not only had the Democrats, by commanding margins, taken the White House and held on to the Congress; George W. Bush was slinking out of Washington a conspicuous failure, leaving behind a shattered economy and a discredited war of choice still raging in Iraq. (Few voters were happy about the Afghan war, either, but most saw it as having been forced on Bush.)

More fundamentally, Obama's election underscored the growing racial and ethnic diversity of the electorate, a transformation that clouded the future of the overwhelmingly white GOP. The record turnout at Obama's inauguration – about 1.8 million spectators braved sub-freezing temperatures for the occasion – further spooked Republican leaders, causing many to feel like members of an endangered species. On inauguration night, a small group of Republican congressional leaders dined at the Caucus Room, a Washington steakhouse, and agreed that their party's salvation lay in waging a cohesive and tenacious struggle against the new administration. "The only way we'll succeed," said Paul Ryan of Illinois, the ranking member of the House Budget Committee, "is if we're united." Kevin McCarthy, the third-ranking Republican in the House, agreed. "If you act like you're the minority you're going to stay in the minority," he said. "We've gotta challenge them on every single bill and challenge them on every single campaign."

Some Republicans surely would have preferred to cooperate with Obama on certain issues, but they faced growing pressure to give him the cold shoulder. Such urgings came not just from within congressional walls. In early 2009, a constellation of rightwing protest movements known as the Tea Party (named for the 1773 protest by American colonists in Boston Harbor) quickly achieved national prominence. Though more or less spontaneous in origin, the Tea Party rebellion gained early recognition and support from FreedomWorks, a well-heeled conservative advocacy group, and from prominent figures in conservative media and the Republican Party; it was both a grassroots and an "AstroTurf" phenomenon. Tea Party activists often called themselves nonpartisan, and some had harsh words for the financial bailouts President Bush had spearheaded on his way out of office. Overwhelmingly, though, the movement focused its wrath on Obama's early economic policies, denigrating them as "big government" or even socialist encroachments on private enterprise. A small subset of Tea Partiers advanced social-conservative causes, such as outlawing abortion and restoring prayer to public schools. In a succession of multi-city rallies over the course of 2009 – on April 15 (Tax Day), on the Fourth of July, and on September 12 (invoking the patriotic spirit that had prevailed immediately after the terrorist attacks of September 11, 2001) – Tea Party activists voiced their antipathy to the new president and threatened political reprisals against congressional Republicans willing to work with him.

A conspicuous minority of Tea Partiers expressed that disdain in xenophobic or racist terms. They stressed Obama's Kenyan origins and pointedly referred to him as Barack *Hussein* Obama, sneering out a middle name the president himself almost never used. Like others on the right, some Tea Party activists circulated the baseless charge that Obama had been born outside the United States and thus was ineligible to serve as president. (The claim had first surfaced during the 2008 presidential campaign. Obama had sought to debunk it by releasing a scan of his Hawaii birth certificate, which conspiracy theorists dismissed as a forgery.) Inscriptions like "Obama-Nomics: Monkey See, Monkey Spend!" and "WE DON'T WANT SOCIALISM, YOU ARROGANT KENYAN!" occasionally appeared on signs at Tea Party rallies, causing some embarrassment to the movement's national spokespeople.

Less vituperatively, left-leaning Democrats faulted Obama for not responding more boldly to the financial calamity, such as by nationalizing the banks or prosecuting the Wall Street titans whose recklessness had helped to capsize the economy. But Obama believed that such measures would only compound his administration's burdens and alienate the very institutions whose help he needed in finding a way out of the crisis. That said, he did champion the 2010 Dodd–Frank Act (named for Senator Christopher Dodd of Connecticut and Representative Barney Frank of Massachusetts, both Democrats), which reorganized federal agencies charged with regulating financial institutions, barred banks from engaging in certain risky practices, and created a new Consumer Financial Protection Bureau to keep a closer eye on financial actors.

Obamacare

Shortly before Obama took office, an economic adviser told him, "Your accomplishment is going to be preventing a second Great Depression." "That's not enough for me," the president-elect protested. Indeed, his ambitions went well beyond staving off disaster and included enacting far-reaching reforms in health care, immigration, the environment, and other policy areas. First and foremost, Obama sought to overhaul the nation's health insurance system, a decades-long goal of previous Democratic (and some Republican) presidents. By now, about forty-five million Americans lacked health insurance, and those who did have it paid an inordinate share of their income for policies that – they often discovered only after being plunged into devastating health crises – failed to cover large portions of staggering medical bills. Moreover, millions of Americans with preexisting health conditions, such as diabetes or asthma, had to pay higher insurance premiums or were denied coverage altogether. Obama was determined to tackle this issue early in his presidency. "I figured that scoring a victory on the item that most affected people's day-to-day lives," he later wrote, "was our best shot at building momentum for the rest of my legislative agenda." So, even as the new president scrambled to forestall an economic collapse, he pressed Congress to enact comprehensive health care reform.

Republicans and Tea Partiers accused Obama of pushing "socialized medicine." Actually, his health care plan drew on ideas floated twenty years earlier by the Heritage Foundation, a conservative think tank, and enacted in the mid-2000s by Mitt Romney, Massachusetts's Republican governor. In essence, Obama proposed a grand bargain with the nation's health insurance companies, whose opposition had helped to torpedo the last effort at comprehensive reform, by Bill Clinton in the 1990s. Under the new plan, the federal government would engineer a vast expansion of the insurance companies' customer base, by making it mandatory for people to buy insurance plans and by providing subsidies to those who could not afford the plans' premiums. In return, the insurance companies would offer more reasonably priced policies and accede to certain federal requirements, such as that they offer the same terms of service to customers with preexisting conditions and allow young people to stay on their parents' plans until they turned twenty-six. Facilitating the scheme would

Figure 14.1 Tea Party protesters on the steps of the state capitol, Denver, Colorado, 2009. Source: Andy Cross / *The Denver Post* / Getty Images.

be a set of "health exchanges": online marketplaces, managed by states, where people could compare and purchase individual insurance policies. Initially, Obama hoped to offer a government-run insurance plan that would compete on the exchanges with the private plans, but conservative Democrats shot this "public option" down.

A clash with insurance companies was not the only Clinton-era misstep that Obama sought to avoid. He also wanted to quiet any accusation that he was presenting Capitol Hill with a fait accompli. After unveiling the broad outlines of his health care plan, he let Congress take the lead in working out the details. This proved to be a misstep in the opposite direction. Congressional Democrats spent months negotiating with their GOP counterparts over the terms of an acceptable plan, only to realize, by the summer of 2009, that the Republicans were determined to thwart any legislation at all. Hostility to health care reform came not just from congressional Republicans but also from Tea Party protesters. One of the more outlandish Tea Party claims, originated by Governor of Alaska and 2008 Republican vice-presidential candidate Sarah Palin, was that the Democrats were scheming to establish "death panels" to determine which patients merited lifesaving treatment – a wild distortion of a proposal to help people navigate living wills and end-of-life care options. Reporters debunked the accusation, but Republican lawmakers recognized its potency and soon were echoing it. "We should not have a government program," declared Iowa Senator Charles Grassley, the ranking member of the Senate Finance Committee and one of the leading Republican negotiators on health care, "that determines if you're going to pull the plug on grandma."

As of the summer of 2009, the Democrats seemed capable of passing a health care bill entirely on their own. They not only controlled both houses of Congress but also had sixty votes in the Senate, just enough to withstand a Republican filibuster.[1] A sad milestone in August, however, complicated the picture. Senator Edward Kennedy of Massachusetts, a legendary figure among Democrats, died of brain cancer at the age of seventy-seven. Kennedy had long championed comprehensive health care reform and had enthusiastically endorsed Obama's initiative. There was poignancy in the giant's demise just as the great legislative quest was being resumed. A more practical consequence of Kennedy's death was a change in the Senate's political composition. A lawyer and politician named Paul Kirk was appointed to fill Kennedy's seat until a special election could be held early in the New Year. On Christmas Eve 2009, Kirk cast the sixtieth vote for the health care bill in the Senate; the House had narrowly passed its own version seven weeks earlier. Health care reform was now close to becoming law.

Close, but not quite there. Before the legislation could be sent to the president for signing, the House and Senate had to resolve the differences between their separate bills by fashioning a new, compromise bill that each chamber would then approve. The Democrats were sure they could cross that hurdle. It was widely assumed that Massachusetts's imminent special election would yield a victory for the Democrats and preserve their filibuster-proof majority in the Senate. But in January the Republican candidate, Scott Brown, stunningly defeated Martha Coakley, the Democratic nominee. Brown had run hard against Obama's health care plan. He would unquestionably furnish the forty-first vote to mount a successful Republican filibuster when the Senate took up the House/Senate compromise. To circumvent that threat, the House Democrats agreed to adopt the Senate version of the bill. Although some funding issues remained to be resolved, Senate rules allowed them to be decided by a simple majority vote. In these ways, in March 2010 Congress passed the Affordable Care Act – or Obamacare, as it would also be called. Not a single House or Senate Republican voted for the ACA. The White House would have preferred a bipartisan bill, but a win was a win, especially considering what had just been achieved: the most ambitious health care reform since the passage of Medicare and Medicaid forty-five years earlier. "Mr. President, this is a big fucking deal!" exulted Vice President Joseph Biden as Obama prepared to speak at the bill's signing ceremony.

The process of implementing the ACA was slow, arduous, and at times nail-bitingly precarious. Congressional Republicans declared war on the new policy, conveniently ignoring its conservative pedigree. In the coming years they would launch repeated, though unsuccessful, legislative efforts to repeal it. Conservative legal advocates challenged Obamacare in court and, in 2012, came within a whisker of persuading the Supreme Court

[1] Technically, as of the summer of 2009, the Senate contained fifty-eight Democrats and two independents, Joseph Lieberman of Connecticut and Bernie Sanders of Vermont, who usually voted with the Democrats. At the start of that legislative session in January 2009, there had been only fifty-six Democratic senators. But two events in the first half of the year raised the number to fifty-eight: Senator Arlen Specter of Pennsylvania switched his party affiliation from Republican to Democrat; and Al Franken, a Minnesota Democrat, was declared the winner of that state's 2008 Senate election, following a months-long dispute over the results.

to overturn it. (In a startling move, Chief Justice John Roberts veered off from his fellow conservative justices and found a novel basis for upholding the ACA, resulting in a five-four vote to preserve the policy.) But one of the most potent attacks on Obamacare was an act of self-sabotage. In October 2013, the Obama administration unveiled the centerpiece of the ACA: the set of health exchanges on which Americans could shop for suitable insurance plans. To the president's acute chagrin, the website hosting the exchanges was nearly impossible to navigate. It took weeks to fix the glitches and get the site working properly. The success of the ACA depended on the voluntary purchase, on the exchanges, of millions of insurance policies; the more policies people bought, the cheaper the premiums could be. At a crucial stage, the website fiasco severely hindered that process. Despite all these challenges, however, by the time Obama left office in January 2017 the ACA was a reasonably well-functioning system, one that had approximately halved the number of the uninsured since the start of its implementation. When the next president tried to dismantle that system, he discovered it was quite a popular one, too.

At the time of the ACA's passage, however, a CNN poll found that only 39 percent of Americans approved of the new law.[2] Many of the Democrats who voted for it (under pressure from party leadership) feared they were jeopardizing their own political futures. The apprehensions were justified. In the 2010 midterm elections, the Republicans gained a stunning sixty-three votes in the House, taking control of that body. The Democrats kept the Senate but lost six seats. At the state level, Republicans gained six governorships, dozens of lesser executive offices, and majority control in twenty legislative houses. That last development was especially consequential: Republican-controlled legislatures could now redraw congressional districts in ways that would favor GOP candidates for years to come. What had happened? In addition to reacting against the ACA, voters were dismayed by the seeming lack of economic improvement. The 2009 stimulus bill had laid the basis for an eventual recovery, but few Americans felt its effects yet. The unemployment rate, which peaked at 10 percent in October 2009, declined somewhat in the months thereafter but was back up at 9.8 percent when voters cast their midterm ballots. Obama's compromises with fiscal conservatives had angered liberals and progressives while winning hardly any cooperation from Republicans, who were unified in branding the president a despotic leftist. Whatever the explanation, Obama had taken what he publicly admitted was "a shellacking" from the electorate.

Nonetheless, the president quickly recovered from the setback and made a surprisingly strong showing in the December 2010 "lame duck" session of Congress. During those last weeks in which the Democrats still controlled the House and enjoyed a large Senate majority, Obama won Senate approval of an updated US–Russian Strategic Arms Reduction Treaty (called New START), which cut each side's nuclear arsenals by a third. He also got

[2] As in previous eras, the political dynamics of health care made sweeping change unpopular. The uninsured, though shockingly numerous, still represented a small share of the population (less than 15 percent in 2010), and the worst shortcomings of existing insurance plans usually became evident only during medical calamities – and only to those immediately affected. When the ACA was passed, most Americans were vaguely dissatisfied with the status quo but fearful that a new system would make things worse.

both houses to pass legislation overturning the Clinton-era "Don't ask, don't tell" policy that barred gays and lesbians from serving openly in the military. Obama had prepared the way for DADT repeal by asking his defense secretary, Robert Gates, and the chairman of the Joint Chiefs of Staff, Navy Admiral Michael Mullen, to conduct a formal review of the policy. In February 2010, as the review neared completion, Mullen voiced his support for repealing DADT, a startling declaration that gave political cover for some lawmakers to shift their own positions. Meanwhile, a survey of 400,000 servicemembers revealed that only a third favored keeping the ban, reflecting a broader transformation in Americans' attitudes toward homosexuality in recent years. In that same lame duck session, Obama struck a deal with Republicans entailing a continuation of jobless benefits for the long-term unemployed, in return for a two-year extension of George W. Bush's tax cuts.

The DREAMers

A fourth issue raised in the lame duck session, an aspect of immigration reform, did not go Obama's way. It concerned the status of young people, mostly of Latin American origin, whose parents had brought them to the United States illegally when they were children. Many of these youths had no real memory of or connection with their countries of origin and spoke English as their first, and perhaps even their only, language. Since 2001, a proposed bill called the Development, Relief, and Education for Alien Minors (DREAM) Act had been repeatedly introduced in Congress. It would grant these young people, whom many called DREAMers, temporary legal residency and a pathway to citizenship. The DREAM Act had never passed, mainly because it was incorporated into broader immigration reform bills that fell by the wayside (see Chapter 13). By the start of Obama's presidency, DREAMers and their supporters were losing patience with the status quo and growing ever more willing to take matters into their own hands.

In January 2010, four undocumented college students – Carlos Roa, Gabriella Pacheco, Juan Rodriguez, and Felipe Matos – began walking on foot from Miami, Florida, to Washington, DC. Extending over 1,500 miles and four months, the Trail of Dreams was designed to publicize the DREAMers' plight. "With this walk," Matos told a reporter for a Mexican newspaper, "we are announcing to the world that we are coming out of the shadows." As they proceeded northward, the four marchers held press conferences, visited sites associated with civil rights campaigns of the 1960s, and documented their journey on blogs. Local activists and supporters cheered them on and accompanied them for short stretches of the route. Not everyone in the immigrants' rights movement was thrilled about the march. Some leaders of the more established organizations worried that excessive attention on DREAMers would divert energy and resources from the struggle for comprehensive immigration reform. Their skepticism softened, however, as the Trail of Dreams gained more notice in the national news media and inspired similar (though shorter) treks in Southern California and the mid-Atlantic states. Perhaps a focus on DREAMers could be a prelude to comprehensive reform, rather than a feel-good substitute for it.

Figure 14.2 Carlos Roa, Gabriela Pacheco, Felipe Matos, and Juan Rodriguez leading the Trail of Dreams, 2010. Source: Courtesy of Isabel Sousa-Rodriguez.

Within Republican ranks, however, sentiment against undocumented immigrants was hardening – partly a response to agitation by the Tea Party's more xenophobic elements. In late April, just days before the Trail walkers' triumphant arrival in Washington, Arizona's Republican-dominated legislature passed, and its Republican governor signed, a law requiring state law enforcement officers to determine the immigration status of any individuals they stopped or arrested, if they had reason to suspect they were in the country illegally; officers were to hold the individuals until federal authorities verified their status. Over the next few months, Republican lawmakers introduced similar "show your papers" bills in several other state legislatures around the country.

During his 2008 campaign, Obama had pledged to pursue a comprehensive immigration reform bill, with the DREAM Act embedded in it. Once he took office, however, economic recovery and health care reform dominated his domestic agenda. He hoped to defer immigration until after the 2010 midterms. But Senate Majority Leader Harry Reid had other plans. The Nevada Democrat faced a tough reelection fight that November; to maximize his Latino support, he promised to bring the DREAM Act up for a Senate vote during the December lame duck session. Reid won his race and, true to his word, added the DREAM Act to the Senate's crowded docket. As with so many other Senate votes by now, success required a sixty-vote supermajority to end a filibuster by the bill's opponents, most of them Republicans insisting that any relief for DREAMers be directly paired with measures to secure the US–Mexican border. As DREAMer activists watched in dismay from the Senate gallery, the bill's supporters (including hastily mobilized members of the Obama administration) failed to muster more than fifty-five votes. Even under full Democratic control, Congress had been unable to provide relief for the most sympathetic members of the undocumented population. Any further legislative attempts would have to be made in a divided Congress.

Following the Senate's rejection of the DREAM Act, pressure mounted on Obama to use his executive authority to provide relief to the DREAMers, by issuing an across-the-board policy that deportation laws would not be applied in their cases. Commentators in Spanish-language media demanded that he take action. In July 2011, the president raised the DREAMers' predicament while addressing a luncheon hosted by the National Council of La Raza, the country's largest Latino advocacy organization. When he said "Now I know some people want me to bypass Congress and change the laws on my own," a handful of activists stood up and chanted, "Yes you can! Yes you can!" – a pointed alteration of Obama's 2008 campaign slogan, "Yes We Can." Many luncheon attendees, who included some of the most prominent Hispanic leaders in the country, briefly took up the cry, clapping in unison. The audience remained friendly, but the urgency of the cause was palpable. In May 2012, ninety-four law professors argued in a public letter that the president, contrary to his own stated view, had the authority to exercise blanket discretion in the DREAMers' cases. In early June, realizing that Colorado, whose Latino population was growing rapidly, would be a battleground state in Obama's effort to win reelection that fall, activists staged a sit-in at his state campaign headquarters in Denver. The action received relatively little English-language media coverage, but others in the movement immediately took notice. Similar protests occurred at Obama campaign offices in California, Michigan, and Ohio.

Obama had repeatedly insisted that his hands were tied on the matter, but he now saw the wisdom of shifting course. Hispanic turnout in the 2010 midterm elections had been lower than that of African Americans and whites, with disastrous results for the Democrats; the president would take no chances with his own reelection. He was also genuinely moved by the DREAMers' cause. Speaking from the White House Rose Garden on June 15, 2012, Obama announced that his administration would no longer deport people who had come to the United States before they had turned sixteen – provided they were now aged thirty or younger; had been in the United States for the last five years; had no criminal records; and were currently in school, or had graduated from high school, or had joined the military. They could stay in the country for the next two years and then apply to renew their status. After all, the president said, DREAMers "are Americans in their heart, in their minds, in every single way but one: on paper." The new policy, known as Deferred Action for Childhood Arrivals, was an executive-branch initiative requiring no congressional action. By year's end, around 350,000 young people had applied for DACA status, and just over 100,000 had obtained it. Yet a broader reform of the immigration system remained elusive.

Foreign Relations in the First Term

On the world stage, Obama labored to distinguish his foreign policy from that of his predecessor – to replace George W. Bush's messianism and hyper-assertiveness with a more modest, low-key, and practical approach. On occasion, Obama publicly acknowledged his nation's past misdeeds (such as its involvement in the overthrow of Iran's constitutional government in 1953) or stressed that US military power alone could solve few international problems. Statements like these caused Republicans to accuse him of conducting an extended "apology tour." Still, Obama proved more than willing to use military force, especially in the form of unmanned aerial "drone" strikes against suspected terrorist operatives in the Middle East, South Asia, and North and East Africa. These drone attacks frequently killed civilian bystanders, too. In 2011, Obama took the unprecedented step of ordering the assassination, via drone strike in Yemen, of a US citizen. The target, Anwar al-Awlaki, was a Yemeni American imam whose online sermons had inspired several actual or attempted violent attacks by Islamist extremists. Meanwhile, Obama forcefully condemned the previous administration's use of torture, even as his Department of Justice dismayed liberals and progressives by declining to prosecute US officials who had authorized that heinous practice. The president also tried to close the US detention facility at Guantánamo Bay, Cuba, and have some of its inmates tried in US courts. He had to abandon the idea, however, after Congress balked at it.

When Obama took office, his most pressing foreign policy objective was ending the two major wars on which Bush had embarked. In Iraq, this meant withdrawing US forces as soon as possible; in Afghanistan, it meant surging more forces into the country, stabilizing the situation, and *then* bringing the troops home. Within the confines of that general Afghan strategy, Obama sparred with military leaders over the size of the surge, with the latter favoring a larger presence than the president thought politically wise. Obama talked the brass down a bit, but by mid-2010 around 100,000 US troops were in Afghanistan, nearly triple the number he had inherited from Bush. Obama hoped for a rapid improvement on the ground, permitting a full troop withdrawal within a few years' time. But the Taliban insurgents were tenacious, and the best Obama could manage was a gradual drawdown. At the end of his two terms, 8,400 US troops remained in the country.

In Iraq, Obama's exit strategy amounted to implementing the agreement that Bush himself had reached with the Iraqi government in 2008, envisioning the withdrawal of all US combat troops by December 2011. Originally, the plan had been for the United States to leave a small residual force in the country to help ensure stability. The Obama administration was unwilling to do this, however, without an Iraqi government commitment that the remaining US troops would continue to enjoy immunity from prosecution in Iraqi courts if they ran afoul of local laws. (The United States had concluded similar agreements with other countries hosting its troops.) Iraq's prime minister, Nouri al-Maliki, offered to make that commitment on his own authority, but Obama's legal advisers insisted that it had to come from Iraq's parliament, which refused to grant immunity. Unable to resolve the issue, the two governments agreed there would be no residual force at all. The US withdrawal, now total, occurred at the end of 2011 as scheduled. Back home, conservatives faulted Obama for not trying harder to reach an immunity agreement that would have allowed some US troops to stay behind. When Iraq descended into anarchy a few years later (see below), that criticism grew much louder. At the time, however, most Americans were relieved to see the last US troops come home.

Elsewhere in the Middle East, a remarkable political drama was under way. In several Arab countries, starting in late 2010 and extending into 2011, ordinary citizens took to the streets in protest, fueled by anger over decades of authoritarian governance and economic stagnation, and by new organizing possibilities afforded by social media platforms such as Facebook and Twitter. In most instances, the upheavals of this "Arab Spring" unfolded without Western intervention. The governments of Egypt, Tunisia, and Yemen were forced out of power; those of the United Arab Emirates and Bahrain, the latter with help from Saudi Arabia, successfully crushed the dissent. But in two nations, Libya and Syria, the internal chaos was so bloody and pervasive that the question of intervention from outside the region arose.

In Libya, violent protests escalated into a full-scale rebellion, which the authoritarian leader Mu'ammar Qaddafi mobilized his forces to crush. In March 2011, fearing a mass slaughter in the city of Benghazi, the center of the uprising, the US, British, and French governments secured UN Security Council authorization to "take all necessary measures," short of military occupation, to protect civilian-populated areas from Libyan government attack. A US-led coalition of NATO countries conducted air strikes against the Libyan military, blocking it from attacking Benghazi and enabling the rebels to take the initiative. By summer, the rebels had overrun Tripoli, Libya's capital, and forced Qaddafi into hiding. In October, they dragged him out of a sewer pipe and beat and stabbed him to death. "We came, we saw, he died," boasted Secretary of State Hillary Clinton. (Partly to heal intraparty wounds, Obama had brought his former rival for the Democratic nomination into his cabinet.) Yet Libya's new government, despite significant US assistance, failed to stabilize the country and faced violent internal dissent from radical Islamist forces. In September 2012, armed Islamists stormed a US diplomatic compound in Benghazi and killed the US ambassador to Libya, Christopher Stevens, and three other American diplomats. Republicans charged Secretary of State Clinton with criminal negligence in failing to protect State Department personnel. Several committees of the Republican-controlled House of Representatives conducted investigations into the tragedy. They found problems with the State Department's procedures for safeguarding diplomats but no personal wrongdoing by Clinton. For Americans, the term "Benghazi" became shorthand for Obama's feckless foreign policy or, alternatively, for Republicans' cynical politicizing of national security.

In Syria, another authoritarian government faced internal dissent from an ideologically diverse range of factions, some of which took up arms. Obama called on Syria's president, Bashar al-Asad, to step down but was unwilling to do much more. Although pundits, members of Congress, and some Obama administration officials favored arming Syrian factions deemed friendly to US interests, Obama refused to do so to any significant degree, fearing that the United States would be drawn into a quagmire or that US-supplied weapons would fall into unfriendly hands. Syria's civil war continued for the remainder of Obama's presidency (with Asad's government eventually gaining the upper hand), killing about 200,000 Syrian civilians and turning millions more into refugees. Critics blamed some of this humanitarian catastrophe on Obama's passivity, but opponents of US intervention could point to the unhappy outcome in Libya and argue that military involvement was no panacea.

As the Obama administration navigated these upheavals in the Arab world, US intelligence agencies had their eye on a residential compound in Abbottabad, a small city in northern Pakistan. In the winter and spring of 2011, aerial photographs depicted a tall man who took regular walks around the yard but never ventured beyond the compound's walls. "Kids would walk with him. They'd be all around," recalled Leon Panetta, the CIA director at the time. "It was clear that people there were giving him deference." American officials thought the man might be the al-Qa'ida leader Osama bin Laden, who had eluded detection for nearly a decade. After months of surveilling the Abbottabad compound, the intelligence analysts remained unsure they had made a positive identification; some rated the likelihood no higher than 50 percent. Despite this uncertainty, and against the counsel of Vice President Biden and several other top advisers, Obama ordered a unit of Navy SEALs (short for Sea, Air, and Land teams) to move secretly against the compound. The operation was scheduled for May 1, 2011.

The night before, the White House Correspondents Association (WHCA) held its annual dinner in Washington, DC, a charity event featuring humorous speeches and skits – and one that, this year, would be linked in the public mind with the Navy SEALs' raid against bin Laden. As presidents customarily do, Obama had agreed to address the gathering, and he now used the opportunity to settle scores with an emerging political antagonist. For some weeks, the old canard that Obama was foreign-born had gained fresh currency in Republican and conservative circles. Donald Trump, the tycoon-turned-television-personality, had loudly taken up the cry, claiming that investigators in his employ were on the ground in Hawaii, uncovering explosive evidence of Obama's fraudulence that would soon be publicly unveiled. Doubtless, Trump was flogging the "birther" issue to generate buzz around his reality show *The Celebrity Apprentice*. But he was also teasing a presidential run to unseat Obama in 2012. Pundits' speculation about that prospect lent all of Trump's utterances, including his wild talk about Obama's origins, broad publicity.

The flurry of interest in birtherism convinced Obama that he needed to do more to put the matter to rest. In late April 2011, he authorized Hawaii's Department of Health to release the official "long form" version of his birth certificate. (The scanned copy released in 2008 had been of the "short form," a summary of the certificate prepared by Hawaii's government.) Although many of Obama's advisers found this a demeaning exercise, the certificate's release did cause the issue to die down among mainstream Republicans, even as fringier elements within the party kept it alive. Trump claimed vindication, boasting that his intervention had finally shed light on the matter (though in the coming years he would occasionally resume his "birtherist" attacks).

Days later, on April 30, Obama addressed the WHCA dinner. As Trump himself sat seething in the audience, the president skewered the brash business icon. With faux earnestness, he saluted Trump's "credentials and breadth of experience," drawing mocking laughter from the crowd. "No, seriously," Obama deadpanned. On a recent episode of *Celebrity Apprentice*, he noted, Trump had shrewdly diagnosed the shortcomings of a men's cooking team. "There was a lot of blame to go around, but you, Mr. Trump, recognized that the real problem was a lack of leadership. And so ultimately you didn't blame Lil Jon or Meat Loaf; you fired Gary Busey" – references to a rap artist, a rock singer, and a Hollywood film actor. "And these are the kind of decisions that would keep me up at night." That last line brought down the house. It would resonate even more powerfully, writes Obama chronicler Peter Baker, when the world "learned what decision *really* was keeping Obama up that night."

The following day, a twenty-three-member SEAL team boarded two helicopters at a US airbase in Jalalabad, Afghanistan, and flew to Abbottabad. Landing at the edge of the compound, team members stormed into the main residence and shot one woman and four men dead, including a tall bearded figure who was assumed, and later confirmed, to be bin Laden. Obama's terse public announcement of the operation stirred jubilation across the country, while also triggering painful memories of that day of carnage nearly ten years earlier in New York City, the Washington, DC, area, and rural Pennsylvania.

In mid-May, Trump announced that he would not run for president in 2012. But he clearly had not given up on seeking the office, which, anyway, would be more attainable in a year in which no incumbent president was on the ballot – a year like 2016. Indeed, some in Trump's inner circle believed that the humiliation of the WHCA dinner only intensified his determination to win the presidency and wipe the sneers off his detractors' faces.

The 2012 Presidential Election

Regarding the more immediate presidential contest, Obama's reelection prospects were mixed. The president could credibly claim to have prevented the economy from sliding into an abyss, and his authorization of the Abbottabad raid played well with the American public. ("Osama bin Laden is dead and General Motors is alive" was Joe Biden's way of summing up those two achievements.) On the other hand, the economic recovery was slow and uneven, with unemployment still hovering above 8 percent for most of 2012. In late 2011 and early 2012, a diffuse rebellion on the left known as the "Occupy" movement – because its activists took over parks and streets close to Wall Street, near state capitals, and in the downtown areas of major cities – trained a spotlight on extreme disparities of wealth. Both implicitly and explicitly, the Occupy movement rebuked Obama for failing to check the power of financial elites. Other critics noted that he had yet to pursue comprehensive immigration reform or take broadly effective action on climate change.

Nevertheless, Obama benefited from the incoherence of his opponent. The Republican presidential nominee, former Governor of Massachusetts Mitt Romney, would have been a highly formidable candidate two or three decades earlier. He was a devoted family man, a stellar success in business, and a politician with a reputation for moderation, competence, and bipartisan effectiveness. His crowning achievement as Massachusetts's governor had been the design and implementation of a widely praised health insurance system that served as a model for Obamacare. In the GOP of 2012, however, many of these assets counted as liabilities, and Romney had to disavow them to gain the party's nomination. The ex-governor struggled to do so convincingly. His self-description as "severely conservative" struck many as a case of protesting too much, as did his insistence that Romneycare and Obamacare were light years apart.

Obama also turned out to have a superior campaign operation. His team blanketed the airwaves with TV ads about Romney's business record, disparaging the challenger as a ruthless plutocrat who squeezed profits from the economic misfortunes of others. The ads began airing at a relatively early stage, solidifying an extremely unflattering image of Romney before he had a chance to present a positive one of himself. (The negative portrait was distorted, but Romney lent it credence when he was secretly recorded, at a fundraising event he thought was off the record, complaining about the "forty-seven percent of the people who will vote for the president no matter what." Such individuals, he said, "are dependent upon government … believe they are entitled to health care, to food, to housing, to you-name-it…. And so my job is not to worry about those people." By this last remark, Romney meant he would never win the votes of the "forty-seven percent" and should concentrate instead on the rest of the electorate, but it sounded as if he was writing them off as human beings. The recording aired on television and deeply damaged Romney's campaign.) To get its voters to the polls, Team Obama flooded organizers into the swing states, vastly exceeding Romney's on-the-ground effort. In Ohio, the president's campaign fielded 130 offices and 700 paid staff members, as compared with just 40 offices and 157 staff members working for Romney. Obama's "get out the vote" effort also benefited from much more extensive and sophisticated use of digital tracking technologies and social media.

It all paid off on Election Day, when the president prevailed with 51 percent of the popular vote while his opponent received (with poetic justice) 47 percent. The Electoral College result was 332 to 206. Obama's 2008 victory had been more decisive, but 2012 furnished important validation. "In some ways this one is sweeter than 2008," the president told an aide. "Folks know you pretty well after four years." In the congressional races, Democrats made small gains in each chamber, but the overall balance remained the same, with Republicans holding the House and Democrats the Senate.

The Drive for Marriage Equality

During 2012, the issue of marriage quality – that is, the question of whether same-sex couples should enjoy the same legal right to marry as heterosexual couples – briefly but dramatically arose. In recent years, the matter had become increasingly important to activists in what was now known as the LGBTQ community (lesbian, gay, bisexual, transgender, and queer; letters and symbols for additional orientations would later be appended). This had not always been a pressing issue. Gay and lesbian activist organizations of the 1960s, 1970s, and 1980s had generally dismissed same-sex marriage as either too quixotic a goal to justify major exertion or too emblematic of the smothering traditionalism they were trying to escape. Even so, hundreds and possibly thousands of lesbian and gay couples had, on their own, persuaded sympathetic county clerks or clergy members to formalize their unions, and a growing number of lawyers and activists publicly advocated for marriage equality. The onset of the AIDS crisis in the 1980s raised new questions about the status of same-sex relationships. Could gay people wield power of attorney on behalf of their gravely ill partners, or receive survivors' benefits after their partners died? In 1989, the New York Supreme Court ruled that landlords in the state must allow the same-sex domestic partners of deceased tenants to inherit the tenants' leases. Activists and public intellectuals increasingly argued, some from an avowedly conservative perspective, that granting gays and lesbians the full benefits and dignity of marriage would be a stabilizing force in American life.

In the 1990s and 2000s, a curious dynamic unfolded. At first, same-sex marriage remained a low-priority issue, sometimes even an unwelcome one, for most LGBTQ organizations. But, because some members of the community *were* raising the matter, the Christian right mobilized to vanquish the marriage equality idea – prompting more and more LGBTQ activists to rally to its defense. In 1996, catering to social-conservative sentiment, Congress passed the Defense of Marriage Act (DOMA), which declared that, in all matters relating to federal legislation or policy, "the word 'marriage' means only a legal union between one man and one woman." In both houses, the bill passed with lopsided majorities, reflecting the reality that the traditional definition of marriage was still too popular for many liberal Democrats to challenge. President Clinton, seeking reelection that fall, quietly signed DOMA into law. Over the next decade and a half, twenty-five states outlawed same-sex marriage by statute or constitutional amendment. In response, in liberal-leaning states and cities across the country, marriage equality advocates enacted *their* vision, whether by winning the legalization of same-sex marriage or by staging "rogue weddings" for same-sex couples. In February 2004, San Francisco Mayor Gavin Newsom invited Phyllis Lyon and Del Martin, who nearly fifty years earlier had founded the pioneering lesbian organization the Daughters of Bilitis, to exchange marriage vows in his city hall office. Over the next month, nearly four thousand same-sex wedding ceremonies occurred in San Francisco, before the California Supreme Court ordered a halt to them. Across the nation, support for marriage equality was increasingly the expected stance in LGBTQ circles.

All the same, most Democratic politicians at the national level continued to oppose marriage equality, usually with the qualification that same-sex couples should be permitted to enter into civil unions offering most of the legal benefits of marriage. These were the positions Obama held when he ran for president in 2008, and they remained substantially unchanged during his first term. In the space of those four years, however, public support for marriage equality grew markedly, surpassing the 50 percent threshold in national opinion polls in 2011. As the 2012 election approached, Obama sought a graceful way to reverse his position and thereby catch up to his own supporters. In the spring of that year, White House staffers arranged for the president and his wife, First Lady Michelle Obama, to appear on *The View*, a daytime television talk show hosted by a panel of women, on which the topic of same-sex marriage would come up seemingly spontaneously, in an atmosphere underscoring Obama's qualities as a compassionate family man keeping up with the times.

Before that could happen, however, Vice President Biden, who like Obama had heretofore opposed marriage equality, appeared on the television news program *Meet the Press* and was asked for his own view on the matter. Never one to be coy when garrulousness was an option, Biden revealed that he now supported same-sex marriage. The news media buzzed over an apparent rift at the top of the Democratic ticket. In a hastily arranged interview on *Good Morning America*, Obama aligned himself with Biden's position. It was a matter of simple justice, the president said, especially for members of the military "who are out there fighting on my behalf, and yet feel constrained, even now that Don't Ask, Don't Tell is gone, because they're not able to commit themselves in a marriage." Some White House aides were annoyed that Biden had inadvertently spoiled the carefully choreographed about-face, but Obama himself seemed relieved to have shed what had become, for mainstream Democrats, a retrograde stance. (Mitt Romney, by now the presumptive Republican nominee, remained committed to opposing marriage equality. In a sign of the times, however, he found it prudent to avoid raising the issue.)

On Election Day, not only was Obama returned to office, with LGBTQ voters supporting him three to one, but marriage equality prevailed in four state elections. (Voters in Maine, Maryland, and Washington state approved ballot measures permitting same-sex marriage, while Minnesota's electorate defeated a constitutional amendment that would have outlawed it.) Although many more states still banned same-sex marriage than permitted it, the political and legal momentum now clearly favored marriage equality. In its June 2013 decision *The United States v. Windsor*, the US Supreme Court overturned a provision of DOMA denying federal recognition to same-sex marriages. (In another sign of the times, the Obama Department of Justice had refused to defend DOMA in the case.) The *Windsor* ruling unleashed a series of court challenges to state same-sex marriage bans. Technically, *Windsor* did not bear directly on the arguments underlying the state bans, but the decision's language was so clear and forceful that it furnished powerful legal and political ammunition to marriage equality proponents. In rapid succession, federal district judges overturned state bans. Although some of these decisions were reversed or stayed on appeal, by June 2015 thirty-seven states allowed same-sex marriage. That same month, in its landmark ruling *Obergefell v. Hodges*, the Supreme Court invalidated all state bans on same-sex marriage, saying they violated the due process and equal protection clauses of the Fifth and Fourteenth Amendments. Same-sex couples, wrote Justice Anthony Kennedy in the majority opinion, "ask for equal dignity in the eyes of the law. The Constitution grants them that right."

Reform Efforts on Guns and Immigration

Obama had ambitious plans for his second term. He wanted to build on the achievements of his first four years, such as by implementing the Affordable Care Act and boosting the sluggish economic recovery, and to tackle issues he had been unable to address more frontally, like immigration and climate change. Unexpectedly, however, the opening months of his second term were dominated by an effort to combat gun violence. The issue intruded in the

Figure 14.3 People leaving the staging area outside Sandy Hook Elementary School in Newtown, Connecticut, December 14, 2012. Source: *New York Daily News* Archive / *The New York Daily News* / Getty Images.

worst possible way. In December 2012, a mentally disturbed young man with a semiautomatic rifle entered the Sandy Hook Elementary School in Newtown, Connecticut, and killed twenty children, all aged six or seven, along with six adult staff members; two teachers were injured. The gunman, who had fatally shot his mother earlier that morning, committed suicide as first responders arrived. It was the largest school shooting in US history.

Several mass shootings had already occurred during Obama's first term. In November 2009, an army psychologist killed thirteen and wounded more than thirty at the Fort Hood army base in Central Texas. In January 2011, in a Tucson, Arizona, parking lot, a gunman killed six and wounded thirteen, including Democratic Representative Gabrielle Giffords, who suffered permanent brain damage. In July 2012, another gunman killed twelve and injured seventy in a movie theater in Aurora, Colorado. But Sandy Hook was different. The deliberate targeting of elementary school students stunned and horrified Americans, especially those with young children. Obama, whose own two daughters were aged eleven and fourteen, was visibly grief-stricken. After each previous shooting, the president had deplored the violence, reiterated his support for "commonsense gun reform," and then, mindful of political realities, moved on to other matters. This time, he surprised his aides by vowing to push for meaningful gun legislation, whatever the political consequences.

The odds were against such an endeavor. True, polls suggested that most Americans favored moderate reforms to keep guns out of dangerous hands and curb the circulation of military-style assault weapons. But the minority opposing gun restrictions was far more passionate and mobilized than was the majority supporting them. The chief organizer of the nay-sayers, the National Rifle Association, saw any gun control reform, however modest, as an unacceptable infringement on Americans' Second Amendment right to keep and bear arms. The NRA exerted enormous influence over Republican members of Congress – and had some Democrats running scared as well. Largely for that reason, Congress had passed no major gun control legislation since the ban on military-style assault weapons in 1994 (see Chapter 12).

Nonetheless, Obama and other gun control advocates, who now poignantly included some of the parents of the murdered Sandy Hook children, hoped the nation's shock over the killings would force action on Capitol Hill. In January 2013, Obama urged Congress to reinstate the assault weapons ban, which had expired in 2004; to outlaw armor-piercing bullets and large-capacity magazines; to require expanded criminal background checks for all firearms purchases; and to close loopholes that permitted criminals to evade existing background checks by purchasing weapons at gun shows or from private sellers. No one expected the NRA and other gun rights supporters to accede to these proposals, but the audacity, ferocity, and ultimate effectiveness of their counterattack were startling. Schoolchildren could be protected, the NRA insisted, not by restricting the general public's access to guns but by arming teachers or stationing police officers at schools. "The only thing that stops a bad guy with a gun," said NRA executive vice president Wayne LaPierre, "is a good guy with a gun." LaPierre also called for an "an active national database of the mentally ill," glossing over the fact that the vast majority of mentally ill people are nonviolent. From the far right fringe, the radio talk show host Alex Jones alleged that the US government had faked the Sandy Hook shootings to build public support for gun control. Listeners inflamed by Jones harassed and threatened family members of Sandy Hook victims, accusing them of complicity in the fraud.

Republican lawmakers steered clear of Jones's wild theories, but few were willing to buck the NRA. "President Obama is targeting the Second Amendment rights of law-abiding citizens," said Florida Senator Marco Rubio, "instead of seriously addressing the real underlying causes of such violence," by which Rubio meant the antisocial propensities of criminals and the mentally ill. Senator Joe Manchin of West Virginia, a right-leaning Democrat from a red state, worked with Senator Pat Toomey of Pennsylvania, a conservative Republican from a purple state, to craft legislation containing some of Obama's ideas. But in April 2013 their bill failed to clear the sixty-vote threshold for withstanding a filibuster. "[T]his was a pretty shameful day in Washington," Obama said of the spectacle on the Senate floor. Five months later, a gunman fatally shot twelve people at the Washington Navy Yard in the nation's capital. Grisly mass shootings continued to punctuate Obama's presidency.

If the failure of the gun control drive came with any consolation, it was that the effort collapsed only three months into Obama's second term, enabling his administration to pivot to another, seemingly more achievable project: a long-delayed overhaul of the nation's immigration policies. A period of rare introspection within the Republican establishment, occasioned by Mitt Romney's 2012 defeat, had furnished an opening. In March 2013, channeling the views of many party leaders and strategists, Republican National Committee chair Reince Priebus issued a 100-page document officially entitled the "Growth and Opportunity Project" but colloquially known as the "Autopsy." It called on the party to modernize itself by making better use of digital technology and working harder to win over women and racial and ethnic minorities, groups that had drifted away from the GOP in recent election cycles. The Autopsy was especially keen on outreach to Hispanics, whose disaffection from the party had been unusually sharp. In 2004, 40 percent of Latinos had voted to reelect George W. Bush; in 2012, only 27 percent voted for Romney. According to the Autopsy, the problem lay squarely in immigration politics: "If Hispanic Americans hear that the GOP doesn't want them in the United States, they won't pay attention to our next sentence." Explicitly, the Autopsy confined itself to urging that Republicans adopt a more inclusive "tone" when discussing immigration. Implicitly, the message was that the party's substantive positions should be more welcoming, too. Republican leaders generally praised this admonition as clear-eyed and bracing. Others in the party were less persuaded, and their political clout was underappreciated at first.

Meanwhile, immigration rights advocates were enjoying a surge of self-confidence. Latino voters had been key to Obama's reelection victory; the president and other Democrats now owed them a large debt. This development, combined with the Autopsy, suggested that the moment to renew the push for comprehensive immigration reform had finally arrived. In the Senate, a "Gang of Eight" consisting of four Democrats and four Republicans hammered out a bill that, like the failed bills of the previous decade, combined beefed-up security measures with efforts to normalize the status of those already in the country illegally. The 2013 version, which the Senate passed in June by a vote of sixty-eight to thirty-two, increased funding for border control; contained a guest worker program that made it easier for companies to hire (and for the federal government to track) temporary foreign laborers; and provided pathways to legal status and US citizenship for many undocumented immigrants, with DREAMers granted the speediest path (DACA having furnished them only stopgap relief).

The focus now shifted to the House, which, unlike the Senate, was under GOP control. Speaker of the House John Boehner, an Ohio Republican, wanted to pass an immigration bill but realized that most House Republicans disdained the Senate version as ceding too much to the undocumented. (Few of these members represented districts with large Latino populations; they were generally immune to the political pressure besetting the party's national leadership.) Boehner could have passed the Senate bill by combining Democratic votes with those of a minority of Republican members, but the resulting rebellion within his caucus might well have cost him his speakership. So Boehner refused to bring the Senate bill to a floor vote. Instead, he allowed pro-reform House Republicans to try to craft an alternative bill that could somehow pass muster with the Republican caucus while still signaling the party's friendliness to Hispanics.

For months, the House negotiations dragged on inconclusively. By early 2014, many immigrants' rights advocates had despaired of legislative action and were again calling on Obama to use his executive authority. They demanded that he apply "deferred action" not just to DREAMers but to all undocumented immigrants, except those guilty of serious violent crimes. They also decried the stepped-up deportations occurring on his watch. In five years, the Obama administration had deported close to two million people, nearly as many as the previous administration had removed over two terms. (The administration was implementing a Bush-era directive that US Immigration and Customs Enforcement cooperate with local law enforcement to deport more undocumented immigrants with criminal records. Obama declined to reverse this policy, he later wrote, so as not "to provide ammunition to critics who claimed that Democrats weren't willing to enforce existing immigration laws – a perception we thought could torpedo our chances of passing a future reform bill.") In March 2014, National Council of La Raza president Janet Murguía called Obama the "deporter in chief." The epithet became a staple of pro-immigrant demonstrations and commentaries. Though stung by their rebukes, Obama was moving in his critics' direction. If Congress failed to pass an immigration bill by summer, he warned, his administration would act unilaterally.

For a while, the president's threat seemed to be working. Behind closed doors, the pace of congressional negotiations quickened, and informed insiders reported genuine progress. In June 2014, however, a political earthquake struck. Representative Eric Cantor, the Republican majority leader, lost what should have been an effortless race for renomination in his Virginia district. The victor was David Brat, an obscure Tea Party-ish college professor who had painted Cantor as soft on illegal immigration. (Cantor was plenty hawkish on the issue, but like other Republicans he had shown some sympathy for DREAMers.) Cantor's defeat sent a shiver of fear through Republican ranks, ending all prospects of a grand bargain on immigration. Boehner told Obama that the House would pass no bill in 2014.

Obama had planned, in the event of Congress's failure to act, to unveil an executive policy change that summer, but outside events intruded. Over the previous year, tens of thousands of unaccompanied children, most of them from Central American countries stricken by poverty and gang violence, had arrived at the southern border seeking entry into the United States; this human surge peaked in the summer of 2014. US officials placed the young migrants in improvised detention centers, granting asylum to some of them and sending others back into Mexico. The influx eased in the late summer and fall. At its height, though, Obama feared that any declaration of a new policy showing leniency to the undocumented would draw more migrant children to the US–Mexican border. Meanwhile, Democratic congressmembers up for reelection in swing districts and states, fearing the same wrath that had just felled Eric Cantor, urged the president to delay his announcement until after the November 2014 midterms. Obama complied. A couple of weeks after the elections – which went terribly for the Democrats anyway (see below) – he announced a broadening of DACA. Now, the parents of DREAMers, and all other undocumented immigrants whose children were US-born citizens or legal residents, would be similarly exempted from deportation.

Or so, at least, Obama intended. Twenty-six states, all with Republican governors, promptly sued in federal court to block the new policy, known as Deferred Action for the Parents of Americans. A federal district judge in Texas issued an injunction against DAPA, pending a ruling on its constitutionality. The policy remained tied up in the courts for the rest of Obama's presidency.

Second-Term Foreign Policy

During his second term, as during his first, Obama enjoyed greater freedom of action in foreign affairs than he did at home, though pressures and criticisms mounted by fellow Americans could scarcely be ignored. A diplomatic flareup in August 2013 over civil-war-wracked Syria was a case in point. The previous summer, US intelligence agencies had reported that the Syrian government had taken some chemical weapons out of storage, prompting Obama to issue a public warning that the use of such weapons would cross a "red line." Obama had zero appetite for enforcing this ultimatum but felt he had no choice but to deliver it. Some of his advisers wished he had not done so. A year later, US and European intelligence agencies confirmed that a Syrian government sarin gas attack against Ghouta, a rebel-held suburb of Damascus, had killed an estimated 1,400 men, women, and children. With palpable reluctance, Obama began preparing the nation for a "limited, tailored" military operation in Syria to uphold the norm against using CWs. Few in the American public, on Capitol Hill, or in the international community hankered for US military action, either. When Obama announced that he was prepared to strike but would do so only if Congress authorized it – ostensibly a gesture of constitutional deference and scruple – lawmakers of both parties were furious to see the onus of decision descending on *them*. It seemed probable that Congress would deny authorization and thereby damage the president's domestic and international credibility.

For Obama, political and diplomatic salvation came from an unlikely quarter. Russia's president, Vladimir Putin, said he could persuade Syria, a close ally of Russia, to surrender its CW stockpiles if the United States refrained from military action. Obama practically leapt at the offer. Over the following year, under UN supervision, Syria destroyed what appeared to be all of its CW stockpiles. Soon after Obama left office, however, the Asad government – drawing on stores that had either escaped detection or been freshly assembled – resumed its CW attacks on civilians, prompting President Donald Trump to order limited air and missile strikes against Syrian military targets.

Obama succeeded, then, in postponing a US military confrontation with the Damascus regime until after he stepped down. But he could not avoid taking military action of his own against other, nonstate adversaries operating within Syria. This turn of events grew out of the nexus between the Syrian civil war and the destabilization of neighboring Iraq. In the latter country, the US troop surge of 2007–2008 and the accompanying strategy of placating Sunni communities had significantly weakened Iraqi militias affiliated with al-Qa'ida (see Chapter 13). From 2012 to 2014, however, three developments reversed that trend. First, the withdrawal of US troops in December 2011 had left a security vacuum in the country. Second, Iraq's US-backed prime minister, Nouri al-Maliki, a Shia, infuriated Iraqi Sunnis by excluding them from governing and law enforcement institutions, jailing some of their leaders, and violently suppressing their political activities. In response, Sunnis again turned to al-Qa'ida-affiliated militias for protection, allowing those militias to recover their strength. Third, amid the chaos of Syria's civil war, al-Qaida-affiliated groups from Iraq established a foothold in Syria, making common cause with Syrian jihadists and building a power base that, in short order, lent cross-border support to jihadi military operations back in Iraq.

By 2013, the combined Iraqi and Syrian militants were calling themselves the Islamic State in Iraq and al-Sham (an Arabic word for Syria) and were expanding rapidly across a broad swath of ungoverned territory spanning those two nations. As its name suggested, ISIS aspired to the status of a territorial state, not simply of a militant Islamist organization like al-Qa'ida. Indeed, ISIS declared itself to be the Caliphate, heir to a succession of Islamic states that had governed different parts of the Middle East from the seventh century through the early twentieth century (the last Caliphate being the Ottoman Empire, based in Turkey, which held the title from 1517 until its official dissolution in 1923). The twenty-first-century Islamic State behaved with stunning brutality, executing enemy combatants en masse and terrorizing civilians who fell under its control. Non-Muslims faced the choice of conversion or slaughter. ISIS also gained notoriety for beheading hostages and even burning them alive; it posted videos of these grisly acts on the internet. In 2014, ISIS beheaded three captured Americans: journalists James Foley and Steven Sotloff and aid worker Peter Kassig.

The rise of ISIS forced the Obama administration to reenter the fray. In the fall of 2014, it pressured al-Maliki to resign the premiership in favor of another Shia politician, Haider al-Abadi, who took a more conciliatory stance toward Iraqi Sunnis. Earlier that year, the United States began conducting airstrikes against ISIS positions in both Iraq and Syria, as part of a multilateral effort (involving the air and ground forces of several nations and a hodgepodge of local militias, many of these actors mutually antagonistic) to halt and reverse ISIS's terrifying spread. The campaign to defeat ISIS would succeed a couple of years after Obama left office, but its necessity mocked his earlier pledge to end America's "forever wars" in the Middle East.

Obama had greater success in dealing with Iran, though his actions generated considerable controversy. Since the early 2000s, the United States had sought to curb Iran's nuclear energy program. The Iranians claimed the program was intended solely for civilian purposes, but their withholding of crucial information about it from the International Atomic Energy Agency aroused suspicions that they were pursuing a nuclear weapons capability. Strident public statements by Iranian leaders menacing Israel's security and casting doubt on the truth of the Nazi Holocaust alarmed and outraged the Israeli government, which threatened unilateral military action against Iran's nuclear facilities. Prodded by Washington, the UN Security Council imposed increasingly stringent economic sanctions against Iran, which insisted on its right to keep enriching uranium.

During Obama's second term, the United States joined with Russia, China, Britain, France, and Germany (a group known as the "P5+1," for the five permanent members of the UN Security Council plus Germany) to negotiate a resolution with Iran. In the resulting Joint Comprehensive Plan of Action (JCPOA), signed in July 2015, Iran accepted limits on its ability to acquire and enrich nuclear fuels in exchange for the easing of economic sanctions. Israeli prime minister Benjamin Netanyahu blasted the JCPOA, charging that it asked far too little of Tehran and would only abet its nuclear ambitions, a view shared by many Americans, especially in the Republican Party. In March 2015, Republican leaders invited Netanyahu to attack the anticipated agreement in a speech before a joint session of Congress, a startling breach of political and diplomatic norms. Saudi Arabia, another strategic foe of Iran, also strongly opposed the JCPOA. But the Obama administration stayed the diplomatic course, insisting that a shunned and isolated Iran would be much more dangerous to its neighbors.

In all of these actions in the Middle East, Obama relied on a measure of Russian cooperation. It was Vladimir Putin who furnished Obama with a face-saving exit from his "red line" predicament over Syria. Putin's Russia also enlisted in the anti-ISIS campaign and participated in the negotiations leading to the JCPOA. Overall, though, US–Russian relations sharply deteriorated in Obama's second term, due largely to Putin's intensified efforts to reassert Moscow's dominance over former Soviet republics.[3] In early 2014, Russia annexed Crimea, in southern Ukraine. The merits of the case were not entirely clear-cut. Russia had annexed Crimea in 1783, and the Soviet Union had made it a separate Soviet republic in 1921. In 1954, Moscow transferred Crimea to the Ukrainian Soviet Socialist Republic, and Ukraine kept it after gaining independence in 1991. Still, the brazenness of Putin's move shocked international observers. Weeks later, Russia fomented a separatist rebellion in eastern Ukraine, supporting the uprising with arms, training, logistics, propaganda, and, surreptitiously, some of its own troops. The United States and other Western nations imposed economic sanctions against Russia. The Group of Eight (G-8), an intergovernmental forum for the leading democracies to discuss global issues, became the G-7 by expelling Russia from its ranks. Obama gave Ukraine nonlethal military equipment but resisted calls from Congress and from within his own administration to arm that country or take other strong action on its behalf. "We're not going to send in the Eighty-Second Airborne, Joe," he told Vice President Biden. Obama's restraint averted a proxy military confrontation, but the United States and Russia appeared to be sliding into a new cold war.

Wielding Executive Authority

Against the backdrop of these turbulent developments, Americans voted in the November 2014 midterm elections and handed the Democrats another "shellacking." The Republicans significantly expanded their majority in the House and also took control of the Senate. Although each individual result reflected local circumstances, the electorate as a whole appears to have been swayed by a sense that the Democratic standard-bearer had lost control of events. The rampages of ISIS, the provocations of Putin, the surge of migrant children at the border, the terrifying Ebola crisis mentioned at the start of this chapter – it all formed an impression of a cocky president suddenly out of this depth. A handful of domestic outrages and missteps – a scandal at the Veterans Administration, where officials had falsified records

[3] Some analysts attributed Putin's aggressive stance on former Soviet republics to anxiety over NATO's eastward expansion, especially the decisions to admit Poland, Hungary, and the Czech Republic in 1999 and the Baltic states of Lithuania, Latvia, and Estonia in 2004. Yet Putin's later actions, especially his military assault on Ukraine in early 2022 (see Epilogue), suggested a more basic drive to dominate Ukraine and perhaps eliminate its independence entirely.

to conceal long delays in granting doctors' appointments to veterans; the botched unveiling of the Obamacare website in 2013, still a fresh memory – completed the picture of a flailing administration. In an era when congressional races were increasingly nationalized, perceived shortcomings at the top affected all Democratic candidates. "No member of the Democratic caucus screwed up the rollout of that health-care Web site," complained an aide to Senate Majority Leader Harry Reid, "yet they paid the price – every one of them." The rejoinder that Obama had handled the Ebola crisis, at least, with steadiness and skill, whereas Republicans had reacted hysterically, consoled few congressional Democrats now facing across-the-board minority status.

Obama himself was less discouraged by the setback than one might have expected. He realized he could effectuate a good deal of policy change without Congress's help, much as he had done in providing relief to DREAMers. Since the start of his administration, Obama had, like all modern presidents, resorted to executive orders and executive agreements (agreements with other countries requiring no Senate ratification), but these mechanisms now became more central to his governance. The main advantage of executive actions is that they bypass the obstructionism of hostile Congresses. Their principal drawback is that they are much easier for future presidents to undo.

A clear candidate for the executive approach was climate change policy. As recently as the mid-2000s, a handful of leading Republicans had acknowledged that humankind's increased emissions of carbon dioxide, methane, nitrous oxide, and other compounds were very likely altering the earth's climate in ways that threatened future generations. (Collectively, these emissions are known as "greenhouse gases," because they contribute to the "greenhouse effect" of trapping heat within the earth's atmosphere.) By the time of Obama's presidency, however, the combined influence of the fossil fuel industry and conservative pressure groups had virtually eliminated such sentiment within the GOP. The only acceptable position these days was outright denial of any human impact on climate or an insistence that the jury was still out on the matter. Some Democratic congressmembers from oil- and coal-producing states were also susceptible to such thinking. (Ironically, politicians' rejection of the theory of human-caused climate change coincided with a rapid accumulation of evidence supporting it.) The 2009 stimulus bill, passed with hardly any Republican votes, contained $90 billion in subsidies for technologies aimed at reducing greenhouse gas emissions. These investments dramatically boosted wind, solar, and other "green" forms of energy, reducing their costs to the point that they started becoming commercially viable. After the 2010 midterms, however, it was all but impossible to promote green energy legislatively. So the Obama administration turned increasingly to executive action, issuing regulations that tightened fuel efficiency and emissions standards for cars, buses, and trucks. The cumulative impact of all of these measures was a marked reduction in US greenhouse gas emissions, which never returned to their peak 2007 level.

In 2015, Obama's executive action strategy grew more ambitious. For all the progress achieved in reducing greenhouse gas emissions, a major component of the problem remained unaddressed: power plants, which accounted for 40 percent of all such emissions. In August, the Obama administration issued the Clean Power Plan. Drawing on authority granted in the 1970 Clear Air Act (and thus requiring no new legislation), the Plan imposed an individualized cap on each state's power plant emissions, while granting states leeway in how they adhered to their limits. Working together, the caps were designed, by 2030, to reduce all power plant emissions by 32 percent from their 2005 levels.

Meanwhile, recognizing the global nature of the challenge, Obama engaged with other nations to curb greenhouse gas emissions. The People's Republic of China, which was industrializing at a furious rate and had overtaken the United States in carbon emissions (albeit with a far larger population, meaning its per capita contribution to the problem was much smaller), had a special status in Obama's diplomacy. Since emerging as an economic powerhouse late in the twentieth century, the PRC had refused to join international efforts to limit industrial pollution, noting, accurately enough, that in the nineteenth and twentieth centuries Western nations had industrialized *their* economies utterly heedless of environmental impacts. If the PRC could be turned around on this issue, Obama administration officials reasoned, other industrializing countries might more readily accept limits on their greenhouse gas emissions. Actually, the PRC was itself coming to see the value of clean energy: its cities were already choked with pollution, and "green diplomacy" could enhance Beijing's international prestige. In 2013 and 2014, the PRC reached bilateral agreements with the United States whereby each nation pledged to curb its harmful emissions.

The "China first" strategy succeeded. In the Paris Climate Agreement of December 2015, the United States, China, and nearly 200 other nations pledged to work toward the goal of keeping global temperatures at well below 2 degrees Celsius, and preferably at 1.5 degrees C, above preindustrial levels by the middle of the twenty-first century. They would also try to achieve "net zero" – the condition in which greenhouse gas emissions do not exceed the ability of trees, soil, and oceans to absorb them – by 2050. Instead of imposing hard limits on signatories, the Paris Agreement committed them to setting voluntary goals, in the expectation that these goals would grow more ambitious over time. Critics objected that the terms were too vague and soft. The agreement's defenders countered that a certain looseness was key to achieving progress on such a massive, intricate, and contentious issue. Previous climate agreements had imposed firm limits that nations failed to meet, creating an aura of futility around the diplomacy. A more voluntary system would encourage signatories to work toward success. Proponents also argued that the green energy revolution under way since around 2010 made it more economically feasible for nations to meet their self-proclaimed targets.

From a US standpoint, the main weakness of the Paris Agreement was that the Obama administration had entered into it as an executive agreement. There had been no other way. A treaty would have required the approval of two-thirds of the Senate; it would have been hard enough to get that back in 2009, let alone after 2014. But the lack of congressional endorsement rendered the Paris Agreement vulnerable. Like the Clean Power Plan – or, for that matter, the JCPOA over Iran's nuclear capabilities – it was subject to unilateral revocation by a future president, a threat that would materialize a good deal sooner than many expected.

Black Lives Matter

Throughout Obama's public performance of the presidency, questions of race were never far below the surface, and sometimes, of course, they were in plain view. In the early years, Obama had stepped carefully around the topic, seeking to avoid appearing excessively attuned to the concerns of fellow African Americans – a stance that disappointed and sometimes angered many Black activists and commentators. From about 2012 on, however, the age-old issue of excessive police violence against African Americans became much more prominent and pressing, and Obama grew bolder about sounding racial themes. Inseparable from these developments were rapid advances in digital technology and changes in the media landscape. The proliferation of smartphones, and of digital cameras attached to the dashboards of police cars and the bodies of officers, made it much easier to record cops' interactions with ordinary people. The growing popularity of social media platforms, and the fact that newspapers and television programs now operated websites onto which they uploaded video clips, meant that recordings of police officers in action, including ones in which they brutalized and sometimes killed African Americans, could be widely posted and shared. Even altercations not captured on film were endlessly dissected and debated in the new, high-velocity social media environment.

One of the early incidents to gain viral notoriety not only wasn't recorded; it involved an amateur rather than a paid officer of the law. In February 2012, twenty-eight-year-old George Zimmerman, a neighborhood watch volunteer for his gated community in Sanford, Florida, shot and killed Trayvon Martin, an unarmed Black seventeen-year-old. Zimmerman, who was of white American and Peruvian parentage (and thus lacked a clear racial identity in media coverage), claimed he had fired his gun in self-defense during a scuffle in which Martin had gained the upper hand. The Sanford police initially accepted this account and let Zimmerman walk free. Outraged by the inaction, Martin's parents started an online petition publicizing the killing and demanding Zimmerman's arrest. National media outlets picked up the story, and protest demonstrations occurred in several cities. Black athletes, entertainers, public intellectuals, and officeholders urged an investigation of the homicide. President Obama echoed the call, saying, "If I had a son, he'd look like Trayvon." In response to the pressure, Zimmerman was arrested, and a special prosecutor appointed by Florida's governor charged him with second-degree murder. But in July 2013 a jury acquitted him, citing insufficient evidence for conviction on such a serious charge.

Opinions about the Trayvon Martin case varied, but African American and left-of-center commentators generally agreed that Zimmerman had killed Martin unjustly and done so out of the same punitive, racist zeal that characterized all too many urban police forces. (An aspiring criminologist, Zimmerman had a history of calling 911 dispatchers to report suspicious activities, often by African American men.) In a Facebook post, an Oakland, California, labor activist named Alicia Garza condemned Zimmerman's acquittal and closed with the words "Our lives matter." Garza and two other activists, Patrisse Cullors and Opal (later Ayọ) Tometi, then launched the social media hashtag #BlackLivesMatter, which became an online rallying cry for critics of excessive

Figure 14.4 Black Lives Matter protesters in St. Louis, Missouri, 2014. Source: Jewel Samad / AFP / Getty Images.

police violence and vigilantism, high incarceration rates for African Americans, and other manifestations of institutional racism.

At first mainly a social media phenomenon, Black Lives Matter (BLM) grew into a much more concrete and visible movement in the summer of 2014. In July, New York City police accused a forty-three-year-old Black man, Eric Garner, of illegally selling loose cigarettes on the street. An officer wrestled Garner to the ground and placed him in an unauthorized chokehold as other cops handcuffed him. An onlooker filmed the incident on his cellphone. Eleven times, Garner, who was overweight and suffered from asthma, could be heard to plead "I can't breathe." He lost consciousness and died soon thereafter. Across the country, Garner's killing sparked angry protests, which intensified in December, when a local grand jury declined to indict the officer who had choked Garner.

Meanwhile, an incident in Ferguson, Missouri, a suburb of St. Louis, aroused national and even international notoriety. In August 2014, a white police officer shot and killed Michael Brown, an unarmed Black eighteen-year-old he had stopped on suspicion of robbery. There was no film recording of the altercation. The officer, Darren Wilson, claimed that Brown had charged at him with his right hand at his side, as if to draw a gun (which Wilson could not have known was nonexistent). Some witnesses corroborated Wilson's account, while others claimed that Brown had been shot with upraised hands. Dorian Johnson, a friend of Brown's who was at the scene, told a television interviewer that the slain teenager's last words were "I don't have a gun, stop shooting!" In the weeks of protest following the killing, in Ferguson itself and in cities across the nation, the slogan "Hands up, don't shoot!" gave voice to the vulnerability and terror so many Black Americans experienced in their day-to-day dealings with law enforcement.

As with the Trayvon Martin case, however, the stark and morally clear narrative put forward by activists proved difficult to sustain legally. Although Wilson lost his job at the Ferguson police department, a grand jury convened by the St. Louis County prosecutor determined that there was not enough evidence to indict him. The Obama Department of Justice, too, looked into the matter and concluded it could not credibly charge Wilson with violating Brown's civil rights. The DOJ's publicly released report so fully vindicated Wilson's account that *Washington Post* columnist Jonathan Capehart, a champion of BLM protests, ruefully concluded that the "Hands up, don't shoot" storyline "was wrong, built on a lie."[4] Yet Capehart went on to make a larger and more disturbing point: "[T]he false Ferguson narrative stuck because of concern over a distressing pattern of other police killings of unarmed African American men and boys around the time of Brown's death." In addition to Eric Garner, killed a few weeks earlier, these victims included twenty-two-year-old John Crawford III, shot dead in August 2014 near Dayton, Ohio, while holding a BB air rifle that was for sale at a Walmart store; and twelve-year-old Tamir Rice, killed that November in Cleveland, Ohio, by a policeman who thought his toy gun was real. In September, a South Carolina highway patrolman shot and wounded thirty-five-year-old Levar Jones as he reached for his driver's license during a traffic stop. And these were just the high-profile cases, all clustered in the second half of 2014.

Moreover, the Michael Brown killing, however misconstrued, shed a harsh light on broader police practices. When some of the Ferguson protesters began looting, setting fires, and throwing bricks and bottles at police, the latter responded with startling militarism, deploying armored vehicles, assault weapons, rubber bullets, and tear gas. It turned out that many of these menacing items were surplus military equipment furnished to the Ferguson police by a bloated Pentagon, and that numerous other urban police forces had overarmed themselves in this way. A chastened Obama administration banned federal agencies from providing certain military items to local police departments. The public soon learned other disturbing facts about law enforcement in Ferguson – and presumably elsewhere. In parallel with its inquiry into Brown's death, the Obama Department of Justice investigated the city's general police practices. Even as it effectively exonerated Officer Wilson, the DOJ found that the Ferguson police had systematically exploited the city's Black majority, especially through the issuing of traffic tickets. African Americans comprised 67 percent of Ferguson's population yet accounted for 86 percent of all drivers pulled over by the police, who wantonly fined Black motorists for all conceivable offenses, even the most trivial. Failure to pay a fine could result in arrest and imprisonment. Ferguson's entire law enforcement apparatus was built on

[4] The version of events offered by the Department of Justice report diverged significantly from the one generally presented in national media stories. Initially, several onlookers gave accounts to reporters that reinforced the "Hands up, don't shoot" narrative. After reviewing sworn testimony, however, the DOJ concluded that the most credible witnesses tended to be ones who claimed that Michael Brown had charged at Darren Wilson. Some of these witnesses had previously declined to share these accounts with the news media or the police for fear of antagonizing other members of the community. One reluctant witness "expressed concerns because there were signs in the neighborhood [of the shooting] stating, 'snitches get stitches.'"

these shakedowns, which were a major source of municipal revenue. Under the pressure of a DOJ lawsuit, the city government pledged to end its obnoxious treatment of residents.

Such practices may have been especially brazen in Ferguson, but few doubted that versions of them existed elsewhere. In late 2014, Obama convened a Task Force on Twenty-First Century Policing to explore ways to improve relations between law enforcement and local communities. The Task Force's report, issued in May 2015, offered a range of recommendations, from gathering fuller data on police shootings, to providing officers with sensitivity training, to increasing the racial and ethnic diversity of police forces, to demilitarizing the police presence at protest demonstrations. By the summer of 2015, twenty-four states had passed new laws regulating law enforcement's treatment of citizens. By mid-2017, according to one count, some 40 percent of the nation's largest police departments had adopted more community-friendly policies and training methods. Of course, reforms on paper were no guarantee of changes in police culture.

And shocking killings of African Americans kept coming to light, recorded by police car "dashcams" and bystanders' smartphones. In Tulsa, Oklahoma, in April 2015, Eric Harris was shot in the back by an officer who mistakenly drew his gun instead of his taser. "I'm losing my breath," Harris gasped, before succumbing to his wound. "Fuck your breath," a second cop snapped. In July 2016, Philando Castile was shot dead in his car, in front of his girlfriend and her four-year-old daughter, by a Minneapolis-area policeman who erroneously believed Castile was reaching for a gun. Not all of these homicides involved firearms. In April 2015, Baltimore police placed twenty-five-year-old Freddie Gray, hobbling and crying out in pain, into the back of a police van and failed to secure him properly. In the careening ride to the police station, Gray suffered severe neck and spine injuries and a crushed voice box; he slipped into a coma and died a week later. Black Baltimoreans erupted in protest, reacting not just to Gray's killing but to a pattern of Ferguson-like abuses by a police force seemingly bent on targeting and exploiting Black residents.

To be sure, most victims of police killings were, and continue to be, white. With non-Hispanic whites comprising nearly 60 percent of the US population, this is no surprise. Horrifying instances of excessive police violence against whites can easily be cited, and often have been by dissenters from the BLM narrative. That said, studies have shown that African Americans are about two and a half times as likely as whites to die at the hands of law enforcement. *Why* this is so is no simple matter. White police officers have occasionally been revealed to participate in racist subcultures, such as by sharing hateful memes on social media; some of these cops (and perhaps other cops free of overt bias) may well be more trigger-happy when confronting Black suspects. Still, one's chances of being killed by police seem more directly a function of class than of race. The percentage of Black people living in poverty is, again, about two and a half times as large as the percentage of whites in that condition. Residents of poor neighborhoods, whatever their race, are more likely to find themselves in hostile encounters with law enforcement, a tiny but now highly visible share of which turn deadly. African Americans are disproportionately killed in these encounters largely because they are disproportionately poor. Of course, the high levels of Black poverty are themselves a legacy of historical racism.

Although most Black victims of police violence are male, a substantial minority have been female. In the years of BLM's emergence, these included Rekia Boyd, killed in March 2012 by an off-duty Chicago policeman who mistook her companion's cellphone for a gun; Yvette Smith, who in February 2014 called 911 to report an altercation near her home, only to be shot dead by a Texas deputy dispatched to the scene; and Tanisha Anderson, a Cleveland, Ohio, woman with bipolar disorder who died in November 2014 after police forcefully subdued her during a manic episode. Because such cases received hardly any national attention, in 2015 the African American Policy Forum (AAPF), a social justice think tank, launched the hashtag #SayHerName and sponsored a vigil in New York City to publicize police violence against Black women and girls.

Weeks after the AAPF event, the case of twenty-eight-year-old Sandra Bland trained a national spotlight on the treatment of Black women in police custody. Pulled over for a minor traffic violation in Waller County, Texas, Bland argued with the cop, who barked commands at her, threatened to tase her, and pinned her to the ground. Bland was arrested for assaulting a police officer and held in the county jail, where she struggled to make bail. Three days later, she was found hanging in her cell, an evident suicide. Although some BLM activists alleged foul play by prison authorities, the more common charge was that a psychologically vulnerable young woman (Bland had faced mental health challenges) had been casually tossed into a Kafkaesque labyrinth. "[T]he entire possibility is that had she been white," remarked law professor and AAPF founder Kimberlé Crenshaw, "she would not have been in that jail cell in the first place." As with the DOJ's exposure of broader law enforcement practices in Ferguson, the Sandra Bland case suggested that police killings were merely the most blatant manifestation of a far larger, more complicated, and more mundane pattern of official abuse, consisting of thousands of small interactions that almost never made news.

Nor, of course, was law enforcement the only source of anti-Black violence. In June 2015, against the backdrop of ongoing BLM protests, a young white man entered a bible study session at the Emanuel African Methodist Episcopal Church in Charleston, South Carolina, and murdered nine Black parishioners. The gunman, apprehended the next day, was twenty-one-year-old Dylann Roof, a self-proclaimed white supremacist intent on starting a race war. The details of the tragedy were wrenching. Roof, the nation learned, had been welcomed by the parishioners and sat with them for nearly an hour before drawing his gun. The killings dragged on for six minutes. At the bond hearing, where a live image of Roof was displayed in the courtroom via closed-circuit television, the defendant stood impassively as family members of the slain tearfully forgave him. (Roof was later convicted and sentenced to nine consecutive life prison terms.) At a memorial service in the same church, President Obama eulogized one of the victims, pastor and state senator Clementa Pinckney, whom he had met while campaigning in South Carolina. "Our pain cuts that much deeper because it happened in a church," Obama observed. "The church is and always has been the center of African American life"; a place, he said – gently referencing the movement then roiling the country – "where children are loved and fed and kept out of harm's way and told that they are beautiful and smart and taught that they matter." The president closed by unexpectedly breaking into "Amazing Grace," some shaky notes at the beginning underscoring his humble fellowship with the gathered mourners, who joined him in song.

News reports that Roof's social media posts had featured the Confederate flag reignited long-smoldering controversies over official displays of that symbol. In 1961, in defiance of the civil rights movement, South Carolina's government had placed the Confederate flag atop the statehouse dome. In 2000, in a small concession to African Americans and others who found it offensive, the flag was relocated to the capitol grounds. After the Charleston church massacre, politicians and commentators of all backgrounds demanded that this emblem of slavery be banished altogether. The state's Republican governor, Nikki Haley, who had previously avoided the issue, now joined the call and quickly secured legislation in the state's Senate and House of Representatives, both of them Republican-controlled, for the flag's removal from the capitol grounds. In large part, the gesture responded to the growing racial and ethnic diversity of South Carolina, a reality highlighted by the fact that Haley herself was the daughter of Sikh Indian immigrants. Haley was a rising star in the Republican Party, one of a handful of prominent nonwhite Republican officeholders – such as Louisiana Governor Bobby Jindal, another Indian American, and South Carolina Senator Tim Scott, an African American – whom proponents of the GOP's 2013 Autopsy liked to tout. The failure to pass immigration reform in 2014 had been a conspicuous setback for the Autopsy's strategy of minority outreach. Perhaps South Carolina Republicans' quick action after the Charleston murders, and the applause it was drawing from Republicans everywhere, meant that the party really was starting to transcend its white base.

***

Or perhaps not. On June 16, 2015, the day before the Charleston church massacre, Donald Trump announced his candidacy for president in 2016. In rambling remarks delivered in the marble basement of Trump Tower, the Manhattan high-rise doubling as his business headquarters and personal residence, the magnate blasted the incumbent president's performance and presented himself as America's salvation. Receiving the widest attention were Trump's statements suggesting that most Mexican immigrants were drug dealers and rapists. Trump was tapping an all too evident vein of Republican sentiment on immigration, but it was unheard of for a credible major-party presidential aspirant to discuss the issue in such vulgar terms. Most pundits assumed, therefore, that Trump had no real shot at the nomination and was running mainly to make mischief, feed his ego, and generate publicity for his business ventures.

Startlingly, however, Trump raced to the front of the pack, acquiring a fervid base within the GOP surpassing that of any other Republican candidate. His harsh antiimmigrant statements, and his refusal to appease political tastemakers by disavowing the support of racists and white nationalists, were plain assets in his drive for the nomination. Many rank-and-file Republicans were drawn to Trump because of these qualities, not in spite of them. The GOP Autopsy would soon be swept off the table for good, and the nation's governing institutions plunged into an existential crisis unlike any other in their two-and-a-quarter-century history.

READING QUESTIONS

1. Although President Obama's Affordable Care Act drew on ideas previously embraced by conservatives, it elicited unanimous opposition from congressional Republicans. Why was that the case? What broader political outlook and strategy did that opposition exemplify?
2. What circumstances in the first half of the 2010s gave advocates for undocumented immigrants leverage in their quest for immigration reforms? What obstacles did those advocates face? How did both the opportunities and the obstacles evolve during those years?
3. How and why, in the 1990s and 2000s, did attitudes about the issue of marriage equality change within the LGBTQ activist community? How, in the 2010s, did national institutions respond to those shifting views?
4. Why, after about 2012, did the issue of excessive police violence against African Americans become so prominent? How did national, state, and local officials respond to activism surrounding that issue?

SUGGESTIONS FOR FURTHER READING

Alberta, Tim. *American Carnage: On the Front Lines of the Republican Civil War and the Rise of President Trump*. New York: Harper, 2019.

Alter, Jonathan. *The Center Holds: Obama and His Enemies*. New York: Simon & Schuster, 2013.

Baker, Peter. *Obama: The Call of History*. New York: New York Times, 2017.

Chait, Jonathan. *Audacity: How Barack Obama Defied His Critics and Created a Legacy that Will Prevail*. New York: William Morrow, 2017.

DeSipio, Louis, and Rodolfo O. de la Garza. *US Immigration in the Twenty-First Century: Making Americans, Remaking America*. Boulder, CO: Westview Press, 2015.

DiMaggio, Anthony. *Rebellion in America: Citizen Uprisings, the News Media, and the Politics of Plutocracy*. New York: Routledge, 2020.

Frank, Nathaniel. *Awakening: How Gays and Lesbians Brought Marriage Equality to the Nation*. Cambridge, MA: Belknap Press, 2017.

Hillstrom, Laurie Collier. *Black Lives Matter: From a Moment to a Movement*. Santa Barbara, CA: ABC-CLIO, 2018.

Kaufman, Burton I. *Barack Obama: Conservative, Pragmatist, Progressive*. Ithaca, NY: Cornell University Press, 2022.

Lacombe, Matthew J. *Firepower: How the NRA Turned Gun Owners into a Political Force*. Princeton, NJ: Princeton University Press, 2021.

Lowery, Wesley. *They Can't Kill Us All: Ferguson, Baltimore, and a New Era in America's Racial Justice Movement*. Boston: Little, Brown, 2016

Obama, Barack. *A Promised Land*. New York: Crown, 2020.

Wides-Muñoz, Laura. *The Making of a Dream: How a Group of Young Undocumented Immigrants Helped Change what it Means to Be American*. New York HarperCollins, 2018.

15 Crossfire Hurricane

The Trump Years, 2015–2021

Introduction

"Let us in! Let us in!" the crowd chanted as it confronted the thin line of police officers at the Capitol entrance. The protesters wore jackets, sweatshirts, vests, and other thick garments in the brisk morning air. Some draped themselves in American flags or sported red caps bearing President Donald Trump's "Make America Great Again" slogan. Others, many of them white men with long, unkempt beards, wore camouflage, bulletproof vests, and similar military attire. A few carried rifles on their shoulders. On the lawn and streets behind them, fellow protesters displayed signs reading "Don't Tread On Me" and "Make treason punishable by hanging." Someone had brought a Confederate flag.

The demonstrators were angry but peaceful. Some were allowed to enter, and even carry their guns into, the lobby of the State Capitol in Lansing, Michigan. They had gathered on that day in April 2020 to protest the stay-at-home orders that Democratic Governor Gretchen Whitmer had imposed to contain the deadly Covid-19 pandemic. They claimed that Whitmer's measures were arbitrary and draconian, stifling personal freedoms and destroying precious livelihoods. Although the Trump administration, following expert advice, had encouraged Michigan and other states to lock down their economies, the protesters had good reason to believe that the president himself embraced their cause. In a recent tweet, Trump had told Michiganders, "your Governor, Gretchen 'Half' Whitmer is way in over her head, she doesn't have a clue." Following an earlier anti-lockdown protest at the Michigan Capitol, during which many more Confederate flags, along with some nooses, had been spotted in the crowd, Trump tweeted "LIBERATE MICHIGAN!" After this second Capitol demonstration, Trump again ignored the protesters' menacing gestures and tweeted that Whitmer "should give a little, and put out the fire. These are very good people, but they are angry." It was neither the first time nor the last that Trump openly defied the very policies over which he was presiding, or did so in ways that nurtured insurrectionist impulses.

Michigan's lockdown wars erupted during the fourth year of Trump's tumultuous presidential term, an extraordinary interlude that revealed both the dysfunction of the nation's political system and the capacity of American institutions to surmount, or at least cope with, novel and frightening challenges. Trump was the first president to serve without prior experience in political office or the military. This in itself was no disqualification, but Trump had little understanding of the issues he was charged with addressing and still less desire to become better informed about them. Worse, he lacked even a rudimentary commitment to serve the broader interests of the nation, or to operate within its constitutional limits and political norms. Republican leaders had long recognized many of these qualities and, from mid-2015 to mid-2016, proclaimed their determination to keep Trump from becoming their standard-bearer. But they were unable to prevent his nomination, and then the vagaries of the electoral system allowed him to slip into the presidency. Once in office, Trump completed his capture of the Republican Party; the task of blocking his abuses fell almost entirely to the Democratic opposition. In the end, it was a presidential election, held amid a global pandemic and domestic social unrest, that ousted the domineering and lawless incumbent, whose desperate efforts to overturn that verdict presented the scariest test of all.

Donald Trump's Pursuit of the Republican Nomination

As soon as Trump launched his presidential bid in June 2015, he surged to the front of the Republican primary field. His disparaging remarks about Mexican immigrants posed no impediment to his advance, and neither did a host of ensuing outbursts that, under normal political rules, would have ended a presidential campaign. In July, Trump opined that Senator John McCain of Arizona, who had spent five and a half years as a prisoner of war in North Vietnam, was no hero. "I like people who weren't captured," Trump said, drawing thunderous denunciation from the Republican establishment and veterans' groups but no evident disapproval from his rank-and-file supporters. During the first Republican primary debate, in August 2015, Trump sparred with one of the moderators, Megyn Kelly of the right-leaning Fox News network. Recounting the exchange to a CNN reporter the next day, Trump said, "You know, you could see there was blood coming out of her eyes, blood coming out of her ... wherever." Many conservative commentators condemned this statement and rallied to Kelly's defense. Fox News chair Roger Ailes demanded that Trump apologize to Kelly, but the candidate refused and kept on attacking her, mainly via his choice medium of Twitter. In the coming weeks, seeing that Trump would not back down and remained at the head of the Republican pack, Fox made its peace with him. Soon thereafter, the network emerged as his avid booster.

How did Trump win over so many Republican base voters? In part, he skillfully exploited the resentment that a large swath of white Americans, many but by no means all of them lacking college education, harbored toward the elites of both parties who dominated national policy. He tapped into those voters' anger over the loss of good manufacturing jobs (hardly a new problem, but one whose very longevity yielded a sort of compounded rage); over the perception that the United States was losing trade wars against the People's Republic of China and other economic competitors; over the fact that large swaths of rural America were economically stagnant and ravaged by a growing opioid crisis;[1] and over a belief that illegal immigration was out of control.

This last issue dovetailed with unsettling international events to create a sense of heightened vulnerability. By 2015, turmoil in Afghanistan, Iraq, and Syria, was propelling hundreds of thousands of refugees into the nations of the European Union, straining their material resources and their commitment to generous asylum policies. Many Americans feared that the refugee waves would soon break upon their own shores. During that same year, as the multilateral campaign against the Islamic State in Iraq and al-Sham gathered force (see Chapter 14), ISIS reacted by sponsoring and inspiring violent attacks around the world, including a set of coordinated assaults in Paris in November that killed 137 people, and a shooting rampage in San Bernardino, California, in December that killed sixteen. Days after the San Bernardino attack, whose perpetrators were a Pakistani American and his Pakistani wife, Trump called for "a total and complete shutdown of Muslims entering the United States until our country's representatives can figure out what the hell is going on." Leaders of both parties criticized this statement, but a poll found 59 percent of Republicans supporting it, and Trump remained the frontrunner. His pledges to reinstate torture, kill the family members of terrorists, and "bomb the shit out of" ISIS drew lusty cheers from Republican crowds.

Trump also exploited the bewilderment and resentment with which many older, white, nonurban voters greeted cultural changes occurring in universities, the national news media, and other realms where liberals tended to predominate. Starting around 2014, national media outlets ran stories about "trigger warnings," "safe spaces," "microaggressions," and other newfangled terms and concepts circulating on college campuses. To many in red America, these developments were bizarre and incomprehensible, especially when seen through the distorting prism of conservative media, which highlighted the most flamboyant and off-putting manifestations of the evolving academic culture. It was at about this time that Black Lives Matter, a movement many non-Black Americans found strident and divisive – why only Black lives? Didn't all lives matter? – became nationally visible, along with a host of new rules and taboos governing public discussion of race, ethnicity, gender, and sexuality. More boldly than any other Republican candidate, Trump defied these emerging norms (and plenty of established norms, too), cultivating a "politically incorrect" persona that rank-and-file Republicans, and many others not tied to the party, found liberating.

Trump had another asset that pundits often underestimated. For well over a decade, he had starred in two popular reality TV shows, *The Apprentice* and *The Celebrity Apprentice*. On both, he sat behind an imposing desk and made crisp, commanding, executive decisions. The content was scripted and edited, of course, to make him seem much more disciplined

[1] Since the late 1990s, doctors had increasingly prescribed synthetic drugs known as opioids (so named because they interact with opioid receptors in the nervous system) to help patients manage acute pain. Some of the medications were highly addictive, and people's overreliance on them produced severe disruptions in their family lives, employment patterns, and physical health. In 2015, more than 33,000 Americans died from opioid overdoses. The crisis was especially prevalent in white rural communities.

and articulate than he actually was. As President Obama had reminded everyone at the 2011 White House Correspondents' Dinner, the issues Trump was resolving were trivial and frequently absurd. But the subliminal impression, received by millions of viewers, was of a forceful decision-maker asserting his control over contentious and chaotic situations. Why *couldn't* he be a national political leader?

Republican leaders were disturbed by the enthusiasm Trump aroused, but most of them assumed he was a novelty candidate whom the party's rank and file might indulge for a while but would eventually forsake for "real" presidential contenders. The other Republican candidates similarly calculated that Trump's campaign would fade at some point. Each rival, in that event, hoped to be the one to inherit Trump's supporters; few wished to jeopardize that prospect by sharply attacking the blustering tycoon. So Trump cruised through the primaries relatively unscathed, all but unstoppable by the time he reached the July 2016 Republican National Convention in Cleveland, where – to the horror of many in the party and many more outside it – he received the nomination. Trump's running mate was Indiana Governor Mike Pence, a former radio talk show host and congressman with close ties to conservative evangelical Christians. Both by enlisting Pence and by promising to appoint socially conservative judges, Trump won the support of millions of conservative Christians who might otherwise have recoiled from the vulgar, profane, and twice-divorced candidate.

That same July, Hillary Clinton, who had stepped down as Barack Obama's secretary of state in 2013, clinched the Democratic nomination at the party's convention in Philadelphia. She did so after defeating an unexpectedly formidable primary challenge from Vermont Senator Bernie Sanders, a self-described socialist who caucused with Senate Democrats. Sanders championed universal health care, expanded federal protection of workers' rights, and aggressive action to combat climate change. The effort to beat back his insurgency drained Clinton's campaign of energy, and it made Clinton herself seem less like a bold shatterer of glass ceilings than like a scripted upholder of the status quo. Clinton was already damaged by the revelation that, as secretary of state, she had conducted official business via a private email server in her home, rather than using the State Department's far more secure system. An FBI investigation found that, of the tens of thousands of emails on Clinton's server, a small number were classified. Shortly before the Democratic Convention, FBI Director James Comey concluded that Clinton should not be criminally charged, though he publicly labeled her conduct "extremely reckless." Despite all these challenges, Clinton consistently ran ahead of Trump in opinion polls, sometimes by wide margins.

The 2016 General Election Campaign

In the ensuing general election campaign, a strange dynamic became glaring: an affinity between Trump and Vladimir Putin, Russia's president. Part of this could be explained by Putin's antipathy to Trump's opponent. As secretary of state during Obama's first term, Clinton had taken a harder line on Russia than the president himself had done, criticizing that nation for bullying its neighbors and failing to observe democratic norms at home. In

December 2011, Russia held parliamentary elections, and it grew evident that state authorities were rigging the vote to favor Putin's party. The Russian people, Clinton declared, "deserve to have their voices heard and their votes counted." Mass protests erupted in Moscow, and Russian authorities harshly suppressed them. Putin charged that Clinton had fomented the unrest to undermine his regime. Four and half years later, he was naturally dismayed to see Clinton emerge as the Democratic nominee and the candidate favored to win the election. He swung into action against her campaign. Initially, it appears, his goal was less to defeat her outright than to tarnish her image and make it harder for her to govern effectively. Later, however, Putin became more affirmatively committed to aiding Trump.

As for Trump's softness for Putin, on one level it can be easily explained: the magnate was delighted to have the support of anyone who so strongly opposed Hillary Clinton. But it went deeper than that. During his real estate career, because of his questionable business practices, Trump had sometimes struggled to get loans from reputable banks. So he turned to other, less reputable sources, including banks favored by Russian oligarchs allied with Putin. Trump also entered into business ventures with Russians in Putin's orbit, projects such as the 2013 Miss Universe Pageant, held in Moscow. During the 2016 campaign itself, Trump was negotiating with the Russian government over a permit to build a Trump Tower in Moscow. Some speculated that Putin possessed derogatory information about Trump and was thus in a position to blackmail him. No hard evidence substantiates this claim, though Trump's refusal to voice even mild criticism of Putin (as distinct from the anti-Russian policies he sometimes followed as president) would arouse considerable suspicion in the years ahead.

In any event, when Trump launched his presidential bid, Putin was all too eager to help. He did this primarily through cyberwarfare. Russian "troll farms" – organizations devoted to spreading disruptive internet content – created thousands of bogus Facebook, Twitter, and Instagram accounts that disparaged Hillary Clinton via false or misleading stories and "memes." Meanwhile, digital saboteurs working for Russia hacked into the email accounts of members of Clinton's inner circle. They turned those emails over to Wikileaks, an antisecrecy organization run by Julian Assange, an Australian activist who, like Putin, loathed Clinton. Wikileaks publicly posted the stolen emails, which consisted of candid exchanges that, when published in the news media, embarrassed Clinton and her advisers and threw her campaign off its stride.

Did Trump help Russia do these things? From 2017 to 2019, former FBI Director Robert Mueller headed an investigation into the matter and determined that there was insufficient evidence to conclude that Trump or his campaign engaged in a criminal conspiracy with Russian agents. But Mueller did find that the Trump campaign knew what the Russians were up to and enthusiastically welcomed their help. "[T]he investigation," he wrote in his 2019 report, "established that the Russian government perceived it would benefit from a Trump presidency and worked to secure that outcome, and that the Campaign expected it would benefit electorally from information stolen and released through Russian efforts."

Certainly, members of Trump's inner circle *tried* to collude with Russia. In June 2016 Robert Goldstone, a British publicist with close ties to Putin, emailed Trump's son, Donald

Trump, Jr., to say the Russians had derogatory information about Hillary Clinton to share with the Trump campaign; it was "part of Russia and its government's support for Mr. Trump." "If it's what you say I love it," Don Jr. replied, "especially later in the summer," meaning after his father had secured the Republican nomination. Days later, Don Jr. and other Trump campaign officials held a meeting at Trump Tower with representatives of Putin's government. Nothing apparently came of the encounter because, on this occasion, the Russians had no useful dirt to share. As noted, however, Russia did assist Trump by flooding cyberspace with anti-Clinton content and providing Wikileaks with hacked emails from Clinton's inner circle. Wikileaks published the first batch of those emails in July 2016.

During that summer, US intelligence agencies learned that Moscow was interfering on Trump's behalf. Advisers urged Obama to issue a public statement alerting the American public to Russia's meddling, but the president worried about appearing to play favorites in the election. He approached the Republican leaders in Congress, Speaker of the House Paul Ryan and Senate Majority Leader Mitch McConnell, to enlist them in a bipartisan statement about Russian interference. Ryan was amenable, but McConnell refused, suspecting an effort to sabotage Trump. Obama resigned himself to saying nothing at all. Clinton seemed headed for a win anyway; why taint her victory by taking action many would see as an unfair attack on her opponent? Obama's advisers kept pressing for a public statement. Finally, in early October, Obama authorized Director of National Intelligence James Clapper and Secretary of Homeland Security Jeh Johnson to issue a joint public statement. Released on October 7, it conveyed the intelligence community's conclusion that Russia was behind Wikileaks's recent dumps of hacked emails.

The statement was quickly overshadowed, however, by a much more dramatic story breaking that same day. *The Washington Post* released a piece of video recorded in 2005, when Trump appeared on the television entertainment program *Access Hollywood*. In some pre-show banter, Trump could be heard boasting to the male host about his practice of sexually assaulting women: "You know, I'm automatically attracted to beautiful – I just start kissing them . . . . And when you're a star, they let you do it. You can do anything. Grab 'em by the pussy. You can do anything." The *Access Hollywood* tape was a massive story that, for a time, dwarfed all other news items, including the one about Clapper's and Johnson's statement. To be sure, the tape's release was a terrible development for Trump. His crude words were condemned across the political spectrum, and many top Republican leaders withdrew their support, all but conceding the race to Clinton. Still, the significance of Russia's election interference did not register with the news media or the public as powerfully as it should have.

A third thing happened on October 7: Wikileaks started posting thousands of emails hacked from the account of Clinton campaign chairman John Podesta – additional servings of in-house gossip that embarrassed and distracted the candidate and her staff. Though far less explosive than the *Access Hollywood* tape, the mortifying revelations dribbled out over a longer period of time, eroding the campaign's credibility. Moreover, although these emails had nothing to do with the ones on Clinton's private server, they constantly reminded voters of that other security breach.

And then, on October 28, as if seeking to hammer that reminder home, FBI Director Comey suddenly announced that he was revisiting the case of Clinton's State Department emails. Back in July, Comey had seemingly put the matter to rest by announcing that Clinton's conduct, while reckless, did not warrant criminal charges. Now, Comey disclosed that additional emails discovered on the laptop of the husband of Clinton's top aide, Huma Abedin, had to be examined before the case could be finally closed. On November 6, just two days before the election, Comey announced that a study of the emails failed to alter his initial conclusion that Clinton should not be charged. But the late-breaking resurrection of the server issue deeply damaged Clinton's campaign.

Even so, as Americans went to the polls on November 8, Clinton remained the overwhelming favorite. Democrats scheduled election-night viewing parties to celebrate Trump's banishment from the national stage, and the belated ending of a too-close-for-comfort stress test of the nation's civic institutions. By the small hours of the next day, however, it was clear that Clinton had suffered a stunning defeat. Although she received nearly three million more popular votes than Trump did, Trump won the Electoral College 304 to 227. A margin of 800,000 votes in Pennsylvania, Michigan, and Wisconsin ensured this victory. The Clinton campaign had taken those and other battleground states for granted, underestimating Trump's ability to turn out rural white voters and the willingness of rank-and-file Republicans to back their party's nominee, regardless of his glaring flaws. In a further blow to shellshocked Democrats, Republicans kept control of both houses of Congress.

Trump's Assumption of the Presidency

For millions of Americans, and for millions more watching anxiously around the world, Trump's transition into the presidency was a surreal spectacle. Many had hoped that the imminent prospect of high office would inspire the president-elect to adopt a more dignified manner, but he continued to tweet wild attacks against his adversaries and made it clear he would keep doing so from the White House. Observers had assumed that ethics requirements would compel Trump to divest himself of his business holdings or at least place them in a "blind trust" that blocked him from managing them while serving as president. Instead, he turned those holdings over to the control of his two adult sons, Don Jr. and Eric, who remained enmeshed in their father's political activities. Trump had discovered to his delight that US presidents are exempt from many of the conflict-of-interest laws constraining other federal office holders. Previous presidents had generally avoided blatant conflicts less for legal reasons than because they assumed such forbearance was expected of them. (Once in office, Trump dropped even the pretense of separation from some of his businesses. He openly encouraged foreign dignitaries and other favor-curriers to patronize his pricey hotels and clubs.) Many of Trump's cabinet picks were wealthy business executives whose track records suggested, and whose performances in office all too often confirmed, a determination to reduce the powers of their own departments if doing so benefited private interests.

The public had seen business-friendly administrations before, but other features of the new order were unprecedented and bizarre. As Trump prepared to take office, news stories appeared about US intelligence agencies' recent investigation of the then candidate's ties to Russia. Among the leads the agencies had pursued were salacious (and unsubstantiated) claims involving Trump and Russian prostitutes. Trump accused the intelligence community of deliberately leaking those details. "I think it's a disgrace," he told reporters. "… [T]hat's something that Nazi Germany would have done." Trump entered the White House still castigating the intelligence agencies he was about to oversee. He was also feuding with journalists over the size of his Inauguration Day crowd. When news outlets reported (and photographs clearly showed) that many fewer spectators attended Trump's swearing-in than had been at Barack Obama's first inauguration, the new president forced his press secretary to insist to reporters that the Trump inaugural audience had been the largest on record. Comedians delighted in Trump's obsession with crowd size, but something profound and disturbing had just happened. The president had compelled a public servant to tell a blindingly obvious lie about a matter of little significance. The incident portended that brazen falsehoods would be a regular feature of the nation's official record, inserted at the whim of an overbearing and psychologically needy head of state.

A chaotic episode erupting a week into Trump's presidency offered a more substantive glimpse of what was in store. In a January 27, 2017, executive order, Trump abruptly barred entry into the United States to travelers from Iran, Iraq, Libya, Somalia, Sudan, Syria, and Yemen – all Muslim-majority countries – for ninety days. Clearly, this was a partial implementation of the "Muslim travel ban" Trump had advocated on the campaign trail. Drafted by Steve Bannon and Stephen Miller, two of Trump's more zealously nativist advisers, the executive order had not been cleared with the Departments of State or Homeland Security, whose officials and employees scrambled to implement the carelessly written edict. (An example of shoddy drafting: the order initially applied to permanent residents of the United States traveling abroad; they were quickly exempted in response to the resulting outcry.) Acting Attorney General Sally Yates, an Obama administration holdover minding the store until Trump's pick for attorney general could be confirmed, called the travel ban unlawful and refused to enforce it; Trump promptly fired her. Charging religious discrimination, multiple plaintiffs sued to block the executive order, which a handful of district courts agreed was unconstitutional. By now, large crowds had gathered at major US airports to protest the travel ban, and thousands of lawyers were working pro bono to defend and advise Muslim travelers. In mid-February, the Ninth Circuit Court of Appeals upheld the district court decisions. Protesters cheered as travelers were finally cleared through customs.

The Trump administration rescinded the travel ban and replaced it with a modified one, which the courts also rejected. A third attempt, which removed some Muslim-majority nations from the forbidden list and added non-Muslim countries such as North Korea and Venezuela, was, yet again, stayed by lower courts. But in December 2017 a divided Supreme Court overturned the stays, effectively approving the revised travel ban. By then, the onrush of other outrages and stunners had been so relentless that the initial travel ban felt like ancient history.

Figure 15.1 Opponents of President Donald Trump's Muslim ban gather at Los Angeles International Airport, February 2017. Source: Anadolu Agency / Getty Images.

Continuing Investigation of Trump's Ties with Russia

Dominating the Trump administration's early months was the lingering fallout from Russia's involvement in the recent presidential election. Like most FBI directors since 1976, Jim Comey had been appointed to a ten-year term, his starting in 2013. He thus expected to keep his job well into Trump's presidency. But Trump soured on Comey soon after the 2016 election, mainly because the FBI continued to pursue the Russia collusion allegations. In March 2017, Comey publicly confirmed that the FBI was investigating "whether there was any coordination between the [Trump] campaign and Russia's efforts" to interfere in the 2016 election. Trump was agitated by the statement and insisted that the FBI publicly declare that he was not personally under investigation. Officially, he was not, and Comey privately assured him of this. But FBI officials could not rule out that new information might put Trump in the investigative crosshairs. If that happened, and if they had previously announced that he was not under investigation, they would have to correct the record. It would be better not to address this issue in public at all. Comey fended off the president's demand.

Enraged, in May 2017 Trump abruptly fired the FBI director. Comey's on-again, off-again handling of Hillary Clinton's emails had angered Republicans and Democrats alike, so Trump expected the firing would be popular; he even initially claimed this was his reason for sacking Comey. Instead, the move outraged Democrats and many news analysts, who accused Trump of trying to shut down the FBI's Russia investigation. Jeff Sessions,

Trump's first attorney general, had already recused himself from the investigation because he had advised Trump's 2016 campaign; at least potentially, he was one of the people under investigation. Even with Sessions sidelined, pressure mounted on the Department of Justice to name a special counsel to oversee the Russia investigation, which now *did* include questions about Trump's personal involvement. And so, later that month, Deputy Attorney General Rod Rosenstein appointed former FBI Director Robert Mueller to serve as special counsel. Mueller and his team were to investigate alleged coordination between the Trump campaign and Russia and, subsequent to that, possible efforts by President Trump to obstruct legitimate inquiry into the matter. As during the Watergate scandal of the 1970s, investigators would be partly concerned with documenting, in real time, a sitting president's attempts to impede their work.

Trump and Congressional Republicans

In those early months of his administration, Trump had plenty of Republican defenders on Capitol Hill, but his domination of that caucus was hardly complete. Republican lawmakers made only scattered objections to the FBI's announced investigation into the Russia collusion allegations or to Rosenstein's naming of a special counsel. By the end of 2017, however, Trump had silenced or marginalized his fiercest Republican critics in Congress and had largely bent the GOP to his will. This was a remarkable outcome considering the impulsive, volatile, and ill-informed manner in which the president interacted with members of his own party.

Trump's first venture with congressional Republicans was easy enough: filling a Supreme Court vacancy. Back in early 2016, the conservative justice Antonin Scalia had unexpectedly died, and Obama nominated Merrick Garland, a moderate Appeals Court judge, to replace him. Much to Democrats' fury, however, Republican Senate Majority Leader Mitch McConnell refused to hold hearings on the nomination or put it to a vote, citing a dubious "tradition" that the Senate need not fill a Supreme Court vacancy arising during a presidential election year, if the White House and the Senate are held by opposing political parties. Thus Obama's court vacancy became Trump's to fill. In January 2017, Trump nominated Neil Gorsuch, an appellate judge recommended by the Federalist Society, a conservative legal organization. The Senate confirmed Gorsuch in April by a vote of fifty-four to forty-five, with three Democrats joining the Republican majority.

Trump's next congressional endeavor – seeking to vanquish the Affordable Care Act, Obama's signature health care reform – proved a much taller order. Repeatedly during Obama's presidency, congressional Republicans had tried to repeal the ACA. But these were easy, consequence-free efforts, mounted in the certain knowledge that they would fail, either because the repeal legislation could not pass in both houses or because Obama would veto it if it did. That all changed in January 2017. With Republicans now holding the White House, the Senate, and the House, it was "put up or shut up" time.

Trump, eager to keep his own campaign promise to kill Obamacare, demanded that congressional Republicans quickly repeal it; he was all but indifferent to the content of whatever remained in its place. But Republican lawmakers could not ignore substance, and the "repeal and replace" effort exposed divisions in their ranks. In May 2017, the House narrowly passed the American Health Care Act. Strongly influenced by the House Freedom Caucus (a group of conservative and libertarian Republicans who earlier in the decade had allied with the Tea Party), the AHCA would abolish the ACA's individual and employer mandates, pare back the Medicare component of the ACA, and eliminate many of the taxes on which the program relied. A giddy Trump staged a celebration in the White House Rose Garden, only dimly grasping that mere approval by the House hardly guarantees a bill's final passage. Republican Representative Tom Cole of Oklahoma remembered thinking, "I'm not sure it's wise to be spiking the football at the fifty-yard line, but what the heck."

Indeed, many Republican senators disliked the House bill, which had provoked angry protests from citizens unwilling to see Obamacare dismantled. (That spring, for the first time, a Gallup poll recorded that a majority of Americans supported the ACA.) Insisting on crafting their own bill, Senate Republicans labored for several weeks to find a "repeal and replace" formula on which enough of them could agree. The best they could manage was a bill informally known as the "skinny repeal," because it would eliminate only the individual and employer mandates. In July 2017, the skinny repeal failed by a single vote, dramatically cast by an ailing John McCain, who would die of brain cancer a year later. Though critical of the ACA, McCain was even more dismayed by the rushed and haphazard process the Senate had followed in the repeal effort. Obamacare remained the law of the land. A public, intraparty spat ensued, with Trump calling the failed repeal drive "a disgrace" and Mitch McConnell, more circumspectly, lamenting the president's "excessive expectations about how quickly things happen in the democratic process."

Trump's relations with Republican leaders soon got much worse. In August 2017, a coalition of white supremacist, neo-Nazi, neo-Confederate, and other far right groups descended on Charlottesville, Virginia, to protest the city council's decision to take down a statue of Confederate General Robert E. Lee. (Following the 2015 murder of nine Black parishioners in Charleston, South Carolina [see Chapter 14], jurisdictions across the South had begun removing statues and monuments celebrating the Confederacy.) The Charlottesville protests started with an evening rally on the University of Virginia campus, where torch-bearing marchers chanted, "You will not replace us!" and "Jews will not replace us!" The next day, far right protesters gathered at the site of the Lee statue, squaring off against, and at times brawling with, a larger group of antiracist counter-protesters. A white supremacist rammed his car into a crowd of counter-demonstrators, killing one woman and wounding twenty-eight other people.

Hours later, Trump spoke to the nation about the tragedy, reading from a prepared text. After intoning the line, "We condemn in the strongest terms this egregious display of hatred, bigotry, and violence," he ad-libbed, "on many sides. On many sides." The comment caused an uproar, which intensified a few days later when, at a combative press conference, the president insisted that the Charlottesville standoff had featured "very fine people, on both sides . . . . You had people in that group who were there to protest the taking down of, to them, a very, very important statue," not to espouse extremist politics. (It was a fanciful claim. If such gentle antiquarians *were* present at Charlottesville, they were indistinguishable from the marchers shouting racist and anti-Semitic slogans. Trump evidently offered this disingenuous argument so as to avoid a rupture with white supremacists, whom he wanted to keep in his political base.) The chorus of criticism of Trump grew louder, and many prominent Republicans joined in. "No, not the same. One side is racist, bigoted, Nazi. The other opposes racism and bigotry," tweeted 2012 Republican presidential nominee Mitt Romney. "There are no good neo-Nazis," McConnell declared.

The president, however, had the Republican base on his side, and he could use this fact to punish GOP politicians who crossed him. Senator Jeff Flake of Arizona had opposed Trump in 2016. In the summer of 2017, he published a book charging that Republicans under Trump had surrendered themselves to "a sugar high of populism, nativism, and demagoguery." Trump retaliated by tweeting his approval of Kelli Ward, a rightwing politician running to unseat Flake in Arizona's 2018 primary election. Ward surged ahead in the polls, and Flake decided not to seek reelection. Another Republican senator, Bob Corker of Tennessee, told reporters in August 2017 that Trump had failed to demonstrate the "stability" and "competence" his office demanded. "Strange statement by Bob Corker," Trump tweeted, with a hint of menace, "considering that he is constantly asking me whether or not he should run again in '18. Tennessee not happy!" Realizing that Trump was correct – at least insofar as Tennessee Republicans were concerned – Corker, too, bowed out of his reelection race. Trump's enemies relished Corker's taunt that "the White House has become an adult day care center," but there was no denying that the "Toddler in Chief," as one commentator dubbed him, was getting his way. In the House, thirty-nine Republicans, many of them Trump critics fearing primary challenges, chose not to run in 2018. Most were succeeded by pro-Trump Republicans.

Even so, as of the fall of 2017, Trump had failed to preside over any major legislative accomplishments. To rectify this, Congressional Republicans hastily passed the Tax Cuts and Jobs Act, which the president signed in December. Like many previous conservative tax bills, the TCJA reduced rates across the board but disproportionately benefited corporations and wealthy individuals. It also was a budget buster: the Congressional Budget Office estimated it would enlarge the deficit by $1.9 trillion over the next eleven years. At another football-spiking ceremony at the White House – this one celebrating a genuine political touchdown – Republican lawmakers took turns at the microphone to heap praise on Trump, whose role in the achievement had in truth been modest. "[S]omething this profound could not have been done without exquisite presidential leadership," said House Speaker Paul Ryan. "You're one heck of a leader," gushed Utah Senator Orrin Hatch, "… and we're going to make this the greatest presidency that we've seen, not only in generations but maybe ever." The terms of the bargain were clear: fawning deference toward the president in exchange for his nomination of conservative judges and his thick, spiky signature on conservative bills. At least in Congress, the embers of Republican resistance to Trump had mostly gone cold.

The "Me Too" Movement

As Trump tightened his hold over congressional Republicans, an extraordinary drama convulsed the wider culture. In October 2017, *The New York Times* and *The New Yorker* reported that more than a dozen women in the entertainment industry, some of them prominent actors, others less well known, had accused the acclaimed movie producer Harvey Weinstein of various kinds of sexual misconduct. Some said that he had pressured them to have sex; others alleged outright sexual assault or even rape. The women had previously complained about Weinstein's behavior but had been induced to remain silent; some had reached secret settlements with Weinstein's production company. The producer's predatory qualities had been an open secret within the film industry, a topic of jokes and sly references but never frank acknowledgment. Once this first set of accusations appeared in the news, however, they quickly dissolved the taboo and encouraged other victims to come forward. Eventually, more than eighty women made allegations against Weinstein. He was tried in New York City for some of these offenses and, in 2020, convicted and sentenced to twenty-three years in prison.

Throughout the fall of 2017 and into the next year, the charges against Weinstein opened the floodgates of accusation against scores of other prominent men, in the entertainment industry, the news media, business, and politics. Alleged perpetrators included the radio personality Garrison Keillor, the comedian Louis C. K., the television journalists Matt Lauer and Charlie Rose, and the Michigan congressman John Conyers. Women who had previously feared that people would never believe their stories, or would discount them if they did, were emboldened to share their experiences. A key vehicle for encouraging them to come forward was the Twitter hashtag #MeToo. The phrase had circulated for about a decade, but it now became, worldwide, an instantly recognized statement of solidarity. There was of course nothing new about accusations of sexual misconduct. Distinguishing *this* moment were the sheer volume of the allegations and the fact their consequences were swift, visible, and concrete. Most of the accused men, if their guilt seemed undeniable, were unable to brush off the charges or escape with mere apologies. They were forced to resign their positions, and some completely vanished from public life.

The first group of female accusers associated with #MeToo tended to be white and at least middle-class (and in some cases quite wealthy); news coverage of the phenomenon perpetuated that socioeconomic bias. But the movement's visibility boosted preexisting efforts by lower-income women, many of them nonwhite, to wage their own struggles against unwanted sexual attention. In September 2018, McDonald's employees staged a nationwide walkout to protest sexual harassment in the chain's restaurants, often perpetrated by male managers against female workers. "Hold your burgers, hold your fries. Keep your hands off my thighs," chanted strikers in a suburb of St. Louis, Missouri. Chicago strikers wore blue duct tape over their mouths inscribed with the letters "MeToo." McDonald's responded by establishing sexual harassment training programs and an anonymous reporting hotline. Strikers acknowledged the efforts but insisted they were only a first step.

Figure 15.2 A "Me Too" demonstration in Hollywood, 2017. Source: AFP / Getty Images.

Trump, of course, was already notorious for behavior of this sort. His alleged victims formed a mini-"Me Too" movement in and of themselves. Right after the release of the *Access Hollywood* tape, several women publicly charged that Trump, at different points over the preceding four decades, had forcibly kissed, groped, or fondled them. Other women came forward in the coming years, and by late 2020 the accusers numbered twenty-six. In 2019, the advice columnist E. Jean Carroll claimed that Trump had raped her in a department store dressing room in the mid-1990s. Trump or his spokespeople categorically denied most of these allegations, ignoring the rest.

A couple of other cases involving Trump were consensual, but sordid. In early 2018, news reports surfaced that, during the 2016 campaign, Trump had paid hush money to two women with whom he had had affairs: Stephanie Clifford, a pornographic film actress better known as Stormy Daniels; and Karen McDougal, an actress and model. The White House denied the reports, but they soon received dramatic confirmation. In April 2018, the FBI raided the New York office of Trump's lawyer, Michael Cohen, executing a search warrant obtained by Special Counsel Robert Mueller, who, in the course of his probe, had uncovered evidence of fraudulent business practices by Cohen. A few months later, Cohen pleaded guilty in a Manhattan federal court to several charges, including arranging the bribes to Daniels and McDougal on Trump's behalf. The president's chief response to the revelation was to call Daniels "Horseface" on Twitter. He had done this sort of thing before: disparaging a woman's physical appearance as if to prove he could not have been intimate with her.

"Ladies and Gentlemen, may I present your president," Daniels tweeted in response. "In addition to his ... umm ... shortcomings, he has demonstrated his incompetence, hatred of women and lack of self control .... And perhaps a penchant for bestiality."

The politics of "Me Too" played out in the judicial confirmation process, too. In the summer of 2018, Trump nominated Brett Kavanaugh, a conservative appellate judge, to fill a second Supreme Court vacancy. A psychology professor named Christine Blasey Ford came forward with an explosive allegation: that in the early 1980s, when she and Kavanaugh were teenagers, the future judge had sexually assaulted her at a social gathering in suburban Maryland. The accusation convulsed the nation. In a replay of the Clarence Thomas/Anita Hill controversy of 1991, women's advocates rallied to Ford's support. The case raised complex issues, giving backers of each party plenty to talk about. As Ford herself acknowledged (with keen professional insight), there were gaps in her memory of the alleged assault. Still, she recounted it in ways that many found highly believable. There were no corroborating witnesses – or at least none available to testify: Ford claimed that another boy, Mark Judge, had participated in the attack, but the Republican-controlled Senate Judiciary Committee declined to subpoena Judge, who was permitted to deny Ford's account in writing. Kavanaugh was seventeen years old at the time, and some worried about the unfairness of penalizing adults for youthful missteps. On the other hand, the alleged act was a serious crime; if Kavanaugh *was* guilty as charged, he could at least be asked to reflect on his conduct and offer some sort of symbolic restitution to Ford (the legal statute of limitations having long since expired). But Kavanaugh was categorically denying the allegation. What if he was telling the truth?

Within days, additional accusations against Kavanaugh surfaced. They tended to weaken Ford's case. A social worker named Deborah Ramirez claimed that Kavanaugh had exposed himself to her at a drunken party when they were both undergraduates at Yale University. Yet her account, too, lacked corroboration, and Ramirez had even been uncertain for a time that Kavanaugh was the culprit. Michael Avenatti, the publicity-craving lawyer representing Stormy Daniels, claimed that another of his clients, Julie Swetnick, was prepared to testify that Kavanaugh and his friends had drugged and "gang-raped" young women at parties in the early 1980s. Swetnick's allegations were internally inconsistent, however, and many journalists questioned her veracity. Ford's story was more credible than both of these accounts, but it suffered from association with them. Republicans on the Senate Judiciary Committee, mindful of the new "Me Too" climate, had responded cautiously, even deferentially, when Ford was the only known accuser. After the other two women emerged, the Republicans treated all of the allegations as a coordinated Democratic assault on a conservative nominee, around whom they rallied. Kavanaugh himself angrily charged from the witness table that the accusations were a "calculated and orchestrated political hit ... on behalf of the Clintons," who refused to accept the 2016 election results. Trump, who had found Ford's testimony disconcertingly impressive, was delighted by the judge's counterattack. "This is why I nominated him," he exulted to aides. Kavanaugh was confirmed in October by a vote of fifty to forty-eight.

Trump on the World Stage

Abroad, Trump's behavior was no less impulsive and self-serving than it was at home. As he had done during the 2016 campaign, the president couched his ideas about foreign relations under the heading "America First," indifferent (or perhaps oblivious) to the slogan's origins in a long-defunct isolationist organization with anti-Semitic baggage.[2] For all its many flaws, US foreign policy since 1945 had been largely rooted in the concept of enlightened self-interest – the insight that actions serving the needs of others are likely to redound to the benefit of oneself. American leaders had helped to build global economic, commercial, and collective security systems that, though hardly free of exploitation, coercion, and appalling violence, were sufficiently stable and attractive that countries around the world sought their opportunities and protections. As the most powerful and prosperous nation within those systems, the United States benefited the most, both materially and in its enjoyment of global prestige. Pretty much all of this was lost on Trump. Unable to grasp the holistic value his nation derived from its international alliances and commitments, he frequently expressed contempt for them, demanding to know how, in the narrowest sense, they served the United States. And "serving the United States" was often synonymous with serving Trump's individual political or psychological needs. Unmoored from the traditions of US foreign policy, the president lurched unpredictably between belligerence and appeasement, upending multinational protocols and cutting bilateral deals as his pride, gut, or political instincts dictated. Sometimes, however, advisers who *had* been socialized in US diplomatic norms prevented Trump from acting on his wildest impulses.

Relations with North Korea illustrated many of these patterns. Since that nation's acquisition of a nuclear-weapons capability in the mid-2000s, the focus of US diplomacy had been to prevent Pyongyang from developing long-range delivery systems. Obama's policy of "strategic patience" ratcheted up pressure on North Korea, in the form of stepped-up economic sanctions and military cooperation with South Korea, to compel it to negotiate over its own arsenal. Instead, North Korea's young president, Kim Jong-un (the grandson of Kim Il-sung, the nation's first leader), launched a flurry of missile tests during the closing months of Obama's presidency. In the summer of 2017, with Trump now in office, North Korea tested an intercontinental ballistic missile capable of reaching the continental United States. Sharply reversing "strategic patience," Trump warned that North Korea "will be met with fire and fury like the world has never seen" if it threatened the United States. Addressing the United Nations General Assembly in September, he proclaimed that in the event of conflict "we will have no choice but to totally destroy North Korea. Rocket Man" – Trump's derisive nickname for Kim Jong-un – "is on a suicide mission for himself

[2] In 1940 and 1941, after World War II had broken out but before the United States entered it, an organization called the America First Committee agitated against US involvement in the conflict. The group's chief spokesman, the famous aviator Charles Lindbergh, charged in September 1941 that American Jews were seeking to drag the United States into war. "Their greatest danger to this country," he said, "lies in their large ownership and influence in our motion pictures, our press, our radio, and our government."

and for his regime." North Korea's state media released a statement by Kim vowing to "tame the mentally deranged US dotard with fire." Kim's advanced vocabulary bemused English-speaking observers, but the standoff was genuinely frightening.

Fortunately, both sides stepped back from the brink, and within months Trump and Kim were exchanging cordial messages and preparing to meet in Singapore. No previous sitting US president had met with his North Korean counterpart, and some American progressives applauded Trump's willingness to cast aside stale taboos in a bold effort for peace. But Trump attended the June 2018 Singapore summit with no evident strategy apart from reaching a high-profile agreement, and with no demonstrated interest in, or grasp of, the issues at stake. When Kim said he was committed to the "denuclearization of the Korean Peninsula" – meaning that, if the United States concluded a peace treaty with North Korea and ended its alliance with South Korea, Pyongyang could scale back its arsenal – Trump treated this as a pledge of unilateral disarmament. "He's denuking the whole place, and he's going to start very quickly," Trump enthused on *Good Morning America.* To his fifty-three million Twitter followers, he proclaimed, "There is no longer a Nuclear Threat from North Korea." To rallygoers, the president confided that he and Kim "fell in love." But US intelligence agencies detected no sign of North Korean denuclearization, and soon Trump himself had to acknowledge that the deal wasn't quite sealed. A second Trump–Kim summit, held in Hanoi, Vietnam, in February 2019, could not even match the empty atmospherics of the first. Trump cut the meeting short when no agreement was forthcoming. A few months later, he ratcheted up the cinematic drama by shaking hands with Kim at the Demilitarized Zone separating North and South Korea. Still no deal.

Even when in the throes of his "fire and fury" phase, Trump muddied his stance by questioning the value of his nation's alliance with South Korea. He believed the $3.5 billion Washington spent annually to station 28,000 troops in the country was wasted, and he wondered why the South Koreans themselves were not paying for a US missile defense system deployed on their soil. Trump thought this way about America's alliances in general. During the 2016 campaign, he said of NATO members, "The countries we are defending must pay for the cost of this defense, and if not, the US must be prepared to let these countries defend themselves." Once in office, Trump often sounded this refrain, implying that the United States might pull out of NATO if the other members failed to step up. Behind closed doors, he reportedly voiced this threat explicitly.

The burden-sharing issue was not new. For decades, successive US administrations had urged the NATO allies to spend more on defense and thus reduce the US obligation, which was indeed disproportionate. But no previous American president had suggested that US membership of NATO hinged on this question. The allies had granted the legitimacy of Washington's position, and since 2014 each NATO member had begun working toward the goal of devoting 2 percent of its gross national product to defense. This evolution continued during Trump's presidency, and NATO's secretary general, Jens Stoltenberg, shrewdly allowed the US president to take credit for it. "Our NATO partners," Trump publicly boasted in 2020, "... were very far behind in their defense payments, but at my strong urging ... they upped their payments . . . . Secretary General Stoltenberg, who heads

NATO, was amazed after watching for so many years and said that President Trump did what no one else was able to do." That Trump did not, in the end, pull out of NATO was primarily a result of pressure exerted by his aghast foreign policy advisers. But Stoltenberg's ego-stroking certainly helped.

On other international commitments, Trump was willing to pull the plug. In mid-2017, he announced his intention to withdraw from the 2015 Paris Climate Agreement, a move applauded by most Republicans. But the rules of the agreement prevented signatories from leaving immediately. Thus the US exit did not take effect until November 4, 2020, one day after the presidential election, which Trump lost to former Vice President Joseph Biden. Immediately upon his inauguration on January 20, 2021, Biden signed an executive order reentering the nation into the climate agreement. Over the preceding four years, Trump had issued executive orders of his own curbing regulations on greenhouse gases, even as many individual states, especially ones governed by Democrats, promoted green energy. Greenhouse gas emissions continued to decline during the Trump years, but at a significantly slower rate than Obama had pledged upon signing the Paris Agreement.

In May 2018, Trump pulled the United States out of another 2015 agreement, the Joint Comprehensive Plan of Action, informally known as the Iran nuclear deal. The agreement had done what it was supposed to do. Iran scaled back its nuclear activities, extending the "breakout period" (the time it would take for it to build a nuclear weapon, should it suddenly throw caution to the winds and race to acquire that capability) from a few months to at least a year. In return, the United States, Britain, France, Russia, China, and Germany agreed to the easing of economic sanctions on Iran. The Trump administration, however, claimed that the JCPOA was a failure, because it did not prevent Iran from supporting Middle Eastern regimes and organizations Washington saw as malign and disruptive – an issue the agreement was never meant to address. After withdrawing from the Iran nuclear deal, the United States resumed its economic sanctions, not just against Iran but also against non-US companies doing business with it. The sanctions inflicted severe hardship on Iran but failed to induce a more conciliatory attitude on nukes. Just the opposite: Tehran stepped up its enrichment of uranium, bringing its "breakout period" back down to an estimated six months by the summer of 2020 and mere weeks by early 2022.

Elsewhere in the Middle East, Trump did achieve some notable successes, albeit at a stiff cost to many Middle Easterners. He continued the campaign against ISIS that Obama helped to launch in 2014. In March 2019, the group was ousted from its last territorial stronghold, in Syria. The following October, Trump authorized a special US Army commando operation in Syria that resulted in the death of ISIS's leader in hiding, Abu Bakr al-Baghdadi. But in fighting ISIS, and in targeting other nonstate adversaries, the Trump administration dispensed with some of the precautions the Obama administration had taken to minimize "collateral damage," yielding a marked increase in civilian casualties.

In the fall of 2020, the Trump administration unveiled a series of bilateral agreements between Israel and four Arab countries, the United Arab Emirates, Bahrain, Sudan, and Morocco, each of which formally recognized Israel after decades of refusing to do so. Proponents of these "Abraham Accords," which were brokered by Trump's son-in-law Jared

Kushner, argued that they demonstrated the wisdom of the administration's inclination to sideline the Palestinian issue. Look at what could be accomplished, they said, when regional diplomacy was no longer held hostage to that tiresome and insoluble conflict! (Since the late 1970s, US administrations had generally treated an accommodation between Israel and the Palestinians, even a very limited one, as a necessary component of any broader Arab–Israeli peace prospects.) Critics replied that Israel's continued subjugation of the Palestinians remained a pressing international concern that should not be swept under the rug just because a handful of Arab governments seemed willing to do just that.

In Central Asia, Trump made a decision that was little noticed at the time but whose consequences became glaring several months into the term of his successor. After surging more US troops into Afghanistan at the start of his presidency (much as Obama had done), Trump opted in early 2020 for a negotiated exit. In a February 29 agreement with the Taliban, in which the Afghan government took hardly any part, the United States committed to withdraw all of its troops by May 1, 2021, in exchange for the Taliban's pledge not to allow al-Qa'ida or similar groups to operate in areas under Taliban control. The Trump administration unveiled and began implementing the agreement just as the Covid-19 pandemic became a consuming issue for Americans (see below), and few journalists paid much attention to the deal. Those who did expressed skepticism that the Taliban were actually breaking with al-Qa'ida. Secretary of State Michael Pompeo brushed the concerns aside, telling a Fox News interviewer, "I looked them in the eye. They revalidated that commitment." The Trump administration briskly withdrew US troops, who numbered 2,500 when Trump left office. President Biden's manner of completing the withdrawal would, for the first time in nearly two decades, make Afghanistan top of mind for many Americans (see Epilogue).

On US–Russian relations, Trump's actions struck many as contradictory, but they became more comprehensible when one distinguished between policy matters that affected him personally and those that did not. Overall, the Trump administration took a hard line on Russia, treating it more sternly than the Obama administration had done. Trump declined to extend the New START nuclear agreement that Obama had negotiated in 2010, saying it favored Russia. In 2019, the Trump administration pulled out of the Intermediate Range Nuclear Forces Treaty, forged between the United States and the Soviet Union in 1987, claiming, accurately enough, that Russia had violated it by deploying a new class of medium-range nuclear missiles targeting Western Europe.

On the other hand, Trump repeatedly cast doubt on the conclusion, reached by US intelligence analysts, that Russia had interfered on his behalf in the 2016 election. Under the most benign reading, Trump was simply resisting a narrative that suggested his victory was not legitimate. Less charitably, he wanted to obscure his past collusive behavior in the hope of repeating it in 2020. In July 2018, Trump met with Vladimir Putin in Helsinki, Finland. At a joint press conference following the meeting, an American reporter challenged Trump to "denounce what happened in 2016" and "warn [Putin] to never do it again." Trump acknowledged that his top intelligence officials had accused Russia of meddling in the election. But he added, "I have President Putin [standing next to me]. He just said it's not Russia. I will say this: I don't see any reason why it would be." The spectacle of Trump, in

Putin's presence, flatly siding with the Russian leader over US intelligence analysts sparked outrage back home, with some Democrats openly charging the president with treason. In a brief – very brief – replay of Charlottesville, several congressional Republicans allowed that Trump was in the wrong. Trump tried to quell the furor by claiming he had misspoken; he really meant to say, "I don't see any reason why it *wouldn't* be" Russia. But in context such a statement would have made no sense. Nor, of course, was it clear how any of this amounted to putting "America First" – except perhaps in a universe in which Trump's personal needs were synonymous with the national interest.

Immigration and the Southern Border

On immigration, Trump's policies were less idiosyncratic, fitting within a familiar tradition of nativist restrictionism. In addition to limiting new arrivals from the Muslim world, the president was preoccupied with stanching illegal immigration across the US–Mexican border and with cracking down on undocumented people already in the United States. In September 2017, the Trump administration announced that Deferred Action for Childhood Arrivals, the policy Obama had launched by executive order to provide relief to DREAMers (see Chapter 14), would be rescinded in six months' time. Congress thus had a window in which it could pass legislation that superseded executive action, but it failed to do so. Instead, DACA advocates sued in federal court, and in 2018 several district and appellate courts temporarily stayed the program's cancellation. In June 2020, the Supreme Court ruled that the administration's rescission of DACA had been "arbitrary and capricious," though it did not address the legality of DACA itself. In January 2021, President Biden reinstated DACA by executive order. But the program's opponents pursued their own litigation, and the issue remained mired in the courts. Of course, DACA's political and legal vicissitudes caused enormous anxiety to DREAMers, for whom the specter of deportation – or, short of that, ineligibility for college financial aid programs and similar benefits – loomed painfully large.

High on Trump's priority list was "building the wall," or expanding the barrier across the US–Mexican border. Through both executive action and requested legislation, Trump hammered relentlessly on this project. When Congress failed to fund it to his satisfaction, he employed various gambits – such as forcing a government shutdown to extract more funding, or diverting money from Department of Defense programs – to promote wall construction. Many of these efforts were blocked by Congress or the courts. By the end of his presidency, Trump claimed to have built more than 400 miles of border wall. This was technically accurate, but less than fifty miles of this construction amounted to new barriers where none had stood before; the rest merely replaced or reinforced preexisting fences or walls. The barrier now extended some 700 miles along the 1,954-mile border.

One feature of Trump's border policies was tragically consequential. A recurring challenge for US immigration authorities, long preceding the Trump administration, had been the arrival at the southern border of families and unaccompanied children seeking entry into the country. A 1997 federal court settlement agreement, as interpreted by a later court, prohibited the detention of migrant children for longer than twenty days. To comply with this restriction, US border authorities had generally released all families and unaccompanied children from immigration custody, allowing them to remain in the United States until immigration courts could decide whether they should be admitted. Although the vast majority of released migrants appeared for their court hearings, the fact that a small number did not caused critics to allege that the policy furnished a loophole for illegal entry into the country. Trump claimed, preposterously, that only 2 percent of these migrants showed up in court; the figure was more like 90 percent. To many, of course, that was still too low.

In May 2018, the Trump administration launched a "zero tolerance" policy. Border officials detained and prosecuted all adults seeking to enter the country illegally. As migrant children could not be imprisoned as well, they were separated from their parents and placed in shelters operated by the Office of Refugee Resettlement. At home and around the world, the new policy provoked a storm of outrage. American television news programs played heartbreaking video of migrant children, many of them toddlers, crying for their mothers and fathers. Some of the separated children were infants just a few months old. In June, Trump bowed to the criticism and rescinded "zero tolerance." Stunningly, however, administration officials had failed to keep track of the children and were unable to reunite most of them with their families. Many deported parents had to leave their children in the United States. Eleven months after Trump left office, following concerted efforts by the Biden administration to undo the damage, roughly 1,150 of the 5,500 separated children remained unaccounted for. If Trump was ever troubled by the debacle, he gave no sign of it.

House Democrats and the Russia Investigation

As the 2018 midterm elections approached, pundits predicted a "blue wave" that would sweep the Democrats back into power in the House, though probably not in the Senate, too. Democrats' determination to check Trump's power was sky-high, and Democratic candidates in swing districts were waging focused, disciplined campaigns that emphasized bread-and-butter issues such as economic fairness and health care. (The Republicans' failed effort to repeal Obamacare and their successful effort to cut taxes for the rich were in many races liabilities for the GOP.) At the start of election night, it appeared that Democrats might be heading for disappointment, but the tide turned in their favor, and they kept picking up wins as the votes were slowly counted in the days after the election. In the end, the Democrats gained forty-one House seats and took control of that chamber, though the Senate stayed Republican.

The Democrats' capture of the House made it possible for that body to conduct aggressive investigations into the many controversies swirling around Trump, including the big one relating to the 2016 election. All eyes were on Special Counsel Robert Mueller, who would soon complete his inquiry into allegations that Trump had colluded with Russia and then tried to obstruct legitimate investigation of his actions. Since May 2017, Mueller and his team had labored behind a shroud of mystery, emerging only to issue tantalizing indictments: against Russian operatives for waging cyberwarfare and against various Trump associates for lying to investigators, tampering with witnesses, and similar obstruction-of-justice offenses. Trump had repeatedly claimed, sometimes in all-caps tweets fired off at dawn, that Mueller's investigation was a "WITCH HUNT!" and a "hoax." Trump's allies did uncover, and incessantly trumpet, some flaws in "Crossfire Hurricane," the FBI's evocatively named inquiry into the matter, launched during the 2016 election campaign.[3] The Bureau had cut corners in obtaining judicial warrants to investigate a minor Trump campaign official; two FBI agents conducting an extramarital affair had exchanged private text messages about their disdain for Trump, even as they investigated his campaign. The Department of Justice's inspector general later sternly criticized these irregularities but found no evidence that they compromised the overall FBI investigation.

In March 2019, Mueller submitted his long-awaited report to William Barr, Trump's new attorney general, who a month later publicly released a redacted version of it. On Russian collusion, as we have seen, the report stated that the investigation found insufficient evidence to charge a criminal conspiracy but concluded that the Trump campaign knew about and welcomed Russia's interference. On obstruction of justice, Mueller's investigation "found multiple acts by the President that were capable of exerting undue influence over law enforcement investigations." (Those acts included Trump's orders to White House Counsel Don McGahn that he fire Mueller and to then Attorney General Jeff Sessions that he "un-recuse" himself from, and presumably protect Trump's interests in, the Russia collusion investigation. In each case, the recipient of the order refused to carry it out.) Nonetheless, because the DOJ had determined decades earlier that a sitting president cannot be indicted, the investigation "did not draw ultimate conclusions about the President's conduct" in the matter. "At the same time," the report continued, "if we had confidence … that the President clearly did not commit obstruction of justice, we would so state . . . . [T]his report … does not exonerate him."

Between the lines, Mueller was almost certainly saying that Trump had abused his office but that the criminal justice system could not supply a remedy; only Congress could do that. A growing number of House Democrats wanted to impeach Trump, but Nancy Pelosi, the new Speaker of the House, resisted these calls, fearing that such a step would politically backfire against the party. Pro-impeachment Democrats hoped that Mueller's planned testimony before the House Judiciary and Intelligence Committees would help them build a public case for moving against Trump. Although few Americans could be expected to plow through Mueller's 448-page report and parse its measured and complex prose, millions *would* likely tune in to watch the chief investigator explain the implications of his findings, hopefully in forceful and plainspoken terms.

Yet when the seventy-four-year-old Mueller appeared on Capitol Hill on July 24, 2019, his presentation was dry and halting. Democrats tried to draw him out on the report's highlights and get him to offer a ringing oral indictment, but his responses were terse and generally unhelpful. The Trump camp was jubilant. Donald Trump, Jr., shared a tweet by the

[3] The name came from a line in the Rolling Stones' 1968 song "Jumpin' Jack Flash."

rightwing commentator Dinesh D'Souza, who asked, "Is it possible that the Republicans have kidnapped the real Robert Mueller and substituted a mentally retarded look-alike in his place?" Tim Murtaugh, the communications director for Trump's reelection campaign, gloated that the Democrats "took a big swing at it with these hearings and they whiffed." Impeachment advocates insisted that Mueller's testimony, which did include some damaging statements about Trump, actually strengthened their case, but Speaker Pelosi made it clear it was time to move on.

Ukraine and the First Trump Impeachment

Trump could not agree more. Having gotten away with encouraging foreign meddling in the 2016 election, he was already soliciting outside interference in the next presidential race. On July 25, 2019, just one day after Mueller's congressional testimony, Trump spoke on the telephone with Volodymyr Zelensky, Ukraine's new president. Since 2014, Ukraine had contended with a Russian-backed secessionist movement in its eastern regions. In 2018, the Trump administration had begun supplying Ukraine with antitank missiles and other weapons, a shift away from the previous US policy of providing only nonlethal military aid. Zelensky saw the continuation of this assistance as a vital national imperative. Not surprisingly, the topic came up in the Trump–Zelensky phone conversation, with Trump observing (in tones vaguely reminiscent of a mafia don) that "the United States has been very good to Ukraine," and Zelensky replying, "You are absolutely right . . . . I would ... like to thank you for your great support in the area of defense." Zelensky expressed his eagerness to acquire additional antitank missiles from the United States.

Trump's immediate answer to this request would shortly become notorious: "I would like you to do us a favor though." In fact, Trump was seeking two favors in exchange for continued US aid, one retrospective and the other prospective. Looking backward, Trump wanted Zelensky's help in establishing that a previous Ukrainian government had interfered in the 2016 US election to boost Hillary Clinton (a discredited theory promoted by Trump and his supporters to draw attention away from Russia's known interference on Trump's behalf). The forward-looking request, and by far the more explosive one, was that the Ukrainian government investigate former Vice President Joe Biden and his forty-nine-year-old son Hunter Biden for alleged acts of corruption inside Ukraine. The younger Biden, who had struggled with substance abuse and other personal demons, had indeed engaged in questionable business practices in Ukraine, but no wrongdoing of this sort could be credibly pinned on his father. Trump's chief reason for targeting Joe Biden was, of course, that Biden was seeking the presidency in 2020. As of the summer of 2019, Biden was the frontrunner for the Democratic nomination. Although pundits expected he would soon face stiff competition from other, more liberal contenders, many agreed that, if Biden *did* get the nomination, he would be a tough candidate for the president to beat. Trump appeared to believe this, too.

In a way (though almost certainly unwittingly), Trump was taking a page out of Richard Nixon's Watergate playbook. As we saw in Chapter 7, back in early 1972 Nixon had feared that Maine Senator Edmund Muske, a mainstream Democrat widely seen as Nixon's most formidable potential opponent in that year's general election, would win the Democratic nomination. So Nixon's minions executed a "dirty trick" in the form of a forged letter containing explosive allegations, setting in motion a chain of events that eventually drove Muskie from the race. It is exceedingly unlikely that Trump had any memory or knowledge of this episode, but he faced a similar political threat in the moderate Joe Biden, and he was just as willing as Nixon had been to interfere in the Democratic Party's primary election process. If the Ukrainian government could conduct – or, really, just announce – an anticorruption investigation of the Bidens, news coverage of that development might throw the former vice president on the defensive, perhaps harming his electoral prospects. (Zelensky's reply to Trump's request, which the Ukrainian had heard before, was deferential but noncommittal: Ukraine's "next prosecutor general will be 100% my person, my candidate . . . . He or she will look into the situation … you mentioned.")

It was highly improper, of course, for a US president to request such a crass political favor from another head of state, and to try to extract it by using the enormous powers of his office.[4] Several other US officials were listening in on the call, and word of Trump's transgression caused immediate consternation among professional staff members within the National Security Council and the intelligence community. On August 12, a CIA officer submitted an anonymous "whistleblower" complaint to Michael Atkinson, the inspector general of the intelligence community. After some delay, Atkinson alerted several congressmembers to the document's existence. Senate Republicans, who held the majority in their chamber, were predictably incurious, but a number of committees of the Democratically led House launched aggressive investigations into the Ukraine matter, which by late September was the top national news story. Amid this flurry of public concern, the Trump administration was obliged to declassify a memorandum of the July 25 phone call, along with other relevant documents. These materials, combined with the closed-door (and quickly leaked) testimony of some administration officials, revealed that Trump's obsession with investigating the Bidens had pervaded US–Ukrainian relations. The severity of the alleged misconduct, combined with Democrats' rising calls for action, finally overcame Nancy Pelosi's resistance. On September 24, the House speaker announced the launch of an impeachment inquiry.

In November 2019, several US officials involved in Ukraine policy publicly testified before the House Intelligence Committee. One of the most electrifying moments occurred during the testimony of former US Ambassador to Ukraine Marie Yovanovitch, whom Trump had recalled in April 2019, after she obstructed an earlier effort by him to get Ukrainian officials to investigate Joe Biden. As Yovanovitch sat in the witness chair, the president publicly

[4] To pressure Ukraine to announce an investigation of the Bidens, Trump ordered that $400 million in congressionally appropriated military aid to that nation be blocked. After Congress discovered and started investigating this action in September, however (see main text, below), Trump was obliged to release the aid. Trump had also dangled a White House visit by Zelensky (a prized asset to any Ukrainian leader seeking to deter Russian aggression) in exchange for an announced investigation of the Bidens. Zelensky never got his White House visit, though he briefly met with Trump at the United Nations in New York in September 2019.

attacked her, insisting he had been right to pull her out of Ukraine. "Everywhere Marie Yovanovitch went turned bad," he tweeted. "She started off in Somalia, how did that go? Then fast forward to Ukraine, where the new Ukrainian President spoke unfavorably about her in my … phone call with him." Intelligence Committee chair Adam Schiff, a California Democrat, read the tweet aloud to a rattled Yovanovitch and arranged to have an image of it displayed on a large monitor in the committee room, in further evidence of the president's bullying nature.

In December, the House voted to impeach Trump, charging him with abuse of power and obstruction of Congress (in trying to hinder the House's pursuit of the impeachment inquiry itself). The case proceeded to the Senate, where, everyone knew, the Republicans would wield their majority powers to protect the president. The only real question was whether the Senate trial would include new witness testimony. Former National Security Adviser John Bolton, whom Trump had sacked a few months earlier, signaled that he could provide incriminating information about the president and Ukraine. No one expected Bolton's testimony to produce a conviction, which would require a two-thirds supermajority. The best-case scenario, for those seeking to rid the nation of Trump, was a full airing of the president's misdeeds that persuaded a handful of Senate Republicans to vote for conviction. This would make his inevitable acquittal more tenuous and, presumably, weaken the case for his reelection in 2020.

Senate Republicans were evidently thinking along similar lines. At the impeachment trial, which took place in late January and early February 2020, the Senate voted fifty-one to forty-nine against hearing new witnesses. All of the Republicans but two, Susan Collins of Maine and Mitt Romney, now a senator from Utah, took this position. All of the Democrats, plus the two independents who caucused with them, Bernie Sanders of Vermont and Angus King of Maine, voted to call witnesses. "I don't need to hear any more evidence to decide that the president did what he's charged with doing," said Republican Senator Lamar Alexander of Tennessee, explaining his no-witnesses vote. "So if you've got eight witnesses saying that you left the scene of an accident, you don't need nine." In other words: guilty as charged, but we already knew that.

Trump's journalistic defenders had talked themselves into a similar conclusion. In January 2020, Fox News commentator Steve Doocy argued that Bolton's corroboration of the quid pro quo would be superfluous: "[W]e heard [Trump] say in the transcript he wanted President Zelensky to look into the Bidens … so is this a big, big, big story?" Back in September, that same Doocy, first hearing of the allegation and not yet convinced of its validity, had remarked, "If the president said, you know, 'I'll give you the money, but you've got to investigate Joe Biden,' that is really off-the-rails wrong. But if it's something else … it would be nice to know what it is." Such goalpost-shifting had become an essential survival skill in Trump World.

On February 5, the Senate acquitted Trump by a vote of fifty-two to forty-eight on the abuse of power charge (with Romney casting the only Republican vote for conviction) and fifty-three to forty-seven on obstruction of Congress (with Romney joining the rest of the Republicans). Most Senate Republicans, even those conceding that Trump had misbehaved, said that the ultimate judgment of his conduct should be left to the voters in November. "While that logic is appealing to our democratic instincts," Romney acknowledged in a speech explaining his stance, "it is inconsistent with the Constitution's requirement that the Senate, not the voters, try the president." And the evidence conclusively revealed the president to be "guilty of an appalling abuse of the public trust." That the sole Republican vote for conviction was being cast by the party's standard-bearer in 2012 spoke volumes about the GOP's transformation in the intervening years.

Prior to the Senate vote, Adam Schiff, leader of the "House managers" (the team of Democratic House members advocating in the Senate trial on behalf of the articles of impeachment), had also answered the "let the voters decide" argument: "Now, you may be asking, 'How much damage can [Trump] really do in the next several months until the election?' A *lot*. A lot of damage." Schiff warned that Russia might again interfere in a presidential election; or maybe China would do so this time. Under such a scenario, "you know you can't trust this president to do what's right for this country. You can trust he will do what's right for Donald Trump." Schiff did not mention the possible public health implications of Trump's continuation in office. Nor did he speculate about the harm Trump might do *after* the 2020 votes had been cast.

The Covid-19 Pandemic

Since the first days of 2020, US public health officials had anxiously monitored an unfolding crisis in Wuhan, a large inland city in the People's Republic of China. The PRC government was saying very little, but scattered unofficial reports indicated that a previously unknown viral infection had broken out in the city, possibly the result of animal-to-human transmission in a food market selling live animals. (Some analysts would later hypothesize that the virus had, through human error, escaped from a Wuhan laboratory that specialized in studying viruses found in bats.) People contracting the virus suffered pneumonia-like symptoms, or maladies associated with the most severe seasonal flus. The Chinese government said there was no evidence of human-to-human transmission, but the growing number of infections belied that claim. In the second half of January, China's officially reported cases climbed into the hundreds, and at month's end there were more than a hundred confirmed deaths. US intelligence reports painted an even direr picture of overwhelmed hospitals and filled-up morgues. By now, cases were cropping up in other countries, too. The United States had six as of January 31. Secretary of Health and Human Services Alex Azar and other public health officials were trying to get Trump to focus on the crisis, with little success.

The president's earliest responses to the coronavirus pandemic, or Covid-19, as it also was called, were filtered through his preoccupation with trade. Trump had come into office determined to confront what he saw as unfair trading practices by many nations, especially China. He substantially raised tariffs on Chinese imports, prompting the PRC to retaliate in kind. Undaunted, Trump tweeted in March 2018, "[T]rade wars are good, and easy to win." Actually, not so easy. The standoff damaged both countries' economies, with American farm exports especially hard hit. To address the problem – which, if left unattended, could harm Trump's reelection prospects in Midwestern battleground states – the president approved large increases in federal farm subsidies. In January 2020, he pursued a more rational remedy: an agreement with PRC President Xi Jinping, who pledged that his nation would buy $200 billion in American products, mainly agricultural, in exchange for a significant reduction in US tariffs on Chinese imports. Covid-19 began looming as a threat to the United States just as Trump was negotiating and then touting his trade deal with the PRC. He saw concerns about the virus and about China's secretive behavior as an unwelcome intrusion on this positive storyline. In late January, Trump assured the public that the virus was "under control" and praised China's "efforts and transparency" in addressing the situation.

During February, Covid-19 spread rapidly in South Korea and Italy, and the caseload in the United States rose to sixty-nine, including the first confirmed American death. The US news media started paying closer attention. Trump was no longer shielding China; in fact, on January 31 he had banned flights from that country, a move endorsed by many public health experts. But, overall, he continued to downplay the virus, fearful of sparking a Wall Street panic that might damage him politically. "It's going to disappear," Trump declared. "One day – it's like a miracle – it will disappear." He predicted Covid-19 would be no worse than the flu and would probably vanish when the weather warmed in April. Speaking privately in early February to *Washington Post* reporter Bob Woodward, however, Trump fretted that the virus was "more deadly than even your strenuous flus."

Everything changed in March, especially its second week. With American cases spiking from the scores to the thousands, stores, restaurants, libraries, museums, theaters, schools, and universities started shutting down around the country – sometimes in response to state or local government edicts, often as a result of private decisions. Major League Baseball canceled spring training; the American Football League, the National Hockey League, the Big Ten Conference, and other athletic associations canceled or suspended their seasons. Anxious shoppers cleared grocery shelves of toilet paper, cleaning products, canned goods, and hand sanitizer. Classes, meetings, and other group events began shifting to Zoom. The term "social distancing" entered the lexicon. Now, even Trump had to take the virus seriously. In a March 13 televised speech, he announced a ban on commercial flights from Europe. Unfortunately, because he neglected to mention that US citizens were exempted, panicked American travelers rushed to board US-bound planes before the ban took effect, producing congested, chaotic, and probably contagious scenes at airports on both sides of the Atlantic. Rates of infection and death were on a terrifying ascent. As of March 31, more than 189,000 Americans had contracted Covid-19 and 3,815 had died of it. By the end of April, the respective figures were over a million and 55,225. The disease was especially deadly to the elderly and to those whose immune systems were already compromised by other health conditions. Thankfully, it afflicted very few children.

The Covid-19 pandemic, which continues as of this writing, severely disrupted the US economy. In April 2020, as shuttered businesses lost the ability to pay workers, unemployment shot up to 14.8 percent, the highest recorded rate since the Great Depression. The Coronavirus Aid, Relief, and Economic Security (CARES) Act, a $2.2 trillion relief

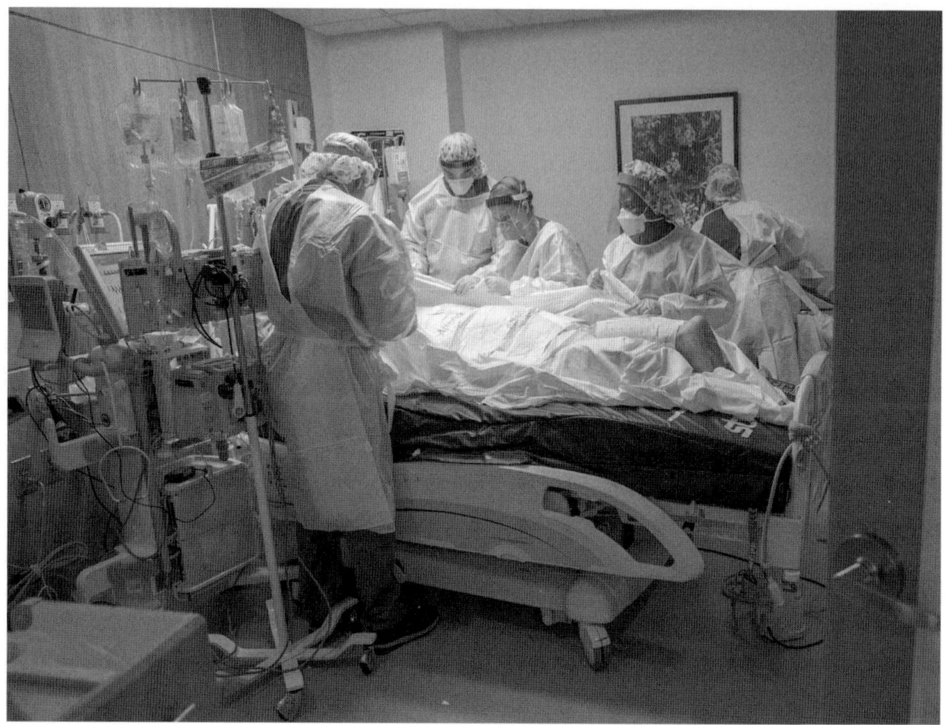

Figure 15.3 A medical "prone team" turns over a Covid-19 patient to ease labored breathing, Stamford, Connecticut, 2020. Source: John Moore / Getty Images News / Getty Images.

and stimulus bill passed by Congress in late March, extended unemployment benefits to individuals and subsidies to employers. Thanks to the latter provision, the unemployment rate began steadily declining that spring and was down to 6.7 percent by year's end.

Still, the crisis exposed and exacerbated the nation's class and racial disparities. Although many white-collar employees were laid off, most were able to keep their jobs by working remotely from home. Employees in more menial positions lacked that luxury; if not laid off, they were required to work on site, often in close, poorly ventilated quarters presenting serious risk of infection. These "frontline workers" – grocers, meatpackers, factory workers, farm laborers, sanitation workers, truck drivers, cleaners, hospital orderlies, and others – performed essential labor that could not be offloaded to cyberspace. The Centers for Disease Control and Prevention reported that, adjusting for age, both African Americans and Latinos were 4.6 times more likely than non-Hispanic whites to be hospitalized for Covid-19. American Indians and Native Alaskans were 5.3 times more likely.

Trump got some things right. The European travel ban, though ineptly executed, was a public health necessity. It was part of a broader Trump administration policy, announced in mid-March 2020, of encouraging a temporary shutdown of the non-essential economy, also clearly imperative. Later that spring, the administration launched Operation Warp Speed, a public–private partnership to coordinate knowledge and resources to hasten development of a Covid-19 vaccine. Critics mocked the razzle-dazzle name, but OWS facilitated what proved to be stunningly rapid progress. Trump said a vaccine would be ready in a matter of months, whereas most public health experts projected a timeline of at least a year or eighteen months. Trump's prediction was closer to the truth: the first vaccines received US government approval in December 2020 – a rare instance in which his penchant for bluster and self-promotion approximated reality.

Mostly, though, Trump got in the way. For some weeks in the spring of 2020, he enjoyed holding forth at televised daily meetings of the White House coronavirus task force that he had established, engaging in public colloquies with medical professionals on combating the virus. But his suggestion that Covid-19 patients might be treated with injections of disinfectant drew widespread ridicule, and he petulantly stepped back from this public forum. Although Trump had made a wise call in shutting down the economy, he soon began pushing for a premature reopening, defying experts' advice. He needled and harassed Dr. Anthony Fauci, the long-serving director of the National Institute for Allergy and Infectious Diseases, whose bias toward caution obstructed Trump's drive to declare an end to the pandemic and focus on his reelection. The president refused to wear a mask in public, complaining it made him look weak.

Trump's extraordinary hold on the Republican base and other right-leaning elements made his statements and behavior downright dangerous. Following his comments about injecting disinfectant, medical hotlines fielded numerous calls about the efficacy of swallowing bleach. Trump's resistance to mask-wearing and obvious displeasure over his own administration's public health measures gave aid and comfort to "anti-lockdown" protests that, like the demonstrations at the Michigan Capitol in April, sometimes took a menacing turn. His "LIBERATE MICHIGAN!" tweet was accompanied by nearly identical tweets about Minnesota and Virginia, two other states in which clamorous anti-lockdown movements stymied the efforts of Democratic governors. "I don't think it's helpful," Maryland's Republican governor, Larry Hogan, delicately observed, for Trump to "encourage people to go against the president's own policy."

The George Floyd Protests

On May 28, 2020, Americans marked a grim milestone: 100,000 US deaths due to Covid-19. Days earlier, another kind of horror, much more immediate and graphic, had unfolded before the nation. In Minneapolis, Minnesota, police arrested George Floyd, a forty-six-year-old Black man, on suspicion of using a counterfeit $20 bill. As Floyd lay on the street, a white officer, Derek Chauvin, knelt on his neck for nine minutes, ignoring Floyd's pleas that he could not breathe. Two other officers helped to restrain Floyd while a fourth held back onlookers, who demanded, futilely, that Chauvin ease the pressure. Floyd lost consciousness and was shortly pronounced dead.

In the ensuing hours and days, cellphone and security camera video of Floyd's excruciating death circulated on social media, provoking intense and quickly widening outrage. Chauvin was arrested and charged with third-degree murder and second-degree manslaughter. (A state court would later convict him of third- and second-degree murder.) Chauvin's arrest failed to quell the rising protests, which were fueled by a belief that the problem was systemic and required remedies much broader and deeper than the disciplining of individual officers. First in Minneapolis and then in cities across the nation (and even abroad), people of all racial and ethnic backgrounds staged demonstrations, rallies, and prayer vigils to protest excessive police violence, especially against African Americans. Earlier in 2020, Black Lives Matter protests had gathered momentum, galvanized by the cases of Ahmaud Arbery, a twenty-five-year-old Black jogger in Brunswick, Georgia, attacked by three white men and fatally shot by one of them; and of Breonna Taylor, a twenty-six-year-old Black emergency room technician killed in her home by Louisville, Kentucky, police officers conducting an ill-conceived drug raid. The George Floyd protests drew on the outrage these killings aroused, and probably also on the fact that millions of Americans had grown restless after several weeks of Covid-19 lockdowns. Many had also, one suspects, been radicalized by the social injustices laid bare by the pandemic. Over the next several months, somewhere between fifteen million and twenty-six million people are believed to have joined in George-Floyd-related protests in the United States.

Although the vast majority of these protesters were peaceful, some did engage in rioting, looting, and clashes with law enforcement. Cops occasionally used excessive force to subdue crowds. About twenty-five people died in the disturbances, and property damage ran in the hundreds of millions of dollars. Conservatives were quick to condemn protesters' violence, while liberals and progressives generally downplayed it, or contextualized it in ways that made it seem more defensible. Some to the left of center criticized this tendency, noting that many of the shopkeepers whose livelihoods had been destroyed were themselves people of color, both immigrant and native-born. The dissenters also warned that the Democratic Party might suffer in the 2020 elections if voters perceived it to be "soft on rioting."

Like many Americans, Trump was both shaken by the video of Floyd's murder and angered by the sight of violent protests. Characteristically, the latter reaction was much more visible to the nation. "These THUGS are dishonoring the memory of George Floyd," Trump tweeted early on the morning of May 29, after protesters set fire to a Minneapolis police station. He added that, "when the looting starts, the shooting starts," repeating a line first used by a Miami police chief in 1967 and occasionally cited in the years since as an emblematic – and heavily racialized – "law and order" maxim. Trump grew more agitated over the next few days, as boisterous demonstrators besieged the north end of the White House. He demanded that the US Army be deployed to restore order, alarming his top military advisers. To placate him, they not only agreed to bring some National Guard units to Washington but also helped him stage a bizarre photo opportunity. On June 1, federal police using tear gas, batons, and other riot gear violently removed the protesters at the White House's north end. The president, accompanied by Attorney General Bill Barr, Defense Secretary Mark Esper, Chairman of the Joint Chiefs of Staff General Mark Milley, and other officials, then walked across the cleared area to St. John's Episcopal Church, which had suffered fire damage during protests the night before. Awkwardly holding up a bible, Trump posed for pictures at the church's boarded-up entrance. The stunt was widely panned, and General Milley soon publicly regretted that his participation in it had "created a perception of the military involved in domestic politics."

In the wake of Floyd's killing, much of US society embarked on a "racial reckoning," an intensification of an effort, already under way for some years, to bear witness to the destructive impact of racism on past and present American life, especially regarding African Americans. Journalistic, educational, governmental, and cultural institutions, along with many for-profit companies, became more vigilant about identifying, acknowledging, and addressing manifestations of racism or racial insensitivity within their ranks, both historically and in the present. The names of historical figures who had championed racism, such as the Confederate leaders Jefferson Davis and Robert E. Lee and US Presidents Thomas Jefferson and Woodrow Wilson, were removed from schools, universities, streets, and parks. Some chapters of the reproductive health organization Planned Parenthood formally repudiated the eugenicist views of Margaret Sanger, the group's early twentieth-century founder. The white editor of *Bon Appétit*, a cooking magazine, resigned when an old photograph of him in brownface surfaced on social media. The white country music trio the Dixie Chicks changed their name to the Chicks. Institutions also reallocated resources to examine and recognize African American experiences, outlooks, and accomplishments. Colleges and universities created new teaching positions in African American studies and history. Fashion magazines featured more Black models on their covers and published stories about antiracist activism. Macy's, Old Navy, Sephora, and other retailers signed the "15 Percent Pledge," a commitment to devote that much of their shelf space to products from Black-owned businesses.

The "racial reckoning" was not universally applauded. Some dismissed it as little more than lip service – a cheap, feel-good substitute for grappling with the hard realities of structural poverty, over-policing, mass incarceration, and persistent health disparities between races. Others objected that the reckoning had created an excessively censorious climate, in which people had to walk on eggshells and risked ostracism or even unemployment if they deviated from "woke" orthodoxies. There was no shortage of excesses to cite: an analyst fired from a data consulting firm for sharing an article suggesting that the riots following Martin Luther King's 1968 assassination had been politically damaging to Democratic candidates; a business professor suspended from teaching after uttering a Chinese word that sounded like a racial slur in English. Of course, one could also point to individuals who had been punished for antiracist speech, such as the untenured history professor whose contract was not renewed after he criticized his university's "powerful, racist donors." All of these cases underscored the complexity of the racial moment, and the fact that the impulse to silence could come from many points on the political spectrum.

The fact that the George Floyd protests coincided with a major pandemic had a further polarizing impact on the nation. As the demonstrators took to the streets, they received warm encouragement from public health professionals who in recent weeks had scolded other Americans, especially anti-lockdown protesters, for congregating in large numbers. The medical experts justified these disparate reactions in two main ways. First, they noted that many George Floyd protesters wore masks, whereas lockdown opponents generally refused to do so. Second, they maintained that racial injustice was itself a public health scourge and that prioritizing antiracism over pandemic control could be a defensible and even a laudable choice. Though not without validity, both arguments struck many Americans, including some liberals, as glib and disingenuous. True, large numbers of antiracist protesters were masked, but plenty of others chanted and sang in close quarters without any face coverings. (In the end, the antiracist protests appear not to have caused significant Covid-19 spread, but that could not be confidently predicted at the time.) Furthermore, although public health, in the fullest sense, clearly does encompass broader social realities, medical experts had often dismissed such holistic reasoning when critics used it to challenge lockdown measures, such as by citing the harmful mental health consequences of extended unemployment and school closures. The abrupt shift in messaging eroded the credibility of public health experts, with ominous implications for future efforts to contain the virus.

Election and Insurrection

At the Democratic National Convention in August 2020, held physically in Milwaukee, Wisconsin, and virtually across the nation, Joe Biden received the party's presidential nomination. Six months earlier, this had hardly been the predicted outcome. Although Biden consistently led in the national polls, he generated little evident enthusiasm in the early primaries and caucuses. In February, he finished fourth and fifth in Iowa and New Hampshire, respectively, and eked out a second-place showing in Nevada. Everything changed in South Carolina's primary on February 29. Thanks to overwhelming support from African Americans in the state, Biden crushed his closest competitor, Bernie Sanders. The momentum quickly shifted to Biden, who won most of the states in the "Super Tuesday" cluster of races held on March 3. By month's end, most of the other Democratic contenders had dropped out and endorsed Biden. In April, Sanders did so, too, making Biden the presumptive nominee. Accepting the nomination in August, the seventy-seven-year-old Biden promised to bring the pandemic under control, restore the stricken economy, and make long-delayed investments in the nation's infrastructure and human capital. Less tangibly, he pledged to fight for "the soul of this nation" and strive to end "this chapter of American darkness." Senator Kamala Harris of California, who had vied with Biden for the presidential nomination, became his running mate. A woman of Afro-Caribbean and South Asian background, Harris would shatter several barriers if the ticket succeeded.

Holding a national election during a global pandemic was a novel and sometimes disorienting experience. Trump staged numerous campaign rallies at which largely maskless attendees sat close together. He brushed off medical experts' warnings that these could well be "super-spreader" events. Few were surprised when Trump himself contracted Covid-19 and was briefly hospitalized. For some hours, the president was in genuine peril. With the help of experimental drugs not yet approved for general use, however, he made a rapid recovery – leaving him even surer that he was invincible and that the pandemic's dangers were overblown. "Don't be afraid of Covid," Trump exhorted his Twitter followers upon leaving the hospital. "Don't let it dominate your life. We have developed, under the Trump Administration, some really great drugs & knowledge. I feel better than I did 20 years ago!" By now, the pandemic had taken more than 200,000 American lives.

Postal voting, increasingly common over previous election cycles, now took a quantum leap, as states and other jurisdictions prepared for an election in which many, and in some places all, of the ballots would be submitted by mail. Trump bitterly opposed mail-in voting, fearing that more Democrats than Republicans would use that system, harming his chances in November. "There is NO WAY (ZERO!) that Mail-In Ballots will be anything less than substantially fraudulent," he tweeted in May. "This will be a Rigged Election." Fact checkers debunked the notion that mail-in ballots were especially susceptible to fraud, but Trump sounded this alarm right up until Election Day (and beyond). In the summer of 2020, Trump's postmaster general, Louis DeJoy, began decommissioning postal sorting machines (ostensibly to replace them with new ones) and altering the procedures for processing mail. Many suspected he was trying to gum up the postal system to boost Trump's reelection chances. A combination of public pressure and legal action compelled DeJoy to rescind or delay some of these measures, and in the end mail-in voting unfolded with few hiccups.

It took little acumen to guess why Trump kept going on about "a Rigged Election." He was laying the ground for challenging the November result if things did not go his way. And they did not. At the end of Election Day, November 3, the outcome remained uncertain, but Biden could be cautiously optimistic that, of the battleground states yet to be called, enough would eventually land in his column to make him the victor. Shortly before 2:30 a.m. the following day, a livid Trump appeared on national television to insist that *he* had won and declare the vote-counting process "a fraud on the American public." He said he would appeal to the Supreme Court to end the travesty. "STOP THE COUNT!" he tweeted on November 5. Two days later, Pennsylvania officials got through enough of their vote count to award the state to Biden, who thus cleared the 270-vote hurdle for winning the Electoral College. (The final result would be 306 Electoral College votes for Biden and 232 for Trump. Biden received seven million more popular votes than Trump did.) The television networks called the race for Biden.

This is the moment when, in a typical presidential election, the loser graciously concedes defeat and wishes the victor well. Of course, no election with Trump on the ballot could ever be typical. He continued to contest the election result, instructing his lawyers, of whom former New York Mayor Rudolph Giuliani was the most visible (and manic), to file suits in every conceivable jurisdiction. Focusing on battleground states such as Arizona, Michigan, Pennsylvania, and Wisconsin, the attorneys tried to invalidate votes in counties with large Democratic populations. In court after court, state judges dismissed the suits, sometimes remarking on the shoddiness of the lawyers' cases, or on their failure to mount any case at all. (Outside of court, the lawyers would spin lurid conspiracy theories involving stuffed ballot boxes, hacked electronic voting machines, Italian satellites, and Chinese saboteurs. Once in front of judges, however, they usually declined to present that bogus evidence, for fear of incurring professional penalties. "I am not going to lose my fucking law license because of these idiots," a Trump lawyer privately vowed, referring to more zealous members of Trump's "Stop the Steal" campaign. Trump, of course, wholly embraced the wild theories and was infuriated by his lawyers' failure to get anywhere with them.) In late December and early January, Trump pressured DOJ officials to declare the election fraudulent. He urged Georgia's Republican secretary of state "to find 11,780 votes" to put him over the top in that state. To the incalculable benefit of the nation, these GOP officials resisted the president's entreaties.

Trump did render one public service. In pursuing his bankrupt challenges, he gave the nation a crash course in the archaic procedures that, every four years, translate a collection of state-run elections into the inauguration of a new presidential term – rituals the American public almost never sees because they merely ratify a predetermined outcome. A key ritual occurred on December 14, with the vote of the Electoral College; mask-wearing electors convened in state capitols and confirmed Biden's victory. Mitch McConnell publicly congratulated Biden, calling him "president-elect" for the first time. (Like most Republican lawmakers, McConnell had until then privately acknowledged Biden's victory but refrained from doing so openly to avoid angering Trump. A substantial minority of Republicans had publicly proclaimed Trump the winner since November 3 and continued to do so after December 14.) Trump, still refusing to concede, turned his attention to the next key date: January 6, 2021, when Congress was scheduled to certify the Electoral College votes. Several House Republicans had already pledged to object to the certification of votes from Arizona, Georgia, Michigan, Nevada, New Mexico, Pennsylvania, and Wisconsin, states where Trump alleged fraud. A handful of Senate Republicans shortly promised to do the same. The president encouraged his supporters from around the country to gather in Washington on that date to back the challenges. "Big protest in D.C. on January 6," he tweeted. "Be there, will be wild!"

According to the Constitution and an 1887 federal statute, the president of the Senate, a role usually played by the vice president, oversees the certification of Electoral College votes. Trump demanded that Vice President Mike Pence, at the January 6 certification, "reject fraudulently chosen electors" and thus block Biden's election. At the president's behest, a law professor named John Eastman had worked out some convoluted scenarios for the sixth. Under one of them, Pence was to discard the electoral votes from the disputed states, a move that would yield a Trump victory in the Electoral College. When congressional Democrats predictably objected, Pence was to switch gears and declare that, as neither candidate had received 270 electoral votes, the Constitution required that the matter be settled in the House of Representatives, where, according to arcane rules, Trump was again assured of victory. Under an alternative scenario, Pence and congressional Republicans were to engineer a stalemate on Capitol Hill, giving pro-Trump state legislators in the contested states more time to agitate for their candidate.

Pence's ostentatious deference to Trump had long been a subject of mockery. But the vice president knew he was legally powerless to execute any of Eastman's wild schemes, and he said so to Trump at a White House meeting on January 5. "You don't understand, Mike," the president replied. "You *can* do this. I don't want to be your friend anymore if you don't do this." Although he failed to change Pence's mind, Trump issued a false public statement that evening claiming that he and Pence were "in total agreement that the Vice President has the power to act" to reject Electoral College votes.

Figure 15.4 Trump supporters clash with police and security forces at the US Capitol, January 6, 2021. Source: Roberto Schmidt / AFP / Getty Images.

At about 1:00 p.m. on the following day, January 6, Trump addressed tens of thousands of supporters on the Ellipse, a park near the White House. He exhorted them to march the two miles to the Capitol "to try and give our Republicans, the weak ones, … the kind of pride and boldness that they need to take back our country." Throngs proceeded to Capitol Hill, where a large group of Trump supporters was already pushing through the temporary barricades the Capitol Police had erected at the west entrance. The crowd, which heavily outnumbered the police, included people wearing military gear and wielding pipes, batons, baseball bats, and bear spray. They engaged the police in hand-to-hand combat, pushing their way toward the Capitol doors. Inside, a joint session of Congress had begun the certification process. Pence, who earlier that day had announced he would honor the Electoral College result, presided. As rioters broke into the building – some of them chanting "Hang Mike Pence!" – Secret Service and Capitol Police officers whisked the vice president and the congressional leaders out of the chamber, forcing Congress into recess. Congresspeople and staff scrambled into various hiding places in the Capitol Hill complex, while rioters roamed the halls and ransacked offices. A police officer shot and killed a female rioter as she tried to break into a hallway adjoining the House chamber. A second female protester, initially thought to have been trampled, died of a drug overdose. Three other deaths, of a policeman and two protesters, were indirectly linked to the traumas of that day. Scores were injured.

It is unclear if Trump intended or expected a violent insurrection of this sort. He may simply have wanted a raucous and menacing crowd to surround the Capitol and thereby pressure Pence and Congress not to certify Biden's election. Once Trump saw live television coverage of the mayhem, however, he was thrilled by the spectacle of so many ardent supporters battling on his behalf. It took three hours for aides, friends, besieged Republican lawmakers, and his daughter Ivanka to persuade Trump to urge the rioters to go home. No one, it appears, saw any point in involving the president in the mustering of National Guard units to help restore order. In that effort Pence, from his hiding place under the Capitol, played the commanding role. Determined to complete the certification that same day, he ordered Acting Defense Secretary Chris Miller to get forces to the scene immediately. The first National Guard personnel reached the Capitol at 5:40 p.m. Shortly after 8:00 p.m., the certification process resumed in the newly secured building; it ended well past 3:00 a.m. with the confirmation of Biden's election. The shock of the insurrection had caused a handful of Republicans to drop their objections to certification, but eight senators and 139 House members still voted to overturn some of the Electoral College results. Once the certification was official, Trump released a statement in which he finally pledged "an orderly transition on January 20th." But he added, "While this represents the end of the greatest first term in presidential history, it's only the beginning of our fight to Make America Great Again!"

To Democratic House members, it was a foregone conclusion that Trump had to be impeached all over again, and this time some Republican members agreed. On January 13, all 222 House Democrats and ten House Republicans voted to pass a single article of impeachment: incitement of insurrection. When the Senate trial got under way on February 9, Trump had been out of office for nearly three weeks, so one of the standard penalties of a Senate conviction had already been levied by the calendar. But another available penalty was the prohibition against holding federal office again, a sanction many Americans were eager to see imposed in Trump's case. The House managers' presentation included searing video of insurrectionists shooting bear spray into officers' faces, dragging a DC policeman down a stairway, and crushing another in a doorway as he screamed in agony. Once again, the Senate acquitted Trump, but by a closer margin. Fifty-seven senators, ten shy of the required two-thirds supermajority, voted to convict. Six other Republicans joined Mitt Romney in finding Trump guilty. The former president's grip on the GOP had loosened, but not by much. It would tighten back up in the months ahead.

***

To say that Trump was unceremoniously removed from the White House is almost literally accurate. He removed himself from the premises early on the morning of January 20, 2021, so as to be absent from the midday ceremony marking his successor's inauguration. Joe Biden became the oldest person to enter the presidency, and Kamala Harris the first woman, the first African American, and the first South Asian American to serve as vice president. Like all such rituals, the inauguration evoked a range of public emotions, but a mood of relief was prevalent and palpable. The United States had – for the moment – survived its brush with banana republicanism; its constitutional mechanisms were battered but intact. Americans now faced the daunting tasks of addressing the vast substantive challenges, domestic and foreign, besetting their nation, and of attending to the rancorous divisions that had brought it to this state of chaos and disrepute.

READING QUESTIONS

1. Assess candidate and then President Trump's relationship with the Republican Party leadership from mid-2015 to late 2017. Whereas Trump aroused vocal opposition from party leaders at the start of this period, he had won most of them over by its end. How do you explain the transformation?
2. On what basis did many political observers conclude, or at least strongly suspect, that Trump had conspired with the Russian government to improve his chances in the 2016 presidential election? What obstacles did these critics encounter, both during the campaign itself and while Trump was president, in trying to make this case?
3. Prior to the onset of Covid-19, some political observers speculated that it would take a national emergency on the order of a global pandemic to cause Americans to transcend their bitter political and cultural divisions. Clearly, Covid-19 did not have that unifying effect. Why not?
4. Some analysts maintain that the events of late 2020 and early 2021 have starkly exposed the fragility and dysfunction of the nation's system for electing presidents. What features of the system can critics cite to make this argument? Is it a persuasive case? What might a contrary argument look like?

SUGGESTIONS FOR FURTHER READING

Edwards, George C., III. *Changing Their Minds? Donald Trump and Presidential Leadership*. Chicago: University of Chicago Press, 2021.

Frum, David. *Trumpocalypse: Restoring American Democracy*. New York: HarperCollins, 2020.

Gurtov, Mel. *America in Retreat: Foreign Policy under Trump*. Lanham, MD: Rowman & Littlefield, 2021.

Hillstrom, Laurie Collier. *Family Separation and the US–Mexico Border Crisis*. Santa Barbara, CA: ABC-CLIO, 2020.

Kantor, Jodi, and Megan Twohey. *She Said: Breaking the Sexual Harassment Story that Helped Ignite a Movement*. New York: Penguin Books, 2019.

Poniewozik, James. *Audience of One: Donald Trump, Television, and the Fracturing of America*. New York: W. W. Norton, 2019.

Rucker, Philip, and Carol Leonnig. *A Very Stable Genius: Donald J. Trump's Testing of America*. New York: Penguin Books, 2020.

I Alone Can Fix It: Donald J. Trump's Catastrophic Final Year. New York: Penguin Books, 2021.

Schwab, William A. *Dreams Derailed: Undocumented Youth in the Trump Era*. Fayetteville, AR: University of Arkansas Press, 2019.

Stelter, Brian. *Hoax: Donald Trump, Fox News, and the Dangerous Distortion of Truth*. New York: Atria, 2020.

Wolff, Michael. *Landslide: The Final Days of the Trump Presidency*. New York: Henry Holt & Company, 2021.

Woodward, Bob, and Robert Costa. *Peril*. New York: Simon & Schuster, 2021.

Epilogue

They met up at a Houston Walmart store: Abdul Aman Sediqi with his wife and two sons; Dr. Tram Ho with some of her own family. Days earlier, the Sediqis had arrived as refugees from war-ravaged Afghanistan, whose US-backed government had just succumbed to the Taliban insurgency. Sediqi had worked in mine clearance for the US military. In recognition of that service, he and his family were issued Special Immigrant Visas to resettle in the United States. They now wheeled a shopping cart down Walmart's abundantly stocked aisles, selecting furnishings for the apartment that local philanthropic organizations had rented for them with US government support. Tram Ho, who was paying for the shopping trip, helped the Sediqis pick out dinner plates, utensils, appliances, and clothing, including Superman-themed apparel for the boys, who were one and three years old.

Sediqi was at first puzzled by Ho's insistence on purchasing items for his family. Through an interpreter, Ho explained that she and her own loved ones had once walked in the Sediqis' shoes. As a teenager forty years earlier, she had fled with her family from Vietnam, where her father, a former officer in the South Vietnamese navy, had been imprisoned and persecuted by the communist regime that overran the South in 1975. Ho's family settled in Houston, and Ho now worked there as a physician. "We were lucky when we came to America in 1981 to establish a new life here, and the Americans have opened their arms to help us," she told a television news crew recording the Walmart errand. "And we're doing the same for the Afghans."

Tram Ho's gesture was part of a nationwide outpouring of assistance to Afghan refugees by Vietnamese Americans, in the days and weeks following the Taliban's August 2021 seizure of power. From Seattle, a grassroots initiative called 75 Viets for 75 Afghan Families set out to recruit seventy-five Vietnamese American families – the number signified the year in the twentieth century in which the exodus of Vietnamese refugees had begun – to serve as temporary hosts to seventy-five Afghan refugee families or to help them secure affordable housing; more than a hundred Vietnamese American households around the country volunteered. A benefit concert in Southern California featuring Vietnamese American and Afghan American performers raised $160,000 for refugee aid. Daklak Cao Do of Springboro, Ohio, pledged to hire at least fifteen Afghan refugees at his automotive and aerospace supply company and help sponsor their families. Do told a reporter that, after he had found refuge in Ohio as a young man in the early 1980s, a dishwashing job at a Bob Evans restaurant had been the first rung on his ladder of economic success. He was grateful to the Americans who granted him that leg-up, "and that's why I want to return that to the people who are just like I was."

These efforts fit into a still broader mosaic of generous acts toward the new Afghan migrants, performed by Americans of all backgrounds and walks of life. As *The New York Times* panoramically observed in early September, "In rural Minnesota, an agricultural specialist has been working on visa applications and providing temporary housing for the newcomers, and she has set up an area for halal meat processing on her farm. In California, a group of veterans has sent a welcoming committee to the Sacramento airport to greet every arriving family. In Arkansas, volunteers are signing up to buy groceries, do airport pickups and host families in their homes." A *Washington Post*/ABC News poll found that 68 percent of Americans favored admitting Afghan refugees who had been subjected to security screening, which the new arrivals did routinely undergo.

Of course, it was not all sweetness and light. Americans opposed to welcoming Afghans compensated for their minority position by cranking up the volume of their objections. Especially noisy were politicians clamoring for recognition within the Republican Party's ultra-Trumpian wing. The author and venture capitalist J. D. Vance, seeking the Republican nomination for one of Ohio's US Senate seats in 2022, sounded the alarm against admitting "people who believe they should blow themselves up at a mall because somebody looked at their wife the wrong way." Not to be outdone, Vance's main rival for the Senate nomination, former Ohio Treasurer Josh Mandel, warned Ohioans that Afghan refugees would "bring child brides and Sharia Law to your neighborhood."

Meanwhile, a host of logistical obstacles impeded the resettling of Afghan refugees. The previous administration of Donald Trump had downsized federal agencies charged with refugee issues, leaving the Joseph Biden administration ill equipped to handle the influx (though critics rightly noted that the new administration had had several months to prepare for it). A nationwide housing shortage slowed the process of finding homes for new arrivals. Antiquated computer systems in federal offices further gummed up the works, as did the extra precautions necessitated by the ongoing Covid-19 pandemic. Two months after the Taliban takeover, more than 50,000 Afghan refugees remained housed in cramped barracks on eight military bases across the United States. "I don't want to complain because we are in the U.S., and they are doing their best," said Sahar Mohammad, languishing with his wife and five children at Fort Dix, an army base in New Jersey. "But it is hard . . . . We feel like we are not free." By February 2022, fewer than 10,000 refugees remained on military bases. Still, nearly half of the 80,000 Afghans who had entered the country since August had been granted only temporary status and faced possible deportation once it lapsed. Congress could pass legislation to allow these Afghans to apply for permanent status, an accommodation it had made for previous refugee populations, but as of mid-March 2022 it had not done so.

The drama of the Afghan refugees captured several key features of American life in 2021 and early 2022: the compassion and vibrancy of an ever-changing population; the creative partnering of public and private institutions to advance broadly shared values and goals; but also the deeply ingrained attitudes of intolerance and xenophobia; and the aura of shabbiness and dysfunction surrounding so many public endeavors. At the same time, the overseas crisis eliciting these contradictory responses underscored the violence, oppression, trauma, and misery besetting so many areas of the world, dislocations in which the US government had often been implicated and from which the US public could not hope to remain aloof. Russia's stunning military assault on Ukraine in February 2022 brought such global realities into painfully sharp relief. This bewildering jumble of qualities and circumstances both propelled and stymied Americans' efforts to overcome the paralyzing divisiveness of the previous quarter-century, and especially the last half-decade, to build a more cohesive, productive, and humane future for their nation and wider world.

***

In the 2020 elections, the Democrats had not only captured the White House; they had also retaken control on Capitol Hill – but just barely. They now had a margin of five votes in the House, and the Senate was tied fifty-fifty, with Vice President Kamala Harris able to break ties in the Democrats' favor. On most issues the Senate Republican minority could, if it wished, filibuster Democratic bills. To pass them, Democrats would have to peel off enough Republicans to achieve a sixty-vote supermajority. Many Democrats favored abolishing the Senate filibuster, which could be accomplished by a simple majority vote. But two Senate Democrats, Joe Manchin of West Virginia and Kyrsten Sinema of Arizona, openly opposed this course, and a handful of other Democratic senators quietly agreed with them. The issue of the filibuster overshadowed most of the Democratic legislative agenda in 2021. In February and March, Biden and congressional Democrats managed to pass a $1.9 trillion economic stimulus package on a straight party-line vote, but this was a rare occasion when Senate rules forbade the use of the filibuster. Few other pieces of legislation could be passed without substantial Republican support or the filibuster's elimination or revision. The Democrats' legislative wish list – voting rights guarantees, infrastructure, immigration reform, green energy, an increased minimum wage, paid family leave, subsidized preschool and community college, and more – seemed in jeopardy.

Some Republicans did favor investing in the nation's infrastructure, and in August 2021 the Senate passed, in a filibuster-proof vote of sixty-nine to thirty, a $1.2 trillion infrastructure bill. This was a modified version of a bill previously passed in the House, yet the House did not move to finalize the legislation – at least, not at first. Most Democrats in that body, along with most Senate Democrats and President Biden as well, had their sights on a much larger bill, commonly known as the Build Back Better (BBB) Bill, which contained investments in health care, education, green energy, and other social goods. At the urging of progressives in the party, Biden and other Democratic leaders refused for some weeks to advance the infrastructure bill unless it was paired with BBB. But getting BBB through the obstacle-strewn Senate was no easy matter. Senate rules allowed Democrats to pack a large number of legislative items into a single massive bill that could be voted on without interference by filibuster. Democrats could not, however, agree among themselves on the size or contents of the BBB Bill. A flurry of intraparty skirmishes and negotiations failed to resolve the matter, leaving many Democrats despondent. Even with control of the White House and both congressional chambers, they seemed powerless to advance a basic legislative agenda.

Tacitly acknowledging defeat, the Democratic leadership decoupled the infrastructure bill from BBB; the former passed the Congress in early November 2021 and was signed into law on the 15th. Democrats vowed to continue the fight for BBB, but as of March 2022 the effort remained stalled.

Republican leaders, meanwhile, were sliding back into the Trumpian maw. Immediately after the January 6, 2021, insurrection, many observers expected Trump's influence within the Republican Party to wane. Even though the vast majority of congressional Republicans had been unwilling to impeach or convict Trump, pundits reasoned, those lawmakers surely recognized how toxic his influence was and would quietly drift away from him – especially now that Trump, ensconced in his garish Florida estate, had been banished from Twitter and Facebook for spreading disinformation. Into the spring and summer of 2021, however, the former president's hold on the party base remained as strong as ever, and congressional Republicans found it prudent to renew their own fealty. Hours after the insurrection ended, Senator Lindsey Graham of South Carolina, who had been one of Trump's strongest supporters, appeared to have reached his limit: "Trump and I, we've had a hell of a journey. [But] count me out. Enough is enough." Two months later, though, Graham was telling a reporter, "I want us to continue the policies that I think will make America strong. I believe the best way for the Republican Party to do that is with Trump, not without Trump." In September 2021, Graham said he wanted Trump to run for president in 2024. Elected Republicans at all levels of government strongly echoed this sentiment, and Trump gave every indication that he would seek the presidency again. The party's renomination seemed his for the asking.

In May 2021, after the House voted to create an independent, nonpartisan commission to investigate the January 6 attack, Senate Republicans filibustered the parallel bill in their chamber. Not only would such a commission have kept the memory of January 6 alive (and in a manner difficult to dismiss as partisan); it might well have uncovered links between insurrectionists and some Republican lawmakers. In the summer of 2021, the House created its own committee to investigate January 6. But the committee's ability to compel the testimony of Republican House members or former Trump administration officials, or to rebuff Republicans' charges that it was conducting a partisan witch hunt, remained uncertain. By now, some congressional Republicans were downplaying the severity of the insurrection (or, if they acknowledged its seriousness, baselessly claiming that the worst offenders had been leftwing agitators impersonating Trump supporters). Trump himself grew increasingly insistent that January 6 was, in every way, a patriotic outpouring in the service of a vital, heroic, and ongoing cause. If elected president again, Trump declared at a January 2022 rally, he would gladly pardon Capitol rioters facing criminal prosecution.

Meanwhile, in states dominated by Republicans, and with Trump's open encouragement, GOP legislators were systematically removing some of the obstacles that had prevented Trump from overturning the 2020 presidential election. They whittled away at the powers of secretaries of state (who, though members of political parties, were expected to oversee elections independently) and made it more conceivable that their own bodies – the highly partisan state legislatures – would ultimately determine which presidential electors to send to Congress for certification. Republican-dominated legislatures also passed new laws that turned minor election irregularities into felonies, for the evident purpose of creating more situations in which election fraud could be alleged. Arizona, for example, made it a felony to send an unrequested mail ballot to anyone not on a permanent list of absentee voters. If an election official erred and committed that minor infraction, the legislature could now claim that fraud had occurred and use that as a pretext for overturning an election result. At the same time, Trump took a keen interest in the various state primary elections for the office of secretary of state (many of them scheduled for 2022), and he threw his support behind Republican candidates who most forcefully insisted that the 2020 presidential election had been stolen. If elected, such figures would presumably use their offices to try to engineer Trump's election in 2024. These machinations unfolded more or less openly, alarming not just Democrats but a wider array of political observers concerned about the fate of American democracy.

Another source of general dismay was the continuing potency of the Covid-19 pandemic. Biden had taken office amid hopeful news on that front. In December 2020, two Covid-19 vaccines, associated with the pharmaceutical companies Pfizer and Moderna, respectively, had been approved for use in the United States. A third vaccine, by Johnson & Johnson, shortly followed. The vaccines had been developed in record time, and Trump's Operation Warp Speed deserved credit for facilitating this progress (though Trump himself was too fixated on overturning the 2020 election to take a victory lap). The vaccines also were remarkably effective. As the Biden administration worked with states, local jurisdictions, and the private sector to ramp up vaccine production and get "shots into arms," infection rates dropped, raising hopes that the ordeal would very shortly end. But a new strain of the virus, the Delta variant, prevalent in the United States by the early summer of 2021, proved unusually contagious. By mid-summer, hospitalizations and deaths were again on the rise, though the latter increase was slower, thanks to the vaccines. This new wave of infection peaked in late September and began declining with the onset of fall. But by early December still another Covid-19 mutation, the Omicron variant, was circulating the globe. Omicron, which peaked in the United States in mid-January, was even more contagious than Delta, but also considerably less severe. It became quite common for vaccinated people to contract Covid-19, though most experienced relatively mild symptoms.

As of February 2022, 64 percent of eligible Americans (consisting of all residents above the age of five) were fully vaccinated, a disappointing rate to public health officials. African Americans were somewhat less likely than whites, Asians, or Latinos to get vaccinated, partly because vaccines, though free, were less accessible to Black communities and partly because these communities tended to be less trusting of medical authorities. Among whites, "vaccine hesitancy" was more likely to be a function of partisan politics. Just as rank-and-file Republicans had often disdained masks during the pre-vaccine period (and later), so a good many of them now refused to get "vaxxed." Some Republican governors and legislatures catered to this sentiment by refusing to promote vaccines and by barring businesses from requiring employees and customers to be vaccinated. Rightwing media stars, though in most cases almost certainly vaccinated themselves, cast doubt on the vaccines' efficacy and treated the Biden administration's promotion of them as sinister overreach. Antivaccine rhetoric grew harsher in September 2021, when Biden issued executive orders mandating that health care workers in facilities participating in Medicare or Medicaid be vaccinated and that employees of large companies be vaccinated or regularly tested. (In January 2022, the Republican-dominated Supreme Court upheld the mandate for health care workers but invalidated the one for general employees.)

Most vaccine hesitancy, it would appear, resulted from efforts by conservative polemicists to disrupt what they saw as statist liberal schemes. But liberals and progressives had unwittingly exacerbated the problem. In the summer of 2020, as we saw, many public health experts damaged their own credibility by applauding public gatherings aimed at protesting racialized police violence. Meanwhile, Democratically aligned teachers' unions championed school closures with a zeal that infuriated millions of parents, including some with liberal leanings. This latter action was not directly tied to the vaccine issue, but it bolstered the rightwing narrative that Covid-19 was more of a "Dem panic" than a pandemic.

***

A shocking setback overseas further compounded Biden's difficulties and aroused genuine anguish in the nation. Biden had inherited Trump's 2020 agreement on Afghanistan: a pledge to withdraw all US troops from the country by May 1, 2021, in exchange for the Taliban's promise to deny sanctuary to al-Qa'ida and similar groups. Biden, who as vice president had futilely urged President Barack Obama to end the Afghan venture, was not about to repudiate Trump's decision, though he pushed the withdrawal date back to August 31. Biden and his advisers hoped that the US-backed Afghan government would survive in power after the American pullout, at least for a time. But anticipation of the impending withdrawal triggered a wholesale collapse within the Afghan military. Across the country, local commanders cut private deals with the Taliban, surrendering positions and weapons to the insurgents in exchange for promises of safety for themselves and their families. In the summer of 2021, the Taliban made rapid territorial gains against an Afghan army mounting hardly any defense. In the first half of August, they launched a final surge, seizing one regional capital after another. On August 15, the national capital, Kabul, fell to the insurgents.

Stunned by the debacle, US officials arranged a massive airlift out of the country of US citizens and vulnerable Afghans, including those who had worked as translators for the US military or had assisted the US presence in other ways. In scenes reminiscent of the fall of Saigon in 1975, thousands of ordinary Afghans flocked to Kabul's international airport, parts of which remained under US control for a couple of weeks after the capital's surrender. Desperate to avoid falling under Taliban rule, the Afghan civilians clamored for places on the departing transport planes, some even clinging to the sides of the aircraft as they taxied down the runway. At least two people who had stowed away in the undercarriages of planes fell to their deaths shortly after takeoff. Toward the end of the sixteen-day airlift, a suicide bomber detonated his explosive vest in the crowded airport, killing 183 people, most of them Afghan civilians and thirteen of them US servicepeople. An organization known as the Islamic State in Iraq and al-Sham–Khorasan Province (ISIS–K), an avowed enemy of both the United States and the Taliban, claimed responsibility. The attack suggested that, although the Taliban had easily defeated the Afghan army, they would now face an insurgent challenge from an even more ruthless Islamist group. Within forty-eight hours, the US military launched a drone strike against a suspected ISIS-K member believed to be planning another attack. It was later revealed that the strike killed ten Afghan civilians, none of them ISIS-K members and seven of them children.

In one of the largest airlifts in history, the US military evacuated more than 100,000 people from Afghanistan. Yet thousands of Afghans wishing to flee were unable to get onto planes, either because they lacked the requisite documentation or because they could not push their way through the desperate throngs at the airport gates. Heartbreaking messages posted by terrified Afghans left behind to contend with Taliban rule – especially women and girls now facing severe threats to their freedom of movement, to their ability to work and study, to their personal and sexual autonomy, and to their physical safety – flooded social media. American commentators blasted the Biden administration for abandoning Afghanistan or, alternatively, for failing to execute the inevitable abandonment with greater foresight and care. Some observers were startled by the coldness with which the famously empathic Biden publicly greeted the wrenching tableau; in this case, the president's determination to quit Afghanistan overcame his impulse to grieve. A September 2021 poll indicated that 77 percent of Americans supported the US withdrawal from Afghanistan, but most of those favoring a pullout disapproved of Biden's handling of it. As we have seen, most Americans welcomed the approximately 80,000 Afghan refugees admitted into the country in the late summer and fall, and many Americans displayed extraordinary generosity and resourcefulness. Yet a vocal minority warned that terrorists or Islamist fanatics could be lurking in the refugees' ranks, even though the new arrivals had undergone extensive vetting.

A host of other crises crowded in that fall. There were fresh surges of migrants at the US–Mexico border, not just Mexicans and Central Americans but now also Haitians, displaced by years of poverty and political turmoil and a recent earthquake. The Biden administration's attempt to balance border security with humanitarianism antagonized Americans both left and right. Meanwhile, pandemic-related disruptions of commercial supply chains caused shortages of consumer goods and spiking prices. Some expected cargoes failed to turn up at US ports. Others arrived but could not be unloaded because too many American dockworkers and warehouse employees had left their jobs to care for ailing family members, to take better-paying work, or for other reasons. A shortage of truck drivers that had preceded the pandemic significantly worsened on account of the health crisis.

All of these developments – the ineffectual maneuverings to pass BBB, the chaotic retreat from Afghanistan, the delayed reopening of public schools, rising consumer prices, and other perceived failings – generated significant unhappiness with the status quo and ate into the Democrats' popularity. By late 2021, most pundits agreed that the Republicans would almost certainly take back the House, and possibly also regain the Senate, in the 2022 midterm elections. And, with Biden's approval ratings now dipping into the forties, many wondered if the president could be reelected in 2024 (assuming he chose to run again; he would be almost eighty-two at election time). Perhaps Republicans would not even need to tinker with the electoral machinery. As the journalist Matthew Yglesias sarcastically tweeted in December 2021, "Dems are tackling the threat to democracy by becoming sufficiently unpopular that the GOP can win fair and square."

Through it all, the pandemic kept exacting its toll. The Omicron spike had rapidly subsided after its January 2022 peak, and by early spring federal and state government agencies were relaxing some of their Covid-19 restrictions, especially masking requirements. Increasingly, official attitudes were settling around the notion that Covid-19 would be an endemic feature of American life whose effects for the foreseeable future could be mitigated, not eliminated. As of mid-March 2022, however, the pandemic was still killing an average of 1,000 Americans each day, most of them unvaccinated. Nearly a million Americans had succumbed to the two-year-old disease. Worldwide, the death toll exceeded six million.

***

By now, the world had been plunged into a frightening new crisis. In late February 2022, after weeks of threats and ominous troop mobilizations, Russian President Vladimir Putin launched a military invasion of neighboring Ukraine. To justify the move, Putin cited his long-standing fear that Ukraine, if left to its own devices, would join NATO and thereby menace Russian security. But he also spoke dismissively of Ukrainian independence in ways that suggested a desire to annex, or at least thoroughly dominate, that nation. Should any outside power interfere in the Ukraine operation, Putin warned, "Russia will respond immediately, and the consequences will be such as you have never seen in your entire history," an unmistakable – and jolting – reference to nuclear retaliation.

It quickly became clear that Putin had miscalculated. Unlike in 2014, when Russia's annexation of Crimea had met with hardly any military opposition, this time the Ukrainian army tenaciously resisted the invasion. Ukrainian President Volodymyr Zelensky – the same figure Trump had pressured to investigate then Vice President Biden and his son in 2019 – bravely stood his ground, vowing in frequent social media posts to stay in Ukraine with his people and fight to the bitter end. Ordinary Ukrainians rallied to their nation's defense, gaining worldwide admiration for their courage, resourcefulness, and morale. The Russian military operation was poorly planned and ineptly executed, and many of the Russian soldiers on the ground seemed bewildered as to its purpose. Russian tanks and armored cars advanced at a glacial pace, stalled by frequent equipment failures and paramilitary ambushes. Just a couple weeks into the war, an estimated 5,000 Russian soldiers had been killed. Internationally, Putin's action elicited swift and nearly universal condemnation. European countries that had been fairly lackluster members of NATO overnight became full-throated boosters of the alliance. The United States and European nations poured military aid into Ukraine and imposed punishing economic sanctions on Moscow, including a

Figure E.1 Refugees wait for an evacuation train in Zaporizhzhia, a city in southeastern Ukraine, March 2022. Source: Future Publishing / Getty Images.

US ban on Russian oil imports and a halt to a major gas pipeline project linking Russia and Germany. By early March, the Russian economy was in turmoil and the ruble quickly losing its value. None of this, however, meant that Putin would stop trying to subdue Ukraine, or that his effort would fail.

Nor, of course, were Russians the only ones suffering the consequences. By mid-March, thousands of Ukrainian soldiers and hundreds of Ukrainian civilians had lost their lives. More than 2.5 million people had fled the country, mostly to neighboring Poland. A Russian siege of the southern city of Mariupol deprived tens of thousands of residents of food, running water, electricity, and medical care, while subjecting them and their physical surroundings to devastating bombardment. Even if the war could be kept to a matter of weeks, a herculean rebuilding effort awaited. Yet there was no foreseeable end to the crisis, and good reason to fear that it might expand beyond Ukraine's borders. Zelenksy was pleading with friendly nations to establish no-fly zones over his country – portions of Ukrainian airspace through which Russian military aircraft would be forcibly prevented from flying – so that humanitarian relief efforts, and perhaps Ukrainian military operations, could be protected from aerial attack. All knew that a US-imposed no-fly zone would make a direct shooting war between the United States and Russia a terrifying possibility, and Biden declined the request as dangerously escalatory. Even so, influential voices within US military and foreign policy circles were urging Biden not to dismiss Zelensky's pleas out of hand. Such calls were likely to grow louder and more numerous the longer Ukraine's agony continued.

***

In the early spring of 2022, the Ukraine crisis understandably dominated US news coverage. Over the longer term, however, the nation faced daunting challenges that Americans ignored at their peril. One of them, impinging not just on Americans but on all of humanity, was accelerating climate change, a process driven – an ever-growing scientific consensus maintained – by greenhouse gas emissions. In recent years, environmentalist groups, scientific bodies, United Nations agencies, and even the US Department of Defense had issued progressively dire warnings about melting ice caps, rising sea levels, worsening droughts, and a host of other effects that, unless reversed, would fuel impoverishment, civil and military conflict, destabilizing migrations, mass extinctions, and similar global calamities in the years to come. Some climate-related consequences, such as increasingly frequent and severe hurricanes and forest fires, had already upended thousands of American lives.

In the 2010s, as we have seen, the Obama administration and the US private sector had made considerable headway in reducing greenhouse emissions – progress matched and in some cases exceeded by other industrialized nations. The US reductions continued under Trump, though at a slower rate on account of his efforts to reverse Obama's climate policies. In 2020, the worldwide lockdowns necessitated by Covid-19 had further slowed the rate of carbon emissions. The resumption of robust economic activity in 2021, however, began spewing near-record levels of greenhouse gases into the atmosphere. At a November 2021 climate summit meeting in Glasgow, Scotland, 151 countries, including the United States, made ambitious pledges to slash their carbon emissions. It was an impressive diplomatic achievement, but analysts warned that, even in the highly unlikely event that all of the pledges were fulfilled, the planet's temperature would still rise to 1.8 or 1.9 degrees Celsius above preindustrial levels by the middle of the twenty-first century. Climate scientists had already concluded that any temperature increase exceeding 1.5 degrees C would likely be catastrophic.

In the United States, the crisis was further compounded by climate denialism. In virtually all other major industrialized nations, the mainstream political parties, even staunchly conservative ones, accepted that human activity significantly contributed to climate change. Yet American Republicans either rejected that proposition or insisted the evidence was not yet conclusive. And it was not only Republicans who stood in the way: throughout 2021, in addition to upholding the filibuster, the aforementioned Senator Joe Manchin of coal-rich West Virginia had doggedly opposed efforts by fellow Democrats to insert provisions into the elusive Build Back Better Bill that would help the nation reduce its reliance on fossil fuels.

There were other global sources of worry. Trump's and Biden's shared determination to exit Afghanistan, and the American public's broad support of the policy (as distinct from its unhappiness with Biden's execution of it), suggested a national consensus in favor of avoiding large-scale and open-ended military commitments in troubled regions. But what if Afghanistan again became a launching pad for terrorists of global reach? Would American boots return to Afghan ground? A more diffuse danger was that stressed and impoverished areas of the world, made even more so by the dislocations of climate change, would breed violent conflicts or manifestations of political extremism that eventually provoked new US military ventures. Over the previous couple of decades, the United States had come to regard pilotless drone warfare as a relatively "clean" way of combating security threats emanating from the Middle East, Central Asia, and North and East Africa. As the botched raid in Afghanistan in August 2021 made painfully clear, however, such operations were anything but clean to those on the receiving end. One had to wonder if they created as many terrorists as they killed.

And what about America's more powerful adversaries? The old strategic rivalries with Russia and China had outlasted the cold war in attenuated form and, in recent years, grown more contentious. Now, of course, the attack on Ukraine had brought US–Russian relations to a pitch of hostility seldom seen even at the height of the cold war. In this area, too, the emergency momentarily crowded out long-term thinking. But even if one *could* engage in leisurely contemplation, it seemed fruitless to try to predict what US–Russian relations would look like on the other side of this consuming crisis – except perhaps to surmise that Russia would likely emerge from it in a significantly weakened state.

The People's Republic of China, by contrast, presented a more formidable long-term challenge to the United States. Unlike Russia, it had transformed itself after the cold war into a multifaceted world power, wielding advanced military, diplomatic, technological, and especially economic strength. Sino-US disagreements had recently grown harsher and more overt, raising fears that the two nations were on a collision course. Some analysts warned that an increasingly powerful China would grow less and less tolerant of Washington's continued dominance of the Pacific region, a recipe for sharp and possibly violent conflict. Others countered that China had geopolitically peaked in the 2010s and entered a decline that would make it less able to challenge the United States. Still other analysts agreed that China was past its prime but argued that this in itself made the situation more volatile. In 2021, the international relations scholars Hal Brands and Michael Beckley warned that China might "act more boldly, even erratically, over the coming decade – to lunge for long-sought strategic prizes before its fortunes fade." Perhaps Beijing would seek to dominate sea lanes and infrastructure in the Pacific and Indian Oceans; perhaps it would even try to seize Taiwan. Although Washington might well accede to the former set of moves, it was harder to imagine it tolerating that last one.

Relations with China's neighbor, North Korea, brought up another set of worries – and not just the fact that the United States had spectacularly failed to prevent North Korea from acquiring a nuclear option. There was the possibility that Iran, no longer tethered by the multilateral nuclear agreement, would make a sudden bid to achieve its own nuclear weapons capability within its rapidly shrinking "breakout period." Who could say how Israel, already a nuclear power, might react to such a development? Added to this was the enduring fear that Pakistan, another nation possessing nuclear weapons, would fall under the control of political extremists.

There was also, of course, no shortage of long-term domestic concerns. Disparities of income and wealth, which had markedly narrowed between the late 1920s and the mid-1970s, had widened again over the succeeding four and a half decades. In 1975, the top 20 percent of American households had earned, on average, ten times as much as the bottom 20 percent. In 2021, the former earned fourteen times as much as the latter. In 1976, the top

1 percent of US households possessed less than 20 percent of the nation's wealth; now, they held some 32 percent. It was hard to separate these discouraging trends from the declining status of American workers, after a couple of generations of deindustrialization (with the accompanying loss of well-paying manufacturing jobs) and rapidly shrinking union membership. By 2021, only 6.3 percent of private sector workers were represented by unions, as compared with 24.2 percent in 1973. It had become all too easy for companies to extract concessions from employees by threatening to close down American plants and reopen them in much poorer countries where workers could be paid a pittance. Economic disparities were especially glaring along racial lines. According to a 2020 Brookings Institution study, the median white American family held eight times the wealth of the median Black family and five times that of the median Latino family. The Covid-19 pandemic, as we saw in Chapter 15, made such differences of class and race more visible than before.

No less disturbing was the atrophying of the nation's political culture and institutions. Republican leaders' failure to block Trump's nomination in 2016, and Trump's subsequent takeover of the Republican Party, inflicted extraordinary damage on the American polity. As long as Trump advanced the GOP's core political agenda – often captured in the sardonic shorthand "tax cuts and judges" – there was virtually nothing Trump could do to earn the opposition of more than a handful of Republican lawmakers. Trump's hold on the party was guaranteed by his cult-like following among its base, by his vengeful treatment of any Republicans who strayed from the Trumpian fold, and by the party's institutional powerlessness to hold its leaders to minimal standards. More than a year after Trump's exit from office, these conditions remain wholly in effect and seem destined to wreak havoc on future election cycles – and on much of the rest of the nation's politics and governance. Especially alarming have been efforts by Republican state legislators to gain control over their states' selection of presidential electors, a power that properly belongs to the voters.

Although Trump's ascendancy has been immensely destructive in its own right, it is also symptomatic of a deeper affliction: the hyper-partisan, take-no-prisoners politics that have seized hold of both major parties over the previous generation. The malady is more severe on the Republican side, but Democrats are hardly immune to it. In the 1970s and 1980s, Democratic congresspeople had a much stronger sense of identification with and loyalty to their constitutional branch. Their successors of more recent decades, by contrast, have tended to see themselves as Democrats first and senators or House members second. The change is especially noticeable in the conduct of congressional hearings. Forty and fifty years ago, each party had its share of members who treated public hearings as opportunities for partisan grandstanding. Yet each party also had members who were willing to ask challenging questions of executive branch witnesses from their own party. Nowadays, virtually every substantive question posed at a congressional hearing is designed to gain partisan advantage. Even a question that elicits valuable information is first and foremost political in purpose and would not have been asked if the interrogator feared an inconvenient answer. Republicans, of course, have taken this much further and sometimes refuse to allow adversarial witnesses to respond at all to their almost comically hostile questions.

***

Still, as winter turned to spring in 2022, Americans had grounds for encouragement and even some pride. Although the Covid-19 pandemic had revealed plenty of disturbing things about American politics and society, it had also brought latent strengths to the surface. Americans ostentatiously resisting mask mandates and inveighing against vaccines could be highly disruptive, but they were always a distinct minority. The vast majority cooperated with public health edicts and made the best of a baffling and frightening situation, showing less surliness and obstructionism than some commentators initially feared. Frontline workers, often toiling in poorly ventilated and thus risky environments, maintained the sinews of the national economy. Teachers and parents did what they could to keep children engaged on digital platforms, while other parents homeschooled their kids. Health care workers put in twelve-hour shifts to blunt the impact of the pandemic's rolling surges. American epidemiologists and technicians collaborated with colleagues around the world to produce, in less than a year, a set of remarkably effective vaccines.

George Floyd's brutal murder in May 2020 horrified Americans and trained a national spotlight on excessive police violence, especially against African Americans. Twenty-one months after the killing, it was still too early to assess the long-term impact of the tragedy and the enormous protests it sparked. But there were signs of a modest cultural shift, leading in turn to some valuable reforms. Calls to "defund the police" – voiced by progressive activists after the Floyd killing and, for a time, tolerated by some Democrats not wishing to appear insensitive on the issue – proved politically toxic, and by early 2022 most mainstream liberals had repudiated the slogan. But more moderate schemes to reallocate funding within police departments for more community-oriented purposes (which was what some "defund the police" advocates actually meant anyway) were enacted in a number of American cities. Other jurisdictions increased funding for housing, mental health services, trauma counseling, and similar programs designed to make altercations between residents and police less likely.

The George Floyd protests took place amid an ongoing reassessment of the nation's criminal justice system. The draconian drug laws of the 1980s and early 1990s, and many provisions of the omnibus crime bill of 1994, had massively expanded the nation's prison population. Rates of violent and property crime had peaked shortly before the crime bill's passage. Their significant decline over the next quarter-century gradually altered the political climate surrounding criminal justice. By the late 2010s, Americans of all backgrounds and persuasions, including prominent conservatives, were critical of the "tough on crime" approach. In 2018, an unlikely coalition of conservative Republicans, civil libertarians, and African American activists, all coordinated by Trump's son-in-law Jared Kushner – who in turn was lobbied by the reality TV star Kim Kardashian West – persuaded Congress to pass and President Trump to sign the First Step Act. It reduced federal sentences for certain drug offenses, made it easier for some federal prisoners to gain early release, improved conditions for women and juveniles in federal facilities, and provided funding for state and local rehabilitation programs. Meanwhile, attitudes about marijuana were rapidly shifting, resulting in its decriminalization in numerous jurisdictions in the 2000s and 2010s. By 2022, the recreational use of marijuana had been legalized in nineteen states.

The picture was complicated, however, by a spike in the national homicide rate since 2020 and increases in other forms of violent crime. Experts disagreed on the causes of the surges, with some pointing to the wider circulation of guns, others to the social dislocations of the pandemic, and still others to the excessive lenience of local prosecutors. In conservative quarters, the crisis inspired a resumption of "tough on crime" rhetoric, and some liberals again found themselves on the defensive. Still, there seemed to be little appetite for a return to the harsh drug laws of previous decades, especially now that many Republican lawmakers and governors had white rural constituents struggling with opioid addiction. In this area, at least, Americans had come to recognize the harms that could flow from overly punitive approaches and were seeking a more humane and workable balance.

And, throughout all the turmoil and heartbreak, the United States remained, by world standards, an extraordinarily prosperous, free, open, and vibrant nation, a nation into which migrants of all backgrounds, stations, and faiths never stopped clamoring for entry. "This is a land of opportunity," Tram Ho said to Abdul Aman Sediqi during their Walmart errand. "Just work hard. Your American dream will be fulfilled." Of course, it was not that simple. It never had been. But, like the stirring legend of World War II with which we began our story, this myth offered just enough truth to bind a fractious people within its magic.

Index